AN INTRODUCTION TO THE COMPARATIVE STUDY OF PRIVATE LAW

READINGS, CASES, MATERIALS

JAMES GORDLEY

Shannon Cecil Turner Professor of Jurisprudence
School of Law, University of California at Berkeley

ARTHUR TAYLOR VON MEHREN

Story Professor of Law Emeritus
Harvard Law School

CAMBRIDGE
UNIVERSITY PRESS

CAMBRIDGE UNIVERSITY PRESS
Cambridge, New York, Melbourne, Madrid, Cape Town, Singapore, São Paulo, Delhi

Cambridge University Press
The Edinburgh Building, Cambridge CB2 8RU, UK

Published in the United States of America by Cambridge University Press, New York

www.cambridge.org
Information on this title: www.cambridge.org/9780521118576

First published 2006
This digitally printed version 2009

A catalogue record for this publication is available from the British Library

ISBN 978-0-521-68185-8 hardback
ISBN 978-0-521-11857-6 paperback

Contents

COMPARATIVE PRIVATE LAW: PROPERTY, TORT, CONTRACT, UNJUST ENRICHMENT   139

PART ONE: PROPERTY LAW   141

I. POSSESSION 141

PART TWO: TORT LAW   234

I. THE SCOPE OF THE RIGHTS PROTECTED   234

PART FOUR: UNJUST ENRICHMENT 552

I. THE PRINCIPLE 552

II. UNJUST ENRICHMENT WHEN THE PLAINTIFF DID NOT LOSE 557

III. UNJUST ENRICHMENT WHEN IT IS DOUBTFUL WHAT THE DEFENDANT GAINED 562

Foreword

In his foreword to the second edition of Arthur von Mehren and James Gordley, *The Civil Law System* (1977), André Tunc commented on a sentence written by Roscoe Pound in the foreword to the first edition of that work (1957). Pound had stated categorically that the methods of the jurists "must have a basis in comparison." To what extent, Tunc asked, have we heeded that injunction? His answer was gloomy. He described the story of our efforts aimed at legal unification as sad; and most attempts to improve our domestic laws were also not based on comparative study. Today, nearly thirty years later, we have reason to be more optimistic. Of course, the picture is very different in different areas of the world. But at least in Europe the scene has changed dramatically.

Private law in Europe is in the process of acquiring, once again, a genuinely European character. The Council and the Parliament of the European Communities have enacted a string of directives deeply affecting core areas of the national legal systems. Increasingly, therefore, rules of German, French, or English law have to be interpreted from the point of view of the relevant community legislation underpinning it. The case law of the European Court of Justice, too, acquires an ever greater significance for the development of German private law. The prospect of a codification of European private law is starting to be seriously considered; and as a precursor various "restatements" of specific areas of European private law have been published or are in the process of preparation. The internationalization of private law is also vigorously promoted by the uniform private law based on international conventions which cover significant areas of commercial law. The United Nations Convention on Contracts for the International Sale of Goods, in particular, has been adopted by more than 60 states. It has started to generate a significant amount of case law, and it has shaped national law reform initiatives. The Sales Convention has been elaborated by Uncitral, and it aims at the global harmonization of a core area of private law. But Uncitral is not the only international organization active in this field. Unidroit, too, continues to produce ambitious instruments such as the Principles of International Commercial Contracts which have been widely noted, internationally, and which enjoy increasing recognition as a manifestation of a contemporary lex mercatoria. Every year, thousands of students spend a period of one or two semesters at a law faculty in another Member State of the European Union under the auspices of the immensely successful Erasmus/Socrates programme. Alternatively, or in addition, many students acquire additional, post-graduate qualifications in other countries. More and more law faculties attempt to obtain a "Euro"-profile by offering a broad range of language courses, by establishing international summer schools, or integrated programmes on an undergraduate and post-graduate level, by setting up chairs for, or research centres in, European private law. Legal periodicals have been created that pursue the objective of promoting the development of a European private law. Interest has been rekindled in the "old" ius commune, and legal historians are busy rediscovering the common historical foundations of the modern law and restoring the intellectual contact with comparative law and modern legal doctrine. New approaches to legal scholarship, often emanating from the United States, have gained ground in Europe; the economic analysis of law is probably the most prominent example. Legal practice, at the top level, has been all but revolutionized. A wave of mergers has swept over the legal profession and reflects its ever-growing international orientation.

It is widely accepted today that the Europeanization, or more broadly, the internationalization of private law decisively depends on an internationalization of the legal training provided in the various universities throughout Europe. For if students in their domestic law courses continue to be taught the niceties of their national legal systems without being made to appreciate the extent to which the relevant doctrines, or case law, constitute idiosyncrasies explicable only as a matter of historical accident, or misunderstanding, rather than rational design, and without being made to consider how else a legal problem may be solved, a national particularization that takes the abracadabra of conditions, warranties, and intermediate terms, or of the doctrine of consideration, for granted, threatens to imprint itself also on the next generation of lawyers. Thus, what André Tunc said in 1977 remains true today: the law schools must ask themselves whether they cannot do more to broaden the frame of mind of their students. Courses on comparative law and on legal history play a key role in this context; at the same time, however, the comparative and historical approaches should permeate the ordinary courses in the various substantive areas of private law. This makes it necessary to develop teaching materials which make the most important sources and the most influential texts readily available. James Gordley's and Arthur von Mehren's *Introduction to the Comparative Study of Private Law* meets this need. In contrast to its predecessor on *The Civil Law System* (first edition by Arthur von Mehren, second edition by Arthur von Mehren and James Gordley) it also covers the common law; that makes it a most attractive teaching tool for comparative law courses not only in the Anglo-American world but also in countries such as France and Germany. In addition, it provides texts and materials on the historical development of modern legal doctrine and thus demonstrates the close relationship between legal history and comparative law. And so it can now be said with even greater justification than in 1977 that, for students who read English, this book constitutes "an excellent tool enabling them to view law not parochially but from a wider perspective." For a lawyer in the twenty-first century this kind of intellectual horizon is not only desirable but indispensable.

REINHARD ZIMMERMANN
December 2005

*

Foreword

To Arthur Taylor von Mehren, *The Civil Law
System Cases and Materials for the
Comparative Study of Law* (1st ed. 1957)

Writing in a time in which methodology in the social sciences has
become the prevailing approach, Professor von Mehren speaks of comparative study of law rather than of study of comparative law. That is, he would
make the study of the legal order and of the body of authoritative precepts
and authoritative technique of applying them to the adjustment of relations and ordering of conduct more effective for promoting and establishing
an ideal order among men by comparison of significant features of the two
matured systems of law in the modern world.

Study of the civil law system, of the Roman law and the codes of the
Continental countries and lands in the New World settled by them had
much vogue in America in the eighteenth and fore part of the nineteenth
century. Kent and Story, who were the leaders in the development of our
law in the formative era and along with Blackstone and Coke were its oracles, were learned civilians, and the exigencies of commercial law, for which
Blackstone and Kent furnished no useful material, led to increasing use of
civilian materials by text writers and courts. From commercial law a tendency to cite and rely upon the civilians spread to the private law generally. As late as 1860 the Court of Appeals in New York cited French authority
upon a question of the law of fixtures. As late as 1880 Langdell, trained
under Parsons in the fifties, included a discussion by Merlin in a summary
of the law of contracts. To the Middle Ages the academic ideal of all Europe
as the empire for which Justinian had been the law-giver, made Roman
law was taken to be declaratory of the law of nature. But the great civilian treatises did not deal with the general run of questions which had to
be decided by American courts in the formative era. In the end we developed treatises of our own on the basis of the English common law. The
dominant historical school in the nineteenth century gave up the eighteenth-century law-of-nature idea and so Roman law could no longer be
held declaratory. Moreover, the latter part of that century developed a cult
of local law. For a time comparative law was in decadence.

With the passing of the hegemony of historical jurisprudence at the
close of the last century there came a revival of comparative law. An idea
of a comparative science of law got currency in America through Lord Bryce's
Studies in History and Jurisprudence. In fact all methods of jurisprudence must be comparative. But the use of civilian treatises by English
and American analytical and historical jurists had led to attempts to force

common-law institutions and doctrines into civilian molds which retarded their effective development. What has called for comparative method throughout the world is general economic unification and new means and methods of transportation and communication which have been making the whole world one neighborhood.

Jhering, emphasizing the effect of trade and commerce in liberalizing the strict law, vouched the introducing of Greek mercantile custom into the law of the old city of Rome. In the same way the law merchant, a characteristic product of the medieval faith in a universal law, was taken over into the common law in an era of general commercial development. In America increasing economic unification has put an end to the cult of local law. Today worldwide economic unification is challenging the self-sufficiency of systems of law.

Conditions of transportation and communication today make every locality all but the next door neighbor of every other. What happens anywhere is news in the next morning's paper everywhere. The world has become economically unified and law transcending local political limits is an economic necessity. Moreover, since the First World War we have been seeing attempts at political unification of the world and setting up of a world legal order.

Even more the worldwide development of industry, carried on with instrumentalities and under conditions increasingly dangerous to life and limb, and the mechanizing of every activity of life likewise threatening injury to every one, have been creating new legal problems calling for revision of old doctrines and finding of new means of promoting and maintaining the general security. Experience, which is no longer merely local, must be subjected to the scrutiny of reason and developed by reason, and reason, which in its very nature transcends locality, must be tested by experience. The wider the experience, the better is the test. Thus the science of law must increasingly be comparative. Whether we are dreaming of a world law or thinking of the further development of our own law, to suit it to the worldwide problem of the general security in the present and immediate future, the methods of the jurist must have a basis in comparison.

Not the least problem of legal education today is what to leave out of the regular curriculum. Above all the fundamentals of the lawyer's technique and the basic principles by which he must weigh the everyday controversies in which he is to assist clients in maintaining their rights and realizing their just claims, must be thoroughly mastered. Nothing should be allowed to detract from this minimum. But the many difficult and complicated problems confronting the law, the lawmaker, the judge, and the practising lawyer of today call for a science of law beyond what was required of the simpler jurisprudence of the past, and, it must be repeated, the method of that science, whether primarily analytical, historical, philosophical, or sociological, must use comparative law as its main instrument. For jurist, law teacher, and judge it is becoming more than a part of his general culture. As to the practising lawyer, in our polity he is potentially law-writer, law teacher, legislator, or judge. Moreover, law is or ought to be a learned profession and at least an awareness of the technique, institutions, and organization of the legal systems of the other half of the legal world is part of what should make a learned lawyer.

It remains to note that Professor von Mehren gives us, not a setting side by side of detailed rules of law for comparison presumably to enable us to determine which is "the right rule." It was this sort of thing which brought comparative law into disrepute in the last century. He gives us instead material for comparison of the Continental codes with our system of judicially established and developed law, of comparing the administering method of the Continent with our own, and finally what is crucial for the development of our Anglo-American law to meet the conditions of maintaining the general security in the society of our time, materials for comparing with our own the reaction of the civil-law jurisdictions to social and economic change.

ROSCOE POUND

*

Foreword

To Arthur Taylor von Mehren and James Russell Gordley,
The Civil Law System An Introduction to the
Comparative Study of Law **(2d ed. 1977)**

In the masterly foreword that, as a token of esteem and friendship for the author, Dean Roscoe Pound gave to the first edition of this book, one sentence deserves our special attention and, indeed, should give us some concern: "Whether we are dreaming of a world law or thinking of the further development of our own law, to suit it to the worldwide problem of the general security in the present and immediate future, the methods of the jurists must have a basis in comparison."

They "*must* have a basis in comparison." To what extent in the last twenty years did we heed this injunction?

The story of the efforts to create a "world law" is sad; only disappointingly meager results have been achieved. In the field of civil liberties, jurists have no other weapons than hearts, mouths, and pens with which to oppose the frightening machines which crush bodies and minds. But there are other fields, such as trade law, where a "world law" is needed and does not encounter political obstacles. In these fields, parochialism is the impediment to unification of the law. This has proved, by itself, an often insuperable roadblock.

Have we then, at least, based on comparative study our efforts to improve our domestic laws to make them more responsive to the legitimate expectations of our citizens and to the needs of the future?

A totally negative answer would be unfair. In some special fields of law—securities regulation, for instance, under the influence of United States law—and even in more general fields such as torts or family law, juristic thinking has become increasingly international. For many countries, furthermore, encouraging examples could be given of valuable and sometimes systematic studies of foreign laws or institutions and of careful research on the lessons to be derived from such studies.

It remains true, however, that jurists use a comparative approach very little when one considers the importance that, rationally, such an approach should have. Of course, a deliberate effort is required to overcome the psychological difficulties, the language barriers, and the logistic problems that such an approach implies. But, just as no individual can claim to be wise by himself, no legal system can be regarded as so advanced that it has little to gain from the study of foreign schools of thought.

Logistic problems have just been mentioned. They are, of course, very important. However, the *International Encyclopedia of Comparative Law,* when it is completed, will give to every English-speaking jurist easy access, not only to the laws, but to the trends of the laws of a great many countries. As the logistic difficulties are overcome in this and other ways, the law schools must ask themselves whether they cannot do more to broaden the frame of mind of their students and to equip them for a world where, as Dean Roscoe Pound had foreseen, international affairs occupy an increasingly large place.

The answer seems clear: much more is desirable. Much more could and should be done to cross-fertilize our legal systems and, above all, the minds of our students.

The first edition of this book has done a great deal to enlighten students trained in the common law about the civil-law system, as typified by the French and German legal orders. The author, Professor Arthur T. von Mehren, has performed the same task in his teaching. He deserves the gratitude of both common lawyers and civilians. In the preface of the first edition, he explained the way he had conceived the book. Very wisely, the second edition remains basically faithful to the original conception. For the second edition, Professor von Mehren has been joined by Dr. James R. Gordley, a young scholar with particular interest in comparative law. They have not merely brought the first edition up to date—which is already a rather formidable task—but have expanded the treatment of some subjects and treated some others for the first time. This has required the condensation or omission of certain topics handled in the first edition. Of greater interest and importance is the fact that at many points the authors have replaced quoted material by their own discussion of the matter in question. Due to such improvements, the book is, even more than in its first edition, a fortunate combination of technical, historical, and functional approaches.

Let us hope that an awakening to what is needed to prepare our students for the approaching 21st century will everywhere broaden the place given to the comparative study of law. For students who read English, this book will be an excellent tool enabling them to view law not parochially but from a wider perspective.

ANDRÉ TUNC

*

Preface

Arthur von Mehren wrote, in the Preface to his 1957 work on *The Civil Law System* that "[t]his book had its beginning almost ten years ago" when he left the United States to study law at Zurich, Berlin, and Paris. Its "fundamental purpose was to give a student, having some common law training, an insight into the workings of the civil law system as typified by the French and German legal systems." He and I produced a second edition in 1977. This is not a third edition. It now covers only private law. It has been expanded to give an overview of private law rather than a deeper view of selected topics. It includes materials on law in the United States and England. It may therefore be of use in teaching comparative law in continental countries. It may also raise questions about to what extent one can oppose the "common law" of England and the United States to the "civil law" of France and Germany.

While it is not a third edition, it is a continuation of the spirit of the original work. Although it contains some introductory readings, the core of the book is still the statutes, codes and judicial decisions of the jurisdictions it covers. The inspiration is that of von Mehren's original book: that in these materials, law and the differences among laws are to be found, not in easy generalities about what the law of a particular jurisdiction may be or how "common law" and "civil law" may differ.

I am grateful to Christian Beinecke, Ole Lando, and Reinhard Zimmermann for their valuable suggestions and to Eva Vogt for her help in research.

JAMES GORDLEY

This book has many differences from the two earlier volumes than the discussions in the first, and more particularly the second editions of the civil law system contained. Professor Gordley's approach to the subject matter is somewhat different and reflects more recent developments in areas that were touched upon in the earlier volumes. There are, obviously, important differences in the coverage and analysis of the several volumes. Professor Gordley has provided an insightful and cosmopolitan view of the problems and institutions he described. Time and circumstances make it impossible for me to analyze the new materials; suffice it to say that Professor Gordley's work will be very useful for scholars and practitioners of international law.

ARTHUR T. VON MEHREN

*

In memoriam

———————

Less than a month after writing this preface, Arthur von Mehren died at the age of eighty-three. It was privilege to have worked with him. If one could dedicate a book to a co-author, I would dedicate this one to him and to the spirit of his work.

JAMES GORDLEY

Acknowledgments

The authors and publisher would like to thank the following for permission to reproduce copyright material: John Dawson, *The Oracles of the Law* (University of Michigan, 1968); Peter Stein, *Roman Law in European History* (English language translation © Cambridge University Press) (Cambridge University Press, 1999) (originally published in German by Fischer Taschenbuch); John H. Langbein 'The German Advantage in Civil Procedure' *University of Chicago Law Review 52* (1985) (University of Chicago Law School, 1985), 823; Konrad Zweigert and Hein Kötz *An Introduction to Comparative Law* (Tony Weir, trans., 3rd edition) (Oxford University Press, 1998) (originally published as *Einführung in die Rechtsvergleichung* (3rd Edition) (Mohr Siebeck, 1996); George A. Bermann, Roger J. Goebel, William J. Davey and Eleanor Fox, *Cases and Material on European Union Law* (2nd edition) (West Publishing, 2002).

*

Table of Abbreviations

A.	Atlantic Reporter
All E.R.	All England Law Reports
Am. Dec.	American Decisions
App.	Appellate Court
App. Div.	Appellate Division
BB	Betriebs-Berater
B. & C.	Barnewell and Creswell's Reports
Barn. & Adl.	Barnewell and Adophus' Reports
Best & S.	Best and Smith's Reports
BGHSt.	Entscheidungen des Bundesgerichtshof in Strafsachen
BGHZ	Entscheidungen des Bundesgerichtshof in Zivilsachen
Bull. civ.	Bulletin des arrêts de la Cour de cassation, chambres civiles
Burr.	Burrow's Reports
BVerfG	Entscheidungen des Bundesverfussungsgericht
C.A.	Court of Appeal
Cai.	Caines' Reports
Cal. App.	California Appellate Reports
Cal. Rptr.	California Reporter
Ch.	Chancery
ch. civ.	chambre civile
ch. Crim	chambre criminelle
ch. req.	chambre des requêtes
ch. soc.	chambre sociale
CLR	Commonwealth Law Reports
COM	Commission Proposal
D.	Recueil Dalloz
D.A.	Recueil Dalloz Analytique
D.C.	Recueil Dalloz Critique
D.H.	Recueil Dalloz Hebdomadaire de Jurisprudence
Dig.	Digest of Justinian
DLR	Dominion Law Reports
D.P.	Recueil Dalloz Périodique et Critique
DR	Deutsches Recht
D.S.	Recueil Dalloz Sirey
EBVerfG	Entscheidungen des Bundesverfassungsgerichts
Eng. Rep	English Reports
Ex.	Exchequer
F.	Federal Reporter

Fed. Cas.	Federal Cases
F.R.D.	Federal Rules Decisions
F. Supp.	Federal Supplement
Gaz. Pal.	Gazette du Palais
Gray	Gray's Reports
H.L.	House of Lords
Inst.	Institutes of Justinian
IR	Informations rapides
J	Jurisprudence
JCP	Juris Classeur Périodique
JR	Juristische Rundschau
JZ	Juristen-Zeitung
K.B.	King's Bench
L.R.	Law Reports
Met.	Metcalf's Reports
Mun. Ct.	Municipal Court
N.E.	Northeastern Reporter
NI	Northern Ireland Law Reports
NJW	Neue Juristische Wochenschrift
NJW-RR	Neue Juristische Wochenschrift-Rechtsprechungs-Report Zivilrecht
N.W.	Northwestern Reporter
N.Y.S.	New York Supplement
O.J.	Official Journal of the European Union
P.	Pacific Reporter
pan.	panorama de jurisprudence
P.C.	Judicial Committee of the Privy Council
Q.B	Queen's Bench
Rev. trim. dr. civ	Revue trimestrielle du droit civil
RGSt	Entscheidungen des Reichsgerichts in Strafsachen
RGZ	Entscheidungen des Reichsgerichts in Zivilsachen
S.	Recueil Sirey
S.C.	Session Cases
So.	Southern Reporter
S.E.	Southeastern Reporter
Super.	Superior Court
S.W.	Southwestern Reporter
Strange	Strange's Reports
T.L.R.	Times Law Reports
U.S.	United States Reports
VersR	Versicherungs Recht
W.L.R.	Weekly Law Reports

*

Table of Cases

Table of Legislation

Table of Restatements and Kindred Sources

Table of EU Legislation and Kindred Sources

Table of Roman and Canon Law Sources

Roman law

Digest of Justinian

1.1.9, 414
2.14.1.3, 414
4.4.16.4, 461
7.47.1, 542
8.1.8, 198
8.1.15, 198
8.3.3.2, 198
8.3.5.1, 198
8.4.13, 198
8.5.8.5, 168, 169, 171
8.5.8.6, 168
8.6.14.1, 213
9.2.2, 214
9.2.5.3, 237
9.2.7.4, 237
9.2.11, 354
9.2.31, 354
9.2.49.1, 213
10.4.19, 213
13.6.17.3, 414
13.6.18, 495
18.1.9, 448, 456
18.1.11.1, 449
19.1.1, 528
19.2.22.3, 461
42.1.13.1, 528
43.27.1, 213
44.7.1.4, 495
45.1.137, 495, 498

47.2.21.7, 236
47.2.43, 144
47.10.15.1, 236
47.10.15.2, 236
47.10.15.20, 236
47.10.15.21, 236
47.10.15.22, 236
47.10.15.27, 236
47.10.15.29, 236
47.10.15.34, 236
47.10.44, 168
50.17.185, 495
50.17.206, 552

Institutes of Gaius

3.88, 236
4.5, 382

Institutes of Justinian

1.2.1, 414
2.1 (12), 141
2.1 (13), 141, 142
2.1(39), 146
3.13.22–26, 413
3.14, 413

Canon law

Decretum of Gratian

C. 3, q. 1., c. 3., 154
C. 22, q. 2., C. 14, 503
D. 1, c. 2, 213
D.47, c. 8, 214

INTRODUCTORY READINGS

INTRODUCTORY READINGS

These readings are merely background for the materials that appear later on the law of property, tort, contract, and unjust enrichment.

It has often been said that there are two major differences between the common law and the civil law traditions. First, the common law was created by English courts. The civil law emerged from Roman law. Second, the common law is still largely case law. Civil law, in most continental countries, has been codified. To what extent they matter will be studied when we turn to the law of property, tort, contract and unjust enrichment. These initial readings will merely introduce them.

They will also introduce the courts and lawyers who administer the law in common and civil law jurisdictions as well as the authorities of the European Union who now have considerable influence in shaping private law.

I. HISTORY: ENGLISH LAW AND ROMAN LAW

1. English law

a. The early English legal profession

John Dawson, *The Oracles of the Law* (1968), 1–6, 38–39

The royal judges who succeeded in organizing the English common law so rapidly were always few in number. Their success was primarily due to the exceptional strength of the monarchy they served, but so much could not have been done by so few if effective means had not been invented for organizing their own work. By delegating and subdividing the judicial function, the central court judges relieved themselves of many time-consuming and burdensome tasks while retaining general supervision and effective power to coordinate. It thus became possible for a very small group of judges and, when it emerged, a very small group of expert pleaders to administer the central controls of the whole common law system of remedies. As their work rapidly became extremely technical and highly specialized, the judges and the most expert pleaders grew together in a remarkable kind of partnership. The English legal tradition was carried forward by this small elite group, in which the judges were acknowledged leaders but merely as first among equals. This group acquired a dominant role by expertise in a very special and narrow function and did much to ensure that the common law would be narrow, insular, and incapable of responding to newly emerging needs.

1. *The Formative Period*

Before the death of Henry II in 1189 the main institutions had been devised through which, in less than a century, a national common law would be created. One of the main institutions was the Court of Common Pleas, with which this account will be much concerned. A group of men who specialized in judicial business emerged from the king's entourage in the 1170s. It rapidly developed a separate record and organized its procedure, though jurisdictional boundaries were not yet defined. It ceased to follow the king on his travels and came to be held in "a certain place," as Magna Carta, in 1215, required. The place was usually Westminster. But Henry II had devised expedients by which trials could be decentralized. Routine cases were heard in the localities where the disputes arose. The more difficult and interesting cases were reported back for decision, or at least for discussion, at Westminster. This ingenious system of itinerant justices helped greatly to promote the popularity and effectiveness of the new royal remedies, but it also preserved uniformity in their administration and made the law that was built around the new remedies a truly national law.[1]

The law developed so rapidly that Bracton, writing in the middle decades of the thirteenth century, was able to describe a great system of law and procedure, manufactured out of native materials. Legislation had played a minor part in producing it. The solid core was English custom, a synthesis or abstraction that was derived from the usages of many English communities, but did not coincide precisely with any of these. The reiterated experience of royal judges in deciding cases and their frequent, informal consultation brought consistency and structure and made the rules into a system. It is therefore no exaggeration to say that the English common law from the very beginning was created by the royal judges who administered the new royal remedies.

One striking thing about it was that these royal judges at all times were so few. A contrast with France will make this more clear. By 1297 the highest royal court in France—the Parlement of Paris—had 51 judges. The total rose to 80 in the following century and to 240 in the eighteenth century. By the eighteenth century, however, twelve other Parlements had been created and the total membership of all thirteen of these high appellate courts was over 1,200. In addition, there were at least 5,000 judges in the inferior royal courts in France and to them could be added some tens of thousands of judges (many of them part-time) in the seignorial courts of the feudal lordships.[2] But in thirteenth century England the Court of Common Pleas ordinarily numbered four or five judges and the King's Bench when it emerged as a separate court, usually had only

1. Frederick Pollock & Frederic William Maitland, History of English Law (2d ed., 1898), I 153–56, 169–70 [hereafter cited as Pollock & Maitland, H.E.L.]; Sir William Holdsworth, History of English Law, I 264–84 [hereafter cited as Holdsworth, H.E.L.].

2. J.P. Dawson, A History of Lay Judges (Cambridge, Mass., 1960), 69–71, 79.

three.[3] In later times the total membership of the two courts remained about the same—seven or eight—though with variations from year to year.[4] Then in the sixteenth century, when the court of Exchequer acquired a general common law jurisdiction, its complement of judges (four or five) should be added to the total of common law judges. If we ignore the specialized jurisdictions like the Admiralty and the church courts but if the two judges of the Chancery are added, one can make the point shortly by saying that from 1200 to 1800 the permanent judges of the central courts of common law and Chancery, all taken together, rarely exceeded fifteen.

Our present concern is not with the surfeit of judges in France but with the strict economy in judicial manpower that was practiced in England. This strict economy was maintained not only during the rapid growth of the thirteenth century but, as I have said, for centuries thereafter. On first view it would seem a miracle that seven or eight (or later, twelve or thirteen) common law judges could handle all the trials and appellate review of an entire country.

The explanation is partly found in the fact that the coverage of the common law system of remedies was for long severely limited. In the ordering of English society it was a matter of the utmost importance that the crown acquired early a monopoly over prosecutions for major crime, but there remained an enormous range of minor offenses that were punished in the hundred courts, the courts of the manors and towns, and later by the justices of the peace, over whom the central courts exercised a control that was at most sporadic. Civil litigation dealt with the affairs of the relatively prosperous. For most of the population the 40 shilling limit of value on actions brought in royal courts was an effective barrier; forty shillings in the late Middle Ages was a considerable sum of money.[5] In the thirteenth century records so far published, civil litigation was primarily concerned with title to and possession of freehold land, but it seems unlikely that at that time

---

3. Maitland gave lists of the Common Pleas judges under Henry III (1216–72) in his introduction to Bracton's Note Book (Maitland ed., London, 1887), I 139–45. The numbers ranged from 2 to 8 (in one term 9 are listed). There were frequent changes both in numbers and names from term to term, though in the latter part of the reign the membership became more stabilized. Of the 181 terms listed by Maitland, there were 66 in which 5 or more judges were listed, mostly in the early years, but the number of judges that appeared most frequently was 4 (49 terms). The next most frequent was 3 (45 terms), and there were only 2 judges in 32 terms. It is interesting and significant that the strong tendency was for the numbers to diminish rather than to increase with the enlarged workload of the later years.

For the reigns of Edward I (1272–1307) and Edward II (1307–27) lists of judges are given by Sayles, Introduction, Select Cases in the Court of King's Bench (Selden Society),

I cxxix–cxli. Under Edward I the Common Pleas had either 4 or 5 judges, and the King's Bench 3 during most of the terms. Under Edward II the Common Pleas had 5 as a rule (though about one-third of the time there were 6), and the King's Bench was stabilized at 3.

4. Sayles, King's Bench (Selden Society), VI li–lxxxi, gives lists which show in the King's Bench from 1341–99 either 2 or 3 judges in 104 of the 114 terms listed, but in 76 of these terms there were only 2. From 1399–1422 the King's Bench had 3 judges in 31 out of 47 terms and 4 judges in the other 16 terms. In both these periods the Common Pleas was much more variable; in two terms it had only one judge and in 13 it had 7, but in almost four-fifths of the terms between 1340 and 1422 its membership ranged between 4 and 6.

Professor Sayles has been most obliging in allowing me to see these lists in advance of publication.

5. Dawson, Lay Judges, 228–29.

much more than half the occupants of thirteenth century English land held by freehold tenure.[6] Disputes over land between unfree tenants, like most disputes of other kinds, were settled in the local courts of county, hundred, manor, and town. Many types of disputes were wholly excluded because no royal writ had been devised. Altogether one can say that at the time of its creation the common law system was remarkable for its range, for its impact on English society and for the power that it mobilized, but that it captured only the key controls, over matters of paramount interest to the crown. In later centuries the emphasis shifted,[7] new types of interests were recognized, and the coverage of the writs expanded somewhat. But the expansion was gradual and through most of the later Middle Ages the disputes and misdeeds of most Englishmen were still remitted to local courts.

A second major explanation can be found in the measures adopted to economize on judges' time. It will be remembered that in the thirteenth century witnesses did not testify before jury and judges in open court. It was for the jurors themselves to find answers to the questions asked them, using their own private knowledge, gossip in the community, or such other sources as they could tap. By the use of a collective verdict, the sources of their knowledge and the ignorance or dissent of individual members were all effectively buried. This meant that trials could mainly consist of asking the jury the appropriate questions and compelling them to give their answers. It also meant that for many trials no royal justice was needed at all. And so the practice developed in the thirteenth century of appointing judicial commissions of local gentry, "knights of the shire." There were several types. For criminal cases the most common commissions were *oyer* and *terminer* (giving authority to "hear and determine" the classes of criminal cases specified) and gaol delivery (giving authority to hear the accusations and render judgment against prisoners already confined in designated jails). For civil cases the most common commission was the commission of assize, giving authority to hear the possessory assizes, such as novel disseisin or mort d'ancestor. The commissions could be fairly inclusive (all the cases of a certain class that were pending in a certain county) or could designate a case between particular persons. Very large numbers of commissions were issued; in the year 1273 alone some 2,000 commissions of assize were issued.[8] In many of these, it seems quite clear, no central court judge was included at all. Or if one was included, he would share with local gentry the burden of conducting trials, the burden itself being immensely reduced by casting on the jury so large a share of the principal task.

---

6. G.O. Sayles, Medieval Foundations of England (Philadelphia, 1950), 433 estimates that in the manorialized areas (central, eastern and southern England) the ratio of freeholders to unfree tenants was about 4:6. On the other hand, in the north and west the percentage of freeholders was probably somewhat larger.

7. The tabulations of Miss Neilson in The English Government at Work, 1327–36 (ed. Dunham, Cambridge, Mass., 1950), III 259 and 273, indicate that in the 1300s disputes over possession of or title to land were

becoming a smaller percentage of the workload. Out of some 6,000 cases pending in the Common Pleas in Hilary term, 1332, over 1550 cases were actions of account, about 1,000 were actions of debt, and detinue and trespass were about 500 each. Similar conclusions are expressed by Sayles, King's Bench (Selden Society), IV xxxviii. By 1470 debt and trespass cases had apparently come to predominate. Neilson, Introduction, Y.B. 10 Edw. IV and 49 Henry VI (Selden Society), xix, xxiv.

8. Pollock & Maitland, H.E.L., I 200–01.

And so it was no miracle that so much was accomplished by so few men. The judicial function in thirteenth century England was in effect divided up and distributed through the community. The finding of facts—the most troublesome and time-consuming function of all—was entrusted to the jury, "the voice of the countryside." [9] Direction of the jury, the framing of the questions they must answer, the extraction and recording of the answers they gave, were entrusted in large measure to responsible laymen, often without help from any judges at all. In the fourteenth century, as we shall see, the trial commission came to include a larger professional element. But even then, and for centuries thereafter, the basic arrangements of the formative years persisted. Their net result was that a small group of professional judges could handle the work quite well. The great bulk of routine litigation did not require their attention at all, or at most would require them to extract a verdict from jurors on disputed issues of fact. In the select group of cases that called for joint action by the judges, their task was primarily to supervise the process by which issues of fact were reached. They could concentrate on the difficult problems that preceded or followed resort "to the country." They were mainly concerned with framing and applying rules of law. At this they became superbly skilled.

Not much is known of the training and background of the earliest royal judges. One thing is clear—most of the regular judges were churchmen. Some were bishops, there was even an archbishop, and many held minor church offices. How much canon law they knew is a question, though a normal career reaching through the lower orders up to high office in the church would almost surely have meant some exposure to canonist ideas.[10] In any case it is hard to imagine what other legal training they could have had, for the rules that governed the royal remedies were in process of being manufactured by the judges themselves. As the system developed, until 1250 at least, the crown continued to draw on the clergy as the principal source of educated and able men. Bracton himself was a cleric, as were his heroes, Raleigh and Pateshull. But like other clerical judges of that early period whose careers are known, they must have expended most of their energies, not on the cure of souls, but in the king's service and especially on their own judicial duties.

---

9. The phrase is that of Maitland in Pollock & Maitland, H.E.L., II 624.

10. The problem as to how much canon law was known by the early justices has been much debated, for it is part of the larger problem of the extent of direct borrowing from Roman law, with which any well-trained canonist was bound to be broadly familiar. The argument for Roman influence has been strongly put by H.G. Richardson, "The Oxford Law School under John," 57 L.Q.R. 319 (1941), who pointed out (at p. 323) that Hubert Walter, archbishop of Canterbury and justiciar under Richard I, was one of the Englishmen who studied Roman law at Bologna. But his argument in this article and by Richardson and Sayles, Introduction, Select Cases of Procedure without Writ (Selden Society), lix–lx, cviii–cxxxiv, tends mainly to show that Roman law conceptions were filtering in through the work of notaries and draftsmen of pleadings. As to the royal justices themselves, Maitland's comment still seems persuasive: "We attribute to these clerical justices in general no more than a superficial acquaintance with the canon law, an acquaintance with its main principles and methods. But this much we must attribute to them, and it means a great deal . . . Viewed therefore from one point, the effect produced on English law by its contact with the romano-canonical learning seems immeasurable, or measured only by the distance that divides Glanvill's treatise from the *Leges Henrici*." Pollock & Maitland, H.E.L., I 133–34.

The volume of judicial business and the complications of the legal system rapidly grew so great that close study and special competence were plainly needed. Whether or not Bracton himself had formal training in Roman law, he had acquired mastery of English law and procedure. It may well be that for him, as for others, the path to learning was a kind of apprenticeship to older royal judges.[11] It seems quite clear in any case that the active and able judges of this early time were acquiring on-the-job training of a very high order. As Bracton's treatise showed, Roman law could give enormous help in organizing this fund of knowledge and without this help the work of organization might have been long postponed. But the knowledge itself was certainly for the most part English. When Bracton stopped writing in 1256 a great structure had been erected by English judges with almost no help from practicing lawyers and with amazing speed—in less than 100 years.

Even in Bracton's life time, however, practicing lawyers had begun to appear and more would clearly be needed.

* * *

Deep obscurity surrounds the process by which the common lawyers developed their own system of vocational training. It seems plain enough that from an early time—certainly by the late 1200s—young men were attracted to London to study law. A "crib" was reserved for infant lawyers within earshot of the Common Pleas bench.[3] They were probably true "apprentices," in the sense that they attached themselves to older lawyers and watched their work, did some drafting under supervision, and in return picked up scraps of legal knowledge. Like others who shared common interests—like the students in the universities—they probably gathered in small guilds, eating, sleeping, and talking together. These groups for some time must have made their own arrangements, renting houses, then disbanding or shifting from place to place among the houses and taverns of Holborn. Through the fourteenth century there were scattered references to buildings in which "apprentices" lived.[4] We can only guess

---

11. This suggestion that Bracton was trained through his clerkship to Raleigh was made by Pollock & Maitland, H.E.L., I 205–06, and developed by Lady Stenton, Introduction, Rolls of the Justices in Eyre for Lincolnshire and Worcestershire (Selden Society), xv–xxiv, and T.F.T. Plucknett, Early English Legal Literature (Cambridge, England, 1958), 44–48. Richardson presented an opposing view in "Azo, Drogheda and Bracton," 59 Eng. Hist. Rev. 22 (1944), and Bracton, The Problems of His Text (London, 1965), 3–8, arguing that Bracton was probably trained by studying Roman and canon law at Oxford. This question in turn becomes tangled up with the continuing dispute as to how good a Romanist Bracton was. Recent writings on this subject are reviewed by Plucknett, Early English Legal Literature, 61–79.

3. Above, section 2, note 8.

4. In 1329 one of the judges referred to the apprentices leaving their "hostels." R.V. Rogers, "Law Reporting and the Multiplication of Law Reports in the Fourteenth Century," 66 Eng. Hist. Rev. 481, 482 (1951).

In 1356 a Year Book argument referred to an exception that had never been allowed in the Common Pleas "but we have heard it often among the apprentices in the hostels." Y.B. 29 Edw. III, Mich., 47.

W.B. Odgers, "A Sketch of the History of the Four Inns of Court," Essays in Legal History (ed. Sir Paul Vinogradoff, London, 1913), 233, 243–49, has shown that Coke misread the will of John Tavy, armorer, who in 1349 devised a house "in which the apprentices used to dwell." The apprentices referred to were not apprentices of law but young men who had studied under Tavy to be armorers.

when it was that they settled down in the locations that were to be permanent. By 1381 at least one such location had been occupied, for a chronicle reports that the rebels in the Peasants' Revolt sacked "the Temple Bar where dwelt the apprentices of the law." [5]

As with the Order of the Coif, the Inns of Court became so familiar a feature of the English tradition, that there has been a strong inclination to assign them great antiquity, though no one has yet claimed that they preceded the Norman Conquest.[6] Yet their very uniqueness, which has been to Englishmen a source of pride, should give one pause. In the countries of Europe whose experience will be here reviewed, there is hardly a trace of a similar phenomenon—organized instruction in law conducted by practitioners in technical schools under their own control. One can well understand why young men who were ambitious to be lawyers in late medieval England felt an urgent need for guidance through the jungle that lay before them. For some time, however, there were real questions whether and how the need would be met.

We grope in darkness in attempting to discover how the roving guilds of students in the fourteenth century secured from senior lawyers the guidance and help they needed. For any kind of organized instruction the vacations would be the time. Then both practitioners and students would be free from the distractions of court attendance. An older lawyer, inspired by family friendship or personal interest, might assemble a few young men and spare them some time in the vacations, running through important statutes and perhaps some Year Book cases. By 1363, at least, it seems that for young men with serious intent the period of study stretched through most of the year, not merely the seventeen weeks of the terms of court.[7] Over decades many experiments must have been tried, with many variations in subjects and methods of instruction. It could even be that patterns of teaching developed and were passed along through groups of younger men that were tied by family connections or common geographical origin. Sustained leadership was probably not given by the most eminent pleaders nor was it to be later by the serjeants of the Coif, who formally terminated membership in their Inns of Court on assuming the rank of serjeant. Even by the mid-1300s the most eminent pleaders

5. Holdsworth, H.E.L., II 495. But the fuller quotation from the same chronicle in Dugdale, Origines Juridiciales, c. 57, p. 145 indicates that the attack was not inspired by the usual first impulse of revolutionaries to "kill the lawyers" but by hatred of one Robert Hales, who evidently resided there.

6. For example, Bolland, "The Training of a Medieval Justice," in Cambridge Legal Essays (1926), 57, asserted that by 1250 "at the latest" there were organized law schools whose certificates the judges accepted as qualification for the right of audience. A statement that has had great influence is that of Sir Frederick Pollock, "The Origins of the Inns of Court," 48 L.Q.R. 163, 166 (1932): ". . . the constitution of the Inns of Court was settled about the middle of the fourteenth century on the lines which in all essentials are much the same as at this day." R.J. Fletcher, Introduction, Pension Book of Gray's Inn (London, 1901), ix–xv, is more conservative, claiming no more than that the Inns were fully organized by the middle of the fifteenth century.

7. In 1363 one Richard of Norwich was granted a royal exemption from service as coroner because he was "staying at London the greater part of the year as an apprentice of the Common Bench upon his education among other apprentices thereof." Cal. Close Rolls, 1360–64, 481.

had little free time in vacations, when they were heavily engaged in conducting trials.

b. The writ system

F.W. Maitland, *The Forms of Action at Common Law* (A.H. Chaytor & W.J. Whittaker ed. 1909), Lecture I.

I propose to begin by speaking briefly of the Forms of Action, with especial relation to those which protected the possession and ownership of land. It may—I am well aware of it—be objected that procedure is not a good theme for academic discussion. Substantive law should come first—adjective law, procedural law, afterwards. The former may perhaps be studied in a University, the latter must be studied in chambers. As to obsolete procedure, a knowledge of it can be profitable to no man, least of all to a beginner. With this opinion I cannot agree. Some time ago I wished to say a little about seisin, which still, with all our modern improvements, is one of the central ideas of Real Property Law; but to say that little I found impossible if I could not assume some knowledge of the forms of action. Let us remember one of Maine's most striking phrases, "So great is the ascendancy of the Law of Actions in the infancy of Courts of Justice, that substantive law has at first the look of being gradually secreted in the interstices of procedure." [1] Assuredly this is true of our real property law, it has been secreted in the interstices of the forms of action. The system of Forms of Action or the Writ System is the most important characteristic of English medieval law, and it was not abolished until its piecemeal destruction in the nineteenth century.[2]

What was a form of action? Already owing to modern reforms it is impossible to assume that every law student must have heard or read or discovered for himself an answer to that question, but it is still one which must be answered if he is to have more than a very superficial knowledge of our law as it stands even at the present day. The forms of action we have buried, but they still rule us from their graves. Let us then for awhile place ourselves in Blackstone's day, or, for this matters not, some seventy years later in 1830, and let us look for a moment at English civil procedure.

Let it be granted that one man has been wronged by another; the first thing that he or his advisers have to consider is what form of action he shall bring. It is not enough that in some way or another he should compel his adversary to appear in court and should then state in the words that naturally occur to him the facts on which he relies and the remedy to which he thinks himself entitled. No, English law knows a certain number of forms of action, each with its own uncouth name, a writ of right, an assize of novel disseisin or of *mort a'ancestor*, a writ of entry "*sur disseisin*" in the *per* and *cui*, a writ of *besaiel*, of *quare impedit*, an action of covenant, debt, detinue, replevin, trespass, assumpsit, ejectment, case. This choice is

---

1. Maine, Early Law and Custom, 389.   2. See Post, p. 301.

not merely a choice between a number of queer technical terms, it is a choice between methods of procedure adapted to cases of different kinds. Let us notice some of the many points that are implied in it:

(i) There is the competence of the court. For very many of the ordinary civil cases each of the three courts which have grown out of the king's court of early days, the King's Bench, Common Pleas and Exchequer is equally competent, though it is only by means of elaborate and curious fictions that the King's Bench and the Exchequer can entertain these matters, and the Common Pleas still retains a monopoly of those actions which are known as real.

(ii) A court chosen, one must make one's adversary appear; but what is the first step towards this end? In some actions one ought to begin by having him summoned, in others one can at once have him attached, he can be compelled to find gage and pledge for his appearance. In the assize of novel disseisin it is enough to attach his bailiff.

(iii) Suppose him contumacious, what can one do? Can one have his body seized? If he cannot be found, can one have him outlawed? This stringent procedure has been extending itself from one form of action to another. Again, can one have the thing in dispute seized? This is possible in some actions, impossible in others.

(iv) Can one obtain a judgment by default, obtain what one wants though the adversary continues in his contumacy? Yes in some forms, no in others.

(v) It comes to pleading, and here each form of action has some rules of its own. For instance the person attacked—the tenant he is called in some cases, the defendant in others—wishes to oppose the attacker—the demandant he is called in some actions, the plaintiff in others—by a mere general denial, casting upon him the burden of proving his own case, what is he to say? In other words, what is the general issue appropriate to this action? In one form it is *Nihil debet*, in another *Non assumpsit*, in another "Not guilty," in others, *Nul tort, nul disseisin*.

(vi) There is to be a trial; but what mode of trial? Very generally of course a trial by jury. But it may be trial by a grand or petty assize, which is not quite the same thing as trial by jury; or in Blackstone's day it may still conceivably be a trial by battle. Again in some forms of action the defendant may betake himself to the world-old process of compurgation or wager of law. Again there are a few issues which are tried without a jury by the judges who bear witnesses.

(vii) Judgment goes against the defendant, what is the appropriate form of execution? Can one be put into possession of the thing that has been in dispute? Can one imprison the defendant? Can one have him made an outlaw? or can he merely be distrained?

(viii) Judgment goes against the defendant. It is not enough that he should satisfy the plaintiff's just demand; he must also be punished for his breach of the law—such at all events is the theory. What form shall this punishment take? Will an amercement suffice, or shall there be fine or imprisonment? Here also there have been differences.

(ix) Some actions are much more dilatory than others; the dilatory ones have gone out of use, but still they exist. In these oldest forms—forms invented when as yet the parties had to appear in person and could only appoint attorneys by the king's special leave—the action may drag on for years, for the parties enjoy a power of sending essoins, that is, excuses for non-appearance. The medieval law of essoins is vast in bulk; time is allowed for almost every kind of excuse for non-appearance—a short essoin *de malo veniendi, a long* essoin *de malo lecti.* Now-a-days all is regulated by rules with a wide discretion left in the Court. In the Middle Ages discretion is entirely excluded; all is to be fixed by iron rules. This question of essoins has been very important— in some forms, the oldest and solemnest, a party may betake himself to his bed and remain there for year and day and meanwhile the action is suspended.

These remarks may be enough to show that the differences between the several forms of action have been of very great practical importance— 'a form of action' has implied a particular original process, a particular mesne process, a particular final process, a particular mode of pleading, of trial, of judgment. But further to a very considerable degree the substantive law administered in a given form of action has grown up independently of the law administered in other forms. Each procedural pigeon-hole contains its own rules of substantive law, and it is with great caution that we may argue from what is found in one to what will probably be found in another; each has its own precedents. It is quite possible that a litigant will find that his case will fit some two or three of these pigeon-holes. If that be so he will have a choice, which will often be a choice between the old, cumbrous, costly, on the one hand, the modern, rapid, cheap, on the other. Or again he may make a bad choice, fail in his action, and take such comfort as he can from the hints of the judges that another form of action might have been more successful. The plaintiff's choice is irrevocable; he must play the rules of the game that he has chosen. Lastly he may find that, plausible as his case may seem, it just will not fit any one of the receptacles provided by the courts and he may take to himself the lesson that where there is no remedy there is no wrong.

The key-note of the form of action is struck by the original writ, the writ whereby the action is begun. From of old the rule has been that no one can bring an action in the king's courts of common law without the king's writ; we find this rule in Bracton—*Non potest quis sine brevi agere.*[3] That rule we may indeed say has not been abolished even in our own day. The first step

3. Bract. F. 413b.

which a plaintiff has to take when he brings an action in the High Court of Justice is to obtain a writ. But there has been a very great change. The modern writ is in form a command by the king addressed to the defendant telling him no more than that within eight days he is to appear, or rather to cause an appearance to be entered for him, in an action at the suit of the plaintiff, and telling him that in default of his so doing the plaintiff may proceed in his action and obtain a judgment. Then on the back of this writ the plaintiff, in his own or his adviser's words, states briefly the substance of his claim— 'The plaintiff's claim is £1,000 for money lent,' 'The plaintiff's claim is for damages for breach of contract to employ the plaintiff as traveller,' 'The plaintiff's claim is for damages for assault and false imprisonment,' 'The plaintiff's claim is to recover a farm called Blackacre situate in the parish of Dale in the county of Kent.' We can no longer say that English law knows a certain number of actions and no more, or that every action has a writ appropriate to itself; the writ is always the same, the number of possible endorsements is as infinite as the number of unlawful acts and defaults which can give one man an action against another. All this is new. Formerly there were a certain number of writs which differed very markedly from each other. A writ of debt was very unlike a writ of trespass, and both were very unlike a writ of *mort a'ancestor* or a writ of right. A writ of debt was addressed to the sheriff; the sheriff is to command the defendant to pay to the plaintiff the alleged debt, or, if he will not do so, appear in court and answer why he has not done so. A writ of trespass is addressed to the sheriff; he is to attach the defendant to answer the plaintiff why with force and arms and against the king's peace he broke the plaintiff's close, or carried off his goods, or assaulted and beat him. A writ of *mort a'ancestor* bade the sheriff empanel a jury, or rather an assize, to answer a certain question formulated in the writ. A writ of right was directed not to the sheriff but to the feudal lord and bade him do right in his court between the demandant and the tenant. In each case the writ points to a substantially different procedure.

In the reign of Henry III Bracton had said *Tot erunt formulae brevium quot sunt genera actionum.*[4] There may be as many forms of action as there are causes of action. This suggests, what may seem true enough to us, that in order of logic Right comes before Remedy. There ought to be a remedy for every wrong; if some new wrong be perpetrated then a new writ may be invented to meet it. Just in Bracton's day it may have been possible to argue in this way; the king's court and the king's chancery—it was in the chancery that the writs were made—enjoyed a certain freedom which they were to lose as our parliamentary constitution became definitely established. A little later though the chancery never loses a certain power of varying the old formulas to suit new cases and this power was recognized by statute, still it is used but very cautiously. Court and chancery are conservative and Parliament is jealous of all that looks like an attempt to legislate without its concurrence. The argument from Right to Remedy is reversed and Bracton's saying is truer if we make it run

---

4. Bract. F. 413b. A whole group of these forms is ascribed to Bracton's master, W. Raleigh—one might well have spoken of *actions Raleighamae.*

Tot erunt actiones quot sunt formulae brevium—the forms of action are given, the causes of action must be deduced therefrom.

Of course we must not for one moment imagine that seventy years ago or in Blackstone's day litigation was really and truly carried on in just the same manner as that in which it was carried on in the days of Edward I. In the first place many of the forms of action had become obsolete: they were theoretically possible but were never used. In the second place the words 'really and truly' seem hardly applicable to any part of the procedure of the eighteenth century, so full was it of fictions contrived to get modern results out of medieval premises: writs were supposed to be issued which in fact never were issued, proceedings were supposed to be taken which in fact never were taken. Still these fictions had to be maintained, otherwise the whole system would have fallen to pieces; anyone who would give a connected and rational account of the system was obliged—as Blackstone found himself obliged—to seek his starting point in a very remote age.

We will now briefly notice the main steps by which in the last century the forms of action were abolished. First we must observe that there was a well-known classification of the forms: they were (1) real, (2) personal, (3) mixed. I shall have to remark hereafter[5] that this classification had meant different things in different ages; Bracton would have called some actions personal which Blackstone would have called real or mixed. But at present it will be sufficient if we note Blackstone's definitions.[6]

Real actions, which concern real property only, are such whereby the plaintiff, here called the demandant, claims title to have any lands, or tenements, rents, commons, or other hereditaments in fee simple, fee tail or for term of life.

Personal actions are such whereby a man claims a debt, a personal duty, or damages in lieu thereof; and likewise, whereby a man claims a satisfaction in damages for some injury done to his person or property.

Mixed actions are suits partaking of the nature of the other two, wherein some real property is demanded, and also personal damages for a wrong sustained.

Now in 1833 the real and mixed actions were swept away at one fell swoop by the Real Property Limitation Act of that year, 3 and 4 Will. IV, c. 27, sec. 36. That section sets out the names of 60 actions and says that none of these and no other action real or mixed—except a writ of right of dower, a writ of dower, *unde nihil habet, a quare impedit*, or an ejectment—shall be brought after 31 December, 1834. Practically for a very long time past the action of ejectment, which in its origin was distinctly a personal action, had been made to do duty for all or almost all the actions that were now to be abolished. The *quare impedit* had become the regular action for the trial of all disputes about advowsons, and, as ejectment was here inapplicable, this had to be spared. There were special reasons for saving the two writs of dower, since the dowress could not bring ejectment until her dower had been set out. But they were abolished in 1860 by the Common Law Procedure Act of

---

5. See lecture V, *post.*   **6.** Bl. Comm. III, 117, 118.

that year (23 and 24 Vic., c. 126, sec. 26), and a new statutory action of a modern type was provided for the doweress. By the same Act, sec. 27, the old *quare impedit* was abolished and a new statutory action was put in its place.

Meanwhile in 1832 a partial assault had been made on the personal forms. The principal personal forms were these—Debt, Detinue, Covenant, Account, Trespass, Case, Trover, Assumpsit, Replevin. By 2 Will. IV, c. 39 (1832) "Uniformity of Process Act"—the process in these personal actions was reduced to uniformity. The old original writs were abolished and a new form of writ provided. In this writ, however, the plaintiff had to insert a mention of one of the known forms of action. Another heavy blow was struck in 1852 by the Common Law Procedure Act, 15 and 16 Vic., c. 76. It was expressly provided (sec. 3) that it should not be necessary to mention any form or cause of action in any writ of summons. But still this blow was not heavy enough—the several personal forms were still considered as distinct.

The final blow was struck by the Judicature Act of 1873 and the rules made thereunder, which came into force in 1875. This did much more than finally abolish the forms of actions known to the common law for it provided that equity and law should be administered concurrently. Since that time we have had what might fairly be called a Code of Civil Procedure. Of course we cannot here speak of the details of that Code; but you will not misunderstand me if I say that the procedure which it enjoins is comparatively formless. Of course there are rules, many rules.

We cannot say that whatever be the nature of the plaintiff's claim the action will always take the same course and pass through the same stages. For instance, when the plaintiff's claim falls within one of certain classes he can adopt a procedure[7] whereby when he has sworn positively to the truth of his claim the defendant can be shut out from defending the action at all unless he first makes oath to some good defence. So again there are cases in which either party can insist that the questions of fact, if any, shall be tried by jury; there are other cases in which there will be no trial by jury. Again, I must not allow you to think that a lawyer cannot do his client a great deal of harm by advising a bad or inappropriate course of procedure. Though it is true that he cannot bring about a total shipwreck of a good cause so easily as he might have done some years ago. The great change gradually brought about and consummated by the Judicature Acts is that the whole course of procedure in an action is not determined for good and all by the first step, by the original writ. It can no longer be said, as it might have been said in 1830 that we have about 72 forms of action, or as it might have been said in 1874 that we have about 12 forms of action. This is a different thing from saying that our English law no longer attempts to classify *causes* of action, on the contrary a rational, modern classification of causes of action is what we are gradually obtaining—but the forms of action belong to the past.

Since the Judicature Acts there are, of course, differences of procedure arising out of the character of the various actions, whether for

---

7. Commonly called (from the Order which authorizes this procedure) "Going under Order XIV."

divorce, probate of a will, specific performance of a contract: such differences there must be, but they can now be regarded as mere variations of one general theme—procedure in an action in the High Court of Justice. It was entirely otherwise in the Middle Ages, then lawyers say very little of the procedure in *an* action, very much of the procedure in some action of a particular kind, e.g. an assize of *mort d'ancestor* or an action of trespass. Knowledge of the procedure in the various forms of action is the core of English medieval jurisprudence. The Year Books are largely occupied by this. Glanvill plunges at once into the procedure in a writ of right. Bracton, with the Institutes scheme before him, gives about 100 folios to Persons and Things and about 350 to the law of Actions.

We can now attempt to draw some meagre outline of the general history of these forms of action, remembering however that a full history of them would be a full history of English private law.

Now I think that our first step should be to guard ourselves against the notion that from the very beginning it was the office or the king's own court or courts to provide a remedy for every wrong. This is a notion which we may but too easily adopt. In the first place it seems natural to us moderns, especially to us Englishmen, that in every decently governed country there should be some one tribunal, or some one definitely organized hierarchy of tribunals, fully competent to administer the whole law, to do right to every man in every case. In the second place it is true that in England such a scheme of centralized justice has existed from what, having regard to other countries, we may call a very remote time; it has existed for some five hundred years. Ever since Edward I's time, to name a date which is certainly not too recent, the law of England has to a very large extent been the law administered by the king's own courts, and to be without remedy in those courts has commonly been to be without any remedy at all. A moment's reflection will indeed remind us that we must use some such qualifying words as 'to a very large extent' when we lay down these wide propositions. Think for one moment of the copyholder, or of his predecessor the tenant in villeinage; he was not protected in his holding by the king's court, still to regard him as without rights would be a perversion of history. And then think of the ecclesiastical courts with their wide jurisdiction over matrimonial and testamentary causes; at least until the Reformation they were not in any sense the king's courts; their power was regarded as a spiritual power quite independent of the temporal power of the state. But in the third place we may be led into error by good masters. So long as the forms of action were still in use, it was difficult to tell the truth about their history. There they were, and it was the duty of judges and text writers to make the best of them, to treat them as though they formed a rational scheme provided all of a piece by some all-wise legislator. It was natural that lawyers should slip into the opinion that such had really been the case, to suppose, or to speak as though they supposed, that some great king (it matters not whether we call him Edward I or Edward the Confessor, Alfred or Arthur) had said to his wise men 'Go to now! a well ordered state should have a central tribunal, let us then with prudent forethought analyze all possible rights and provide a remedy for every imaginable wrong.' It was difficult to discover, difficult to tell, the truth, difficult to say that these forms of action belonged to very different ages, expressed very different and sometimes discordant theories of law, had been twisted and tortured to inappropriate uses, were the monuments of long forgotten political struggles; above all it was difficult to say of them that they had their origin and their explanation in a time when the king's court was but one among many courts. But now, when the forms of action are gone, when we are no longer under any temptation to make them more rational than they were, the truth might be discovered and be told, and one part of the truth is assuredly this that throughout the early history of the forms or action there is an element of struggle, of struggle for jurisdiction. In order to understand them we must not presuppose a centralized system of justice, an omni-competent royal or national tribunal; rather we must think that the forms of action, the original writs, are the means whereby justice is becoming centralized, whereby the king's court is drawing away business from other courts.[8]

Note: As Maitland mentions, the forms of action were abolished in the 19th century. Supposedly, despite the changes, judges still gave relief only in those cases in which the plaintiff would previously have been entitled to it. But during the 19th and early 20th centuries, the common law was recast into a form that is far more familiar today. In large part, the recasting was the work of treatise writers and courts who were sympathetic to their work. Before the 19th century, there were few treatises. The prevalent type of little legal literature were the reports and abridgements of decided cases. Blackstone's *Commentaries on the Laws of England* were the first attempt to describe the common law systematically.[1] The first treatise on the common law of contracts was written by Powell in 1794. The first treatise on the common law of torts was written by Hilliard in 1861.[2] Neither had the common law been taught in universities, again, with the exception of Blackstone. The treatise writers and university professors of the 19th and early 20th century treatise claimed that they were merely explaining what the judges had been doing all along. But, as we will see, this process meant that the substantive law was changed. It changed because in devising explanations for traditional rules, the treatise writers changed the rules themselves. It also changed because, in seeking explanations, they borrowed a vast amount from continental law which already had a systematic doctrinal structure. What they borrowed will be seen later, when we deal with property, tort, contract and unjust enrichment.

---

8.   As an example of the theory against which it is necessary to protest, see Blackstone's account of Alfred's exploits, Comm. IV. 411; "To him we owe that masterpiece of judicial polity, the subdivision of England into tithings and hundreds, if not into counties; all under the influence and administration of one supreme magistrate, the king; in whom as in a general reservoir, all the executive authority of the law was lodged, and from whom justice was dispersed to every part of the nation by distinct, yet communicating ducts and channels; which wise institution has been preserved for near a thousand years unchanged form Alfred's to the present time."

1.   William Blackstone, Commentaries on the Laws of England (1765–69).

2.   Francis Hilliard, The Law of Torts or Private Wrongs (1861), 83–4.

2. Roman law

John Dawson, *The Oracles of the Law* (1968), 100–09

If we reverse our time-machine and circle back to Roman law, we discover a landscape that could hardly seem more strange. None of the shapes with which we are familiar appear on first inspection. Instead of making judges into monumental figures, it seems that the Romans hid them in caves. In their places were various artifacts that depict our own experience no better than the stone carvings of Easter Island.

Many minds and much devotion have been applied to the reconstruction of Roman law. Each generation that has engaged in this continuing task has added elements from its own experience. Especially in examining the main foundations of the rebuilt structure, one finds it difficult to separate evidence as to origins from the driftings and accumulations of that long stretch of time—more than 800 years—since the study of Roman law was resumed in medieval Italy. A striking example of the intermixture that persists is a statement, heavily glossed with modern ideas, which purports to give the message of Roman law as modern society should understand it. The statement was made by Engelmann, a German legal historian, and was published in 1938:

> Precedent-justice is not only illogical but pernicious, because it interferes with the wiser conclusion of a later judge through the "prejudice" of the earlier judge and serves the comfort of the indolent judge. Its sway marks a lack of legal culture. (Precedent-justice rules where there is no scientific knowledge or theory to enrich and guide legal practice and legislation—it exists where legal practice teaches legal practice, as in England. Judges lacking independence favor it, since it is comfortable and saves effort, work and personal responsibility.) A mark of Rome's high legal culture is its systematic prohibition.[1]

This statement is no doubt extreme and seems to us perverse; surely few modern Germans would subscribe to it. It suggests, however, that Roman law has helped to maintain in western Europe some attitudes that still differ sharply from our own.

To discover what actually happened in Roman law it will be necessary again to travel rapidly. Between two important relics of Roman law, the Twelve Tables and Justinian's Code, the interval is nearly 1,000 years. For the present purpose most interest attaches to the classical period of Roman law (roughly 27 B.C.–235 A.D.).[2] The late empire up to the completion of the Corpus Juris (235 A.D.–535 A.D.) can be discussed more briefly. I will then consider some developments in medieval Italy, where

---

1. Woldemar Engelmann, Die Wiedergeburt der Rechtskultur in Italien (Leipzig, 1938), 29. The passage placed in parentheses appears in Engelmann's book in a footnote.

2. This conventional dating, fixing the start of the classical period at the advent to power of Augustus, is necessarily arbitrary. If "classical" method and style are traced to the great jurists of the republic, one can push the classical period back to 150 B.C. Franz Wieacker, "Ueber das Klassische in der römischen Jurisprudenz," in Vom römischen Recht (2d ed., Stuttgart, 1961), 161.

the main conclusions of Roman law were revised, adapted, and prepared for the use of later generations.

1. *The Relations of Iudex and Praetor in Classical Law*

The first point to note is that classical Roman law was mainly based on a procedural system that provided no place for professional judges. In the standard type of civil action, proceedings began with a hearing before a praetor, one of a group of magistrates who were elected annually. The purpose of this hearing was to define the issues in dispute. There followed a second, separate stage—a trial before a *iudex*, who was chosen ad hoc by consent of the parties and empowered by the praetor to render judgment. Both praetor and *iudex* usually lacked any training in law. Likewise in the other tribunals that were used under the late Republic judicial duties were assigned to laymen. In criminal cases the question of guilt was answered by assemblies of laymen, perhaps forty or more. There were other courts for civil cases, one type with some thirty to forty members and another with only three or five, but they were composed of laymen who were much more than jurors. They not only found the facts, as do our jurors, but they heard and rendered judgment on the whole case. This assignment of laymen to judicial duties is a central feature of Roman procedure at the time when Roman law was approaching full maturity but was still in its most creative phase.[1]

It was the praetorian order of civil procedure that the classical lawyers mainly discussed, even under the later principate when new forms of procedure had already emerged. It is therefore essential to examine the functions of praetor and praetorian *iudex* if one is to see why the surviving sources of Roman law make judges seem such shadowy figures.

In litigation between Roman citizens in the city of Rome, the governing principle was that any sane male citizen over the age of 25 could be chosen as *iudex* if the parties agreed. In practice the choice was usually made from a list of high-ranking citizens, prepared in advance. This list or panel, called the *album*, was established in the last century of the Roman Republic. At first it was used only for criminal cases and contained 450 members. The methods of choosing the membership changed from time to time and remained for fifty years a bitterly contested issue of Roman politics. Then in 70 B.C. a compromise was reached. Thereafter for several decades the *album*, prepared each year by the urban praetor, contained 900 members drawn equally from the three highest social classes—senators, knights, and *tribuni aerarii*, a commercial class that ranked in wealth just below the knights. The total of 900 was raised by Augustus to 4,000 and later by Caligula to 5,000, but property qualifications ensured that the persons certified as eligible were men of at least considerable wealth. This was the list, annually revised, from which the members of the assembly courts in criminal cases were exclusively chosen and the

---

1. A fuller discussion of this whole matter, with references, appears in Dawson, Lay Judges, 14–29. The functioning of Roman trial procedure in the classical period is referred to in a more recent account that is mainly concerned with post-classical developments. M.C. Ferguson, "A Day in Court in Justinian's Rome," 46 Iowa L. Rev. 732 (1961).

one-man *iudex* in civil cases was normally chosen.[2] Men on the *album* usually were not lawyers but men of wide experience in public or commercial affairs. They were drawn from the highest ranks of Roman society. Their trustworthiness and capacity were further ensured by the requirement of consent to their choice by the interested parties themselves.

It may have been partly for these reasons that the proceedings before the *iudex* were left so free of formal controls. There were no rules of evidence to restrict the inquiries of the *iudex* and there was no review of his findings of fact.[3] Furthermore, there was no appeal. Flagrant departures from procedural fairness (for example, bribery of the *iudex* or his failure to hear one of the parties at all) could invalidate the judgment rendered or lead to its cancellation through exceptional intervention by the praetor.[4] There was one other recourse. The *iudex* could become personally liable to the losing party if he had accepted a bribe or, perhaps, if he acted with manifest favoritism. But so far as surviving evidence indicates, this form of control, like the control reserved to the praetor himself, was rarely used in classical times. If his actions conformed to the formula which conferred his powers, the *iudex* in performing his judicial duties was almost wholly unhampered by procedural rules or appellate review. He was thus under no compulsion to formulate reasons or write an opinion. Judgments were rendered orally. So far as we know there was no effort made to state, much less to preserve, the grounds of the *iudices* for their decisions.

2. *The Case Law of Iudex and Praetor*

The apparent absence of a reporting system is at least an indication that the Romans of the classical period did not look to judicial decisions as an important source of innovation. For clearly if a decision by a praetorian *iudex* had been worth reporting, means could have been found. Written records were kept for many other purposes, by lawyers and others. But when one measures the gain against the effort involved, it seems plain enough why judicial reporting was not worth the effort. Each *iudex* was appointed to serve only in the particular case. Some might have been called on frequently; when called on it was their duty to serve, for the office of *iudex* was a public office which could be declined only for valid reasons. But for men of affairs, on whose time and energy there were many demands, service as *iudex* was a burden that had to be distributed and that many sought to escape.[1] Without some continuity of tenure there was little chance to develop expertise. As the *album* grew longer and came to comprise a multitude (a multitude that changed somewhat with each year's revision), communication of their experiences would face increasing difficulties. Furthermore, many issues of interest to lawyers were settled

2. Jean Mazeaud, La Nomination du Iudex Unus sous la Procédure Formulaire à Rome (Paris, 1933), 1–48; Leopold Wenger, in his review of Mazeaud, 55 Zeitschrift der Savigny-Stiftung für Rechtsgeschichte (rom.), 425 (1935) [hereafter cited Z.S.S. (rom.)]; Pauly-Wissowa, Realencyclopädie, VI 289–301 (*Equites Romani*).

3. Leopold Wenger, Institutionen des römischen Zivilprozessrechts (Munich, 1925), sec. 18.

4. Wenger, sec. 19.

1. Mazeaud, La Nomination du Iudex Unus, 78–87, referring to evidence from the principate.

by decisions of the praetor in drawing up the formula. The two-stage split of praetorian procedure meant that adjudication itself was divided in fractions that varied from case to case. Why should the Romans have erected monuments to these thousands of men—men of distinction though they were—who came and went on short-term service, with powers that were often limited, and who were so greatly trusted that they were put under no compulsion to explain their decisions?

Yet monuments are not the only measure of useful and lasting contribution. It many be that anyone trained in American law who searches the record of that distant time is handicapped by his own prejudice. From our own experience we have acquired the prejudice—indeed the conviction—that the application of rules of law over a broad-band of problems necessarily includes some new creation. If there is any truth in this, then these half-judges of the Roman praetorian system must have added some content to the rules they applied. That this occurred is made more likely by the honored status of many of the men that were called on to serve as *iudices*. Let us suppose that we had a system in which Nicholas Murray Butler or Bernard Baruch could be required to accept a special appointment to decide a case under the law of sales between Sempronius Jones and Titius Smith. The gentlemen so selected would have had few occasions to formulate or administer legal rules but they would have acquired, surely, some notions of respectable conduct that were too deeply absorbed to require discussion and were only remotely dependent on legal sources. For a praetorian *iudex* in Roman procedure, the scope accorded these private ideas would largely depend on the formula which appointed him and defined his authority. But as the praetorian system developed it became increasingly common for the praetor to include in the formula some highly generalized standards—the judge was directed to decide according to "good faith" or "equity" or in a manner that would prevent "fraud." The moral ideas that were thus cast into the crucible were likely to reflect in some degree the usages and expectations of the upper ranks of Roman society. It seems more than likely that decisions in particular cases would help to precipitate these expectations and to shape them into specific rules that could be then adopted as law. In surviving sources there is one instance where this process can be traced to the decision of a particular *iudex*. It might have occurred much more often in cases of which no record survives.[2] In short, the negative evidence is not conclusive. Though the unrecorded judgments of these transient laymen were not a promising source of legal doctrine, they may well have produced case law of a kind, disguised and almost unrecognized.

---

2. Paul Collinet, "Le Role des Juges dans la Formation du Droit Romain Classique," Receuil d'Études sur les Sources du Droit en Honneur de François Gény (Paris, 1923), I 23. In this interesting study eighteen instances are mentioned in which prominent persons under the late Republic and early principate were chosen to serve as *iudices*. In one of them P. Mucius Scaevola, consul and later *pontifex maximus*, was quoted by a classical jurist for the proposition, adopted by Mucius when serving as a *iudex*, that total property lost by a husband through the husband's "fault" must be restored to the wife (D.24.3.66.pr.). Professor Collinet also suggested that the liability of a seller for undisclosed defects in the object sold was first established through decisions to the effect that a seller who failed to disclose defects known to him did not act in "good faith."

The innovations of the Roman praetors are much better known and have been often discussed. The praetors were high magistrates, elected to office for terms of one year. Under the late Republic there were six, later eight, most of whom were engaged in provincial administration. It was the *praetor urbanus* who outranked all the others and was chiefly responsible for litigation in the city of Rome.[3] As chief administrative officer of the judicial system that was used in litigation between Roman citizens, the *praetor urbanus* had a central position. The formal source of the praetor's power was his control over the grant or refusal of remedies to individual litigants. Being free either to grant or deny, he claimed power to fix terms; by changes in the formula that defined the issues at the trial, the praetor could inject new terms or qualifications that departed widely from existing law. Innovations introduced by these means clearly transformed the Roman legal system. The period of greatest activity for the praetors extended for about 200 years (roughly 150 B.C. to 50 A.D.), the period in which the rapid expansion of Roman imperial power brought great changes in Roman society. All this was done without much legislation, by a gradual process of piecemeal change.

Was this case law? It surely was, if we can free our own minds of some prepossessions, disregard the theories of the Romans themselves, and measure solely by results. The praetors, as has been said, were seldom lawyers. They were elected public officials, most of whom viewed the praetorship as a stage of the course of public honors in which ambitious men competed. They were high magistrates, invested with an important share of the governmental power of the Roman people. They could certainly not be asked to write opinions or give public statements of the reasons that guided them in particular cases. Even more certainly they were not bound by decisions of their predecessors. The praetor's edict, issued at the beginning of each praetor's term, stated in generalized language the policies that he proposed to follow during his term of office. But until 67 B.C. even the praetor who had issued it was not bound to follow his own edict and a statute passed in that year, which directed each praetor to follow his own edict, left each succeeding praetor free to depart from the edicts of his predecessors. Certainly in matters not governed by his edict, each praetor remained entirely free in individual cases to decide as he thought best. Indeed the whole program of praetorian reform depended on the principle that a high magistrate with *imperium* could disregard existing law in administering his office. Constitutional theory made it hard for a Roman lawyer to conceive of the praetor as a judge at all. It excluded altogether the notion that he was limited by rules that had somehow emerged from the theories or the practice of his predecessors.

Yet the record is clear—continuities did in fact develop. New terms inserted in praetorian formulas were copied and used in other cases. Copies of the formulas that were commonly used were kept by clerks attached to the praetor's office and were available there for public

---

3. H.F. Jolowicz, Historical Introduction to the Study of Roman Law (2d ed., Cambridge, Eng., 1954), 46–48 [hereafter cited as Jolowicz, R.L.].

inspection. New phrases that were introduced as experiments became stereotyped elements in these standard formulas. As their use became predictable, it became apparent that the praetor's actions were being guided by new rules, of which notice was often given by the praetor's edict. The freedom to recast the edict, possessed by each praetor in theory, was exercised in practice with great restraint; the main provisions were carried over from year to year. But the edict was usually cast in general terms: "I will uphold pacts agreed upon; what has been done by threat I will not hold valid; if something is said to have been done by fraud, if there is no other remedy and just cause appears, I will give a remedy." Even more than the edict itself, the provisions of the standard formulas gave guidance to litigants and their legal advisers. The whole system of praetorian law, in short, was built up through patterns of action that were firmly maintained. This was done without judicial opinions or disclosure of reasons, without citation of cases, and with a constitutional theory that excluded any theory of precedent. Thus, with none of the trappings of modern case law lay magistrates remade Roman law through the storing up of solutions reached in individual cases.[4]

It was important and in some respects most beneficial that the key function of adjudication was thus entrusted to informed and responsible laymen in both branches of these two-stage courts. The praetors, like the *iudices*, ordinarily came from the upper ranks of Roman society. Their use in combination insured that Roman law could respond to developing needs and changing values, as perceived by the nation's leadership. This meant that urgently needed, major reform could be accomplished without appeal to a separate source of authority, like that of the Chancellors in England who were also high magistrates and also for centuries untrained in law—untrained at least in the common law system for which their remedies were correctives. But in Roman law there was nothing really comparable to the Anglo-American split between the older law and the new equity. The praetors presided over the whole judicial system of the capital city. The changes they made were absorbed within the existing system and their praetorian origin became a matter merely of historical interest. All this was fortunate for Roman law and for the societies which it was later to influence so greatly. The constant exposure to lay opinion surely helped to produce a painless adjustment between ancient rules and emerging needs in a time of drastic change in Roman society.

To say this, however, is merely to compound the problem—how could adjudication produce an ordered system of law when conducted by these untrained men, whose work was so ephemeral? Who would remember what they did? They must have had reasons for what they did, but who would note the reasons, formulate and preserve them, and organize them under some rational plan? Who, in short, were the oracles? The answer is plain from the most casual reading of Roman texts. The custodians of the

---

4. Allen, Law in the Making (6th ed., London, 1958), 160–61, makes a similar comment on the development of the praetorian system: "There could be no more instructive example than this of a whole body of law built up by judicial practice."

Roman legal tradition, the men who gave guidance and direction, were a special and highly honored group—the jurists.

3. *The Social and Political Status of the Classical Jurists*

To understand the role of the jurists one must go back to earlier times, before law had been separated from religion. Knowledge of law was then reserved to the priests who served the religious cults. To discover the appropriate forms of procedure, the methods of framing valid legal transactions, or the rules of legal interpretation, it was necessary to consult a member of a pontifical college. The priest consulted on a question of law issued a *responsum*, of which a copy was kept in the college archives. Such a *responsum* was considered binding, even on Roman magistrates.[1] But no attempt was apparently made to produce an atmosphere of divine inspiration, expressed through some kind of Delphic frenzy. As one writer has put it, the Roman pontiffs were not "clairvoyants, rainmakers, or medicine men," or "'men of god' whose divine character was derived from some mysterious personal endowment." Membership in the priesthood came from high birth or public service.[2] Its monopoly over knowledge of law was destroyed about 300 B.C., the later tradition being that this was done by a publication of the priestly secrets on the initiative of one Appius Claudius. But the change was probably gradual, a secularizing process that lasted for decades. In any event it did not at once destroy the dominance of the pontiffs or reduce the authority of the legal opinions they rendered. For at least another 150 years most of the persons whose views on legal matters have survived were members of one of these aristocratic priesthoods.[3]

The priesthoods indeed merely symbolized the social and political predominance of the Roman aristocracy. Until their power was challenged by the Gracchi in the late second century B.C., the great families of Rome, perhaps 20 in number, had almost a monopoly of the major public offices, commanded the armies and through their membership in the Senate controlled the main course of governmental policy. The circle was not completely closed, for some new families won their way to high public office and thereby joined the controlling caste. The political influence of the high nobility was extended into Roman society by patron–client relationships which gave mutual aid and protection and an exchange of services and favors between the great families and large numbers of dependent clients.[4] Included among the services that the heads of families rendered their clients was the giving of advice on legal as well as personal matters. Even after the time of troubles initiated by the Gracchi these practices survived. Cicero, writing in the first century B.C., described a great man strolling through the Forum or seated in his home, giving advice not only

---

1. A *responsum* by an individual priest could, however, be overruled by vote of his college. Leopold Wenger, Die Quellen des römischen Rechts (1953), 476. The subject is also discussed by Paul Jörs, Römische Rechtswissenschaft zur Zeit der Republik (Berlin, 1888), 15–50; Fritz Schulz, Roman Legal Science (Oxford, 1946), 16–18,

the latter giving examples of pontifical responsa.
2. Schulz, 6–7.
3. Wolfgang Kunkel, Herkunft und Stellung der römischen Juristen (Weimar, 1952), 45–57.
4. Howard H. Scullard, Roman Politics, 220–150 B.C. (Oxford, 1951), 8–13.

on questions of law but also "concerning a prospective marriage of a daughter, the purchase of a house, the tilling of land and every conceivable kind of duty and transaction."[5] For this advice, naturally, no great aristocrat would expect to be paid. The giving of legal opinions was indistinguishable from all the other services by which a nobleman brought honor to himself and his family and bound others through ties of gratitude.

It was in this milieu that the jurists emerged. As law was increasingly secularized and the rules of law became more complex, some specialization was needed. Among the nobility there were some men whose views on legal matters were entitled to special respect. Their views would be quoted and would carry weight if they showed exceptional knowledge, judgment, and acuteness in giving advice on legal matters, among the many matters on which the great men gave advice.

There came a time, during the civil wars that destroyed the Republic, when it was not so pleasant to be a great man. The patrician class was decimated in the civil wars, and for a time the knights—wealthy merchants and new men from other parts of Italy—supplied most of the prime legal talent. But the new men fell readily into the established role and their functions and authority were essentially unchanged. Then when Augustus rebuilt an aristocracy and made it one of the pillars of his own political power, a source of supply was re-established. Of the well-known jurists in the period 1–150 A.D., the overwhelming majority were members by birth of the reorganized aristocracy.[6]

In all their manifold services to Roman law and Roman society, the jurists—at least until the time of Augustus—were private citizens who acted without sanction of public authority. Many were senators, but being a senator did not make one a jurist. Conversely, there were some exceptional men who were recognized as leading jurists but never achieved senatorial rank. The jurists in effect selected each other through tests that were never precisely defined. Young men learned about law by attaching themselves to some great man, watching and listening, asking occasional questions, gathering around him when he sat in the Forum or conversed after dinner. It was an extremely informal tutorial system, but it did produce lawyers. For great success it was necessary to have not only aptitude but high social rank. The lawyers were not peculiar in this. Roman society was organized around its aristocracy. Its power and influence were greatly undermined in the civil wars that destroyed the Republic, but the principate of Augustus, in purporting to revive the ancient Republic, restored its social hierarchy.

Peter Stein, *Roman Law in European History* (1999), 16–21, 32–36, 43–54, 71–74

THE JURISTS IN THE CLASSICAL PERIOD

The main agency of legal development in the classical period was the literature produced by the jurists, both those in the imperial service and

---

5. Kunkel, 56–58.   **6.** Kunkel, 272–80.

those conducting a private practice. The jurists as a class were favoured by the emperors; already Augustus granted to certain jurists the right to give opinions with the emperor's authority, perhaps in order to relieve the pressure created by the demand for rescripts from the imperial chancery. A century later Hadrian laid down that if the opinions of all the jurists with this right were in agreement what they held was to have the force of a *lex*. What this means is not clear, but it may well refer to a practice that had grown up of citing as precedents juristic opinions given in similar cases in the past.

The jurist-law of the classical period was marked by certain characteristics, which may be summarised as follows. First, there was a continuous succession of individuals, all dedicated to the law and each familiar with and building on the efforts of his predecessors, whose views they cited, especially when they agreed with them but sometimes when they disagreed. Secondly, they alone could be said to have a comprehensive knowledge of private law. The praetor held office for only a year, the *iudex* was concerned only with the facts of the cases in which he was chosen to preside and the advocates put skill in argumentation above expertise in law. Indeed, there was a tendency, exemplified by Cicero, who was a successful advocate, to sneer at jurists precisely because they seemed to be immersed in legal minutiae, such as the right to let rainwater from one's roof fall on to one's neighbour's roof. Thirdly, the jurists were concerned with the day-to-day practice of the law and could recognise when modifications or reform of the rules were needed. Although they usually had pupils, they were not academics cut off from 'the real world.' Finally, they enjoyed complete freedom to express divergent opinions. Where legal discussion is concerned with cases, it is inevitably controversial, if only because there are at least two sides to every legal dispute and each side wants a legal opinion in his favour. This is not to say that the jurists twisted the law to suit the client who was consulting them but rather that they were ready to test the limits of every legal rule.

The classical law was thus the product of disputation. The techniques used differed according as the law was in written or unwritten form. Where the jurists were dealing with the text of a *lex* enacted by the republican assembly or of the praetorian edict or the text of a contract or a testament, problems had to be solved by the interpretation given to particular phrases in the text and a number of stock arguments were deployed. Should the strict letter of the text or rather its spirit prevail? Should the actual intention of the author be decisive, even when he has expressed it ambiguously, and, in that case, how should his intention be ascertained? Where the law was in unwritten form, stated in juristic opinions which did not involve a fixed authoritative text, the jurists had more scope for reformulating the law.

In the course of the transmission of our sources, much of the evidence of disagreement has not survived (minority views tend to disappear from the sources), but we do know of the existence of two schools or sects among the jurists in the first and early second centuries AD, known as the Proculians and the Sabinians. There is much scholarly debate about the basis of the differences of these schools, but they seem to have been less concerned with substantive issues than with methods. The Sabinians tended to justify their opinions by referring to traditional practice and to the authority of earlier jurists. They were primarily concerned with finding just solutions in individual cases, even if this meant abandoning logic and rationality. When interpreting texts, they were not worried if the same words were given different meanings in different texts. The Proculians, on the other hand, favoured strict interpretation of all texts and insisted that words and phrases should in every case be given an objective, consistent meaning. In the case of the unwritten law, they assumed that it was a logically coherent system of rules and looked behind the rules for the principles that lay behind them. In that way they could extend the rules by analogy to other cases falling under the same principle. Whatever their affiliation, the jurists distrusted broad statements of principle. This was not because they were unable to formulate them but because they understood that the wider the statement, the more there would be exceptions to its application and so there was a danger that the law would be uncertain and unpredictable.

THE ORDERING OF THE LAW

The elaboration of classical law remained largely centred on cases, either real cases or hypothetical cases devised in the schools. Inevitably a casuistic system becomes intricate and complex and in need of categorization and systematization. The process of putting the law in some form of order began in the late republic under the influence of Greek methods of classification. The Greeks themselves had not applied these techniques to law, for they had no professional class of jurists and their legal procedure did not lend itself to technical legal development.

About 100 BC the jurist Quintus Mucius Scaevola had published a small treatise on civil law as a whole. It begins with wills, legacies and intestate succession, which occupy about a quarter of the whole work. Problems arising out of the succession to the inheritance of someone who had died produced more disputes than any other kind of case. The social order was based on the family as a unit and the main purpose of a will was to designate the heirs who, on the death of the family head, would take his place and continue the family into the next generation. Apart from nominating his heirs in his will, a testator might grant legacies, appoint tutors for his children under puberty and free slaves. Since property was concentrated in the family rather than in the individual, it is not surprising that succession on death loomed so large in the law. Apart from succession, Mucius grouped the methods of acquiring ownership and possession of property together but the remaining subjects of private law seemed to be jumbled up without any recognizable order.

A century later another jurist, Masurius Sabinus, who gave his name to the Sabinian school, built on Mucius's scheme and brought together other topics, which were beginning to be recognised as having a relationship with each other. For example, Mucius treated theft of property and damage to property as quite separate from each other, but Sabinus brought them together, thus recognizing a category of wrongdoing (delict), which have the victim a civil action for a penalty against the wrongdoer. Sabinus, however, perceived no equivalent category of contract and dealt with the different ways in which two parties could create a binding obligation between themselves quite separately from each other.

Most classical jurists presented their collections of opinions either in the form of a commentary on Sabinus's treatise on the civil law or of a commentary on the (now codified) praetorian edict. It was not until the middle of the second century that a major advance was made in arranging the substance of private law, but it was noticed only in academic circles. The author was an obscure jurist, known simply as Gaius (without the full Roman complement of three names), who was a law teacher. Earlier jurists had had pupils but their main work was concerned with their practice. Gaius, however, seems to have been exclusively a teacher and as such lacked recognition in his own time.

The scheme of his student's manual, the Institutes, is based on a classification of all the law into three parts. Trichotomy was especially attractive to teachers as being a manageable number, suitable for students with a short attention span. The three parts of the law in the Gaian scheme relate to persons, things and actions. The first category was concerned with different kinds of personal status, considered from three points of view, namely, freedom (is the individual a freeman or a slave?), citizenship (is he a citizen or a peregrine?) and family position (is he a paterfamilias or is he in the power of an ancestor?).

The second category, things, bore the main brunt of the classification. It included anything to which a money value could be attributed and comprehended both corporeal and non-corporeal things. Physical things, whether moveable or immoveable, had always been recognised as things. Under the new class of incorporeal things, Gaius put first collectivities of things, which pass *en bloc* (*per universitatem*) from one person to another, such as the inheritance of a deceased person, which passes *en bloc* to his heirs. Such collectivities may include corporeal things but are themselves incorporeal. The other component which Gaius brought under the head of incorporeal things was that of obligations. The notion of obligation had been used to describe the various ways in which one person could become indebted to another and had normally been looked at from the point of view of the person obligated, the debtor. Thus one who entered into a formal promise to another to pay him money became obligated to him; one who received something from another, to secure an existing debt, became obligated to him to return the security when the debt was paid. Sometimes the praetor treated parties as obligated to each other merely on the strength of an agreement reached between them. The main example was an agreement for the sale of goods. Once the parties unconditionally committed themselves to the sale, in that the seller agreed to deliver the thing sold and the buyer agreed to pay the price, they were obligated to each other.

Jurists before Gaius had seen that most obligations were derived from a prior agreement between the parties, even though what made them binding at law might be something more than mere agreement. So most obligations were seen to have a common feature in that, whatever gave them binding force, there had been an agreement between the parties. The category of contracts, imposing duties on the parties, had been born. Gaius now viewed an obligation in a new way; he saw it not just as a burden on the debtor but also as an asset in the hands of the creditor. By treating the creditor's right to sue the debtor as an obligation, Gaius was able to expand the notion of obligations and include in the category not only contracts but also civil wrongs, delicts, as sources of obligations.

The third part of the law in the Gaian scheme was actions. This part was concerned not so much with the procedure for suing in court but rather with the different kinds of action, such as those that can be brought against anyone, as, for example, actions to claim property, in contrast with those that can be brought only against particular individuals, such as actions to enforce obligations.

By the time of Gaius, the heyday of the classical period, the contents of private law were more or less fixed, and he could identify its component elements. His scheme contained several novel features. He included actions among the legal phenomena to be classified, on a par with persons and things; he recognised incorporeal things as falling in the same category as physical things; he classified inheritances and obligations as incorporeal things; and he recognised both contracts and delicts as sources of obligations.

The Institutional scheme was destined to have enormous influence on law in the future but at the time it had little impact outside the schools. The professional jurists did not need a systematic order.

THE CULMINATION OF CLASSICAL JURISPRUDENCE

At the beginning of the third century, the Emperor Antoninus Caracalla enacted a significant edict which had the effect of turning most of the residents of his empire into Roman citizens, whether they liked it or not. The *Constitutio Antoniniana* of 212 AD was promulgated not with any liberal intention but probably for fiscal reasons, to apply the inheritance tax levied on the estates of citizens to more people. Another result was that many people who had not considered themselves Roman, and who might not even have known Latin, were now expected, as Roman citizens, to follow the forms of the civil law.

The classical period reached its climax, in the decade after the *Constitutio Antoniniana*, in the work of three jurists whom later ages were to consider the most distinguished, Papinian, Paul and Ulpian. Each of them held the highest imperial office, that of praetorian prefect, and was both the emperor's principal legal officer and his chief of staff. They all wrote prolifically on the law. Papinian excelled in the analysis of particular cases and his solutions to legal problems show a keen moral sense and a desire to reach a just result. Paul and Ulpian are known for their great commentaries, which synthesised the work of their predecessors and passed it on in a mature, but still very complex form, to later generations.

In an elementary institutional work, Ulpian made for the first time a clear distinction between private law and public law. Hitherto the phrase "public law" had no precise meaning and was often used to indicate those civil law rules which could not be altered by private agreement, by contrast with those that could be altered by the parties. Ulpian now applied the term to the law that was primarily of public concern, such as the powers of magistrates and the state religion, by contrast with the law that concerned the interests of private individuals. What his aim was can only be conjectured but the fact that the work appeared just after the *Constitutio Antoniniana* is significant. Ulpian probably wanted to protect the traditional civil law from imperial interference and to re-assure the new citizens to whom it now applied that the civil law was something quite distinct from public law. The distinction was to have momentous consequences.

With the murder of Ulpian, at the hands of mutinous guards, in 223 AD (Papinian had been executed on the orders of Caracalla a decade earlier), the classical period ended. The second century AD had been a period of unusual peace and stability for the Roman empire. The eighteenth-century historian Edward Gibbon called it "the period in the history of the world during which the condition of the human race was most happy and prosperous" (*Decline and Fall of the Roman Empire*, ch. 3). The third century, by contrast, was a period of considerable social disorder. Although the imperial rescripts show that efforts were made, at least in the imperial chancery, to maintain the standards of the earlier law, there was little legal writing of the quality needed to justify a claim of vitality in the law.

* * *

JUSTINIAN AND THE CORPUS IURIS

The collapse on the western empire had left the eastern empire relatively unscathed and indeed the second half of the fifth century saw a revival of legal learning in the law schools of Constantinople and Beirut. The texts were, of course, all in Latin but they were expounded in Greek. In 527 there ascended the imperial throne a man whose name is for ever associated with Roman law. Justinian was born near Naissus (Niš in modern Serbia), also the birthplace of Constantine. He was a native Latin-speaker (the last eastern emperor to be such) but enjoyed a Greek education at Constantinople, which now reverted to its old name of Byzantium. His legal work was part of an ambitious programme to renew the ancient glory of the Roman empire in all its aspects. A man of great nervous energy and command of detail, like Napoleon he required little sleep. He was much influenced by his wife Theodora, a former actress, and after her death in 448, he was less active as a ruler. Through the efforts of his generals, Narses and Belisarius, he recovered North Africa from the Vandals and re-established imperial authority over the Ostrogothic kingdom in Italy. He resisted the claims of the Pope to equal authority with the emperor and regarded himself as holding supreme religious as well as supreme temporal power. The symbol of his religious authority was the great church of Hagia Sophia in Byzantium, in the building of which he claimed to have surpassed Solomon.

In his legal work Justinian was fortunate in having a brilliant minister, Tribonian, to execute his plans. Whether his ideas were influenced by what the Visigothic king had done, it is not possible to say, for Justinian would never have admitted it. Whereas Alaric's aim was to give his Roman subjects a law suitable for sixth-century Gaul, Justinian consciously looked back to the golden age of Roman law and aimed to restore it to the peak it had reached three centuries before. Rather inconsistently he also wanted a law that could be applied in the Byzantine empire of his own time.

One part of his project was modest enough: to bring the Theodosian Code up to date. The main agency of legal development had been imperial constitutions and there had been many "Novels" in the previous century. Justinian's Code arranges the constitutions in chronological order in titles and covers twelve books. In the course of the general overhaul of the law, many controversies, unresolved since the time of the classical jurists, came to light and were settled by his own constitutions.

The most important part of Justinian's compilation was quite unprecedented. This is the Digest (Latin *Digesta*; Greek *Pandectae*), an anthology of extracts from the writings of the great jurists. The five jurists of the Law of Citations are given pride of place, over one-third of the Digest being taken from Ulpian and a sixth from Paul, but there are extracts from earlier jurists of repute, even the jurists of the late republic. The whole forms an immense legal mosaic, about one and a half times the size of the Bible, but it represents, Justinian says, only a twentieth of the material with which its compilers began. The extracts are arranged in titles, each title being devoted to a particular topic and the titles arranged in fifty books. Where a subject could not easily be divided up, such as legacies, a single title might extend over three books. Normally, however, division was preferred, as with the contract of sale which is covered in eight titles: a general title and special titles dealing with particular aspects of sale. The order of the titles is the traditional order of the praetorian edict, but the fragments within each title seem to be arranged quite haphazardly.

The compilers were instructed to attribute each fragment to its source by an appropriate inscription. In the nineteenth century, the German scholar Bluhme showed, from a study of these inscriptions, that extracts from particular works appear in three groups and that within each group the extracts normally appear in the same order, although the groups themselves were not arranged in the same order in every title. He therefore concluded that the compilers, under pressure from the emperor to speed up the work, must have divided themselves into three committees, each of which took a bundle of works to extract. They then brought chains of fragments to a plenary session, at which the order of the respective chains was agreed for each title and a few specially significant fragments moved out of order into a more prominent position. Recent research, based on computerised study of the text, has further refined Bluhme's conclusions.

The Digest was produced in three years and the compilers must have had their work cut out just abbreviating the material at their disposal and making the resulting extracts as coherent as possible. Although they gave the source of each extract, we cannot assume that what they attributed to the jurist is what he actually wrote. This is partly because the original discussion has been cut down, but also because the compilers were expressly instructed to eliminate all contradictions and to avoid repetitions. Much evidence of disagreement among the classical jurists was therefore excised.

The compilers were also authorised to make whatever substantive changes were necessary to ensure that the final work expressed the law of sixth-century Byzantium. It is the extent of such alterations which has been a main concern of Digest study in the twentieth century. The changes in the texts have been known since the sixteenth century as *emblemata Triboniani* and more recently as interpolations, whether they subtract from, add to, or just alter the original text.

The Code and the Digest are the main parts of Justinian's compilation, but they were too complex to put into the hands of students at the beginning of their studies, and Justinian ordered that they be supplemented by a new Institutes, based on Gaius's Institutes of nearly four centuries earlier. Although an elementary textbook, it was given equal status with the Digest and Code. The Digest and Institutes became law on 31 December 533 and a revised edition of the Code a year later.

The materials out of which Justinian's compilation was forged were of differing origin, some, the contents of the Code, being derived from legislation and others, the juristic writings, enjoying only the authority derived from the author's reputation. Justinian made the whole work his own, converting it into statutory form. Defending the changes that had been made in his name, he observed that he who corrects what is not stated accurately deserves more praise than the original writer (*Constitutio Deo auctore*, 6). He prohibited any reference to the original material and tried to ban commentaries on the text on the ground that it was crystal clear as it stood.

Justinian continued to issue constitutions until his death in 565. These Novels, many of them written in Greek, were collected together privately and added to the other three parts of what came to be called the Corpus iuris civilis, the body of the civil law, by contrast with the canon law of the Church. The whole collection marked the culmination of a millennium of legal development. Without Justinian's compilation we would know very little about the earlier law. Little classical law has survived directly, the main example being Gaius's Institutes, the full text of which was discovered only in 1816.

The extraordinary fact about Justinian's work is that, despite the fanfare with which it was published, it attracted relatively little attention. Being written in Latin, it was unintelligible to many Greek-speaking Byzantine lawyers. One of the compilers of the Institutes, Theophilus, produced a Greek version of that work known as the Paraphrase. In the eighth century a shorter official collection in Greek appeared, called the *Ecloga*, which sought to modify Justinian's law in the direction of current Byzantine practice. About 900 Emperor Leo the Wise sponsored a large Greek restatement of Justinian's law, the *Basilica*, which wove the contents of Digest, Code, Institutes and Novels into a single whole. The texts were supplemented with scholia, notes mainly derived from the comments of the jurists of Justinian's own time and therefore sometimes of value in elucidating the original Latin text. Shorter versions of the *Basilica* were produced in the following centuries, the most influential being the *Hexabiblos* (six-book work), published in 1345, which was still recognised as the basis of the law of modern Greece until replaced by the code of 1940.

In 1453 the Byzantine empire, which had been gradually contracting in size, finally succumbed to Turkish attack, but Byzantine Roman law in Greek dress survived in the Balkans and in Russia, whose emperors liked to regard themselves as the successors of the Byzantine emperors.

* * *

THE REDISCOVERY OF THE DIGEST

In the later eleventh century the level of legal culture began to rise and there is evidence of a new interest in Justinian's law; notaries in their documents and advocates in their pleadings now refer accurately to technical Roman legal institutions. Five hundred years after its compilation, Justinian's Digest came to be used in Western Europe as a source of rules and arguments. No doubt there had been manuscripts lurking in Italian libraries but their bulk and the difficulty of understanding them had hitherto deterred potential readers. All surviving manuscripts of the Digest today derive ultimately from a sixth-century codex in Pisa, which was seized as war booty by the victorious Florentines in 1406 and is now in the Laurentian library in Florence. The relationship is not direct but through a lost, amended, copy made in the eleventh century and known as *Codex secundus*. This version was the source of the *vulgata* or *litera bononiensis*, that came to be studied in the twelfth-century schools.

The recovery of the entire Corpus iuris civilis was a slow process, extending over much of the twelfth century. The Digest became available in three parts, known as *Vetus*, *Infortiatum* and *Novum*. The division bears little relation to the original structure, *Vetus* being Books 1 to 24.2, *Infortiatum* Books 24.3 to 38 and *Novum* Books 39 to 50. The origin of the division, and in particular the designation *Infortiatum* for the middle section, is unknown and was a mystery to the twelfth-century doctors themselves. It probably reflects the order in which the parts of the Digest became generally available. Eventually the complete Digest could be added to the Institutes and to the first nine books of the Code. Later the *Tres libri* (the last three books of Justinian's Code) were discovered but were kept separate rather than integrated into the rest of the Code; and a better version of the Novels than the *Epitome Juliani*, known as the *Authenticum*, became available. The latter was grouped into nine *Collationes* in imitation of the Code. The Institutes, *Tres libri*, and *Authenticum* were placed in a fifth volume, after the three volumes of the Digest and the (nine books of the) Code. This so-called *volumen parvum* formed a receptacle, which also incorporated some non-Justinian material, such as twelfth-century imperial legislation.

The churchmen were perhaps even more eager than secular lawyers to exploit the newly discovered texts to justify the new ideas that churchmen were proposing. Ninety-three extracts from the Digest, ninety of them from the *Digestum vetus*, appear in a canonist collection known as *Collectio Britannica*, an Italian work from about 1080, now known only in a single manuscript in the British Library. The immediate source of these

Digest texts is not known but the compilers may well have found them in archives in Rome or perhaps in the great Benedictine monastery of Monte Cassino. The French canonist Ivo of Chartres is known, for example, to have been working on his own collections in Rome in the 1090s. The *Collectio Britannica* itself became the source of local canonist collections made north of the Alps.

It is difficult to overrate the significance of the rediscovery of the Digest. Knowledge of the outlines of Roman law could readily be obtained from the Roman law of the Visigoths and from Justinian's Institutes and Code. As F. W. Maitland observed, however,

> The Digest was the *only* book in which medieval students could obtain a knowledge of Roman law *at its best*. The Institutes are a slight text book. The Code is made up of detached ordinances. The Novels are not merely detached ordinances but are penned in a pompous, verbose style, likely to do as much harm as good . . . but for the Digest Roman law could never have reconquered the world . . . Men would never have become *enthusiastic* students of other books . . . the man who first teaches the Digest is the man who first teaches what the modern world has meant by Roman law . . . it was only in the Digest that men could get any notion of keen and exact legal argument, precise definition etc. (*Letters*, vol. II, ed. P. Zutshi, Selden Soc. supp. ser. 11, 1995, nr 37)

The major secular law school in the eleventh century was that of Pavia, the capital of the Lombard kingdom. The jurists of Pavia were primarily concerned with Lombard law, as contained in the *Liber Papiensis*, a collection of the edicts of the Lombard kings before the Frankish conquest and of Frankish capitularies. In their exposition of this text, the jurists of Pavia were the first jurists to use the method of the gloss alongside the text. On matters of substance they formed two groups, the *antiqui* and the *moderni*. The former adhered to the traditional understanding of the Lombard texts, whereas the latter were characterised by their readiness to refer to Roman law as a general law to supplement and interpret the Lombard law. The modernist contribution is summed up in the *Expositio* to the *Liber Papiensis*, which appeared about 1070. It refers to the sources that had been available in Italy for some time, that is, Institutes, Code and *Epitome Juliani*, but it also contains nine extracts from the Digest.

The jurists of Pavia did not give particular attention to the Digest, because Roman law was not their prime concern. Their concern was the law of the Lombard kingdom and their aim was to ensure that judges and advocates in the Lombard courts were properly prepared. They recognised the value of Justinian's texts in inculcating a sense of legal reasoning but they did not study those texts for their own sake. They were interested less in the juristic arguments of the Digest than with what could be gleaned from the Roman sources about the nature and purpose of law in general. The *Expositio* shows that jurists were no longer satisfied simply with making summaries of texts. They now wanted to interpret them in depth. Where adherence to the letter of a text would lead to injustice, the *Expositio* stressed that its rationale, the *ratio legis*, must be identified and the text understood in the light of that *ratio*.

THE CIVIL LAW GLOSSATORS

The school of Pavia pointed the way to a new approach to the study of legal texts but the honour of producing the first expositors of Justinian's compilation belongs not to Pavia but to Bologna. The first law teacher at Bologna was said to be a *causidicus*, or consultant judge, called Pepo, in the last decades of the eleventh century. According to the English theologian Ralph Niger, writing a century later, his teaching was based on the texts of the Code and the Institutes, but he was apparently in a position to cite the Digest in his forensic arguments. For example, in 1076 the court of Beatrice, Marchioness of Tuscany, held at Marturi, had to deal with a dispute over the entitlement to a piece of land between a monastery, which claimed ownership by virtue of a prior grant, and a long-standing possessor. The latter relied on forty-year prescription to retain the land but the court was persuaded that the prescription had been interrupted, since there had been a *restitutio in integrum* in favour of the monastery, in accordance with Digest 4-5.26, cited by Pepo.

Whatever Pepo's claims to have taught Justinian's law, it was Irnerius who marked the separation between the science of law and the practice of law. He had been a teacher of grammar and began his study of the legal texts with explanations of difficult terms that they contained. Then he moved on to whole passages. His comments were originally in interlinear glosses, which gradually expanded into the margins of the text. Irnerius was thus the first of a line of doctors at Bologna, known, from their characteristic method of expounding the texts, as the glossators.

The new approach was marked by a debate on how law fits into the general scheme of knowledge. The traditional view, expressed by Isidore of Seville, was that, since law deals with human behaviour, it must be categorised under ethics. Now it was said that this was only true so far as the content of the rules was concerned. In so far as it concerns the interpretation of words in a text, law is part of logic. Logic embraced all three arts of that part of the traditional education known as the trivium, namely, grammar, dialectic and rhetoric. The scholastic techniques developed in these disciplines were exploited by the masters of Bologna. For them law was a higher study, only to be undertaken by those who had already mastered the arts of the trivium.

The glossators regarded Justinian's texts as sacred and ascribed to them almost biblical authority. They accepted without question Justinian's assurance that the texts contained no contradictions that could not be reconciled by one who tackled them with a subtle mind (*Constitutio Tanta*, 15) and they took it for granted that the compilation as a whole contained all that was necessary to answer any conceivable legal problem. The opening fragment of the Digest says that jurists are called priests and a succeeding fragment defines jurisprudence as "the knowledge of things human and divine." Does this mean, asked the glossators, that the jurist should study theology? The answer was no, since 'everything is found in the Corpus iuris.'

One of the main difficulties they faced was the appalling lack of coherence in the arrangement of the texts. The same matters were dealt with in the Institutes, Digest and Code, but without any order. The Bolognese glossators did not tamper with the order of the texts approved by Justinian. They supplied cross-references to all the texts which dealt with a particular topic, explaining differences and marshalling the arguments for and against a particular result. Their familiarity with the texts as a whole is indicated by the fact that they could cite every fragment in the Corpus iuris by its first words. No later generation of Roman law scholars has had a closer familiarity with the texts. They used all the techniques of dialectic to squeeze the correct meaning from a text. For them every text, indeed every separate clause in every text, having been approved by the Emperor Justinian, had equal authority.

Various types of legal literature developed out of the glosses on individual texts. Summaries of the content of particular titles of the Digest or Code evolved into *summae* of the content of a whole part of the Corpus iuris, especially the Code and the Institutes. An *apparatus* was a collection of glosses covering the material contained in a particular title in a fuller manner than in a *summa*. A particular favourite for this treatment was the last title of the Digest, 50.17, *de diversis regulis iuris antiqui*, which contained over two hundred 'rules,' many in the form of general maxims. The glossators delighted in *distinctiones*, elaborate classifications with many divisions and subdivisions, sometimes illustrated by diagrammatic tables. There were collections of opposing views on particular points (*dissensiones dominorum*) and collections of *quaestiones*, disputed points, with arguments for each view set out with its supporting texts and usually a *solutio*. Whatever the form, however, everything they wrote revolved around Justinian's texts in all their complex entirety. The glossators worked in an incremental way, each generation imposing a new layer on that laid down by its predecessors.

Irnerius was succeeded by the generation of the Four Doctors, of whom the most distinguished were Bulgarus and Martinus Gosia. Bulgarus was pre-eminent at Bologna, where he was known as 'the golden mouth.' Martinus favoured a more liberal approach. They differed over the kind of interpretation of the texts that would produce sensible and just results. Bulgarus assumed that Justinian's law was equitable and that the interpreter's function, in relation to any text, was to seek out the *ratio legis*, the purpose of the particular rule. In order to find this, other texts might be consulted, so long as they related to the same subject matter. For Martinus, on the other hand, that was not enough. The apparent meaning of a rule, when taken in isolation, could be modified by reference to equity. This was not merely a general idea of fairness (*equitas rudis*), but the equity which was to be gleaned from a consideration of the Corpus iuris as a whole (*equitas constituta*). In interpreting a particular text, therefore, one was not limited to a consideration of other texts dealing with the same topic but could take into account any text which seemed to throw light on the problem.

Bulgarus was succeeded as leader of the Bolognese school by his pupil Johannes Bassianus, who perfected the method of expounding the texts. In his view a proper treatment of a difficult text should have four stages. First, there should be a bare statement of the problem without any elaboration. Secondly, the teacher should cite contrary texts and the *solutiones* which had been suggested. Thirdly, the matter should be projected on to a wider plane by the citation of general propositions that were relevant to the case. Such propositions, Bassianus said, were popularly known as brocards. Finally, there should be a broad discussion of the problem, either immediately in class or in the evening, when more time was available. This method started from the individual text and broadened the discussion outwards, first to other relevant texts on the same matter and then to the law as a whole.

One of the aims of glossatorial scholarship was to discover the general principles, or brocards, inherent in the Corpus iuris. Some of them were already assembled in the last title of the Digest, dedicated to maxims. Others were detached from their original context and were used as part of an argument on any matter to which they could be made relevant. Their function in litigation was to establish a presumption in favour of the party relying on them, but their exact scope was undefined and frequently they could be met by a counter-proposition, which put forward an opposing view. Collections of brocards appear in the last quarter of the twelfth century. They always introduced strings of texts, which either supported or denied the proposition adopted by the brocard. Although apparently a civil law invention, they were taken up with enthusiasm by the canonists. They directed the busy lawyer quickly to the textual authorities, with which he could embellish his argument and impress the judge; often they were used to 'blind the judge with science.'

Bassianus's pupil Azo began the task of synthesising the detailed case discussions of the previous generations of glossators. His *summa* on the Code was to have enormous influence, so that it came to be regarded as indispensible for legal practice; the adage was 'who does not have Azo, should not go to court.' Finally, a century after Irnerius, between 1220 and 1240, the opinions of the whole school of civil law glossators were collected together by Azo's pupil, Accursius, in what became the standard *Glossa ordinaria* to Justinian's texts. It contains over 96,000 separate glosses, immediately superseded all earlier work and was always copied, and later printed, together with the original texts.

Without the help offered by Accursius's Gloss, it was thought, the texts could only offer partial guidance. For centuries, the Accursian Gloss was the basis of any doctrine which claimed to be derived from Roman law. The maxim came to be accepted that 'What the Gloss does not recognise, the Court does not recognise.' It is only in the last decades of the twentieth century that serious study of pre-Accursian writing has revealed the wealth of ideas produced by the generations between Irnerius and Accursius. The authority of the Gloss is the origin of the idea, still characteristic of the continental civil law, that authoritative academic comment on a legal text is itself an authentic source of law.

CIVIL LAW AND CANON LAW

Canon law was soon added to civil law as a subject of study at Bologna. It started with the disadvantage that, by contrast with the civil law, it lacked an authoritative body of texts, comparable to Justinian's corpus. There were various unofficial collections of material of different kinds, statements from the Bible, decisions of Church councils, opinions of Church Fathers, decisions (decretals) of Popes and fragments of Roman law. At first the civil lawyers regarded this disparate jumble with disdain, as unworthy of consideration as an autonomous discipline.

A dramatic change followed the publication by the monk Gratian, about 1140, of his *Concordantia discordantium canonum*, an authoritative collection, which sought to reconcile apparent contradictions. Unlike earlier compilers, Gratian provided explanations of the texts he had selected for inclusion in what came to be known as his *Decretum*. It superseded earlier canonist collections and was quickly accepted as an appropriate subject for glossatorial exegesis by canonists. Unlike the civil law, however, the texts of the canon law were continuously increasing with the promulgation of new papal decretals, which themselves had to be collected in new compilations.

The immediate reaction of orthodox civil lawyers to Gratian's achievement was negative. They continued to treat canon law as an inferior discipline to their own. In their view, Gratian was trying to do the impossible and was giving a spurious air of harmony to self-contradictory material. In their opinion, only the civil law provided all the techniques necessary for understanding any kind of law, including canon law. By the 1160s the civil lawyers had to recognise canon law as a parallel discipline to civil law, with parity of esteem, but they tended to keep their studies separate from canon law, even when the subject that they were discussing was covered by both systems, such as marriage or usury.

The civil law was a self-contained system, which had no need of supplementation from any other system. On the other hand, it was not applied exclusively in any court but only where the local law was lacking. Canon law, by contrast, was applied in the courts of the Church in all matters that appertained to ecclesiastical jurisdiction (the precise limits of the latter were much disputed and varied from country to country). For Gratian, canon law was a divine law, on a par with the law of the Gospel itself. It had to be admitted, however, that canon law did not have the answers to all legal questions, as the civil law claimed to do. The *Decretum* itself stated that in matters left undefined by the canons, the civil law should be followed (D.10 p.c.6). How this applied in practice was a matter of keen debate among the early canonists, known as decretists.

The question of filling gaps in the canon law from the civil law was tied up with two wider issues, that of the legislative power of the Pope, as having equal authority with that of the emperor, and that of the nature of the proceedings in ecclesiastical courts. Should they anticipate the judgment of God, by applying moral rules in the tradition of the Penitentials, or were they public proceedings which had to follow similar rules to those of other public courts? Some canonists, such as the Frenchman Stephen of Tournai, held that civil law applied wherever it was not contrary to canon law. Others were less deferential to the authority of the civil law. In this formative period of their law, however, all canonists paid close attention to the debates among their senior partners, the civil law glossators.

At the beginning of the thirteenth century the decretists made a conscious effort to elucidate the precise legal effect of the canons by making comparisons with Roman law. This applied even in the sacramental parts of the canon law. For example, Laurentius Hispanus in his *Glossa Palatina* to the *Decretum* discusses the question whether a heretic can administer a valid baptism. He cites Inst. 2.8.1 to the effect that a non-owner can sometimes transfer ownership, as when he sells a security given to him by a debtor and the debt has not been paid. Similarly, argues Laurentius, a heretic can confer spiritual grace, even though he lacks that grace himself (*ad De consecratione*. D.4 c.23 *v*. Romanus).

Between 1188 and 1226, five compilations of papal decretals appeared. Then, in 1234, Pope Gregory IX promulgated a large collection of extracts from papal decretals, based partly on these older compilations. The work was edited by the Spanish Dominican Raymond of Peñaforte, and was known as the *Liber extra* because it was outside (*extra*) Gratian's *Decretum*. It contains 1,971 chapters, arranged in five books. The order of treatment was cited by students according to the mnemonic verse 'judex, judicium, clerus, connubia, crimen,' that is, judges and their powers, legal proceedings, clerical matters, marriages and crime. The Decretals were intended to form, with the *Decretum*, the law of the universal church. In 1298 a further collection appeared, promulgated by Boniface VIII and known as *Liber sextus*, since it supplemented the five books of the *Liber extra*.

The earlier compilations had concluded with a title containing general legal maxims, in imitation of the concluding title of Justinian's Digest. But where Justinian found 202 examples, Gregory's *Liber extra* only included eleven. The popularity of maxims and brocards increased in the thirteenth century and the *Liber sextus* concludes with a title of eighty-eight. Many were transferred from the corresponding title of the Digest (50.17), in some cases with the wording made more pithy. Some were abstracted from other parts of the Corpus iuris and, removed from their original context, acquired greatly extended meaning.

Thus a famous principle, much bandied about in political debate, is *quod omnes tangit debet ab omnibus approbari* ('what touches all should be approved by all'), which is *reg*.29 in the *Liber sextus*. Originally this statement was part of a ruling in which Justinian explains that, where there were several guardians of the same ward, their joint administration of the ward's property could not be ended without the consent of all (C. 5.59.5.2). The canonists saw nothing strange about transferring the maxim from a private law context first to procedure and then to public law. Its authority came from the fact that it appeared somewhere in the texts of Justinian's law.

Certain other additions were made to the texts of authoritative canon law and by the end of the fourteenth century the Church had what came to be known as the Corpus iuris canonici, a compilation on a scale worthy of standing next to the Corpus iuris civilis of Justinian.

The compendious expression *utrumque ius*, 'both laws,' was used as a qualification for those who had studied both systems. It also indicated a relationship between them that became increasingly close as time went on. By the thirteenth century the two systems were on an equal footing and the civil lawyers sought to keep them in distinct spheres. The civil law was concerned with the common good of man on earth and the canon law with keeping him from sin and ensuring the salvation of his immortal soul. Accursius (*gl. conferens generi ad Auth. Coll.1.6, quomodo oportet episcopos*) states that the Pope should not meddle with temporal matters nor the emperor with spiritual matters.

As later civil lawyers pointed out with exasperation, however, by reason of its concern with sin the Church usurped to itself jurisdiction over everything. From the time of the *Liber extra*, canon law covered many matters which were treated in Justinian's law. It included a large part of criminal law, from adultery and perjury to forgery and homicide; it touched private law at many points where a party might be tempted to sin, such as loan, the taking of interest, sale and real and personal security for debt. Because marriage was a sacrament, it was regulated by canon law and, as a result, all questions of family status fell within its purview.

Already in the twelfth century, problems arose in connection with the computation of degrees of blood relationship. This was crucial in ascertaining whether the parties to an apparent marriage were within the prohibited degrees of kinship. Civil law counted the degrees merely upwards from the parties to the common ancestor, whereas canon law counted them from one party up to the common ancestor and then down to the other party. As a result, many more cousins found that, under canon law, they were within the prohibited degrees, and so needed papal dispensations to marry, than would have been the case under civil law. The Fourth Lateran Council limited the prohibited degrees to four.

The glossators had tended to ignore such differences, but by the fourteenth century the two laws came to be dealt with together, even by civilian commentators. Many canonists were laymen and a qualification in both laws (*in utroque iure*) became quite common. The phrase 'both laws' began to refer to two aspects of what in many respects was regarded as a single system, a *ius commune* for the whole of Europe.

THE ATTRACTION OF THE BOLOGNA *STUDIUM*

By the end of the twelfth century the position of Bologna as the legal centre (or 'mother of laws') of Europe was unchallenged and the *studium* had thousands of law students from all over Europe. They were grouped in 'nations' according to their country of origin. For the first time since the fall of Rome, law in the West was an autonomous discipline, whose special techniques had to be learned over several years of rigorous study, at the conclusion of which a professional qualification was received.

The law students not only attended lectures. They cut their teeth as lawyers by participating in disputations on set topics, in which each side presented an argument with supporting texts, after which the master presiding gave his solution to the problem. They were expected to equip themselves with a personal set of the more important texts. Authorised booksellers, known as *stationarii exempla tenentes*, held certified copies of the texts, which they hired out to students so that they could make their own copies. When their period of study was over, they would have the basic material to take with them. In this way former students were able to disseminate a knowledge of what they had learned in their own countries.

Although the emphasis of the Bologna law school was academic rather than practical, the students who flocked there were not all motivated by a disinterested love of learning. The Gregorian reforms had stimulated many disputes of a quite unprecedented character. They could not be settled by sheer force, as had been the case in earlier centuries. There was a yearning for power to be legitimated, but standard collections of laws, whether of Roman or Germanic origin, offered little guidance on fundamental questions of jurisdiction and the like. Bishops and secular princes alike looked for men who could deploy arguments, based on principles which were objective and rational and had a universal authority. Only the Roman texts could provide such principles. The new legal learning provided its students with qualifications which won them positions of responsibility both in episcopal and princely establishments. Enlightened bishops sent their promising young chaplains to Bologna to acquire at least some knowledge of the new learning, while princes and nobles seeking to legitimate their power sought to ensure that its results were also available to them.

The University of Bologna was not founded by a deliberate act. It emerged out of the need, felt by the students of law, to organise themselves for the purpose of ensuring that they received the most effective teaching and obtained a recognised qualification. In contrast with the other twelfth-century universities of Paris and Oxford, established and governed by masters, Bologna became the model of a university governed by students, who employed the professors to teach them. Although other higher subjects, such as theology and medicine, were also taught there, law, both civil and canon, remained dominant.

Both the imperial and the papal authorities endeavoured to find favour with the Bolognese *studium*, by supporting it in its dealings with the municipal authorities of the city. The influx of students had created serious problems for the citizens but they did not want to lose the economic advantages that the students' presence brought them. The young Emperor Frederick Barbarossa, on his way to Rome for his coronation in 1155, stopped at Bologna to meet the leading doctors of law and to seek their support, in justifying certain laws that he wished to enact. Having obtained their assistance, he promulgated the *Constitutio habita*, in which he conferred privileges on law students coming to Bologna, whom he described as "pilgrims for the sake of study." In particular Frederick recognised corporations of students, who were to be allowed to govern themselves in the manner of craft guilds. This concession enabled the students to negotiate with the professors but it also gave the *studium* as a whole a certain independence from the commune of Bologna.

By the beginning of the thirteenth century, the students were sufficiently strong that they could often get their way by threatening to secede from the town. The commune reacted by trying to keep them and it was now the turn of the papal authorities to intervene on the students' behalf. In 1217 Pope Honorius III pointed out that, instead of trying to compel the students to stay, it would be better for the commune to adopt measures that would encourage them to remain there of their own free will. Two years later, the Pope granted the archdeacon of Bologna the power to confer on successful students the right of teaching everywhere, thus indirectly subordinating the university to the Church.

The success of Bologna ensured its imitation through the foundation of law schools in other parts of Italy. There was a law school at Modena in 1175. The *studium* at Padua was begun in 1222, and the example was followed by other Italian centres, such as Pavia, where the old school of Lombard law developed into a school of civil and canon law. In 1224 the Emperor Frederick II founded the university of Naples, largely for the study of Roman civil law, and sought to ensure its success by commanding his subjects to study there rather than in Bologna. At first the order applied only to those in the kingdom of Sicily, but, in the course of his dispute with the Lombard League, to which Bologna adhered, he extended the ban on studying at Bologna to his subjects in his Lombard dominions and to those in Germany and Burgundy. This might have proved disastrous for Bologna but again Pope Honorius III stepped in and obtained a revocation of the ban.

* * *

THE COMMENTATORS

Bartolus, who gave his name to the school which dominated the study of the civil law during the fourteenth and fifteenth centuries, was born in 1313 or 1314 in Sassoferrato, a small village in the Marches, and died in 1357. He began his studies of law, at the age of thirteen or fourteen, at Perugia under Cinus and later went on to Bologna, where he took his doctorate at the age of twenty. He was a judge in the small town of Todi and then devoted himself to teaching, first at Pisa and then at Perugia, where he died. His short life was completely absorbed by the law and his output was phenomenal: apart from treatises on particular topics, he wrote exhaustive commentaries on all parts of the Corpus iuris, which in the early printed editions fill nine folio volumes.

True, much of the material consisted of citation of his predecessors but Bartolus always added something of his own, usually a clear path through the thickets of earlier debates, indicating a practical solution to a problem. Under his influence the study of the civil law became less purely academic and more orientated towards the legal problems of the day. He and his followers continued to expound the texts in the form in which they were transmitted but their aim was no longer to explain the meaning of those texts as they stood. Rather they sought to find in them rules which would be appropriate for late medieval society but would still carry the authority of imperial law.

Bartolus realised that the law had to be accommodated to the facts. On the question of the emperor's power over the Italian cities, he was able to build on Azo's views. Although in law the emperor was lord of the world, Bartolus observed that in practice many peoples did not obey him. In the Italian city-states, the people recognised no superior, they made laws as they chose and so, he concluded, they possessed *imperium*, with as much power within their territories as the emperor had generally. If they had been exercising this power for a long time, they need not prove any concession from the emperor. Indeed, when the people confer power on their rulers, the latter are the delegates of the people, who retain ultimate authority.

Bartolus's practical tendency can be illustrated from his approach to the problems that arose where different laws came into conflict: between civil law and local law, between one local law and another and between civil law and canon law.

Bartolus confronted the issue of a conflict between civil law and local law in a discussion of a custom of Venice. This custom accorded validity to a will if it had three witnesses, which was directly contradictory of the Roman rule that required a minimum of five witnesses (C.6.23.31). Bartolus sought the reason for holding a local custom to be void, if it conflicted with imperial law, and concluded that it must be that it was thereby presumed to be a bad custom. The Roman emperors, however, are known to have allowed conflicting local customs to exist by way of privilege. It follows that it must have been possible to rebut the presumption that a conflicting custom is necessarily a bad custom. Justinian's law could only invalidate customs already in existence in his time. It is possible to prove that a later custom is good, even if it conflicts with Justinian's law. The Venetians knew their own needs best. If they thought it unreasonable to expect five merchants to interrupt their business activities in order to witness a will, a rule according validity to a will with only three witnesses should be valid or else testators' last wishes would be frustrated. In this way Bartolus used Roman arguments to stand Justinian's rule on its head.

Although Bartolus had to justify the existence of a particular law (*ius proprium*) alongside the *ius commune*, he gained acceptance for the notion that local statues must be interpreted according to the methods established by the *ius commune* and in such a way as to derogate as little as possible from the *ius commune*. There are no rules in the Corpus iuris which deal expressly with the conflict between different secular laws. In Justinian's time almost all those living in the Roman empire were Roman citizens, so that problems of conflict did not arise. In the complex world of fourteenth-century Italian city-states, on the other hand, such problems were pressing and general rules were sorely needed. The glossators had held that a person's law is that of the community of which he is a citizen, but problems arose when two merchants from different cities made a contract with each other.

Bartolus took specific cases reported in the Corpus iuris and generalised their rulings, producing a coherent set of convenient rules, nowhere expressly stated in the Corpus iuris but claiming the authority of that law. The procedure in a civil action must always be governed by the law of the court in which the action is brought. As to the rules to be applied, however, the form of the contract must be governed by the law of the place where it was made, whereas any issue concerning the performance of the contract must be ruled by the law of the place where it should have been carried out.

The conflicts between civil law and canon law had to be dealt with by conciliatory methods. One problem, in which the two laws came into conflict, was that involving a will that the testator had confirmed by an oath, in which he swore not to change its terms in a subsequent will. The canonists considered the vital element to be the oath. For Durandus, for example, there was no problem. Every oath, which could be carried out without prejudice to one's immortal soul, had to be observed. The civilians emphasised the principle of freedom of testation. A testator must be free to change his mind and revoke the earlier will, by making a new will, at any time before he dies. The oath is not binding on him since, by purporting to limit this freedom, it is contrary to the law.

Later jurists, particularly the Orleans masters, made valiant efforts to reconcile the two positions, by allowing validity to a later will under certain conditions. The basic question was whether the law should allow an irrevocable will. Bartolus was determined that it should not but, unlike some of his predecessors, he could not just ignore canon law. In his view an attempt to deprive the testator of his freedom of testation was immoral (*contra bonos mores*) and as such was not binding, even by canon law. His conclusion was stated in the general rule that whatever is disapproved by the authority of the law is not validated by the force of an oath. Eventually Bartolus's accommodation of civil and canon law was accepted.

By making explicit the rationale that seemed to lie behind the spare rulings of the Roman texts, Bartolus was able to produce a set of new rules, which could claim to enjoy the authority of imperial law. Jurists were agreed that henceforth no one could be a lawyer who was not a Bartolist (*nemo jurista nisi Bartolista*). His methods were followed by a whole school, known as Commentators, of whom the most distinguished was his pupil Baldus de Ubaldis.

Baldus dominated the second half of the fourteenth century, dying in 1400. He commented not only in the civil law but also canon law and feudal law and perfected the opinion (*consilium*), a discussion of the legal issues raised by a particular case. This form of legal literature completed the adaptation of the civil law to contemporary problems.

By the fourteenth century the *ius commune* consolidated its position as part of a common Christian culture of Europe. It is this unity of culture which explains why law and religion were so closely related in late medieval writing.

Note: Roman law after the medieval commentators.

For the most part, the medieval professors of Roman law thought that their task was, so far as possible, to reconcile logically every text of the *Corpus iuris civilis* of Justinian and the *Corpus iuris canonici* with every other. Philosophy was studied in the medieval universities. After the 13th century, it was commonly the philosophy of Aristotle. But the medieval jurists did not try to explain Roman law in philosophical terms.

That enterprise began in the early 16th century. A group of jurists centered in Spain and known to historians as the "late scholastics" embarked on a project which was fundamentally different.[1] Some of the leading figures were not only jurists but Catholic theologians: for example, the Dominican Domingo de Soto (1494–1560), and the Jesuits Luis de Molina (1535–1600) and Leonard Lessius (1554–1623). They self-consciously tried to synthesize Roman and Canon law with the philosophy of their intellectual heroes, Aristotle and Thomas Aquinas. In the process, they gave private law a theory and a systematic doctrinal structure for the first time. Instead of writing commentaries on the texts of Roman or Canon law, they wrote books with sections on property, contract and tort. The sections would begin by describing the fundamental principles that should govern these fields of law. These principles were then used to explain as many Roman rules as possible. For examples, these authors explained that contracts require the consent of the parties, and then discussed the effect on consent of mistake, fraud, and duress.[2] In the *Corpus iuris civilis*, mistake is discussed in couple of texts that appear under the law of sales, and fraud and duress in discussions of the Roman actions *de dolo* and *quod metus causa*. The Romans had discussed different kinds of contracts and torts without ever trying to define what a contract or tort was. The late scholastics equated contract and tort with the two kinds of commutative justice described by Aristotle. In an act of voluntary commutative justice, the parties exchanged resources voluntarily but at a price at which neither profited at his own expense. In an act of involuntary commutative justice, one party had enriched himself at another's expense against the will of his victim. Justice required that he make compensation. Having identified these philosophical ideas with contract and tort as known to Roman law, the late scholastics then used them to explain Roman rules.

In the 17th and 18th century, Aristotelian philosophy fell into disfavor in large part through the attacks of the founders of modern critical philosophy. Paradoxically, however, many of the conclusions of the late scholastics were spread throughout Europe by the northern Natural Law School founded by Hugo Grotius (1583–1645) and Samuel Pufendorf (1632–94). The members of the school were steadily more vague about the philosophical principles that underpinned these conclusions. Thus the conclusions drifted on without the principles that had originally inspired them.

Other 17th and 18th century jurists had a more practical turn of mind. They continued to write commentaries on Roman texts which were often quite learned but had little philosophical content at all. Many of the most famous of them came from Holland or Germany, and so their work is often said to belong to a Dutch-German school of law. Leaders were Arnold Vinnius (1588–1657), Samuel Stryk (1640–1710), Johannes Voet (1647–1713) and Cornelis van Bykershock (1673–1743).

---

1. James Gordley, *The Philosophical Origins of Modern Contract Doctrine* (1991), 68–111.

2. For example, Domenicus Soto, *De iustitia et iure libri decem* (1553), lib. 8, q. 2, a.1; Ludovicus Molina, *De iustitia et iure tractatus* (1614), disp. 352; Leonardus Lessius, *De iustitia et iure, ceterisque virtutibus cardinalis libri quatuor* (1628), lib. 2, cap. 17, dubs. 5–6.

The question of how far modern law owes its specific doctrines to the Roman jurists and the schools that followed them will be faced when we turn to the law of property, tort, contract and unjust enrichment.

II. CODIFICATION

1. Codification in France

a. The enactment of the French Civil Code

Arthur von Mehren & James R. Gordley, *The Civil Law System* (2d ed., 1977), 48–51

Plans for a unified law for France predate the enactment of the Code Civil.[136] But, except for the three Ordinances of Chancellor D'Aguesseau drafted between 1731 and 1747, the private law of France remained as essentially diverse at the end of the 18th century as it had been at the beginning of the 15th. Voltaire described the situation tersely: The traveler changed his law as often as he changed his horses. The reasons why legal diversity persisted in the face of considerable political and economic unity are varied. Of particular importance was the fact that the tradition of local independence remained strong in the provinces[137] and, as central control became more effective in some areas of life, increasingly found expression in local legal practices and through provincial institutions, especially the Parliaments.

The French Revolution of 1789 shattered the old institutional structures; in particular, the Parliaments were eradicated. Political power and the machinery of government were now centralized to a degree never before known in France.

Codification efforts began at once. On July 5, 1790, the Constituent Assembly voted "that the civil laws would be reviewed and reformed by the legislators and that there would be made a general code of laws simple, clear and appropriate to the constitution."[138] The first Title of the Constitution of 1791 concluded with the promise that "a Code of civil laws common to the whole Kingdom will be enacted." However, the Constituent Assembly and its short-lived successor the Legislative Assembly, never found time to undertake the task of codification.

Actual work on codification began under the Convention (1792–1795). Its Committee on Legislation was directed in June 1793 to prepare a draft

---

136. A useful and detailed discussion in English of the preparation and enactment of the Code Civil is contained in A General Survey of Continental Legal History 279–84 vol. I of the Continental Legal History Series, 1912.

137. "The spirit of the province always caused these projects [for a uniform civil law] to fail: each fraction of the nation regarded its particular laws as a heritage guaranteed by the pact that had incorporated it into France." 1 J. Locré, La Legislation civile, commerciale et criminelle de la France 69 (1827).

138. Quoted in P. Fenet, Recueil complet des travaux préparatoires du Code Civil xxxvi (1827).

code within a month.[139] In August, Cambacérès presented an incomplete draft of 715 articles.[140] The Convention ultimately rejected this draft "as too complicated; one wanted simpler and more philosophic conceptions." [141] After Robespierre's downfall, a second draft of only 297 articles was presented by Cambacérès on 23 fructidor An II.[142] A few articles were approved[143] but ultimately nothing came of the project. The Convention itself realized that the draft "was too concise and was more a table of contents than a Code of civil laws . . ." [144]

The codification effort continued under the Directory (1795–1799). Cambacérès presented a draft of 1104 articles to the Council of Five Hundred on 24 prairial An IV. But political tensions prevented further action.[145] Real progress toward codification began only under the Consulate (1799–1804).[146] Bonaparte as First Consul had concentrated great power in his hands and harbored the ambition to be known by history as a great lawgiver. By an arrêt of 24 thermidor An VIII (13 August 1800),[147] he appointed a commission of four to prepare a draft by November. The commission's members were Tronchet, president of the Tribunal de cassation; Bigot-Préameneu, a Commissaire du gouvernement in a Prize Court; and Malleville, a judge of the Tribunal de cassation who served as secrétaire rédacteur.[148] The three Cambacérès drafts and the Jacqueminot draft—presented to the Legislative Committee of the Council of Five Hundred on 30 frimaire An VIII (21 December 1799)—were transmitted to the commission pursuant to article 3 of the arrêt.

A portion of the subject matter to be covered by the code was assigned to each of the commission's members; in four months they had prepared a

---

139. See id. xxxvi–xxxvii.

140. See id. 15–98. The report by Cambacérès that accompanied the draft appears in id. 1–16. The convention's debates on the draft are contained in id. xxxvii–xlvi.

141. Id. xlvii.

142. See id. 110–39 for the draft; Cambacérès's report presenting it appears in id. 99–109.

143. See id. xlvii–xlviii.

144. Id. xlvii. The objections mentioned in the text to the two Cambacèrés drafts are those noted by Cambacérès in presenting his third draft to the Council of Five Hundred. See id. lii, at liv.

145. See id. xlix. Cambacérès's report on the draft was made in the month of messidor An IV. See id. 170–77. The draft is contained in id. 178–326. The debates on the third Cambacérès's draft in the Council of Five Hundred are given in id. lii–liv.

After the coup d'état of 18–19 brumaire An VII (November 9–10, 1799), had replaced the Directory by a Commission Consulaire Exécutive, a fourth draft of seven hundred and fifty-seven articles—this time prepared by Jacqueminot—was presented to the Commission Législative du Conseil des Cinq-Cents, the successor to the Council of

Five Hundred. The draft is given in id. 333–462; Jacqueminot's report on the draft is in id. 327–32. No significant consideration was given to this draft by the Commission Legislative.

146. The Consulate first functioned under the Constitution of the Year VIII (December 25, 1799). For the circumstances surrounding the replacing of the Constitution of the Year III by that of the Year VIII, see J. Godechot, Les Constitutions de la France depuis 1789, 143–50 (1970). In 1802, the powers of the First Consul were considerably augmented by the Sénatus-consulte organique de la Constitution du 16 thermidor An X (August 4, 1802). See id. 163–66. The so-called Constitution of the Year X did not, however, fully supplant the Constitution of the Year VIII. The basic structure of government there established is assumed and continued. The later document thus explicitly refers to the earlier one as "la Constitution." See, e.g., arts. 31, 54, 55, 61, 63.

147. See 1 Fenet, loc. cit. supra note 138, lxii–lxiii.

148. See article 2 of the arrèt; article 7 provided that Malleville, unlike the other three commissioners, would not attend the Council of State's discussions of the draft.

draft.[149] This draft was submitted for comment to the Tribunal de cassation and the courts of appeal, which responded quickly and thoughtfully.[150] The complex legislative process required by the Constitution of the Year VIII then began.[151] The General Assembly of the Council of State first considered the draft on 28 messidor An IX (17 July 1801).[152] Upon completion of discussion of a segment of the draft, the Council's recommendation—uniformly favorable—was transmitted to the First Consul, who submitted it to the Tribunate.

Difficulties were encountered in the Tribunate, however. This body was composed of 100 members, appointed by the Senate, and had the function of debating drafts proposed by the government, ultimately recommending approval or disapproval to amending the draft submitted to it. However, its negative recommendation presented by three of its members to the Legislative Body could influence significantly the latter's vote.

The Legislative Body was composed of 300 members chosen by the Senate from lists of national notables.[153] This body could not amend bills and voted 'in secret and without any discussion by its members . . .'[154] If a measure was approved, the First Consul promulgated the law ten days later unless, within that period, either the Tribunate or the government challenged the law's constitutionality by referring it to the Sénat conservateur.[155]

---

149. See the statement of Malleville, quoted in 1 Fenet, op. cit. supra note 138, lxiii.

150. For the observations of the Tribunal de cassation, see 1 Fenet, op. cit. supra note 138, 415 ff.; for those of the cours d'appel see 3–5 id.

151. See the Constitution of the Year VIII, arts. 25–37.

152. The Council of State first considered the drafts of the Civil Code in its legislation section whose members were Boulay de la Meurthe, Berber, Emmery, Portalis, Réal, and Thibaudeau. See 1 Fenet, op. cit. supra note 138, lxiv. After the section had considered a draft, the proposal was referred to the First Consul by whom it was then submitted to the General Assembly of the Council.

The General Assembly's discussions continued until 14 nivôse An X (January 4, 1802) when they were suspended until 22 fructidor An X (September 4, 1802). The final discussion on the Civil Code in the General Assembly was held on 26 ventôse Am XII (March 17, 1804). See 1 Locrè, op. cit. supra note 137, 74.

153. National notables comprised one-tenth, selected by co-option, of the departmental notables. These latter were selected in a comparable manner from among the communal notables. Communal notables were elected by universal suffrage. See Constitution of the Year VIII, arts. 6–14. The Constitution provided for drawing officials at each level of government from a list of notables established for that level. This complex system was devised by Sieyès to permit universal suffrage while avoiding the tendency towards anarchy that had characterized the period of the Convention. See Godechot, op. cit. supra note 146, 146–48. The system never functioned effectively and was abolished by the Constitution of the Year X. See id. 148, 165. Thereafter, only cantonal assemblies were elected by universal suffrage. The cantonal assemblies selected electoral colleges for the arrondissement and for the department. Members of these colleges served for life and, in the case of the departmental college, were selected from among the six hundred largest tax-payers of the department. The function of the electoral colleges was to nominate candidates for various offices; each college nominated, for example, two candidates for the list from which the members of the Legislative Body were named by the Senate. See Constitution of the Year X, arts. 4–38, 59; Constitution of the Year VIII, art. 20.

154. See id. arts. 9, 19, 20, 31. The lists from which members of the Legislative Body were chosen were also used by the Senate in electing "les tribuns, les consuls, les juges de cassation, et les commissaires à la comptabilité." Id. art. 20.

155. Id. art. 34.

Many political opponents of Bonaparte were members of the Tribunate. They attacked the code drafts as a servile imitation and vapid compilation.[156] The Tribunate was either persuaded by these arguments or desired to embarrass the First Consul; accordingly, their recommendations to the Legislative Body on the first two drafts were negative.[157] The first draft was rejected,[158] and the second was in jeopardy when Bonaparte decided to withdraw it. A message to the Legislative Body dated 13 nivôse An X (3 January 1802) announced that:

> Legislators, the government has decided to withdraw the drafts of the Civil Code. . . . It regretfully finds itself compelled to defer until another time the laws which the nation awaits with such interest, but is convinced that the time has not yet arrived when the calmness and unity of purpose required can be employed in these important discussions.[159]

Bonaparte promptly set about securing the desired calmness and unity of purpose by removing those who disagreed with him. Article 76 of the Constitution of the Year X[160] reduced the Tribunate's membership to fifty; the reduction in size was accomplished by eliminating Bonaparte's opponents.[161] The Tribunate's capacity to frustrate the government's purpose was further restricted by dividing it into three sections: legislation, internal affairs, and finances.[162] In addition, provision was made for "semi-official communications" between the Council of State and the Tribunate.[163] When these two bodies had reached agreement on a draft, it was transmitted by the First Consul to the Legislative Body, which then formally transmitted the proposal to the Tribunate to obtain its views.

---

156. Id. arts. 21, 37. Once the law had been promulgated no further constitutional challenge was possible. Id. art. 37. The Sénat Conservateur's members served for life. Id. art. 15. They were selected by the Sénate Conservateur from a panel of three for each vacancy, one candidate being proposed by each of the following: the Legislative Body, the Tribunate, and the First Consul. Id. art. 16. To the extent that the proposers agreed upon candidates, the Senate's power of selection was restricted. Ibid.

157. See 1 Locré, op. cit. supra note 137, 85–87. Locré believes that the Tribunate was motivated both by the desire to retain legislative supremacy and by political and personal opposition to Bonaparte. See id. 85–86.

158. The Tribunate's recommendation on the third draft—the last considered by it before Bonaparte withdrew the drafts—was favorable. See 1 Fenet, op. cit. supra note 138, lxxvii.

159. Ibid.

160. Article 77 provided for renewal of the entire membership of the Tribunate or of the Legislative Body, respectively, when the Senate ordered dissolution. Although the Sénat Conservateur appeared to receive substantial new powers (see arts. 54–65), these were illusory because of the First Consul's hold over the body's personnel. See Godechot, op. cit. supra note 146, 166.

161. For the constitutional and political arrangements that made this purge possible, see notes 153 and 160 supra.

162. A sénatus-consulte of August 19, 1807 abolished the Tribunate; committees corresponding to its three sections were established in the Legislative Body.

163. This is the so-called communication officieuse, provided for by the arrêt of 11 germinal An X (April 1, 1802) and 18 germinal An X (April 8, 1802), set out in 1 Fenet, op. cit. supra note 138, lxvii, as distinguished from the communication officieuse, required by the Constitution, from the Legislative Body to the Tribunate to obtain the latter's views. The introduction of the communication officieuse was designed, at least in part, to make consultation with the Tribunate more useful and flexible by affording that body an opportunity to suggest changes in drafts. See 1 Locré, op. cit. supra note 137, 88–89.

Proceeding in this fashion, the draft Civil Code, between March 1803 and March 1804, was voted and promulgated in 36 separate laws. A law of 30 ventôse An XII (21 March 1804) consolidated these separate laws into a single Code civil des Français of 2281 articles.

b. The interpretation of the code

The earlier understanding: Portalis

Portalis, "Discours préliminaire prononcé lors de la présentation du projet de la Commission du gouvernement" in P.A. Fenet, *Recueil complet des travaux préparatoires du Code civil* (1827), I, 461 at 467–72

At the beginning of our meetings we were struck by the view, which is so generally widespread, that a few precise texts on each subject would be enough for the redaction of the Civil Code, and that the great art is to simplify everything while foreseeing everything.

To simplify everything is a work on which one must agree. To foresee everything is a an end which it is impossible to achieve.

We do not need useless laws. They weaken necessary laws and compromise the certainty and majesty of legislation. But a great state such as France, which is both agricultural and commercial, which consists of so many different professions and which offers so many different types of activity, cannot have laws as simple as those of a society which is poor or more restricted.

* * *

In despotic states where the prince is the owner of the entire territory or where all commerce is done in the name of the head of state and for his profit, where individuals have neither liberty nor choice nor property, there are more judges and executioners than laws: but wherever the citizens have goods to preserve and protect, wherever they have political and civil rights, wherever honor counts for something, one must have a certain number of a laws to address all the problems.

The different types of goods, the different varieties of activity, the various situations of human life demand different rules. The care of the legislator must be proportionate to the multiplicity and importance of the matters to be governed. Whence comes, in the codes of civilized nations, that scrupulous foresight which multiplies particular cases and seems to make an art of reason itself.

We have not therefore thought it our duty to simplify the laws to the point of leaving citizens without a rule and without a guarantee of their greatest interests.

Equally, we have preserved ourselves from the dangerous ambition of wanting to regulate everything and foresee everything. Who could think that there are those, often the ones to whom a code would always appear too large, who would dare imperiously to prescribe for the legislator the terrible task of leaving nothing for the determination of the judge?

* * *

The task of the law is to establish in broad perspective the general principles of the law, to establish principles that are fertile in consequences, and not to descend into detail into the questions which each topic may raise.

It is for the magistrate and the jurist, penetrated with the general spirit of the laws, to direct their application.

Whence, among all civilized nations, one always sees the formation, by the sanctuary of the laws and under the surveillance of the legislator, of a deposit of principles, of decisions, and of doctrines which are daily purified by practice and by the clash of legal argument, a deposit which increasingly grows with all the knowledge acquired and which has constantly been seen as the supplement of legislation.

Those who profess the study of law have been criticized for multiplying subtleties, compilations, and commentaries. That criticism may be well founded. But in what art, what science, is one not open to the same charge? Should one accuse a particular class of men for what is only a general malady of the human spirit? There are times when one is condemned to ignorance because there is a lack of books; there are other times when it is difficult to learn because there are too many of them.

If one can pardon intemperance in commenting, discussing and writing, it is above all in the study of law. To believe without hesitation that it is so, one need only reflect on the innumerable links which bind citizens, on the development and progression in turn of the matters with which the magistrate and the jurist are obliged to deal, on the course of events and the circumstances which modify social relations in so many ways, and, finally, on the continual action and reaction of all of the different passions and interests. One can hardly blame subtleties and commentaries which become in a personal case the most subtle and fastidious of guides.

No doubt it would be desirable if everything could be governed by statutes.

But absent a precise text on each subject, an old continuous and well-established usage, an uninterrupted line of similar decisions, an opinion or an accepted principle takes the place of statute. When no direction is to be found in anything established or known, when it is an absolutely new event, one returns to the principles of natural law. For if the foresight of legislators is limited, nature is infinite; it applies to everything in which men may be interested.

All this presupposes compilations, collections of cases, treatises, many volumes of research, and dissertations.

The people, some say, cannot disentangle in this maze what they must avoid and what they must do for the security of their possessions and their rights.

But would a code, even the simplest, be within reach of all the classes of society? Would passions not be perpetually engaged in twisting their sense? Isn't a certain experience necessary to make a wise application of statutes? What nation can one find in which a small number of simple statutes proved sufficient for long?

It would therefore be an error to think that a body of laws could exist which could foresee all cases in advance and nevertheless be within the grasp of the least citizen.

In the state of our societies, it is only too fortunate that the study of law constitutes a science which can attract talent, flatter *amour-propre*, and inspire emulation. An entire class of men devotes itself to this science, and this class, dedicated to the study of laws, gives advice and defense to citizens who cannot direct and defend themselves. It becomes like a seminary of judges.

It is only too fortunate that there are collections of cases and a received tradition of usages, principles and rules because one must decide today as one decided yesterday, and there must be no other changes in public decisions than those which are caused by the progress of thought and by the force of circumstances.

It is only too fortunate that the judge's need to learn, to do research, and to delve into the questions presented before him never lets him forget that if there are matters left open to his reason, nothing is left purely to his caprice or his will.

In Turkey, where legal studies are not an art, where the *bacha* can rule as he will when higher orders displease him, litigants ask and receive justice only in fear. Why is there not the same anxiety before our judges? It is because they are experienced in matters, because they have insight and knowledge, and because they believe that they are unceasingly obliged to rely on that of others. One can understand how far this habituation to science and reason moderates and governs power.

The later understanding: The exegetical school

Charles Aubry & Charles Rau, *Cours de droit civil français* 1 (4th ed. 1869), §§ 1–2

Law (*droit*) is the body of rules or precepts of conduct by observation of which it is permitted to restrain man by external or physical coercion. Precepts relating only to purely interior acts escape such coercion by their nature and by that fact are outside the sphere of law. Precepts relating to exterior acts can legitimately become the object of physical coercion whenever the acts involved are of such a nature that their performance or omission offends the moral sense of a people in a given epoch, and thus provokes formal reprobation by the public conscience. . . . The body of precepts or rules of conduct which, according to the nature of the acts they govern, may legitimately become the object of external coercion constitute what one terms natural law. One calls positive law the body of precepts which in fact have been recognized or declared susceptible of such coercion by custom . . . or statute (*loi*).

[The following explanation is added in a footnote.] The criterion of determining the precepts legitimately susceptible of becoming the object of external coercion resides in the collective consciousness of each people, and the moral sense of a nation modifies itself according to its degree of civilization; hence, in our view, natural law does not constitute a complete body of absolute and immutable precepts, anterior and superior to all positive legislation, such as, for example, the personality of man, the right of property, the constitution of the family, the liberty and binding force of contracts, and the necessity of the State. It merely appears to us to be impossible to determine a priori the rules destined to organize and develop these principles, rules which themselves present on a contingent and variable character.

Note: If the rules in force have only a contingent and variable character, how can one determine what they are, absent a clear text of the Code? Presumably, not in the way Portalis suggested. Many French jurists concluded that, therefore, these rules must be interpretations of the texts of the Code. In the following passage, Aubry and Rau explain how interpretation is possible. In fact, for centuries, jurists had given similar descriptions of how particular statutes were to be interpreted. Statutes, however, had been interstitial. Now, these methods were supposedly capable of establish all the rules of private law.[1] That conviction led to attitudes like the one expressed by Demolombe in the passage following the next one. The texts of the Civil Code, exegetically interpreted, were the civil law. Whether it has been possible for French courts to interpret them in this way, and whether they have actually tried to do so, is a question we will confront issue by issue in dealing with property, tort, contract, and unjust enrichment.

Charles Aubry & Charles Rau *Cours de droit civil français* 1 (4th ed., 1869), § 40

The Napoleonic Code does not contain rules for the interpretation of laws, but those which it gives. . . . for the interpretation of contracts may be applied by analogy. Laws, in fact, are the expression of the will of the legislator, as contracts are the expression of the will of the parties.

One may have recourse to interpretation of the law in two distinct cases:

(1) When the phrasing used by the legislator does not present a clear and complete meaning taken alone, whether because of the more or less vague significance of the words, or because of a more or less defective phrase construction.

(2) When that phrasing, although presenting a clearly determined sense, does not exactly express the thought of the legislator.

---

1. I am indebted for this insight to P.G. Monatieri.

In the first case, interpretation is absolutely necessary; in the second it is legitimate, insofar as it pursues the single goal of finding the true thought of the legislator with the aim of arriving at the exact application of a legal text. . . .

Commonly, interpretation is called grammatical if it is designed to discover the true sense of an obscure or incomplete law with the aid of linguistic usage and rules of syntax. . . . The opposing concept is logical interpretation, which includes all other means of interpretation. . . .

The principal means by which logical interpretation proceeds are the following:

(1) Juxtaposition of the text being interpreted with other legal dispositions relating to the same or analogous matters.
(2) Discovery of the motives or end of the law, i.e., the spirit of the law, whether from preparatory work that led to the code or from previous law.
(3) Evaluation of the consequences to which the application of the law would lead if it were given either an extended or a restricted sense.

These different procedures do not have an equal value, and do not give results of an equal certitude. The surest is without doubt the first. As to the last, one must only have recourse to it with great reserve, and not to give it decisive weight unless it leads to rejecting an application of a law that would lead to manifest iniquity. . . .

Charles Demolombe, *Traité publication, des effets et de l'application des lois en géneral, preface* (ed. 4, 1869)

My motto, my profession of faith is this: The texts before all else! I am publishing a treatise on the Napoleonic Code; my aim is, accordingly, to interpret and explain the Napoleonic Code itself, considered as living law, as applicable and obligatory law.

2. Codification in Germany

a. The initial opposition

Friedrich Karl von Savigny, *The Vocation of our Age for Legislation and Jurisprudence* (trans. A. Hayward, 1831), 24, 28, 38–42

We first inquire of history, how law has actually developed itself amongst nations of the nobler races; the question—What may be good, or necessary, or, on the contrary, censurable herein—will be not at all prejudiced by this method of proceeding.

In the earliest times to which authentic history extends, the law will be found to have already attained a fixed character, peculiar to the people, like their language, manners and constitution. Nay, these phenomena have no separate existence, they are but the particular faculties and tendencies of an individual people, inseparably united in nature, and only wearing the semblance of distinct attributes to our view. That which binds them into one whole is the common conviction of the people, the kindred consciousness of an inward necessity, excluding all notion of an accidental and arbitrary origin.

* * *

With the progress of civilization, national tendencies become more and more distinct, and what would otherwise have remained common becomes appropriated to particular classes; the jurists now become a more and more a distinct class of the kind; law perfects its language, takes a scientific direction, and, as formerly it existed in the consciousness of the community, it now devolves upon the jurists, who thus, in this department, represent the community. Law is henceforth more artificial and complex, since it has a two-fold life; first, as a member of the community, which it does not cease to be, and secondly, as a distinct branch of knowledge in the hands of the jurists.

[Savigny observes that this development can proceed with only occasional intervention from the legislature, and does not require that the whole body of law be rethought or codified. He then criticizes codes.]

As regards the substance, the most important and difficult part is the completeness of the code, and upon this point we have only fully to comprehend the following proposition, in which all agree.

The code, then, as it is intended to be the only law-authority, is actually to contain, by anticipation, a decision for every case that may arise. This has been often conceived, as if it were possible and advantageous to obtain, by experience, a perfect knowledge of the particular cases, and then to decide each by a corresponding provision of the code. But whoever has considered law-cases attentively, will see at a glance that this undertaking must fail, because there are positively no limits to the varieties of actual combinations of circumstances. In all the new codes, indeed, all appearance of an attempt to obtain this material perfection has been given up, without, however, establishing any thing in its stead. But there is certainly a perfection of a different kind, which may be illustrated by a technical expression of geometry. In every triangle, namely, there are certain data, from the relations of which all the rest are necessarily deducible: thus, given two sides and the included angle, the whole triangle is given. In like manner, every part of our law has points by which the rest may be given: these may be given: these may be termed the leading axioms. To distinguish these, and deduce from them the internal connection, and the precise degree of affinity which subsist between all juridical notions and rules, is amongst the most difficult of the problems of jurisprudence. Indeed, it is peculiarly this which gives our labours the scientific character. If then the code be formed in a time which is unequal to this art, the following evils are inevitable: The administration of justice is ostensibly regulated by the code, but really by something else, external to the code, acting as the true dominant authority. This false appearance, however, is productive of the most disastrous effects. For the code, by its novelty, its connection with the prevailing notions of the age, and its external influence, will infallibly attract all attention to itself, away from the real law-authority; so that the latter, left in darkness and obscurity, will derive no assistance from the moral energies of the nation, by which alone it can attain to a satisfactory state. That this is no groundless apprehension, will appear further on when we come to treat of the new codes: and it will be seen that not only the substance itself, but the very notion and general nature of this true governing source of law is misunderstood, as it then appears under the most opposite names, sometimes as natural law (Naturrecht), sometimes as jurisprudence, sometimes as analogical law. If to this imperfect knowledge of the leading principles, be added the above-mentioned aim at material completeness, particular decisions unnoticed by the framers, will be constantly crossing and contradicting each other, which will gradually come to light by practice only, and, in the case of a bad administration of justice, not even by that.[1] This result would be clearly inevitable, so far as contemporaries are concerned, were an age, without being fully qualified, to fix its legal notions by legislative authority in this manner; but the effect of it would be no less injurious to succeeding times. For if, in these, circumstances should be favourable for a revision of the law, nothing would be more conducive to the end in view than the being extensively connected with preceding intelligent times; but the code now stands between, impeding and throwing difficulties in the way of this connection on all sides. Besides, in the partial dealing with an established positive law, there is the risk of being overwhelmed by mere texts, and every sort of relief must, on the other hand, be very welcome: an imperfect code, however, more than any thing else, must confirm the supremacy of this dead spiritless mode of treating the law.

But, besides the substance, the form of the code must be taken into consideration, for the framer may have fully studied the law on which he is at work, and his production may, notwithstanding, fail of its end, if he have not with all the art of exposition. What this exposition ought to be, is better shown by instances of successful or unsuccessful application, than by general rules. It is commonly required that the language of the law should be particularly distinguished by brevity. Certainly brevity may be extremely effective, as is clear from the examples of the Roman Decrees and Edits. But there is also a dry, inexpressive brevity, adopted by him who does not understand the use of language as an instrument, and which remains wholly ineffective; numerous examples of it are to be found in the laws and records of the middle ages. On the other hand, diffuseness in law authorities may be very exceptionable, nay, wholly intolerable, as in many of the constitutions of Justinian, and in most of the novels of the Theodosian Code; but there is also an intelligent and very effective diffuseness, and this is discernible in many parts of the Pandects.

---

1.   Hugo, Naturrecht, S. 130. N. 7. "Were all law questions to be decided by the higher judicial authorities, the decisions would be so numerous that it would hardly be possible to know them all; and for the undecided cases, of which no small number are sure to remain, there would be but the more contradictory analogies."

Putting together what has been said above concerning the requisites of a really good code, it is clear that very few ages will be fund qualified for it.

b. The enactment of the German Civil Code

Arthur von Mehren & James R. Gordley, *The Civil Law System* **(2d ed., 1977), 75–79**

The Constitution of the German Reich of 1871 did not give the federal government power over the entire field of private law; federal power extended only to commercial law, bills of exchange, and obligations. Efforts, led by Miquel and Lasker, were immediately begun in Parliament to amend the Constitution so that federal legislation would be possible for the whole field of private law. These efforts were opposed by conservatives and by proponents of state's rights. However, in 1873 the desired amendment was obtained. The Federal Council appointed in 1874 a Pre-Commission (Vorkommission), consisting of four judges from higher courts and a representative of the ministry of justice.[211] This committee recommended that the drafting of the civil code be entrusted to a large group of legal scholars and practitioners from all parts of the Empire. The drafting commission was given three tasks: The first was to survey the private-law rules and principles in force within the Empire and its constituent states and to analyze their respective usefulness, validity, and logical coherence. The commission was next to consider to what extent the law should be made uniform where different rules and principles were in force. The commission's third task was to consider "with utmost care" what the form and structure of the new code should be.

In 1874 the Federal Council approved the report of the Pre-Commission and appointed the so-called First Commission. Its eleven members consisted of six judges from higher courts, three government officials, and two law professors, Bernhard Windscheid and Gotlieb Planck.[212] The commission easily and quickly decided that the code should have five parts, the first of which would be a general part. Five members of the commission were assigned responsibility for preparing drafts for the commission's consideration. The commission met regularly for the next thirteen years but did not make its work available to the legal profession or to the academic world. By the end of 1887, the draft was completed. The political reaction to the published draft was relatively mild for two reasons. In the first place, controversial matters affecting the upper classes, by and large, were not dealt with in the draft but were viewed as matters to be regulated by state law. Secondly, the political and social thinking opposed to the positions taken in the draft did not enjoy strong political representation at the time. However, the draft did provoke a tremendous amount of legal writing; more than 600 monographs and articles soon appeared.[213] Relatively

---

211. See generally G. Planck, Bürgerliches Gesetzbuch xxi (ed. 4, 1913).

212. Windscheid's influence was particularly important for the Code's structure; Planck was more concerned with the practical applications of the Code's rules. See id. vi.

213. For a collection of this literature, see volumes 1–3 of Bekker & Fischer, op. cit. supra note 207.

little adverse criticism was directed to the general structure of the draft
or to individual provisions. But there was an almost unanimous agreement that the language used was too abstract and often not understandable; objection was also made to the frequent cross-references in the draft.
The draft was condemned as being intended for lawyers, not laymen.

The division between the Germanists and Romanists is reflected in
the discussion of the draft. Otto von Gierke (1841–1921) developed the
position of the Germanists very effectively in his pamphlet. The Draft for
a Civil Code and the German Law (Der Entwurf eines Bürgerlichen
Gesetzbuchs und das Deutsche Recht) (1889). For Gierke the draft, especially in its basic structure and approach, embodied Romanist ideas developed by the Pandektenwissenschaft. In his view, a code thus inspired
could never really be accepted by the German people. Gierke also objected
to the draft on the grounds that liberalism and individualism dominated,
and little attention had been paid to social considerations; this criticism
was further elaborated on by Anton Menger in The Civil Law and the Poor
Classes (Das bürgerliche Recht und die besitzlosen Klassen) (1891). The
Romanists defended the draft and its reliance on Romanist thinking as a
continuation of an advanced legal culture.

In view of the criticism, the Federal Council appointed a second commission to review and revise the first draft. This second commission consisted of ten permanent and twelve nonpermanent members. The ten
permanent members were all from the legal profession, including two law
professors—Planck and von Mandry, who had replaced Windscheid—both
members of the first commission, six representative of the government,
and one lawyer. The twelve nonpermanent members, who had the right to
be present and vote at any time, but were obligated to attend only if asked
by the chairman, basically represented business interests; the members
included owners of large farms, a bank director, a director of a brewery, a
professor of economics, and a professor of law.

In order to give the commission the benefit of the public's reactions to
its work, a drastic change in procedure was made. The First Commission
had made its deliberations and their results public only when the draft
was complete; the Second Commission published weekly reports. Planck,
who has been called the "father of the BGB," emerged as the most influential member of the Second Commission. (Windscheid had resigned from
the First Commission and was not a member of the second.) The First
Commission, following its terms of reference, had sought to draft a code
that harmonized in a balanced fashion existing rules and principles; the
Second Commission sought both to adapt the first draft to modern needs and
to give greater recognition to considerations of social justice.[214] The language
was made somewhat less formal but was not generally rewritten; the
number of cross-references was reduced. However, the basic structure of
the first draft was not changed.[215]

After almost five years of work, the Second Commission completed the
second draft in October 1895. A draft of the Civil Code was now for the first

---

214. Cf. BGB §§ 617, 618, 950.   **215.** See Planck, op. cit. supra note 211, xliv.

time referred to the legislature. The upper house—the Bundesrat—made significant changes in two areas: it liberalized the law of associations and transferred the provisions dealing with international private law form the sixth book to the introductory book. The resulting draft, often called the third draft, was now sent to the Reichstag, accompanied by a memorandum prepared by the Ministry of Justice. The Reichstag concentrated its attention on the relatively few parts of the draft that were politically controversial at the time. The law of associations was further liberalized; the law of marriage was partially rewritten to reflect a more conservative view. Unlike the former drafts, a will in the form of a declaration written and signed by the testator was recognized (§ 2747). The particular interests of farmers were reflected in some minor changes dealing with the liability of animal keepers (§ 833), the liability for damage done by wild animals (§ 835), and, in four new paragraphs (§§ 961–65), the law is migrating swarms of bees.

The stormiest debates in the Reichstag were over the rights that the states wanted to retain—despite the constitutional amendment of 1873—in the field of private law. The states obtained significant concessions reflected in articles 56 to 152 of the Introductory Law (Einfuhrungsgesetz); these articles have been called a "catalogue of lost German legal unity." They made it possible for a state to preserve local customs. Subsequently, some of the exempted areas—e.g., the rights of certain landowners and nobles—lost all practical importance while others—e.g., the regulation of insurance companies—were made subject to federal regulation. The states still have power to regulate water and mining.

The legislature's work on the BGB was finished in the summer of 1896.[216] The law enacting the code passed on July 1, 1986 by a vote of 222 to 48 (mostly Socialists), with 18 abstentions, and was signed by the Kaiser on August 18, 1896. The code came into force on January 1, 1900.

If one characterizes and evaluates the BGB from a contemporary perspective,[217] the BGB does not seem a revolutionary product but a reflection of the sober, business-minded mood of the late 19th century. The BGB differs significantly from late 18th- and earlier 19th-century codifications such as the Prussian ALR (Allgemeines Landrecht). The very detailed, situational approach of the ALR and its non-technical language contrast sharply with the BGB's complex and interrelated system of rules and principles set out in technical language. The ALR and the BGB are connected by the rationalist view that a code can regulate completely the sphere of life to which it is directed. In the one hundred years between the ALR and the BGB

---

216. For the legislative history of the BGB, including the work done by the commission, see the five-volume work of Mugdan, Die gesamten Materialien zum BGB (1899). See also Schwartz, Die Geschichte des privatrechtlichen Kodificationsbestrebungen in Deutschland und die Entstehungsgeschichte des Entwurfs eines bürgerlichen Gesetzbuchs für das Deutsche Reich, 1 Archiv für Bürgerliches Recht 1 (1899); Sohm, Die Entstehung des deutschen Bürgerlichen Gesetzbuchs, 5 Deutsche Juristenzeitung 6

(1900); Thieme, Aus der Vorgeschichte des Bürgerlichen Gesetzbuchs für Enstehung des Positivismus, 39 Deutsche juristenzeitung 968 (1934); Wieacker, op. cit. supra note 37, 468.
217. Cf. Schmidt, Das Bürgerliches Gesetzbuch aus heutiger Sicht, in H. Soergel & W. Siebert, BGB, Allgemeiner Teil 3 (1967); Wieacker, op. cit, supra note 37, 479–84; K. Larenz, Allgemeiner Teil des Bürgerlichen Rechts 19 (1960); P. Boehmer, Einführung in das Bürgerliche Recht 70 (ed. 2, 1965).

Pandekten legal science had, however, completely changed thinking with respect to the structure and arrangement of a code. In particular, the division of the code into five parts—already seen in the Saxon Code of 1865—reflected the arrangement of the standard 19th-century Pandekten treatises.[218] The idea of a general part, placed as Book I before the Books II to V, dealing with specific substantive fields (obligations, property, family, and inheritance), emerged at the end of the 18th century.[219] The Romanist school, starting with Savigny, was attracted by the logic of the arrangement, and it is used in practically all 19th-century Pankekten treatises. The basic structure of the BGB is thus a legacy from 19th-century Pandekten science. The same is true of the view that a code, systematically using precise legal terms, could provide for a comprehensive and gapless system of justice.

The political values of 19th-century liberalism determined in large measure the contents of the rules contained in the BGB. The individual and his need for freedom are central to the code's approach. The BGB views the individual as homo oeconomicus;[220] relatively little attention is paid to the social consequences of individual conduct. Accordingly, the BGB gives parties great freedom in the fields of contracts and of property, thus reflecting the liberal view that equal freedom for all individuals would ensure a well-functioning system of social justice.[221] The BGB was drafted at a time when far-reaching changes were occurring within Germany; an agrarian society was changing to an industrial society; big business was replacing small business; towns were becoming big cities. But, although the social and economic order was thus being fundamentally changed, the drafters of the BGB did not seek to take these changes into account.

The BGB was not written for laymen but for the legal profession. The structure of the BGB makes it difficult, if not impossible, for a nonlawyer to find in the code the solution to a given problem. For example, in order to determine one's legal rights upon discovering that a newly purchased cow is sick, five different parts of the code must be consulted.[222] The technical language of the first draft was not basically changed by the Second Commission; those members who did not come from the legal profession simply deferred to the jurists on most questions.[223] The drive towards precise solutions and predictability of outcome, which dominated 19th-century legal thinking, left little room for popular language with undefined connotations. For all these reasons the BGB is often said to reflect the end rather than the beginning of an era. Its structures, the choices made, and the code's underlying values all come from the 19th century.[224]

---

218. See I/1 Enneccerus & Nipperdey, op. cit. supra note 191, 47; Wieacker, op. cit. supra note 37, 475 ("This is not a fortunate arrangement.").

219. The first author to use this scheme was probably Christoph Dabelow in his System des gesamten heutigen Civilrechts (ed. 2, 1796); see Boehmer, op. cit. supra note 217–71. Wieacker, op. cit. supra note 37, 486–88.

220. See Boehmer, op. cit. supra note 217, 83.

221. The drafters of the BGB looked to a growing economy—not to the law—to ensure social justice.

222. See Boehmer, op. cit. supra note 217, 77.

223. See Wieacker, op. cit. supra note 37, 471.

224. See Boehmer, op. cit. supra note 217, 83; Wesenberg, op. cit. supra note 37, 174; Wieacker, op. cit. supra note 37, 479.

Note: The 19th century values that influenced the Code are described below in a note on codification and the will theories.

c. The interpretation of the Code

Motive zu dem Entwurfe eines Bürgerlichen Gesetzbuches für das Deutsche Reich 1 (1888), 14–17

III. Interpretation. Analogy.

(1) The texts of the Roman law contain countless expressions of general legal truths which are very important for the logical activity of interpretation and whose inner worth arises form an importance that is independent of their validity as positive law. The Prussian Code provides in § 46: "In deciding disputed cases the judge cannot give any meaning to the law (*Gesetz*) other than the meaning which clearly arises either from the words and context of the law or from the clear grounds of the law"; the Saxon Code § 22: "In other cases" (that is to say other than the following case of authentic interpretation) "the laws are to be interpreted according to their literal meaning and, if the words leave a doubt, according to the otherwise expressed intention of the legislator"; § 23: "In case of doubt, a law is to be interpreted in the way which best corresponds to general legal principles"; § 24: "Statutory provisions, which are set forth as the consequences of expressly indicated assumptions, remain restricted to these assumptions." Compare also the Austrian Code § 6, the Italian Law, article 3(1). The French Civil Code contains no provision dealing with interpretation; but article 4 ("the judge who refuses to decide a case, on the pretext that the law (*loi*) is silent, obscure or insufficient, may be prosecuted as being guilty of a denial of justice") makes it clear that the judge is both justified and obligated to give a free interpretation.

   In this draft such a definite provision is not contained. A provision that would seek only to recognize that the interpreter may not be bound to the literal words is unnecessary because this is clear without a special provision. But special provisions, which were intended to make interpretation easier and to guarantee the correctness of its result, could only express guiding conceptions, whose investigation and exposition belong to legal theory. The legislator who attempts to include such articles in the text of a law does not order (*disponieren*) but instructs (*unterweisen*). In addition, the correct formulation of general jurisprudential principles in the short form of a law has to contend with difficulties that are hard to overcome; instead of assisting the process of interpretation such provisions can easily become problems of interpretation. Also the decision over differences in opinion as to the limit of allowed and required interpretations must be left to the case law (*Jurisprudenz*) without the restrictions of positive provisions of law. The Commercial Code, the Criminal Code and the Code of Procedure, all of them comprehensive codifications of German law, have preceded the Civil Code. It can be seen from the science and practice that has grown up around them that the problems of interpretation have been solved with excellent results without special code provisions. . . .

(2) Authentic interpretation is likewise not considered in the draft. It is clear that the legislator can interpret the law (*Gesetz*); it follows from the conception of law (*Gesetzbegriffe*) that such a claim on the part of the legislator has validity. . . .

(3) No law (*Gesetz*) can be complete in the sense that it has for every conceivable relationship falling within the limits of the legal material handled by it an obvious, directly applicable provision. It would be a mistake to strive for such completeness. The Civil Code must, in case of need, be enlarged out of itself, out of the system of law (*Rechtssysteme*) that it contains. It does not contain a dead mass of legal principles placed in conjunction with each other, but instead an organic structure of innerly related norms. The principles that are basic to the Code carry the germ of further development in themselves. This development is by way of analogy. If a case is not regulated in the law but a legally similar case is regulated, then this provision is decisive in the deciding of the first case (*Gesetzesanalogie*). Semper quasi hoc legibus inesse credi oportet, ut ad eas quoque personas et od eas res pertinerent, quae quandoque similes sunt (1. 27 D. de leg. 1.3). If no result can be reached through this process of analogy then the decision must be drawn form the spirit of the whole law (*Recht*) considered as one system (*Rechtsanalogie*). To give decisive importance to the natural law here (. . . § 7 of the Austrian Code) is precluded because this "law (*Recht*) found by an a priori construction, whose content in each case is only what the person construing it considers to be true," does not permit objective legal norms to be derived from it. Nor can the law varying by territory, which was in force at the time of enactment of the Code, or one of the territorial laws, be considered as a subsidiary law. If new relationships arise in the course of time, or if the existing relationships so alter themselves in the flux of life that the assumptions under which a provision of the Code was made applicable to them no longer exist, then the *Rechtsanalogie*, insofar as the *Gesetzesanalogie* is not applicable, suffices for handling the relationships. The consideration of the so-called nature of the thing is not excluded by this, but the decision may not be based upon considerations which lie outside of the positive law (*das positive Recht*). The factual nature of the relationship must be placed under the norm which arises logically from the principles basic to the positive law and from the factual situation considered in its particularity. Of course, the rejection of former law as subsidiary

law does not reject the rich treasure of general truths contained in the sources of the common law (*gemeines Recht*). . . . The acceptance of the provisions of section 1 is designed to oppose from the very beginning any straying and to ensure the development of the Code in its own spirit.

Note: Here, as in the passage quoted from Aubry and Rau earlier, it seems that the Code is to be interpreted out of itself—in "its own spirit" and "not by considerations which lie outside the positive law." Again, whether German courts have been able to do so, or have tried to do so, is a question that will be confronted issue by issue later on.

d. A note on codification and 19th century will theories

The 19th century jurists broke with the natural law theories that had dominated previous centuries. The innovation was not the concept of the will. It was to use that concept exclusively, without introducing any other concept that could limit what legitimately could be willed. In contrast, in the natural law theories of the late scholastics and northern natural lawyers, such limits were thought to be part of the institutions of contract and property.

Having defined contract in terms of the will or consent or agreement of the parties without any attempt to circumscribe what could legitimately be willed,[1] 19th century will theorists regarded the will as the source of all the terms of the contract. They no longer claimed that these terms rested on the principle of equality or the nature of the parties' agreement. Some said vaguely that will was the source of all the parties' obligations.[2] Laurent thought that the provisions of the French Civil Code governing various types of contracts were merely those the parties would have thought of themselves. The Code listed them "to dispense the parties from writing them into their instruments. . . ."[3] Some jurists suggested that even though the parties would not have thought of these terms, they willed their obligations to be those the law would read into their contract. At the turn of the century, one critic caricatured: "Question, what does the law will? Answer: What the parties will. What do the parties will? What the law wills!"[4]

---

1. Charles Demolombe, *Cours de Code Napoléon*, 24 (3d ed., 1882), § 12; Léon Larombière, *Théorie et pratique des obligations* 1 (1857), § 41; François Laurent, *Principes de droit civil français*, 15 (3d ed., 1875), §§ 424–27; Georg Friedrich Puchta, *Pandekten* (1844), §§ 49, 54; Friedrich Carl von Savigny, *System des heutigen römischen Rechts* 3 (1840), § 134; Bernhard Windscheid, *Lehrbuch des Pandektenrechts* 1 (7th ed.

1891), § 69. See generally James Gordley, *The Philosophical Origins of Modern Contract Doctrine* (1991), 161–213.
2. Puchta, *Pandekten*, § 58.
3. Laurent, *Principes*, 16: § 182
4. Siegmund Schlossmann, review of Ernst Zitelmann, "Irrthum und Rechtsgeschäft," *Zeitschrift für das Privat- und öffentliche Recht der Gegenwart* 7 (1980), 562.

Similarly, the will theorists defined property as the power of the owner to dispose of what belonged to him according to his will.[5] Thus, as in the case of contract, they had no principle to look to other than the will of the owner to explain the rules of property law. They found limits that the law placed on what the owner could do to be theoretical inexplicable.

French jurists claimed to find these ideas in the French Civil Code. That is an unlikely.[6] The drafters drew continually on the works of the 17th century jurist Jean Domat and the 18th century jurist Robert Pothier who themselves had been heavily influenced by the natural law writers, Grotius and Pufendorf. None of them were will theorists.

The French will theorists read their theory of contract into art. 1134 of the Code which states: "Agreements lawfully formed take the place of law for those who have made them." That statement paraphrased one by Domat[7] which he had taken from a collection of papal letters promulgated by the medieval Pope Boniface VIII,[8] who had taken it from the *Corpus iuris civilis* of Justinian.[9]

They read will theories of property into art. 544 which states: "Property is the right to enjoy and dispose of things in the most absolute manner provided that one does not make a use of them in a manner that is prohibited by statutes or regulations." This passage paraphrases one in Pothier who, interesting enough, was describing the rights of a French feudal tenant before the Revolution who could freely use and alienate his land provided he paid feudal rents and duties to his "lord."[10]

Meanwhile, German jurists were extracting will theories from their Roman texts. In contrast to France, these theories had time to flourish before a civil code was enacted. As has often been noted, the German Civil Code shows their influence. At the last minute, some changes were made in defiance of the will theories. For example, the draft was amended to allow relief in some cases in which a contract was unfair (§ 138(2)) and to permit a person in great need to use an owner's property against his will (§ 904).

In the 20th centuries, will theories are out of favor. One of the tasks of courts and jurists has been to escape from some of the conclusions of their predecessors. In Germany, the great escape valve has been the use of the so-called "general clauses" or vaguest terms of the Code. The great example is § 242 which provides that a contract must be performed in "good faith." Courts have read more into this clause than the drafters could have imagined, let alone intended. How successful courts have been in finding avenues of escape will be seen later when we deal with contract law.

5. Charles Aubry & Charles Rau, *Cours de droit civil français d'après la méthode de Zachariae* (4th ed., 1869), § 190; Laurent, *Principes* 6: § 101; Demolombe, *Cours* 9: § 543; Windschied, *Lehrbuch* 3: § 167.

6. *See generally*, James Gordley, "Myths of the French Civil Code," *American Journal of Comparative Law* 42 (1994), 459 at 460–83.

7. Jean Domat, *Les Loix civiles dans leur ordre naturel* (1713), liv. prim., introduction.

8. *Liber Sextus* V.13.85.

9. Dig. 50.17.23.

10. Robert Pothier, *Traité du droit de domaine de propriété* § 4 in *Oeuvres de Pothier* 9 (Bugnet ed., 1861).

III. INSTITUTIONS

1. Germany and the United States

John H. Langbein,* "The German Advantage in Civil Procedure," *University of Chicago Law Review* **52 (1985), 823–65**

Our lawyer-dominated system of civil procedure has often been criticized both for its incentives to distort evidence and for the expense and complexity of its modes of discovery and trial.[1] The shortcomings inhere in a system that leaves to partisans the work of gathering and producing the factual material upon which adjudication depends.

We have comforted ourselves with the thought that a lawyerless system would be worse.[2] The excesses of American adversary justice would seem to pale by comparison with a literally nonadversarial system—one in which litigants would be remitted to faceless bureaucratic adjudicators and denied the safeguards that flow from lawyerly intermediation.

The German advantage. The main theme of this article is drawn from Continental civil procedure, exemplified for me by the system that I know reasonably well, the West German.[3] My theme is that, by assigning judges rather than lawyers to investigate the facts, the Germans avoid the most troublesome aspects of our practice. But I shall emphasize that the familiar contrast between our adversarial procedure and the supposedly nonadversarial procedure of the Continental tradition has been grossly overdrawn.

To be sure, since the greater responsibility of the bench for fact-gathering is what distinguishes the Continental tradition, a necessary (and welcome) correlative is that counsel's role in eliciting evidence is greatly

* Max Pam Professor of American and Foreign Law, University of Chicago Law School; Russell Baker Scholar (1985). Scholars, judges, and practitioners in the U.S. and Germany have favored me with suggestions for research or have commented on prepublication drafts. Among those whose help has most proximately affected this paper, although not always in directions that they would have preferred, are Albert Alschuler, Erhard Blankenburg, Mauro Cappelletti, Gerhard Casper, Mary Ann Glendon, Geoffrey Hazard, Benjamin Kaplan, Robert Keeton, Hein Kötz, John Merryman, Henry Monaghan, Richard Posner, Martin Redish, Mathias Reimann, Erich Schanze, William Schwarzer, Steven Shavell, Geoffrey Stone, Cass Sunstein, and Arthur von Mehren. I am grateful to learned audiences who reacted to this paper in earlier versions at law school workshops at Cornell, Harvard, and Northwestern; at the 1984 meeting of the American College of Trial Lawyers; at the 1985 meeting of the litigation section of the Association of American Law Schools; and at a session of the National Academy of Sciences' Committee on National

Statistics, Panel on Statistical Evidence in the Courts.

1. *E.g.*, Jerome Frank, Courts on Trial: Myth and Reality in American Justice (1949); Frankel, *The Search for Truth: An Umpireal View*, 123 U. Pa. L. Rev. 1031 (1975); Brazil, *The Adversary Character of Civil Discovery: A Critique and Proposals for Change*, 31 Vand. L. Rev. 1295, 1298–1303 (1978).

2. *E.g.*, Stephan Landsman, The Adversary System: A Description and Defense 38, 40–41, 43 (1984).

3. A somewhat similar account of Continental practice could be based upon other Western European systems, although details would differ, particularly as one moves from the Northern European systems that have been most influenced by Austrian–German legal culture, to the systems of Southern Europe, where judicial domination of fact-gathering is less prominent and where less adequate resources have been devoted to developing and motivating the bench. *See* Cappelletti, *Social and Political Aspects of Civil Procedure—Reforms and Trends in Western and Eastern Europe*, 69 Mich. L. Rev. 847, 858–59 (1971).

restricted. Apart from fact-gathering, however, the lawyers for the parties play major and broadly comparable roles in both the German and American systems. Both are adversary systems of civil procedure.[4] There as here, the lawyers advance partisan positions from first pleadings to final arguments. German litigators suggest legal theories and lines of factual inquiry, they superintend and supplement judicial examination of witnesses, they urge inferences from fact, they discuss and distinguish precedent, they interpret statutes, and they formulate views of the law that further the interests of their clients. I shall urge that German experience shows that we would do better if we were greatly to restrict the adversaries' role in fact-gathering.

Convergence. The concluding theme of this article directs attention to recent trends in American civil procedure. Having developed the view that judicialized fact-gathering has immense advantages over traditional American practice, I point to the growing manifestations of judicial control of fact-gathering in certain strands of federal procedure. The *Manual for Complex Litigation*[5] is infused with notions of judicial management of fact-gathering for the multi-party Big Case, but there has been no natural stopping place, and these techniques have been seeping into the conduct of ordinary litigation in the development that has been called "managerial judging."[6]

In principle, managerial judging is more compatible with the theory of German procedure than with our own. Having now made the great leap from adversary control to judicial control of fact-gathering, we would need to take one further step to achieve real convergence with the German tradition: from judicial control to judicial conduct of the fact-gathering process. In the success of managerial judging, I see telling evidence for the proposition that judicial fact-gathering could work well in a system that preserved much of the rest of what we now have in civil procedure.

I should emphasize, however, that the main concern of this article is not the sprawling Big Case, but the traditional bipolar lawsuit in contract, tort, or entitlement. The Big Case is testing and instructive but quantitatively unimportant. Ordinary litigation is the place to compare and to judge civil procedural systems.[7]

Outline. After sketching the main features of German civil procedure (Part I), I contrast the striking shortcomings of American procedure: the wastefulness and complexity of our division into pretrial and trial

---

4. Von Mehren remarks that, especially by contrast with criminal procedure, where adversarial components are thoroughly subordinated in the Continental tradition, "the civil-procedure systems of France, Germany and the United States were—and remain—adversarial." Von Mehren, *The Significance for Procedural Practice and Theory of the Concentrated Trial: Comparative Remarks*, in 2 EUROPÄISCHES RECHTSDENKEN IN GESCHICHTE UND GEGENWART: FESTSCHRIFT FÜR HELMUT COING 361 n.3 (N. Horn ed. 1982). When writers take the shortcut and

speak of German or other Continental civil procedure as "nonadversarial" (a usage that I think should be avoided although I confess to having been guilty of it in the past), the description is correct only insofar as it refers to that distinctive trait of Continental civil procedure, judicial conduct of fact-gathering.

5. MANUAL FOR COMPLEX LITIGATION (5th ed. 1982).

6. Resnik, *Managerial Judges*, 96 HARV. L. REV. 376 (1982).

7. Regarding the role of the Small Case in these developments, see *infra* note 138.

procedure (Part II), and the truth-defeating distortions incident to our system of partisan preparation and production of witnesses (Part III) and experts. I devote special attention to the German practice in obtaining impartial expert testimony (Part IV). I pause to notice how flimsy are the theoretical justifications that have been advanced in support of adversary domination of fact-gathering in civil litigation (Part V). Because a more judge-centered fact-gathering process would direct attention to the powers of the bench, I describe the incentive structure of the German career judiciary (Part VI) and the appellate safeguards for litigants (Part VII). Finally, I point to the potential for the convergence of the two systems arising from the appearance of managerial judging in the United States (Part VIII).

I. OVERVIEW OF GERMAN CIVIL PROCEDURE[8]

There are two fundamental differences between German and Anglo-American civil procedure, and these differences lead in turn to many others. First, the court rather than the parties' lawyers takes the main responsibility for gathering and sifting evidence, although the lawyers exercise a watchful eye over the court's work. Second, there is no distinction between pretrial and trial, between discovering evidence and presenting it. Trial is not a single continuous event. Rather, the court gathers and evaluates evidence over a series of hearings, as many as the circumstances require.[9]

---

8. Readers interested in the detail of the German system will find, in addition to the indigenous treatises, a surprisingly rich English-language literature. The remarkable mini-treatise, Kaplan, von Mehren & Schaefer, *Phases of German Civil Procedure* (pts. 1 & 2), 71 HARV. L. REV. 1193, 1443 (1958) [hereafter cited as Kaplan-von Mehren], although approaching its thirtieth anniversary, remains fundamentally accurate. *See also* 2 E.J. COHN, MANUAL OF GERMAN LAW 162–248 (2d ed. 1971). For comparative observations growing out of the Kaplan-von Mehren study, see Kaplan, *Civil Procedure— Reflections on the Comparison of Systems*, 9 BUFFALO L. REV. 409 (1960) [hereafter cited as Kaplan]. William B. Fisch updated the Kaplan–von Mehren article, with particular attention to the 1977 amendments that are discussed *infra* note 9, in Fisch, *Recent Developments in West German Civil Procedure*, 6 HASTINGS INT'L & COMP. L. REV. 221, 236–60 (1983). On the 1977 reforms see also Gottwald, *Simplified Civil Procedure in West Germany*, 31 AM. J. COMP. L. 687 (1983). Regarding the appellate system, see Meador, *Appellate Subject Matter Organization: The German Design from an American Perspective*, 5 HASTINGS INT'L & COMP. L. REV. 27 (1981). On the differing roles of lawyers, judges, and other legal professionals, see Kötz, *The Role and Functions of the Legal Professions in the Federal Republic of Germany*, in DEUTSCHE LANDESREFERATE ZUM PRIVATRECHT UND HANDELSRECHT, XI INTERNATIONALER KONGRESS FÜR RECHTSVERGLEICHUNG 69 (U. Drobnig & H. Puttfarken ed. 1982) [hereafter cited as Kötz, *Legal Profession*]; *see also* DIETRICH RUESCHMEYER, LAWYERS AND THEIR SOCIETY: A COMPARATIVE STUDY OF THE LEGAL PROFESSION IN GERMANY AND IN THE UNITED STATES 27–62 (1973).

9. Reforms enacted in 1976 and in force since 1977, based on practice pioneered in Stuttgart and widely known as the "Stuttgart Model," encourage the courts to dispose of a case in a single hearing when circumstances permit. *See, e.g.*, LEO ROSENBERG & KARL-HEINZ SCHWAB, ZIVILPROZESSRECHT § 84, at 456–60, § 107, at 614–17 (13th ed. 1981); *see id.* § 107, at 614 for bibliography. For English-language discussion, see Bender, *The Stuttgart Model*, in 2 ACCESS TO JUSTICE: PROMISING INSTITUTIONS 433 (M. Cappelletti & J. Weisner ed. 1979).

As modified, the code reads: "Ordinarily (*in der Regel*), the case should be resolved in a single hearing, comprehensively prepared." ZIVILPROZESSORDNUNG [ZPO] (Code of Civil Procedure) § 272(I). In aid of this comprehensive preparation, ZPO § 273, formerly ZPO § 272(b), authorizes the court to take various steps in advance of the hearing (for example, requiring the parties to clarify

Initiation. The plaintiff's lawyer commences a lawsuit in Germany with a complaint. Like its American counterpart, the German complaint narrates the key facts, sets forth a legal theory, and asks for a remedy in damages or specific relief.[10] Unlike an American complaint, however, the German document proposes means of proof for its main factual contentions.[11] The major documents in the plaintiff's possession that support his claim are scheduled and often appended; other documents (for example, hospital files or government records such as police accident reports or agency files) are indicated; witnesses who are thought to know something helpful to the plaintiff's position are identified. The defendant's answer follows the same pattern. It should be emphasized, however, that neither plaintiff's nor defendant's lawyer will have conducted any significant search for witnesses or for other evidence unknown to his client. Digging for facts is primarily the work of the judge.[12]

Judicial preparation. The judge to whom the case is entrusted examines these pleadings and appended documents.[13] He routinely sends for relevant public records. These materials form the beginnings of the official dossier, the court file. All subsequent submissions of counsel, and all subsequent evidence-gathering, will be entered in the dossier, which is open to counsel's inspection continuously.

When the judge develops a first sense of the dispute from these materials, he will schedule a hearing and notify the lawyers. He will often invite and sometimes summon the parties as well as their lawyers to this

positions, obtaining documents, summoning parties and witnesses to the hearing). Many simpler cases do lend themselves to one-hearing disposition, either through court-aided settlement or by judgment. When this happens the German procedure resembles the American pattern of pretrial preparation followed by a concentrated trial. However, even in such cases, because the court has the option to schedule further hearings if developments at the initial hearing seem to warrant further proofs or submissions, German procedure is devoid of the opportunities for surprise and tactical advantage that inhere in the Anglo-American concentrated trial. *See infra* text accompanying note 23.

For cases that do not lend themselves to one-hearing resolution, the 1977 amendments have not altered the episodic character of the procedure. Further hearings may be ordered as necessary. *See, e.g.,* ZPO § 278(IV). "The whole procedure up to judgment may therefore be viewed as being essentially a series of oral conferences." Kötz, *Civil Litigation and the Public Interest,* 1 Civ. Just. Q. 237, 243 (1982) [hereafter cited as Kötz, *Civil Litigation*].

German procedure recognizes something called the *Konzentrationsmaxime,* which, if translated as the "principle of concentration" and equated with the rule of concentrated trial in Anglo-American law, is a serious

false cognate. The *Konzentrationsmaxime* expresses nothing more than the general efficiency value that the court should handle the case as rapidly as possible, and where possible in a single hearing. *See, e.g.,* Adolf Baumbach, Zivilprozessordnung § 253, Übersicht at 634, ¶ 2(E) (43d ed. 1985).

10. *See* ZPO § 253 (complaint); *id.* §§ 271, 274(II) (service on the defendant).

11. ZPO § 253(IV) invokes ZPO § 130, including § 130(5), calling for the party to designate the means of proof he thinks will support his contentions of fact. For a specimen complaint and other items of record from a hypothetical lawsuit rendered in English, see 2 E. Cohn, *supra* note 8, at 191–97.

12. For English-language discussion of this point, which is so striking to those of us bred in the Anglo-American tradition, see Kaplan–von Mehren, *supra* note 8, at 1206–07, 1247–49.

13. In former times there was greater use of collegial first-instance courts, but by 1974 the tradeoff between dispatch and safeguard was resolved in favor of dispatch, and ZPO § 348 now presupposes a single-judge court in most circumstances. For background in English see Fisch, *supra* note 8, at 227–36; on the former practice, see Kaplan-von Mehren, *supra* note 8, at 1206–07, 1247–49.

or subsequent hearings. If the pleadings have identified witnesses whose testimony seems central, the judge may summon them to the initial hearing as well.[14]

Hearing. The circumstances of the case dictate the course of the hearing. Sometimes the court will be able to resolve the case by discussing it with the lawyers and parties and suggesting avenues of compromise. If the case remains contentious and witness testimony needs to be taken, the court will have learned enough about the case to determine a sequence for examining witnesses.

Examining and recording. The judge serves as the examiner-in-chief. At the conclusion of his interrogation of each witness, counsel for either party may pose additional questions, but counsel are not prominent as examiners.[15] Witness testimony is seldom recorded verbatim; rather, the judge pauses from time to time to dictate a summary of the testimony into the dossier.[16] The lawyers sometimes suggest improvements in the wording of these summaries, in order to preserve or to emphasize nuances important to one side or the other.

Since the proceedings in a difficult case may require several hearings extending across many months, these summaries of concluded testimony—by encapsulating succinctly the results of previous hearings—allow the court to refresh itself rapidly for subsequent hearings. The summaries also serve as building blocks from which the court will ultimately fashion the findings of fact for its written judgment. If the case is appealed, these concise summaries constitute the record for the reviewing court. (We shall see that the first appellate instance in German procedure involves review de novo, in which the appellate court can form its own view of the facts, both from the record and, if appropriate, by recalling witnesses or summoning new ones.[17])

Anyone who has had to wade through the longwinded narrative of American pretrial depositions and trial transcripts (which preserve every inconsequential utterance, every false start, every stammer) will see at once the economy of the German approach to taking and preserving evidence.[18] Our incentives run the other way; we pay court reporters by the page and lawyers mostly by the hour.

A related source of dispatch in German procedure is the virtual absence of any counterpart to the Anglo-American law of evidence. German law exhibits expansive notions of testimonial privilege, especially for potential witnesses drawn from the family.[19] But German procedure

---

14. The nineteenth-century tradition that one of the parties had to nominate a witness before the court could examine him (*Verhandlungsmaxime*) has long been something of a fiction, since a party usually detects a strong incentive to follow judicial suggestion in nominating some line of proof. The reforms of the 1970s directed to accelerating the procedure have further accentuated the court's authority to investigate independent of party nomination. For recent complaint from the bar that the bench is straining too far in this direction, see Birk, *Wer führt den Zivilprozess—der Anwalt oder der Richter?* 38 NEUE JURISTISCHE WOCHENSCHRIFT 1489, 1496 (1985).

15. *See* ZPO §§ 395–97.

16. *See* Kötz, *Civil Litigation, supra* note 9, at 240.

17. *See infra* text accompanying notes 115–20.

18. *But see infra* text accompanying note 79.

19. ZPO §§ 383–89. *See generally* A. BAUMBACH, *supra* note 9, §§ 383–389, at 1018–29.

functions without the main chapters of our law of evidence, those rules (such as hearsay) that exclude probative evidence for fear of the inability of the trier of fact to evaluate the evidence purposively. In civil litigation German judges sit without juries (a point to which this essay recurs[20]); evidentiary shortcomings that would affect admissibility in our law affect weight or credit in German law.

Expertise. If an issue of technical difficultly arises on which the court or counsel wishes to obtain the views of an expert, the court—in consultation with counsel—will select the expert and define his role. (This aspect of the procedure I shall discuss particularly in Part IV below.)

Further contributions of counsel. After the court takes witness testimony or receives some other infusion of evidence, counsel have the opportunity to comment orally or in writing. Counsel use these submissions in order to suggest further proofs or to advance legal theories. Thus, nonadversarial proof-taking alternates with adversarial dialogue across as many hearings as are necessary. The process merges the investigatory function of our pretrial discovery and the evidence-presenting function of our trial. Another manifestation of the comparative efficiency of German procedure is that a witness is ordinarily examined only once. Contrast the American practice of partisan interview and preparation, pretrial deposition, preparation for trial, and examination and cross-examination at trial. These many steps take their toll in expense and irritation.

Judgment. After developing the facts and hearing the adversaries' views, the court decides the case in a written judgment that must contain full findings of fact and make reasoned application of the law.[21]

II. JUDICIAL CONTROL OF SEQUENCE

From the standpoint of comparative civil procedure, the most important consequence of having judges direct fact-gathering in this episodic fashion is that German procedure functions without the sequence rules to which we are accustomed in the Anglo-American procedural world. The implications for procedural economy are large. The very concepts of "plaintiff's case" and "defendant's case" are unknown. In our system those concepts function as traffic rules for the partisan presentation of evidence to a passive and ignorant trier. By contrast, in German procedure the court ranges over the entire case, constantly looking for the jugular—for the issue of law or fact that might dispose of the case.[22] Free of constraints that arise from party presentation of evidence, the court investigates the dispute in the fashion most likely to narrow the inquiry. A major job of counsel is to guide the search by directing the court's attention to particularly cogent lines of inquiry.

Suppose that the court has before it a contract case that involves complicated factual or legal issues about whether the contract was formed, and if so, what its precise terms were. But suppose further that the court quickly

20. *See infra* text accompanying notes 144–53.

21. For discussion of the importance of those safeguards, see *infra* text accompanying notes 110–14.

22. For English-language discussion, see Kaplan–von Mehren, *supra* note 8, at 1208–31, especially 1224–28.

recognizes (or is led by submission of counsel to recognize) that some factual investigation might establish an affirmative defense—illegality, let us say—that would vitiate the contract. Because the court functions without sequence rules, it can postpone any consideration of issues that we would think of as the plaintiff's case—here the questions concerning the formation and the terms of the contract. Instead, the court can concentrate the entire initial inquiry on what we would regard as a defense. If, in my example, the court were to unearth enough evidence to allow it to conclude that the contract was illegal, no investigation would ever be done on the issues of formation and terms. A defensive issue that could only surface in Anglo-American procedure following full pretrial and trial ventilation of the whole of the plaintiff's case can be brought to the fore in German procedure.

Part of what makes our discovery system so complex is that, on account of our division into pretrial and trial, we have to discover for the entire case. We investigate everything that could possibly come up at trial, because once we enter the trial phase we can seldom go back and search for further evidence.[23] By contrast, the episodic character of German fact-gathering largely eliminates the danger of surprise; if the case takes an unexpected turn, the disadvantaged litigant can count on developing his response in another hearing at a later time. Because there is no pretrial discovery phase, fact-gathering occurs only once; and because the court establishes the sequence of fact-gathering according to criteria of relevance, unnecessary investigation is minimized. In the Anglo-American procedural world we value the early-disposition mechanism, especially summary judgment, for issues of law. But for fact-laden issues, our fixed-sequence rule (plaintiff's case before defendant's case) and our single-continuous-trial rule largely foreclose it.

The episodic character of German civil procedure—Benjamin Kaplan called it the "conference method"[24] of adjudication—has other virtues: It lessens tension and theatrics, and it encourages settlement. Countless novels, movies, plays, and broadcast serials attest to the dramatic potential of the Anglo-American trial. The contest between opposing counsel; the potential for surprise witnesses who cannot be rebutted in time; the tricks of adversary examination and cross-examination; the concentration of proof-taking and verdict into a single, continuous proceeding; the unpredictability of juries and the mysterious opacity of their conclusory verdicts—these attributes of the Anglo-American trial make for good theatre. German civil proceedings have the tone not of the theatre, but of a routine business meeting—serious rather than tense. When the court inquires and directs, it sets no stage for advocates to perform. The forensic skills of counsel can wrest no material advantage, and the appearance of a surprise witness would simply lead to the scheduling of a further hearing. In a system that cannot distinguish between dress rehearsal and opening night, there is scant occasion for stage fright.

---

23. For discussion of the parallels to discovery waves under the *Manual for Complex Litigation* and to bifurcated trials under Federal Rule of Civil Procedure 42, see *infra* text accompanying notes 134–35.

24. Kaplan, *supra* note 8, at 410.

In this business-like system of civil procedure the tradition is strong that the court promotes compromise.[25] The judge who gathers the facts soon knows the case as well as the litigants do, and he concentrates each subsequent increment of fact-gathering on the most important issues still unresolved. As the case progresses the judge discusses it with the litigants, sometimes indicating provisional views of the likely outcome.[26] He is, therefore, strongly positioned to encourage a litigant to abandon a case that is turning out to be weak or hopeless, or to recommend settlement. The loser-pays system of allocating the costs of litigation gives the parties further incentive to settle short of judgment.[27]

25. ZPO § 279 imposes upon the court the duty to explore the possibility of a settlement at every stage of the proceeding. "Settlement is sometimes prized as the crown of the judicial function, as the goal for which a healthy legal system continually strives." OTHMAR JAUERNIG, ZIVILPROZESSRECHT § 48 (VII), at 171 (20th ed. 1983). Kaplan and his coauthors remark: "The intensity and candor of the court's drive toward settlement will astonish an American observer. In few cases does settlement go unmentioned and it is the judge who generally initiates the discussion." Kaplan–von Mehren, *supra* note 8, at 1223.

In 1977 I spent some time observing the conduct of civil cases in the main first-instance court (Landgericht, or LG) in Frankfurt. In one case, involving the amount of child support, the presiding judge told a defendant who was resisting the settlement recommended by the court: "If we have to go to judgment, I assume that the judgment would not look much different than the suggested settlement." He settled.

Settlement has many advantages, especially in the eyes of judges who promote it:

1. It accelerates resolution of the case.
2. No one is stigmatized as the loser.
3. The court is spared writing a judgment, which is a considerable attraction in a legal system that takes the contents of the written judgment so seriously, *see infra* text accompanying notes 111–13. Kötz warns in this regard that "an activist judge who applies pressure in order to persuade the parties to accept a settlement may be motivated, not so much by a desire to end the litigation in a peaceable manner and thereby to protect the public interest in reducing delay in the courts but, instead, by a wish to reduce his workload." Kötz, *Civil Litigation, supra* note 9, at 238.
4. Because settlement precludes appeal, the court knows that if it embodies its result in a settlement rather than a judgment, there is no possibility of being reversed. (Regarding reversal rates as a factor affecting progress in judicial careers, see *infra* text accompanying note 95.)

The Kaplan–von Mehren article makes the instructive comparative point that the greater judicial involvement in settlement in German procedure reflects the German judge's early and active role in developing the facts. "In American practice, on the other hand, a large percentage of settlements are concluded with the judges playing no part, for barring preliminary motions or a pretrial conference, cases commonly do not appear before the judges until the stage of trial." Kaplan-von Mehren, *supra* note 8, at 1223 n.120. On the correlation between the growing involvement of American judges in pretrial discovery and their larger role in promoting settlement, see *infra* text accompanying notes 124–32 & note 132.

26. The presiding judge is required to discuss the factual and legal aspects of the case with the parties, ZPO § 139(I), and to advise the parties of his doubts, ZPO § 139(II).

27. ZPO § 91 announces the basic principle, although the details extend across several special statutes, including the Kostenordnung [KOSTO] (Statute on Costs) and the Bundesrechtsanwaltsgebührenordnung [BRAGO] (Federal Statute on Lawyers' Fees). *See generally* 1 STEIN-JONAS, KOMMENTAR ZUR ZIVILPROZESSORDNUNG § 91 Vorbemerkungen at 293–304 (20th ed. 1984). For brief treatment in English, see 2 E. COHN, *supra* note 8, at 182–90; Kaplan-von Mehren, *supra* note 8, at 1461–70; *see also* Pfennigstorf, *The European Experience with Fee Shifting*, LAW & CONTEMP. PROBS., Winter 1984, at 37; *infra* note 78.

In a valuable recent analysis of the effects of cost-shifting regimes, Steven Shavell makes the point that cost-shifting actually increases the parties' propensity to litigate in the situation where each overvalues his chances of prevailing. Shavell, *Suit, Settlement, and Trial: A Theoretical Analysis under Alternative Methods for the Allocation of Legal Costs*, 11 J. LEGAL STUD. 55, 65–66 (1982). The German effort at active judicial clarification of the facts and issues is a counterforce likely to correct such misperceptions much of the time.

III. Witnesses

Adversary control of fact-gathering in our procedure entails a high level of conflict between partisan advantage and orderly disclosure of the relevant information. Marvin Frankel put this point crisply when he said that "it is the rare case in which either side yearns to have the witnesses, or anyone, give *the whole truth*." [28]

If we had deliberately set out to find a means of impairing the reliability of witness testimony, we could not have done much better than the existing system of having partisans prepare witnesses in advance of trial and examine and cross-examine them at trial. Jerome Frank described the problem a generation ago:

> [The witness] often detects what the lawyer hopes to prove at the trial. If the witness desires to have the lawyer's client win the case, he will often, unconsciously, mold his story accordingly. Telling and re-telling it to the lawyer, he will honestly believe that his story, as he narrates it in court, is true, although it importantly deviates from what he originally believed. [29]

Thus, said Frank, "the partisan nature of trials tends to make partisans of the witnesses." [30]

Cross-examination at trial—our only substantial safeguard against this systematic bias in the testimony that reaches our courts—is a frail and fitful palliative. Cross-examination is too often ineffective to undo the consequences of skillful coaching. Further, because cross-examination allows so much latitude for bullying and other truth-defeating stratagems, it is frequently the source of fresh distortion when brought to bear against truthful testimony. [31] As a leading litigator boasted recently in an ABA publication: "By a carefully planned and executed cross-examination, I can raise at least a slight question about the accuracy of [an adverse] witness's story, or question his motives or impartiality." [32]

When we cross the border into German civil procedure, we leave behind all traces of this system of partisan preparation, examination, and cross-examination of witnesses. German law distinguishes parties from

28. Frankel, *supra* note 1, at 1038 (emphasis in original).

29. J. Frank, *supra note* 1, at 86.

30. Id.

31. Wigmore's celebrated panegyric—that cross-examination is "the greatest legal engine ever invented for the discovery of truth"—is nothing more than an article of faith. 5 John H. Wigmore, Evidence § 1367, at 29 (3d ed. 1940). Judge Frankel explains why: "The litigator's devices, let us be clear, have utility in testing dishonest witnesses, ferreting out falsehoods, and thus exposing the truth. But to a considerable degree these devices are like other potent weapons, equally lethal for heroes and villains." Frankel, *supra* note 1, at 1039.

For a well-known discussion of deliberately misleading techniques of examination and cross-examination, drawn mostly from how-to books, see J. Frank, *supra* note 1, at 81–85. For recent discussion (by a booster of adversary procedure) of the shortcomings of cross-examination as a remedy for coaching, see Landsman, *Reforming the Adversary Procedure: A Proposal Concerning the Psychology of Memory and the Testimony of Disinterested Witnesses*, 45 U. Pitt. L. Rev. 547, 570–71 (1984). In the hands of many of its practitioners, cross-examination is not only frequently truth-defeating or ineffectual, it is also tedious, repetitive, time-wasting, and insulting.

32. Hanley, *Working the Witness Puzzle*, Litigation, Winter 1977, at 8, 10.

witnesses. A German lawyer must necessarily discuss the facts with his client, and based on what his client tells him and on what the documentary record discloses, the lawyer will nominate witnesses whose testimony might turn out to be helpful to his client. As the proofs come in, they may reveal to the lawyer the need to nominate further witnesses for the court to examine. But the lawyer stops at nominating; virtually never will he have occasion for out-of-court contact with a witness. Not only would such contact be a serious ethical breach, it would be self-defeating. "German judges are given to marked and explicit doubts about the reliability of the testimony of witnesses who previously have discussed the case with counsel or who have consorted unduly with a party." [33]

No less a critic than Jerome Frank was prepared to concede that in American procedure the adversaries "sometimes do bring into court evidence which, in a dispassionate inquiry, might be overlooked." [34] That is a telling argument for including adversaries in the fact-gathering process, but not for letting them run it. German civil procedure preserves party interests in fact-gathering. The lawyers nominate witnesses, attend and supplement court questioning, and develop adversary positions on the significance of the evidence. Yet German procedure totally avoids the distortions incident to our partisan witness practice.

IV. EXPERTS

The European jurist who visits the United States and becomes acquainted with our civil procedure typically expresses amazement at our witness practice. His amazement turns to something bordering on disbelief when he discovers that we extend the sphere of partisan control to the selection and preparation of experts. In the Continental tradition experts are selected and commissioned by the court, although with great attention to safeguarding party interests. In the German system, experts are not even called witnesses. They are thought of as "judges' aides." [35]

Perverse incentives. At the American trial bar, those of us who serve as expert witnesses are known as "saxophones." This is a revealing term, as slang often is.[36] The idea is that the lawyer plays the tune, manipulating the expert as though the expert were a musical instrument on which the lawyer sounds the desired notes. I sometimes serve as an expert in trust

---

33. Kaplan–von Mehren, *supra* note 8, at 1201. Kötz has written lately in a similar vein: "German attorneys will be highly reluctant to talk with prospective witnesses. This results in part from an ethical standard as expressed in the canons promulgated by the German Bar Association where it is said: 'Questioning of witnesses out of court is advisable only when special circumstances justify it. In such questioning even the appearance of attempting to influence the witness must be avoided.' [Citing *Richtlinien der Bundesrechtsanwaltskammer für die Ausübung des Anwaltsberufs*, § 4 (May 11, 1957).] If any attorneys were prepared to wink at this standard, which is doubtful, they would have to take account of the further fact that German judges would take an extremely dim view of the reliability of witnesses who previously had discussed the case with counsel." Kötz, *Civil Litigation, supra* note 9, at 241.

34. J. FRANK, *supra* note 1, at 80.

35. *E.g.*, KURT JESSNITZER, DER GERICHTLICHE SACHVERSTÄNDIGE 72, 78 (7th ed. 1978).

36. Equally revealing is the slang used to describe the preparation of ordinary witnesses: "sandpapering" and "horseshedding." For remarks on the latter, see MARVIN E. FRANKEL, PARTISAN JUSTICE 15 (1980).

and pension cases, and I have experienced the subtle pressures to join the team—to shade one's views, to conceal doubt, to overstate nuance, to downplay weak aspects of the case that one has been hired to bolster. Nobody likes to disappoint a patron; and beyond this psychological pressure is the financial inducement. Money changes hands upon the rendering of expertise, but the expert can run his meter only so long as his patron litigator likes the tune. Opposing counsel undertakes a similar exercise, hiring and schooling another expert to parrot the contrary position. The result is our familiar battle of opposing experts. The more measured and impartial an expert is, the less likely he is to be used by either side.[37]

At trial, the battle of experts tends to baffle the trier, especially in jury courts. If the experts do not cancel each other out, the advantage is likely to be with the expert whose forensic skills are the more enticing. The system invites abusive cross-examination. Since each expert is party-selected and party-paid, he is vulnerable to attack on credibility regardless of the merits of his testimony. A defense lawyer recently bragged about his technique of cross-examining plaintiffs' experts in tort cases. Notice that nothing in his strategy varies with the truthfulness of the expert testimony he tries to discredit:

> A mode of attack ripe with potential is to pursue a line of questions which, by their form and the jury's studied observation of the witness in response, will tend to cast the expert as a "professional witness." By proceeding in this way, the cross-examiner will reap the benefit of a community attitude, certain to be present among several of the jurors, that bias can be purchased, almost like a commodity.[38]

Thus, the systematic incentive in our procedure to distort expertise leads to a systematic distrust and devaluation of expertise. Short of forbidding the use of experts altogether, we probably could not have designed a procedure better suited to minimize the influence of expertise.[39]

37. Advertisements like the following (from the journal of the trial lawyers' association) conjure up a vision more of the huckster than of the scientist: "EXPLODING BOTTLES FLYING CAPS[:] expert with 20 years worldwide experience . . . 100% success to date." TRIAL, Feb. 1985, at 92.

One excuse for the litigation-biased expert is the claim that "there is no such thing as a neutral, impartial [expert] witness. . . . [He] is bound to be biased and partial, and strongly motivated towards advocacy of his particular prejudiced point of view." Diamond, *The Fallacy of the Impartial Expert*, 3 ARCHIVES OF CRIM. PSYCHODYNAMICS 221, 229–30 (1959), *reprinted in* DAVID W. LOUISELL, GEOFFREY C. HAZARD, JR. & COLIN C. TAIT, CASES AND MATERIALS ON PLEADING AND PROCEDURE 842, 846 (5th ed. 1983). However, it is important not to confuse litigation-bias (hiring somebody to conform his views to the needs of your lawsuit) with the good faith differences of opinion that can develop in scientific fields or in other areas of expertise concerning questions that have not been authoritatively resolved. It is true that bias may provoke a difference of opinion; it is false to reason that a difference of opinion must reflect bias.

38. Ryan, *Making the Plaintiff's Expert Yours*, FOR THE DEFENSE, Nov. 1982, at 12, 13; *see also* Trine, *Cross-examining the Expert Witness in the Products Case*, TRIAL, Nov. 1983, at 86 (taking as its leitmotif the advice from a fisherman's manual that "[t]he concept behind playing a trout is to tire him to the point where he may be easily handled or netted, yet is not at the portals of death").

39. See, for example, the trial judge's account of a proceeding that concerned an issue of Salvadoran law: "[T]he experts for the respective sides contradict each other in every material respect." Corporacion Salvadorena de Calzado, S.A. v. Injection Footwear Corp., 533 F. Supp. 290, 293 (S.D. Fla. 1982), *cited in Merryman, Foreign Law as a Problem*, 19 STAN. J. INT'L L. 151, 158 n.10 (1983).

The Continental tradition. European legal systems are, by contrast, expert-prone.[40] Expertise is frequently sought. The literature emphasizes the value attached to having expert assistance available to the courts in an age in which litigation involves facts of ever-greater technical difficulty.[41] The essential insight of Continental civil procedure is that credible expertise must be neutral expertise. Thus, the responsibility for selecting and informing experts is placed upon the courts, although with important protections for party interests.

Selecting the expert. German courts obtain expert help in lawsuits the way Americans obtain expert help in business or personal affairs. If you need an architect, a dermatologist, or a plumber, you do not commission a pair of them to take preordained and opposing positions on your problem, although you do sometimes take a second opinion. Rather, you take care to find an expert who is qualified to advise you in an objective manner; you probe his advice as best you can; and if you find his advice persuasive, you follow it.

When in the course of winnowing the issues in a lawsuit a German court determines that expertise might help resolve the case, the court selects and instructs the expert. The court may decide to seek expertise on its own motion, or at the request of one of the parties.[42] The code of civil procedure allows the court to request nominations from the parties[43]— indeed, the code requires the court to use any expert upon whom the parties agree[44]—but neither practice is typical. In general, the court takes the initiative in nominating and selecting the expert.

The only respect in which the code of civil procedure purports to narrow the court's discretion to choose the expert is a provision whose significance is less than obvious: "If experts are officially designated for certain fields of expertise, other persons should be chosen only when special circumstances require."[45] One looks outside the code of civil procedure, to the federal statutes regulating various professions and trades, for the particulars on official designation.[46] For the professions, the statutes typically authorize the official licensing bodies to assemble lists of professionals deemed especially suited to serve as experts. In other fields, the state governments designate quasi-public bodies to compile such lists. For example, under section 36 of the federal code on trade regulation, the state governments empower the regional chambers of commerce and industry (Industrie- und Handelskammern) to identify experts in a wide variety of

40. *See generally* INSTITUT DE DROIT COMPARÉ DE PARIS, L'EXPERTISE DANS LES PRINCIPAUX SYSTÈMES JURIDIQUES D'EUROPE (1969).

41. *E.g.*, Arens, *Stellung and Bedeutung des technischen Sachverständigen im Prozess*, in EFFEKTIVITÄT DES RECHTSSCHUTZES UND VERFASSUNGSMÄSSIGE ORDNUNG 299 (P. Gilles ed. 1983). For a volume of conference proceedings largely devoted to this topic, see DER TECHNISCHE SACHVERSTÄNDIGE IM PROZESS (F. Nicklisch ed. 1984) (*see especially id.* at 273 ff., for the editor's English-language general report).

42. *See* ZPO § 404(I); K. JESSNITZER, *supra* note 35, at 97.

43. ZPO § 404(III).

44. ZPO § 404(IV).

45. ZPO § 404(II).

46. For a list of statutes that authorize licensing and similar bodies to designate experts, see 2 STEIN-JONAS, KOMMENTAR ZUR ZIVILPROZESSORDNUNG § 404(II), at 1674–75 (19th ed. 1972); *see also* K. JESSNITZER, *supra* note 35, at 122–23.

commercial and technical fields. That statute directs the empowered chamber to choose as experts persons who have exceptional knowledge of the particular specialty and to have these persons sworn to render professional and impartial expertise.[47] The chamber circulates its lists of experts, organized by specialty and subspecialty, to the courts. German judges receive sheaves of these lists as the various issuing bodies update and recirculate them.

Current practice. In 1984 I spent a little time interviewing judges in Frankfurt about their practice in selecting experts.[48] My sample of a handful of judges is not large enough to impress statisticians, but I think the picture that emerges from serious discussion with people who operate the system is worth reporting. Among the judges with whom I spoke, I found unanimity on the proposition that the most important factor predisposing a judge to select an expert is favorable experience with that expert in an earlier case. Experts thus build reputations with the bench. Someone who renders a careful, succinct, and well-substantiated report and who responds effectively to the subsequent questions of the court and the parties will be remembered when another case arises in his specialty. Again we notice that German civil procedure tracks the patterns of decision-making in ordinary business and personal affairs: If you get a plumber to fix your toilet and he does it well, you incline to hire him again.

When judges lack personal experience with appropriate experts, I am told, they turn to the authoritative lists described above. If expertise is needed in a field for which official lists are unavailing, the court is thrown upon its own devices. The German judge then gets on the phone, working from party suggestions and from the court's own research, much in the fashion of an American litigator hunting for expertise. In these cases there is a tendency to turn, first, to the bodies that prepare expert lists in cognate areas; or, if none, to the universities and technical institutes.

If enough potential experts are identified to allow for choice, the court will ordinarily consult party preferences. In such circumstances a litigant may ask the court to exclude an expert whose views proved contrary to his interests in previous litigation or whom he otherwise disdains. The court will try to oblige the parties' tastes when another qualified expert can be substituted. Nevertheless, a litigant can formally challenge an expert's appointment only on the narrow grounds for which a litigant could seek to recuse a judge.[49]

Preparing the expert. The court that selects the expert instructs him, in the sense of propounding the facts that he is to assume or to investigate, and in framing the questions that the court wishes the expert to address.[50] In formulating the expert's task, as in other important steps in

---

47. GEWERBEORDNUNG [GEWO] (Code on Trade Regulation) § 36.

48. I wish especially to acknowledge rewarding discussions with Dr. Erika Bokelmann, Richterin am Oberlandesgericht Frankfurt; Dr. Heinrich Götzke, Vorsitzender Richter am Landgericht Frankfurt; and Dr. Ernst Windisch, Richter am Bundesgerichtshof.

49. ZPO § 406(I). *See generally* A. BAUMBACH, *supra* note 9, § 406, at 1047–49.

50. *E.g.*, PETER ARENS, ZIVILPROZESSRECHT 203 (2d ed. 1982).

the conduct of the case, the court welcomes adversary suggestions. If the expert should take a view of premises (for example, in an accident case or a building-construction dispute), counsel for both sides will accompany him.[51]

Safeguards. The expert is ordinarily instructed to prepare a written opinion.[52] When the court receives the report, it is circulated to the litigants. The litigants commonly file written comments, to which the expert is asked to reply. The court on its own motion may also request the expert to amplify his views. If the expert's report remains in contention, the court will schedule a hearing at which counsel for a dissatisfied litigant can confront and interrogate the expert.

The code of civil procedure reserves to the court the power to order a further report by another expert if the court should deem the first report unsatisfactory.[53] A litigant dissatisfied with the expert may encourage the court to invoke its power to name a second expert. The code of criminal procedure has a more explicit standard for such cases, which is worth noticing because the literature suggests that courts have similar instincts in civil procedure.[54] The court may refuse a litigant's motion to engage a further expert in a criminal case, the code says,

> if the contrary of the fact concerned has already been proved through the former expert opinion; this [authority to refuse to appoint a further expert] does not apply if the expertise of the former expert is doubted, if his report is based upon inaccurate factual presuppositions, if the report contains contradictions, or if the new expert has available means of research that appear superior to those of a former expert.[55]

When, therefore, a litigant can persuade the court that an expert's report has been sloppy or partial, that it rests upon a view of the field that is not generally shared, or that the question referred to the expert is exceptionally difficult, the court will commission further expertise.[56]

A litigant may also engage his own expert, much as is done in the Anglo-American procedural world, in order to rebut the court-appointed expert. The court will discount the views of a party-selected expert on account of his want of neutrality, but cases occur in which he nevertheless proves to be effective. Ordinarily, I am told, the court will not in such circumstances base its judgment directly upon the views of the party-selected expert; rather, the court will treat the rebuttal as ground for engaging a further court-appointed expert (called an *Oberexperte*, literally an "upper" or "superior" expert), whose opinion will take account of the rebuttal.[57]

---

51. K. Jessnitzer, *supra* note 35, at 183.

52. ZPO § 411(I) authorizes the court to require the expert to report in writing. The language of the statute may make this look exceptional ("If a written report is ordered . . ."), but in practice ordering the report is quite the norm. *See* K. Jessnitzer, *supra* note 35, at 166–67.

53. ZPO § 412(I).

54. *See, e.g.*, K. Jessnitzer, *supra* note 35, at 232.

55. Strafprozessordnung [StPO] (Code of Criminal Procedure) § 244(IV). *See generally* 3 Löwe-Rosenberg, Die Strafprozessordnung und das Gerichtsverfassungsgesetz § 244 (IV), ¶¶ 143–150 (23d ed. 1978).

56. *See* K. Jessnitzer, *supra* note 35, at 231–32.

57. *Cf. id.* at 235–36.

To conclude: In the use of expertise German civil procedure strikes an adroit balance between nonadversarial and adversarial values. Expertise is kept impartial, but litigants are protected against error or caprice through a variety of opportunities for consultation, confrontation, and rebuttal.

The American counterpart. It may seem curious that we make so little use of court-appointed experts in our civil practice, since "[t]he inherent power of a trial judge to appoint an expert of his own choosing is virtually unquestioned"[58] and has been extended and codified in the Federal Rules of Evidence[59] and the Uniform Rules of Evidence (Model Expert Testimony Act).[60] The literature displays both widespread agreement that our courts virtually never exercise this authority, and a certain bafflement about why.[61]

While "simple inertia"[62] doubtless accounts for much (our judges "are accustomed to presiding over acts initiated by the parties"[63]), comparative example points to a further explanation. The difficulty originates with the locktight segmentation of our procedure into pretrial and trial compartments, and with the tradition of partisan domination of the pretrial. Until lately, it was exceptional for the judge to have detailed acquaintance with the facts of the case until the parties presented their evidence at trial. By then the adversaries would have engaged their own experts, and time would no longer allow a court-appointed expert to be located and prepared. Effective use of court-appointed experts as exemplified in German practice presupposes early and extensive judicial involvement in shaping the whole of the proofs. It seems possible that the rise of managerial judging (discussed below in Part VIII) may at last achieve that precondition for effective use of court-appointed experts in our system.[64]

V. SHORTCOMINGS OF ADVERSARY THEORY

The case against adversary domination of fact-gathering is so compelling that we have cause to wonder why our system tolerates it. Because there is nothing to be said in support of coached witnesses, and very little to be said in favor of litigation-biased experts, defenders of the American status quo are left to argue that the advantages of our adversary procedure counterbalance these grievous, truth-defeating distortions. "You have to take the bad with the good; if you want adversary safeguards, you are stuck with adversary excesses."

The false conflict. This all-or-nothing argument overlooks the fundamental distinction between fact-gathering and the rest of civil litigation. Outside the realm of fact-gathering, German civil procedure is about as adversarial as our own. Both systems welcome the lawyerly contribution

58. FED. R. EVID. 706 advisory committee note.
59. FED. R. EVID. 706.
60. UNIF. R. EVID. 706, 13 U.L.A. 319 (1974).
61. *See, e.g.,* 3 JACK B. WEINSTEIN & MARGARET A. BERGER, WEINSTEIN'S EVIDENCE ¶ 706[01], at 706-8 to -12 (Supp. 1985).

62. Merryman, *supra* note 39, at 165.
63. *Id.*
64. *See infra* text accompanying note 130.

to identifying legal issues and sharpening legal analysis.[65] German civil procedure is materially less adversarial than our own only in the fact-gathering function, where partisanship has such potential to pollute the sources of truth.

Accordingly, the proper question is not whether to have lawyers, but how to use them; not whether to have an adversarial component to civil procedure, but how to prevent adversarial excesses. If we were to incorporate the essential lesson of the German system in our own procedure, we would still have a strongly adversarial civil procedure. We would not, however, have coached witnesses and litigation-biased experts.

The confusion with criminal procedure. Much of the rhetoric[66] celebrating unrestrained adversary domination of judicial proceedings stems from the criminal process, where quite different policies are at work.[67] It has been argued that partisan fact-gathering is appropriate to the special values of criminal procedure—the presumption of innocence, the beyond-reasonable-doubt standard of proof, and the privilege against self-incrimination.[68] Bestowing upon the criminal accused the right to conduct his own fact-gathering, despite the risk that he may misuse this power in truth-defeating ways, can be understood as one more way of adjusting the scales to protect the accused. "The specter of capital punishment and the often barbaric conditions of our penal institutions in the past and present, as well as the unique stigma of conviction of a crime, have had a profound impact upon the protections accorded the defendant and the freedom of action accorded the defense lawyer in a criminal case." [69] While I happen to disagree that adversary procedure is a particularly effective way to implement our concern for safeguard in the criminal process,[70] my present point is simply that regardless of right or wrong, that concern is absent in the world of civil procedure. In civil lawsuits we are not trying systematically to err in favor of one class of litigants.

Equality of representation. The German system gives us a good perspective on another great defect of adversary theory, the problem that the Germans call "Waffenungleichheit"—literally, inequality of weapons, or in

---

65. *See supra* text accompanying note 4.

66. The obligatory illustration is Lord Brougham's speech in the defense of Queen Caroline: "[A]n advocate, in the discharge of his duty, knows but one person in all the world, and that person is his client. To save that client by all means and expedients . . . is his first and only duty. . . ." 2 TRIAL OF QUEEN CAROLINE 8 (J. Nightingale ed. 1821), *cited in* Fried, *The Lawyer as Friend: The Moral Foundations of the Lawyer–Client Relation*, 85 YALE L.J. 1060, 1060 n.1 (1976).

67. Monroe Freedman's well-known book, LAWYERS' ETHICS IN AN ADVERSARY SYSTEM (1975), typifies this viewpoint. Regarding limiting this policy to criminal as opposed to civil procedure, see, e.g., Luban, *The Adversary System Excuse*, in THE GOOD LAWYER: LAWYERS' ROLES AND LAWYERS' ETHICS

83, 91–92 (D. Luban ed. 1984); Schwartz, *The Zeal of the Civil Advocate*, 1983 AM. B. FOUND. RESEARCH J. 543, 548–50.

68. *See, e.g.*, Garner v. United States, 424 U.S. 648, 655 (1976), asserting that "the preservation of an adversary system of criminal justice" is "the fundamental purpose of the Fifth Amendment."

69. Schwartz, *supra* note 67, at 550.

70. It seems unlikely that privatized fact-gathering favors the accused in American criminal procedure. In the typical case the prosecution's greater resources disadvantage the accused by comparison with the nonadversarial fact-gathering of German criminal procedure. For a discussion of German criminal procedure, see Langbein, *Land Without Plea Bargaining: How the Germans Do It*, 78 MICH. L. REV. 204, 206–12 (1979).

this instance, inequality of counsel. In a fair fight the pugilists must be well matched. You cannot send me into a ring with Muhammed Ali if you expect a fair fight. The simple truth is that very little in our adversary system is designed to match combatants of comparable prowess, even though adversarial prowess is a main factor affecting the outcome of litigation. Adversary theory thus presupposes a condition that adversary practice achieves only indifferently. It is a rare litigator in the United States who has not witnessed the spectacle of a bumbling adversary whose poor discovery work or inability to present evidence at trial caused his client to lose a case that should have been won. Disparity in the quality of legal representation can make a difference in Germany, too, but the active role of the judge places major limits on the extent of the injury that bad lawyering can work on a litigant.[71] In German procedure both parties get the same fact-gatherer—the judge. (I discuss below (in Part VI) the incentives and safeguards designed to attract and motivate able judges.)

Prejudgment. Perhaps the most influential justification for adversary domination of fact-gathering has been an argument put forward by Lon Fuller: Nonadversarial procedure risks prejudgment—that is, prematurity in judgment.[72] Fuller worried that the judge would make up his mind too soon:

> What generally occurs in practice is that at some early point a familiar pattern will seem to emerge from the evidence; an accustomed label is waiting for the case and, without awaiting further proofs, this label is promptly assigned to it. . . .
>
> An adversary presentation seems the only effective means for combatting this natural human tendency to judge too swiftly in terms of the familiar that which is not yet fully known. The arguments of counsel hold the case, as it were, in suspension between two opposing interpretations of it. While the proper classification of the case is thus kept unresolved, there is time to explore all of its peculiarities and nuances.[73]

This passage obtains much of its force from the all-or-nothing contrast that so misdescribes German civil procedure. In a system like the German, which combines judicial fact-gathering with vigorous and continuing adversarial efforts in nominating lines of factual inquiry and analyzing factual and legal issues, the adversaries perform just the role that Fuller

---

71. The active role of the German judge extends to matters of law as well as fact. The discussion of this point in the Kaplan-von Mehren article remains quite sound: There is "an overriding principle of German law, *jura novit curia*, the court knows—and is bound to apply—general law without prompting from the parties." Kaplan-von Mehren, *supra* note 8, at 1224–25 (discussing ZPO § 139); *cf. id.* at 1227–28.

72. Fuller's argument is usually cited to a speech text, Fuller, *The Adversary System*, in TALKS ON AMERICAN LAW 30 (H. Berman ed. 1961). *See, e.g.*, Schwartz, *The Professionalism and Accountability of Lawyers*, 66 CALIF. L. REV. 669, 672 n.5 (1978) (citing that

work as "[t]he first successful attempt to analyze the adversary system"). Fuller's argument first appeared in the report of a body known as the Joint Conference on Professional Responsibility. *Professional Responsibility: Report of the Joint Conference*, 44 A.B.A. J. 1159 (1958) [hereafter cited as Fuller]. Randall cosigned the report for the ABA but must have had nothing to do with writing it. Portions of Fuller's argument were republished in the posthumously assembled work that appeared as Fuller, *The Forms and Limits of Adjudication*, 92 HARV. L. REV. 353, 383 (1978).

73. Fuller, *supra* note 72, at 1160.

lauds, helping hold the decision in suspension while issues are framed and facts explored.

In German procedure counsel oversees and has means to prompt a flagging judicial inquiry; but quite apart from that protection, is it really true that a "familiar pattern" would otherwise beguile the judge into investigating too sparingly? If so, it seems odd that this asserted "natural human tendency" towards premature judgment does not show up in ordinary business and personal decision-making, whose patterns of inquiry resemble the fact-gathering process in German civil procedure. Since the decision-maker does his own investigating in most of life's decisions, it seems odd to despair of prematurity only when that normal mode of decision-making is found to operate in a courtroom. Accordingly, I think that Fuller overstates the danger of prematurity that inheres in allowing the decision-maker to conduct the fact-gathering; but to the extent that the danger is real, German civil procedure applies just the adversarial remedy that Fuller recommends.[74]

Depth. Fuller's concern about prematurity shades into a different issue: how to achieve appropriate levels of depth in fact-gathering. Extra investment in search can almost always turn up further proofs that would be at least tenuously related to the case. Adversary domination of fact-gathering privatizes the decision about what level of resources to invest in the case. The litigants who are directly interested in the outcome decide how much to spend on search. In German procedure, by contrast, these partisan calculations of self-interest are subordinated, for a variety of reasons. The initiative in fact-gathering is shared with the judge; and the German system of reckoning and allocating the costs of litigation is less sensitive to the cost of incremental investigative steps than in our system where each side pays for the proofs that it orders.[75] On the other hand, the German judge cannot refuse to investigate party-nominated proofs without reason,[76] and this measure of party control greatly narrows the difference between the two systems.

Writing in 1958, Kaplan and his co-authors recorded their "impression" that German civil "proceedings do not in practice serve as an engine of discovery comparable in strength to the modern American methods,"[77] in part because German courts are hostile to fishing.[78] Further, the authors worried

---

74. The assumption that adversary procedure corrects for the dangers of prejudgment needs itself to be probed. I have known American litigators to complain of particular judges tending to make up their minds too soon, even on the pleadings.

75. *See* sources cited *supra* note 27.

76. A. BAUMBACH, *supra* note 9, § 286, at 749–51, ¶¶ 3(B)(a)-(1).

77. Kaplan–von Mehren, *supra* note 8, at 1246.

78. *Id.* at 1247.

The extreme form of fishing that our discovery process invites, viz., bringing a lawsuit in order to discover whether you might actually have one, is unknown not only in Continental procedure, but in English procedure as well. *See, e.g.,* Jolowicz, *Some Twentieth Century Developments in Anglo-American Civil*

Procedure, in 1 STUDI IN ONORE DI ENRICO TULLIO LIEBMAN 217, 241–44 (1979).

The absence of fishing-type lawsuits is more a function of the loser-pays cost-shifting principle common to all major legal systems except our own than it is a function of different investigative procedures. In this connection see Kaplan's remarks on aspects of discovery in England:

[R]epresenting a possible loser, the solicitor is interested in holding down the expenses on his own side and in seeing to it that his opponent's reimbursed expenses are kept well within reason; representing a potential winner, he is still concerned lest he incur expenses that will be found inessential and thus will not be reimbursed.

that the technique of recording witness testimony in succinct summaries could bleach out "[f]ine factual differentiations."[79] They found German procedure to be "far less preoccupied than the American with minute investigation of factual detail of reliability of individual witnesses."[80]

Defenders of the American status quo may take too much comfort from these observations. A main virtue of German civil procedure, we recall, is that the principle of judicial control of sequence works to confine the scope of fact-gathering to those avenues of inquiry deemed most likely to resolve the case. Fact-gathering occurs when the unfolding logic of the case dictates that investigation of particular issues is needed. That practice does indeed contrast markedly with the inclination of American litigators "to leave no stone unturned, provided, of course, they can charge by the stone."[81] The primary reason that German courts do less fact-gathering than American lawyers is that the Germans eliminate the waste. Likewise, when American observers notice that there is less harrying of witnesses with "those elaborate testings of credibility familiar to American courtrooms,"[82] I incline to think that the balance of advantage rests with the Germans, since so much of what passes for cross-examination in our procedure is deliberately truth-defeating.[83]

Kaplan, *An American Lawyer in the Queen's Courts: Impressions of English Civil Procedure*, 69 MICH. L. REV. 821, 822 (1971).

Hostility to fishing is not confined to other legal systems, nor based solely on considerations of efficiency. Judge Rifkind lamented a decade ago that

> the power for the most massive invasion into private papers and private information is available to anyone willing to take the trouble to file a civil complaint. A foreigner watching the discovery proceedings in a civil suit would never suspect that this country has a highly-prized tradition of privacy enshrined in the fourth amendment.

Rifkind, *Are We Asking Too Much of Our Courts?* 70 F.R.D. 96, 107 (1976).

Although the Kaplan–von Mehren article correctly observes that German hostility to fishing is a tension point in the contrast with American practice, the example that the authors choose to illustrate the point is wrong. Without citation to authority, they say: "Suppose an eyewitness to an occurrence, testifying in court, states that another person was present: is it permissible [for the court or the adversaries] to ask him then and there to give up the person's name? The answer commonly given is no." Kaplan–von Mehren, *supra* note 8, at 1247. However, the authors continue, "there is no bar to a party's asking the witness the same question in the court corridor," *id.*, after which, presumably, that side would nominate the newly-identified witness for subsequent judicial examination.

I have put this example to countless German legal professionals familiar with German civil procedure, and I have never found one who thought it was other than flatly wrong. Whatever the etiquette may have been in Hamburg in the 1950s when Kaplan and his coauthors were at work, there is today no convention restricting judge or counsel from following up such leads during the course of courtroom examination of a witness.

79. Kaplan–von Mehren, *supra* note 8, at 1236.

80. *Id.* at 1237. In a similar vein the authors observe that the German judge's "questing attitude" toward developing the case, encouraged by ZPO § 139 (on which, see *supra* note 71), tends "to debilitate German lawyers by providing them with an inward excuse for sloppy work," although "it would be hard to say whether in the long run this is outweighed by benefits, such as helping the party represented by an ineffective lawyer." Kaplan–von Mehren, *supra* note 8, at 1228. Followers of the public speeches of Chief Justice Warren Burger are aware that concern about the extent of sloppy lawyering is not confined to Germany. Sloppiness aside, it is certainly the case that, because German judges bear the main responsibility for fact-gathering, German lawyers do less (and get paid less) than American lawyers. See *infra* note 89.

81. Rhode, Ethical Perspectives on Legal Practice, 37 STAN. L. REV. 589, 635 (1985).

82. Kaplan–von Mehren, *supra* note 8, at 1236.

83. *See supra* note 31.

Interestingly, detractors of Continental procedure have also voiced the opposite criticism—complaining of excessive rather than inadequate depth. Stephan Landsman, for example, defending American adversary practice against the complaint that it sets too low a value on the discovery of material truth, warns against inquisitorial zeal. "The weakness of human perception, memory, and expression will often render the discovery of material truth impossible. To become preoccupied with truth may be both naive and futile. It is to the advantage of the adversary system that it does not define its objectives in such an absolute and unrealistic fashion." [84] This argument overlooks a crucial distinction—between the case with unknowable facts and the case in which the truth-defeating excesses of American adversary fact-gathering cause knowable facts to be obscured. The former scarcely excuses the latter. I side with Blackstone in thinking that fact-finding is the central task of civil litigation. "[E]xperience will abundantly shew," he wrote, "that above a hundred of our lawsuits arise from disputed facts, for one where the law is doubted of." [85] Resolve the facts, resolve what actually happened, and the law usually takes care of itself.

The choice between adversarial and judicial conduct of fact-gathering need not correlate strongly with the level of search achieved in a legal system. Factors unrelated to that choice, such as the clarity of the substantive law or the attitude toward fishing, will influence the levels of search. If the Germans saw any virtue in the American practice of allowing the adversaries to cascade each other with undigested files and records, they could in principle incorporate our luxuriant fishing tradition into their procedure (perish the thought) while still preferring court-appointed experts and forbidding adversary contact with nonparty witnesses. Furthermore, within the realm of judge-conducted fact-gathering, we would expect the levels of search to vary significantly among legal systems, depending upon the incentives for judicial diligence, the scope of adversary oversight, and the effectiveness of appellate review.

VI. JUDICIAL INCENTIVES

Viewed comparatively from the Anglo-American perspective, the greater authority of the German judge over fact-gathering comes at the expense of the lawyers for the parties. Adversary influence on fact-gathering is deliberately restrained. Furthermore, in routine civil procedure, German judges do not share power with jurors. There is no civil jury.[86]

---

84. S. LANDSMAN, *supra* note 2, at 36.

85. 3 WILLIAM BLACKSTONE, COMMENTARIES ON THE LAWS OF ENGLAND 330 (1768). This emphasis on fact-finding as the central function of the civil procedural system remains, I believe, the dominant view both in the Anglo-American tradition and in Continental civil procedure. I think that the work of John Thibaut and Laurens Walker, *A Theory of Procedure*, 66 CALIF. L. REV. 541 (1978), does not represent a true departure from this view. When the authors call it a "misconception that the fundamental objective of the legal process is the discovery of truth," *id.* at 556, they are not denying that the proper work of the legal system is typically to establish the sequence of past events. Rather, they are pointing out that the experimental method for ascertaining truth in the sciences must be largely foreclosed to the law, in part because legal disputes so characteristically do arise out of past facts.

86. *See infra* text accompanying notes 144–53.

Because German procedure places upon the judge the responsibility for fact-gathering, the danger arises that the job will not be done well. The American system of partisan fact-gathering has the virtue of its vices: It aligns responsibility with incentive. Each side gathers and presents proofs according to its own calculation of self-interest. This privatization is an undoubted safeguard against official sloth. After all, who among us has not been treated shabbily by some lazy bureaucrat in a government department? And who would want to have that ugly character in charge of one's lawsuit?

The answer to that concern in the German tradition is straightforward: The judicial career must be designed in a fashion that creates incentives for diligence and excellence. The idea is to attract very able people to the bench, and to make their path of career advancement congruent with the legitimate interests of the litigants.

The career judiciary. The distinguishing attribute of the bench in Germany (and virtually everywhere else in Europe) is that the profession of judging is separate from the profession of lawyering. Save in exceptional circumstances, the judge is not an ex-lawyer like his Anglo-American counterpart. Rather, he begins his professional career as a judge.

In Germany judges and lawyers undergo a common preparatory schooling. After completing a prescribed course of university legal education that lasts several years,[87] the young jurist sits a first state examination. After passing this examination satisfactorily, he enters upon an apprenticeship that now lasts two and one-half years. He clerks for judges in the civil and criminal courts, assists in the prosecutor's office, and works in a lawyer's office. At the conclusion of this tour of duty, the young jurist sits a second state examination, remotely akin to our bar examination, which concludes the certification process. Thereafter, the career lines of judge and lawyer diverge.

Recruitment. Although West Germany is a federal state, the state and federal courts comprise an integrated system. The courts of first instance and the first layer of appellate courts are state courts, while the second (and final) layer of appellate jurisdiction operates at the federal level.[88] Thus, even though the basic codes of civil and criminal law and procedure are federal codes, the state courts have exclusive jurisdiction until the final appellate instance. It follows that most judges are state judges;[89] and since

87. For good English-language accounts see RUDOLF B. SCHLESINGER, COMPARATIVE LAW: CASES, TEXT, MATERIALS 157–82 (4th ed. 1980); Griess, *Legal Education in the Federal Republic of Germany*, 14 J. SOC'Y PUB. TCHRS. L. 166 (1978).

88. For detailed discussion in English, see Meador, *supra* note 8.

89. Data for 1983 appears in STATISTISCHES BUNDESAMT, STATISTISCHES JAHRBUCH 1984 FÜR DIE BUNDESREPUBLIK DEUTSCHLAND 338 (1984). Table 15.2, "Judges in State and Federal Service," shows 16,429 state and 493 federal judges.

Using data for the year 1973, Kötz estimates that about one German lawyer in five

is a judge. "To the foreign observer," he notes, "the most conspicuous feature of the German legal profession is perhaps the very large judiciary. . . ." Kötz, *Legal Profession, supra* note 8, at 71. The size of the German bench is, of course, no mystery. "The real reason that the Germans need more judges is the same reason that they need fewer lawyers: their civil procedure assigns to the judiciary much of the workload that we leave to private counsel." Langbein, *Judging Foreign Judges Badly: Nose Counting Isn't Enough*, JUDGES' J., Fall 1979, at 4, 6.

appointment to the federal bench is by way of promotion from the state courts,[90] all entry-level recruitment to the bench occurs at the state level.

In each of the eleven federal states, the ministry of justice is responsible for staffing the courts. Entry-level vacancies are advertised and applications entertained from young jurists. The judiciary is a prized career: influential, interesting, secure, and (by comparison with practice of the bar) prestigious and not badly compensated. "[O]nly the graduates with the best examination results have any chance of entering the judicial corps."[91]

Advancement. A candidate who is accepted begins serving as a judge without any prior legal-professional experience, typically in his late twenties.[92] At the outset his position is probationary, although he must be promoted to tenure or dismissed within five years.[93] His first assignment may be to a court of petty jurisdiction (Amtsgericht), or else he will become the junior member of a collegial chamber of the main court of general jurisdiction (Landgericht, hereafter LG), where he can receive guidance from experienced judges.[94]

The work of a German judge is overseen and evaluated by his peers throughout his career, initially in connection with his tenure review, and thereafter for promotion through the several levels of judicial office and salary grades. A judge knows that his every step will be grist for the regular periodic reviews that will fill his life-long personnel file. His "efficiency rating"[95] is based in part upon objective factors, such as caseload discharge rates and reversal rates, and in part on subjective peer evaluation. The presiding judge of a chamber has special responsibility for evaluating the work of the younger judges who serve with him, but the young judges are rotated through various chambers in the course of their careers, and this reduces the influence of an aberrant rating from any one presiding judge. These evaluations by senior judges pay particular regard to (1) a judge's effectiveness in conducting legal proceedings, including fact-gathering, and his treatment of witnesses and litigants; and (2) the

90. Except for the federal constitutional court, discussed *infra* text accompanying note 101.

91. Manfred Wolf, *Ausbildung, Auswahl und Ernennung der Richter*, in HUMANE JUSTIZ: DIE DEUTSCHEN LANDESBERICHTE ZUM ERSTEN INTERNATIONALEN KONGRESS FÜR ZIVILPROZESSRECHT IN GENT 1977, at 73, 77 (P. Gilles ed. 1977).

92. *Id.* For English-language discussion of the recruitment and promotion process in Bavaria, see Meador, *German Appellate Judges: Career Patterns and American-English Comparisons*, 67 JUDICATURE 16, 21–25 (1983).

93. DEUTSCHES RICHTERGESETZ [DRiG] (Statute on the German Judiciary) § 12(2). DRiG § 22 governs the grounds for dismissing an untenured judge; *see* GÜNTHER SCHMIDT-RÄNTSCH, DEUTSCHES RICHTERGESETZ § 22, at

202–08 (3d ed. 1983). There are special rules limiting the competence of untenured judges, DRiG §§ 27–29, in order to assure litigants that major decisional responsibility will be in the hands of tenured (i.e., unquestionably independent) judges. *See* EDUARD KERN & MANFRED WOLF, GERICHTSVERFASSUNGSRECHT 138–39 (5th ed. 1975).

94. Although much of the work of a LG chamber is now assigned to a single judge for discharge without collegial participation, *see supra* note 13, the basic unit of organization remains the collegial chamber, and there is still an important residue of collegial first-instance business.

95. Herrmann, *The Independence of the Judge in the Federal Republic of Germany*, in CONTEMPORARY PROBLEMS IN CRIMINAL JUSTICE: ESSAYS IN HONOUR OF PROFESSOR SHIGEMITSU DANDO 61, 73 (1983).

quality of his opinions—his success in mastering and applying the law to his cases.[96]

This meritocratic system of review and promotion is meant to motivate the judge to perform at his best. In the main first-instance court (LG), which is sectioned into many three-judge panels called chambers, the judge aspires to advance to the position of presiding judge of a chamber, a job of greater importance and status with corresponding salary improvement. From there the main career path leads to the first appellate instance (Oberlandesgericht, hereafter OLG), which is also divided into many chambers, each led by a presiding judge who is promoted to that job after distinguishing himself as an ordinary judge of the court.[97] And the final appellate instance, the federal supreme court for nonconstitutional law (Bundesgerichtshof, hereafter BGH), is staffed almost entirely with judges who have been promoted from the OLG.[98]

Meritocratic review and promotion are meant to reward and thereby to inspire judges to be diligent in fact-gathering, to stay current in the law, and to be fair and accurate in the conduct of hearings and the rendering of judgments.

Specialization. I have been speaking throughout this article of the ordinary courts. Of the 17,000 judges who were sitting in Germany as of 1983, the most recent year for which the statistics are published, 13,000 sat in the ordinary courts.[99] The others served in the specialized court systems for administrative law, tax and fiscal matters, labor and employment law, and social security.[100] Furthermore, the Germans operate a separate supreme constitutional court (Bundesverfassungsgericht), to which the other courts refer some contentious constitutional business. Appointment

---

96. These factors were mentioned to me repeatedly in 1984 when I had occasion to inquire about the promotion process in interviews with German judges and with German law professors specializing in civil procedure and judicial administration. *See also infra* note 113 and accompanying text.

97. Wolf, *supra* note 91, at 77; *see also* Meador, *supra note* 92, at 22–23.

98. Meador, *supra* note 92, at 24–25. The BGH now has more than a hundred judges and a dozen chambers. Call to that court is perhaps not quite the prize that we might imagine the pinnacle to be. There has been some concern that not enough of the best OLG judges aspire to join the BGH, despite the enhancement in rank, authority, and compensation that promotion to the BGH entails. The opportunity for promotion to the BGH usually comes when a judge is well into his forties or fifties and long settled in his home state. The BGH sits in Karlsruhe, an unexciting city on the southwestern fringe of the country. Some prominent OLG judges decline to exile themselves and their families to Karlsruhe from life in Munich, Dusseldorf, Frankfurt, or Hamburg. We can

imagine the problem in American terms by supposing that we had created a supreme court of nonconstitutional law and sited it in Akron, Boise, or Macon; perhaps we would have found Learned Hand and Henry Friendly not too anxious for that last round of promotion. But laying aside this peculiarity about the BGH, it can be said with great confidence that most German judges aspire to maximize their chances for promotion through the lower levels of the pyramid.

99. STATISTISCHES BUNDESAMT, *supra* note 89, at 338 (Table 15.2).

100. For discussion in English, see ARTHUR T. VON MEHREN & JAMES R. GORDLEY, THE CIVIL LAW SYSTEM 133–37 (2d ed. 1977); Meador, *supra* note 8, at 31–34. Continental specialized court systems are distinguished from ours by having their own appellate systems. In the United States, appeal lies from the specialized tax court to the regular courts of appeal, and thereafter to the Supreme Court. In Germany, appeal lies from the tax court to the supreme court for tax matters, with no possibility of review by the federal supreme court of ordinary jurisdiction (BGH).

to the constitutional court is by design highly political; members are seldom part of the career judiciary that I have been describing.[101]

The specialized courts and the constitutional court siphon off business that Americans would expect to see in the ordinary courts. Within the German ordinary courts of first instance there are special divisions that have counterparts in our tradition—for crime, for what we would call probate, for domestic relations. In addition, commercial law matters are removed to specialized chambers.[102] Thus, the German ordinary courts of first instance have a somewhat narrower diet than our own.

At the appellate level, including the first appellate instance (OLG) that proceeds by review de novo, there is extensive specialization. An OLG is quite large by our standards, sometimes staffed with more than a hundred judges, who sit in chambers containing four or five judges. Cases are allocated among these chambers on the basis of subject matter.[103] All the medical malpractice cases go to one chamber, the maritime cases to another, and so forth. This system permits the judges to develop over the years just that sort of expertise in legal subspecialties that we expect of lawyers, particularly lawyers in large-firm practice, in the United States. The litigants get judges who know something about the field, in contradistinction to the calculated amateurism of our appellate tradition.[104]

Political influence. Judicial appointments and promotions issue in the name of the state or federal minister of justice, who is an important political official, usually a member of the state or federal parliament and of the cabinet. The minister acts in consultation with an advisory commission of senior judges;[105] in some of the German states that commission has a formal veto power.

Directly political concerns appear to be very subordinated in the selection and advancement of judges. Because this subject is not much ventilated in the literature, I have inquired about it when talking with German judges and legal academics. The impression I have gained is that political considerations do not materially affect appointment or promotion until the level of the federal supreme court (BGH).[106] Party balance is given weight in BGH

101. For an English-language account, now a little dated, see DONALD P. KOMMERS, JUDICIAL POLITICS IN WEST GERMANY: A STUDY OF THE FEDERAL CONSTITUTIONAL COURT 113–59 (1976).

102. GERICHTSVERFASSUNGSGESETZ [GVG] (Statute on the Organization of the Courts) §§ 93–95. *See generally* OTTO R. KISSEL, GERICHTSVERFASSUNGSGESETZ §§ 93–95, at 894–911.

103. For commentary in English, see Meador, *supra* note 8, at 44–72.

104. The case for the generalist judiciary is argued anew in RICHARD A. POSNER, THE FEDERAL COURTS: CRISIS AND REFORM 147–60 (1985). It would entail a large digression in the present article to detail all of my disagreements with Judge Posner's treatment of this subject. I find particularly unpersuasive Posner's central claim that

specialized courts are unworkable in fields where differences of view persist among the specialists. "It is remarkable in how few fields of modern American law there is a professional consensus on fundamental questions." *Id.* at 153. This is an exaggeration, and one that resembles in an eerie way the all-law-is-politics theme of a contemporary legal-academic movement with which Posner is ordinarily not associated. The truth is that even in fields like constitutional law or torts (Posner's examples) where much is unsettled, there are vast areas of consensus. The work of legal doctrine is to forge consensus. The more learned the court, the more likely is the court to do that job well.

105. For discussion of Bavarian practice, see Meador, *supra* note 92, at 22–23.

106. *See* Wolf, *supra* note 91, at 77–78.

appointments, but political connections do not substitute for merit. Positions on the BGH go to judges who have distinguished themselves on the OLG.

We must remember that the decision to isolate important components of constitutional and administrative-law jurisdiction outside the ordinary courts in Germany lowers the political stakes in judicial office, by comparison with our system, in which every federal district judge (and for that matter, every state judge) purports to brandish the Constitution and thus to be able to wreak major social and institutional change.

American contrasts. If I were put to the choice of civil litigation under the German procedure that I have been praising in this article or under the American procedure that I have been criticizing, I might have qualms about choosing the German. The likely venue of a lawsuit of mine would be the state court in Cook County, Illinois, and I must admit that I distrust the bench of that court. The judges are selected by a process in which the criterion of professional competence is at best an incidental value.[107] Further, while decent people do reach the Cook County bench in surprising numbers, events have shown that some of their colleagues are crooks. If my lawsuit

---

107. The following remarks by Justice Seymour Simon of the Illinois Supreme Court, made in an unpublished speech, deserve wide attention:

For 15 years I was an elected ward committeeman in the nation's most publicized local political party organization, the Democratic Party of Cook County. As a committee member, I attended slate-making sessions for judges as well as other candidates—sessions which, until recent years, always were held behind closed doors. There, I have seen those seeking to be picked as judges sponsored and praised by their committeemen, but praised not for their learning and experience in the law, praised not for their academic backgrounds or legal achievements, but praised instead for their loyalty to their political party, for their work in the precincts or, in the political lingo that became standard usage in appraising the quality of judicial aspirants, "for remembering from whence they came." Recently a committeeman who was also an alderman was quoted as favoring an aspirant because he would be an "alderman's judge." I have heard would-be judicial candidates asked to pledge their support to all the other candidates on their party's ticket even though they had no idea who these candidates would be. Sometimes judgeships were parceled out to ward organizations because it was "their turn" or as a reward for performance in previous elections. . . .

. . .

John Gilligan, Governor of Ohio from 1971 to 1975 . . . , wrote this about

judicial elections: "It's a murderous ordeal to go through. It takes a full year out of your life handing out matchbooks and going to wiener roasts. There are lawyers who would be very fine judges who simply would not subject themselves to that. . . ."

. . .

Of still greater concern is the unfortunate truth that the all-pervasive need for campaign funds in modern politics intertwines judicial elections with political fundraising. . . . Although under our Supreme Court Rules and those of the ABA a [campaign] committee ostensibly shields a candidate from the identity of his campaign contributors, a candidate is not prohibited from attending his own fundraising parties where he can observe who shows up and who doesn't. For that matter, I wonder how many judicial candidates turn down checks handed to them by acquaintances who meet them on the street. And, all campaign contributions, including names of contributors of more than $150, must be reported by the fundraising committee so that anyone who is curious, including the candidate or his friends or family, can examine these reports. And there is no rule against examining an opponent's reports.

S. Simon, After "Greylord" What? Address at the Chicago Bar Association and Illinois State Bar Association 1983 Dinner Honoring Illinois Supreme Court 4–5, 6–7, 10–11 (November 4, 1983) (unpublished speech; copy on file with *The University of Chicago Law Review*).

may fall into the hands of a dullard or a thug, I become queasy about increasing his authority over the proceedings.

German-style judicial responsibility for fact-gathering cannot be lodged with the Greylord judiciary. Remodeling of civil procedure is intimately connected to improvement in the selection of judges. I do not believe that we would have to institute a German-style career judiciary in order to reform American civil procedure along German lines, although I do think that Judge Frankel was right to "question whether we are wise" to disdain the Continental model, and to "wonder now whether we might benefit from some admixture of such [career judges] to leaven or test our trial benches of elderly lawyers." [108] The difference in quality between the state and federal trial benches in places like Cook County is sufficient to remind us that measures far short of adopting the Continental career judiciary can bring about material improvement.[109]

Americans will long remain uncomfortable at the prospect of a more bureaucratic judiciary. We have not had good experience attracting and controlling an able career bureaucracy in the higher realms of public administration, although we have scarcely tried. Some observers point to that elusive construct, national character. Europeans in general and Germans in particular are thought to be more respectful of authority, hence better disposed toward the more bureaucratic mode of justice that judicialized fact-gathering entails.

Cultural differences surely do explain something of why institutional and procedural differences arise in different legal systems. The important question for present purposes is what weight to attach to this factor, and my answer is, "Not much." It is all too easy to allow the cry of "cultural differences" to become the universal apologetic that permanently sheathes the status quo against criticism based upon comparative example. Cultural differences that help explain the origins of superior procedures need not restrict their spread. If Americans were to resolve to officialize the fact-gathering process while preserving the political prominence of the higher bench, we would probably turn initially to some combination of judges, magistrates, and masters for getting the job done. Over time, we would strike a new balance between bench and bar, and between higher and lower judicial office.

The rise of American managerial judging (discussed in Part VIII below) should put us on notice that we may no longer have the leisure to decide whether we want more judicial authority over civil litigation. If greater judicial control of civil proceedings is inevitable, greater attention

---

108. Frankel, *supra* note 1, at 1033.

109. Part of what makes the federal bench more attractive—that the supremacy clause makes federal judges more powerful—is beyond emulation. But other attributes of the federal judicial career that could be copied must affect the quality of the recruits. For example, the federal salary scale, while hardly munificent, is significantly better than at the state level, especially when account is taken of the generous federal judicial pension scheme. Lifetime tenure makes the federal judicial career more attractive, sparing federal judges from the career uncertainty and indignity to which state trial judges are exposed through the elective process, on which see *supra* note 107. The appointive process for selecting judges enhances the influence of the organized bar and other interest groups that have some concern to assure professional competence in the judiciary.

to safeguarding litigants' interests against abuse of judicial power must follow. The German model should inspire attention to the way judicial career incentives (above all, meritocratic selection, review, and promotion) can serve as safeguards for litigants.

VII. APPELLATE REVIEW

Like the career incentives that encourage good judicial performance, the German appellate process is designed to protect litigants from caprice, error, or sloth. The adversarial component of lawyerly oversight, to which this article has so often referred, ultimately depends for its effectiveness upon the threat of appellate review. From the standpoint of comparison with American procedure, two attributes of German appellate practice appear especially noteworthy: (1) the requirement, meant to facilitate review, that the first-instance court disclose in writing its findings of fact and reasons of law; and (2) the de novo standard of review.

Disclosure of grounds. Unless the first-instance court is successful in encouraging the parties to settle,[110] it must decide the case by means of a written judgment containing findings of facts and rulings of law.[111] The thoroughness of the German judgment is legendary.[112] Empirical study has shown how seriously the first-instance courts take their judgment-writing responsibility.[113] Judges know that they will be judged on the quality of their opinions. Good opinions reduce the reversal rate and win esteem in the peer evaluation process. Judges know that the reviewing court will have convenient access to the whole of the evidence and the submissions received at first-instance, since the dossier goes up with the appeal. Especially when coupled with searching review by an appellate court of great ability, the requirement of written findings and reasons is a bulwark against arbitrary or eccentric adjudication. In our system, by contrast, the conclusory general verdict of a jury is the antithesis of a reasoned judgment; nor do we insist on much better in the realm of bench trials.[114] Fact-finding in American courts all too often resembles Caligula dealing with vanquished gladiators: thumbs up or thumbs down, yours but to wonder why.

Review de novo. Ultimately, it is the prospect of appellate review in German civil procedure that makes the other safeguards effective, both as deterrents and as correctives. The dissatisfied litigant has the right of appeal de novo (Berufung) in the first appellate instance (typically the OLG).[115] No presumption of correctness attaches to the initial judgment.

---

110. *See supra* note 25.

111. ZPO § 313(I)(5)–(6); see 2 STEIN-JONAS, *supra* note 46, § 313(IV)–(V), at 1279–84.

112. *See* Weyrauch, *The Art of Drafting Judgments: A Modified German Case Method,* 9 J. LEG. ED. 311, 316–26 (1956).

113. In a considerable sample of nondivorce cases that went to judgment (i.e., that resisted settlement) in the main first-instance court (LG), an average 43% of the total time devoted to all aspects of the courts' work (including review of the dossier, fact-gathering, and oral hearings) was spent on writing the judgment. 2 BUNDESRECHTSANWALTSKAMMER, TATSACHEN ZUR REFORM DER ZIVILGERICHTSBARKEIT: AUSWERTUNGEN 64–65 (1974).

114. *See* Leubsdorf, *Constitutional Civil Procedure,* 63 TEXAS L. REV. 579, 630 & n.311 (1984).

115. Appeal de novo lies from the court of petty jurisdiction (Amtsgericht) to the court of general jurisdiction (LG). For the LG, which is

What makes this astonishingly liberal system of appellate review possible is the extreme economy of the technique, previously discussed, of recording in pithy summaries the evidence gathered at first instance.[116] Retrial becomes for the most part only rereading.

The OLG "may choose to rehear evidence and is likely to do so when demeanor of a witness seems important or when the record fails to give sufficient detail."[117] The main task in review de novo is not, however, gathering new evidence, but considering afresh the record and the judgment from below. OLG review guarantees to the dissatisfied litigant a second look by a panel of long-experienced judges on all matters of law and fact. In other words, for a litigant who wishes it, fact-finding will be reassigned from the court that did the primary fact-gathering (and this is another way in which German procedure may be said to respond to Lon Fuller's concern about the danger of prejudgment in the investigating court[118]). OLG review is collegial; a panel of several judges decides the case.[119] And because the OLG panels are specialized by subject matter, chances are that some of the judges who decide the case will be masters of the particular field of law.

From the OLG there is a further level of review (by the BGH) according to a standard of review (Revision) that approximates the Anglo-American notion of review for error.[120]

Adequacy of safeguards. There is no denying the power of the German judge, yet complaints about the misuse of judicial power are extremely rare. The career incentives and the system of appellate review have been designed to deter and correct abuse. Experience suggests that they work.

VIII. AMERICAN MANAGERIAL JUDGING: CONVERGENCE?

Important changes have occurred in recent years that diminish the contrast between German and American civil procedure. Under the rubric of case management, American trial judges are exercising increasing control of the conduct of fact-gathering. Although many American courtrooms remain untouched by the new developments, the changes have occurred broadly enough to have about themselves the look of the future.

The Manual. Managerial judging arose in the federal courts as a response to the increasing quantity of so-called "complex litigation"— cases that involve "unusual multiplicity or complexity of factual issues."[121] The *Manual for Complex Litigation* was created to deal with these cases,

---

the main first-instance court, the OLG is the court with responsibility for review de novo.

Following are some figures that give a feel for the frequency of appeal de novo to the OLG from the LG. In 1981 the LGs had a first-instance caseload of 574,860 cases and the OLGs had a caseload of 85,021. The LGs decided 106,538 cases by full judgment ("streitiges Urteil"), which is the main cohort of cases that can give rise to appeal de novo; in the same year the OLG decided 25,299 cases by "streitiges Urteil." STATISTISCHES BUNDESAMT, *supra* note 83, at 339 (Table 15.4.1).

116. *See supra* text accompanying notes 15–18.

117. Kaplan–von Mehren, *supra* note 8, at 1451; *see id.* at 1453 (discussing the purposes of review de novo).

118. *See supra* text accompanying notes 72–74.

119. *See* Kaplan–von Mehren, *supra* note 8, at 1451.

120. *Id.* at 1454.

121. MANUAL, *supra* note 5, § 0.22.

but because complexity is a matter of degree, managerial judging was hard to confine to the Big Case. The *Manual* identifies antitrust, securities, mass disaster, product liability, class action, and multiparty cases, among others, as typical.[122] In cases with many parties and many issues, the feeling grew that court-centered control was needed to prevent the confusion and duplication that would result if the adversaries were "left to themselves, each pursuing the course that is most favorable to his particular client."[123] Accordingly, "[t]he essence" of what the *Manual* propounds "is the exercise of judicial control over complex litigation plus a positive plan for discovery and pretrial preparation."[124]

The *Manual* effects judicial control over adversary fact-gathering through a set of interconnected measures:

(1) The judge uses pretrial conferences to explore the case with counsel and to identify key issues.[125]

(2) The judge is expected to promote settlement from the earliest opportunity.[126]

(3) The judge also helps sharpen the issues. "To the extent feasible the judge should narrow the issues in the course of the first pretrial conference and limit discovery accordingly."[127]

(4) Issue definition leads to the regulation of discovery. The court convenes discovery conferences and breaks discovery into "waves."[128] Thus, the court decides what subjects may be investigated in what sequence. This power has now been codified for the ordinary Federal Rules of Civil Procedure in revised rule 26(f): "Following the discovery conference, the court shall enter an order tentatively identifying the issues for discovery purposes, establishing, a plan and schedule for discovery. . . ."[129]

(5) The *Manual* recommends that the court explore the need for expert testimony early, in part in order "to determine whether court appointment of an expert is desirable."[130]

Convergence. What makes the *Manual* look "proto-Germanic" in the eyes of the comparative lawyer is the informal feel of "the conference

---

122. *Id.*
123. *Id.* § 1.10.
124. *Id.* (italics deleted).
125. *Id.* § 1.20. The *Manual* also encourages "the practice of obtaining counsel's views of the case by requiring the filing before discovery of initial pretrial briefs containing all the legal and factual contentions of the parties." *Id.* We have seen that it is characteristic of German practice that counsel may guide the court's work by submitting written commentary on issues of law or fact. *See supra* text between notes 20 and 21.
126. MANUAL, *supra* note 5, § 1.21.
127. *Id.* § 1.30.
128. *Id.* § 0.50 ("Ordinarily, in a complex case, use of sequential discovery—first wave,

second wave, and special issue—promotes efficiency, orderliness, and early completion of all permissible discovery."); *see also id.* § 1.50.
129. FED. R. CIV. P. 26(f). "Rule 26(f) mandates the holding of a discovery conference upon proper motion by a party. In the complex case, however, the judge should not ordinarily wait for the filing of such a motion. . . ." MANUAL, *supra* note 5, § 1.95. Judge Schwarzer has expressed "dissatisfaction" that the *Manual* is inadequately directive. WILLIAM W. SCHWARZER, MANAGING ANTITRUST AND OTHER COMPLEX LITIGATION: A HANDBOOK FOR LAWYERS AND JUDGES § 1-1, at 4 (1982).
130. MANUAL, *supra* note 5, § 2.60; *see also id.* § 3.40.

method;"[131] and the active judicial role in defining issues, promoting settlement,[132] and fixing the sequence for fact-gathering.

To be sure, managerial judging in the pretrial process leaves adversary domination of the trial (especially jury trial) largely unaffected. But the vast preponderance of cases settle or are dismissed before trial; pretrial procedure is the whole procedure for most of our caseload.[133]

Moreover, judicial control of the pretrial process interacts with certain features of trial procedure. Early identification of issues and issue-specific discovery can lead to issue-specific trial, that is partial trial, under rule 42(b).[134] One could envision manipulating these powers to replicate something of the German court's control over the sequence of issue-identification and fact-gathering in the development of a lawsuit.[135] And under rule 53(c), which empowers the court to refer issues to a master for investigation and report,[136] one could imagine further movement toward judicial conduct of fact-gathering. That is, however, still a glimmer; the important trend has been toward judicial control of the adversaries' conduct of the investigatory function, not judicial conduct of the investigation.

Thus, while managerial judging leaves untouched some of the worst abuses of our trial procedure such as coached witnesses and partisan experts, it has reoriented pretrial procedure away from adversary domination; and in a legal system that actually tries only a tiny fraction of its civil caseload, judicial capture of pretrial could become more important than continuing adversary control of trial.

The importance of managerial judging ought not to be overstated. Managerial judging is prevalent in the federal courts, but less evident in the state systems where complex litigation is less prevalent. (Many of the state systems also lack an essential predicate for managerial judging, the continuous-case-management system in which a case remains assigned to the same trial judge from initial docketing to final judgment.) Moreover, even within the federal system, managerial judging is routine only for

---

131. *See supra* note 24 and accompanying text. Judith Resnik remarks on the informality of managerial judging, noticing that these conferences resemble "ordinary business meetings." Resnik, *supra* note 6, at 407.

132. Resnik, who popularized the term "managerial judging," observes the similarity to the German practice in promoting settlement as it was described in the Kaplan–von Mehren article. "Ironically, their description of the German judge—6 '. . . as insistent promoter of settlements'—now seems apt for the American judge as well." Resnik, *supra* note 6, at 386 (citing Kaplan–von Mehren, *supra* note 8, at 1472).

133. "[O]ver ninety percent of the cases in most courts terminate through settlement or dismissal prior to trial." Miller, *The Adversary System: Dinosaur or Phoenix?* 69 MINN. L. REV. 1, 14 (1984); *see id*. at 4 n.7

(citing ADMINISTRATIVE OFFICE OF U.S. COURTS, ANNUAL REPORT OF THE DIRECTOR 1983, at 142 (Table 29)).

134. FED. R. CIV. P. 42(b).

135. *See supra* text accompanying notes 22–27.

136. FED. R. CIV. P. 53(c). *But see* Brazil, *Referring Discovery Tasks to Special Masters: Is Rule 53 a Source of Authority and Restrictions?* 1983 AM. B. FOUND. RESEARCH J. 143. For an account of the work of the court-appointed masters in managing pretrial procedures in the mammoth AT&T antitrust case, see Hazard & Rice, *Judicial Management of the Pretrial Process in Massive Litigation: Special Masters as Case Managers*, in WAYNE D. BRAZIL, GEOFFREY C. HAZARD, JR. & PAUL R. RICE, MANAGING COMPLEX LITIGATION: A PRACTICAL GUIDE TO THE USE OF SPECIAL MASTERS 77 (1983).

complex cases that require to be dealt with under the *Manual*. Outside the realm of the Big Case, the litigant gets managerial judging only if, by the fortuity of the case-assignment wheel, he draws a managerial judge. If you get assigned to Robert Keeton or Prentice Marshall or William Schwarzer, you get managerial judging. If you draw a traditional federal district judge, you get old-style adversary domination of the pretrial process. It is hard to imagine that our system can long continue to leave such fundamental choices to luck and whim.

Safeguards. Not only does whim determine whether a litigant gets managerial judging, but whim can surface in the conduct of managerial judging. Judith Resnik observes:

> [M]anagerial responsibilities give judges greater power. Yet the restraints that formerly circumscribed judicial authority are conspicuously absent. Managerial judges frequently work beyond the public view, off the record, with no obligation to provide written, reasoned opinions, and out of the reach of appellate review.
>
> . . .
>
> . . . [B]ecause managerial judging is less visible and usually unreviewable, it gives trial courts more authority and at the same time provides litigants with fewer procedural safeguards to protect them from abuse of that authority.[137]

Viewed from the perspective of comparative law, therefore, American managerial judging displays contrasting tendencies. On the one hand, it exhibits convergence toward the Continental model of judicial domination of the fact-gathering process. On the other hand, the haphazard growth of managerial judging has not been accompanied by Continental-style attention to safeguarding litigants against the dangers inherent in the greatly augmented judicial role. The career incentives for our judiciary are primitive, and the standards of appellate review barely touch the pretrial process.

The trend toward managerial judging is irreversible,[138] because the trend toward complexity in civil litigation that gave rise to managerial

---

137. Resnik, *supra* note 6, at 378, 380. Under the rubric of "managerial judging," Resnik brings two trends: the one that so interests us in the present article, the growth of judicial participation in the fact-gathering work of the pretrial process; and the phenomenon to which Chayes directed attention a decade ago, the increasing judicial responsibility for devising and adjusting complex remedial orders in the post-trial process, primarily for public law litigation. Chayes, *The Role of the Judge in Public Law Litigation*, 89 HARV. L. REV. 1281 (1976).

138. Resnik's article, which is so instructive in pointing to the dangers that lurk in unconstrained managerial judging, sometimes conveys the impression that

managerial judging is a foible that the judiciary might be persuaded to abandon. *E.g.*, Resnik, *supra* note 6, at 445 (the federal bench has been "[s]educed by controlled calendars, disposition statistics, and other trappings of the efficiency era and the high-tech age"; further, "[n]o one has convincingly discredited the virtues of disinterest and disengagement, virtues that form the bases of the judiciary's authority"). This yearning for the golden age of judicial passivity exaggerates the potential for retracing our steps, because it does not give due weight to the factors that gave rise to managerial judging: the growth in complex litigation and the difficulty of distinguishing the Big Case from slightly smaller cases.

judging is irreversible. If we were to learn from the success of the long established German tradition of managerial judging, we would not only improve our safeguards, we would encourage more complete judicial responsibility for the conduct of fact-gathering. For example, we might have the judge (or a surrogate such as a master or a magistrate) depose witnesses and assemble the rest of the proofs, working in response to adversary nomination and under adversary oversight as in German procedure. We might then be able to forbid the adversaries from contact with witnesses—in other words, we could abolish the coaching that disgraces our civil justice. We would also be able to routinize the use of court-appointed experts. And if we were to concern ourselves with devising a standard of appellate review appropriate to the seriousness of managerial judging, we might want to experiment with the German technique of succinct recordation of evidence.[139]

Concentration. When Kaplan sought "the grand discriminant, the watershed feature, so to speak, which shows the English and American systems to be consanguine and sets them apart from the German, the Italian, and others in the civil-law family," he found it in our "single-episode trial as contrasted with discontinuous or staggered proof-taking" on the Continent.[140] Arthur von Mehren has advanced a similar view, showing in a recent article how extensively the concentrated trial has affected the rest of our civil procedure.[141]

For the future, however, I doubt that the contrast between systems of concentrated and discontinuous trial will have such prominence in thinking about comparative civil procedure. The tendency of our pretrial process to

In emphasizing the Big Case as the origin of managerial judging in American procedure, I do not mean to imply that I think that managerial judging ought to be confined there. To the contrary, I agree with the point that Hein Kötz has long asserted, most recently in Kötz, *Zur Funktionsteilung zwischen Richter und Anwalt im deutschen und englischen Zivil-prozess,* in FESTSCHRIFT FÜR IMRE ZAJTAY 277, 290–91 (R.H. Graveson et al. eds. 1982), that the German advantage in civil procedure is at its greatest in the Small Case, where the costliness of adversary fact-gathering is intolerable. *See also* Jolowicz, *supra* note 78, at 270 (cited by Kötz, predicting that the Anglo-American systems will experience "an abandonment of the adversary process, even if only for small claims"). For cogent evidence of the judicial hand in small claims litigation, see Galanter, Palen & Thomas, *The Crusading Judge: Judicial Activism in Trial Courts,* 52 S. CAL. L. REV. 699, 706–08 (1979).

A full account of the decline of adversary fact-gathering in the real practice of modern American dispute resolution would also give due attention to the rise of administrative decision-making. *See, e.g.,* JERRY L. MASHAW, BUREAUCRATIC JUSTICE: MANAGING SOCIAL SECURITY DISABILITY CLAIMS (1983), describing one corner of the field:

There are perhaps 5,600 state agency personnel (supported by 5,000 more) whose sole function is to adjudicate disability claims. Over 625 federal administrative law judges hear administrative appeals from state agency denials. This total of more than 6,000 adjudicators approaches the size of the combined judicial systems of the state and federal governments of the United States. And the claims that these officials adjudicate are not small. The average, present, discounted value of the stream of income from a successful disability application is over $30,000. Disability claims, on the average, thus have a value three times that required by statute for the pursuit of many civil actions in federal district courts.

Id. at 18.

139. MANUAL, *supra* note 5, § 2.711, relying upon FED. R. EVID. 1006, notices the possibility of using summary rather than verbatim testimony for "[v]oluminous or complicated data." On the parallel to German techniques of recording and consulting testimony, see *supra* text accompanying notes 15–18.

140. Kaplan, *supra* note 78, at 841.

141. Von Mehren, *supra* note 4.

displace the trial, a phenomenon long evident in American criminal procedure,[142] is now increasingly manifest in civil procedure as well. Between discontinuous trial in the Continental tradition and our system of discontinuous pretrial proceedings followed by concentrated trial, the difference need not be all that great, especially since so few of our cases actually go to trial. Although ostensibly conducted in preparation for the concentrated trial, managerial judging in its more important aspects is directed toward suppressing the trial. Managerial judging succeeds best when pretrial clarification produces settlement, capitulation, or dismissal.

Even when civil cases do advance to trial in our system, much of what has made the trial so consequential is the latitude for adversary distortion in the fact-adducing process. Accordingly, I incline to point to a different "grand discriminant" between the two legal cultures—not concentration, but adversarial versus judicial responsibility for gathering and presenting the facts. If our concentrated trial occurred after nonadversarial fact-gathering in the pretrial process, our trial might ultimately resemble somewhat the current German review-de-novo proceeding for first appeals.[143] At trial the court would recall and examine key witnesses afresh, while facts not in serious controversy would be elicited from the pretrial dossier.

The jury. "The common law system," writes von Mehren, "had to concentrate trials because of the jury. . . . The presence of a jury makes a discontinuous trial impractical."[144] Historically, it is surely correct that concentration of the trial eliminated the problems of reassembling and controlling groups of laymen across long intervals, problems that would otherwise have bedeviled a system of routine but discontinuous jury trial. "Moreover, at least until relatively modern times, there was probably no way in which material presented at widely separate points in time could have been preserved in a form that would have enabled the jury to refresh its recollection when it ultimately came to deliberate and render the verdict."[145] In an age of stenographically reported and now videotaped testimony, however, those concerns look less fundamental.[146]

Although civil jury trial is a comparative rarity within the declining subset of our cases that go to any kind of trial,[147] the jury entitlement is enshrined in the seventh amendment and in comparable state constitutional guarantees. There is a substantial body of opinion that the civil jury is a

142. I have discussed the origins and the shortcomings of our nontrial plea bargaining procedure in Langbein, *Understanding the Short History of Plea Bargaining*, 13 L. & Soc'y Rev. 261 (1979), and Langbein, *Torture and Plea Bargaining*, 46 U. Chi. L. Rev. 3 (1978).

143. *See supra* text at note 116. Note further that developments in German procedure have also been undermining the contrast between concentrated and discontinuous trial. Regarding the German effort to limit discontinuity, see *supra* note 9; *see also* von Mehren, *supra* note 4, at 370–71.

144. Von Mehren, *supra* note 4, at 364 (note omitted).

145. *Id.* at 364–65.

146. *See, e.g.*, M. Frankel, *supra* note 36, at 109–14, discussing the Ohio experiment in which judicially edited videotaped evidence is replayed for the trial jury. Frankel observes the potential for this technique to help liberate us from the concentration requirement, and thus to bring us closer to Continental civil procedure. *Id.* at 113–14.

147. Two decades ago Kenneth Culp Davis gathered data indicating that "[f]ive out of six trials in courts of general jurisdiction are without juries." Davis, *An Approach to Rules of Evidence for Nonjury Cases*, 50 A.B.A. J. 723, 723 (1964).

worthwhile safeguard, and that view can scarcely be gainsaid as long as our trial bench remains, at the margin, so unreliable.

The question arises, therefore, whether the jury guarantee will continue to dominate our increasingly juryless practice. In the context of comparative civil procedure, the question is whether the jury tradition that underlies the Anglo-American concentrated trial is a true "grand discriminant," capable of preventing convergence toward Continental procedure. An initial cause for doubt is that the Anglo-American tradition has been for half a century decisively sundered in the matter of the jury entitlement. The English effectively abolished civil jury trial in 1933.[148] Paradoxically, however, theirs is the more faithful adherence to the tradition of the concentrated trial, because their pretrial process is less developed. What has continued to unite English and American civil procedure, therefore, is adversary domination of fact-gathering.[149]

But must the American jury entitlement ultimately defeat convergence toward the German model? In other words, is judicial responsibility for fact-gathering incompatible with lay adjudication? We have little direct experience, since European legal systems do not share our preoccupation with the jury in civil procedure. The Germans employ juror-like lay judges for first-instance proceedings in various of the specialized courts (labor, social, commercial, administrative, tax) and in the courts that handle cases of serious crime.[150] The lay judging system combines lay and professional judges in a single panel (a "mixed court") that deliberates and decides together. I have elsewhere had occasion to describe the German mixed court, and to contrast it with our jury court in the realm of criminal procedure.[151] I came to the conclusion that while each form of court structure has advantages, the two are broadly comparable in serving the main purposes of the jury guarantee.[152] Elsewhere in Europe, true jury courts have been incorporated into criminal procedural systems that retain strongly nonadversarial pretrial processes.[153] Key witnesses who have been examined in the officialized pretrial are simply recalled for the jury. Accordingly, the indications are that judicial conduct of fact-gathering could be smoothly integrated into the jury tradition.

Abridging adversary theory. It is curious that managerial judging took hold so easily in a legal system supposedly governed by the counterprinciple

148. ADMINISTRATION OF JUSTICE (MISCELLANEOUS PROVISIONS) ACT, 1933, 23 & 24 Geo. 5, ch. 49, § 6. *See* Ward v. James, [1966] 1 Q.B. 273, 279–303, for discussion of the minute residual sphere of civil jury trial in England.

149. At least for the present, the Americans do not find English companions on the early steps of the path of convergence toward German-style judicial responsibility for fact-gathering. The predicate is lacking— the English have not followed us into managerial judging. The English have restricted in a variety of ways the growth of complex multi-party litigation, the phenomenon that gave rise to American managerial judging. English substantive law is narrower, their pretrial system is primitive, their multi-party practice is less permissive, and their loser-pays

cost-shifting rules deter adventurous litigation. *See* R. Prichard, A Systemic Approach to Comparative Law: The Effect of Cost, Fee, and Financing Rules on the Development of the Substantive Law, J. LEGAL STUD. (forthcoming); Jolowicz, *supra* note 78, at 226–57, especially 242–44.

150. *See generally* EKKEHARD KLAUSA, EHRENAMTLICHE RICHTER: IHRE AUSWAHL UND FUNKTION, EMPIRISCH UNTERSUCHT (1972).

151. Langbein, *Mixed Court and Jury Court: Could the Continental Alternative Fill the American Need?* 1981 AM. B. FOUND. RESEARCH J. 195.

152. *Id.* at 215–19.

153. *See* GERHARD CASPER & HANS ZEISEL, DER LAIENRICHTER IM STRAFPROZESS 9–10 (1979).

of judicial inactivity.[154] Because managerial judging imposes such major limits on partisan autonomy in fact-gathering, it is in principle irreconcilable with that branch of adversary theory that purports to justify adversary fact-gathering.

Regardless of where managerial judging is headed for the future, it has already routed adversary theory. I take that as further support for the view advanced in Part V that adversary theory was misapplied to fact-gathering in the first place. Nothing but inertia and vested interests justify the waste and distortion of adversary fact-gathering. The success of German civil procedure stands as an enduring reproach to those who say that we must continue to suffer adversary tricksters in the proof of fact.

2. France

Konrad Zweigert & Hein Kötz, *An Introduction to Comparative Law* (Tony Weir, trans., 3d ed., 1998), 119–31

I

Just as the French Code civil has served as a model for the private law of many countries of the Romanistic legal family, so has the French *system of courts*. We shall concentrate here on the *Court of Cassation*, the highest French court in civil and criminal matters, which deserves special attention, since it differs in characteristic respects from the comparable supreme courts of the Anglo-American and German legal families.

The Court of Cassation was created by the legislation of the French Revolution. Under its original title 'Tribunal de Cassation', its first function was to assist the legislature rather than to act as a court: its task was to see that the courts did not deviate from the text of the laws and so encroach on the powers of the legislature. In those days even the *construction* of a statute ranked as a 'deviation' from its text, as did the judicial completion of an incomplete law. This was because the provincial courts of the *ancien régime*—the 'Parlements'—had often used the device of construction to evade or restrict the reforming laws of the king. Furthermore it seemed to conflict with the principle of separation of powers for the judges to be empowered to construe statutes; so courts were allowed to refer doubtful questions of construction to the legislature—the 'référé facultatif'. The fact that the Tribunal de Cassation was originally outside the courts system proper had two consequences: first, it could only quash ('casser') the decisions of the courts, not substitute its own decision on the merits; secondly, the courts were not bound by the decisions of the Tribunal de Cassation, but could decide the matter on remand exactly as they had done the first time; if this second decision was questioned, the Tribunal de Cassation was bound to lay the question in dispute before the legislature for final solution—the 'référé obligatoire.'

The revolutionary distrust of judicial legal development in all its forms evaporated fairly quickly; the courts never used the 'référé facultatif', and

---

154. *See* Miller, *supra* note 133, at 21–22, for some interesting conjectures on why the bar has not resisted the rise of managerial judging. For the cheering endorsement of the American College of Trial Lawyers, see AMERICAN COLLEGE OF TRIAL LAWYERS, RECOMMENDATIONS ON MAJOR ISSUES AFFECTING COMPLEX LITIGATION (1981).

the text of the Civil Code itself recognizes the need for judicial interpretation . . . so the Tribunal de Cassation, which NAPOLEON renamed the 'Cour de Cassation', itself gradually took over the task of construing the statute and of quashing the judgments of lower courts which had misconstrued it. The principle still remains, however, that the Court of Cassation cannot itself render a decision on the merits, but can only quash the decision under attack and remit the matter for rehearing to another court of the same level. Even today that court is not bound to follow the view of the Court of Cassation: if it refuses to do so and this second judgment is brought to the Court of Cassation, the combined chambers of the court of Cassation decide the matter. if the second decision is quashed, the matter is remitted to a third court, which is then bound to follow the view of the law laid down by the Court of Cassation.

In *Italy* this rather cumbrous procedure is simplified. There also the Corte di Cassazione may only quash the decision under attack, but the court to which the matter is remanded is thereupon bound to follow the view of the law laid down by the Court of Cassation; see art. 384, par. 1 Codice di procedura civile.

It should be noticed that in principle every decision of a French court is liable to attack before the Court of Cassation, provided that other remedies are unavailable or have been exhausted. Thus decisions which are unappealable, because of their low monetary value, for example, may be taken to the Court of Cassation which may therefore have to review the decision of a *tribunal d'instance*. If the preconditions are satisfied the Cour de Cassation is *obliged* to render a decision: it has no power to select cases of special significance. In consequence the Court is grossly overworked, delivering about 18,000 decisions on applications for review every year in civil matters alone.

In *Italy* the right to have judicial decisions reviewed by the Court of Cassation is laid down in the *Constitution* of 1948: see art. 111. It is true that the Codice di procedura civile of 1942 denies review to judgments of *juges de paix* which are not subject to appeal (art. 360), but art. 111 of the Constitution, as construed by the courts, permits review by the Court of Cassation even in these cases; see Cass. 9 Feb. 1962, n. 271, Giust. Civ. Rep. 1962, s. v. "Cassazione civile" n. 163.

In principle the Court of Cassation only answers *questions of law; questions of fact* are left to the 'uncontrolled judgement of the judges of fact' (*appreciation souveraine des juges de fait*). Of course the distinction between questions of law and questions of fact is notoriously difficult, so the Court of Cassation can very often determine the extent of its activities. The principal factor it considers is whether any decision it makes will be of general significance and so help to maintain uniformity in the courts. Contrariwise, the Court of Cassation adopts a position of restraint when it appears that a legal development is still in full flood; in such a case it often leaves the issue unresolved, saying that it is (ostensibly) a question of fact on which the trial judge has the final say.

For the French Court of Cassation, foreign law is in principle a question of fact; it therefore refuses to quash a judgment on the ground that

foreign law has been wrongly applied, but it reserves the right to intervene in a case where the court below has wholly failed to apply foreign law
as required by a rule of French conflicts law, or where a very gross error
has been made in applying foreign law, or where it is a question of general
significance (compare ZAJTAY, *Zur Stellung des ausländischen Rechts im
französischen internationalen Privatrecht* (1963)). —The construction of
contracts is also in principle a matter for the trial courts, but the Court of
Cassation may intervene when general conditions of business or standard
form contracts are being construed, or when the trial judge has "dena-
tured" the contract by his construction, or has attributed to it a meaning
inconsistent with the words of a clause 'claire et precise' (see Ch. 30 II)—
Art. 360 par. 5 Codice di procedura civile puts the Italian Court of Cassation
in a similar position to indulge in covert appreciation of questions of fact.

The French Court of Cassation has six chambers. Three chambers deal
with litigation arising out of the general private law, a fourth deals with
trade and economic law, the fifth with labour and social security matters,
and the sixth with criminal law. Each civil chamber has at least fifteen
judges, so that in the Court of Cassation as a whole there are about a hundred judges, in addition to about thirty-five 'conseillers référendaires', junior judges who do preparatory work on the cases for decision and take part
in the decision-making process, though usually without a vote. A quorum of
five judges is required in the civil and criminal chambers, in simple cases
three. With such a large number of judges there is a risk that different
benches may adopt different methods of judging cases, so when there may
be contradictory decisions or when there is a 'question de principe' to solve
the President of the Court or the individual chambers can remit a decision
to a 'Chambre Mixte'. The 'Chambre Mixte' is made up of judges from the
chambers concerned in the matter in question, each chamber sending its
President, its senior judge, and two other judges. Judges chosen in this way
from *all* the chambers constitute the 'Assemblée Plénière' (formerly the
Chambres Réunies). Apart from ceremonial occasions, the Assemblée
Plénière meets only when a decision is up for review a second time, because
of the refusal of the lower court to which the matter was remanded after
being quashed on the first occasion to adopt the view of the law enunciated
by the Court of Cassation (see PERDRIAU, ["La Chambre Mixte et l'assemblée
plénière de la Cour de cassation, *JCP* 1994.I.3798]). The Court of Cassation
also has a special team of state attorneys, led by the Procureur Général,
who co-operate not only in criminal matters, but in all civil matters as well;
the French view is that at the level of the Court of Cassation the public,
whom the state attorney represents, has an interest in the maintenance of
law even in *civil* matters. In lower courts the participation of a state attorney in civil suits is necessary only in questions involving status and
guardianship, though there is a right of intervention in all cases.

The content, structure, and phraseology of the decisions of the Court
of Cassation, and to a lesser extent those of lower courts, are extremely
characteristic of the particular style of French legal thought. From the
external point of view every decision of a French court consists of a single
sentence, which in the case of the Court of Cassation reads either 'The

court . . . dismisses [the demand for cassation]' or 'The Court . . . quashes [the judgment under attack] and remits the matter to the Court of . . .'. All the reasons for the judgment are to be found between the subject and predicate of this sentence, in the form of a string of subordinate clauses, all beginning with the formula 'attendu que . . .' ('whereas . . .'). There is no particular section devoted to the facts of the case or the history of the litigation; indeed, the facts are referred to only so far as may be necessary to clarify the particular grounds on which cassation is urged ('moyens'), the reasoning of the lower court or the particular view of the Court of Cassation, and even then the reference may be very allusive. Furthermore, especially in the Court of Cassation, every effort is made to make the text of the judgment as dense and compact as possible. Subsidiary considerations are eschewed; and when the decision must be quashed on one ground, other grounds are not even considered. Asides, divagations, and efflorescences are never to be found in the Court of Cassation, and hardly ever below; nor are there references to the background of the case, legal history, legal policy, or comparative law. In a widely used guide to the style of judgments MIMIN wrote:

> Extrajuridical arguments which do not assist in the solution of a case are among those which lend a merely sophistical appearance to a decision. To invoke considerations of economics, sociology or diplomacy is to confuse different types of arguments and to conceal the correctness of sound reasoning [citation omitted].

Judgments of the Court of Cassation never contain references to previous decisions made by itself or any other court, or even references to legal writing; such references occasionally appear in the judgments of lower courts, but MIMIN regards them as objectionable even there [*Le style des jugements* (4th edn. 1978), pp. 473 ff.]. In consequence, decisions of the Court of Cassation are very rarely longer than 4–5 pages of typescript, and are often no more than a few lines long. They are generally marked by polished elegance, formal clarity, and stylistic refinement; often, however, they seem to be frozen in a pedantic ritual of empty formalism, inappropriate to the uniqueness of the concrete facts of life behind the case, which indeed can often only be guessed at. It is difficult to believe that these decisions are the work of judges of flesh and blood who ever indulged in the luxury of doubt; it seems to be required by the 'majesté de la loi' that a judgement should appear in perfect purity as the act of an anonymous body.

The style of judgments in the Cour de Cassation has been criticized by French writers as well as by foreigners (see DAWSON, *The Oracles of the Law* (1968) 375, 410 f.; KÖTZ, *Über den Stil höchstrichterlicher Entscheidungen* (1973)). TOUFFAIT/TUNC ["Pour une motivation plus explicite des decisions de justice, notamment de celles de la Cour de Cassation", *Rev. trim. dr. civ.* 72 (1974) 487] have shown that because the judgments generally give only the decision and not the real reasons behind it, no dialogue between the Cour de Cassation and the legal public is possible and they make clear with a wealth of examples how trying it is for a French lawyer to have to venture a view on the possible scope of a terse and cryptic judgment without any expectation that the court will ever respond to what he says. They therefore propose that the Procrustean method of giving decisions in the form of 'attendus' be abandoned and that the judges should be required 'to give their reasoning, with an explanation why they decided in the way they did, and without concealing any of the relevant considerations'. To similar effect is WITZ, *Rev. trim. dr. civ.* 91 (1992) 737. Needless to say, these proposals have had no effect so far; indeed, they have been roundly dismissed (see BRETON ["L'Arrêt de la Cour de Cassation," *Ann. Université des Sciences Sociales de Toulouse* 23 (1975) 5]).

Since the reforms of 1958 the French courts system below the level of the Court of Cassation is of the two-tier model familiar elsewhere in Continental Europe. Civil matters are decided at first instance by a single judge in the *tribunaux d'instance*, of which there are 471 in the whole of France, an average of 5 for each of the 90 departments. They can hear cases whose monetary value does not exceed 30,000 francs; their decision in litigation involving up to 13,000 francs is unappealable, though recourse to cassation is always possible. All other civil suits go first of all to one of the 180 *tribunaux de grande instance*, where three judges sit. Commercial cases, whatever their value, are first heard by *tribunaux de commerce* set up by governmental decree as required in the centers of commerce. At the moment there are about 230 of them. Three judges also sit on a *tribunal de commerce*, but instead of being career judges they are indirectly elected by the tradesmen of the jurisdictional area. Many of them, of course, have a basic knowledge of law, since in France legal education is nothing like as specialized as it is in Germany, and many educated laymen know some law. Labour disputes go first of all to the *conseil de prud'hommes*, which are also staffed by honorary lay judges. A bench is normally constituted by equal numbers of employers and workmen, but in the event of disagreement a judge with a casting vote is called from the *tribunal d'instance*. Special first instance tribunals exist for litigation arising out of tenancies, social security, and eminent domain.

Although, as we have seen, there are several special tribunals at first instance, alongside the general civil courts, on appeal the principle of unified jurisdiction is observed; since the reforms of 1958 all appeals to go to the *cours d'appel*, no matter whether the judgment in question was rendered by a *tribunal d'instance*, a *tribunal de grande instance*, or one of the special tribunals; the only exception is for some social security cases. If the sum in issue is less than 13,000 francs no appeal is possible, even in commercial or labour disputes. As there are only 35 courts of appeal this makes justice in France very centralized. Most of them serve two to four departments, though the court of appeal of Bastia hears appeals only from the department of Corsica. The Court of Appeal of Paris is especially important, for its catchment area includes nearly a fifth of the whole population of France; it has nearly 200 judges whose prestige, position, and pay are greater than those of the judges in the provinces. Courts of Appeal sit in chambers with three judges, which may specialize in particular areas of law, especially in the larger courts.

II

Judges in France, like those in Italy and Germany, are *career judges*; they opt for a judicial career early in life, they are appointed by the state after passing the necessary examinations, and they are generally promoted to more important positions in higher courts on the basis of their performance and years of service. Here is RENÉ DAVID's picture of the career of the judge and the state attorney, both of whom in France are called 'magistrats':

> In France it is often family tradition or personal inclination which attracts people to the career of magistrat. In addition, it also appeals to some people who are not very ambitious, who prefer the security of a modest but assured salary to the risks of competition or the uncertainties of a life in business. A person who chooses to be a magistrat can count on a quiet life whose early years at any rate will be spent in a provincial town, and this life will not be troubled by undue responsibility: a judge in France sits alone only in very small cases, private or public; matters of any importance come before a tribunal with several members, whose decisions, in accordance with a principle of French law, are anonymous [*Le Droit français I: Les Données fondamentales du droit français* (1960) pp. 49f.].

In France lawyers of different branches follow different systems of training. Certainly future advocates, notaries, judges, and state attorneys must all follow the same four-year law course in a university, which leads to the 'maîtrise en droit' once the university examination is passed. But then the paths diverge. The future 'magistrat' has to pass a further, rather difficult examination conducted by the state, success in which gives him the right to attend the 'École Nationale de la Magistrature' in Bordeaux. This school was founded in 1958 on the model of the famous 'École Nationale d'Administration,' and it admits about 200 young lawyers a year. They are sworn in as 'auditeurs de justice' and are paid by the state during their period of training which lasts two and a half years. They spend time at different courts and state attorney's offices, and receive intensive instruction to develop their specialist legal knowledge, including disciplines like forensic medicine, criminology, and business accounting. This period of training culminates in a further examination, and then the successful candidates, of whom for many years about 60 per cent have been women, take up posts as judges and state attorneys; the range of choice available to them depends on their performance in the final examination.

French judges are guaranteed complete independence: they cannot be removed or even promoted against their will. The promotion of judges depends principally on the decision of a central committee on promotion, which contains prominent judges as well as officials of the Ministry of Justice and has before it the annual reports submitted by Presidents of Courts on the performance of the judges set under them. When judges are to be named to the Court of Cassation the Conseil supérieur de la Magistrature plays an important part; this is a committee of eminent judges whose members are chosen by the President of the Republic from a list prepared by the superior courts. This procedure more or less ensures that the political views of judges play no part in their promotion; if, on the other hand, men of a very independent cast of mind are not very likely to be promoted, this is not a fault of the French system in particular, but one which exists whenever the bridge between 'inferior' and 'superior' judges has to be crossed on the basis of a superior's evaluation of an inferior's performance in office.

In contrast to the judge in the Anglo-American legal system, the judge in France can hardly ever make a name for himself during his professional career. Only on trivial cases in the lowest courts does he sit alone; if he is one of a bench of judges, he is not permitted to deliver a dissenting opinion, and even if he writes the decision of the court the rigorous style of judgments in France requires him to repress all his personal characteristics. Yet this obviously reflects the internal attitude of French judges.

'Judges in France do not like to put themselves forward as creating rules of law. In practice, of course, they have to do so; it is not, and could not be, the function of a judge mechanically to apply well-known and predetermined rules. But judges in France make every effort to give the impression that this is how it is: in their decisions they keep claiming to be applying a statute; only rarely, if ever, do they put forward unwritten general principles or maxims of equity which might suggest to observers that judges were being creative or subjective' (DAVID, above, p. 50). In fact judges all over the world like to be seen as "applying" the law rather than as forming it, even interstitially, in a creative manner. MAX WEBER concluded that 'the very judges who, objectively speaking, are the most "creative" have felt themselves to be just the mouthpiece of legal rules, as merely interpreting and applying them, latent though they may be, rather than as creating them.' (*Wirtschaft und Gesellschaft* II (4th edn., 1956) 512).

III

Until recently the business of advising and representing parties in legal affairs, which has long been done in Germany by the unified profession of the *Rechtsanwalt*, was in France divided between *avocat, avoué*, and *conseil juridique*. Although the sole profession to survive the reforms of 1971 and 1990 is that of *avocat* we shall give a brief description of the different types of lawyer that used to exist, partly because traces of the distinctions remain and partly because the present rules would otherwise be incomprehensible.

(1) *Avocat* and *avoué*. For a long time a major distinction was drawn in France between the preparation of a case, essentially regarded as a ministerial matter, and the presentation of the facts and questions of law to the court, which was thought to be a task calling for special eloquence, grasp of doctrine, liberal education, and mental and professional distance from the minutiae of the proceedings. The former task fell to the *avoué*, the latter to the *avocat*.

The old-style *avocat* did all the oral pleading; the rest of the trial, the written part, fell to the *avoué*. The *avoué* did what was needed to get the court proceedings started, he drafted the statement of claim or the defence and any other documents, he saw to the distribution of the judgment, entered the appeal, supervised the execution, and so on. The task of the *avocat* was said to be *la plaidoirie*, while that of the *avoué* was *la procédure, l'écriture et la postulation*. The functions of *avocat* and *avoué* were mutually exclusive: neither could trespass on the prerogatives of the other. The *avocat* was a member of a liberal profession, the *avoué* an *officier ministériel*, holder of an office, as was evident from the fact that his fees, unlike those of the *avocat*, were fixed by an official tariff, not by negotiation with the client, and that the number of *avoués* admitted to any court was strictly limited.

The distinction between the functions of *postulation* and *plaidoirie* came under increasingly heavy criticism. The litigant could not see why he had to engage two professionals in even the simplest case. The duplication delayed the proceedings and rendered it more costly, since both were doing much the same work. The division of roles in the trial itself was also problematical, since assembling and presenting the facts in writing is not rationally separable from oral argument on the applicable legal rules. Indeed it often happened, especially in big cities, that the documents handed in to court were drafted by the *avocat* and simply signed by the *avoué* on his headed paper. For all these reasons the two professions were combined in 1971 in the '*nouvelle profession d'avocat*'. Now it is only before the appellate courts that the prior division of labour obtains. In other courts all procedural steps are taken by the 'nouvel avocat'. Indeed it is only in the *tribunal de grande instance* and the higher courts that an attorney is required at all, for in other courts the parties may be represented by other persons. But in one respect the old distinction between *avocat* and *avoué* is retained in the *tribunal de grande instance*: although the *avocat* may plead before any *tribunal de grande instance* in France, he is like the *avoué* before him in being unable to take the purely procedural steps in a lawsuit except in the court in whose area he has his chambers. Thus a person who wants a Paris attorney to represent him in litigation in Bordeaux has to retain an attorney with chambers in Bordeaux as well, so that he may do what was previously done by the *avoué*. It is different in the *tribunaux d'instance* and the commercial and labour courts, where the *avocat* may conduct the entire lawsuit irrespective of geographical considerations. The *avocat* may not appear before the Cour de Cassation or the Conseil d'État, where the representation of litigants is still entrusted to a special group of lawyers, who, like the former *avoués*, are *officers ministériels* rather than independent professionals. So far as remuneration goes, the old distinction between 'postulation' and 'plaidoirie' has been maintained. For purely procedural steps the *avocat* receives payment in accordance with a fixed tariff (just like the former *avoué*), but he can negotiate the honorarium for advice and pleading with his client without reference to any tariff.

(2) *Avocat* and *conseil juridique*. Only an *avocat* may address a state court on behalf of a litigant, but until recently it was open to others to give legal advice. These other legal advisers, called 'conseils juridiques', were in brisk competition with the *avocats* and won a good deal of work away from them; they concentrated on giving advice to businesses and were readier to meet the increasing demand for expertise in specialist areas of

law as well as business management, tax matters, and international affairs. The *conseil juridique* had to be registered, just like the *avocat*, but all that was needed for this was a degree in law or business management. Foreigners thus qualified were automatically admitted to practise as *conseils juridiques*, though only to give advice on foreign and international law. This liberal attitude made Paris a veritable Mecca for foreign lawyers and law firms for twenty years or so, but the distinction between *avocat* and *conseil juridique* was at odds with the position elsewhere in Europe where only one kind of legal adviser was known, and decisions of the European Court of Justice on freedom of establishment and the provision of legal services made legislative intervention imperative. The Law of 31 December 1990 accordingly merged the professions of *avocat* and *conseil juridique* (for details see BÉNABENT ["Avocats: Premières vues sur la 'nouvelle profession', *JCP* 1991.I. 3499]) and added to the twenty thousand or so *avocats* in France in 1990 approximately five thousand *conseils juridiques*. All these are members of one of the 180 chambers of advocates (*barreaux*) and practise as *avocats*, so that now for the first time in France no one may give legal advice for reward unless he has first been admitted as avocat.

(3) The two reforms have also made major changes in the professional life of lawyers. Traditionally the French *avocat* was a sole practitioner, a generalist able to deal with business of all kinds. Nowadays, however, thanks to economic and social developments in France as elsewhere, a client can only get proper advice from someone with specialist knowledge and expertise, which no attorney can possess in all areas of law at the same time. Furthermore, a modern attorney's office requires staff and equipment such as no sole practitioner could afford. There was thus an increasing need for new forms of co-operation between attorneys. Laws of 1971 and 1990 therefore opened up a whole range of other forms of co-operation between lawyers. Various forms of office-sharing are possible, as well as legal partnerships of the kind known in Germany, and one can even incorporate a company of attorneys (*société civile professionnelle*). Such a company has independent legal personality, its own firm name, and its own capital, but the personal liability of the attorneys who are members of it remains unlimited.

Whereas Germany still clings to the ideal of the all-purpose lawyer (*Einheitsjurist*) and insists that all lawyers undergo the same training, whatever branch of the profession they propose to enter—a training far too prolonged, geared to training judges, and heavily regulated by the state—the system in France is like that in the rest of Europe. After spending four years studying law at University and gaining the *maîtrise*, a youngster planning to be an attorney or commercial lawyer will, if well advised, spend a further year acquiring specialist knowledge and taking the 'Diplome d'études supérieures' (DESS). If he still wants to become an attorney he must gain admittance to a 'Centre national de formation professionnelle', where he spends a year doing practical exercises and following courses given by professors, attorneys, and judges. On passing the final examination he will be awarded the 'Certificate d'aptitude pour la profession d'avocat' (CAPA), and must then spend two years in the office of an *avocat* as an *avocat stagiaire*. During this period he is permitted to give legal advice and appear in court, and at the end of it he is qualified, without any further examination, to appear as *avocat* before any court in France other than the Conseil d'État and the Cour de Cassation.

IV

One may often throw some light on the characteristic style of a legal system by asking which *type of lawyer* it regards as representative. France and Germany are alike in not having developed the type of the wise judge which other people find so remarkable in the Anglo-American systems. But France and Germany differ, if we are right, in that in France the representative type of lawyer is the *avocat*, the lawyer who pleads before the courts, while the ideal German lawyer is the learned Doctor Iuris, the trained scholar who is to be found in all legal careers, especially among professors, but among judges and barristers as well.

In France the lawyer most often in the public eye is the *avocat* with his brilliant oratory and his special prestige. Although the traditional view that the *avocat* has no monetary contractual relationship with his client is virtually without significance today, the social prestige of the *avocat* still rests on the belief that when he appears in court he comes not so much as the agent of a particular party as in the exercise of a kind of public office. There are historical reasons for the high reputation of the *avocat*, for he is the representative of the self-confident French bourgeoisie which emerged triumphant from the Revolution of 1789. From that Revolution, like the July Revolution of 1830, the French lawyer learnt that one has to fight for the rights of the individual not in the study, but in the forum, on the floor of Parliament, and in the halls of justice. This explains the public standing of the French *avocat* and his importance in French politics. For a long time one could justly say that the Parliament of France consisted half of mayors and half of advocates. Thus the revolutionary spirit of the French bourgeoisie has lived on in the advocate for two hundred years. It is true that like the French bourgeoisie, these advocates are by our standards today rather conservative, but theirs is a conservatism rooted in the belief that one should act with energy and commitment for the protection of freedom once won, for the maintenance of rights which have been earned, of 'droits acquis'. The German lawyer, on the other hand, is typical of a bourgeoisie which is the product of revolutions which failed to succeed or failed to occur. While the impression of the French Revolution and the War of Liberation was fresh the German lawyer was still ready enough to leap on the barricades—consider the dispute between THIBAUT and SAVIGNY—but after 1848 he withdrew from public life like the rest of the bourgeois intelligentsia. At the time, towards the beginning of the nineteenth century, when the lawyers in France were constructing the noble edifice of administrative law—especially through the jurisprudence of the Conseil d'État—to protect the freedoms of the citizens against high-handed intervention by the state, the German lawyer was turning to the meditative cultivation of private law, supposed to be 'unpolitical'. At the turn of the century in Germany lawyers who had theretofore abstained from public life and politics and had shut themselves up in the ivory tower of legal learning began to co-operate with the established powers; but this was the very time in France when the conscience of the nation was shocked by the Dreyfus affair. It is significant that ÉMILE ZOLA's famous article in *L'Aurore* of 13 Jan. 1898 started with the words: 'J'accuse . . .' and continued in the style of a prosecutor's speech in court; this is a further indication of how the methods of thought and speech characteristic of the *avocat* are consciously used in France in the interests of maintaining the standards of law and morality in the public life of the nation.

One can also see marked differences when one asks which *legal virtues* are regarded as specially important in Germany and France. The ideal qualities of a German lawyer are expressed by ideas such as thoroughness, exactitude, learnedness, a strong tendency to tolerate academic disputes and the ability to construct concepts of law with which to master the variety of legal life. The French lawyer, especially the *avocat*, but also the judge, aims at clarity and brevity of expression, eloquence, style, effect, and form. This form is not something purely external, but structural in legal thought itself: 'La forme donne l'être à la chose.' French lawyers have no time for pedantry, for the 'querelles d'Allemand', for the urge to be right in trivia irrelevant to the solution of actual problems. The German lawyer, on the other hand, willingly dons the cloak of learning and is eager to widen his knowledge. This is immediately obvious when one compares the style of judgments of German and French courts. The superior German court gives reasons which are wide-ranging and loaded with citations like a textbook, while the French Court of Cassation goes in for lapidary 'whereas'-clauses. But the same conclusion follows from the characteristics of the legal language in the two countries. STENDHAL may, according to tradition, have read the Code civil frequently in order to improve his style, but one could hardly advise a German novelist to attend to the Prussian General Land Law or the BGB. Indeed, one has the impression that in France there is very little room for a special legal language and that the French legal writer is the equal of the great masters of the French novel in writing in a manner which is clear and unpretentious and often brilliantly elegant. Germany, on the other hand, has developed a specialist legal language in which obscurity too often rates as profundity and which, even when it is not pure jargon, still makes it more difficult for the intelligent citizen to know what is going on in the law than is really desirable for public faith in its activities.

This also helps to explain why in France, unlike Germany, legal studies are part of a *general education*, why the Frenchman regards a basic legal knowledge—as RENÉ DAVID writes (above, p. 40)—as an 'élément presque normal de la culture générale'. Many young people at French universities study law without having any intention of taking up a legal career: laws is not just the object of a special training but an area in which one can learn to think clearly, to express oneself lucidly, and to practise oratorical skills. The other side of the coin is that the teaching of law in France is often a matter of rarefied principle, of not being occupied with the practical question of finding the right legal solution for the problems of social reality. But to study law in this general, unpractical, and rather 'literary' manner is a way of furthering the education of young people who are not going to be lawyers. Therefore among educated Frenchmen one often meets with a certain familiarity with basic legal ideas. It may or may not be true, as one says, that the French peasant keeps a copy of the Code civil next to his Bible. But it does seem as if SOREL was right to say: 'There is, so far as I know, no other country where the private law has entered so deeply into the customs of the country, and forms so intimate a part of its intellectual, emotional and literary life' (*Livre du Centenaire du Code Civil* I (1904) p. xxxv).

3. England

Konrad Zweigert & Hein Kötz, *An Introduction to Comparative Law* (Tony Weir, trans., 3d ed., 1998), 205–17

I

Lawyers from other countries have long been fascinated by the institutions of English legal life and by the men who run them. This fascination has not always conduced to objectivity of judgment about English justice. The European who addresses himself to this theme often has in his mind's eye the romantic picture of a judge, robed in scarlet and heavily bewigged, holding court in a splendidly paneled hall and making law with wise authority from fat volumes of reports. People are especially surprised to be told that an industrial state like England with nearly 50 million inhabitants can get by with only a few dozen judges. One sometimes hears the view that this tiny number of judges is explained by the fact that lawyers' fees and court fees are so exorbitant in England that law is only open to plutocrats, or the view that Bench and Bar conspire to preserve a legal system which has lots of old world charm but is seriously in need of reform, or the view that young English lawyers are trained exclusively in offices, on the theory that a university education in law is not only unnecessary but actually harmful. There may or may not be a grain of truth in these views but they certainly give a one-sided and false impression of English justice; in the following section we shall try to present a picture, necessarily only in outline, which is rather nearer the truth.

II

The English citizen who is involved in civil litigation normally comes into contact not with the High Court in London, much less the Court of Appeal or the House of Lords, but with the Magistrates' Courts or the County Courts which are spread throughout the land.

(1) *Magistrates' courts* are staffed by 'Justices of the Peace', magistrates without any legal training, three of whom constitute a bench under a chairman chosen by themselves. Only in the larger towns are there professional paid 'stipendiary magistrates' who have legal training and who sit alone. Justices of the Peace, of whom at the moment there are about 30,000 in England, divided between about 1,000 courts, are nominally

appointed by the Queen but really chosen by the Lord Chancellor from lists provided by local commissions. The choice is normally made from people who have shown some interest in public affairs by being active in local government, trades unions, professional organizations, chambers of commerce, or in some other way; but party political considerations also play some part in the selection of magistrates. To be a Justice of the Peace is not a full-time job and many of them are retired; it is an honorary position which attracts only a small payment for expenses. But the social prestige attaching to the position is considerable: persons of rank in provincial towns and even tycoons see it as an honour to be a Justice of the Peace and to be able to put the initial JP after their names.

The Jurisdiction of Magistrates' Courts is mainly in *criminal law*, where they deal with all minor offences, especially the vast number of traffic offences. Their procedure is summary, without a jury, and is very swift, especially since the defendant in trivial cases often pleads guilty and no evidence need be called.

For more serious crimes where a jury is called for, there is a special court, the Crown Court. Depending on the gravity of the charge, cases in the Crown Court are tried either before a full-time judge or before a 'Recorder', an experienced barrister or solicitor in professional practice who is commissioned to serve as judge from time to time. The Crown Court may also contain up to four Justices of the Peace.

So far as *private law* is concerned, the jurisdiction of Magistrates' Courts is principally in matters of family law: they hear claims for maintenance between spouses and between parents and children, legitimate or illegitimate, issue separation orders, apply the laws about the care of children, agree to adoptions, supervise guardians, and have extensive competence in matters concerning the protection of children.

Although for some time Justices of the Peace have been required on nomination to follow courses which introduce them to the most important legal questions likely to arise, it is nevertheless necessary to have a skilled lawyer constantly at their side to advise them. In the Magistrates' courts this function is performed by the so-called 'clerk to the justices', a solicitor whose task it is, part-time or, in the larger towns, full-time, to supervise the administration of the court, to see to the procedure in court, and above all to advise the Justices when problems arise during a sitting. For this purpose the clerk may, should the justices so wish, take part in the deliberations prior to judgment.

(2) *County Courts* were introduced in England by statute 'only' in 1846. The aim was to provide within easy reach of the parties courts which could determine private law disputes involving relatively low sums at rather small cost.

There are about 270 County Courts in England, so situated in the country that everyone is within easy distance of one. The courts are manned by a single judge, called 'Circuit Judges'. There are also 'District Judges' in the County Courts who hear cases involving £5,000 or less in simple and informal proceedings. To these Circuit and District Judges, approximately 770 in number at present, must be added the 'Recorders' who sometimes sit in the County Court; these are usually practicing barristers charged by the Lord Chancellor to take on occasional judicial functions.

County Courts deal with civil matters involving £25,000 or less, and may hear cases involving larger sums, for cases of up to £50,000 are only heard by the High Court if they are particularly difficult or raise questions of special importance. In equity cases the County Courts' jurisdiction rises to £30,000. Furthermore, modern social legislation has reserved for the County Courts a whole series of very important matters, notably those arising from housing law and legislation protecting tenants. The practical importance of the County Courts is shown by the fact that about 85 per cent of all civil actions are first heard in these courts: If we consider that from a social point of view the importance of a court is the number of *persons* whose affairs it deals with, there can be no doubt that County Courts are the most important civil courts in the country (JACKSON/SPENCER [*The Machinery of Justice in England* (7th edn. 1989), p. 33]).

(3) When people abroad or even in England speak of English justice, they think in the first place of the *High Court of Justice* in London. This court consists today of three divisions: the Queen's Bench Division, the Chancery Division, and the Family Division. The number of High Court judges has risen from only 25 in 1925 to 97 at the present time, and it will probably increase still more. Each judge is attached to one of the three divisions mentioned. Today there are 63 in the Queen's Bench Division, presided over by the Lord Chief Justice, 15 in the Chancery Division under the Vice-Chancellor, and a further 19 in the Family Division under the President. Except for appeals from judgments of lower courts and for some proceedings of an administrative nature, all cases in the High Court are decided by a single judge.

The division of business in the High Court allocates to the Queen's Bench Division the cases which before 1873 fell within the jurisdiction of the old Common Law courts. These include claims for damages for tort (mainly traffic or industrial accidents) and for breach of contract. The Queen's Bench Division has several specialized subdivisions, the 'Commercial Court' which hears disputes between businessmen and enterprises in commercial matters, the 'Admiralty Court', concerned with maritime collisions, maritime creditors' rights, cargo claims, and arrest of vessels, and the 'Divisional Court', which applies administrative law. Judges in the *Chancery Division* hear cases affecting the administration of estates, bankruptcy, and the property of incapable persons, and resolve questions of trust law, company law, and intellectual property; accordingly that division has a strong equity flavour. Family matters are dealt with in the *Family Division*.

A number of important judicial tasks in the High Court are performed by the many 'masters' and 'registrars', who are chosen from barristers or solicitors with a certain professional experience. They perform many varied tasks (see DIAMOND, 76 *LQ Rev.* 504 (1960)) of which the main one is to work closely with parties and their legal advisers in the preliminary steps of procedure so that when the matter comes before the judge, it can be decided without delay in a single oral hearing. The master also decides, with appeal to a judge, whether the trial should be referred to a County Court, what security, if any, should be given, and questions regarding expert opinions and methods of proof. Furthermore, on proper motion of the parties, he sees to it that before the oral trial begins the parties provide their opponent with full information about the facts they propose to prove and the relevant documents in their possession. The master also tries to get the parties to agree as many facts as possible so as to reduce the amount that must be proved and thereby lighten the task of the judge. Because the trial is so carefully prepared and because the parties must fully disclose what positions they propose to adopt, many suits are terminated by compromise, admission or withdrawal of claim before the oral trial ever starts.

(4) The *Court of Appeal* hears appeals from judgments of the High Court, and, with some limitations, appeals from the County Courts as well. In theory the Lord Chancellor presides but in practice his role is performed by another judge, called the 'Master of the Rolls'—a title borne since the seventeenth century by the Chancellor's senior subordinate in Chancery. In addition to the Master of the Rolls the Court of Appeal consists of 29 'Lord Justices of Appeal', who sit in divisions of three or occasionally two. The Court of Appeal reviews every point of law on which the judgment below was based but often feels itself bound by trial judge's findings of fact, even if they have legal consequences. Thus the Court of Appeal does not hear again the evidence presented at the trial and new evidence is admitted only within very strict limits.

(5) The *House of Lords* is the highest court, not only for England, but also for Scotland (except for criminal cases) and Northern Ireland, which in other respects have their own system of courts. Decisions are made by a special judicial committee which contains, apart from the present Lord Chancellor and predecessors who have demitted office on a change of government, ten judges who bear the title 'Lord of Appeal in Ordinary', called 'Law Lords' for short. The committee is normally composed of five judges and hears appeals from judgments of the Court of Appeal provided that, in view of the importance of the case, leave to appeal has been granted either by the Court of Appeal or by the House of Lords itself.

Brief mention must finally be made of the *Judicial Committee of the Privy Council*. The Privy Council is an advisory body which developed out of the old Curia Regis and the task of its judicial committee is to give the Queen advice, which is invariably followed, on petition made to her as the fount of justice by parties who have unsuccessfully exhausted the legal procedures in the national courts of Commonwealth countries. Appeal to the Privy Council has been abolished by many important members of the Commonwealth: Canada, India, Pakistan, and, in 1982, Australia have all declared that the decisions of their own highest courts are final. But even today it is not uncommon for the Privy Council to hear cases from countries as diverse as New Zealand, Sierra Leone, Bermuda, Gibraltar, and Mauritius, an impressive indication of the world-wide spread of the Common Law tradition.

(6) High Court judges are nominated by the Queen on the proposal of the Lord Chancellor who selects them from among barristers with at least ten years practical experience (the same pool as provides most Circuit and District judges); on appointment they receive the accolade of a knighthood.

As a member of the government, the Lord Chancellor is a politician who has often spent many years in the House of Commons but it must be said that for the last fifty years at least political considerations have played next to no part in the nomination of judges. In the narrow and familiar circle of barristers a *communis opinio* readily determines which of their number are fit for judicial office and a Lord Chancellor would quickly incur public reproach or, worse still, public ridicule if he proposed for a judgeship a barrister who was politically committed but professionally incapable. Once appointed, judges are wholly independent. Under the formula of the Act of Settlement 1701, which is still in force today, a judge holds his office only 'during good behaviour subject to a power of removal by His Majesty on an address presented to His Majesty by both Houses of Parliament', but no English judge has ever been removed from office since that date and no one in England is quite sure how exactly one would set about it (see JACKSON/SPENCER above, pp. 368 ff.). Even desire for promotion, which can temper the independence of judges on the Continent, plays no great role in England. High Court judges have already reached a peak position and for many of them a further move up to the Court of Appeal or the House of Lords would not be very attractive.

All judges, even Circuit Judges, are chosen from among the group of successful and well-regarded barristers ... This ensures that the higher courts are manned by judges who are extremely competent and very experienced in practice, able to command the respect of the whole legal profession. But in the view of many people, this restricted principle of choice has the disadvantage that the English judges tend to be of an extremely conservative temperament: a person who has enjoyed a brilliant professional career will hardly be disposed to criticize and reform the very circumstances which made it possible. This tendency to stability may also be reinforced by the fact that a judge is never appointed before he is 40, and usually not until he is past 50; he retires at age 70. To be more specific, the charge has occasionally been made that the marked individualism of English judges led them, especially until the Second World War, to adopt a perverse attitude to modern social legislation and give an unduly restrictive construction to many of their provisions contrary to the clearly discernible will of Parliament (see JACKSON/SPENCER (above, pp. 377 ff.) and ABEL-SMITH/STEVENS [*In Search of Justice – Society and the Legal System* (1968), pp. 166 ff.]).

Parliament itself has reacted to this. According to many writers, it was in a deliberate attempt to render modern statutes on social security, tax, agricultural holdings, and landlord and tenant 'judge-proof' that Parliament referred disputes in these areas not to the ordinary courts but to special 'tribunals', of which there are now an enormous number; their procedure is relatively simple and cheap, they are often staffed by laymen, and they are often closely linked with relevant government departments. The number of appeals to the Court of Appeal in these areas is small and diminishing. This very fact helps us to understand how England gets by with so relatively small a number of judges, especially when one considers that Germany, for instance, has three levels of separate courts for administrative and social matters.

Whatever one may think of the conservatism of the English judges, it seems clear that England has never been readier for reform or more energetically critical of the existing system than today. Some radicals have demanded the 'nationalization' of all professional lawyers, much as doctors were nationalized in the National Health Service, and would leave no part of the courts system untouched. In present circumstances these proposals may seem unrealistic but it must be granted that an increasing number of leading and influential jurists see the law of procedure and the courts system as in need of drastic reform (see JACOB, *The Fabric of English Justice* (1987) 246 ff., and in particular ZANDER, *A Matter of Justice, The Legal System in Ferment* (1989)). The process was started off by the Courts and Legal Services Act 1990, and further reforms are awaited. So far as the reform of substantive law is concerned, England and Scotland have each had a five-member 'Law Commission' since 1965. They have a well-equipped staff to help them in their demanding task

> to take and keep under review all the law . . . with a view to its systematic development and reform, including in particular the codification of such law, the elimination of anomalies, the repeal of obsolete and unnecessary enactments, the reduction of the number of separate enactments and generally the simplification and modernization of the law (Law Commissions Act 1965 s. 3).

Many of the Law Commission's proposals have resulted in legislation which has modernized and improved English law on important topics. The Law Commission's programme of work originally contained a plan to codify the whole law of contract. This project has been abandoned. The advantages and disadvantages of the codification of English law are discussed in many recent articles of great interest to anyone from a Civil Law jurisdiction: see, for example, SCARMAN, *A Code of English Law?* (1966); HAHLO, "Here lies the Common Law: Rest in Peace", 30 *Mod. L. Rev.* 241 (1967); DIAMOND, "Codification of the Law of Contract", 31 *Mod. L. Rev.* 361 (1968); DONALD, "Codification in Common Law Systems", 47 *Austr. LJ* 160 (1973); KERR, "Law and Reform in Changing Times", 96 *LQ Rev.* 515 (1980); NORTH, "Problems of Codifications in a Common Law Country", *RabelsZ* 46 (1982) 94; ANTON, "Obstacles to Codification", 1982 *Jur. Rev.* 15. Also, from the point of view of a continents observer, KÖTZ, "Taking Civil Codes Less Seriously", 50 *Mod. L. Rev.* 1 (1987).

In recent years various aspects of the English legal system have repeatedly come under investigation by Committee and criticism by writers. It may be that London's importance as a legal center will diminish as the limits on the financial jurisdiction of the County Courts are raised and more criminal cases are heard by the Crown Courts. Noteworthy, too, are the English experiments with novel forms of 'informal' resolution of minor disputes in private law. In non-litigious matters advice to the relatively deprived has been provided not only by solicitors but also, most successfully, by 'Citizens Advice Bureaux'. Such fascination as the English system of justice still exercises on the Continental observer depends now not so much on the admittedly astonishing position of the English judge as on the interesting question how in the years to come England will manage to effect a compromise between its tendency to cling tenaciously to traditional legal institutions and the need which exists in all modern societies to provide effective justice for every citizen.

III

Professional lawyers in England are divided into *solicitors* and *barristers*. This distinction, which has cropped up several times in the preceding pages, is a further peculiar characteristic of English legal life which must now be briefly considered.

(1) The typical English *solicitor* is an independent lawyer who gives legal advice to a client on personal and business affairs. In practice on his own or in partnership with other solicitors, he carries through transactions involving land, drafts contracts and wills, undertakes the administration of estates, and advises his client on tax, commercial, insurance, and company law matters. Solicitors alone are empowered to take the necessary steps prior to trial. They may also act in the name of their client in the procedure which precedes the oral hearing before the judge. In the trial itself they have a right of audience only in the Magistrates' Courts and the County Courts. Although solicitors have for years been campaigning against this restriction, which they regard as unjustified, the bitter resistance of the Bar saw to it that the door was opened only very slightly by the Courts and Legal Services Act 1990: the conditions attached to a solicitor's 'right of audience' are so stringent that no significant change in practice is likely in the foreseeable future.

Most solicitors' offices are naturally not so much concerned in the preparation, initiation, or conduct of trials as with transactions concerning land. Registers of land exist in most areas of the country, but they are not as sophisticated as in Germany. If the title is not registered, the title of a vendor or mortgagor must be investigated carefully by any purchaser or mortgagee. Even if it is registered, most people who are buying and selling houses wish their interests to be protected from the contractual stage to the completion of the transaction. This business, called 'conveyancing', falls mainly to solicitors (who had, indeed, a legal monopoly of it until very recently), and the fees for the conveyancing of houses constitute nearly half of the profession's income.

In 1989 there were about 60,000 registered solicitors in England. About 13,000 of these were employed by local authorities or in business. Of the 9,100 solicitors' firms about 80 per cent have four partners or less, 14 per cent have between five and ten, and the rest more than ten. There is normally one salaried assistant solicitor to every three partners, in large firms one to every two. In 1991 there were 6 firms with more than 500 solicitors.

The professional organization of solicitors is the *Law Society*, of which as many as 85 per cent of all practicing solicitors are members. There is no legal requirement for a solicitor to be a member but the Law Society has statutory power to lay down rules, with the agreement of the Lord Chancellor and other leading judges, regarding the training and admission of solicitors. The Law Society also finances the Solicitors' Complaints

Bureau which can bring disciplinary proceedings before the Solicitors' Disciplinary Tribunal, an independent judicial body. Solicitors' fees in private matters are normally a matter for agreement between solicitor and client. The courts, however, retain the power to review a solicitor's charges in any case involving court proceedings, and in other cases the Law Society will do so if a client complains.

(2) *Barristers* specialize in advocacy before the higher courts, essentially the preparation of written documents and the oral presentation before the court. Here barristers have a monopoly which rests not on the provisions of any statute but on a long-established practice of the judges according to which a party who does not appear *personally* can have no legal adviser in court other than a barrister. Barristers also give oral legal advice or written opinions and draft complicated wills, land contracts, or trust deeds; indeed, some barristers do nothing else. In these areas there is a certain competition between barristers and large firms of solicitors, but it is quite normal for a solicitor in a case of particular difficulty to seek the opinion of a barrister, many of whom specialize in particular topics and therefore have an extremely detailed knowledge of the relevant judicial precedents. One very striking fact is that the etiquette of the Bar forbids any direct contact with the client. Thus a person who wishes to institute a suit in the High Court or to obtain a barrister's opinion must always do so through a solicitor. If a conference becomes necessary between the barrister and the client who is thus brought into contact with him, the barrister is bound by professional etiquette to hold his conference in the presence of the solicitor and in his own chambers, so far as possible. The choice of barrister normally falls to the solicitor since only a few litigants have any preferences, so it follows that a barrister's success depends very much on his links with the large firms of solicitors.

Even today barristers are not entitled to form partnerships. Instead, barristers occupy "sets of chambers" in loose groups of about twelve to fifteen, often specializing in particular areas of law. In London all these chambers are situated in the Inns of Court, in buildings possessed for centuries and steeped in tradition, not far from the High Court. The chief of staff in these sets of chambers is the *clerk*. The clerk makes the contact between solicitors and the barristers in his chambers, fixes appointments, gives information about the individual barrister's programme of work, and agrees with the solicitor on the fee payable to the barrister by the client. The amount of these fees is not fixed by statute but depends on the difficulty and importance of the case as well as the reputation and standing of the barrister in question. Since the clerk receives a fixed percentage of the fees paid to the barristers in his chambers, he is naturally interested in fixing the fee as high as possible, without losing the business to another set of chambers. Until recently it was regarded as unprofessional for barristers and solicitors to have *direct* transactions regarding fees without the clerk as intermediary, and this is still extremely unusual.

The method of fixing fees and the prohibition of partnership make it difficult for young barristers to make a living at the outset of their career, but the more they succeed in obtaining a certain reputation and in maintaining good contacts with firms of solicitors, the more sought-after they become and the higher the fees they can, through their clerk, prescribe. For barristers who are greatly in demand the burden of work can be very heavy, since advocacy can only be performed in person and the barrister is in principle obliged to accept every brief which is offered provided that the stipulated fee is paid. At a certain moment in a very successful career barristers will face the question whether they should not lighten their workload by petitioning the Lord Chancellor to submit their name to the Queen for nomination as *Queen's Counsel* (abbreviated QC). Queen's Counsel form the elite of the Bar from whom High Court and Circuit judges are normally chosen. They stand in high regard in court and in the Inns, and are entitled to wear a robe of silk. For this reason, when a person has recently been promoted to the rank of Queen's Counsel, one says that 'he has taken silk'. Queen's Counsel can demand particularly high fees and normally appear in court in company with a 'junior' barrister, for whom of course the party must pay an additional fee; in consequence of this great expense, Queen's Counsel are briefed only for important and interesting suits. No barrister may *claim* to be appointed Queen's Counsel; whether the Lord Chancellor accepts such a petition and proposes nomination to the Queen depends on whether the petitioner has, in practice at the Bar for at least ten years, achieved the requisite degree of success in his profession and renown among his peers. About one in ten of the 6,500 odd active barristers in 1990 were Queen's Counsel, and of these over 90 per cent had chambers in London.

The professional organizations for barristers are the four *Inns of Court*, all of equal standing, known as 'The Honourable Society of Lincoln's Inn', 'of the Inner Temple', 'of the Middle Temple' and 'of Gray's Inn'. The business of these four Inns is conducted by the so-called 'benchers', not elected by the members of their Inn but co-opted for life by the other benchers. Most of them are now practicing barristers, mainly Queen's Counsel, but some are judges, for judges remain members of their Inn even after appointment.

In addition to running the business of their Inn of Court and administering its property, benchers admit students, who must become members of an Inn before their training, and call them to the Bar once they have completed it. Other institutions are of general importance for barristers. The most important of these is the *General Council of the Bar*. With members elected from the whole Bar, it represents the Bar's interests in public when threatened by legislation, the Law Society, and other organizations. It also lays down guidelines for professional conduct at the Bar. The training of future barristers is organized by the *Council of Legal Education* under the general direction of the Bar Council.

For details on the profession of the barrister and his position in the whole context of English legal life, reference may be made to the works of MEGARRY and ABEL-SMITH/STEVENS (above, p. 205). The former is written from the point of view of a successful Queen's Counsel and gives a clear and flowing account of the activities of English barristers and judges; it conveys the impression that everything is really all for the best in the state of justice in England, and that drastic reforms are unnecessary if not actually harmful. ABEL-SMITH/STEVENS, on the other hand, have done some empirical sociological research and raise the question whether the practice of law in England today is responsive to the demand of a modern society that it should be a 'social service'. The authors give a distinctly negative answer to this question and they do so with details which will give the foreign lawyer pause for thought, especially if he is unduly in love with English law. ZANDER (*Lawyers and the Public Interest, A Study in Restrictive Practices* [1968], p. 212) sees the principal aim of the monopolies and professional duties of English barristers and solicitors, whether fixed by statute or tradition, as being to limit free competition in the production and distribution of legal services. The crucial question is whether these restrictive practices are justified as being in the public interest; the author thinks that by and large they are not . . .

(3) The *training of lawyers* in England also has many features which will surprise the observer from abroad. The training is directed to the profession of *lawyer*, rather than of *judge* as in Germany. This is only natural because there is no such thing as a 'judicial career' in England: one only becomes a judge after many years of successful practice as a barrister. Again, the bifurcation of the legal profession means that there are different methods of training and examination for solicitors and barristers. As one would expect from the historical development of the legal professions in England, these methods of training and examination are the responsibility of the respective professional organizations, the Law Society and the Bar Councils, not of the state or the universities. Of course it is possible to study law in almost all of the British universities and to emerge, normally after three years, as a Bachelor of Laws (Bachelor of Arts in Oxford and Cambridge). It is true that most of those admitted as barristers and solicitors possess a university degree in law, but this is not required, and indeed one can become a solicitor without being a graduate at all. The Inns of Court do require budding barristers to have a degree, but it need not be a degree in law. Many distinguished English judges took a degree in some other subject: LORD DIPLOCK read chemistry, LORD DENNING mathematics, and LORD WILBERFORCE classics before training to be a barrister—*after* leaving the university!

Today a distinction is drawn between the 'academic' and 'professional' stages of legal training. For most people the 'academic' stage consists of three years study of law in a university. Those who graduate in some other discipline before opting for the Bar satisfy the academic stage by taking a one-year course prescribed and overseen by the professional bodies, leading to the Common Professional Examination.

At the 'professional' stage the paths of future solicitors and barristers diverge. The future barrister spends a year at the Inns of Court Law School in London, and the future solicitor takes a comparable course elsewhere in London or in the provinces, the teaching and examining being done largely by judges and practitioners.

The examination passed, the future solicitor must spend two years under a 'training contract' in a solicitors' office. He is then admitted as a solicitor, but must still serve for three years as an assistant solicitor before he can practice on his own or as a partner in a firm of solicitors: in this way the public can be protected from lawyers of undue youth and inexperience.

The further training of a *barrister* is much the same. He must be entered as a 'bar student' in one of the four Inns of Court and spend a year in barristers' chambers as a 'pupil' gaining practical experience under the supervision of a pupil-master.

The bar student must also keep a specified number of 'dining terms'. 'Dining terms', of which there are four per year, are periods of about three weeks during which bar students may take an evening meal in the Dining Hall of their Inn. One 'keeps a dining term' by dining at least three times during it, and one must keep eight terms in this manner, that is, have dined on twenty-four occasions, before one may be admitted as a barrister. The explanation of this institution is that in the old days the communal dinner was an occasion for contact between barristers and youngsters, for conversations on legal matters and for moots. In our times this practice has largely lost its point, especially in view of the large numbers of students: 'Today it is difficult to find any student who can see any value or utility in the ritual of dining in hall. The food, it is said, is poor or scanty or both, and the conversation does no more than pass the time; but the Inn requires it, and so one must go through the pointless ceremony' (MEGARRY [*The Lawyer and Litigant in England* (1962), p. 114] . . .).

After passing his exams the candidate is 'called to the Bar' in a formal ceremony, and thereby becomes a barrister.

(4) Whether the division of the legal profession into two branches should be maintained is the subject of recurrent and lively debate in England. *In favour* of the split, it is said that to have barristers who specialize in advocacy is a great advantage for the parties and for the court: for the *parties* because the barrister is more detached from the case, can see it with fresh eyes, and has special experience in pleading, gained by constant practice; for the *court* because co-operation with lawyers can be made easier, more trusting, and free from fiction if judges have to deal with only a small circle of experienced specialists. *Against* the division of the legal professions one often hears the objection that it greatly increases the expense and duration of legal proceedings, since the same case is being worked on by two lawyers one after the other, and sometimes both together. One thing is sure, that it makes sense to have specialized competences within the legal profession, as, for example, for conveyancing or for the conduct of cases in court. What is in issue is only whether the kind and extent of such specialization should be fixed by compulsory rules as in England, or whether it should not be left, as on the continent and in the United States, to the free play of the forces of the market.

4. The European Union

George A. Bermann, Roger J. Goebel, William J. Davey & Eleanor Fox, *Cases and Materials on European Union Law* (2d ed. 2002), 33–39, 42–51, 54, 58–59; *Supplement* (2004), 21

[The text that follows refers to the ECSC Treaty (the European Coal and Steel Community Treaty) of 1951 which was one of the first steps toward forming the European Community and was allowed to lapse in 2002. It also refers to the TEU (Treaty on European Union) and its "pillars." The TEU and the EC Treaty (Treaty Establishing the European Community) are the "constitutive" documents that establish legal institutions independent of those of the member states. The three "pillars" of the TEU are (pillar one) provisions directed to the goals of the EC Treaty, (pillar two) provisions on a common foreign and security policy and (pillar three) provisions on police and judicial cooperation in criminal matters.]

Focusing on the European Community, we can identify four major institutions.[8] Three of them—the Council, the Commission and the European Parliament—share the political tasks of making and administering Community law at the European level. The fourth is the Court of Justice which, aided by a more recently created Court of First Instance, represents the Community's judicial arm. All four institutions date back to the ECSC Treaty, but since the 1965 Merger Treaty have served the three European Communities in common. TEU Article 5 (ex E) refers to the same institutions as serving the European Union.

Although the institutions still bear a striking resemblance to those of the 1950s, they have undergone a distinct evolution in their respective powers and functions. Much of this evolution—e.g., the steady increase in the administrative power of the Commission and in the doctrinal authority of the Court of Justice—has been gradual. Other aspects stem from structural and procedural reforms brought about by the Single European Act and the Treaties of Maastricht, Amsterdam and Nice, all of which have notably increased the legislative power of the Parliament. This evolution is of course ongoing, and the years ahead will doubtless see further intergovernmental conferences bringing further institutional change.

During this period, a good deal of activity also occurred outside the institutional framework of the European Community. Much of it took place in the hands of the heads of state or government of the EC Member States assembled in an intergovernmental formation that came to be known as the European Council. (The European Council's functions are dealt with in a later section of this chapter.) When the Maastricht Treaty came into effect in 1993, the new European Union, although intergovernmental in nature and lacking legal personality, required some institutional structure in order to operate in pillars two and three. Under both pillars, the Council serves as the decision-making organ, which helps

---

8. EC Treaty Article 7 (ex 4) identifies the Community institutions, including among them the Court of Auditors.

explain why the Council formally changed its name to the Council of the European Union (or EU Council).[9] The Commission (whose official name remains the Commission of the European Communities) shares with the Member States the power of initiative in proposing pillar three actions and may be called upon by the Council to assist in matters under pillar two. The Parliament is to be kept informed of developments under the second pillar and on specified issues must be consulted. (The Court of Justice has no role in pillar two and a very limited one—discussed below in this chapter—in pillar three.)

1. The Council

The Council (or the Council of Ministers, as it is sometimes called to distinguish it from other "Councils") does not have a perfect analogue among conventional government structures at the nation-state level.

Within the framework of the European Community, the Council functions as a kind of collective head of state of the European Community, deciding external trade policies and concluding international agreements. The Council also exercises primary legislative power within the Community, although it now shares that power with the European Parliament through the introduction into the EC Treaty of legislative procedures requiring the participation of both bodies. By virtue of some of this legislation, the Council's legislative authority has been delegated to the Commission. Viewed structurally, the Council consists of representatives of the governments of the Member States, voting in the name of their State and (to the extent qualified majority voting obtains) with a voting strength crudely weighted according to the State's relative population size. The Council thus resembles in some degree a head of state in status, a legislature in function and an assembly of constituent states in structure.

The Council also has significant decisional (though technically not "legislative") authority under the TEU's pillars two and three . . .

. . .

Article 203 (ex 146) of the EC Treaty states that the Council is to be composed of a representative of each Member State "at ministerial level" authorized to commit that member State's government. (Originally, Member States could be represented in the Council only by government ministers, but the term "representative . . . at ministerial level" was introduced by the Maastricht Treaty so as to permit representatives of the German *Lander* to act in the name of Germany in the Council as appropriate.) It is commonly the Ministers of Foreign Affairs who come together as the Council. When they meet as the Council on institutional or internal affairs, they are known as the "General Affairs Council," as distinct from the "Foreign Affairs Council," the name used when they meet for purposes of action under the Common Commercial Policy (i.e. external economic relations) or under pillar two (the Common Foreign and Security Policy). When a meeting concerns a specialized subject, such as transport, agriculture or

9. Council Decision 93/591. O.J. L 281/18 (Nov. 16, 1993).

finance, the Council may consist of the relevant ministers (or pairs of ministers, when two distinct matters—foreign affairs and agriculture, for example—are involved). With the advent of EMU, Council meetings of the economic and finance ministers (known for short as the Ecofin Council) are increasingly common. In April 2000, the Council set at 16 its maximum number of different "compositions."

The Presidency of the Council is held for a six-month term, typically rotating among the Member States in a substantially modified alphabetical order. Article 203 empowers the Council to decide upon the order by unanimous decision Recently, the order has been drawn up to ensure that a large state—France, Germany, Italy, Spain or the UK—holds the Presidency at least once in every third six-month period. Besides increasing the frequency of Presidencies by large states (as was its purpose), the pattern ensures that at least one large state will at all times participate in the Council's "troika" system, described just below. Sweden and Belgium held the Presidency in 2001, and Spain and Denmark will do so in 2002. On the presidency, see B. Schloh, The Presidency of the Council, 25 Syr. J. Int'l L. 93 (1998).

The Council meets when convened by its President, whether on the latter's own initiative or at the request of a Member State or the Commission. It meets frequently, over 80 times a year on the average, usually in Brussels. In recent years, the Presidency has assumed increased importance as each Member State in succession uses its term to advance certain agenda items. In the interest of continuity, a "troika" staff has been established, consisting in part of representatives of the immediate past and future Presidents.

As a legislator, the Council operates under special constraints. In the first place, the Commission has exclusive authority to initiate legislation. Thus, a Commission proposal is required before the Council may consider and adopt virtually any legislative measure. Article 208 (ex 152) allows the Council to instruct the Commission to undertake studies and submit proposals, but this rarely occurs. Further, the Single European Act and the Maastricht, Amsterdam and (prospectively) Nice Treaties have brought the European Parliament into the legislative process in decisive ways. . . . Finally, as we know, the Council does not enjoy plenary legislative power, the scope of its legislative authority being specified in various articles of the EC Treaty.

In international affairs, the Council plays a leading role. As amended, Article 300 (ex 228) authorizes the Council to approve most international agreements between the Community and other states or international organizations. Such agreements may be entered into by the Council by qualified majority vote, except in the case of association agreements under Article 310 (ex 238) or when the agreement covers a field on which the Council can legislate internally only if it acts unanimously. The Council is required to consult the European Parliament before concluding any international agreement, with the exception of commercial agreements under Article 133 (ex 113); in some instances (e.g. agreements by the Community establishing an association involving reciprocal rights and obligations, common actions or special procedures, or agreements having important budgetary implications for the Community), the Parliament must not only be consulted but its assent must be had. Agreements for the accession of new Member States are separately addressed by TEU Article 49 (ex O); both unanimity in the Council and parliamentary assent are required. . . .

Article 202 (ex 145) describes the Council's internal functions in general terms as "ensur[ing] that the objectives set out in [the] Treaty are attained." More specifically, it calls upon the Council to "ensure coordination of the general economic policies of the Member States," to "take decisions," and to "confer on the Commission, in the acts which the Council adopts, powers for the implementation of the rules which the Council lays down"—all of this, however, to be accomplished "in accordance with the provisions of [the] Treaty." Of course, particular articles of the EC Treaty assign the Council still more precise tasks. Every measure is required to be taken in the manner set out in the Treaty articles governing the matter in question, be it agriculture, commercial policy, competition law or the free movement of goods, persons, services or capital. Finally, although the Parliament and the Commission are also importantly involved, the Council has the chief role in the budgetary process described in Chapter 3C.

The EC Treaty specifies the manner of Council voting. On certain matters, such as the procedure for accession of new states or the harmonization of tax legislation, unanimity is still required. In rare non-legislative instances (notably in adopting internal rules of procedure), a simple majority vote suffices. Today, by far the most widespread manner of voting is by qualified majority. Qualified majority voting (QMV) originally applied in a relatively small number of sectors, such as agriculture, transport, competition law and commercial policy. However, every major Treaty amendment starting with the Single European Act (in the area of harmonizing national laws in aid of the internal market) has expanded the scope of application of QMV to the point that it is now the decidedly preponderant voting formula in the Council.

Qualified majority voting is outlined in Article 205 (ex 148) as follows:

(1) Save as otherwise provided in this Treaty, the Council shall act by a majority of its members.

(2) Where the Council is required to act by a qualified majority, the votes of its members shall be weighted as follows:

Belgium	5
Denmark	3
Germany	10
Greece	5
Spain	8
France	10
Ireland	3
Italy	10
Luxembourg	2

The Netherlands	5
Austria	4
Portugal	5
Finland	3
Sweden	4
United Kingdom	10

For their adoption, acts of the Council shall require at least:

– 62 votes in favour where this Treaty requires them to be adopted on a proposal from the Commission,

– 62 votes in favour, cast by at least 10 members, in other cases.

Under qualified majority voting all of a Member State's votes must be cast as a bloc. Since the total number of votes in the Council under qualified majority voting is now 87, the "blocking minority" is set at 26. The formula is designed in part to secure the interests of the larger states. Simple calculation shows that the opposition of three large states will defeat a proposal in a qualified majority vote, but that the opposition of the five smallest ones will not. On the other hand, the support of the five largest states is not sufficient for the passage of legislation; at least three of the smaller states must also support it. Significantly, each time the Community's membership has grown, the numbers in the qualified majority formula have been changed to produce a similar sort of equilibrium. What are the logical premises of the qualified majority voting system? Are they sound? How does the system compare with state representation rules in the US Congress?

Among the Member States' main objectives at the Nice Intergovernmental Conference was to decide upon the future re-weighting of votes in the Council in anticipation of expanded EU membership. The Treaty of Nice provides that, as of January 1, 2005, the weighting of votes among the current Member States should be as follows:

Belgium	12
Denmark	7
Germany	29
Greece	12
Spain	27
France	29
Ireland	7
Italy	29
Luxembourg	4
The Netherlands	13
Austria	10
Portugal	12
Finland	7
Sweden	10
United Kingdom	29

Of this total of 237 votes, at least 170 would be required for the passage of legislation by qualified majority. In addition, where the EC Treaty requires measures to be adopted upon proposal by the Commission, a majority of Member States would have to have cast their votes in favor of the measure. (In the case of all other measures, the fraction rises to 2/3 of the Member States.) Finally, any State could demand verification that the total population among the States supporting the measure constitutes 62% of the total EU population; if verification is demanded and cannot be shown, the measure could not be enacted. In short, adoption would require a *triple* majority: a qualified majority of total Member State votes, a majority (or in some cases a qualified majority) of Member States, and a qualified majority of the EU population.

By increasing the vote allocation of each current Member State, the IGC cleared the way for assigning smaller vote allocations to new Member States having small populations. A Declaration on Enlargement, while keeping vote numbers for the current Member States at the levels prescribed for January 1, 2005, assigns Council votes to the applicant States as follows:

Poland	27
Romania	14
Czech Republic	12
Hungary	12
Bulgaria	10
Slovakia	7
Lithuania	7
Latvia	4
Slovenia	4
Estonia	4
Cyprus	4
Malta	3

Upon the accession of all twelve, the combined total of Council votes would be 345. Passage of legislation by qualified majority would require at least 258 votes, cast by either a majority of Member States (for measures requiring a proposal from the Commission) or 2/3 of the Member States (for all other measures). The requirement that it be shown, upon demand by a Member State, that the supporting States account for 62% of the total EU population, would continue to apply. Obviously, if the twelve applicant States do not all accede at the same moment in time, temporary adjustments in the qualified majority threshold of weighted votes will have to be made.[10]

---

10. See the Declaration on the Qualified Majority Threshold and the Number of Votes for a Blocking Minority, agreed upon at Nice in December 2000. The Declaration recognizes that when some but not all of the applicant States accede to the EU, the percentage of votes constituting a qualified majority will be lower than the percentage required as of January 1, 2005. It provides for the applicable percentage to progressively increase until it reaches 73.4%.

The Council does not consist merely of government ministers (one per State) convening as the occasion requires. The Council is assisted by a large technical and administrative staff of several, based in Brussels. (The Council also has its own Legal Service of over 30 lawyers functioning entirely independently of the Commission Legal Service. Its Director-General Jean-Claude Piris served as general counsel for both the Amsterdam and Nice IGCs.) The Council's highest staff level is known as COREPER, an acronym for the French term for "Committee of Permanent Representatives." As its name suggests, COREPER, whose existence is recognized in EC Treaty Article 207 (ex 151), consists of permanent representatives of the Member States. These representatives conduct a preliminary review of all legislative measures before they go to the Council. COREPER in turn is assisted by both standing and ad hoc working groups of a technical and/or policy character. The advice of these national officials, as well as of ministry staff in the home capitals, informs the permanent representatives and, through them, the ministers who on any given occasion constitute the Council. In many instances, COREPER is able to work out an agreement and forward a proposal for routine approval by the Council; in other cases, COREPER isolates the major unsettled issues and sends them to the Council for their specific resolution if possible. Through their expertise, COREPER and the Council staff enable the Council to scrutinize the technical and policy proposals of the Commission, and their input understandably strengthens the Council in its dealings with the Commission.

As one might expect with such an institution, all Council meetings require simultaneous translation into all official languages, and are canceled or postponed if that is not possible. All draft texts must be presented in all languages.

· · ·

2. The Commission

The European Commission bears a striking but imperfect resemblance to a Government in the usual European sense of the term. Often referred to as the Community's executive organ, the Commission in fact performs tasks commonly identified with the executive: formulating a general legislative program, initiating the legislative process by drafting specific pieces of legislation, exercising the powers delegated to it by the Council, making the decisions and carrying out the administrative tasks assigned to it, and overseeing (and if need be enforcing) compliance with the law. Much of this is captured in the language of Article 211 (ex 155) of the EC Treaty. . . .

Despite its close affinity to a modern Government in the European sense, the Commission has certain structural features that set it apart. The term and mode of appointment of the Commission has changed over time. Under the amended EC Treaty Article 214 (ex 158), the Commission is appointed for a five-year renewable term. The Member State governments nominate by common accord a Commission President, whose appointment is subject to Parliamentary assent. In concert with the nominee, the Member States then nominate the other members of the Commission. (As

amended at Nice, the Treaty would place in the Council, acting by qualified majority, the power to nominate both the Commission President and
the body of Commissioners. In nominating the President, the Council
would sit in the composition of heads of state or government.) The
Commission's total membership is fixed at present by Article 213 (ex 157)
of the EC Treaty at 20, with the understanding that each smaller State
may nominate one member apiece, while the five larger States nominate
two. (As indicated below, the Nice Treaty would bring a change.)

Article 214 of the EC Treaty, as amended at Nice, introduces qualified
majority decision-making into the procedure for the appointment of
Commissioners. The President of the Commission is first nominated by
the Council meeting as the Heads of State or Government and voting by
QMV. When that nomination is approved by the European Parliament,
the Member States then determine the other Commissioners, and the
Council (acting by qualified majority and by common accord with the
nominee for President) adopts this list.

Before assuming office, the Commission must, as a body, receive a
"vote of approval" by the Parliament.[12] In January 1995, the Parliament
made conspicuous use of this then-new power, by expressing reservations
about certain individual Commission nominees before approving the
Commission as a whole. (At the Maastricht IGC, Parliament had unsuccessfully sought the right to approve or disapprove the appointment of
individual commissioners.)

Over the years, starting with the first President, Walter Hallstein,
Commission Presidents have shaped the Commission's agenda and often
exerted great influence over Commission policy. This was decidedly the
case with Jacques Delors, the former French Socialist Minister of Finance
and President of the Commission between 1985 and 1994, who strongly
promoted the Community's 1992 "internal market" program, the EMU,
and further steps toward political union.

The President's authority within the Commission has been progressively strengthened. As noted, he or she participates in the designation of
the other Commissioners. Under the EC Treaty, as amended by the Treaty
of Nice, the President appoints from among the Commissioners, with the
Commission's collective approval, an unstated number of Vice-Presidents.[13]
By virtue of the same amendment, the President is given the power to
allocate and reallocate portfolios among the Commission's members, to dismiss a Commissioner (with the Commission's collective approval), to determine the Commission's internal organization, and more generally to give
the Commission its "political guidance."[14] The current Commission
President is Romano Prodi.

---

12. EC Treaty art. 214 (ex 158).
Following Parliament's approval, the Council,
acting by qualified majority, formally
appoints the Commission and its President.

13. EC Treaty art. 217 (ex 161). Prior to
the amendment at Nice, the Commission
appointed the Vice-President whose number
the Treaty fixed at either one or two.

(Previously the Member States named the
Vice-Presidents, of whom there were
required to be six.)

14. Article 217, as amended at Nice, further requires the Commissioners to "carry
out the duties devolved upon them by the
President under his authority."

As its functions suggest, the Commission may be considered the Community's primary engine of integration. Although its members are effectively selected by nationality, the Commission is expected to act so as to promote the Community's interests and development rather than those of any of its Member States. The Commission's record of performance largely bears out this expectation. The independence of the Commission from the Member States is forcefully guaranteed: Commissioners are required to be "completely independent in the performance of their duties," to "neither seek nor take instructions from any Government or from any other body" and to "refrain from any action incompatible with their duties." [15] The Commission acts by a simple majority of its members and its deliberations are secret.

The Treaty says little about the Commission's relationship to the Council.[16] The Commission's relationship to the Parliament, which is treated, does not fully correspond to what an analogy to parliamentary models of government might lead one to expect. Commissioners neither come from Parliament nor necessarily reflect the political sentiments dominant in that body, though Parliament is entitled to ask questions of the Commission, to receive from it an annual report on Community activities, and to censure the Commission as a body and thus force its resignation. However, the rules of the Parliament provide for "confirmation hearings" on each individual Commissioner, a practice in which the Prodi Commission acquiesced. Moreover, the change of the Commission's term of office from four to five years permitted the Commission's appointment to become congruent with Parliamentary elections. Along with other changes recently made (such as the requirement that Parliament approve the Commission as a whole before it takes office), this is meant to increase the "parliamentary" character of the government while strengthening the Commission's political and popular accountability.

As described in Chapter 1, Commission accountability came conspicuously to the fore in 1998–99 during the Presidency of Jacques Santer, former Luxembourg Prime Minister. Following a period of growing parliamentary disenchantment with the Santer Commission, a report specially prepared for the Parliament concluded that certain Commissioners had behaved improperly (notably through a pattern of favoritism in decision-making) and that the Commission as a whole had failed to exercise sufficient collective responsibility or oversight. As noted, the Commission resigned in the immediate wake of the report, thereby preempting a highly likely vote of censure.

In late March 1999, the European Council in Berlin accepted the Commission's resignation and selected Romano Prodi, former Italian Prime Minister, as the next Commission President, both to complete the 1995–99 term and for the new 2000–04 term. However, it decided that designation of the full Commission should await the June 1999 parliamentary elections on the understanding that Parliament would then promptly consider the nominations. (Meanwhile, Parliament resolved

---

15. EC Treaty art. 213 (ex 157). Article 213 also deals specifically with the limitations on Commissioners' freedom of action during and after office, and their removal from office.

16. "The Council and Commission shall consult each other and shall settle by common accord their methods of cooperation." EC Treaty art. 218 (ex 162).

that the naming of the new Commission should be subject to parliamentary approval in accordance with the amendment to EC Treaty Article 214 (ex 158) introduced by the Amsterdam Treaty.) In May, Parliament approved Mr. Prodi's nomination as President-designate and the Member State's nomination of new Commissioners followed. Parliament conducted its hearings on the proposed Commissioners following the June 1999 elections, and in September the Commissioners were confirmed as a body by a large parliamentary majority both to complete the remainder of the 1995–99 term and to constitute the new 2000–04 Commission.

At its Berlin meeting, the European Council urged that the new Commission reform its organization, management and control, and the new Commission wasted no time. Commissioner *cabinets* were made smaller (but with requirements of nationality and gender balance), and shifts made in the top positions in the Directorates-General. A task force on Commission administrative reform was set up under the direction of Commission Vice-President Neil Kinnock, who was one of only four Commissioners reappointed to the new Commission. The result was a March 2000 White Paper on Reforming the Commission (COM (2000) 200), a plan which has since been acted upon in various respects, including recruitment and promotion (once again to promote nationality and gender diversity, as well as access from persons outside the Commission) and improved financial management for each Directorate-General. Under a new system inaugurated in December 2000, Directors-General and directors of units are evaluated every two years and ordinarily expected to serve in their posts no more than five years prior to reassignment.

With prospects of further EU enlargement, the growing size of the Commission has also become a serious preoccupation. The Amsterdam IGC failed to resolve the "numbers" issue. Only at Nice in December 2000 did the Member States agree on changes in the composition of the Commission, to be reflected in EC Treaty Article 213 (ex 157) as of January 1, 2005. From that date, every State—large and small—would name only a single Commissioner. Then, at the point when the EU has 27 Member States, the number of Commissioners would be set by the Council, acting unanimously, at a number less than the number of States. From then, Commissioners would be chosen according to a rotation system likewise to be decided upon by the Council acting unanimously. While based on the principle of equality,[17] the rotation system would also be required "to reflect satisfactorily the demographic and geographical range" of Member States.

To cope with enlargement, the Accession Treaty introduced interim provisions effective as of the accession of new Member States. (Article 45, O.J. L 236/17 (Sept. 23, 2003)). Pursuant to that, each new Member State in early 2004 nominated a Commissioner who began functioning in the institution immediately upon accession. (Therefore, as of May 1, 2004, the then-current Commission had thirty members and will continue to do so until

---

17. Protocol on the Enlargement of the European Union, agreed upon at Nice in December 2000, art. 4. The Protocol, in art. 4(3)(a), specifies by way of equality that the difference between the total number of terms of office held by any pair of Member States may never be more than one.

the end of its mandate later in the year.) The signing of the Accession Treaty also in effect moved forward the date for the new composition of the Commission. . . . Thus, when chosen on November 1, 2004, the new 2005–09 Commission will no longer include two Commissioners from each of the five largest Member States. Present and new Member States will each nominate one Commissioner, producing a total of twenty-five Commissioners.

To facilitate the entry of the ten new Member States on May 1, 2004 (until the end of the Commission's term on October 31, 2004), a process of "twinning" was announced by President Prodi (Commission press Release, IP/04/233 (Feb. 18, 2003)). Rather than being assigned immediately a specific portfolio, the new Commissioners (each with their own cabinet) are to be twinned or paired with current members of the College. The cabinets of the new Commissioners are to work closely with the cabinets of the Commissioners with whom they are associated. While this may be the only feasible solution, in view of the short remaining limited term of the new Commissioners in the 1999–2004 Commission, it also means that the ten new Member States will have a primarily symbolic representation in the Commission until November 1, 2004. It also remains to be seen how the new Commission President will allocate portfolios, which must be adjusted to account for the larger College.

The Commission in 1993 published detailed procedural rules for use at its meetings, in its written procedures, and in decision-making by delegation. O.J. L 230/17 (Sept. 11, 1993). The latter two procedures refer to decision-making in the absence of a meeting and to authorization of a single Commissioner to take definitive action in the name of the full Commission. The rules were revised in 1999,[18] so as to incorporate certain reforms provided for by the Amsterdam Treaty, such as the President's power to allocate portfolios and other responsibilities among Commissioners. Also, by a decision of the European Council of December 23, 1992, reiterated in an Amsterdam Treaty Protocol on the Location of the Seats of the Institutions, Brussels has been confirmed as the Commission's permanent seat.

In terms of functions, the Commission is in part a legislative and in part a regulatory body. In a few areas, the EC Treaty gives the Commission certain powers of "primary" or "original" legislative authority. A current example is Article 86 (ex 90), authorizing the Commission to issue directives or decisions to Member States on the application of competition rules to public undertakings or undertakings to which the States may have granted special rights. Indeed, in the case of Spain, Belgium and Italy v. Commission (Competition in the market for telecommunications services), Joined Cases C–271, 281 & 289/90, [1992] ECR I–5833, the Court held that the Commission's issuance of directives setting out the Member States' obligations in relation to their public undertakings does not impinge upon the general legislative powers given to the Council by Articles 83 (ex 87) and 94 (ex 100) of the Treaty. More generally, though, the Commission enjoys the very significant monopoly on the proposal of

---

18.   O.J. L 252/41 (Sept. 18, 1999).

legislation to the Council, which means that it essentially sets the Community's legislative agenda and initially drafts its legal texts.

In addition to exercising original legislative authority under the EC Treaty, the Commission has been delegated extensive rulemaking powers by the Council. Agriculture is a sector in which such delegation occurs with particular regularity. Under the Common Agricultural Policy (CAP), the Community comprehensively regulates product standards, prices and marketing for a great number of different commodities, and these regulations must be adapted at short intervals in response to changed economic circumstances. Lodging rulemaking powers in the Commission allows detailed production, pricing and marketing standards for goods as diverse as cereals, pork and preserves to be devised and regularly modified. Other sectors in which the Council has delegated rulemaking authority to the Commission include competition policy and the harmonization of technical and safety standards.

The Commission's other institutional tasks include drafting the initial annual budget for review and adoption by the Council and Parliament, and administering the Community's finances. (See Chapter 3C below.) The Commission also brings enforcement actions against Member States under Article 226 (ex 169) for their violations of Community law, such as maintaining barriers to trade or failing to adopt the legislation or regulations that Community directives require. Enforcement actions against Member States, which constitute a significant part of the Commission's business, are discussed in Chapter 11.

Certainly not to be overlooked are the myriad specific administrative decisions (typified by rulings on competition law violations or violations of the prohibition on state aids) that the Commission, as the Community's chief executive arm, is called upon to make on a daily basis. Such decisions will appear throughout the substantive chapters of this book. Another prime area of Commission activity is, of course, external relations and trade. Under Article 300 (ex 228), the Commission, upon authorization by the Council, opens and conducts negotiations over international agreements for eventual conclusion by the Council. The Commission also represents the Community in the WTO and other international organizations and enforces the Community's protective trade legislation.

In aid of these many functions, but also independent of them, the Commission performs the vital role of gathering and providing information. The general report on Community activities that the Commission submits to Parliament each year provides a wealth of information and guidance. The Commission also publishes specialized annual reports (e.g., on competition, the environment and social affairs) and numerous economic and social studies and statistics.[19]

19. The Court of Justice has ruled that the Commission must make Community documents (including ones that are ordinarily confidential) available to national judges investigating infringements of Community law, and allow its officials to appear and testify before those judges as necessary. The Court based this conclusion on EC Treaty Article 10 (ex 5), which imposes an obligation of "sincere cooperation" between the Member States and the Community. Zwartveld, Case C–2/88 Imm., [1990] ECR I–3365. The Commission may only avoid the obligation by demonstrating "imperative reasons" for doing so.

To help discharge its far-ranging responsibilities, the Commission has, as of the year 2000, a permanent staff of over 16,400, divided into 24 large sections known as Directorates General (or "DGs"), as well as a number of other services and offices. As recently re-titled, the DGs are named by subject (e.g. competition, agriculture, internal market, enlargement) rather than number I, II, etc. Each DG is further subdivided into subdirectorates and the latter into divisions along policy lines. Most Community activities fall within the portfolio of one of the Directorates General, whether the matter is agriculture, external relations, the internal market, competition, or budget and finance. Each DG is headed by a Director General who in turn reports to one of the Commissioners. Since each Commissioner supervises one or two DGs, he or she has authority over a broad field of action. Each Commissioner also has a personal cabinet headed by a "chef de cabinet". The chefs de cabinet not only perform administrative duties, including liaison with the other Commissioners, but attempt through their weekly meetings to resolve among themselves matters not requiring the Commissioners' personal involvement.

The Commission Legal Service, consisting of some 125 lawyers, reviews the texts of all draft legislation and decisions, renders legal advice, and represents the Commission in litigation before the Court of Justice. Translation of documents and interpretation at meetings alone require a Commission staff of over 1900 in the Translation Service. All measures (including drafts), as well as major reports and studies, must be translated into all eleven official Community languages,[20] and all official meetings require simultaneous translation. These are daunting tasks for the Commission no less than for the other institutions, and they have noticeably slowed the legislative and decisionmaking processes.

Under Article 290 (ex 217), the Council determines unanimously "the rules governing the languages of the institutions." In practice, not only the Official Journal (and all its contents), but also (1) Court judgments and orders, (2) resolutions and proceedings of Parliament and the Communities' advisory bodies, and (3) informational sources like the Commission's annual general and sectoral reports, the Bulletin of the Union, and reports and studies by the Commission, Council and Parliament, appear in all the official languages (with the exception of Irish). Notwithstanding the burdens, no serious consideration has been given up to now to the idea of withholding official status from the languages of the new Member States. In 1995, Parliament adopted a resolution strongly opposing any reduction in the number of official languages.[21] Even with the prospective enlargements and growing linguistic complexity, the situation is unlikely to change.

NOTE ON DELEGATIONS OF POWER TO THE COMMISSION

As noted, and as is hardly surprising, the Commission commonly exercises rulemaking authority delegated to it by the Council. EC Treaty

---

20. Danish, Dutch, English, Finnish, French, German, Greek, Italian, Portuguese, Spanish and Swedish. (Irish is technically also an official language, but Ireland does not require that it be used for translation purposes.)

21. O.J. C 43/91 (Feb. 20, 1995).

Articles 202 (ex 145) and 211 (ex 155) expressly call upon the Council to delegate power to the Commission and direct the Commission to use that power. The advantages of executive legislation—speed, flexibility and expertise—are especially pronounced in the Community, where legislative authority vests chiefly in a Council that sits only intermittently and in different compositions, and where most legislative action now requires a complex and protracted interplay between the Council and Parliament.

The Council often delegates rulemaking powers to the Commission only on condition that the latter first submit its draft rules for an opinion from, and in some cases actual approval by, specialized committees representing the Member States. The most common structure is the so-called "management committee," chaired by a non-voting Commission official, but composed of Member State representatives whose votes are weighted by State in the fashion of the Council itself. Under this system, the Commission's draft legislation is reviewed by the relevant management committee, and if the committee by qualified majority gives a favorable opinion of the legislation or expresses no opinion at all, the draft automatically becomes law. If, on the other hand, the committee by qualified majority disapproves the proposal, its effectiveness is postponed for one month, during which time the Council itself may act to reject it. However, only a vote of disapproval by the Council will prevent the measure from coming into effect; the management committee's disapproval alone is not sufficient.

Variations on the management committee system are the so-called "advisory committees" and "regulatory committees." The former committees, as their name suggests, exercise purely consultative functions in that the Commission is bound to solicit and presumably consider their advice before finally adopting a measure pursuant to delegation. Neither approval by the advisory committee nor by the Council itself is necessary in order for the delegated legislation to become effective. "Regulatory committees" resemble the management committees, but actually go further in restricting the Commission's freedom of action. Under this system, formal committee opposition to a Commission proposal is not needed in order for implementation to be delayed. The measure may not legally come into force until it receives a favorable opinion from the regulatory committee (or the Council itself) acting by a qualified majority vote.

The Court of Justice considered the legality of the management committee system in the case of Einfuhr- und Vorratsstelle für Getreide und Futtermittel v. Köster, Berodt & Co., Case 25/70, [1970] ECR 1161, where it ruled:

> . . . The function of the Management Committee is to ensure permanent consultation in order to guide the Commission in the exercise of the powers conferred on it by the Council and to enable the latter to substitute its own action for that of the Commission. The Management Committee does not therefore have the power to take a decision in place of the Commission or the Council. . . . [The] machinery enables the Council to delegate to the Commission an implementing power of appreciable scope, subject to its power to take the decision itself if necessary.

[1970] ECR at 1171. Does the Court's reasoning also support the validity of the regulatory committee system? The Court subsequently rejected the claim that such a system "[has] the effect of paralyzing the Commission" or has any other feature that would "affect [its] validity." Tedeschi v. Denkavit, Case 5/77, [1977] ECR 1555, 1579–80.

As amended, Article 202 (ex 145) now expressly permits the Council to impose conditions on the Commission's use of delegated powers in accordance with "principles and rules" established by the Council upon proposal by the Commission and advice by Parliament. The Council eventually adopted a so-called Comitology Decision,[22] which established three committee models (plus certain variants) for reviewing the Commission's exercise of delegated powers. That decision has been updated[23] and supplemented by an agreement between the Parliament and Commission which guarantees that the Parliament will receive essential documents (e.g. draft agendas, draft measures) from the Commission at the same time as committee members do. The committee models mirror the advisory, management and regulatory models and operate as a menu from which the Council on any given occasion may freely select a preestablished mode of committee review. The decision thus regularizes the committee system and tends to limit political debate over details of the review procedure to be incorporated by the Council in any given delegation of power.[24]

Questions occasionally arise over the scope of delegations to the Commission. A notable example is ACF Chemiefarma NV v. Commission, Case 41/69, [1970] ECR 661. Acting under EC Article 83 (ex 87), which authorizes it to enact legislation for the implementation of Community competition rules, the Council adopted Regulation 17, which in turn empowered the Commission to issue procedural rules for investigating suspected violations, holding hearings and fining violators. (Regulation 17 is examined in Chapter 20.) A party that had been fined by the Commission under these rules challenged the action on the ground that Regulation 17 delegated powers to the Commission going beyond the "implementation" of Council rules, within the meaning of Article 211 (ex 155). The Court rejected the argument that the Council was required by itself to exercise all the rulemaking authority that Article 83 confers on it. "[T]he rules laying down the procedure to be followed . . ., however important they may be, constitute implementing provisions within the meaning of [former] Article 155." [1970] ECR at 668.

---

22. Council Decision 87/373, O.J. L 197/33 (July 18, 1987).

23. Council Decision 1999/468, O.J. L 184 (June 28, 1999).

24. The Comitology Decision was challenged by Parliament in the Court of Justice, but the suit was dismissed for lack of standing. See page 131 *infra*. The committee system nevertheless continues to come under criticism from the European Parliament. The latter complains that it is denied information about how the committees arrive at their recommendations on how legislation approved by the Council and Parliament should be implemented. This sentiment has spawned proposals for legislation modeled on the U.S. Federal Advisory Committee Act, which requires like committees in the U.S. to announce agendas in advance, to hold public meetings, to publish their minutes, and to disclose their members' financial interests. Among other means invoked in this effort, Parliament blocked the appropriation of the $28 million earmarked in 1996 for the committees' administrative budgets.

. . .

3. THE EUROPEAN PARLIAMENT

While the Commission functions as the principal engine of integration, and the Council as a kind of intergovernmental legislature, the Parliament is designed to express the political sentiments of the Member State populations. The EC Treaty describes the Parliament in Article 189 (ex 137) as composed of "representatives of the peoples of the States brought together in the Community." Contrary to what one might expect from its name, however, the Parliament received from the drafters of the original treaties scant legislative power. (The drafters actually used the term "Assembly," but that body began calling itself the European Parliament in 1962, and the other institutions eventually accepted the term. The Single European Act formalized the name change as of 1987.)

In its original wording, Article 189 (ex 187) specifically referred to Parliament's powers as "advisory and supervisory." Indeed Parliament initially had no decisional role in either the legislative or budgetary process. However, Parliament has continually demanded increased authority and, as Chapter 3 will show, the Single European Act and the Treaties of Maastricht, Amsterdam and Nice have all granted it. For its part, the Maastricht Treaty deleted the terms "advisory and supervisory."

. . .

The European Parliament has proven quite difficult to describe from a functional point of view. Its name notwithstanding, the Parliament enjoys only limited legislative power. It is the Commission, not the Parliament, that proposes legislation, though, by amendment at Maastricht, the EC Treaty (Article 192, ex 138b) now expressly invites Parliament to request that the Commission submit legislative proposals.

More significantly, Parliament originally had at best the right to be consulted, i.e., to give its opinion, before the Council took legislative action, and even then only where expressly provided for in the treaties. (As a matter of practice, the Council, since the 1970s, tended to seek Parliament's advice even when not required to do so.) Particularly since becoming directly elected in 1979, Parliament pressed vigorously for a greater voice in the legislative process, most notably in its own 1984 Draft Treaty Establishing the European Union, which would have required parliamentary assent for the passage of virtually all Community legislation.[28] Instead, the Single European Act devised a new legislative process, called the "parliamentary cooperation procedure," which created a complicated multi-stage process through which Parliament won a substantial legislative voice but still not a legislative veto. The Maastricht Treaty created an additional legislative procedure known as "parliamentary codecision," which made Parliament more of a legislative co-equal. As a result of further EC Treaty amendments at Amsterdam and Nice described in Chapter 3B, codecision has steadily gained ground.

---

28. EU Bull. 7/8-00.

. . .

4. THE COURT OF JUSTICE

The Court of Justice of the European Communities, whose seat is in Luxembourg, is dealt with extensively in the constitutive treaties. Article 220 (ex 164) of the EC Treaty gives the Court responsibility for "ensur[ing] that in the interpretation and application of this Treaty the law is observed."

Suffice it here to say that the Court entertains legal actions against both the institutions and the Member States for their alleged nonobservance of Community law. These are all in the nature of original actions. More significant, in numbers and arguably also in function, is the Court's jurisdiction to render "preliminary rulings" under EC Treaty Article 234 (ex 177) on the interpretation and validity of Community acts at the request of Member State courts.[33]

Through all these forms of action, the Court plays a vital role in securing a Community legal order that is both effective and respectful of the rule of law and of individual rights. The Court's doctrinal contributions include the fundamental concepts of direct effect and supremacy.

More generally, it has sought through its jurisprudence to clarify the Member States' responsibilities under Community law. At the same time, the Court is continually defining the freedom of action of the Community institutions themselves. On all such issues, the Court's understanding of the relevant Community norms is considered authoritative.

---

33. Under EC Treaty Article 300 (ex 228), the Court also has jurisdiction to give an opinion on the compatibility with the Treaty of any proposed international agreement of the Community. The Council, the Commission, a Member State, and (as of the Treaty of Nice) the Parliament have standing to request such an opinion. See Part IV *infra* for examples of such opinions.

COMPARATIVE PRIVATE LAW: PROPERTY, TORT, CONTRACT, UNJUST ENRICHMENT

PART ONE:

PROPERTY LAW

I. POSSESSION

1. Possession as a means of acquiring rights

a. Wild animals

Roman law

Inst. 2.1 (translation from Peter Birks & Grant McLeod, *Justinian's Institutes* **(1987))**

(12) Wild animals, birds and fish, the creatures of land, sea and sky, become the property of the taker as soon as they are caught. Where something has no owner, it is reasonable that the person who takes it should have it. It is immaterial whether he catches the wild animal or bird on his own land or someone else's. Suppose a man enters someone else's land to hunt or to catch birds. If the landowner sees him, he can obviously warn him off. If you catch such an animal it remains yours as long as you keep it under your control. If it escapes your control and recovers its natural liberty, it ceases to be yours. The next taker can have it. It is held to have regained its natural freedom when it is out of your sight or when, though still in sight, it is difficult for you to reach it.

(13) Does an animal become yours when it is wounded and ready to be caught? Some jurists thought it became yours at once and stayed yours till you gave up the chase, only then becoming available again to the next taker. Others thought that it became yours only when you caught it. We confirm that view. After all, many things can prevent you from catching the animal.

Anglo-American law

Young v. Hitchens, (1844) 6 Q.B., 115 Eng. Rep. 228

[Plaintiff had nearly surrounded a school of fish with a net when defendant rowed his boat into the opening and prevented plaintiff from capturing them.]

"It does appear almost certain that the plaintiff would here had possession of the fish but for the act of the defendant: but it is quite certain that he had not possession. Whatever interpretation may be put on such terms as 'custody' and 'possession,' the question will be whether any custody or possession has been obtained here. I think it is impossible to say that it had, until the party had actual power over the fish. It may be that

141

the defendant acted unjustifiably in preventing the plaintiff from obtaining such power: but that would only show a wrongful act, for which he might be liable in a proper form of action."

Pierson v. Post, 3 Cai. 175, 2 Am. Dec. 264 (N.Y. 1805)

[The plaintiff claimed that he "did upon a certain wild and uninhabited heath, find and start one of those noxious beasts called a fox. . . ." But while he was pursuing it, the defendant "well knowing the fox was so hunted and pursued . . . did . . . kill and carry it off."]

"It is admitted that a fox is an animal *ferae naturae*, and that property in such animals is acquired by occupancy only. The admissions narrow the discussion to the simple question of what acts amount to occupancy, applied to acquiring rights to wild animals.

If we have recourse to the general principles of law, the judgment below [for the plaintiff] is obviously erroneous. Justinian's Institutes lib.2, tit. 1, s. 13 and Fleta lib.3, c. 2, p. 175, adopt the principle, that pursuit alone vests no right or property in the huntsman, and that even pursuit, accompanied by wounding, is equally ineffectual for that purpose, unless the animal be actually taken. The same principle is recognised by Bracton, lib. 2, c. 1, p. 8.

Puffendorf lib. 4, c. 6, s. 2, and 10, defines occupancy of beasts *ferae naturae* to be the actual possession of them and Bynkershoek is cited as coinciding in this definition. It is indeed with hesitation that Puffendorf affirms that a wild beast mortally wounded, or greatly maimed, cannot be fairly intercepted by another, whilst the pursuit of the person inflicting the wounds continues. The foregoing authorities are decisive to show that mere pursuit gave Post no legal right to the fox, but that he became the property of Pierson, who intercepted and killed him."

Note: Suppose a hunter killed or captured an animal while trespassing on another person's land. The common law rule is that the animal belongs to the landowner, not the hunter. *Churchward v. Studdy*, (1811) 6 East. 49, 104 Eng. Rep. 596 ("if A start a hare in the ground of B and hunt and kill it there, the property continues all the while in B. . ."). On the law in the United States, see Ray A. Brown, *The Law of Personal Property* (3d ed., 1975), 17.

French law

French Civil Code art. 715

The right to hunt or fish . . . is regulated by particular statutes.

François Terré & Philippe Simler, *Droit civil Les biens* (6th ed., 2002), no. 415

"The Civil Code regards hunting as the acquisition of game: according to art. 715, the "right to hunt" is governed by particular statutes. . . .

The *right to hunt* constitutes an attribute of the right of property which belongs in principle to the one who one who owns the land. . . . But the acquisition of game is independent of the right of property to the land and of the right to hunt there. . . .

The hunter acquires property in the game killed or captured by virtue of his right of occupation, and without any distinction as to whether he has acted on his own land or the land of another, and even when he was hunting without a permit, although he may be liable in a criminal action and may owe civil damages or be subject to a confiscation, which has sometimes been declared."

German law

German Civil Code

§ 958 [ACQUISITION OF OWNERSHIP OF UNOWNED OBJECTS]

(1) One who takes an unowned moveable object into his own possession acquires ownership of the object.

(2) Ownership is not acquired when its acquisition is prohibited by statute or when the taking of possession injures the rights of acquisition of another.

German Civil Code

§ 960 [WILD ANIMALS]

(1) Wild animals are ownerless as long as they remain free. Wild animals in zoos and fish in ponds and other enclosed private waters are not ownerless.

(2) A wild animal that recovers its freedom becomes ownerless unless the owner of the animal is in immediate pursuit or when he abandons pursuit.

(3) A tame animal becomes ownerless when it gives up the habit of returning to a definite place.

Federal Hunting Law (Bundesjagdgesetz)

§ 7

(1) A personal hunting preserve is a continuous parcel or property with surfaces of land or forest or water suitable for fishing which are at least 75 hectares belonging to the same person or to an unincorporated partnership.

* * *

(4) In a personal hunting preserve, the owner is the one entitled to exercise the right to hunt. In his place, the right is exercised by the holder of a usufruct when the usufruct includes the entire area.

§ 8

(1) All parcels of land which are public or whose boundaries are particularly designated which do not belong to a private hunting preserve for a public hunting preserve when they encompass at least 150 hectares of land.

Note: Although the Federal Hunting Law does not explicitly say so, some German jurists believe that it qualifies the provisions of sections

958 and 960 of the German Civil Code, so that an animal caught in violation of another's hunting rights belongs to the holder of those rights, not to the hunter. Fritz & Jürgen Baur, *Lehrbuch des Sachenrechts* (16th ed., 1992), § 27 VIII. Other jurists believe that the animal continues to be ownerless until it is taken by the person to whom the hunting right belong. RGSt 39, 427; Harm Peter Westermann, *Sachenrecht Ein Lehrbuch* (7th ed. 1998), § 58 IV.

b. Found objects

Roman law

Dig. 47.2.43 (translation from Alan Watson, ed., *The Digest of Justinian* (1985))

(6) Even if the taker only thought [an object was] abandoned when it was not, he would not be liable for theft.

(7) And if he picked up a thing, just lying there, which was not, and which he did not think to be, abandoned, with the object not of personal profit but of returning it to the owner, he would not be guilty of theft.

(8) That being so, let us consider the case where, not knowing whose it was, he took it, intending to return it to the person who claimed it, or proved that it was his: is the guilty of theft? I think not. For there are many who do this sort of thing and put up a notice saying that they have found the thing and will return it to the claimant. Such persons have shown that they have no theftuous intent.

(9) But what if the finder claim a reward . . . ? I do not think that even he commits theft although his asking for something is conduct not to be condoned.

Anglo-American law

Armory v. Delamire, 1 Strange 505 (K.B. 1772)

[The plaintiff, a chimney sweeper's boy, found a jewel which he took to the shop of a goldsmith—the defendant here—to find out what it was, and left it with the goldsmith's apprentice. The goldsmith took out the jewels to weigh them, and offered the boy a half pence. When the boy refused, he was given back the socket of the ring but without the stones.]

"And now in trover against the master these points were ruled.

(1) That the finder of a jewel, though he does not by such finding acquire an absolute property or ownership, yet he has such a property as will enable him to keep it against all but the rightful owner, and hence can maintain trover.

(2) That the action well lay against the master, who gave a credit to his apprentice and is answerable for his neglect.

(3) As to the value of the jewels several of the trade were examined to prove what a jewel of the finest water that would fit the socket would be worth; and that the Chief Justice (Pratt) directed the jury, that unless the defendant did produce the jewel, and show it not to be of the finest water,

they should presume the strongest against him, and make the value of the best jewels the measure of their damages, which accordingly they did."

Ray A. Brown, *The Law of Personal Property* **(3d ed. 1975), 26**

"[T]he title of the finder is good against all the world except the true owner. . . ."

French law

French Civil Code

ARTICLE 717

Rights over objects of whatever nature which are thrown into the sea, or washed in from the sea and over plants and vegetation on the shores of the sea are governed by special legislation.

So also are objects which are lost when the owner does not identify himself.

ARTICLE 2279

In the case of moveable property, possession is as good as title.

Nevertheless, a person whose property was lost or stolen can claim it back within three years, counting from the day it was lost or stolen, against any person who has it, although that person does not lose any right he has against the one from whom he obtained the object.

François Terré & Philippe Simler, *Droit civil* *Les biens* (6th ed., 2002), no. 409

"By the name of property that is lost (*épave*, which literally means lost in a wreck), all moveable objects are meant which were lost by their owner. It is important not to confuse these objects with those which have been abandoned (*res derelictae*) which are *res nullius* [things belonging to no one]. In contrast to treasure, on the one hand, these objects have not been concealed or buried, and, on the other, their owner may identify himself one day. In fact, he did not renounce his property right even though he may often be ignorant that he lost his object. The object is a briefcase found on a street, some pieces of wood caught in the flow of a stream, or a some of money of which no one knows the origin.

. . .

Article 717 par. 2 of the Civil Code leaves rights to these things to be dealt with by special legislation, absent which, the following rules have been adopted:

The person who finds an object does not have the right to appropriate it. He commits a theft if he merely takes it, and he will not be the owner even if the thirty year period of prescription runs. Almost all towns have established a 'lost and found bureau.' A municipal ordinance requires the finders of lost objects to leave them with this bureau where their owners may claim them, and after a certain time has passed, generally a year and a day, objects which have not been claimed are returned to the finder. This administrative measure does not make him their owner but merely their possessor.

Some authors believe that this case should be treated as one of a possessor in good faith because one may presume that the owner gave up his right, and so one can apply by analogy art. 2279 par. 2 of the Civil Code which prevents the owner from claiming his property three years after its loss. That solution entails a very dubious assimilation of the rights of the finder to those of the possessor in good faith within the meaning of art. 2279."

German law

German Civil Code

§ 965 [DUTY OF THE FINDER TO GIVE NOTICE]

(1) One who finds and takes an lost object has the duty to give immediate notice to the loser, the owner, or other person who has the right to have it.

(2) If the finder does not know the person with the right to have the object or is unaware of his whereabouts, then he must immediately make the finding and the circumstances relevant to the discovery of that person known to the authorized bureau. If the object is worth less than ten euros, notice is not necessary.

§ 967 [DUTY OF DELIVERY]

The finder is required to deliver the object [or an appropriate sum of money] to the authorized bureau.

§ 971 [REWARD FOR THE FINDER]

The finder can claim a reward from the person entitled to have the object. [Further provisions fix the amount of the reward.]

§ 973 [ACQUISITION OF OWNERSHIP BY THE FINDER]

(1) When six months have passed since notice of the finding was given to the authorized bureau, the finder acquires ownership of the object unless the presence of the person who has a right to have it has become known or his right has been reported to the bureau. With the acquisition of ownership, previous rights to the object are extinguished.

c. Treasure

Roman law

Inst. 2.1 (translation from Peter Birks & Grant McLeod, *Justinian's Institutes* (1987))

39. The Emperor Hadrian, deciding in accordance with natural justice, allowed treasure found by a man on his own land to go to the finder, with the same ruling for chance finds on sacred or religious land. For a find on land of a private owner, so long as the land was found by chance and not by deliberate search, he allowed the owner half; and, correspondingly, for a find on imperial property he ruled that half should go to the finder and half to the emperor.

Anglo-American law

**Bruce Welling, *Property in Things in the
Common Law System* (1996), 202–203**

"[T]he law of treasure trove . . . has survived in many jurisdictions. Special rules apply when certain types of gold and silver buried things are found. 'Treasure trove is the name given by the early common law to any gold or silver in coin, plate or bullion found concealed in the earth or in any other private place, but not lying on the ground, the owner of the discovered treasure being unknown.'[179] The common law position was simple: treasure trove was owned by the king, anyone digging up something meeting the description,[180] or diving for sunken treasure in coastal waters, is likely to have it confiscated, though rewards are usually paid.

In America, the concept of royal prerogative died with the revolution. No state has a claim to treasure trove unless created by local legislation.[181] Where no state claim exists, some have suggested that the holder of an estate in land where the treasure trove was found can have no claim.[182] This makes no sense. The constitutional abolition of a state claim would make treasure trove the same as other things for purposes of property analysis. Whether an estate holder has a claim depends on whether he can prove prior possesssion.[183]"

French law

French Civil Code

ARTICLE 716

Property in a treasure belongs to the person who finds it on his own land. If the treasure is found on the land of another person, half belongs to the discoverer and half to the owner of the property.

Treasure is anything hidden or buried which no one can prove to be his property and the discovery of which is the result of pure chance.

German law

German Civil Code

§ 984 [THE FINDING OF TREASURE]

If an object is discovered that has been concealed for so long that its owner can no longer be determined (treasure), and possession is taken of

---

179. *Weeks* v. *Hackett* 71 A 858 (Me 1908) per Whitehouse, J. Similarly, see *A-G* v. *British Museum Trustees* [1903] 2 Ch 598 (Eng). Things hidden above ground level are included: *Hurley* v. *City of Niagara Falls* 254 NE 2d 917 (NY 1969). The definition is analyzed by Emden, "The Law of Treasure Trove, Past and Present" 42 LQR 369 (1926).

180. See *Lord Advocate* v. *University of Aberdeen* 1963 SC 533 (Scot).

181. *Weeks* v. *Hackett* 71 A 858 (Me 1908), citing "a substantially uniform line of

decisions in the American states", reaffirmed in *Campbell* v. *Cochrane* 416 A 2d 211 (Del 1980).

182. *Weeks* v. *Hackett* 71 A 858 (Me 1908); *Vickery* v. *Hardin* 133 NE 922 (Ind 1922); *Groover* v. *Tippins* 179 SE 634 (Ga 1935); *Zornes* v *Bowen* 274 NW 877 (Iowa 1937); *Niederlehner* v. *Weatherly* 69 NE 2d 787 (Ohio 1946).

183. *Schley* v. *Couch* 284 SW 333 (Texas 1955) per Calvert, J [extensive quotation from the decision omitted].

it after its discovery, the ownership belongs half to the discoverer and half to the owner of the property on which the object was concealed.

d. Adverse possession and prescription

Roman law

J.A.C. Thomas, *Textbook of Roman Law* (1976), 164–65

"Being an institution of the civil law, *usucaptio* [an older means of acquiring title through passage of time] was applicable only to those who had *commercium*, the right to exercise Roman civil processes. . . . It consequently did not apply to provincial land. . . . There thus developed, in the later Principate, *longi temporis prescriptio*, an innovation introduced by imperial enactment. . . .

In principle, *longi temporis prescriptio*, unlike the acquisitive *usucaptio*, was extinctive; that is to say, it did not give the current possessor ownership (where it was possible) of what he held; it simply prevented the person entitled from effectively asserting his claim to it. But long before Justinian, it had become no less acquisitive than *usucaptio*: if the person primarily entitled was barred from asserting himself, no one else could have effectively deprived the current holder. . . .

This development in turn produced the requirement that the possession concerned should have a *bonum initium*, a valid beginning, which would appear to be a compendious expression for the requirement of *bona fides* [good faith] and *iusta causa* [just cause] in *usucaptio*.

· · ·

Justinian in effect fused *longi temporis prescriptio* and *usucaptio*, mainly along the lines of the former. Henceforth, in respect of immovables, *longi temporis prescriptio* was exclusively applicable, the period of possession being ten or twenty years. . . . [citation omitted]"

English law

**Michael Harwood, *Modern English Land Law*
(2d ed. 1982), 505–506**

"A right of action to recover possession of land is generally extinguished 12 years from the date on which the right of action accrues.

In general, time does not begin to run until

(a) the claimant is entitled to possession, and

(b) there is someone in adverse possession (the squatter or adverse possessor).

· · ·

Whether or not there is adverse possession is a question of fact. Exclusive occupation and use of the land is generally sufficient. . . .

· · ·

If the owner does not take steps to regain possession, within the limitation period, his action is barred. It is no excuse for inaction that he does not know of the possession; or that he does not know that it is adverse. Nor is it any excuse that he has no immediate use for the land and that the possession is not inconveniencing him. . . ."

Sir Robert Megarry & H.W.R. Wade, *The Law of Real Property* (4th ed. 1975), 1014–15

"As already explained, a squatter has a title based on his own possession, and this title is good against everyone except the true owner. Accordingly, if a squatter who has not barred the true owner sells the land he can give the purchaser a right to the land which is as good as his own.

. . .

If a squatter is himself dispossessed, the second squatter can add the former period of occupation to his own as against the true owner. This is because time runs against the true owner from the time when adverse possession began. . . ."

Law in the United States

American law is generally like that of England. American courts have said that possession must be "open and notorious" and "hostile," but these requirements add little to the English requirement that it be exclusive. One difference is that American courts differ over whether the adverse possessor must have taken possession in good faith. Another is that the adverse possessor who dispossesses another adverse possessor cannot simply add together the time periods during which the owner was dispossessed. He must show he derived his claim from a grant from the previous adverse possessor.

William B. Stoebuck & Dale A. Whitman, *The Law of Property* (3d ed. 2000), 856–60

" 'Open and notorious possession' usually means possession that gives visible evidence to one on the surface of the possessed land. The purpose of this requirement is to afford the owner opportunity for notice. . . .

. . .

'Hostility' is the very marrow of adverse possession; it has even redundantly been called adversity. To say that possession is hostile should mean nothing more than that it is without permission of the one legally empowered to give possession, usually the owner. . . .

. . .

This brings us to the most difficult, thoroughly maddening, question in all adverse possession, whether an adverse possessor's subjective state of mind, imprecisely often called 'intent,' can destroy hostility. It is the view here, along with that of most decisions and of nearly all scholars, that what the possessor intends should have nothing to do with it. Yet in many decisions a variety of states of mind, too many to explore more than leading examples here, have purportedly defeated adverse possession. An extreme view is that an adverse possessor must have a 'a bona fide claim . . . that he has got a right as owner.' . . .

The final element, that adverse possession be 'continuous,' means that it must continue without significant interruption for a solid block of time at least as long as the period of limitation. . . .

An interesting question within the subject of continuity is 'tacking': the adding together of periods of possession that are continuous but by different persons. This is allowed, provided there is a sufficient nexus, often called 'privity,' between the successors. This nexus is provided if the earlier possessor gives the next one a colorable title document that describes the area possessed or if the next one is the heir of the first. To ask how it is an adverse possessor, who has not yet title, can pass anything by a deed or will is to conjure up musty questions about whether possession is the source of title or is itself vestigal title. The answers are too wonderful (not to say to lengthy) too work out here."

French law

French Civil Code

ARTICLE 2220

For prescription to occur, there must be continuous, uninterrupted and peaceable possession which is public and unequivocal and under color of right (*à titre de propriétaire*).

ARTICLE 2230

A person is always presumed to possess for himself and under color of right unless he is proven to have begun possession for another person.

ARTICLE 2231

When a person has began to possess for another, he is always presumed to possess by that authority unless proof is made to the contrary.

ARTICLE 2232

Acts which are merely permissive or acts of tolerance are not a basis either for possession or for prescription.

ARTICLE 2233

Acts of force cannot be a basis for possession which can ripen into prescription.

ARTICLE 2234

The actual possessor who proves that he was in possession in the past is presumed to have been in possession in the intervening time absent proof to the contrary.

ARTICLE 2235

To complete prescription, a person can join to his possession that of another person in such a way that he has succeeded that person, whether by a universal or a particular right, or whether by an exchange or a gratuitous transfer.

ARTICLE 2262

All actions, whether to recover property or against a person, are barred by prescription at the end of thirty years, without any requirement that the person alleging prescription show title, or that he can be attacked on the grounds of his bad faith.

German law

German Civil Code

§ 937 [PRESUMPTIONS]

(1) A person who has a moveable object in his possession for ten years acquires ownership (prescription).

(2) This prescription is excluded when the acquisition is not in good faith or when his subsequent experience shows that he was not the owner.

§ 938 [PRESUMPTION OF ONE'S OWN POSSESSION]

If someone has an object in his own possession at the beginning and the ending of a period of time, it is presumed that his possession also existed in the intervening time.

§ 943 [SUCCESSION]

If the object is obtained by succession to the possession of another person, then the period of possession of the predecessor can be counted by his successor.

§ 900 [PRESCRIPTION IN THE LAND REGISTER]

(1) One who is entered as the owner of a parcel of land entered in the land register [*Grundbuch*] but has not acquired ownership becomes the owner when the entry remains for thirty years and he has the land in his possession for this period of time.

§ 927 [PROCEDURE FOR PUBLIC NOTICE]

(1) An owner may, when his land has been in the possession of another for thirty years, assert his rights by giving public notice. The time for possession is to be determined in the same way as that for a moveable object. If an owner is listed in the land register, then the public notice is only effective if that person is dead or missing and no entry in the land registry which relates to his rights has been made for thirty years.

(2) A person who has given notice of the exclusion of the right of another acquires ownership when he is listed as owner in the land registry.

2. The protection of possession against non-possessors

a. Legal remedies

Anglo-American law

It is often said that civil law and common law take a radically different view of the relationship between ownership and possession. Supposedly, while the common law blurs these concepts, "[c]ontinental law makes a sharp distinction."[1] Anglo-American jurists—and particularly the English—say that the common law "never bothered much with the idea of ownership,"[2] "never applied the conception of ownership to land,"[3] "never really disentangled [the concept of ownership] from that of possession."[4] In the common law, supposedly, ownership or title to land is based on the fact of possession or the best right to possession.[5] Title is therefore relative. The person with possession has title against anyone who does not have a better right.[6] A "better right" is a right based on still earlier possession.[7]

That theory, as we will see, was not part of ancient common law learning but was invented by Sir Frederick Pollock in an attempt to answer a question that perplexed continental jurists: why the law protected a possessor at all. A few words need to be said about common law remedies for loss of possession to make it clear that this conception had little to do with them historically.

In the Middle Ages, a person could recover land by showing that he had "seizin" and had been "disseized" by the other party. If so, he could bring a writ of "novel disseizen." If he claimed through an ancestor who had died seized of the land, he could bring a writ of "mort d'ancestor." The closest thing to an action based on ownership was the "writ of right," but even this was an action to protect seizin since the party who prevailed was the party who could trace his claim to the earliest person to have seizin.[8] These writs, however, fell into disuse. Eventually, both an owner and a possessor recovered property by bringing the same action: an action in ejectment. The action of ejectment originally protected a lessee of land. Historically, this action happened to have procedural advantages. Consequently, both owners and possessors took advantage of it, with the

---

1. Jacob Houdyn Beekhuis, "Civil Law," in "Chapter 2 Structural Variations in Property Law," 3 at 18 in *International Encyclopedia of Comparative Law* 6 *Property and Trust* (Frederich Henry Lawson, ed. 1973).

2. Michael Harwood, *Modern English Land Law* (2nd ed. 1982), 503.

3. Edward Hector Burn, *Cheshire and Burn's Modern Law of Real Property* (16th ed. 2000), 26.

4. Robert Megarry & H.W.R. Wade, *The Law of Real Property* (5th ed. 1984), 104.

5. *See* Megarry & Wade, *Real Property* 104; Burn, *Real Property* 26; Harwood, *Land Law* 503.

6. Megarry & Wade, *Real Property* 106; Burn *Real Property* 26–27; Harwood, *Land Law* 503; K.J. Gray & P.D. Symes, *Real Property and Real People Principles of Land Law* (1981), 49; Kevin Gray, *Elements of Land Law* (1987), 65, 752–53.

7. *See* Megarry & Wade, *Real Property* 107; Harwood, *Land Law* 503.

8. A.W.B. Simpson, *A History of the Land Law* (2d ed. 1986), 38.

blessing of the courts, by alleging fictitiously that they had leased their land to someone, and that the lessee was the plaintiff.

Fifty years ago, two eminent English historians argued over whether the rise of the action of ejectment marked a change in "theory" from the older notion of seizin to an civilian-like notion of ownership and possession. Sir William Holdsworth claimed that it did.[9] A.D. Hargreaves challenged him, arguing that the concept of seizin still mattered although the English courts were losing sight of it "in a fit of absentmindedness."[10]

Neither opinion explained the English cases through the mid-19th century.[11] From the 17th century onward, English judges had said that to recover in ejectment, the plaintiff must have title. Lord Holt said so in the 17th century,[12] and Lord Mansfield in the 18th.[13] But it does not follow that Holdworth was right that the plaintiff had to prove title to recover. It was not clear, in the cases just mentioned, that either party did have title. Moreover, in a subsequent case, even though the plaintiff could not prove he had been in possession for the twenty year period necessary to obtain title, Lord Mansfield allowed the jury to infer possession for the requisite twenty years.[14] Moreover, while courts said the plaintiff must have title, they allowed him to recover if he proved forcible dispossession[15] and sometimes if he merely proved possession[16] on the grounds that he had produced evidence from which title could be inferred. If Hargreaves were right, these courts should not have mentioned title since what mattered was not title but seizin. If Holdsworth was right, they should have insisted that plaintiff actually prove title.

Instead, the courts had been reaching results pragmatically without any clear theory in mind. They might have done so indefinitely except that, in the mid-19th century, some cases finally came before them in which the plaintiff plainly did not have title. They could no longer say that his prior possession or forcible dispossession was evidence of title. They had to say either that he could not recover or that he need not have title to do so. Initially, in 1849, in *Doe dem. Carter v. Barnard*, they gave the first answer.[17] Then, in 1865, in *Asher v. Whitlock*,[18] they flip-flopped and gave the second. While *Asher* made it clear that a prior possessor without title could recover his land, that proposition is accepted by civil law systems as well. It hardly commits the common law to a distinct theory about the

9. Sir William Searle Holdsworth, *History of English Law* 7 (1926), 57–81.

10. Anthony Dalzell Hargreaves, "Terminology and Title in Ejectment," *L. Quar. Rev.* 56 (1940), 376, 398.

11. James Gordley & Ugo Mattei, "Protecting Possession," *Am. J. Comp. L.* 44 (1996), 293.

12. Stokes v. Berry, 2 Salk 421, 91 Eng. Rep. 366 (K.B. 1699) ("plaintiff recovers because the possession of twenty years shall be a good title").

13. Roe dem. Haldane & Urry v. Harvey, 4 Burr. 2484, 2487, 98 Eng. Rep. 302, 304 (K.B. 1769) ("plaintiff can not recover but on the strength of his own title").

14. Denn ex dem. Tarzwell v. Barnard, Cowp. 595, 98 Eng. Rep. 1259 (K.B. 1777).

15. Doe dem Hughes v. Dyeball, M. & M. 345, 173 Eng. Rep. 1184 (N.P. 1829); Doe dem. Humphrey v. Martin, Carr & M. 32, 174 Eng. Rep. 395 (N.P. 1841); Davison v. Gent, 1 H. & N. 744, 156 Eng. Rep. 1400 (Ex. 1857).

16. *Compare* Doe dem. Smith & Payne v. Webber, 1 Ad. & E. 119, 10 Eng. Rep. 1152 (K.B. 1834) (plaintiff recovers) *with* Doe dem. Wilkins v. Marquis of Cleveland, 9 B. & C. 864, 109 Eng. Rep. 321 (1829) (plaintiff does not recover).

17. 13 Q.B. 945, 116 E.R. 1524 (1849).

18. L.R. 1 Q.B. 1 (1865).

relationship of ownership and possession. Even if it had, theory would have emerged only in 1865.

Continental law

Following Roman law, civil law systems have traditionally distinguished between two kinds of remedies. One can be brought by an owner to reclaim his property. The Romans called this action a *vindicatio*. Other actions to protect possession. Roman law granted what were called possessory interdicts. A possessor could bring the interdict *unde vi* to recover land. He could bring the interdict *uti possedetis* if he had not lost possession of the land but his possession was threatened or disturbed. He could bring the interdict *utrubi* to recover or protect the possession of moveable property. During and after the Middle Ages, these Roman remedies were supplemented, and sometimes displaced, by one developed in Canon law which the secular courts adopted and preserved even in protestant countries. The remedy was called the *actio spolii*. It provided that one who had been dispossessed by another must have his possession restored before the question of who had title to the property in question could be raised.[19]

Remedies for possession such as these appear in a simpler form in modern codes.

French law

French Civil Code

ARTICLE 2282

Possession is protected without regard to whether it is based on right against disturbance which threatens or menaces it.

ARTICLE 2283

Possessory actions are available according on the terms provided by the Code of Civil Procedure to those who possess or peacefully detain property.

German law

German Civil Code

§ 861 [CLAIM FOR THE LOSS OF POSSESSION]

(1) If the possessor loses possession by the unlawful force of another then he can claim restoration of possession from the person who has a possession which is defective by comparison with his own.

§ 862 [CLAIM FOR THE DISTURBANCE OF POSSESSION]

(1) If the possession of the possessor is disturbed by the unlawful force of another, he can demand that this person cease the disturbance. If further disturbance is to be feared, he can have an action against it.

---

19. Gratian, *Decretum* C. 3, q. 1, c. 3.

b. The debate over why possession should be protected

Savigny

Friedrich Karl von Savigny, *Das Recht des Besitzes Eine Zivilistische Abhandlung* (7th ed., repr. Wien 1865, repr. Aalen 1990), § 6

"[T]o what class of rights does possession belong? [Savigny explains that he does not mean possession that gives rise to title but possession which is protected by the possessory interdicts.] This question can be answered perfectly well without getting into the classification of all of private law which would necessarily interrupt the course of our inquiry. One can see that possession belongs to the law of obligations [a civil law category including contract and tort], a concept which can be taken to be fully defined by Roman law. When one divides the law that concerns what belongs to a person [*Vermögensrecht*] into the law of property and the law of obligations, then it is evident in itself that possession must be separated from the law of property. Anyone who rejects this division must make a special classification in which he can place possession.

Since the right of the possessory interdicts belongs to the law of obligations, it follows that this principle must apply to all of these interdicts. To be merely more precise, they must be obligations *ex maleficiis* [obligations that arise from wrongdoing]. . . .

If the basis of the possessory interdicts is an obligation *ex maleficiis*, why are they not classified as such in Roman law? The reason is simply that the Romans developed their classifications on procedural grounds.

. . .

To us, possession appears principally as a purely factual dominion over a thing, and so as something that is not a right (as distinguished from a violation of right), that is, as something which is legally indifferent. Consequently, it is protected against various injuries, and this protection is given by various rules governing the gain and loss of possession, just as though it were a right. The task is to state the basis for this protection by which it is treated like a right. This basis lies in the link between every factual situation regarding the person in possession and the immunity from injury which covers him against injuries that may pertain to a person. To be specific, the person must simply be secure against all exercise of force. When force is used, that is itself unlawful. This unlawfulness can take different forms. We can consider the two extreme cases. In one, the force is brought to bear on the person, and nothing outside him. In the second, the force is brought to bear on a right belonging to the person, for example, on an object that is his property. . . . In the middle, between these two extremes, the force inflicted on a person disturbs or deprives him of possession. In this case, an independent right belonging to the person is not injured but the condition of the person is nevertheless altered to his disadvantage, and so the unlawfulness, which consists in the application of force to this person, must have its consequences completely eliminated. That can only be done by the production or protection of the factual situation to which force has been applied. That is the true basis for the possessory actions. . . ."

Ihering

Rudolf Jhering, *Ueber den Grund des Besitzschutzes* (2nd ed. 1869), 45–46, 54–55

"I come now to my own position. I can summarize it in the principle: the protection of possession as the actuality of ownership is a necessary completion and supplement to the protection of ownership, an easing of the burden of proof in favor of the owner, which, however, will necessarily be of benefit to a non-owner.

The thought that possession is bound up with ownership is not a new one. It is 'the exercise of ownership,' 'presumptive possible initiation of ownership,' 'in constant relationship with ownership' [citations omitted], and even Savigny, as little as he shared this view, nevertheless saw that it had a certain truth. . . . But the way in which writers have tried to explain this connection is, in my judgment, unsatisfactory, and in what follows I will strike a new course.

. . .

The concept of the protection of possession developed here regards possession as dependant on ownership, as an outwork of ownership. It is not valued for itself but for the sake of ownership.

. . .

To want ownership is therefore to want the protection of possession. But one cannot provide it to the owner without allowing the non-owner to participate. For once one no longer relaxes a genuine requirement of proof of ownership and allows a showing of the exercise of ownership, then the relaxation of the proof required, then the benefit is reaped by anyone who can take advantage of this presumption. Possession thus acquires an identity and independence with regard to property which makes it possible, not only that property is served, but that it is disserved. The same advantage that possession provides to the owner who is in possession, so that he can more easily protect himself against the attack of others, is likewise provided to the non-owner who is in possession and denied to the owner who is not in possession.

. . .

The defense of this viewpoint is that the relationship to the purpose of possession to me leads to unpleasant but unavoidable consequences: that there is a price that the law must pay in order to provide the owner with the easier protection of his ownership which he is granted."

Pollock

Sir Frederick Pollock, *A First Book of Jurisprudence for Students of the Common Law* (6th ed. 1829), 184–86, 192–93

"Possession and use being the common outward signs of ownership, it is reasonable to presume, in the absence of proof to the contrary, that existing peaceable possession is rightful, and further to infer ownership from the right to possess which we have thus presumed. Hence we treat the actual possessor not only as legal possessor but as owner, as against everyone who cannot show a better right. As English lawyers say concerning interests in land, possession is *prima facie* evidence of seizin *in fee*: that is, not of legal possession or seizin alone, but of seizin coupled with the largest powers of use and disposal allowed by law. Then, if we regard the possessor as rightfully in control, we must allow him the powers of an owner within the limits of his apparent right. Not only his acts of use and occupation but his acts of disposal must be valid against everyone who cannot make out a superior claim. And when the superior claim, if any such there be, ceases to be available, the rights founded on possession will be indistinguishable from the rights of ownership. . . . We have come, then, to distinctly recognising possession as an origin of ownership, a 'commencement of title' as our law calls it. Again, we see that not only have we thus to recognise it, but a system of law can get on without recognising any other origin. Continuous possession is quite capable of being, not merely a possible foundation of ownership, but its only foundation and evidence. . . .

. . .

Further historical and comparative details would be out of place here. Perhaps we have been too much tempted in that direction already. But it may be worth remarking in general terms that relations of ownership in Roman and English law, the difficulties arising out of them, and the devices for obviating these difficulties, offer an amount of resemblance in detail which is much more striking than the superficial and technical differences. We cannot doubt that these resemblances depend on the nature of the problems to be solved and not on any accidental connection. One system of law may have imitated another in particular doctrines and institutions, but imitation cannot find place in processes extending over two or three centuries, and whose fundamental analogies are externally disguised in almost every possible way."

II. OWNERSHIP

1. Rights to natural resources

a. Resources of value in their own right, and not merely complementary to the use of property: the case of minerals and gas

In German law, one needs a permit from the state to prospect (*Erlaubnis*) or to exploit a mineral discovery (*Bewilligung*). He can obtain one even if he is not the owner of the land on which the minerals are located.[1] The owner of that land can grant him a right of exploitation but if he refuses, the person with the permit to exploit them can compel such

---

1. Bundesberggesetz §§ 11–13.

a right to be granted although the owner is then entitled to damages.[2] Jürgen Baur calls this law a form of expropriation that can be required when it serves the public interest.[3] It might be more accurate to say that the former proprietor owns the land without which the minerals cannot be exploited and the state owns the minerals. Thus it is less an expropriation that a means of settling conflicting land rights in favor of the person whose interest is of greater value. It is like accession in which one who paints on another's canvas can keep the painting but must pay compensation for the canvas.

French law is similar. Minerals such as coal, iron, salt, gold, silver, petroleum and natural gas belong to the state, not to the surface owner. The state grants a concession for their exploitation.[4] The holder of the concession must pay the surface owner an annual sum which reflects his interference with the surface owner's use of his land.[5] The courts have held that he is also liable for any damage he causes to the surface owner's property whether he is at fault or not.[6]

English law is much the same. Traditionally, the crown had the right to deposits of gold and silver.[7] Now, coal,[8] oil and natural gas[9] also belong to the state.[10] The state grants licenses to search for and extract such minerals for whatever consideration it sees fit. The land owner is entitled to compensation for whatever ancillary rights are necessary for their exploitation.[11]

The exception is the United States in which, in principle, minerals belong to the owner of the land. Perhaps the explanation lies in the peculiarities of the settlement of the American continent in which it was thought desirable to encourage a small population to exploit an abundance of resources as quickly as possible. Perhaps it lies in a traditional American prejudice against an active role for the state, of which more will be said later.

b. Resources complementary to the use of property: water rights

Anglo-American law

The Traditional Rules

Before the 19th century, English law did not have a clear rule governing a person's right to divert water. His prior use affected his rights but it is not clear how and to what extent. Sometimes plaintiffs won without pleading a prescriptive right or that memory runs not to the contrary. They won

---

2. *Id*. §§ 77 ff.

3. Jürgen Baur, *Sachenrecht* (17th ed. 1999), § 30 II.

4. Decree no. 80-204 of 11 March 1980.

5. *Code minier*, 16 Aug. 1956, as modified by Law of 16 June 1977, art. 37.

6. Gérard Cornu, *Droit civil Introduction Les personnes Les Biens* (4th ed. 1990), no. 1520.

7. Case of Mines, (1568), 1 Plowd. 310, 336, 75 E.R. 472, 510.

8. Coal Industry Act 1994 ss 1(1), 7(3).

9. Petroleum Act 1998 ss 1(a), 2(1).

10. *See generally* Kevin Gray & Susan Francis Gray, *Elements of Land Law* (3d ed. 2001), 21–22.

11. Mines (Working and Facilities and Support) Act 1966 s. 8.

by pleading that they had a mill *ab antiquo*,[1] or the water's former course was *antiquus*[2] or it then flowed "customarily and as it ought" (*consuevisset et debuisset*).[3] Some judges said such words amount to a claim of use from "time immemorial,"[4] and some said that they did not.[5] In any event, the plaintiff won without pleading or proving that his mill had stood immemorially or any particular length of time. The jury was left to decide whether the mill was "ancient" or the water had been flowing "customarily and as it ought." Carol Rose believes these expressions meant that the plaintiff's use must have "been in place for a generation or so."[6] She notes, however, that "ancient" may have meant "something akin to 'former' or 'earlier.'"[7] Indeed, 17th and 18th century authors used the word "ancient" sometimes to refer to the distant past and sometimes to mean "former."[8] Since the final decision was up to the jury, all one can say is that the longer the mill had stood, the greater must have been the plaintiff's confidence that he would win.

Moreover, some plaintiffs won, or courts said that they might, even if their mills were newly erected. Sometimes they won alleging that the watercourse, though not the mill, was ancient, and so gained a considerable advantage, since most watercourses fit that description. But it was not clear that this allegation was necessary.[9] Indeed, in one 17th century case, the plaintiff won despite defendant's objection that he alleged neither the mill nor the watercourse to be ancient.[10] In another, he won without the defendant raising the point.[11] In yet another case, Matthew Hale said by way of dictum that one need not plead one's mill was ancient; one can win if it was newly erected.[12]

Had the law clearly been as Hale thought, then a plaintiff with an older mill would not have bothered to plead that it was "ancient." The plaintiffs who did so must have thought the law was not so clear. Again, they were putting their best foot forward. Plaintiffs with younger mills must have been facing a risk. They could plead their mill was "ancient" and hope the jury would agree, or not do so, and hope that the court would think it did not matter.[13]

1. Russell and Handfords Case, 1 Leo. 273, 74 E.R. 248 (K.B. 1583).

2. Richards v. Hill, 5 Mod. 206, 87 E.R. 611 (K.B. 1695).

3. Anonymous, Cro. Car. 449, 79 E.R. 1031 (K.B. 1638).

4. Tenant v. Goldwin, 2 Raym. Ld.1089, 1094, 92 E.R. 222, 225 (1705).

5. Palmer v. Keeblethwaite, 1 Shower, K.B. 64, 64, 89 E.R. 451, 451 (K.B. 1686).

6. Carol M. Rose, *Property and Persuasion Essays on the History, Theory, and Rhetoric of Ownership* (1994), 169.

7. *Id*. 169 n. 20.

8. For examples, see *Oxford English Dictionary* (1971), v. "ancient" A I 1, A I 2.

9. *Compare* Le Countee de Rutland v. Bowles, Palm. 290, 81 E.R. 1087 (K.B. 1622), where the court did not seem to attach importance to that allegation, *with* Keeblethwait v. Palmes, Comb. 9, 90 E.R. 311 (K.B. 1686), where the point was stressed by

counsel, and it is not clear what the court thought.

10. Sands v. Trefuses, Cro. Car. 575, 79 E.R. 1094 (K.B. 1639).

11. Glyn v. Nichols, Comb. 44, 90 E.R. 333 (K.B. 1687).

12. Cox v. Matthew, 1 Vent. 237 (K.B. 1673). Hale said the result would be different if the defendant "used to turn the stream as he saw cause." It is hard to read that passage as Maass and Zobel do, to mean that priority alone doesn't matter. Arthur Maass & Hiller B. Zobel, "Anglo-American Water Law: Who Appropriated the Riparian Doctrine?" in C.J. Friedrich & S.E. Harris, *Public Policy A Yearbook of the Graduate School of Public Administration, Harvard University* 10 (1960), 109 at 127.

13. Thus, unlike Lauer, I don't think one can describe the case law in terms of direction and development. Lauer, "Common Law Background" 81–96.

The Duel in the Early 19th Century

In the early 19th century, both English and American jurists struggled to decide which of two rules should govern water rights. One rule respected prior appropriation. Whoever first put water to a beneficial use could continue to do so, even if this right diminished that of other proprietors to use the same amount of water later on. The second rule treated all proprietors equally, whenever they began using water. None of them had a right to use more water simply because he began using it first, unless he could show that other proprietors had granted him this right, or that he had used it so long that it became his by prescription. This second rule eventually won out but only after a contest.

Prior appropriation: the rule that lost

William Blackstone, *Commentaries on the Laws of England* 2 (London, 1766), 403

"If a stream be unoccupied, I may erect a mill thereon, and detain the water; yet not so as to injure my neighbour's prior mill, or his meadow: for he hath by the first occupancy acquired a property in the current."

Williams v. Morland, 2 B. & C. 910, 107 Eng. Rep. 620 (K.B. 1824)

[The plaintiff claimed that he owned land along a stream, and that the defendant had erected a dam higher up along the stream and diverted the water from running in its usual course.]

Bayley J. "My judgment in this case is founded on the nature of flowing water, and the manner in which an exclusive right to it is obtained. Flowing water is originally *publici iuris*. So soon as it is appropriated by an individual, his right is coextensive with the beneficial use to which he appropriates it. Subject to that right all the rest of the water remains *publici iuris*. The party who obtains a right to the exclusive enjoyment of the water does so in derogation of the primitive right of the public." [Plaintiff was denied recovery on the grounds that he had not yet appropriated water to a beneficial use but was merely objecting to its usual flow.]

Carey v. Daniels, 49 Mass. (8 Met.) 466 (1844)

[Plaintiff claimed that he owned two acres of land along the Charles River with a water mill, and that the defendant had then built a dam across the river below the plaintiff's mill which raised the water above its usual height. As a result, the water flowed back against plaintiff's mill wheel, obstructing its operation.]

Shaw C.J. "[E]ach proprietor is entitled to such use of the stream, so far as it is reasonable, conformable to the usages and wants of the community, and having regard to the progress of improvement in hydraulic works, and not inconsistent with a like reasonable use by the other proprietors of land, on the same stream, above and below. This last limitation of the right must be taken with one qualification, growing out of the nature of the case. The usefulness of water for mill purposes depends as well on its fall as its volume. But the fall depends upon the grade of the land over which it runs. The descent may be rapid, in which case there may be fall enough for mill sites at short distances; or the descent may be so gradual as only to admit of mills at considerable distances. In the latter case, the erection of a mill on one proprietor's land may raise and set the water back to such a distance as to prevent the proprietor above from having sufficient fall to erect a mill on his land. It seems to follow, as a necessary consequence from these principles, that in such case, the proprietor who first erects his dam for such a purpose has a right to maintain it, as against the proprietors above and below; and to this extent, prior occupancy gives a prior title to such use. It is a profitable, beneficial, and reasonable use, and therefore one which he has a right to make. If it necessarily occupy so much of the fall as to prevent the proprietor above from placing a dam and mill on his land, it is damnum absque injuria. . . . It is, in this respect, like the right in common, which any individual has, to use a highway; whilst one is reasonably exercising his own right, by a temporary occupation of a particular part of the street with his carriage or team, another cannot occupy the same place at the same time."

Equal rights and reasonable use: the rule that won

Tyler v. Wilkinson, 24 Fed. Cas. 472 (case no. 14312)

[Plaintiff complained that he owned a mill and that defendant had subsequently built one upstream that interfered with the operation of his own.]

Story J. "Prima facie every proprietor upon each bank of a river is entitled to the land, covered with water, in front of his bank, to the middle thread of the stream, or, as it is commonly expressed, usque ad filum aquae. In virtue of this ownership he has a right to the use of the water flowing over it in its natural current, without diminution or obstruction. But, strictly speaking, he has no property in the water itself; but a simple use of it, while it passes along. The consequence of this principle is, that no proprietor has a right to use the water to the prejudice of another. It is wholly immaterial, whether the party be a proprietor above or below, in the course of the river; the right being common to all the proprietors on the river, no one has a right to diminish the quantity which will, according to the natural current, flow to a proprietor below, or to throw it back upon a proprietor above. This is the necessary result of the perfect equality of right among all the proprietors of that, which is common to all. The natural stream, existing by the bounty of Providence for the benefit of the land through which it flows, is an incident annexed, by operation of law, to the land itself. When I speak of this common right, I do not mean to be understood, as holding the doctrine, that there can be no diminution whatsoever, and no obstruction or impediment whatsoever, by a riparian proprietor, in the use of the water as it flows; for that would be to deny any valuable use of it. There may be, and there must be allowed of that, which is common to all, a reasonable use. The true test of the principle and extent of the use is, whether it is to the injury of the other proprietors or not. There may be a diminution in quantity, or a retardation or acceleration of the natural current indispensable for the general and valuable use of the water, perfectly consistent with the existence of the common right. The diminution, retardation, or acceleration, not positively and sensibly injurious by diminishing the value of the common right, is an implied element in the right of using the stream at all. The law here, as in many other cases, acts with a reasonable reference to public convenience and general good, and it is not betrayed into a narrow strictness, subversive of common sense, nor into an extravagant looseness, which would destroy private rights. The maxim is applied, 'Sic utere tuo, ut non alienum laedas.'

But of a thing, common by nature, there may be an appropriation by general consent or grant. Mere priority of appropriation of running water, without such consent or grant, confers no exclusive right. It is not like the case of mere occupancy, where the first occupant takes by force of his priority of occupancy. That supposes no ownership already existing, and no right to the use already acquired."

Mason v. Hill, 3 Barn. & Adl. 304, 110 Eng. Rep. 114 (K.B. 1833)

[The plaintiff had erected a dam upstream which prevented the water from flowing "along its usual and proper course" and now interfered with the operation of the plaintiff's mill.]

Lord Tenterden C.J. "[F]or the defendants it was insisted that, they having first appropriated the water beneficially to their use at a time when the appropriation was not injurious to the plaintiff, had a right to the water and to the use of it, notwithstanding the diversion had become by subsequent acts of the plaintiff injurious to him. The plaintiff, on the other hand, insisted that the defendants did not, nor could not by law, acquire the right to the water by a diversion or enjoyment for a period of short of twenty years [the time required to acquire a right by prescription]. . . . [The decision of a similar case in Wright v. Howard, 1 Stim. & Stu. 190] is expressed in language so perspicuous and comprehensive that I shall here quote it. 'The right to the use of water rests on clear and settled principles. . . . Every proprietor has an equal right to use the water that flows in the stream; and consequently no proprietor can have the right to use the water to the prejudice of any other proprietor. Without the consent of the other proprietors, who may be affected by his operations, no proprietor can either diminish the quantity of water which would otherwise descend to the proprietors below, nor throw the water back on the proprietors above. Every proprietor who claims a right either to throw the water back above, or to diminish the quantity of water which is to descend below, must, in order to maintain his claim, either prove an actual grant or license from the proprietors affected by his operations, or must prove an uninterrupted enjoyment of twenty years. . . .'

We all agree in the judgment thus delivered. . . ."

Note: As we have seen, Shaw fought a rearguard action in Massachusetts for a rule of prior appropriation. In light of English authority, and authority in other states, he finally surrendered.

Thurber v. Martin, 68 Mass. (2 Gray) 394 (1854)

[The plaintiff produced evidence tending to show that the mill owned and occupied by him was erected fifty or sixty years before any mill was built on the site owned by the defendant, and that it had ever since been in constant use, as far as the supply of water in the stream enabled the successive owners to use it. He claimed that by such use, for such length of time, he acquired an absolute right to have the waters of the stream come to his mill according to their natural flow, without any interruption or disturbance whatever by the defendant in the working and operation of his mill; and requested the presiding judge so to instruct the jury.

But the judge declined to do so, and instead instructed them "that priority of use at any particular point upon a stream, however long continued, could never deprive the owner of lands bounded on the stream, at any point above the millpond of the first occupant, of the right to have and enjoy a similar use of the water as it passed by his lands; . . . but that he was bound to use the water in such way and manner that every riparian proprietor, at points further down the stream, would have the enjoyment and use of it substantially according to its natural flow. . . ."]

Shaw J. "The court are of opinion that the law was rightly stated by the judge at the trial; that it was laid down with fullness and accuracy, and with proper qualifications. Every man has a right to the reasonable use and enjoyment of a current of running water, as it flows through or along his own land, for mill purposes, having a due regard to the like reasonable use of the stream by all other proprietors above and below him. In determining what is such reasonable use, a just regard must be had to the force and magnitude of the current, its height and velocity, the state of improvement in the country in regard to mills and machinery, and the use of water as a propelling power, the general usage of the country in similar cases, and all other circumstances bearing upon the question of fitness and propriety in the use of the water in the particular case. If any party claims a special right to the use of the water, more beneficial to himself, and more burdensome to the riparian proprietors above or below, than what may be called the natural or general right to the reasonable use of the stream, he must establish such right by grant or prescription."

Note: The rule that won is sometimes called the "reasonable use" doctrine. In principle, all owners are entitled to make a reasonable use of the water, regardless of who used it first. What is a reasonable use can be unclear.

Restatement (Second) of Torts

§ 850A (1979)

Reasonable depends on "consideration of the interests of the riparian proprietor making the use, of any riparian proprietor harmed by it and of society as a whole." Factors affecting reasonableness include: "(a) [t]he purpose of the use, (b) the suitability of the use to the watershed or lake, (c) the economic value of the use, (d) the social value of the use, (e) the extent and amount of harm it causes, (f) the practicality of avoiding the harm by adjusting the use or the method or use of one proprietor or the other, (g) the practicality of adjusting the quantity of water used by each proprietor, (h) the protection of existing values of water uses, land, investments and enterprises, and (i) the justice of requiring the user causing harm to bear the loss."

Note: The "Restatements" are attempts by a private organization, the American Law Institute, to state the American common law in the form of a series of rules like those of a code. They have no official status. They are neither case law nor legislation nor do they have a government endorsement. Nevertheless, they have great prestige and often receive deference from American courts, in part because each Restatement is approved by a highly qualified body of academics, judges, and practitioners.

What rule really won?

Law in the United States

For the most part, western American states have rejected the common law rule of apportioning water among each owner as long as each makes a "reasonable use" of it. The eight most arid states (Arizona, Colorado, Idaho, Montana, Nevada, New Mexico, Utah, and Wyoming) repudiated this doctrine very early and entirely.[1] They adopted a prior appropriation system in which the right to use water belongs to the first to put the water to a beneficial use. In most of these states, water rights can then be transferred to another person.[2]

While most states in the east have retained the reasonable use doctrine, sixteen have modified it by enacting permit systems.[3] Typically, a permit must be granted for all pre-existing uses. A pre-existing use is a vested right, and it cannot be taken without compensation.[4] In some states, permits are granted in perpetuity; in others, for terms deemed to be sufficiently long to allow the holder to recoup his investment.[5]

Even with such rules in place, however, some courts have protected the mill which was disturbed by the latecomer. The latecomer has been told that party who first built a mill was entitled to have the water flow in its accustomed manner.[6] Or he has been told that he diverted too much because the water was needed by the old mill.[7] In one case, he was told he could not divert water from a mill for steam locomotives, because different rules applied when he was not merely diverting water but taking it away.[8] When a salt company diverted water from a mill, the court said that its use was not "reasonable." What struck the court as unreasonable was that to allow the diversion when a party came "long afterward and with knowledge of the facts established its plant . . . would amount to a virtual confiscation of the property of small owners in the interest of a strong combination of capital."[9] In all of these cases, though the court claimed to be applying riparian rights doctrine, it protected the prior user.

1. David H. Getches, *Water Law* (1984), 85.

2. Richard R. Powell & Michael Allan Wolf, *Powell on Real Property* (2000), § 65.07[7].

3. *Powell on Real Property* § 65.09[3][c].

4. William Goldfarb, *Water Law* (2d ed. 1988), 26, 27–28.

5. *Id.* 28–29.

6. Mason v. Whitney, 78 N.E. 881 (Mass. 1906)(dicta); Cox v. Howell, 65 S.W. 868 (Tenn. 1901); Woodin v. Wentworth, 23 N.W. 813 (Mich. 1885); Thunder Bay River Booming Company v. Speechly, 31 Mich. 336 (1875); Harding v. The Stamford Water Company, 41 Conn. 87 (1874); Burden v. Stein, 27 Ala. 104 (1855); Parker v. Griswold, 17 Conn. 288, 300 (1845); King v. Tiffany, 9 Conn. 162 (1832); M'Calmont against Whitaker, 3 Rawle 84 (Pa. 1831).

7. Timm v. Bear, 29 Wis. 254, 268 (1871).

8. Garwood v. N.Y. Central & Hudson R. R.R. Co., 83 N.Y. 400 (1881).

9. Strobel v. The Kerr Salt Company, 58 N.E. 142 (N.Y. 1900).

English law

English riparian rights law has largely been replaced by a statutory scheme initially enacted by the Water Resources Law of 1991. Under the Law, a person who abstracts water or obstructs its flow must have a license[1] unless he owns contiguous land and takes less than twenty cubic meters a day for domestic or agricultural purposes other than spray irrigation.[2] The license specifies the quantity of water[3] and purposes for which it may be used.[4] Anyone with land next to a watercourse, or a right of access to the water, can apply for a license.[5] The National Rivers Authority can then grant it on such terms as it deems appropriate.[6] Nevertheless, it may not grant a license which derogates from a "protected right."[7] "Protected rights" are those to take up to twenty cubic meters a day for domestic or agricultural purposes[8] and those of people already holding licenses.[9] If the Authority derogates from a "protected right," it is liable in damages for breach of statutory duty.[10] The Authority can modify or revoke a license.[11] If it does so, however, the Authority must pay compensation if the license holder:

(a) has incurred expenditure in carrying out work which is rendered abortive by the revocation or variation; or

(b) has otherwise sustained loss or damage which is directly attributable to the revocation or variation. . . ." [12]

French law

Antoine D'Espeisses, *Traicté de l'ordre iudiciare observé ez causes civiles* tit. v, art. 3, sec. ix, no. 6, in *Les Oeuvres de M. Antoine D'Espeisses* 3 (Lyon, 1677)

"One who has a mill cannot prevent another person from building one in a lower place provided that he does not hinder the flow of the water or cause damage directly to the first mill. That is so even though the income of the first mill may be diminished. . . . For it is permitted to each person to improve his own condition event to the detriment of that of another provided he does him no wrong."

Note: The drafters of the French Civil Code drew heavily on the work of the 17th century jurist Jean Domat and the 18th century jurist Robert Pothier. Neither of them mentioned the rule just quoted. Neither of them discussed water rights in their works on private law. Domat did so in a work on public law. This passage dealt with the right of state officials to regulate navigable rivers.

---

1. Water Resources Act, 1991 c. 57 §§ 24–45.
2. *Id.* § 27(3)–(4).
3. *Id.* § 46(2).
4. *Id.* § 46(4).
5. *Id.* § 35(2).
6. *Id.* § 38.
7. *Id.* § 39(1).
8. *Id.* §§ 39(3), 27(6).
9. *Id.* §§ 39(3), 48(1).
10. *Id.* § 60(2).
11. *Id.* §§ 52–54.
12. *Id.* § 61(1).

Jean Domat, *Loix civiles dans leur ordre naturel: Le Droit public liv.* i, tit. viii, sec. ii, § 11 (nouv. ed., Paris, 1713)

"[A]lthough one can divert water from a stream or river to water one's meadows or other land, or for mills or other uses, he must use that freedom in such a way that he does no harm either to the navigation in the river whose water he diverts, or in another that is made navigable by the water of the first, or to some other public use, or to neighbors who have a similar need and a like right. And if there is not enough water for all, or if the use that some make of it is injurious to others, all will be provided for, according to need, by the officers who have that responsibility."

Note: Without discussion, so far one can tell from the drafting history, the drafters adopted a similar provision to govern private law, one which conferred on private law judges a discretionary power like that of royal officials enjoyed in regulating navigable waters. It is a power which, as French scholars have noted,[1] is unparalleled elsewhere in the Code.

French Civil Code

ARTICLE 644

A person whose property lies alongside flowing water, other than one which belongs to the public domain according to article 538 on the distinction of goods, may use the water for the irrigation of his land.

A person whose land is crossed by this water can use it while it is there but must return it to its ordinary course when it leaves his property.

ARTICLE 645

If there is a dispute among owners to whom this water may be useful, the courts, in resolving the dispute, must reconcile the interest in agriculture with the respect due to ownership, and, in any event, local and particular rules on the flow and use of the water must be observed.

Note on the Code provisions and prior use. As in the United States, French courts have refused to allow latecomers to build dams which impaired the flow of water to a prior user's mill. They have said that the prior user has the right to have the water flow according to its "natural course and level" (*son cours et son niveau naturel*)[2] or "ordinary course" (*cours ordinaire*).[3]

Consider, in reading the following cases, the extent to which courts have paid attention to who was the prior user despite the provisions of the Code.

Cour d'appel, Rennes, 15 Feb. 1980, D.S. 1983.I.R.13

"The use of water constitutes a quasi-possession which can give rise to a possessory action on the part of the person with land along a river who uses the water within the limits of the right conferred on him by art. 644 of the Civil Code. The terms of that article are declarative of the right

1. Alex Weill, François Terré & Philippe Simler, *Droit civil Les Biens* (3rd ed. 1985), no. 224.

2. Cass., ch. civ., 15 Feb. 1860, D. 1860.1.347.

3. Cass., 3e ch. civ., 12 Oct. 1978, D.S. 1979.I.R.58.

and not a limitation on it, and so allow a principle to be applied not only to irrigation but to other agricultural uses which include the watering of flocks, as well as domestic and industrial uses. . . .

In particular, by placing a pipe with a diameter of 48 cm and a length of 48 meters on the bed of a river, which would operate whatever the height of the water, the defendant was not able to restore the previous level to the fields of the downstream owner. The defendant thereby diminished the volume of water available to him without employing any lawful means."

Cour de cassation, 3e ch. civ., 14 October 1980, D.S. 1981.IR.511

[Downstream owners brought suit when a laundry was started upstream which diverted their water. They recovered below.] "The . . . *Cour d'appel* correctly determined that having done the work in common of constructing water courses, various owners who enjoyed the right to use the water, adding that the establishment of an industrial enterprise was not a dominant estate in relation to the properties along the river and others having the right to take water from it."

German law

In Germany, the permit (*Bewilligung*)[1] entitles a person to use a certain amount of water for a certain purpose.[2] A permit is not necessary if the water can be used without an essential reduction of the flow.[3] If the grant of a permit will adversely affect the right of another, and there is no way to avoid the adverse effect, then the permit can still be granted "on the grounds of the general welfare" but the person who loses his right to water must be compensated.[4] The federal statute does not say who is to make compensation, but the laws of many German federal states provide that it is the person benefitted.[5] The statutes of most German federal states also provide that once a permit has been granted, the right to use water is to be protected in the same way as a property right under the German Civil Code.[6] Consequently, a person who interferes with such a right will be ordered to desist and be held liable for damages in tort.[7]

2. Interference with neighboring property

a. Origins

In the continental tradition, the problem common lawyers call "nuisance" was dealt with for centuries by interpreting a small number of Roman texts. Here are the most important:

> Aristo states in an opinion given to Cerellius Vitalis that he does not think that smoke can lawfully be discharged from a cheese shop onto

---

1. Gesetz zur Ordnung des Wasserhaushalts in der Fassung der Bekanntmachung vom 12. November 1996 (BGBl. I S. 1696) (*Wasserhaushaltsgesetz* or WHG). § 2. Alternatively, he can obtain "permission" to use the water (*Erlaubnis*) but then his use is less completely protected.

2. *Id.* § 8(1).

3. *Id.* § 24(1).

4. *Id.* § 8(3).

5. Paul Gieseke, Werner Wiedemann & Manfred Czychowski, *Wasserhaushaltsgesetz Kommentar* (6th ed. 1992), to § 20 no. 12.

6. *Id.* to § 8 no. 7.

7. *Id.* no. 8.

the buildings above it, unless they are subject to a servitude to this effect, and this is admitted. He also holds that it is not permissible to discharge water or any other substance from the upper onto the lower property, as a man is only permitted to carry out operations on his own premises to this extent, that he discharge nothing onto those of another; and he adds that one can discharge smoke just as well as water. Thus, the owner of the upper property can bring an action against the owner of the lower, asserting that the latter does not have the right to act in this way. (Dig. 8.5.8.5.)

A doubt is raised by Pomponius in the forty-first book of his *Readings*, as to whether a man can bring an action alleging that he has a right or that another has no right to create a moderate amount of smoke on his own premises, for example, smoke from a hearth. He says that the better opinion is that such an action cannot be brought, just as an action cannot be brought to maintain that one has a right to light a fire or sit or wash on one's own land. (Dig. 8.5.8.6.)

If the owner of the lower premises creates smoke to fumigate those of his neighbor above, or if the owner of the upper premises throws or pours anything on to those below, Labeo says that the action for *iniuria* does not lie. I think this wrong, if it were done with the intention to offend. (Dig. 47.10.44.)

The medieval jurists were not sure what to make of these texts. They readily agreed that an action would lie for interference such as smoke and water that were intended to injure another: that was the meaning of Dig. 47.10.44. They were less sure what to do when such an intention was absent. If bothering the upstairs neighbor with smoke was really like bothering the downstairs neighbor with water, what was the difference between smoke from a hearth and smoke from a cheese shop? The 13th century jurist Accursius who wrote the *Ordinary Gloss* to the *Corpus iuris civilis* failed to see how to distinguish smoke from smoke.[1]

Other medieval jurists developed three different solutions which were repeated by others long after the Middle Ages. Accursius' contemporary Odofredus said that one cannot use one's land in a way that bothers others.[2] The same solution eventually was given by Blackstone although the Latin phrase was bit different: "sic utere tuo ut neminem laedere" ("use what is yours so as not to injure another").[3] That maxim has been repeated countless times by common law judges. Critics claim it is meaningless. Everything

---

1. He said that smoke was different from water because "smoke naturally disperses." But that did not distinguish the smoke from the hearth and the cheese shop. He concluded that the text about the cheese shop could not mean what it said. Instead, "the person with the upper premises is required to bear the smoke, and on that account not to have windows." *Glossa ordinaria* to Dig. 8.5.8.5 to *de iure*. As his critic Iacobus de Ravanis noted

pointed out, the text about the cheese shop "says the complete opposite of what the *Gloss* says." (His opinion is described by Albericus de Rosate Bergamensis, *In primam ff. veter. part. Commentarii* to Dig. 8.5.8.5 no. 5 (1585).

2. *Lectura super digesto veteri* to Dig. 8.5.8.5 (1550) ("unusquisque debet facere in suo quod non officiat alieno").

3. William Blackstone, *Commentaries on the Law of England* 2 (1979), *306.

that bothers another person is not actionable, and the maxim does not tell us which uses should be.

Later in the 13th century, Iacobus de Ravanis said that one cannot discharge anything onto another's property that disturbs the owner. He was picking up on Aristo's remark that one must "discharge nothing onto [the premises] of another." His solution was repeated by the great 14th century jurist Baldus de Ubaldis and eventually by many others.[4] But it did not explain why the owner of the hearth was allowed to discharge smoke on his neighbor's property.

Still another explanation was given of Bartolus of Saxoferato, who may have been the greatest medieval jurist. Here is his commentary to Dig. 8.5.8.5:

> The owner of the lower premises cannot discharge smoke into the upper premises by the law of servitudes, and the owner of the upper premises cannot discharge water into the lower unless there is an agreement to the contrary, and for these interferences they can bring actions and the possessory interdicts [Roman actions available to one whose possession has been disturbed]. It may be objected that one is permitted to make a fire in his own premises, and one is not bound if the smoke ascends to those of another unless that happens with an intention to offend. Dig. 8.5.8.5. . . .

> I think the following is to be said: Sometimes the owner of the lower premises makes fire in the usual way for the ordering of his family, and then he may do it lawfully, and he is not liable if the smoke ascends unless he acts with an intention to offend. In the same way, if the owner of the upper premises lets water flow as is normal, for his water clock, he is not liable if some descends unless he acts with an intention to injure. But if the owner of the lower premises wants to make a shop or inn where he is continually making a fire and a great deal of smoke, he is not allowed to do so, as in this text (Dig. 8.5.8.5). In the same way, if the owner of the upper premises lets water flow beyond what is normal, he is not allowed to do so, as this text says.[5]

Thus what mattered to Bartolus was the amount of smoke and the normal or abnormal character of the activity.

All three of these solutions not only endured but sometimes can be found side by side in the same author. Here is how the proprietor's rights were described by the eighteenth century French jurist Robert Pothier:

> Being neighbors obligates each of the neighbors to use his property in such a way that it does not injure the other neighbor. . . .

> This rule must be understood in the sense that, whatever liberty each one has to do what seems good on his own land, he may do nothing

---

4. Baldus de Ubaldis, *Commentaria Corpus iuris civilis* to Dig. 8.5.8.5 (1577).

5. *Commentaria in Corpus iuris civilis* to Dig. 8.5.8.5 (1615).

that may result in something going on the land of his neighbor which is injurious (citing Dig. 8.5.8.5).

Because of this same principle, one is not allowed to do anything on one's land that would send into a neighboring house smoke that is too thick or too much of an interference, such as that which issues from a lime kiln or a furnace for burning the dregs of wine (citing Dig. 8.5.8.5). (*Traité du contrat de société* App. 2, *Du voisinage* §§ 235, 241).

Although the drafters of the French Civil Code borrowed many of its provisions from Pothier, the Code does not contain any provisions about these sorts of interferences among neighbors. The reason the drafters were silent was probably not that they thought the landowner should be able to do whatever he wishes on his own property. They included a lot of specific provisions governing where he could put walls, trees, fences, and so forth. Moreover, there is no discussion of nuisance in the many volumes that have been published of the debates during the drafting of the Code. Most likely, with so much to do and so little time, the drafters simply could not cover everything.

Even though no section of the Code mentions the problem, French courts have allowed a action for what they call "interferences by neighbors" (*troubles de voisinage*) since the early 19th century. Nineteenth century French approved even though they found it hard to explain how, in principle, an owner's rights could be limited. As mentioned earlier, they subscribed to a "will theory" of property. Property meant that the owner could do as he wished with what was his. When they talked about "interferences by neighbors" they usually explained that if the owner were allowed to use his rights, there would be disaster. Demolombe said, that if all proprietors can "invoke their absolute right, it is clear that none would have one in reality. What would be the result? It would be anarchy!"[6] Laurent said: "According to the rigor of the law, each proprietor would be able to object if one of his neighbor's released on his property smoke or exhalations of any kind because he has a right to the purity of air for his person and his goods." If that were so, he admitted, towns could not exist.[7]

Similarly, the 19th century German jurists typically wrote as though ownership implied an absolute right although for practical reasons it had to be limited. They described the text about the cheese shop as a limitation of the rights of the owner by positive law.[8] According to Windscheid, the limitation was a good one because "reckless realization of the consequences of the concept of ownership is not possible without serious disadvantages."[9]

In an important article, the 19th century German jurist Rudolph von Ihering claimed that it was not sensible to say that the rights of owners were unlimited. Imagine two property owners, A and B. It is not clear

---

6. C. Demolombe, *Cours de Code Napoléon* 9 (1854–82), § 543.

7. F. Laurent, *Principes de droit civil français* 20 (1869–78), § 144.

8. "gesetzliche Beschränkung des Eigenthum": *e.g.*, G.F. Puchta & A. Rudorff, *Cursus der Institutionen* 2 (3rd ed., 1851), § 231; B. Windscheid, *Lehrbuch des Pandektenrechts* 1 (7th ed. 1891), § 169.

9. Windscheid, *Lehrbuch* § 169.

whether an absolute right of property is supposed to mean that each can do whatever he likes or that each can object to any interference. But neither alternative makes sense. If A could do whatever he wished, he could force his neighbors to sell their property to him for almost nothing by carrying on an activity so obnoxious that it makes their property valueless. For example, he could open a knacker's yard that poisons the atmosphere. If B could object to any interference then A's life will become intolerable, for example, because he can no longer cook or use heat since some odor or smoke will cross the property line.[10]

To arrive at the correct rule, Ihering asked to what extent one property owner should be able to interfere with the other. To answer the question there had to be some standpoint from which one could evaluate the interference. That standpoint could not be purely individual. An hysterical person could not object if bothered by the noise of a smithy. Nor could the standpoint be absolute. Almost any activity should be permissible if it were conducted in a sufficiently remote locality, for example, on top of a high mountain. Ihering concluded that the proper question to ask was whether the interference exceeded that which was normal for the area concerned. As authority for this conclusion he cited the Roman texts quoted earlier. He argued when Dig. 8.5.8.6 spoke of a "moderate" amount of smoke, it must be referring to a normal interference; Dig. 8.5.8.5 was speaking of an abnormal degree of interference, that caused by a cheese shop. Thus his solution resembles that of Bartolus. As we will see, it was eventually enacted as Section 906 of the German Civil Code.

b. Activities that are intended to bother another

English law is unsettled. Sometimes English courts have held a defendant liable because he engaged in an activity only in order to bother some one. In *Christie v. Davey*, [1893] 1 Ch. 316, the court enjoined the defendant from interrupting the plaintiff's music lessons by whistling, shrieking, and banging on the wall separating their apartments. In *Hollywood Silver Fox Farm Ltd. v. Emmett*, [1936] 2 K.B. 468, defendant was held liable for firing guns near plaintiff's land during the season in which plaintiff's silver foxes were breeding in order to harm the foxes which are nervous during that season. On the other hand, in *Bradford (Mayor of) v. Pickles*, [1895] A.C. 587, the defendant was not held liable even though he deliberately drained his land to diminish plaintiff's water supply so that the plaintiff would be forced to buy his own land.

In modern American, French and German law, as in Roman law, the defendant can be held liable even for an activity that would not normally be actionable can become so if he engaged in it to bother someone. For example, in *Flaherty v. Moran*, 45 N.W. 381 (Mich. 1890), the court held that it is a nuisance to build a fence "with no other purpose than to shut out the light and air from a neighbor's window." (Compare *Kuzniak v. Kozmanski*, 65

---

10. "Zur Lehre von den Beschränkungen des Grundeigentümers im Interesse der Nachbarn," *Jahrbücher für die Dogmatik des heutigen römischen und deutschen Privatrechts* 6 (1863), 81, 94–96.

N.W. 275 (Mich. 1895): the court refused to find a nuisance when defendant moved his shed to the edge of his property where it blocked the light and air to plaintiff's windows. Although the defendant acted partly out of malice, the court said that moving the shed served some "useful purpose.")

In such cases, French jurists say there has been an "abuse of right" (*abus du droit*). The concept of "abuse of right" was developed in the nineteenth century. Perhaps the only way the nineteenth century jurists with their will theory of property could conceive of a limitation on the owner's freedom was as an "abuse of right." Some later jurists have questioned whether the expression makes sense if a person is not legally allowed to act a certain way, it seems odd to say he has a right to do so, and consequently that he is abusing it.

Be that as it may, since the mid-nineteenth century, French courts have given a remedy when a landowner has done something solely to injure or interfere with his neighbor. In one famous case, plaintiff recovered when the defendant who had built a false chimney to block the plaintiff's view (Colmar, 2 May 1855, D.P. 1856.II.9.). Similarly, the plaintiff has recovered when the defendant erected towers with spikes to prevent him from taking off and landing in his dirigible (Cass., Req., 3 Aug. 1915, D.P. 1917, I.79), when the defendant excavated with the sole purpose of cutting off his water supply (Cass., Req., 16 June 1913, D.P. 1914.5.23), and when the defendant hung a manakin opposite his window with a "repugnant aspect" representing a person who had been hanged (Chambéry, 21 July 1914, Gaz. Trib. 19 Jan. 1916).

In Germany, the problem is dealt with by § 226 of the Civil Code.

German Civil Code

§ 226 [PROHIBITION ON USING A RIGHT TO
HARM ANOTHER] [*SCHIKANEVERBOT*]

The use of a right is not permitted when it can only have the purpose of causing harm to another.

c. Activities that happen to bother another

Remedies

English law

Miller v. Jackson, [1977] QB 966

A housing development was built next to the village cricket field. Balls would occasionally land in the plaintiff's garden or strike her house even though the defendant took such precautions as building a fourteen foot fence.

Geoffrey Lane L.J. "Was there here a use by the defendants of their land involving an unreasonable interference with the plaintiffs' enjoyment of their land? There is here in effect no dispute that there has been and is likely to be in the future an interference with the plaintiffs' enjoyment of no 20 Brackenridge. The only question is whether it is unreasonable. It is a truism to say that this is a matter of degree. What that means is this. A balance has to be maintained between on the one hand the rights of the individual to enjoy his house and garden without the threat of damage and on the other hand the rights of the public in general or a neighbour to engage in lawful pastimes. Difficult questions may sometimes arise when the defendants' activities are offensive to the senses, for example by way of noise. Where, as here, the damage or potential damage is physical the answer is more simple. There is, subject to what appears hereafter, no excuse I can see which exonerates the defendants from liability in nuisance for what they have done or from what they threaten to do. It is true no one has yet been physically injured. That is probably due to a great extent to the fact that the householders in Brackenridge desert their gardens whilst cricket is in progress. The danger of injury is obvious and is not slight enough to be disregarded. There is here a real risk of serious injury. . . .

Given that the defendants are guilty of both negligence and nuisance, is it a case where the court should in its discretion give relief, or should the plaintiffs be left to their remedy in damages? There is no doubt that if cricket is played damage will be done to the plaintiffs' tiles or windows or both. There is a not inconsiderable danger that if they or their son or their guests spend any time in the garden during the weekend afternoons in the summer they may be hit by a cricket ball. So long as this situation exists it seems to me that damages cannot be said to provide an adequate form of relief. Indeed, quite apart from the risk of physical injury, I can see no valid reason why the plaintiffs should have to submit to the inevitable breakage of tiles and/or windows, even though the defendants have expressed their willingness to carry out any repairs at no cost to the plaintiffs. I would accordingly uphold the grant of the injunction to restrain the defendants from committing nuisance. However, I would postpone the operation of the injunction for 12 months to enable the defendants to look elsewhere for an alternative pitch."

Lord Denning M.R. [dissenting]. "In our present case, too, nuisance was pleaded as an alternative to negligence. The tort of nuisance in many cases overlaps the tort of negligence. The boundary lines were discussed in two adjoining cases in the Privy Council: The Wagon Mound (No 2)[1] and Goldman v. Hargrave[2]. But there is at any rate one important distinction between them. It lies in the nature of the remedy sought. Is it damages? Or an injunction? If the plaintiff seeks a remedy in damages for injury done to him or his property, he can lay his claim either in negligence or in nuisance. But, if he seeks an injunction to stop the playing of cricket altogether, I think he must make his claim in nuisance. . . .

This case is new. It should be approached on principles applicable to modern conditions. There is a contest here between the interest of the public at large and the interest of a private individual. The public interest lies in protecting the environment by preserving our playing fields in the face of mounting development, and by enabling our youth to enjoy all the benefits of outdoor games, such as cricket and football. The private interest lies in securing the privacy of his home and garden without intrusion or interference by anyone. In deciding between these two conflicting interests, it

---

1.   [1966] 2 All ER 709, [1967] 1 AC 617.   2.   [1966] 2 All ER 989 at 992, [1967] 1 AC 645 at 657.

must be remembered that it is not a question of damages. If by a million-to-one chance a cricket ball does go out of the ground and cause damage, the cricket club will pay. There is no difficulty on that score. No, it is a question of an injunction. And in our law you will find it repeatedly affirmed that an injunction is a discretionary remedy. In a new situation like this, we have to think afresh as to how discretion should be exercised. . . . In my opinion the right exercise of discretion is to refuse an injunction; and, of course, to refuse damages in lieu of an injunction. Likewise as to the claim for past damages. The club were entitled to use this ground for cricket in the accustomed way. It was not a nuisance, nor was it negligence of them so to run it. Nor was the batsman negligent when he hit the ball for six. All were doing simply what they were entitled to do. So if the club had put it to the test, I would have dismissed the claim for damages also. But as the club very fairly say that they are willing to pay for any damage, I am content that there should be an award of £400 to cover any part or future damage."

Law in the United States

Boomer v. Atlantic Cement Co., Inc., 257 N.E.2d 870 (N.Y. 1970)

"Defendant operates a large cement plant near Albany. These are actions for injunction and damages by neighboring land owners alleging injury to property from dirt, smoke and vibration emanating from the plant. A nuisance has been found after trial, temporary damages have been allowed; but an injunction has been denied. . . .

Effective control of air pollution is a problem presently far from solution even with the full public and financial powers of government. In large measure adequate technical procedures are yet to be developed and some that appear possible may be economically impracticable.

It seems apparent that the amelioration of air pollution will depend on technical research in great depth; on a carefully balanced consideration of the economic impact of close regulation; and of the actual effect on public health. It is likely to require massive public expenditure and to demand more than any local community can accomplish and to depend on regional and interstate controls.

A court should not try to do this on its own as a by-product of private litigation and it seems manifest that the judicial establishment is neither equipped in the limited nature of any judgment it can pronounce nor prepared to lay down and implement an effective policy for the elimination of air pollution. This is an area beyond the circumference of one private lawsuit. . . .

The ground for the denial of injunction [by the court below], notwithstanding the finding both that there is a nuisance and that plaintiffs have been damaged substantially, is the large disparity in economic consequences of the nuisance and of the injunction. This theory cannot, however, be sustained without overruling a doctrine which has been consistently reaffirmed in several leading cases in this court and which has never been disavowed here, namely that where a nuisance has been found and where there has been any substantial damage shown by the party complaining an injunction will be granted.

The rule in New York has been that such a nuisance will be enjoined although marked disparity be shown in economic consequence between the effect of the injunction and the effect of the nuisance. . . .

[T]o follow the rule literally in these cases would be to close down the plant at once. This court is fully agreed to avoid that immediately drastic remedy; the difference in view is how best to avoid it. . . .

For obvious reasons the rate of the research is beyond control of defendant. If at the end of 18 months the whole industry has not found a technical solution a court would be hard put to close down this one cement plant if due regard be given to equitable principles.

[T]o grant the injunction unless defendant pays plaintiffs such permanent damages as may be fixed by the court seems to do justice between the contending parties. All of the attributions of economic loss to the properties on which plaintiffs' complaints are based will have been redressed. The nuisance complained of by these plaintiffs may have other public or private consequences, but these particular parties are the only ones who have sought remedies and the judgment proposed will fully redress them. The limitation of relief granted is a limitation only within the four corners of these actions and does not foreclose public health or other public agencies from seeking proper relief in a proper court.

French law

Cour d'appel, Toulouse, 17 March 1970, JCP 1970.II.16534

Plaintiff brought suit because the factory of the defendant, *Société Péchiney*, was emitting fumes containing fluorine gas which disturbed their use of their property. The court of first instance ordered three experts to conduct a study to determine what preventive measures the defendant might take. They described a series of such measures that the defendant had already taken which had reduced the level of emissions. They observed that it was in defendant's own interest to develop more effective measures because they represented a loss of raw material that was of greater value than the damage done to others. The experts concluded:

> Except for totally rebuilding its factory along different lines, the *Société Péchiney* has made very important efforts to reduce the emissions with which this lawsuit is concerned and it has already spent nearly three million francs toward that end. The *Société Péchiney* is continuing and will continue its research. As of this moment, we are unable to see any other course of action aside from the one in which the *Société Péchiney* is engaged.

The *Cour d'appel* refused to order the defendant to stop emitting fluorine. It ordered the defendant to pay an annual indemnity. The court said: "[I]n the current state of science and its industrial applications and of the most modern equipment of our industries, it is not possible to take better measures than those of the *Société Péchiney* to avoid the discharge of fluorine products. . . . [A]s a result it is appropriate, as the judges did below, to reject the request of the Fourniers and the other [plaintiffs] to take whatever measures are appropriate to prevent the discharge from the factory."

German law

German Civil Code

§ 903 [AUTHORITY OF THE OWNER]

The owner of a thing can deal with it as he pleases and exclude others from any dealing with it insofar as statutes and the rights of a third party are not to the contrary.

§ 906 (AS AMENDED IN 1960) [DISCHARGE
OF UNWEIGHABLE MATERIAL]
[*ZUFÜRUNG UNWÄGBARER STOFFE*]

The owner of land may not prohibit the discharge upon it of gas, steam, odors, smoke, soot, heat, noise, vibrations, and any similar interferences from the operations conducted on other land insofar as the use of his own property is not impaired or not substantially impaired. . . .

The same applies insofar as a substantial impairment is caused by a use of other land that is normal for the area and cannot be prevented by measures which are commercially feasible for activities of this type. If the owner must suffer some interference on this account, then he can require an appropriate compensation in money from the person using the other land when the interference prevents a use of his own land or its product that is normal for the area to an unreasonable degree.

Note: Before the 1960 amendment, if an interfering activity was in an appropriate place, nearby landowners had to tolerate it without compensation.

German Civil Code

§ 1004 [ORDER TO CEASE AND DESIST]

If ownership is impaired in any other way than by taking away or withholding possession, the owner can require the disturber to cease impairing it. If there is concern about further impairment, the owner can have an order that he desist.

This claim is not allowed when the interference is one that the owner is obligated to suffer.

The character of the neighborhood

English law

St. Helen's Smelting Co. v. Tipping, (1865) 11 H.L. Cas. 642 (H.L.)

The plaintiff brought suit for damages caused to his estate by defendant's smelter, located a mile and a half away. At trial, Mellor J. charged the jury: "That every man is bound to use his own property in such a manner as not to injure the property of his neighbour unless, by the lapse of a certain period of time, he has acquired a prescriptive right to do so. But the law does not regard trifling inconveniences; every thing must be looked at from a reasonable point of view; and, therefore, in an action for nuisance to property by noxious vapours arising on the land of another, the injury to be actionable must be such as visibly to diminish the value of the property and the comfort and enjoyment of it. That, in determining that question, the time, locality, and all the circumstances should be taken into consideration; that in counties where great works have been erected and carried on, which are the means of developing the national wealth, persons must not stand on extreme rights, and bring actions in respect of every matter of annoyance, as, if that were so, business could not be carried on in those places." Plaintiff recovered £362 18 s. 4½ d. Defendant appealed. Held, the instruction was correct.

Lord Westbury L.C. "My Lords, in matters of this description it appears to me that it is a very desirable thing to mark the difference between an action brought for a nuisance upon the ground that the alleged nuisance produces material injury to the property, and an action brought for a nuisance on the ground that the thing alleged to be a nuisance is productive of sensible personal discomfort. With regard to the latter, namely, the personal inconvenience and interference with one's enjoyment, one's quiet, one's personal freedom, anything that discomposes or injuriously affects the senses or the nerves, whether that may or may not be denominated a nuisance, must undoubtedly depend greatly on the circumstances of the place where the thing complained of actually occurs. If a man lives in a town, it is necessary that he should subject himself to the consequences of those operations of trade which may be carried on in his immediate locality, which are actually necessary for trade and commerce, and also for the enjoyment of property, and for the benefit of the inhabitants of the town and of the public at large. If a man lives in a street where there are numerous shops, and a shop is opened next door to him, which is carried on in a fair and reasonable way, he has no ground for complaint, because to himself individually there may arise much discomfort from the trade carried on in that shop. But when an occupation is carried on by one person in the neighbourhood of another, and the result of that trade, or occupation, or business, is a material injury to property, then there unquestionably arises a very different consideration. I think, my Lords, that in a case of that description, the submission which is required from persons living in society to that amount of discomfort which may be necessary for the legitimate and free exercise of the trade of their neighbours, would not apply to circumstances the immediate result of which is sensible injury to the value of the property.

Now, in the present case, it appears that the plaintiff purchased a very valuable estate, which lies within a mile-and-a-half from certain large smelting works. What the occupation of these copper smelting premises was anterior to the year 1860 does not clearly appear. The plaintiff became the proprietor of an estate of great value in the month of June 1860. In the month of September 1860 very extensive smelting operations began on the property of the present appellants, in their works at St. Helen's. Of the effect of the vapours exhaling from those works upon the plaintiff's property, and the injury done to his trees and shrubs, there is abundance of evidence in the case.

My Lords, the action has been brought upon that, and the jurors have found the existence of the injury; and the only ground upon which your Lordships are asked to set aside that verdict, and to direct a new trial, is this, that the whole neighbourhood where these copper smelting works were carried on, is a neighbourhood more or less devoted to manufacturing purposes of a similar kind, and there it is said, that inasmuch as this copper smelting is carried on in what the appellant contends is a fit place, it may be carried on with impunity, although the result may be the utter destruction, or the very considerable diminution, of the value of the plaintiff's property. My Lords, I apprehend that that is not the meaning of the word 'suitable,' or the meaning of the word 'convenient,' which has been used as applicable to the subject. The word 'suitable' unquestionably cannot carry with it this consequence, that a trade may be carried on in a particular locality, the consequence of which trade may be injury and destruction to the neighbouring property."

Law in the United States

Bove v. Donner-Hanna Coke Corp., 258 N.Y.S. 229 (N.Y.App. Div. 1932)

In 1910 plaintiff purchased two vacant lots in Buffalo and two years later built a house on them. She rented the apartments on the second floor. Defendant then built a large coke oven across the street.

"The result [of the operation of the coke oven] is a tremendous cloud of steam, which rises in a shaft and escapes into the air, carrying with it minute portions of coke and more or less gas. This steam and the accompanying particles of dirt, as well as the dust which comes from a huge coal pile, necessarily kept on the premises, and the gases and odors which emanate from the plant, are carried by the wind in various directions, and frequently find their way onto the plaintiff's premises and into her house and store. According to the plaintiff, this results in an unusual amount of dirt and soot accumulating in her house, and prevents her opening the windows on the street side. She also claims that she suffers severe headaches by breathing the impure air occasioned by this dust and these offensive odors, and that her health and that of her family has been impaired, all to her very great discomfort and annoyance. She also asserts that this condition has lessened the rental value of her property, and has made it impossible at times to rent her apartments. . . .

One who chooses to live in the large centers of population cannot expect the quiet of the country. Congested centers are seldom free from smoke, odors, and other pollution from houses, shops, and factories, and one who moves into such a region cannot hope to find the pure air of the village or outlying district. A person who prefers the advantages of community life must expect to experience some of the resulting inconveniences. . . .

With all the dirt, smoke, and gas which necessarily comes from factory chimneys, trains, and boats, and with full knowledge that this region was especially adapted for industrial rather than residential purposes, and that factories would increase in the future, plaintiff selected this locality as the site of her future home. She voluntarily moved into this district, fully aware of the fact that the atmosphere would constantly be contaminated by dirt, gas, and foul odors, and that she could not hope to find in this locality the pure air of a strictly residential zone. She evidently saw certain advantages in living in this congested center. This is not the case of an industry, with its attendant noise and dirt, invading a quiet residential district. It is just the opposite. . . .

Today there are twenty industrial plants within a radius of less than a mile and three-quarters from appellant's house, with more than sixty-five smokestacks rising in the air, and belching forth clouds of smoke. Every day there are one hundred and forty-eight passenger trains, and two hundred and twenty-five freight trains, to say nothing of switch engines, passing over these various railroad tracks near to the plaintiff's property. Over ten thousand boats, a large portion of which burn soft coal, pass up and down the Buffalo river every season. Across the street, and within three hundred feet from plaintiff's house, is a large tank of the Iroquois Gas Company which is used for the storage of gas.

The utter abandonment of this locality for residential purposes, and its universal use as an industrial center, becomes manifest when one considers that in 1929 the assessed valuation of the twenty industrial plants above referred to aggregated over $20,000,000, and that the city in 1925 passed a zoning ordinance putting this area in the third industrial district, a zone in which stockyards, glue factories, coke ovens, steel furnaces, rolling mills, and other similar enterprises were permitted to be located."

German law

Reichsgericht, 10 March 1937, RGZ 154, 161

"The plaintiff is a farmer in Oberhausen. He has rented the Ripshorst estate which is about 20 *Morgens* in size [1 *Morgen* = 25.53 acres] from Freiherr von B. and owns arable land nearby. The estate is surrounded in a northerly and westerly direction by the industrial installations of the defendant: furnaces, steel mills, rolling mills, and mines with boilers. The Rhine-Herne Canal runs on the north side of the estate. The Frintrop railroad station is located to the south. The plaintiff claims that an excessive and therefore impermissible emission of smoke, soot and dust comes onto the land he cultivates from the installations of the defendant which seriously interferes with his agricultural activities and harms the condition of his cows. He claims the defendant is legally responsible and asks the sum of 11,662 Reichsmarks in compensation for the losses suffered in the years 1924 and 1925. . . . The defendant claims that the emissions from his installations take place within the normal boundaries of a large industrial area. The estate is affected by the emissions of other installations, by the passage of ships along the canal, and by the railroad station at Frintrop. . . .

The decision turns on . . . whether the defendant was within his rights under § 906 of the Civil Code in discharging the gas and dust from his works onto the estate cultivated by the plaintiff. The lower court committed no legal error in finding in the plaintiff's favor that the interference *substantially* impaired the agricultural use of his land. Against the plaintiff, however, the court below found that the interference was caused by a use of the land by the defendant that was normal with regard to the location of the properties. . . .

It is true that there are other industrial operations in Oberhausen. Nevertheless, the area near Ripshorst is dominated by the enterprises of the defendant. They give the city a distinctive character. The people living there see it as an industrial area of the first rank. The individual operations of the defendant are not accidentally or haphazardly located but are organically connected to each other in a manner that is commercially expedient and based naturally on the presence of coal. They are no differently organized and no more intensive than is the case with other enterprises of the same kind. Immediately on the boundaries of defendant's installations are also farms which are parts of small, medium and large-scale agricultural enterprises. The areas cultivated are spread to the south, east and north. . . .

The legal treatment of this case must be influenced by the fact that . . . significant agricultural enterprises are located in the neighborhood. . . .

[I]t would contradict the ideas of our people's community (*Volksgemeinschaft*) if industry were permitted to construct works that admittedly are well planned and correspond to a natural development but are particularly intensive without a duty to compensate the agricultural enterprises that are also enterprises which are not inappropriate to the place and have their own natural conditions for living; industry should not be allowed to interfere them in such a manner that the farms are the only ones to suffer. . . .

In the area around Oberhausen that is of primary relevance here, and especially in the neighborhood of the defendant, not only is the use of property for industrial installations normal, but so also is their use for farming. . . . A balancing of the interests of both is called for when an agricultural enterprise which is in a condition to operate is affected in a way that endangers its existence by interference from the works nearby. This balancing is only possible as a practical matter only if a percentage share of the harm caused by the emissions is borne by the injurer and the other part is suffered without compensation. The apportionment is a task for the judge which is difficult but not insoluble with appropriate discretion." The *Reichsgericht* remanded the case for findings on this issue.

Note: Decisions from the Nazi era often contain expressions such as "people's community" (*Volksgemeinschaft*) which show at least outward allegiance to Nazi principles and may or may not be relevant to the opinion.

French law

Cour de cassation, 3e ch. civ., 3 November 1977, D.S. 1978.434

Thérèse Comys and Phillipe Lavoye owned houses with gardens next to a textile mill belonging to the *Societé Detant-Delplace*. They claimed compensation for harm suffered both because of noise and vibration due to the operations of workers at the mill of *Detant-Delplace*, and because they were deprived of sunlight when a higher wall was built at the mill.

The *Cour d'appel* of Douai reduced the amount of damages awarded Comys and Lavoye for the interference caused by the operation of the factory on the grounds that "the interferences only have an importance that is relative to the level of noise of an industrial quarter." The plaintiffs objected that no text of the Civil Code drew the distinction between a residential quarter in which the plaintiff would have "the right to an absolute assessment of the interference" and an industrial quarter "in which the populace must accommodate itself to the nuisances found there." The plaintiff argued that "to evaluate the abnormality of interferences among neighbors (*troubles de voisinage*) as a function of the characteristics of the surroundings is contrary to the law that gives everyone the same rights to the use of the amenities of the environment wherever they may live with the sole exception of differences instituted by the legislation on urban land use which, in this case, classifies the area in dispute as a residential zone." The plaintiffs also argued that the court below should have specified what "noise level" for the area would be consistent with "the normal inconveniences of having neighbors." The *Cour de cassation* upheld the decision below on the issue of noise and vibration, merely observing that "the judges below are sovereign in their evaluation of the normality of interferences, taking into account the circumstances of time and place."

The portion of the court's opinion dealing with blocking the sunlight appears below.

Priority in time

English law

Miller v. Jackson, [1977] QB 966.

The facts are given on p. 172 above.

Geoffrey Lane L.J. "There is, however, one obviously strong point in the defendants' favour. They or their predecessors have been playing cricket on this ground (and no doubt hitting sixes out of it) for 70 years or so. Can someone by building a house on the edge of the field in circumstances where it must have been obvious that balls might be hit over the fence, effectively stop cricket being played? Precedent apart, justice would seem to demand that the plaintiffs should be left to make the most of the site they have elected to occupy with all its obvious advantages and all its equally obvious disadvantages. It is pleasant to have an open space over which to look from your bedroom and sitting room windows, so far as it is possible to see over the concrete wall. Why should you complain of the obvious disadvantages which arise from the particular purpose to which the open space is being put? Put briefly, can the defendants take advantage of the fact that the plaintiffs have put themselves in such a position by coming to occupy a house on the edge of a small cricket field, with the result that what was not a nuisance in the past now becomes a nuisance? If the matter were res integra, I confess I should be inclined to find for the defendants. It does not seem just that a long-established activity, in itself innocuous, should be brought to an end because someone chooses to build a house nearby and so turn an innocent pastime into an actionable nuisance. Unfortunately, however, the question is not open. In Sturges v. Bridgman[1] this very problem arose. The defendant had carried on a confectionary shop with a noisy pestle and mortar for more than 20 years. Although it was noisy, it was far enough away from neighbouring premises not to cause trouble to anyone, until the plaintiff, who was a physician, built a consulting-room on his own land but immediately adjoining the confectionary shop. The noise and vibrations seriously interfered with the consulting-room and became a nuisance to the physician. The defendant contended that he had acquired the right either at common law or under the Prescription Act 1832 by uninterrupted use for more than 20 years to impose the inconvenience. It was held by the Court of Appeal, affirming the judgment of Jessel MR, that use such as this which was, prior to the construction of the consulting room, neither preventable nor actionable, could not found a prescriptive right. That decision involved the assumption, which so far as one can discover has never been questioned, that it is no answer to a claim in nuisance for the defendant to show that the plaintiff brought the trouble on his own head by building or coming to live in a house so close to the defendant's premises that he would inevitably be affected by the defendant's activities, where no one had been affected previously. See also Bliss v. Hall.[2] It may be that this rule works injustice, it may be that one would decide the matter differently in the absence of authority. But we are bound by the decision in Sturges v. Bridgman and it is not for this court as I see it to alter a rule which has stood for so long."

Lord Denning M.R. [dissenting] "In this case it is our task to balance the right of the cricket club to continue playing cricket on their cricket ground, as against the right of the householder not to be interfered with. On taking the balance, I would give priority to the right of the cricket club to continue playing cricket on the ground, as they have done for the last 70 years. It takes precedence over the right of the newcomer to sit in his garden undisturbed. After all he bought the house four years ago in midsummer when the cricket season was at its height. He might have guessed that there was a risk that a hit for six might possibly land on his property. If he finds that he does not like it, he ought, when cricket is played, to sit in the other side of the house or in the front garden, or go out; or take advantage of the offers the club have made to him of fitting unbreakable glass, and so forth. Or, if he does not like that, he ought to sell his house and move elsewhere. I expect there are many who would gladly buy it in order to be near the cricket field and open space. At any rate he ought not to be allowed to stop cricket being played on this ground."

Law in the United States

With one notable exception, courts in the United States follow the same rule as in England: coming to a nuisance is no defense. Here is the exception.

---

1. (1879) 11 Ch D 852.   **2.** (1838) 4 Bing NC 183.

Spur Industries, Inc. v. Del E. Webb Development Co. 494 P.2d 700 (Ariz. 1972)

The plaintiff was a developer who bought hundreds of acres in a thinly populated agricultural area in Arizona on which he built a retirement community known as Sun City. Residents were bothered by odors from a nearby feed lot owned by Spur. Moreover, Del Webb found it difficult to sell houses near the feed lot. Del Webb asked for an injunction forbidding its operation. The court concluded that Spur could be enjoined. Then it said:

"There was no indication in the instant case at the time Spur and its predecessors located in western Maricopa County that a new city would spring up, full-blown, alongside the feeding operation and that the developer of that city would ask the court to order Spur to move because of the new city. Spur is required to move not because of any wrongdoing on the part of Spur, but because of a proper and legitimate regard of the courts for the rights and interests of the public.

Del Webb, on the other hand, is entitled to the relief prayed for (a permanent injunction), not because Webb is blameless, but because of the damage to the people who have been encouraged to purchase homes in Sun City. It does not equitable or legally follow, however, that Webb, being entitled to the injunction, is then free of any liability to Spur if Webb has in fact been the cause of the damage Spur has sustained. It does not seem harsh to require a developer, who has taken advantage of the lesser land values in a rural area as well as the availability of large tracts of land on which to build and develop a new town or city in the area, to indemnify those who are forced to leave as a result.

Having brought people to the nuisance to the foreseeable detriment of Spur, Webb must indemnify Spur for a reasonable amount of the cost of moving or shutting down. It should be noted that this relief to Spur is limited to a case wherein a developer has, with foreseeability, brought into a previously agricultural or industrial area the population which makes necessary the granting of an injunction against a lawful business and for which the business has no adequate relief.

It is therefore the decision of this court that the matter be remanded to the trial court for a hearing upon the damages sustained by the defendant Spur as a reasonable and direct result of the granting of the permanent injunction."

German law

Reichsgericht, 10 March 1937, RGZ 154, 161

The facts are given above at p. 179. While the court did give relief it said:

"The legal treatment of this case must be influenced by the fact that . . . significant agricultural enterprises are located in the neighborhood. The reason is not that agriculture is older there than industry. According to the law, what matters is the current use and not the historical one. Moreover, all progress would be hindered if one took account of so-called 'preemption.'"

French law

Cour de cassation, 1e ch. civ., 20 February 1968, D.S. 1968.350

In 1958, the plaintiff Gibert built a house on a piece of land next to a factory. He was disturbed by the noise and vibrations it caused. The court below upheld his claim. The defendant argued that the plaintiff "had committed a fault which was the cause of the damage of which he complains." "[T]o construct his building adjoining the wall of a factory presumed to be noisy and to take no precaution to ensure isolation was a grave imprudence which had a cause–effect relationship to the harm suffered from the noise and vibration of the factory."

The *Cour d'appel* decided in the plaintiff's favor. The *Cour de cassation* upheld that decision noting that "the *Cour d'appel* correctly remarked that the priority in the construction of the factory in relation to that of an adjoining house does not create a servitude to the detriment of the neighboring property and that Gibert 'who could not be required to take particular measures to cope with the inconveniences of noise and vibration transmitted by the party wall, made a normal use of his rights and cannot be blamed for any fault.' "

Height

English law

Hunter v. Canary Wharf Ltd., [1996] W.L.J. 348 (C.A.)

Canary Wharf Tower, about 250 meters tall and about 50 meters square, blocked the reception of television broadcasts in hundreds of homes in East London for several years. Occupants of those homes, not all householders, sought damages from the builder.

Pill L.J. "The parties have posed questions to be determined by the court in these appeals. *Is the interference with television reception capable of constituting an actionable private nuisance?* The judge answered this question in the affirmative. The presence of Canary Wharf made it impossible for the plaintiffs to watch television transmissions . . . As an interference with their enjoyment of their premises, it was an actionable nuisance.

Lord Irvine submits that interference with television reception by reason of the presence of a building is properly to be regarded as analogous to loss of aspect. To obstruct the receipt of television signals by the erection of a building between the point of receipt and the source is not in law a nuisance. In *Aldred's Case* (1611) 77 E.R. 816 Wray C.J. said 'for prospect, which is a matter only of delight and not of necessity, no action lies for stopping thereof, and yet it is a great recommendation of a house if it has a long and large prospect. . . . But the law does not give an action for such things of delight' . . . The principle was stated by Lord Blackburn in *Dalton v. Angus* (1881) 6 App.Cas. 740, 824: The distinction between a right to light and a right of prospect, on the ground that one is matter of necessity and the other of delight is to my mind more quaint than satisfactory. A much better reason is given by Lord Hardwicke in *Att.-Gen. v. Doughty* (1752) 28 E.R. 290, where he observes that if that was the case there could be no great towns.

I think this decision, that a right of prospect is not acquired by prescription, shows that, whilst on the balance of convenience and inconvenience, it was held expedient that the right to light, which could only impose a burthen upon land very near the house, should be protected when it had been long enjoyed, on the same ground it was held expedient that the right of prospect, which would impose a burthen on a very large and indefinite area, should not be allowed to be created, except by actual agreement. . . .

I accept the importance of television in the lives of very many people. However, in my judgment the erection or presence of a building in the line of sight between a television transmitter and other properties is not actionable as an interference with the use and enjoyment of land. The analogy with loss of prospect is compelling. The loss of a view, which may be of the greatest importance to many householders, is not actionable and neither is the mere presence of a building in the sight line to the television transmitter. While the authorities which established the limit of the tort of nuisance in this respect are old, the reasoning behind them is not only sound but is applicable to modern conditions. In circumstances such as the present, I would answer the question posed in the negative. Interference with television signals by, for example, the operation of machinery, is a different question which does not arise for determination in the present case . . ."

Law in the United States

Fontainebleau Hotel Corp. v. Forty-Five Twenty-Five, Inc., 114 So. 2d 357 (Fla. App. 1959)

"This is an interlocutory appeal from an order temporarily enjoining the appellants from continuing with the construction of a fourteen-story addition to the Fontainebleau Hotel, owned and operated by the appellants. Appellee, plaintiff below, owns the Eden Roc Hotel, which was constructed in 1955, about a year after the Fontainebleau, and adjoins the Fontainebleau on the north. Both are luxury hotels, facing the Atlantic Ocean. The proposed addition to the Fontainebleau is being constructed twenty feet from its north property line, 130 feet from the mean high water mark of the Atlantic Ocean, and 76 feet 8 inches from the ocean bulkhead line. The 14-story tower will extend 160 feet above grade in height and is 416 feet long from east to west. During the winter months, from around two o'clock in the afternoon for the remainder of the day, the shadow of the addition will extend over the cabana, swimming pool, and sunbathing areas of the Eden Roc, which are located in the southern portion of its property. . . . Plaintiff alleges that the construction would interfere with the light and air on the beach in front of the Eden Roc and cast a shadow of such size as to render the beach wholly unfitted for the use and enjoyment of its guests, to the irreparable injury of the plaintiff. . . .

No American decision has been cited, and independent research has revealed none, in which it has been held that—in the absence of some contractual or statutory obligation—a land-owner has a legal right to the free flow of light and air across the adjoining land of his neighbor. Even at common law, the landowner had no legal right, in the absence of an easement or uninterrupted use and enjoyment for a period of 20 years, to unobstructed light and air from the adjoining land. And the English doctrine of 'ancient lights' has been unanimously repudiated in this country. 1 Am. Jur., Adjoining Landowners, § 49, p. 533.

There being, then, no legal right to the free flow of light and air from the adjoining land, it is universally held that where a structure serves a useful and beneficial purpose, it does not give rise to a cause of action, either for damages or for an injunction under the maxim sic utere tuo ut alienum non laedas, even though it causes injury to another by cutting off the light and air and interfering with the view that would otherwise be available over adjoining land in its natural state regardless of the fact that the structure may have been erected partly for spite.

We see no reason for departing from this universal rule. If, as contended on behalf of plaintiff, public policy demands that a landowner in the Miami Beach area refrain from constructing buildings on his premises that will cast a shadow on the adjoining premises, an amendment of its comprehensive planning and zoning ordinance, applicable to the public as a whole, is the means by which such purpose should be achieved. (No opinion is expressed here as to the validity of such an ordinance, if one should be enacted pursuant to the requirements of law.) But to change the universal rule—and the custom followed in this state since its inception—that adjoining landowners have an equal right under the law to build to the line of their respective tracts and to such a height as is desired by them (in the absence, of course, of building restrictions or regulations) amounts, in our opinion, to judicial legislation."

German law

Bundesgerichtshof, 21 October 1983, BGHZ 88, 344

"The plaintiff is the owner of a property on which a single family house was built on 158 D. Street in H. The defendant erected a hospital during the years 1965–70 which was a nine story high rise that . . . screened (blocked) the waves of television programs so that the reception of television programs on the property of the plaintiff was hardly possible. . . .

The Senate has repeatedly decided, in accord with the current case law (see, e.g., JW 1908; 142 no. 12; JW 1909, 161 no. 10; JW 1913, 267 no. 7, RGZ 98, 15, 16; *id.* 155, 154, 157 ff.) that so-called negative effects through the blocking of things that pass through naturally, such as light and air, are not 'prohibitable' (*unzulässig*) within the meaning of §§ 903, 906, 907, and 1004 of the Civil Code [citations to six cases omitted]. That is in accord with the dominant opinion of the scholarly literature [citations too numerous to reproduce].

The legal distinction in the treatment of positive and negative interferences (*Einwirkungen*) with neighboring property comes from the wording and the system of the law itself. Neither the concept of 'impairment' (*Beeinträchtigung*) (Civil Code § 1004) nor that of 'interference' (*Einwirkung*) (Civil Code § 903) allow one to identify meaningfully the authority of one land owner in relation to that of the owner of neighboring land. The appellate court itself noted pertinently that § 903 in particular says nothing about *what* can be forbidden as an interference and what cannot. A mutual and unlimited right to do as one would like with the property would make a sensible use of both properties as impossible as an unlimited right to prevent the other from any interference. Instead the necessary balancing of interests among neighboring proprietors is done by the statutory provisions that govern the law between neighbors and, in particular, by § 906. According to that section, however, the property owner can only prohibit only the 'discharge upon' the land (*Zuführung*) of so-called 'unweighables' (*Imponderabilien*) (gas, steam, odors, smoke, soot, heat, noise, vibrations) and similar interferences, and then under closely defined circumstances. 'Similar interferences' are to be understood as those which are like the statutory examples, that is, only those which cross the boundary and whose affects are positive and, in general, perceptible to the senses. (See also BGHZ 62, 361, 366; *id.* 70, 212, 220.) If the Civil Code does not contain a rule for so-called 'negative interferences' although there is an obvious need to set limits to the rights of neighboring property owners, it follows that it wishes to leave the matter to the statutory provision on the freedom of the owner (§ 903). In principle, within the boundaries of his land, everyone can do as he likes with his property and does not need a legal justification under § 906.

That can be shown by the drafting history of the Civil Code. The failure to mention so-called negative interferences was the conscious product of the conception then prevailing: the freedom of the owner should not be limited unless the boundaries of the neighboring land are crossed by the sending of 'unweighables' (§ 906) (see *Motive zum Entwurf des BGB*, 2nd ed., vol. 3, pp. 259, 264) [a work containing the drafters' explanations of the provisions they wrote]. The First Drafting Commission accepted the proposal of the drafter Johow . . . and decided expressly between regulating positive limits on ownership in favor of a neighbor (emissions, projections, right of way in case of necessity) and negative limitations (the depth one can dig, the height one can build, dangerous installations)."

French law

Cour de cassation, 3e ch. civ., 3 November 1977, D.S. 1978.434

[The facts of this case are on p. 180 above. The portion of the court's opinion that deals with the blocking of plaintiff's sunlight by defendant's textile mill follows.]

"As to arts. 544 and 1382 of the Civil Code: Whereas the right of an owner to enjoy his property in the most absolute manner except for uses prohibited by statutes and regulations is limited by his obligation not to cause any harm to another that goes beyond the normal inconveniences of having neighbors; whereas in rejecting the claim for compensation for the harm suffered by Comys and Lavoye due to the loss of sunlight on their properties caused by increasing of the height of the wall of the mill belonging to the *Société Detant-Delplace*, the *Cour d'appel* declared that this loss did not violate any servitude or any provision of a statute or regulation and that Comys and Lavoye did not prove any loss of revenue or harm to their goods; whereas in ruling in this way, without investigating whether the harm alleged—which is not limited only to depreciation of their assets in land—exceeded the normal inconveniences of having neighbors, the *Cour d'appel* did not legally justify its decision. . . .

For these reasons, quash [the decision below] and remand to the *Cour d'appel* of Amiens."

Claude Berr & Hubert Groutel, Note to Decision of 3 Nov. 1977, D.S. 1978.435

"In quashing the portion of the decision that dealt with the privation of sunlight, the *Cour de cassation* confirmed that the absence of fault is not enough to prevent the author of an interference with neighbors [*trouble de voisinage*] from being held liable. In rejecting the claim of the neighbors, the *Cour d'appel* based its decision on the fact that the owner of the factory, in making his building higher, did not commit any abuse of his rights, or violate any servitude, any statutory of regulatory provision or any custom. Such a reason is clearly inappropriate. It is settled in the case law that proof of a fault is not necessary to apply the theory of interferences among neighbors (*troubles de voisinage*). (Cass., Civ., 2nd Civ. Ch., 3 Van. 1969, JCP 1969.II.15920, Note Mourgeon; D. 1969.323 [sic.]; Cass., 3rd Civ. Ch., 4 Feb. 1971; two decisions, JCP 1971.II.16781, note Lindon; D. 1971.Somm. 159.)"

Cour de cassation, 2e ch. civ., 3 December 1964, D.S. 1965.J.321

The *Société Grammont* built an eleven story apartment building next to the Lambrigots' three story house. The Lambrigots claim that their chimneys cannot be used because of the difference in height. The court below ordered the *Société Grammont* to pay the cost of making the chimneys longer. The *Cour de cassation* upheld that decision noting that while the court below did not cite art. 1382 of the Civil Code, the court had "found that the harm caused exceeded the normal inconveniences of having neighbors" and therefore "implicitly referred to art. 1382."

Ugliness

Law in the United States

Mathewson v. Primeau, 395 P.2d 183 (Wash 1964)

"This is a neighborhood row, being dignified into a cause celebre. . . .

[The defendants] kept a boar and brood sows. They raised hogs from pigs. It is affirmed, on excellent authority, that 'Pigs is Pigs.' Pigs become hogs, and neither are deodorized. The defendants also accumulated old automobiles and parts thereof, together with crates, lumber, old boxes, and discarded household appliances. The premises were not sightly."

The court gave the plaintiffs some relief on account of the pigs. As to the unsightly condition of the premises, it merely noted:

"That a thing is unsightly or offends the aesthetic sense of a neighbor, does not ordinarily make it a nuisance or afford ground for injunctive relief. Haehlen v. Wilson (1936), 11 Cal. App. (2d) 437, 54 P. (2d) 62;

Livingston v. Davis (1951), 1 243 Iowa 21, 50 N. W. (2d) 592, 27 A.L.R. (2d) 1237; Feldstein v. Kammauf (1956), 209 Md. 479, 121 A.2d 716; Crabtree v. City Auto Salvage Co. (1960), 47 Tenn. App. 616, 340 S. W.2d 940; Vermont Salvage Corp. v. Village of St. Johnsbury (1943), 113 Vt. 341, 34 A.2d 188."

Foley v. Harris, 286 S.E.2d 186 (1982)

Plaintiffs and defendants lived in a residential neighborhood where houses ranged in value from $ 35,000 to $ 75,000. The trial court found that the defendant was keeping "junked, abandoned, or disabled vehicles" on their lot and that "the old, battered, abandoned automobiles on the lot in question . . . definitely 'obstruct[ed] the reasonable and comfortable use of property'" of neighbors, and that it would be "very simple and inexpensive" for the [defendants] to remove the cars. It granted an injunction and the defendant appealed. Held, for plaintiff. "Freedom from discomfort and annoyance while using land, which inevitably involves an element of personal tastes and sensibilities, is often as important to a person as freedom from physical interruption with use of the land itself. The discomfort and annoyance must, however, be significant and of a kind that would be suffered by a normal person in the community."

German law

Bundesgerichtshof, 15 November 1974, NJW 1975, 170

"The *Oberlandesgericht* decided that the plaintiff has no valid claim under §§ 906 and 1004 of the Civil Code for the removal of iron rods and sheets of metal which the defendant put in front of his garage. Certainly, it must not be overlooked with regard to the facts that the wall that the defendant erected out of iron rods and metal sheets affects the total impression made by the plaintiff's house and land in particular in a way that is serious, especially since the area in question is purely residential. Inasmuch as the view affects the aesthetic sensibilities of the plaintiff as a neighbor, there is no "similar interference from the operations conducted on the other land" within the meaning of § 906. Section 906 does not cover purely intangible or immaterial emissions, among which aesthetic interferences are to be reckoned. Moreover, the plaintiff cannot require removal on the grounds that a right has been used to harm another (*Schikane*) [under § 226]. The iron rods and metal plates provide the support for the garage ramp of the defendant's property which is necessary, given the location. On these facts and without other evidence, it cannot be shown that the defendant moved the iron rods and metal plates there to harm the plaintiff. . . .

In its decisions published in BGHZ 51,396 = NJW 1969, 1208 and BGHZ 54, 56 = NJW 1970, 1541, the Senate discussed the question whether conduct or conditions on a property which are optically perceptible from neighboring land and injure the aesthetic sensibilities of neighbors can, for that reason, be ordered to cease or to desist under § 1004. The Senate answered no, basing its decision on § 906. This view has been criticized (see, in particular, Erman, *BGB*, 5th ed., § 1004, no. 11; Palandt, *BGB*, 33rd ed., § 906 no. 2a & § 1004 no. 2d with references; Grunsky, JZ 1970, 785ff.).

Nevertheless, even the opponents of the position of the *Bundesgerichtshof* mean that one can imagine situations which call for regulation. They do not say that every unsightly view can be prevented (Grunsky, *op. cit.*, 786). Here we do not need an explanation in principle of whether the position of the Senate admits of no exceptions and also applies in a particularly gross case. That was not the situation here according to the findings of the judge of the facts based upon photographs that were submitted."

French law

Cour de cassation, 3e ch. civ., 27 November 1979,
Gaz. Pal. 1980.1.pan. 146

The following is all that is reported of this decision: "The decision [below] which found a neighbor's diminished view of the surrounding countryside and less light and sun because of a building, as well as the presence of a blind wall of great height and unaesthetic character enclosing a court, had correctly inferred from these facts that they were interferences that exceeded the normal ones of having neighbors."

Offensive conduct

English law

Laws v. Florinplace Ltd., [1981] 1 All E.R. 659 (Ch.)

Defendant purchased a dress shop in an area that included restaurants, shops, and some homes and put up a two foot illuminated sign "sex centre and cinema club," and began selling hard core pornography and showing sexually explicit films. Plaintiffs are residents seeking an injunction against carrying on such a business. They described the area as "having a marked and attractive village atmosphere" and contended that "defendants' activities would attract undesirable customers who would threaten the ordinary enjoyment of family life in the street and would be an embarrassment and potential danger to young persons, and, in particular young girls who might meet with indecent suggestions." They also introduced evidence that property values would suffer. Defendant introduced evidence by a behavioral psychotherapist that "[p]ersons who feel the need for explicit sexual material of a visual type cannot fairly and properly be described as disturbed individuals on the fringe of society," and by the defendant "that at least 80% of the customers of a sex bookshop, and this one in particular, could be described as constituting well-educated, respectable and normal individuals." Defendant also offered to replace the sign with one that said "Victoria Bookshop and Video Centre," remove all external indications of the nature of its business, and to operate only from noon until 9 P.M. Monday through Saturday.

Vinelott J. "Counsel [for the plaintiff] stressed that cases of nuisance cannot be confined to cases where there is some physical emanation of a damaging kind from the defendants' premises which has occurred or is reasonably feared (such as the smallpox germs, the escape of which was feared in *Metropolitan Asylum District Managers v. Hill*, (1881) 6 App. Cas. 193, [1881–5]). The principle on which the court acts extends to cases in which

the use made by defendants of their property is such that, while not necessarily involving a breach of the criminal law, it is an affront to the reasonable susceptibility of ordinary men and women, and such an affront
that the fact of its being carried on in a way that makes its nature apparent to neighbours and visitors constitutes an interference with the reasonable domestic enjoyment of their property. In this connection, he referred
me to a decision of the Court of Appeals in *Thompson-Schwab v. Costaki*,
[1956] All E.R. 652, [1956] 1 W.L.R. 335 [holding that a house of prostitution may be enjoined as a nuisance]. . . .

[A]s I see it, it is impossible to say that there is not at least a triable
issue whether the existence of a business of this kind, conducted in the way
in which it was initially conducted, so that the nature of the business is
evident to residents of, and visitors to, Longmore Street is not a nuisance
independent of attracting undesirable and potentially dangerous customers,
and of any risk that the shop may in the future prove a plague spot which
will be a source of infection in the neighborhood. . . .

. . . I am not convinced that there is not a serious and triable issue
whether the defendants' business, even if carried on subject to the undertakings that have been offered, would not constitute a nuisance. The business having been started and having been advertised, it may well have
acquired some reputation, and, moreover, even if the name over the shop is
altered to 'Victoria Bookshop and Video Centre,' the way in which the business is conducted, with curtained windows and no outward display, with
soft porn displayed on the shelves inside, the material truly for sale being
concealed on the shelves beneath the counter, may well suggest to any person with experience in the ways of the world the nature of the books and
video cassettes that are being traded in. Furthermore, I cannot disregard
the fact that, however discretely conducted, the business will be in fact the
sale of hard core pornography and will be a business deeply repugnant to
the reasonable sensibilities of most ordinary men and women. If customers
are to use the shop, it must be because the nature of the material sold will be
evident from the name of the shop, coupled with its external appearance.

Lastly, the argument founded on the defendants' evidence as to the
character of 80% of the customers, even if it transpires to be correct, means
that there are a substantial number of others, 20%, some of whom may be, or
are likely to be, persons who are unbalanced and perhaps perverted and who
would be an embarrassment and might be a danger to visitors and residents."

Law in the United States

Mitchell v. Bearden, 503 S.W.2d 904 (Ark. 1974)

"Appellant asserts that the chancery court erred in enjoining him from
constructing a funeral home in Rector on a lot acquired by him for that
purpose. The error, according to appellant, is in the court's finding that the
vicinity in which the funeral home was to be located was an expanding exclusive residential area which was not in transition to business uses, so that the
funeral home would constitute a nuisance. We affirm because we cannot say
this finding was clearly against the preponderance of the evidence.

Decisions recognizing the right of property owners to prevent the intrusion of a funeral home into a residential district are based upon the premise that the continuous suggestion of death and dead bodies tends to destroy the comfort and repose sought by home owners. See Powell v. Taylor [222 Ark. 896, 263 S.W. 2d 906]. The critical factor in determining the application of the general principles appears to be the effect on property values because of the location of the funeral home. Considerable weight is also given to the predominance of either commercial or residential property in the area. We cannot agree with appellant's analysis of our holdings, insofar as he interprets them to turn upon the manner of operation of a funeral home."

Tedescki v. Berger, 43 So. 960 (1907)

"The bill in this case was filed by the appellant against the appellees, and sought to perpetually enjoin the maintaining or continuing of a nuisance, in the shape of a house of prostitution, on the premises adjoining the home of complainant, and also to recover damages on account of the same." Held, for plaintiff.

"The very qualities which have stamped upon the business of keeping a house of ill fame the characteristic of a public nuisance emphasize the fact that to the man whose family residence adjoins such a place it is not only a public nuisance, but a private nuisance of the most offensive kind, rendering his home not only less comfortable, but intolerable, and it necessarily depreciates the value of his property, as it is common knowledge that no one would desire to purchase a home adjoining a house of ill fame. As said by the Supreme Court of Maryland, 'it would be strange indeed if, when the court's powers are invoked for the protection and enjoyment of property, . . . its arm should be paralyzed by the mere circumstance that . . . it might incidentally be performing the functions of a moral censor, by suppressing a shocking vice. . . . And if . . . the court may interfere where the physical senses are offended, the comfort of life destroyed, or health impaired, . . . the present complainants, presenting, as they do, a case otherwise entitling them to relief, should not be disappointed merely because the effect of the process will be to protect their families from the moral taint of such an establishment.' Hamilton v. Whitridge, et al., 11 Md. 128, 147, 148, 69 Am. Dec. 184; Ingersoll, et al. v. Rousseau, 76 P. 513, 35 Wash. 92; Weakley v. Page, 102 Tenn. 178, 53 S.W. 551, 46 L.R.A. 552."

German law

Bundesgerichtshof, 12 July 1985, BGHZ 95, 307

"The plaintiff is the owner of a parcel at 423d C. Street in O. on which a single family row house has been constructed. The defendant rented the neighboring parcel, 423c C. Street, to the married couple T. According to the allegations of the plaintiff, Mrs. T., with the consent of sufferance of the defendant, is running a bordello in the house. The plaintiff claims that a moral injury is being done to his under-age daughter and the under-age children of other neighbors and also that the value of his house is lowered. . . .

The decision below, now under appeal, is correct that the plaintiff cannot successfully raise a claim about the freedom of an owner because of the 'bordello activity' in the neighboring house simply because the moral sensibilities of the neighbors are injured.

Section 1004(1) of the Civil Code presupposes an interference with ownership. In applying this provision to the relations among neighbors, and elucidating the concept of interference under § 906, the *Reichsgericht* had already declared that the neighbor who feels himself disturbed can only forbid such interferences coming from the neighboring property as either damage the property or the things located there or so affect the people on the property that their health is disturbed or they are put in physical discomfort. In contrast, §§ 1004(1) and 906 do not apply when conduct which is visible injures one's sense of shame or aesthetic sensibilities (the basic decision is RGZ 76, 130, 131–32). In developing this case law, the Senate has decided that in any event, creating a view that only injures the aesthetic sensibilities of neighbors cannot give rise to a claim under § 1004(1) (BGHZ 51, 396, 398–99). That position has been maintained in the time that followed despite critical voices in the literature (BGHZ 54, 56, 60; 15 November 1974, ZR 83/73, NJW 1975, 170. In the latter decision, the Senate left the question open whether this position has no exceptions and also is to be followed in a particularly gross case).

The present case is not an occasion for departing from the principles of these decisions.

To speak of intangible—moral or only aesthetic—emissions presupposes that the conduct or situation objected to is perceptible by the senses on the neighboring property. . . . Accordingly, even with conduct that offends one's sense of shame, § 1004(1) cannot be applied when the psychological feelings are not affected by perception of this conduct but only by knowing about it. (See Erman/Hagen, *BGB* 7th ed. § 906 no. 3.) That is also true when awareness of the event which cannot be perceived by the senses injures the general value of the property to the neighbor whose sensibilities are disturbed. (Westermann, *Sachenrecht*, 5th ed. § 36 I 1a.)"

French law

Paul Esmein, Note to decision of 3 December 1964, D.S. 1965.J.321

"The inconvenience most often involved is due to something coming from the defendant's premises that penetrates those of the plaintiff: dust, light, electro-magnetic waves, odors, smoke, vibrations. Nothing of the sort occurs when one increases the height of a building. Nevertheless, there are decisions which allow an action when the annoyance or harm is felt within the property occupied by the plaintiff but it results merely from the view of what is going on at the neighbor's property. (Neighboring house of prostitution: Cass., Req., 3 Dec. 1860; Cass., Civ. ch., 27 Aug. 1861, S. 61.84; Req., 5 June 1882, S. 84.1.71; neighboring theater with mobs of people and piles of filth in front at the door: Cass., Reg., 24 Apr. 1865, S. 66.1.169.)"

Proposed European Council directive on liability for waste

Proposal for a Directive of the European Council on Civil Liability for Damage Caused by Waste

[COM(89) 282 final – SYN 217, O.J. 89/C251/03]

ARTICLE 1

(1) This Directive shall concern civil liability for damage and injury to the environment caused by waste generated in the course of an occupational activity, from the moment it arises.

(2) This Directive shall not apply:

- to nuclear waste covered by national law based on the Convention on Third Party Liability in the Field of Nuclear Energy (Paris, 29 July 1960) and the Convention supplementary to the aforementioned convention (Brussels, 31 July 1963), as well as the Protocols attached to these conventions;

- to waste and pollution covered by national law based on the International Convention on Civil Liability for Oil Pollution Damage (Brussels, 29 November 1969) and the Convention on the Establishment of an International Fund for Compensation for Oil Damage (Brussels, 18 December 1971).

ARTICLE 2

(1) For the purposes of this Directive:

(a) "producer" means any natural or legal person whose occupational activities produce waste and/or anyone who carries out pre-processing, mixing or other operations resulting in a change in the nature or composition of this waste, until the moment when the damage or injury to the environment is caused;

(b) "waste" means any substance or object defined as waste in Article 1 of Council Directive 75/442/EEC[2] [reproduced below];

(c) "damage" means:

(i) damage resulting from death or physical injury;

(ii) damage to property;

(d) "injury to the environment" means a significant and persistent interference in the environment caused by a modification of the physical, chemical or biological conditions of water, soil and/or air insofar as these are not considered to be damage within the meaning of subparagraph (c)(ii).

(2) The following shall be deemed to be the producer of the waste in place of the person defined in paragraph 1(a):

(a) the person who imports the waste into the Community, except where the waste was previously exported from the Community and its nature or composition was not substantially changed prior to its re-importation;

---

2.   OJ No L 194, 25.7.1975, p. 47.

(b) the person who had actual control of the waste when the incident giving rise to the damage or injury to the environment occurred:

   (i) if he is not able within a reasonable period to identify the producer as defined in paragraph I;

   (ii) if the waste is in transit in the Community without having undergone there a substantial change in nature or composition before the occurrence of the incident giving rise to the damage or injury to the environment;

(c) the person responsible for the installation, establishment or undertaking where the waste was lawfully transferred to such installation, establishment or undertaking licensed pursuant to Article 8 of Directive 75/442/EEC, Article 6 of Council Directive 75/439/EEC[1] or Article 9 of Directive 78/319/EEC, or approved pursuant to Article 6 of Council Directive 76/403/EEC.[2]

ARTICLE 3

The producer of waste shall be liable under civil law for the damage and injury to the environment caused by the waste, irrespective of fault on his part.

ARTICLE 4

(1) The plaintiff may take legal action to obtain:

(a) the prohibition or cessation of the act causing the damage or injury to the environment;

(b) the reimbursement of expenditure arising from measures to prevent the damage or injury to the environment;

(c) the reimbursement of expenditure arising form measures to compensate for damage within the meaning of subparagraph (c)(ii) of Article 2(1);

(d) the restoration of the environment to its state immediately prior to the occurrence of injury to the environment or the reimbursement of expenditure incurred in connection with measures taken to this end;

(e) indemnification for the damage.

(2) With regard to the restoration of the environment provided for in paragraph 1(d), the plaintiff, in the case of injury to the environment, may seek such restoration or the reimbursement of expenditure incurred to this end except when:

   – the costs substantially exceed the benefit arising for the environment from such restoration, and

   – other alternative measures to the restoration of the environment may be undertaken at a substantially lower cost.

In this latter case, the plaintiff may seek the implementation of these other measures or the reimbursement of the expenditure incurred to this end.

---

1. OJ No. L 194, 25.7.1975, p. 31.   **2.** OJ No. L 108, 26.4.1976, p. 41.

(3) As regards injury to the environment, the public authorities may take the legal action provided for in paragraph 1(a), (b) and (d).

(4) Where the law in Member States gives common-interest groups the right to bring an action as plaintiff, they may seek only the prohibition or cessation of the act giving rise to the injury to the environment. If, however, they have taken the measures provided for in paragraph 1(b) and (d), they may seek reimbursement of the expenditure resulting from such measures.

(5) This Directive shall be without prejudice to national provisions relating to non-material damage.

(6) The plaintiff shall be required to prove the damage or injury to the environment, and show the overwhelming probability of the causal relationship between the producer's waste and the damage or, as the case may be, the injury to the environment suffered.

ARTICLE 5

Where, under this Directive, two or more producers are liable for the same damage or the same injury to the environment, they shall be liable jointly and severally, without prejudice to the provisions of national law concerning the right of redress.

ARTICLE 6

(1) The producer shall not be liable under this Directive if he shows that the damage or injury to the environment results from force majeure as defined in Community law.

(2) The producer shall not be relieved of liability by the sole fact that he holds a permit issued by the public authorities.

* * *

3. Voluntary changes in the scope of rights: easements, covenants, and servitudes

A landowner may agree that some undertaking of his will bind, not only himself, but anyone who owns his land thereafter. Sometimes, the law will enforce these arrangements. We will first take a general look at them. We will then consider two questions that have often caused trouble: first, whether a landowner can bind himself and his successors to do an affirmative act, rather than simply suffer some interference with his usual rights of ownership; second, whether the beneficiary of the arrangement must be another property owner, or whether it can be someone who owns no land at all. Finally, we will look at a problem each legal system has faced: what happens when the owner of a tract of land subdivides it into parcels, and tries to bind the owner of each parcel, and his successors, to the owner of every other, without binding himself?

a. Overview

Anglo-American law: easements, covenants and equitable servitudes

Easements were enforceable in courts of common law, as distinguished from courts of equity. An easement is "affirmative" if the beneficiary has the right to do something on the burdened property to which its owner could otherwise object. It is "negative" if the owner is prevented from doing something he otherwise could do. It is commonly said that either type of easement must "confer a benefit on the dominant tenant as such" rather than some "personal advantage" on its owner.[1] It cannot "benefit the landowner personally."[2] Traditionally, courts would enforce only a fixed number of negative easements. It would do so when the owner is not to block windows, not to interfere with the flow of air through a defined channel, not to remove support for a building, or not to interfere with the flow of water through an artificial stream.[3] English and American judges have been reluctant to hold that other limits on what an owner can do are enforceable as easements although American courts have occasionally done so.[4] Much of the reason, historically, was that easements could be acquired by prescription and could be enforced against an owner who bought without knowledge of them.[5] It would have been dangerous to say that an owner could not do something on his land merely because he had not done it during the period necessary for prescription to run. It would also have been unfair to subsequent purchasers ignorant of their existence especially because England did not have a system for keeping public records of land titles until 1925. Moreover, new affirmative easements were traditionally permitted only when they resembled those previously recognized. Scholars disagree on whether that traditional rule is still part of English law.[6]

Certain other arrangements called "real covenants" were enforceable in courts of common law, again, as distinguished from courts of equity. A real covenant might prevent the owner from doing something he otherwise could do when such an arrangement was not enforceable as a negative easement. It might require the owner to take some affirmative action. A "real covenant" is enforceable, however, only when the parties who originally created it had were in a special relationship to each other which was termed "privity" (or to be technically accurate, "horizontal privity"). In England, this requirement still means that the parties must be in a "tenurial relationship." In practice, they must be landlord and tenant. Thus one cannot use a real covenant to adjust the rights of nearby landowners. American courts have generally found there to be "horizontal privity" in two other situations as well: when the parties have a mutual interest in the same land (for example, one has an easement in the land owned by the other), or when the covenant was made when one party granted land to the other.[7]

1. Sir Robert Megarry, Sir William Wade & Charles Harpum, *The Law of Real Property* (6th ed. 2000), § 18-045.

2. Peter Sparkes, *A New Land Law* (1999), 574.

3. Jesse Dukeminier & James E. Krier, *Property* (5th ed. 2002), 855.

4. For example, Petersen v. Friedman, 328 P.2d 264 (Cal. App. 1958) recognized an easement protecting a party's view. English courts will not do so. Campbell v. Paddington Corp.

[1911] 1 K.B. 869; Keven Gray & Susan Francis Gray, *Elements of Land Law* (3rd ed. 2001), 470; Sparkes, *New Land Law* 579.

5. Dukeminier & Krier, *Property* 856.

6. *Compare* Gray & Gray, *Land Law* 472 (it still is), *with* Sparkes, *New Land Law* 579 (it is not). Sparkes argues that this rule was in effect abrogated by *Re Ellenborough Park*, [1956] Ch. 131, which recognized an easement to build a private garden.

7 Restatement of Property § 534 (1944).

Yet another kind of arrangement is called an "equitable servitude." It was enforceable in a court of equity, as distinguished from a court of common law. An equitable servitude is not subject to the requirement of privity. It is enforceable, however, against a purchaser who had notice of the servitude. The notice may be "actual"—he really knew about it—or it may be "constructive"—for example, he should have known about it by checking public records. The servitude must also "touch and concern the land," or, as it is sometimes phrased, it must "benefit or accommodate" the dominant estate.[8] In the United States, the drafters of the *Restatement (Third) of Property, Servitudes* have proposed to abolish this requirement.[9]

Continental law: servitudes and kindred relationships

In Roman law, so-called praedial servitudes were always between two parcels of land. They had to be for the general advantage of the owner of the benefitted property, not for the benefit of a particular owner whose needs or wants were relatively unique.[10] While at one time, some servitudes had been recognized which benefit a person who did not own property, eventually they were no longer regarded as servitudes. Nor could an owner be bound by a praedial servitude to perform an affirmative act.[11]

The French Civil Code, in the main, followed these provisions. The German Civil Code extended them.

French law

French Civil Code

ARTICLE 637

A servitude is a charge imposed on one parcel of land for the use and benefit of the land belonging to another proprietor.

French Civil Code

ARTICLE 686

The owners are allowed to establish on their land, and for the benefit of their land, such servitudes as seem good to them, provided, nevertheless, that the servitudes established cannot be imposed either on a person, nor in favor of a person, but only on a property for a property. . . .

German law

German law distinguishes between a *Grunddienstbarkeit* (literally, a "land servitude"), a *beschränkte persönliche Dienstbarkeit* (literally, a "limited personal servitude"), and a *Reallast*. A *Grunddienstbarkeit* is like a servitude in Roman and French law: one property is burdened for the advantage of another. As we will see later on, a *beschränkte persönliche Dienstbarkeit* allows one to go further: a property can be burdened for the

---

8. Gray & Gray, *Land Law* 625.
9. § 3.2 (1991).
10. Dig. 8.1.8 pr.; 8.3.5.1. See Dig. 8.3.3.2; 8.4.13 pr.

11. Dig. 8.1.15 (servitus in faciendo non consistere potest).

advantage of one who does not own property. A *Reallast* allows one to go still further: the owner of the burdened property can be required to perform an affirmative act, whether for whoever owns certain property, or for someone who owns no property at all.

German Civil Code

§ 1018 [CONCEPT (OF A *GRUNDDIENSTBARKEIT*)]

A parcel of land can be burdened in favor of the then owner of another parcel of land in such a manner that this owner is allowed to use the parcel in particular ways, or that certain actions cannot be performed on that parcel, or that the exercise of a right is not permitted that belongs to the ownership of the burdened parcel in relation to the other parcel. (*Grundienstbarkeit*)

§ 1019 [ADVANTAGE TO THE BENEFITTED LAND]

A *Grunddienstbarkeit* can only consist in a burden that advantages the use of the benefited property. The content of such a servitude cannot extend beyond that limit.

b. Burdens for the benefit of one who does not own land

Anglo-American law

London County Council v. Allen, [1914–1915] All E.R Rep. (C.A. 1914)

[An owner of land, having obtained permission of the London County Council to lay out a new street, entered into a covenant promising that he and subsequent purchasers would not "erect, or cause or permit to be erected, any building, structure, or other erection on the land . . . without the previous consent in writing of the council." The council did not own any land adjoining that for the protection of which the covenant was imposed. The plot of land was subsequently sold to the defendant, who had notice of the restrictive covenant, and she built houses on the land without having previously obtained the council's consent.]

Buckley L.J. "By virtue of ss 7 and 9 of the London Building Act, 1894, the London County Council have certain powers of control over land which the owner proposes to form or lay out in streets. But they have no estate or interest in such land. The plaintiffs at the date of the deed of covenant had no estate or interest in any land adjoining or in any manner affected by the observance or non-observance of the covenant contained in the deed. Under these circumstances the defendants Mrs Allen and Norris, who were not covenanting parties, contend upon this appeal that as matter of law, assuming that there has been a breach of the covenant contained in the deed of 24 January 1907, and assuming (although as matter of separate contention they deny it as a fact) that they had notice of that covenant, the plaintiffs cannot as against them maintain any action upon the covenant contained in the deed. The short proposition is that as matter of law a derivative owner of land, deriving title under a person who has entered into a restrictive covenant concerning the land, is not bound by the covenant, even if he took with notice of its existence, if the covenantee has no land adjoining that for the protection of which the covenant was imposed or any land affected by the observance or non-observance of the covenant, they were bound in equity to perform them. That, therefore, is not the principle upon which the equitable doctrine rests. In the present case we are asked to extend the doctrine of Tulk v. Moxhay so as to affirm that a restrictive covenant can be enforced against a derivative owner taking with notice by a person who never has had or who does not retain any land to be protected by the restrictive covenant in question. In my opinion the doctrine does not extend to that case. The doctrine is that a covenant not running with the land, but being a negative covenant entered into by an owner of land with an adjoining owner, binds the land in equity and is enforceable against a derivative owner taking with notice. The doctrine ceases to be applicable when the person seeking to enforce the covenant against the derivative owner has no land to be protected by the negative covenant. The fact that be has notice is in that case irrelevant."

Note: Most American states have preserved the English rule, not as to easements, but as to equitable servitudes[1] although the Third Restatement wants them enforced as well.[2]

One question that therefore arises is what to do when a company wishes to lay pipes underneath the burdened property or to string power or telephone lines across it. It may not own any land which is benefitted. If the arrangement were therefore unenforceable against successors of the owner of the burdened property, the company would have to repurchase them—perhaps at an extortionate price—whenever the land changed hands.

One solution would be to reconsider the rule that allows only the owner of benefitted property to enforce such a burden. American courts have done so in the case of easements. They will not enforce such arrangements, even though they do not benefit the owner of a definite parcel of property, although sometimes they will not allow the beneficiary to assign his rights to others. As Powell noted, however, "almost without exception" American courts have enforced and allowed the assignment of easements "for railroads, for telephone and telegraph and electric power lines, [and] for pipelines . . ."[3] According to Krier, "almost the only easements in gross [that is, easements where the beneficiary does not own specific property] that are not assignable under modern cases are recreational easements (easements for hunting, fishing, boating and camping)."[4] Even then, courts have sometimes upheld the assignment of such a right when the recreational easement was granted for commercial purposes.[5]

1. Richard R. Powell & Michael Allan Wolf, *Powell on Real Property* (2000), § 60,04[3][b]; Uriel Reichman, "Toward a Unified Concept of Servitudes," *S. Calif. L. Rev.* 55 (1982), 1179. That is curious, as James Krier has noted, since the rationale for the refusal to enforce such equitable servitudes in England was the analogy to easements. Jesse Dukeminier & James E. Krier, *Property* (5th ed. 2002), 891–92.

2. § 2.6 Comment d.
3. Powell & Wolf, *Real Property* § 34.16.
4. Dukeminier & Krier, *Real Property* 830.
5. Miller v. Lutheran Conference and Camp Ass'n, 200 A. 646 (Pa. 1938)(noting that "there is an obvious difference . . . between easements for personal enjoyment and those designed for commercial exploitation").

In England, however, the typical solution has been to enact special statutes and ordinances which create what are called "statutory easements." [6] Examples are servitudes for electricity, gas and water lines. [7] Of course, that solution works only when the legislature has perceived the problem and enacted a law. Suppose it has not? One ingenious solution was put forward in the case the following case.

Re Salvin's Indenture, Pitt v. Durham County Water Board, [1938] 2 All Eng. L. Rep. 498 (Ch. Div.)

[The defendant's predecessor, a water company, entered into an agreement with the plaintiff's predecessor in title which allowed it to lay pipes through his land in return for a payment of £ 3 per year. The plaintiff claimed that the arrangement was a personal license, not binding on the grantor's successors.]

Farwell J. "[The plaintiffs say] [i]t is . . . an attempt to create an easement in gross and—and as to this there is no possible doubt—an easement in gross [that is, an easement for the benefit of person who does not own land] is a right unknown to our law. That being so, it may have had the effect that the license that was granted by the grantor may not have been binding on him, but, at any rate, it could not have been binding on any successor of his. As I say, if this be in fact an easement in gross, because it is said—and said quite truly—that in order to create a valid easement, there must be a dominant and a servient tenement, and it is said here that there is no dominant tenement. In my judgment, that is not sound. The undertaking in this case, which is now vested in the defendants, consists of corporeal hereditaments and incorporeal hereditaments, the corporeal hereditaments being the lands which the company acquired for the purpose of its object—that is to say, lands for the erection of reservoirs and other similar purposes—and the incorporeal hereditaments being the rights which it acquired in the lands of others, to lay pipes for other purposes. The undertaking, in my judgment, being composed of both corporeal and incorporeal hereditaments, is capable of being the dominant tenement in a grant such as this. It is plain that the dominant tenement need not be contiguous to the servient tenement."

Note: Some English scholars have said that solutions like the one in *Re Salvin's Indenture* are disingenuous. [1] As Michael Sturley has said, a company that wants rights over a landing pad for its helicopter shuttle should not have to claim that these rights are for the benefit of its West End office. [2]

French law

Cass., 3e ch. civ., 25 March, 1992, 1993 D.S. 64

"[A]ccording to the decision under attack here, . . . the couple Rousselet, who are owners of part of a marsh, deny that Fraud and Bouvier have a

---

6. In addition, "numerous bodies have been given specific authority to enforce restrictive covenants in gross." Kevin Gray & Susan Francis Gray, *Elements of Land Law* (3d ed. 2001), 624.

7. Gray & Gray, *Land Law* 461.
1. Gray & Gray, *Land Law* 461 n. 15
2. Michael F. Sturley, "Easements in Gross," *Law Quarterly Review* 96 (1980), 557 at 567–68.

right, as they claim, as inhabitants of a territory known as the *fraire de Saint-Nervin* by virtue of an agreement concluded on 25 March 1652 with the prior owner of the marsh, to take grass from the property. The couple Rousselet deny that they have this right or the right to graze their flocks there. . . . [F]raud and Bouvier attack the decision below for denying that the right in question is a servitude, though the court did hold it was a proprietary right of a special kind. They claim that the court below failed to recognize 'that a servitude can be instituted for the benefit of limited by territory, so that, without affecting any particular person, it is attached to the territory and benefits its inhabitants, and need have no other characteristic beyond that one, and that in so deciding, the judges violated arts. 637 and 686 of the Civil Code.' . . . [B]ut as it appears that the right of taking grass is a burden on the land of the Rousselet couple, it nevertheless does not benefit any dominant estate but only benefits the inhabitants of a territorial unit, and the exercise of this right does not make one the owner of a servitude over the area in question, therefore, recognizing that the charge in question was not established for the use and utility of another parcel of land, the court of appeal legally justified its decision. . . ." [Nevertheless, the *Cour d'appel* failed to recognize the right to graze as one of a type of property in its own right though not a servitude. The number of types of property that can be recognized in this way is limited by statute.]

Note: Again, however, the problem arises, what to do when a company wants an agreement, that will bind successors, that it can lay pipes through another's land, or string telephone lines across it, or build a ski lift, and use some land for supports, and transport skiers across other land. As in England, one solution has been statutory: to create what the French call *servitudes de l'utilité publique*. Examples are servitudes for electricity, gas and water lines.[1] These enactments allow the beneficiaries to be private companies as well as government entities.[2]

As in England, the problem arises that there is no guarantee the legislature has enacted an appropriate statute. As we have seen, the English courts have sometimes wiggled around the problem by declaring some land, owned by the company, was supposedly benefitted by the arrangement. In one case the *Cour de cassation* was more dogmatic. It held that the operator of a ski lift could not have enforceable servitudes in the properties it crossed.[3] A 1941 statute permitted servitudes for a cable car line[4] but a ski lift was not a cable car. In 1985, the legislature solved the problem by permitting such servitudes in one provision of a statute concerning the protection and development of mountains.[5] Suppose, however, the lift is not on a mountain but across a park or zoo or valley? The legislature cannot think of all possibilities. Indeed, if in some cases, as the legislature evidently thinks, the rule should not be applied, then perhaps it would be better to think to rethink the rule that to wait for the legislature to make exceptions.

---

1. François Terré & Philippe Simler, *Droit civil Les Biens* (5th ed. 1998), no. 332.
2. Terré & Simler, *Les Biens* no. 333.
3. Cass. civ., 3d ch., 12 Dec. 1984, J.C.P. 1985.II.20411.

4. Law of 8 July 1941.
5. Law of 9 Jan. 1985, art. L. 145-1–L. 145-3, Code de l'urbanisme.

German law

German Civil Code

§ 1090 [CONCEPT (OF A *BESCHRÄNKTE PERSÖNLICHE DIENSTBARKEIT*)]

(1) A parcel of land can be burdened in such a manner that the person in whose favor the benefit operates is entitled to use that parcel in certain ways or possesses the kind of authority that can form the content of a *Grunddienstbarkeit* (*beschränkte persönliche Dienstbarkeit*).

* * *

§ 1091 [SCOPE]

In cases of doubt, the scope of a *beschränkte persönliche Dienstbarkeit* is defined according to the personal needs of the person benefitted.

§ 1092 [TRANSFERABILITY . . .]

(1) A *beschränkte persönliche Dienstbarkeit* cannot be transferred. Another person can only be allowed to use of such a servitude when the right to allow such a use was specified.

c. Burdens that require a land owner to do an affirmative act

English law

Haywood v. The Brunswick Permanent Benefit Building Society, [1881] 8 Law Reports 403 (Q.B.)

[Jackson granted a plot of land to Edward. Edward agreed to pay an annual rent of £ 11, to erect, to keep in repair, and if necessary to rebuild, certain buildings on the land. Each party agreed that these obligations would run to their successors.]

"I am clearly of the opinion, both on principle and on the authority of Milnes v. Branch [5 M. & S. 411] that this action could not be maintained at common law. Milnes v. Branch must be understood, as it has always been understood, and as Lord St. Leonard's [Sug. V. & P. 14th ed., p. 590] understood it, and it will be seen, on a reference to his book, that he considers the effect of it to be that a covenant to build does not run with the rent in the hands of an assignee.

That being so, the question is rendered an equitable one. Now the equitable doctrine was brought to a focus in Tulk v. Moxhay [2 Ph. 774], which is the leading case on the subject. It seems to me that the case decided that an assignee taking land subject to a certain class of covenants is bound by such covenants if he has notice of them, and that the class of covenants comprehended within the rule is that the covenants restricting the mode of using the land only will be enforced. It may be also, but it is not necessary to decide here, that all covenants also which impose such a burden on the land as can be enforced against the land would be enforced. Be that as it may, a covenant to repair is not restrictive and could not be enforced against the land; therefore, such a covenant is within neither rule."

Law in the United States

Supposedly, the law of most American states is the exact opposite of that in England. Successors to the burdened property are bound by an agreement to perform an affirmative act provided the act "touches and concerns" the burdened property and, perhaps, the benefitted property as well.[1] In many cases, American courts have followed this rule. Nevertheless, it is more interesting, and more enlightening to see that sometimes they have not given a remedy, even though they acknowledged that the burden was attached to the land. An example is the following case.

Oceanside Community Association v. Oceanside Land Co. 147 Cal. App. 166 (1983)

"Oceana is a 13-unit residential development composed of 932 residences on individual lots and common areas (central club house, swimming pool, recreation areas, administrative offices, streets, walks, covered parking and landscaped areas). The Oceanside Community Association (Homeowners Association) leases the common areas from the Oceanside Land Company (Developer) and assesses its homeowner members for their individual share of the lease.

In September 1965, Developer offered to include a promised golf course in the common area of Oceana, but the homeowners (units I through IV) turned down the offer by a decisive vote at a meeting called by the Homeowners Association. Following this rejection, Developer recorded a declaration of covenants, conditions and restrictions (CC&Rs) on October 13, 1965, restricting certain property adjacent to Oceana to be used as a golf course for 99 years. The CC&Rs stated they created a covenant running with the land and the restriction was imposed 'as heretofore agreed with past purchasers' of units I through IV. Under the CC&Rs homeowners were entitled to play at 75 percent of the rate charged the public and given the right to release the golf course restriction upon a favorable vote of three-fourths of the homeowners.

Developer built the golf course and operated it for several years. Developer's salespersons used the golf course as an inducement to new purchasers. . . .

In November 1970, Developer sold the golf course to the Smiths. . . .

The Smiths operated the golf course until December 1976 at which time they sold the property to Career Knowledge Institute, Inc. (Career Institute) and its president, Phil Plies. . . . Plies did not maintain the golf course. In April 1977 Homeowners Association filed a complaint for damages and injunctive relief against Developer to enforce the covenant.

[The court held that the agreement to operate the golf course was a burden attached to the land. Nevertheless it affirmed the decision of the trial court not to enforce this obligation by an injunction, that is, by an order that the golf course be maintained.]

---

1. Richard R. Powell & Michael Allan Wolf, *Powell on Real Property* (2000), § 60.06[2][c].

The decision to grant or deny an injunction lies within the sound discretion of the trial court; its decision will not be disturbed on appeal absent an abuse of discretion. (*Union Interchange, Inc. v. Savage* (1959) 52 Cal.2d 601, 606 [342 P.2d 249].) The trial court denied the injunction based upon this evidence: By the time Pine Tree acquired the property, the golf course was already badly deteriorated. At the time of trial the estimated cost to restore the course properly was $400,000, or $200,000 if it was done cheaply. The trial court concluded it was not economical for Pine Tree to renovate the course in light of its investment. Additionally, the trial court believed it would be inequitable to hold Pine Tree personally liable (by issuing the injunction) for damage which occurred before it acquired the property and during that time when its title was clouded by Career Institute and Plies. The court was cognizant of the complicated nature of restoring a golf course and of the court supervision necessary to carry out such a decree. Under these circumstances, the trial court's denial of the mandatory injunction was not an abuse of discretion."

French law

In principle, French law follows the old Roman rule that the owner of land subject to a servitude cannot be required to perform an affirmative act.[1] As we will see, however, much can be done by making a creative use of the following provisions of the French Civil Code.

French Civil Code

ARTICLE 697

The one owed an obligation by a servitude has the right to perform all the works necessary to use and preserve it.

ARTICLE 698

These works are not at the expense of the owner of the land that is burdened unless the contrary was specified in establishing the servitude.

Cour de cassation, 9 January 1901, D. 1901.1.450

"[B]y the terms of art. 686 of the Civil Code, a parcel of land can be burdened for the benefit of another parcel with burdens attached to the land (*charges réelles*) of any kind provided that these servitudes are not imposed on a person or created for the benefit of a person, and that they are not contrary to public policy (*ordre publique*). . . . [I]t appears from the statements in the decision attacked here (Montpellier, 5 June 1897), that the right in dispute, created in 1845 and exercised thereafter without interruption, consisted in a power given the glassworks of Bosquet to take the coal necessary for its production from the mines operated by the *Compagnie de Grassac* at a fixed price of 50 centimes per 100 kilograms, that power being limited to the consumption of three ovens. . . . [M]ines, like other real property, are subject to servitudes. . . . [T]he right in dispute was established with no limitation in time. . . . [I]t has produced a benefit, not

---

1. Christian Atias, *Droit Civil Les Biens* (4th ed. 1999), no. 174; François Terré & Philippe Simler, *Les Biens* (5th ed. 1998), no. 746.

to the person of the owners of the glassworks, but in favor of the factory itself.... [T]hat right consists in the taking for operations of products which naturally exist on neighboring land and are indispensable to the working of the factory. Thus, this right combines all the elements of a servitude attached to property.... [T]he fact that this was done by the extraction of the coal to be gathered by the mining company does not modify the nature of this right since art. 698 of the Civil Code allows the parties to entrust the owner of the property with the work necessary for the use of the servitude.... [T]he payments made by the glassworks are of no significance since gratuity is not of the essence of a servitude, and the amount to be paid, fixed once and for all, was merely a condition of the exercise of the right, and serves to diminish the burden placed on the property...." [The *pourvoi* seeking to have the arrangement declared unenforceable as a servitude was rejected.]

German law

German Civil Code

§ 1105 [CONCEPT: SUBJECTIVE PROPRIETARY *REALLAST*]

(1) A parcel of property can be burdened in such a manner that the recurring performances on the parcel are due to the person in favor of whom the burden operates.

(2) The *Reallast* can also be constituted in favor of the then owner of another parcel of property.

§ 1110 [SUBJECTIVE PROPRIETARY RIGHT]

A *Reallast* in favor of the then owner of property cannot be severed from the ownership of this property.

Note: While these provisions of the German Civil Code seem quite permissive, German federal states have imposed their own restrictions on when an obligation to perform an affirmative action is enforceable. In Nordrhein-Westfalen it must be a payment of money.[1] In Baden-Württemberg[2] and Rheinland-Pfalz,[3] the only servitudes that impose affirmative duties and can be established permanently are those to maintain installations for electricity, heat, warm water, or components of the soil, and, in Rheinland-Pfalz, to pay money. In Baden-Württemberg,[4] Bremen,[5] and Rheinland-Pfalz[6] such a servitude can last only for the burdened property owner's lifetime. In Rheinland-Pfalz, if the owner is a juridical person, it can last only 30 years.[7]

1. Preussisches Ausführungsgesetz zum BGB, art. 30, 20 Sept.1899, GS 177.

2. Ausführungsgesetz zum BGB § 33, 26 Nov.1974, Gesetz und Verordungsblatt 498.

3. Ausführungsgesetz zum BGB § 22, 18 Nov. 1976,Gesetz und Verordungsblatt 259.

4. Unless the burden is to maintain installation for electricity, heat, warm water, or components of the soil or to pay money. Ausführungsgesetz zum BGB § 33, 26 Nov. 1974, Gesetz und Verordungsblatt 498.

5. Ausführungsgesetz zum BGB § 26, 18 July 1899, Sammlung des bremischen Rechts 400 a 1.

6. Ausführungsgesetz zum BGB § 22, 18 Nov. 1976, Gesetz und Verordungsblatt 259.

7. Unless the burden is to maintain installation for electricity, heat, warm water, or components of the soil or to pay money. *Id.*

d. The problem of subdivisions

English law

In re Dophin's Conveyance, [1970] Law Reports 654 (Ch. Div.)

[Between February, 1871, and April, 1877, several parcels of land, part of an identified named estate, were conveyed by several conveyances to various purchases by vendors who took from a common owner. Each conveyance required that the land be used for a detached dwelling house built upon at least a quarter acre of land.]

"As Cross J. pointed out in the course of his judgment in *Baxter v. Four Oaks Properties Ltd.* [1965] Ch. 816 . . . the intention that the several purchasers from a common vendor shall have the benefit of the restrictive covenants imposed on each of them, may be evidenced by the existence of a deed of mutual covenant to which all the purchasers are to be parties. That common intention may also be evidenced by, or inferred from, the circumstances attending the sales: the existence of which has often been referred to in the authorities as a building scheme. . . .

What has been argued before me is that here there is neither a deed of mutual covenant nor a building scheme. In the latter connection, it was pointed out that there was not a common vendor, for parcels were sold off, first by the Dolphins, and then by Watts. Nor, prior to the sales, had the vendors laid out the estate, or a defined portion of it, for sale in lots. . . .

In my judgment, these submissions are not well founded. To hold that only where you find the necessary concomitants of a building scheme or a deed of mutual covenant can you give effect to the common intention found in the conveyances themselves, would, in my judgment, be to ignore the wider principle on which the building scheme cases are founded. . . .

The conveyances of the several parts of the estate taking the form they do, and evidencing the same intention as is found in a deed of mutual covenant, I equate those conveyances with the deed of mutual covenant considered by Cross J. in *Baxter v. Four Oaks Properties Ltd.* . . ."

Law in the United States

Sanborn v. McLean, 206 N.W. 496 (Mich. 1925)

"Mr. and Mrs. McLean started to erect a gasoline filling station at the rear end of their lot, and . . . were enjoined by decree from doing so. . . .

Collingwood avenue is a high-grade residence street between Woodward avenue and Hamilton boulevard, with single, double and apartment houses, and plaintiffs who are owners of land adjoining, and in the vicinity of defendants' land, and who trace title, as do defendants, to the proprietors of the subdivision, claim that the proposed gasoline station . . . is in violation of the general plan fixed for use of all lots on the street for residence purposes only, as evidenced by restrictions upon 53 of the 91 lots fronting on Collingwood avenue, and that defendants' lot is subject to a reciprocal negative easement barring a use so detrimental to the enjoyment and value of its neighbors.

Defendants insist that no restrictions appear in their chain of title and they purchased without notice of any reciprocal negative easement. . . .

Is defendants' lot subject to a reciprocal negative easement? If the owner of two or more lots, so situated as to bear the relation, sells one with restrictions of benefit to the land retained, the servitude becomes mutual, and, during the period of restraint, the owner of the lot or lots retained can do nothing forbidden to the owner of the lot sold. For want of a better descriptive term this is styled a reciprocal negative easement. It runs with the land sold by virtue of express fastening and abides with the land retained until loosened by expiration of its period of service or by events working its destruction. It is not personal to owners but operative upon use of the land by any owner having actual or constructive notice thereof. It is an easement passing its benefits and carrying its obligations to all purchasers of land subject to its affirmative or negative mandates. It originates for mutual benefit and exists with vigor sufficient to work its ends. It must start with a common owner. . . .

When Mr. McLean purchased on contract in 1910 or 1911, there was a partly built dwelling house on lot 86, which he completed and now occupies. He had an abstract of title which he examined and claims he was told by the grantor that the lot was unrestricted. Considering the character of use made of all the lots open to a view of Mr. McLean when he purchased, we think he was put thereby to inquiry, beyond asking his grantor whether there were restrictions. He had an abstract showing the subdivision and that lot 86 had 97 companions; he could not avoid noticing the strictly uniform residence character given the lots by the expensive dwellings thereon, and the least inquiry would have quickly developed the fact that lot 86 was subjected to a reciprocal negative easement, and he could finish his house and, like the others, enjoy the benefits of the easement. We do not say Mr. McLean should have asked his neighbors about restrictions, but we do say that with the notice he had from a view of the premises on the street, clearly indicating the residences were built and the lots occupied in strict accordance with a general plan, he was put to inquiry, and had he inquired he would have found of record the reason for such general conformation, and the benefits thereof serving the owners of lot 86 and the obligations running with such service and available to adjacent lot owners to prevent a departure from the general plan by an owner of lot 86."

Neponsit Property Owners' Association, Inc. v. Emigrant Industrial Savings Bank, 15 N.E. 2d 1793 (N.Y. 1938)

"It appears that in January, 1911, Neponsit Realty Company, as owner of a tract of land in Queens county, caused to be filed in the office of the clerk of the county a map of the land. The tract was developed for a strictly residential community, and Neponsit Realty Company conveyed lots in the tract to purchasers, describing such lots by reference to the filed map and to roads and streets shown thereon. In 1917, Neponsit Realty Company conveyed the land now owned by the defendant to Robert Oldner Deyer and his wife by deed which contained the covenant upon which the plaintiff's cause of action is based.

That covenant provides: 'And the party of the second part for the party of the second part and the heirs, successors and assigns of the party of the second part further covenants that the property conveyed by this deed shall be subject to an annual charge in such an amount as will be fixed by the party of the first part, its successors and assigns, not, however exceeding in any year the sum of four ($4.00) Dollars per lot 20 × 100 feet. The assigns of the party of the first part may include a Property Owners' Association which may hereafter be organized for the purposes referred to in this paragraph, and in case such association is organized the sums in this paragraph provided for shall be payable to such association. . . . Such charge shall be devoted to the maintenance of the roads, paths, parks, beach, sewers and such other public purposes as shall from time to time be determined by the party of the first part, its successors or assigns.'

There can be no doubt that Neponsit Realty Company intended that the covenant should run with the land and should be enforceable by a property owners association against every owner of property in the residential tract which the realty company was then developing. The language of the covenant admits of no other construction. Regardless of the intention of the parties, a covenant will run with the land and will be enforceable against a subsequent purchaser of the land at the suit of one who claims the benefit of the covenant, only if the covenant complies with certain legal requirements. These requirements rest upon ancient rules and precedents. The age-old essentials of a real covenant, aside from the form of the covenant, may be summarily formulated as follows: (1) it must appear that grantor and grantee intended that the covenant should run with the land; (2) it must appear that the covenant is one 'touching' or 'concerning' the land with which it runs; (3) it must appear that there is 'privity of estate' between the promisee or party claiming the benefit of the covenant and the right to enforce it, and the promisor or party who rests under the burden of the covenant. . . .

The covenant in this case is intended to create a charge or obligation to pay a fixed sum of money to be 'devoted to the maintenance of the roads, paths, parks, beach, sewers and such other public purposes as shall from time to time be determined by the party of the first part [the grantor], its successors or assigns.' It is an affirmative covenant to pay money for use in connection with, but not upon, the land which it is said is subject to the burden of the covenant. Does such a covenant 'touch' or 'concern' the land? . . .

[I]t seems clear that the covenant may properly be said to touch and concern the land of the defendant and its burden should run with the land. True, it calls for payment of a sum of money to be expended for 'public purposes' upon land other than the land conveyed by Neponsit Realty Company to plaintiff's predecessor in title. By that conveyance the grantee, however, obtained not only title to particular lots, but an easement or right of common enjoyment with other property owners in roads, beaches, public parks or spaces and improvements in the same tract. For full enjoyment in common by the defendant and other property owners of these easements or rights, the roads and public places must be maintained. In order that the burden of maintaining public improvements should rest upon the land benefitted by the improvements, the grantor exacted from the grantee of the land with its appurtenant easement or right of enjoyment a covenant that the burden of paying the cost should be inseparably attached to the land which enjoys the benefit. It is plain that any distinction or definition which would exclude such a covenant from the classification of covenants which 'touch' or 'concern' the land would be based on form and not on substance. . . .

Another difficulty remains. Though between the grantor and the grantee there was privity of estate, the covenant provides that its benefit shall run to the assigns of the grantor who 'may include a Property Owners' Association which may hereafter be organized for the purposes referred to in this paragraph.' The plaintiff has been organized to receive the sums payable by the property owners and to expend them for the benefit of such owners. Various definitions have been formulated of 'privity of estate' in connection with covenants that run with the land, but none of such definitions seems to cover the relationship between the plaintiff and the defendant in this case. The plaintiff has not succeeded to the ownership of any property of the grantor. It does not appear that it ever had title to the streets or public places upon which charges which are payable to it must be expended. It does not appear that it owns any other property in the residential tract to which any easement or right of enjoyment in such property is appurtenant. It is created solely to act as the assignee of the benefit of the covenant, and it has no interest of its own in the enforcement of the covenant. . . .

The corporate plaintiff has been formed as a convenient instrument by which the property owners may advance their common interests. We do not ignore the corporate form when we recognize that the Neponsit Property Owners Association, Inc., is acting as the agent or representative of the Neponsit property owners. . . . Only blind adherence to an ancient formula devised to meet entirely different conditions could constrain the court to hold that a corporation formed as a medium for the enjoyment of common rights of property owners owns no property which would benefit by enforcement of common rights and has no cause of action in equity to enforce the covenant upon which such common rights depend. Every reason which in other circumstances may justify the ancient formula may be urged in support of the conclusion that the formula should not be applied in this case. In substance if not in form the covenant is a restrictive covenant which touches and concerns the defendant's land, and in substance, if not in form, there is privity of estate between the plaintiff and the defendant."

French law

Cour de cassation, 30 June 1936, D.P. 1938.1.68

[In 1861, the city of Paris sold a tract of land in the neighborhood of the Champs-Elysées to Pereire. The contract of sale contained a clause specifying that only family homes could be built on the tract and that no commercial or industrial activity could be undertaken there. Pereire then subdivided and resold the property, inserting clause to that effect in each contract of sale. When one of the purchasers violated this clause, he was sued by other purchasers and by the city of Paris.]

"[I]n the decision below, it was determined that by prohibiting in absolute terms the application of the lands sold to any other use than family homes, both in the original sale and the successive sales, the city of Paris and Pereire, as well and Pereire and his repurchasers, meant, by this general provision, not only to bind the contracting parties personally, but to establish a servitude attached to the land (*servitude réelle*), and not simply for the benefit of the public domain, but in the interest of each party with respect to every other. . . . [O]ne cannot consider that provision to be a denigration of contract, contrary to the claims of the *pourvoi*, since, as it concerns an interpretation of the intention of the parties, the determination of the lower court cannot be reviewed by the *Cour de cassation.* . . . [I]n similar matters, as in every matter so concerned with contract, the lower court has the absolute right to determine the intention of the parties according to the documents and circumstances of the case. . . . [N]or does it appear that by making this determination, the decision under attack . . . has exceeded the limits imposed on servitudes by art. 686 of the Civil Code. . . . The prohibition on the owner of the parcel to use the parcel in any other way than a family home can, according to the circumstances, perfectly have the characteristics of a duty attached to the parcel of land itself in the interest of another parcel. . . . [T]he decision below could consider precisely if that was so in this case, the limitation to use as a family home which the city of Paris wished to bring about in the neighborhood of the Champs-Elysées, and in each parcel in the neighborhood, promoting the desirability of tranquility and elegance. . . . [T]hat desirability indeed takes on the character of a limitation on the rights of property, which, as it is in the interest of every parcel affected, ought normally to promote an increase in their market value." [The *pourvoi* claiming that these restrictions could not be enforced as a servitude was rejected.]

Note (by "M.N.") to Cour de cassation, 30 June 1936, D.P. 1938.1.68

"But granting, with the court below, that the sale of 1861 did not constitute a personal obligation but a servitude, one still must determine the beneficiaries of this provision. The problem here is more difficult to resolve. The sale in question was from the city of Paris to Pereire. It is for the benefit of the city of Paris, the sole owner of the land benefitted, that the servitude was created. And, since the city of Paris never ceded its right to third parties, are those who bought from Pereire entitled to demand respect for a servitude which they do not own, or is there action without any legal foundation?

The objection is serious. But it is more apparent than real. No one can deny that in this case, a legal obligation between the city of Paris and Pereire was created by the contract between these two parties. But it does not necessarily follow that only the city of Paris is entitled to require that the servitude it constituted be respected. The reason is that even if, normally, a servitude is created by the owner of the land benefitted for his own benefit, still, it could be created by a third party acting in the name of the beneficiary or for his advantage, as in the case of a promise to benefit a third party. . . .

This theory of a servitude constituted by a promise for the benefit of a third party has already been accepted by the case law in the case of a subdivision of land. The company selling the land has included in the documents of sale a clause prohibiting the conduct of certain industrial activities. In considering litigation concerning the application of such a clause, the *Cour [d'appel]* of Paris (5 March 1913), interpreting the will of the parties, decided that the prohibition was made in the interest of all those who would become buyers and was created for that purpose, and even though the term 'servitude' never appeared in the sale, it was still a servitude attached to the land, burdening each parcel for the benefit of every other, each parcel being both the land burdened and the land benefited, and this interpretation was upheld by the *Chambre des requêtes* [of the *Cour de cassation*]. . . ."

Cour de cassation ch. civ., 5 May 1919, D. 1923.1.230

"[I]t appears from the statements and explanations of the decision attacked here (Paris, 23 Feb. 1911) that the *Société Civil du domaine de Montfermeil*, as part of the subdivision in 1896 of the lands belonging to this tract and their sale as individual parcels, transferred a certain number of parcels to the parties who are now protesting the decision below. . . . [T]o serve the tract, the sellers organized a network of roads, avenues, squares, and streets for passage to and the use of the parcels sold. . . . [I]t was stipulated that the usability of these roads—the land remaining the property of the *Société*—would be ensured by means of a contribution due from buyers at a set price, and that the maintenance, lighting, and sweeping of these roads would remain the responsibility of the *Société* subject to an annual payment by the buyers of fees proportional to the purchase price of each lot. . . . [T]he rights thus formally established and unlimited in time as to the land used for roads were not created for the benefit of the persons who owned the lots but for the benefit of the lots themselves, and they thus combine all the elements of a servitude attached to the land (*servitude réelle*). . . . [T]he fact that ensuring the usability of these roads and their upkeep are tasks which belong to the *Société* which owns the land, and that certain fees must be paid by the owners of the lands that benefit, does not change the legal nature of these rights. . . . [O]n the one hand, art. 698 of the Civil Code permits one to place on the owner of lands subject to a servitude at the time the servitude is established the charge of the work necessary for the use or preservation of the servitude, and, in this case, that is the character of these works which are a necessary accessory to the servitude and form part of it. On the other hand, gratuity is not of the essence of a servitude, and the amounts paid by the owners of the lands that benefit are the price of the servitude, merely constituting one of the conditions for the exercise of this right." [The *pourvoi* seeking to have these charges declared unenforceable as a servitude was rejected.]

German law

German Civil Code

§ 1196 [CHARGE ON THE LAND FOR THE OWNER]

(1) A charge on the land can also be created for the owner.

(2) For its creation, the owner must make a declaration to the land registry office that charge on the land shall be entered for him in the land registry, and the charge must be so entered. . . .

Note: By analogy to § 1196 (2) of the German Civil Code, the owner of two several parcels of land can register an so called owner's *Grunddienstbarkeit* by analogy to § 1196 II BGB binding each parcel. RGZ 142, 231 (233); BGH WM 1984, 820 (821); BGHZ 41, 209 (210). The owner would need to have an acceptable interest in establishing the *Grunddienstbarkeit*. But his desire to sell the land would constitute an acceptable interest. OLG Frankfurt Rpfleger 1984, 264.

III. THE DOCTRINE OF NECESSITY

1. Origins

Roman lawyers generally approached problems one-by-one, rather than trying to organize their solutions under large doctrines. While they did not speak of a doctrine of necessity, they did discuss cases that later jurists were to see as instances of such a doctrine. Some of them were cases in which one person could enter another's land without permission: for example, to look for a fugitive.[1] Some were instances in which a person preserved his own life or property by destroying that of another: for example, if he pulls down his neighbor's house to save his own from a fire. As we saw, under normal circumstances, if one person damaged another's property, the victim could bring an action under the *lex Aquilia*. What we would call "necessity" was sometimes a defense.[2]

Finally, there were rules allowing the captain of a ship to jettison cargo to save the ship. The passengers whose goods had been saved had to compensate those who goods were thrown overboard. These rules were similar

---

1. Here is how these situations were described by a medieval lawyer (as it happens, a canonist): "There are cases in which one is allowed to pass through another's field: if there is a servitude, C. 3.34.11, or if one wants to dig up one's own treasure, Dig. 10.4.19 (at the end), if my fruit fell into your field, D. 43.27.1, when I am looking for a fugitive, Dig. 11.4.4 . . . and when a public road is destroyed, Dig. 8.6.14.1." *Glossa ordinaria [Ordinary Gloss] to Gratian, Decretum* ad D. 1, c. 2.

2. "What is said about suing under the *lex Aquilia* for damage wrongfully done must be taken as meaning that damage is done wrongfully when it inflicts wrong together with the damage, and this is inflicted, except where it is done under compulsion of overwhelming necessity, as Celsus writes about the man who pulled down his neighbor's house to keep a fire off his own; for he writes that there is no action under the *lex Aquilia*, because he pulled down the adjoining house in the reasonable fear that the fire would reach his own house. Celsus also thinks that there is no action under the *lex* regardless of whether the fire would actually have reached him or been put out first." Dig. 9.2.49.1.

to modern admiralty law, and indeed, were the historical ancestors of that law.[3]

The medieval canon lawyers generalized to formulate a doctrine of necessity. Unlike the Roman lawyers, they were not dealing with the problem of who should pay if cargo was jettisoned or a house destroyed or a fugitive chased onto someone else's land. They were trying to determine when one was guilty of the sin of greed. In one of the texts that Gratian incorporated into his *Decretum*, Saint Ambrose denounced a person who "sees always gold, always silver" and "asks gold even in his prayer and supplication to God." He goes on:

> But, you say, what is the injustice if I diligently care for my own without seizing what is another's? Oh, imprudent saying! Your own you say? What things? From what horde did you bring them into this world? When you came into the light, when you left your mother's womb, stuffed with what possessions and goods, I ask, did you come? . . . Let no one call his own what is common.[4]

Maybe Ambrose merely meant that people shouldn't be piggy. Nevertheless, the literally minded canon lawyers tried to figure out when and in what sense private property can be "common"? They said that property was not meant merely for the benefit of the owner, so that if a person had more than enough for himself, he should give the rest away. They also said that in a state of necessity, property became literally common. In addition to canon law texts, they cited the Roman rules on jettisoning cargo at sea.[5]

While the canonists had formulated a general doctrine of necessity, they explained it only in the way just described: by citing texts. Eventually, a philosophical explanation was found by drawing on Aristotle, whose philosophy dominated the universities until into the seventeenth century. Aristotle had been arguing against the view of his teacher Plato that all property should be in common. If it were, Aristotle said, "[t]hose who labor much and get little will necessarily complain of those who labor little and receive or consume much."[6] In the thirteenth century, building on Aristotle,

---

3. "If goods have been jettisoned, because the ship was in difficulty, the owners who have lost the cargo for whose carriage they contracted may sue the captain on their contracts. Then the captain may bring an action on his contracts of carriage against the others whose goods have been saved, so as to distribute the loss proportionately." Dig. 9.2.2 pr.

4. *Decretum* D.47 c.8.

5. *Glossa Ordinaria* to *Decretum* to D. 47 c.8 to *Commune*. That interpretation seemed to collide with another text that was eventually included in a collection of papal decisions called the *Decretals of Gregory IX*. The text, taken from an early manual for priests prescribing penance to those who confessed their sins, said that "if a person stole food, clothing or money because of necessity, being hungry

or naked, he should do three weeks penance, and if he returned what he stole, he should not be compelled to fast." *Decretals* 5.18.3. The difficulty for the canonists was why a person who stole in time of necessity should have to do penance at all, even a light penance, since by their doctrine all things were in common, and therefore he should not have committed a sin. The standard gloss to the *Decretals* resolved the problem by assuming the text was speaking of moderate necessity: "From the facts that penance is imposed, it may be gathered that the necessity was moderate. Penance would not have been imposed if it had been great . . . for in necessity all things are common." *Glossa ordinaria* ad *Decretals* 5.18.3. to *poenitentia*.

6. *Politics* II. v.

Thomas Aquinas gave a similar explanation.[7] Going beyond Aristotle, he claimed that this account or private property could explain the canonists' doctrine of necessity. In considering "whether it is lawful to steal through stress of need" Aquinas said:

> [T]he division and appropriation of things which are based on human law do not preclude the fact that man's needs have to be remedied by means of these very things. . . . If the need be so manifest and urgent, that it is evident that the present need must be remedied by whatever means be at hand (for instance, when a person is in some imminent danger, and there is no other possible remedy) then it is lawful for a man to succor his own need by means of another's property, by taking it either openly or secretly: nor is this properly speaking theft or robbery.[8]

This explanation was adopted, first by the so-called late scholastics or Spanish natural law school of the sixteenth century, and then by the northern natural law school of the seventeenth and eighteenth centuries.[9] Here is the way it was presented by Hugo Grotius, the founder of the northern natural law school:

> Let us consider whether men have any common right to those things which are already made private property. Some may think that this is a strange question, since property seems to have absorbed all the right which flowed from the common state of things. But this is not so. For we must consider what was the intention of those who introduced private property: which we must suppose to have been, to deviate as little as possible from natural equity. For if even written laws are to be construed

---

7. "[It] is necessary to human life for three reasons. First because every man is more careful to procure what is for himself alone than that which is common to many or all: since each one would shirk the labor and leave to another that which concerns the community, as happens where there is a great number of servants. Secondly, because human affairs are conducted in a more orderly fashion if each man is charged with taking care of some particular thing himself, whereas there would be confusion if everyone had to look after any one thing indeterminately. Thirdly, because a more peaceful state is insured to man if each one is contented with his own. Hence it is to be observed that quarrels arise more frequently where there is no division of things possessed." *Summa theologiae* II-II Q. 66, a. 2.

8. *Summa theologiae* II-II Q. 66, a.7.

9. Here is the way it was presented by Leonard Lessius, one of the leaders of the Spanish natural law school (actually, he was Flemish but he counts because at that time, Spain controlled Flanders, and he worked with the Spanish members): "I say . . . one may take another's thing when one is in extreme necessity because, in extreme necessity, one

needs what is necessary to preserve one's life. This is the common opinion of the doctors. The proof is that in extreme necessity all things are common—which is a received axiom—not that ownership is transferred. . . . All things are common insofar as the right to use them is concerned, and so a person who is pressed by these difficulties can lawfully take them. He has the right to any thing to the extent it is necessary, and he may help himself or another person by its use. The reason for this is that the end of inferior things is to serve men through necessity, so that through them men may preserve and maintain their lives. Therefore this right belongs to all by nature. Nor can the division of things introduced by the law of nations take away this right, for the law of nations presupposes the law of nature and does not destroy it particularly as to what is necessary to preserve life. The division of things must therefore be deemed to have been made with a reservation to each person of this natural right to whatever is necessary to maintain his life. Otherwise the division would not have been done in a rational way." *De iustitia et iure ceterisque virtutibus cardinalis* (1628), lib. 2, cap. 12, dub. 12.

in that sense as far as possible, much more is mere usage, which is not fettered by written words. Hence it follows, that in extreme necessity, the pristine right of using things revives, as if they had remained common: for in all laws, and thus in the law of ownership, extreme necessity is accepted.

Hence the rule, that in a voyage, if the provisions run short, what each one has must be thrown into the common stock. So to preserve my house from a conflagration which is raging, my neighbor's house may be pulled down: and ropes or nets may be cut, of which rules are not introduced by the civil law but by the interpretations of it.

For among theologians also, it is a received opinion, that in such a necessity, if anyone take what is necessary to his life from any other's property, he does not commit theft, of which rule the reason is, not that which some alleged, that the owner of the property is bound to give so much to him that needs it out of charity, but this, that all things must be understood to be a sign to owners with some such benevolent exception of the right thus primitively assigned. For if the first dividers had been asked what was their intention, they would have given such an one as we have stated.

But cautions are to be applied, that this liberty go not too far.

First, that we must endeavor in every way to avoid this necessity in some other manner, as by applying to the magistrate, or by trying whether we cannot obtain the use of things from the owner by entreaty. . . .

Secondly, such liberty is not granted, if the possessor be in like necessity. . . .

Thirdly, that when it is possible, restitution be made.[10]

Explanations of this sort were common on into the eighteenth century. By the nineteenth century, in continental Europe, they had almost vanished. In the nineteenth century, jurists tried to explain property, not by asking about the purposes that property should serve, but by the concept of will. Property, by definition, meant that the will of the owner determined the use to which the property could be put.

Nineteenth century French jurists said that this idea was enshrined in the French Civil Code. Article 544 provided:

Property is the right to enjoy and dispose of things in the most absolute manner provided that one does not make a use of them that is prohibited by statute or regulation.

This sentence had been taken almost verbatim from the eighteenth century jurist Pothier whose conceptions of law were nearly always an unoriginal restatement of the teachings of the natural law school. It is unlikely that when Pothier wrote these words he had in mind any different theory of

10. *De iure belli ac pacis libri tres* (1646), II.ii.2, 6–9.

property than Grotius. It is even more unlikely that the drafting committee of the French Civil Code, in the few months available to it, devised a new theory of property when they borrowed the words of Pothier. Nevertheless, the nineteenth century French jurists claimed that this provision required them to define property solely in terms of the will of the owner.

The nineteenth century German jurists defined property in the same way. According to Bernard Windscheid, one of the greatest jurists of the century:

> To say that a thing belongs to a person is to say that his will is decisive for it in its totality of its relationships. The significance is two-fold: (1) the owner may provide as he will concerning the thing; (2) another person may not provide for the thing in a manner contrary to his will (these are the positive and negative sides of ownership). (*Lehrbuch des Pandektenrechts* § 167)

They concluded that there should not be a doctrine of necessity. The first draft of the German Civil Code provided in what is today § 903:

> The owner of a thing may treat it as he pleases and exclude others from any dealing with it insofar as statutes and the rights of a third party are not to the contrary.

Necessity was not supposed to be an exception.

Nevertheless, as we will see, even in the nineteenth century, the doctrine was accepted in the United States. It is beginning to be recognized in France. Moreover, in Germany, the second drafting commission adopted the doctrine for reasons that were more pragmatic than conceptual. It appears in § 904 of the German Civil Code.

2. The general principle

Law in the United States

Ploof v. Putnam, 71 A. 188 (Vt. 1908)

"It is alleged as the ground of recovery that on the 13th day of November, 1904, the defendant was the owner of a certain island in Lake Champlain, and of a certain dock attached thereto, which island and dock were then in charge of the defendant's servant; that the plaintiff was then possessed of and sailing upon said lake a certain loaded sloop, on which were the plaintiff and his wife and two minor children; that there then arose a sudden and violent tempest, whereby the sloop and the property and persons therein were placed in great danger of destruction; that to save these from destruction or injury the plaintiff was compelled to, and did, moor the sloop to defendant's dock; that the defendant by his servant unmoored the sloop, whereupon it was driven upon the shore by the tempest, without the plaintiff's fault; and that the sloop and its contents were thereby destroyed, and the plaintiff and his wife and children cast into the lake and upon the shore, receiving injuries. . . .

There are many cases in the books which hold that necessity, and an inability to control movements inaugurated in the proper exercise of a strict right, will justify entries upon land and interferences with personal property that would otherwise have been trespasses. A reference to a few of these will be sufficient to illustrate the doctrine.

In Miller v. Fandrye, Phop. 161, trespass was brought for chasing sheep, and the defendant pleaded that the sheep were trespassing upon his land, and that he with a little dog chased them out, and that as soon as the sheep were off his land he called in the dog. It was argued that, although the defendant might lawfully drive the sheep from his own ground with a dog, he had no right to pursue them into the next ground. But the court considered that the defendant might drive the sheep from his land with a dog, and that the nature of a dog is such that he cannot be withdrawn in an instant, and that as the defendant had done his best to recall the dog trespass would not lie.

In trespass of cattle taken in A, defendant pleaded that he was seized of C, and found the cattle there damage feasant, and chased them toward the pound, and that they escaped from him and went into A, and he presently retook them; and this was held a good plea. 21 Edw. IV, 64; Vin. Ab. Trespass, H.a.4 pl. 19. If one have a way over the land of another for his beasts to pass, and the beasts, being properly driven, feed the grass by morsels in passing, or run out of the way and are promptly pursued and brought back, trespass will not lie. See Vin. Ab. Trespass, K. a. pl. 1.

A traveller on a highway, who finds it obstructed from a sudden and temporary cause, may pass upon the adjoining land without becoming a trespasser, because of the necessity.

An entry upon land to save goods which are in danger of being lost or destroyed by water or fire is not a trespass. 21 Hen. VII, 27; Vin. Ab. Trespass, H.a.4, pl. 24, K.a.pl. 3. In Proctor v. Adams, 113 Mass. 376, 18 Am. Rep. 500, the defendant went upon the plaintiff's beach for the purpose of saving and restoring to the lawful owner a boat which had been driven ashore and was in danger of being carried off by the sea; and it was held no trespass.

This doctrine of necessity applies with special force to the preservation of human life. One assaulted and in peril of his life may run through the close of another to escape from his assailant, 37 Hen. VII, pl. 26. One may sacrifice the personal property of another to save his life or the lives of his fellows. In Mouse's Case, 12 Co. 63, the defendant was sued for taking and carrying away the plaintiff's casket and its contents. It appeared that the ferryman of Gravesend took forty-seven passengers into his barge to pass to London, among whom were the plaintiff and defendant; and the barge being upon the water a great tempest happened, and a strong wind, so that the barge and all the passengers were in danger of being lost if certain ponderous things were not cast out, and the defendant thereupon cast out the plaintiff's casket. It was resolved that in case of necessity, to save the lives of the passengers, it was lawful for the defendant, being a passenger, to cast the plaintiff's casket out of the barge; that if the ferryman surcharge the barge the owner shall have his remedy upon the surcharge against the ferryman, but that if there be no surcharge, and the danger accrue only by the act of God, as by tempest, without fault of the ferryman, every one ought to bear this loss, to safeguard the life of a man.

It is clear that an entry upon the land of another may be justified by necessity, and that the declaration before us discloses a necessity for mooring the sloop. But the defendant questions the sufficiency of the counts because they do not negative the existence of natural objects to which the plaintiff could have moored with equal safety. The allegations are, in substance, that the stress of a sudden and violent tempest compelled the plaintiff to moor to defendant's dock to save his sloop and the people in it. The averment of necessity is complete, for it covers not only the necessity of mooring, but the necessity of mooring to the dock; and the details of the situation which created this necessity, whatever the legal requirements regarding them, are matters of proof and need not be alleged. It is certain that the rule suggested cannot be held applicable irrespective of circumstance, and the question must be left for adjudication upon proceedings had with reference to the evidence or the charge. . . .

Judgment affirmed and cause remanded."

Vincent v. Lake Erie Transportation Co., 124 N.W. 221 (Minn. 1910)

The defendant's steamship was moored to the plaintiff's dock unloading cargo when a storm began. Members of the crew kept her tied to the dock, replacing the lines that held the ship there as they became worn. The wind continually threw the ship against the dock, damaging it.

O'Brien J. "The appellant contends . . . that, because its conduct during the storm was rendered necessary by prudence and good seamanship under conditions over which it had no control, it cannot be held liable for any injury resulting to the property of others, and claims that the jury should have been so instructed. An analysis of the charge given by the trial court is not necessary, as in our opinion the only question for the jury was the amount of damages which the plaintiffs were entitled to recover, and no complaint is made upon that score.

The situation was one in which the ordinary rules regulating property rights were suspended by forces beyond human control, and if, without the direct intervention of some act by the one sought to be held liable, the property of another was injured, such injury must be attributed to the act of God, and not to the wrongful act of the person sought to be charged. If during the storm the Reynolds had entered the harbor, and while there had become disabled and been thrown against the plaintiffs' dock, the plaintiffs could not have recovered. Again, if while attempting to hold fast to the dock the lines had parted, without any negligence, and the vessel carried against some other boat or dock in the harbor, there would be no liability upon her owner. But here those in charge of the vessel deliberately and by their direct efforts held her in such a position that the damage to the dock resulted, and, having thus preserved the ship at the expense of the dock, it seems to us that her owners are responsible to the dock owners to the extent of the injury inflicted.

In Depue v. Flatau, 100 Minn. 299, 111 N. W. 1, 8 L. R. A. (N. S.) 485, this court held that where the plaintiff, while lawfully in the defendants' house, became so ill that he was incapable of traveling with safety, the defendants were responsible to him in damages for compelling him to leave the premises.

If, however, the owner of the premises had furnished the traveler with proper accommodations and medical attendance, would he have been able to defeat an action brought against him for their reasonable worth?

In Ploof v. Putnam, 71 Atl. 188, 20 L. R. A. (N. S.) 152, the Supreme Court of Vermont held that where, under stress of weather, a vessel was without permission moored to a private dock at an island in Lake Champlain owned by the defendant, the plaintiff was not guilty of trespass, and that the defendant was responsible in damages because his representative upon the island unmoored the vessel, permitting it to drift upon the shore, with resultant injuries to it. If, in that case, the vessel had been permitted to remain, and the dock had suffered an injury, we believe the shipowner would have been held liable for the injury done.

Theologians hold that a starving man may, without moral guilt, take what is necessary to sustain life; but it could hardly be said that the obligation would not be upon such person to pay the value of the property so taken when he became able to do so. And so public necessity, in times of war or peace, may require the taking of private property for public purposes; but under our system of jurisprudence compensation must be made. Let us imagine in this case that for the better mooring of the vessel those in charge of her had appropriated a valuable cable lying upon the dock. No matter how justifiable such appropriation might have been, it would not be claimed that, because of the overwhelming necessity of the situation, the owner of the cable could not recover its value.

This is not a case where life or property was menaced by any object or thing belonging to the plaintiff, the destruction of which became necessary to prevent the threatened disaster. Nor is it a case where, because of the act of God, or unavoidable accident, the infliction of the injury was beyond the control of the defendant, but is one where the defendant prudently and advisedly availed itself of the plaintiffs' property for the purpose of preserving its own more valuable property, and the plaintiffs are entitled to compensation for the injury done.

Order affirmed.

[dissenting opinion of Lewis, J.] I dissent. It was assumed on the trial before the lower court that appellant's liability depended on whether the master of the ship might, in the exercise of reasonable care, have sought a place of safety before the storm made it impossible to leave the dock. The majority opinion assumes that the evidence is conclusive that appellant moored its boat at respondent's dock pursuant to contract, and that the vessel was lawfully in position at the time the additional cables were fastened to the dock, and the reasoning of the opinion is that, because appellant made use of the stronger cables to hold the boat in position, it became liable under the rule that it had voluntarily made use of the property of another for the purpose of saving its own.

In my judgment, if the boat was lawfully in position at the time the storm broke, and the master could not, in the exercise of due care, have left that position without subjecting his vessel to the hazards of the storm, then the damage to the dock, caused by the pounding of the boat, was the result of an inevitable accident. If the master was in the exercise of due care, he was not at fault. The reasoning of the opinion admits that if the ropes, or cables, first attached to the dock had not parted, or if, in the first instance, the master had used the stronger cables, there would be no liability. If the master could not, in the exercise of reasonable care, have anticipated the severity of the storm and sought a place of safety before it became impossible, why should he be required to anticipate the severity of the storm, and, in the first instance, use the stronger cables?

I am of the opinion that one who constructs a dock to the navigable line of waters, and enters into contractual relations with the owner of a vessel to moor at the same, takes the risk of damage to his dock by a boat caught there by a storm, which event could not have been avoided in the exercise of due care, and further, that the legal status of the parties in such a case is not changed by renewal of cables to keep the boat from being cast adrift at the mercy of the tempest."

English law

Southwark London Borough Council v. Williams, [1971] 1 Ch. 734

"The defendants were in dire need of housing accommodation. One family had to leave their lodging in Deal and came to London to find somewhere to live. The other, for the sake of the family, had left a room in which they lived. [They were a family of four who had been living in one room an eight room damp, rodent infested house where seven other families were living.] They sought the assistance of a squatter's association and made an orderly entry into empty houses owned by the local authority. The houses were two of some hundreds of empty houses to provide housing for the thousands on the local authority's housing list."

Lord Denning M.R. "I will next consider the defence of 'necessity.' There is authority for saying that in case of great and imminent danger, in order to preserve life, the law will permit of an encroachment on private property. That is shown by *Mouse's Case* (1609) 12 Co.Rep. 63, where the ferryman at Gravesend took 47 passengers into his barge to carry them to London. A great tempest arose and all were in danger. Mouse was one of the passengers. The defendant threw a casket belonging to the plaintiff (Mouse) overboard so as to lighten the ship. Other passengers threw other things. It was proved that, if they had not done so, the passengers would have been drowned. It was held by the whole court 'that in case of necessity, for the savings of the lives of the passengers it was lawful for the defendant, being a passenger, to cast the casket of the plaintiff out of the barges. . . .' The court said it was like the pulling down of a house in time of fire, to stop it spreading; which has always been held justified pro bono publico.

The decline so enunciated must, however, be carefully circumscribed. Else necessity would open the door to many an excuse. It was for this reason that it was not admitted in *Reg. v. Dudley and Stephens* (1884) 14 Q.B.D. 273, where the three shipwrecked sailors, in extreme despair, killed the cabin boy and ate him to save their own lives. They were held guilty of murder. The killing was not justified by necessity. Similarly, when a man, who is starving, enters a house and takes food in order to keep himself alive. Our English law does not admit the defence of necessity. It holds him guilty of larceny. Lord Hale said that 'if a person, being under necessity for want of victuals, or clothes, shall upon that account clandestinely, and animo furandi, steal another man's food, it is felony . . .': Hale, *Please of Crown*, i. 54. The reason is because, if hunger were once allowed to be an excuse for stealing, it would open a way through which all kinds of disorder and lawlessness would pass. So here. If homelessness were once admitted as a defence to trespass, no one's house could be safe. Necessity would open a door which no man could shut. It would not only be those in extreme need who would enter. There would be others who would imagine that they were in need, or would invent a need, so as to gain entry. Each man would say his need was greater than the next man's. The plea would be an excuse for all sorts of wrongdoing. So the courts must, for the sake of law and order, take a firm stand. They must refuse to admit the plea of necessity to the hungry and the homeless: and trust that their distress will be relieved by the charitable and the good.

Applying these principles, it seems to me the circumstances of these squatters are not such as to afford any justification or excuse in law for their entry into these houses. . . ."

Edmund Davies L.J. "But when and how far is the plea of necessity available to one who is prima facie guilty of tort? Well, one thing emerges with clarity from the decisions, and that is that the law regards with the deepest suspicion any remedies of self-help, and permits those remedies to be resorted to only in very special circumstances. The reason for such circumspection is clear-necessity can very easily become simply a mask for anarchy. As far as my reading goes, it appears that all the cases where a plea of necessity has succeeded are cases which deal with an urgent situation of imminent peril: for example, the forcible feeding of an obdurate suffragette, as in *Leigh v. Gladstone* (1909) 26 T.L.R. 139, where Lord Alverstone C.J. spoke of preserving the health and lives of the prisoners who were in the custody of the Crown; or performing an abortion to avert a grave threat to the life, or, at least, to the health of a pregnant young girl who had been ravished in circumstances of great brutality, as in *Rex v. Bourne* [1939] 1 K.B. 687; or as in the case tried in 1500 where it was said in argument that a person may escape from a burning gaol notwithstanding a statute making prison-breach a felony, 'for he is not to be hanged because he would not stay to be burnt.' [footnote omitted] Such cases illustrate the very narrow limits with which the pleas of necessity may be invoked. Sad though the circumstances disclosed by these appeals undoubtedly are, they do not in my judgment constitute the sort of emergency to which the plea applies."

W.V.H. Rogers, *Winfield & Jolowicz on Tort* (15th ed. 1998), 880

"Another point not free from doubt is whether, assuming that the defence of necessity has been established, the defendant must make compensation or at least legal restitution for the harm he has inflicted. It is clear that no damage can be claimed in tort where the defendant's act is justified by necessity, but that does not settle the question whether the defendant is liable to make restitution, *i.e.* to restore to its former condition the property of the plaintiff which has been affected by the defendant's act, or, if restoration is impossible, to pay the plaintiff equivalent compensation. Here, the basis of the plaintiff's claim would be restitution, not tort, the practical difference being that compensation payable on a restitutionary claim may be considerably less than damages on a claim in tort. [In the case of] an act done simply in protection of one's own person or property [rather than for the common weal] . . . it is suggested that bare restitution or compensation for the use or consumption of property might be claimed on quasi-contractual grounds: for example, using a neighbour's fire extinguisher to put out a fire on one's own house." [footnotes omitted]

German law

German Civil Code

§ 904 [NECESSITY]

The owner of a thing is not entitled to prohibit another from dealing with the thing when such conduct is necessary to avoid a present danger, and the damage threatened by it is unreasonably large compared to the damage arising to the owner from dealing with his thing. The owner can require compensation for the damage that occurs to him.

§ 228 [STATE OF NEED (*NOTSTAND*)]

One who damages or destroys another's property to avoid a danger which the property poses to himself or another is not acting unlawfully (*widerrechtlich*) if the damage or destruction is necessary to avoid the danger and the harm is not out of proportion to the danger. If the party acting is at fault for the danger, then he is obligated to make compensation for the harm.

Note: The German label for this provision is *Notstand* which means a state of need. German commentators explain that what is really meant is *Verteidigungsnotstand* which means a situation in which one needs to defend oneself or another. More precisely, *Notstand* concerns defense against an object, in contrast to *Notwehr* (dealt with in § 227) which concerns defense against another person.

Note on the legislative history of § 904: As mentioned earlier, the first drafting commission had not included a provision about necessity in the Code. Here is the explanation that the second drafting commission gave for doing so:

> The unacceptability of the legal situation [under the first draft] is apparent without further argument when one considers some practical examples of its application. According to the draft, it is against the law for a drowning man to climb on another's boat to rescue himself. The owner of the boat who is himself not in danger is entitled . . . to push him back in the water. The draft forbids one to tear down another's fence during a

conflagration to permit entry of fire fighting equipment or to break into a neighboring house which is the only possible point from which the work of extinguishing the fire can be directed. In all such cases, the draft will recognize a person's defense as lawful self defense. These results are insupportable and irreconcilable with other principles recognized by law. The draft acknowledges the right [of the owner of property with no access to the public street] to obtain a right of way by necessity . . . , and it permits a person to enter another's property to find and carry off any of his own property that has come there by chance. . . . The most striking example, however, of giving way to lower rights before a higher interest counter to them is the right of expropriation. The fundamental idea of this manifestation of right is that action taken through necessity will be declared to be in accordance with law insofar as it manifests the importance of higher interests over lower ones, that is, to the extent that it is a function performed as a duty to the community. There should be no contradiction between rights and laws of morality. Every private right carries the inherent limitation that it must give way to the general interest, and when such a higher interest is present is decided by the judgment of the community. (*Protokolle der Kommission für die zweite Lesung des Bürgerlichen Gesetzbuches* VI, § 419, 214 (Berlin, 1899)).

French law

The French ignored the problem of necessity for most of the 20th century, as they had in the 19th century. In 1976, Carbonnier, who was one of the few to discuss and approve of it, made the following tentative suggestion:

> One can regard the maxim that necessity has no law as traditional and having the value of customary law. It should only be understood, however, with a good deal of prudence; it only concerns extreme necessity and it imposes on the one who appeals to it the obligation of repairing the damage that he causes. Applied in the area of property law, the maxim amounts to a general right to private requisition. (*Droit civil* § 45.)

He admitted that his position had little support in the case law. He mentioned an old criminal case in which a *Cour d'appel* stretched the text of the Criminal Code to acquit a girl, poor and hungry but not actually starving, who stole bread. The court found that the girl did not have a wrongful intention even though, according to art. 379 of the Criminal Code, all that is necessary is simply the intention to appropriate an object. (Amiens, 22 avr. 1898, S. 1899.II.1.)

In the 1980s, however, the doctrine began finding favor with treatise writers. Here is the way it is now presented in two leading treatises.

Boris Starck, Henri Roland & Laurent Boyer, *Obligations* **1.** *Responsabilité délictuelle* **(4th ed., 1991), §§ 300–301**

"State of necessity

This is the name one gives to the situation in which one can find oneself when, in order to avoid causing a harm, one deliberately causes another. To avoid running down a pedestrian, one prefers to break the window of a car. To end the ferocious behavior of two dogs, one has no other means than to kill them with a rifle shot.[152] In this case there is no fault, and consequently there is no liability under article 1382 because a reasonable man, a *bonus pater familias* [the Roman equivalent of the reasonable person] would have acted in this way.[153]

Such an exemption presupposes that the harm caused voluntarily is less severe than that which one wishes to prevent. One can break into an enclosure to put out a fire. One cannot sacrifice the life of another person to save one's own.

Supposing that the conditions that establish a state of necessity are fulfilled and given the absence of liability of the party who voluntarily caused the harm, one should not lose sight of the fact that there will always be a victim who may be the person who acted or may be someone else. Equity dictates that one make provision for the damage the victim has suffered which has taken the place of the person threatened. There may be [strict liability] for [harm caused by] the act of a thing,[154] or the victim may have other actions based on *gestion d'affaires* when the conditions required for the exercise of these actions are fulfilled."[155]

Note: Strict liability for harm caused by an object is a doctrine we will meet up with later. For the doctrine to apply, an object must have caused the harm. There is no requirement that the object be dangerous. The person who has custody (*garde*) of the object then has to pay.

The doctrine of *gestion d'affaires* allows one who has carried out some necessary service for another without being asked to recover his expenses. For example, if A finds B's horse and feeds it so that it will not starve, B has to pay for the feed. It is not at all clear how the doctrine would apply in this situation.

Francois Terré, Philippe Simler & Yves Lequette, *Droit civil Les obligations* (7th ed. 1999), § 704

"If it is sufficiently clear, a *state of necessity* can also dictate and therefore justify conduct that causes harm. In such a case, one does cause a harm, but in order to avoid one which is more serious whether to oneself or others. Such is the classic case in which a motorist breaks a window to avoid injuring a pedestrian.[2] Inspired by the solutions of criminal law,[3] such a justification does not necessarily exclude, especially on a theory of unjust enrichment, a sort of compensation for the one who had to suffer the act dictated by necessity.[4]

152. Cass., 2nd Civ. Ch., 26 Nov. 1986: D. 1987, I.R. 3.
153. H. Roland & L. Boyer, *Adages*, p. 569.
154. Trib. d'inst. Charolles, 13 mars 1970: JPC 70, II, 16354.
155. Starck, op. cit. pp. 97–116 and R. Pallard, *L'exception de nécessité, Le Tourneau, "La responsabilité civile extra-contrqactuelle" in Études Capitant*, p. 729 ff.
2. See Cass. Civ., 2d Civ. Ch. 8 April 1970, IV, 136.

3. See article 122-2 in the new Criminal Code which provides: "A person is not criminally responsible if he acted under the dominion of force or of a constraint that he could not resist."
4. R. Savatier, "L'état de nécessité et la responsabilité civile extra-contractuelle," *Études Capitant*, p. 729 f.; R. Pallard, *L'exception de nécessité en droit civil*, thèse Poitiers, 1949; J.-Y. Chevallier, "L'état de nécessité," *Mélanges Bouzat*, 1980, p. 117 f.

Note: Here are the cases cited in the two treatises just quoted. Consider whether or not they show that French courts recognize a doctrine of necessity like the one in Germany or like the one the French writers just quoted have described.

Cour de cassation, 2e ch. civ., 26 November 1986, D.S. 1987.

[This brief summary is all that was published of the court's decision.]

"Having observed that two dogs, before anyone could take hold of them, were attacking a spaniel, biting it savagely, and would not desist, and that after searching for the owner and informing the police, [the defendant] had no way to put a stop to their ferocious behavior than to kill them with a rifle shot, the judges of the lower court could infer that this act was done without any fault."

Cour de cassation, 2e ch. civ., 8 April 1970, JCP. 1970.J.136

"A young boy who was visiting at F's house accompanied by his mother shut himself in the bathroom and could not get out. To rescue him, F tried unsuccessfully to break the door, and finally broke the opaque glass pane. A fragment struck the child's eye, and he lost the use of it.

His father, acting as the administrator of the person and goods of his son, sued F for compensation under art. 1382 of the Civil Code.

After having observed that the mother of the child who was present at the accident had consented at least implicitly to everything that F did, and having stated that F's actions were the normal and simple ones of anyone finding himself in such a situation, and adding that since the discomfort of the child could be inferred from his silence, there could be no question of calling a locksmith or of giving the child instructions or even of losing a few moments to check on a small window that was never proven to be adequate, the *Cour d'appel*, given the motives for which he took action, could determine that the action was that of any man exercising ordinary prudence and could justly decided that he had not been at fault."

Tribunal d'instance, Charolles, 13 March 1970, JCP 1970.J.16354

The plaintiff, Géraud, Bonnot was driving his car when he was struck by a truck driven by the defendant Fernand Pras. The truck belonged to his employer the *Societé Café Boca*, also a defendant. The court found that Pras "was constrained to turn left while braking brutally in order to attempt a rescue maneuver to avoid the woman Lagoutte, the wife of Bathiard, who, finding herself on a sidewalk to the right in the direction he was moving, unexpectedly crossed the street at the moment the truck arrived." In fact, the court found that Lagoutte did so in an attempt to commit suicide. The court held that "one cannot complain . . . of [Pras'] attempt at rescue, the sole solution available to him. As a result, he cannot be formally held for a fault as it is defined by art. 1382 of the Civil Code."

Note on the Decision of 13 March 1970: The court found him liable anyway because the accident was caused by the act of an object, namely the car, and liability for the act of an object does not require fault. You may wonder why the plaintiff was not liable as well since his car was an object that contributed to the accident. We'll find out later when we get to this topic.

The plaintiff had sought to recover 500 francs as a *pretium doloris*, what we would call pain and suffering. The court thought this amount was "exaggerated" since the period of his "total incapacity" did not exceed twenty-four hours. It awarded 200 francs for pain and suffering.

You might also wonder why Lagoutte did not have to pay. This court said that she was not at fault. "The intentional component of fault cannot be charged against her, nor can imprudence nor negligence because at that precise moment she no longer had her free will and was deprived of understanding, moved solely by an irrepressible desire for self-destruction." As we will see later, however, a law had been passed which makes insane people liable for their actions: the Law of 3 January 1968, now art. 489-2 of the Civil Code. That law was in force when the accident occurred. As the writer of an anonymous note to this case observed, the judge simply ignored the law.

3. Necessity and land use

English law

Whalley v. Lancashire and Yorkshire Ry. Co., [1884] 13 Q.B. 131

"By reason of an unprecedented rainfall a quantity of water was accumulated against one of the sides of the defendant's railway embankment, to such an extent as to endanger the embankment when, in order to protect their embankment, the defendants cut trenches in it by which the water flowed through, and went ultimately on to the land of the plaintiff, which was on the opposite side of the embankment and at a lower level, and flooded and injured it to a greater extent than it would have done had the trench not been cut."

Lindley L.J. "It seems to me established . . . that if an extraordinary flood is seen to be coming upon land the owner of such land may fence off and protect his land from it, and so turn it away, without being responsible for the consequences, although his neighbors may be injured by it. . . . Of course, there is a difference between protecting yourself from an injury which is not yet suffered by you, and getting rid of the consequences of an injury which has occurred to you." Held: defendants are liable.

Law in the United States

Grant v. Allen, 41 Conn. 156 (1874)

"[T]he plaintiff and defendants were the owners of adjoining lots. . . . The defendants offered evidence to prove that they excavated on their land, and put in their foundation wall for the erection of a block of dwelling-houses, while the ground was filled with frost; that the wall was completed in the month of January, 1873, and formed the west foundation wall of a block of dwelling-houses erected by the defendants, and that it was useless to tamp the wall on the exposed west side while the frost was in the ground; that in the spring season following, as the frost came out of the ground, the ground slightly settled by their wall, from natural causes, with a slope towards the wall, and that the surface water accumulating on the plaintiff's lot from rains ran into this depression, forming a gully by the defendants' wall, and had so increased the same as to cause the water to flow into the defendants' foundations, and endanger the falling of their wall; that they several times requested permission of the plaintiff to enter on his land and fill up the gully, and carefully grade the same at their own expense, but he refused permission, and neglected to take any action in the matter until about the first of August, 1873, when the defendants peaceably entered on the land in the absence of the plaintiff, and filled up the gully with selected and proper soil, and tamped the same in a proper manner, doing no damage whatever to the premises of the plaintiff; and they further offered evidence to prove that such grading was a material benefit to the lot of the plaintiff . . . and that if any water reached the cellar of the plaintiff it was, and always had been, caused by percolation through his soil; and that they had in no way changed the grade of any part of the plaintiff's lot." The plaintiff claimed "that in consequence of the filling and grading the surface water had run into his cellar, and that he had been compelled to raise the walk five inches leading from his front gate to the side entrance to his house, and that the filling and grading had destroyed a grass plat and flower bed along his line." At trial, the defendant asked the judge to charge the jury: "That if the flow of surface water from the lot of the plaintiff was injuring the wall of the defendants, the defendants had a right to enter and abate the same in a reasonable and proper manner, after notice to the plaintiff and neglect or refusal by him to take any action."

Pardee J. "There being in the case before us no grant, express or implied, and no stipulation between the parties concerning the mode in which their respective parcels of land shall be occupied and improved, the defendants could not enter upon the plaintiff's land without his consent, place additional earth upon it, change the grade and burden it with a barrier for the diversion of such water from their own land. He could not compel them to receive it, they could not compel him to withhold it."

Note on use of the power of eminent domain: Suppose a farm owner needs a right of way across adjoining property for an irrigation ditch, or a mine owner needs such a right of way for an aerial bucket line. Under the doctrine of necessity, he will not be entitled to it. Consequently, some states have passed statutes allowing the owner to condemn a right way for which he then must pay the price set by a court. This is an odd use of the power of eminent domain. According to the Fifth Amendment to the United States Constitution, private property can be taken only for a "public purpose." Nevertheless, it was held to be constitutional even in an era where courts regarded private property rights as sacrosanct. Clark v. Nash, 198 U.S. 361 (1905) (irrigation ditch); Strickley v. Highland Boy Gold Mining Co., 200 U.S. 527 (1906) (aerial bucket line).

German law

Reichsgericht, 12 March 1904, RGZ 57, 187

"Plaintiff was the owner of an estate to which two extended meadows belonged, separated by a mill. They were crossed by ditches which, the plaintiff maintained, were planned for drainage and aside from that could be used to breed fish. The defendant had a coal mine and a briquet factory on the property adjoining the estate. The mine had previously belonged to the plaintiff. He had later sold it to an enterprise in which he held an interest, and then the briquet factory was built. When the enterprise went into bankruptcy, the defendant bought the mine and the factory. The water from the mine and factory had previously flowed across the estate of the plaintiff through the ditches just mentioned, across the meadows, and was then carried away by a channel below them. Plaintiff did not want to allow the mine and factory water to pass across his meadows any longer because, he claimed, they would be completely ruined. He denied that the defendant had the right to have the water flow off his land in this way, and he wanted the defendant to be forbidden under penalty to continue."

The first judge dismissed his complaint. He said that it contradicted § 904 of the Civil Code whose presuppositions, he believed, had to be satisfied. The plaintiff's appeal was rejected. The appellate court held that defendant did have the right to have the water flow across plaintiff's land. It was a limitation of plaintiff's ownership provided by a German statute on water law. The *Reichsgericht* remanded on that issue for further findings of fact. On the applicability of § 904, the court said:

"If the flowing of the water across plaintiff's estate is necessary for the operation of the mine, then that matter is regulated exhaustively by the Mine Law (*Berggesetz*) itself in title 5, part 1, §§ 135ff, by which the plaintiff can be compelled to allow the use of his land for the purposes of the mine. To that extent, § 904 of the Civil Code does not apply here. It is true however that the general principle that it contains could be applied in favor of the mine. Nevertheless, as the text of that law provides, it presupposes a 'present danger,' that is, an extraordinary event which alters the existing relations which people take into account so that immediate aid is necessary which includes the use of another's property. It is obvious that an event of that sort could happen to a mine. Nevertheless, the consideration put forward by the [first] judge, below is not a reason to apply § 904: that the plaintiff must permit without contradiction the flow of water necessary to the operation of the mine which can only be drained across his estate, and that the mine will be flooded if the flow of water is now blocked. If the situation is such that the mine must flood if it is no longer possible to drain the mine water across plaintiff's estate—and the factual correctness of this matter was disputed on appeal—it may be that the procedure for expropriation of the mining law can be used against the plaintiff. But if the defendant has no right to use the estate for the draining of his mine water, then he must take account of the possibility that the plaintiff is no longer willing to allow him to do it out of good will, and that does not constitute a 'present danger' within the meaning of § 904."

4. Necessity and intent

One question that will arise in this section is how to draw the boundary line between intentional and negligent conduct. If you aren't already familiar with these concepts, it would be helpful to read pp. 339–353 on intent and pp. 353–363 on negligence.

Law in the United States

W. Page Keeton, Dan B. Dobbs, Robert E. Keeton, David G. Owen, *Prosser and Keeton on Torts* (5th ed. 1984), 74, n. 61

"See also Ruiz v. Formann, Tex. Civ. App. 1974, 514 S.W.2d 817, error dismissed, for a holding that reaches a good result for a questionable reason. There a motorist swerved off the road onto plaintiff's property to avoid a collision. The Court held that the defendant was liable even though he did not intend the invasion since he intended the act that resulted in the invasion. But he intended the invasion to escape greater harm and since he did this to prevent harm to himself he has an incomplete privilege to use plaintiff's property and must pay for any harm done.

Wood v. United Airlines, 1962, 32 Misc.2d 955, 223 N.Y.S.2d 692, affirmed 16 A.D.2d 659, 226 N.Y.S.2d 1022, appeal dismissed 11 N.Y.2d 1053, 230 N.Y.S.2d 207. 184 N.E.2d 180, draws the distinction between a forced but intentional landing, and a plane entirely out of control. In the latter case, it was held that the invasion was not due to any volitional act of the defendant, as where his horse runs away with him. . . . In the former, the invasion might be privileged to a limited extent, but the defendant might be required to pay for any damage which resulted."

German law

Some of the following cases draw upon the German concept of conditional intent. That concept was developed in tort law to explain how a person could be held liable for intentionally causing harm which he did not wish to bring about. Here is the generally accepted description: To have intentionally interfered with another's rights, a "party need not have done so with a 'direct intention'; he need not have the purpose of interfering with these rights or legal interests. Rather, it is enough if he recognized the possibility of such an interference, and proceeds to act despite this knowledge, taking into account that action may occur, although he may even hope that it does not (conditional intent)." Hein Kötz & Gerhard Wagner, *Deliktsrecht* (9th ed. 2001), 44.

Oberlandesgericht, Hamm, 30 May 1940, DR 1940, 1188

"On May 2, 1938, the plaintiff's truck was damaged on highway 63 going from W. to H. by striking a tree when the driver swerved to avoid a horse that had suddenly shied. The defendant came across the highway in a northerly direction sitting in the back seat of a farm cart typical for the region.

He had gone with his horse, a mare, to have it bred in K., and was on the way home in the region O., where a small railway was located on a certain railway embankment on the east side of the highway. One of the railway trains came toward him. The mare shied at the steam that the locomotive gave off and ran straight onto the highway. In the same instant the plaintiff's truck was approaching in an effort to pass the defendant. In order to avoid a collision, witness U., the driver of the truck, swerved the truck to the left, steering it between the trees along a bicycle path on the west side of the street. The truck grazed the horse and cart, giving them some scratches and bruises. It struck one or two of the trees, however, and was seriously damaged.

The accident was not the fault of either the plaintiff or the defendant. The defendant must make compensation for the damage, however, because it was caused by avoiding a serious danger that threatened him. . . .

When the horse shied and brought the cart right across the street, the defendant was in serious danger of losing his life. One cannot blame U. for guiding the heavy truck off the street and onto the bicycle path instead of merely braking. . . . The truck and the people in it were in hardly any danger from a collision with the light, fragile vehicle of the defendant. In any event, no serious injury was to be feared. The defendant's cart, on the contrary, would have been completely destroyed and the defendant and his horse would surely have been injured seriously if, indeed, they were not killed. U. saved him from this danger and thereby damaged the truck.

It would contradict every feeling of justice and equity in this situation to reject the plaintiff's claim for compensation. . . .

. . . U. has dealt with a thing that does not belong to him—the truck—to avoid a danger threatening the defendant, and so the literal text of [§ 904 of the Civil Code] would seem to be satisfied. But one cannot apply that provision directly. The reason is that the truck did not belong to U. and so one cannot find the opposition between the plaintiff as owner of the truck and U. as the person who dealt with it within the meaning of § 904, so as to entitle the plaintiff to recover compensation under the second sentence of § 904. U. was entrusted with driving the truck and therefore also had the duty to do so in conformity with statutes and traffic regulations. In doing so, he must also deliberately incur damages to the truck when, as was the case here, human life was at stake. The damage that U. brought about by swerving the truck therefore came about as part of the task with which the plaintiff entrusted him. It would therefore be a mistake to treat U. as 'another' within the meaning of § 904 whose action the plaintiff must merely permit. Rather, U. stood in the position of the owner. The situation should not be judged any differently than if the owner himself had steered the truck. . . .

If the driver had not been the plaintiff himself, but an unauthorized third party who steered the truck to the side having leapt aboard it and grabbed the steering wheel the plaintiff would have a direct claim against him under § 904. . . .

The plaintiff would always have a claim for compensation if the defendant or a third party had avoided the danger to the defendant instead of his own driver, and so had damaged the truck. The plaintiff ought not to be in a worse position, however, because his driver did not wait for another person to act but, with great presence of mind, guided the truck to the side, and thereby took responsibility for this conduct which was solely in the interest of the defendant. . . .

To counter their arguments, defendant has given the following example. The enraged bull of a farmer attacks a person. To avoid the danger, the farmer shoots the bull. The defendant's point is that if the plaintiff is granted a claim in the present case, the farmer must also have a claim against the person threatened by the bull. But that seems to be incorrect.

The example is not a good one. It differs from the present case in this respect: there, the danger arises from the property of the farmer—the bull—whereas here it stems from the property of the defendant—the horse. The farmer in certain circumstances would have a claim, too, but only if the requirements of § 228 were fulfilled, that is, only if the threatened person were at fault. The plaintiff has a claim under § 904 even when the defendant was not at fault."

Reichsgericht, 29 April 1926, RGZ 113, 301

On the night of June 14–15, 1923, a German naval vessel ran aground. At the request of its captain, a German torpedo boat, "T 151," came to its aid. In effecting a rescue, it dropped anchor and severed an electric cable belonging to the plaintiff. The plaintiff sued the German government.

"The [defendant in its appeal] is not correct in claiming that no one dealt with the cable within the meaning of § 904. This was not a case of purely accidental harm to the cable. Instead, according to the findings of the appellate court, the captain of the torpedo boat threw the anchor over and let it take hold although he knew that the anchor would penetrate the ground and took into account the possibility that the cable would be broken or injured. He tried to avoid or minimize such an injury to the cable. Nevertheless, in the event that these efforts were unsuccessful, he willed the action upon the cable as a consequence of the naval maneuver which he considered to be necessary and had carried out. In this situation, the appellate court without legal error found that he had dealt with the plaintiff's property within the meaning of § 904."

Bundesgerichtshof, 30 October 1984, VersR 1985, 66

"The plaintiff seeks compensation for damages suffered in a traffic accident which took place September 14, 1981, at 11:50 A.M. in S. in Bavaria. The first defendant was driving a small motorcycle insured by the second defendant towards the plaintiff in a southerly direction on the state highway through S. A driver who remains unknown came down the street in an Opel car and, behind him, the plaintiff in her VW Golf. A little in front of the first defendant, the unknown driver suddenly turned left in his direction into a small side street. In order to avoid the frontal collision with this car which was threatening him, the first defendant steered left across the opposing lane. There he struck the plaintiff who was proceeding along the outer right side of his traffic lane. The car suffered physical damage of 4,614.80 DM which the plaintiff seeks in compensation from the first defendant and from the second defendant or insurer.

The *Landgericht* held that the plaintiff's claim was a valid one under § 904, second sentence, of the Civil Code. The *Oberlandesgericht* dismissed the claim.

The plaintiff's appeal (*Revision*) is unsuccessful. . . .

As this Senate held in its Decision of 29 Sept. 1954 (6th Civil Senate, 124/53, VersR 55, 10 at 11) a claim for compensation for harm by an owner under § 904, sentence 2, of the Civil Code is only possible when the defendant knows and wills to deal with the owner's thing under the circumstances of necessity of § 904, sentence 1. For that to be so, the party taking the action must at least conceive of the damage to the object or a possible consequence of his interference with the sphere of legal rights of another, and he must take account of it and consent. The case law has always required, for liability under § 904, sentence 2, that there be such an action for the defendant to have dealt with thing of another—an action which is intended at least conditionally. [citations too numerous to reproduce]

The concept of 'dealing' in § 904, sentence 1, itself indicates the requirement of a purposive action. One can conceive of an intrusion into the legal sphere of another 'to avoid a present danger' only when an action is directed to a goal and accepted by the will, not when the damage to a thing is not willed."

Note: Consider whether the two previous cases are consistent. The following remarks may be of help.

Note to Decision of 10 Oct. 1984 (above) by R. Walter Dunz, VersR 1985, 335

"In this case, a claim under § 904 of the Civil Code was rightly rejected. It is not a criticism that the grounds for the decision cannot be justified by dogmatically watertight arguments. . . .

Taking into account a higher danger to other people's legally protected interests is part of daily life in modern traffic. . . . For example, an ice skater must not have the same consideration for others as a person out walking on a pedestrian street. To that extent, correct conduct is determined by the ambience in which it takes place. It can also be determined by the particular situation. While when the traffic on the streets is undisturbed, one owes every possible consideration for others, and any deviation is culpable, in state of necessity which is not one's fault, conduct is correct even if it endangers others to a considerable extent. One is liable only for mistakes in weighing one thing against another which one is obligated to perform but one normally performs unconsciously.

The legislator certainly did not want a duty to make compensation under § 904 to arise for any kind of conduct which is motivated by a desire to rescue oneself because he undoubtedly did not think about such cases. And the judicial decisions would be going beyond their proper bounds if they made a self-empowered expansion of an exception to include cases such as these which are in many ways attenuated and of almost daily occurrence. . . .

One can doubt the value of drawing the boundary at *dolus eventualis* [that is, what the court called conditional intent], and, at the same time, one can accept it as long as nothing better is found.

Conditional intent is also a vapid idea in criminal law, which is where it originated. What should it be doing here, where the concern with identifying a particular kind of criminal state of mind, but rather with conduct for which no one would reproach the person who caused the harm? Should the far-sighted person be liable for his justifiable conduct but not the thoughtless person?"

PART TWO:

TORT LAW

I. THE SCOPE OF THE RIGHTS PROTECTED

1. Introduction: the structure of tort law

a. Civil law

The Civil Codes

In modern civil codes, much of tort law depends on short, general provisions that say that a person is liable for harm (or certain harms) that he causes through his fault.

French Civil Code

ARTICLE 1382

Any act of a person which causes harm to another obligates the person through whose fault the harm (*dommage*) occurred to make compensation for it.

ARTICLE 1383

A person is liable for the harm that he causes not only by his acts but by his negligence or imprudence.

French commentators explain (correctly) that art. 1381 was meant to govern harm caused intentionally. Taken together, then, these provisions mean that the defendant is liable if he intentionally or negligently causes "harm" to the plaintiff.

Nothing in the French Civil Code or in its drafting history explains what is supposed to count as "harm." French courts have had to work that out for themselves.

The analogous provision of the German Civil Code is a bit different.

German Civil Code

§ 823(1)

A person who intentionally or negligently unlawfully (*widerrechtlich*) injures the life, body, health, freedom, property or similar right (*sonstiges Recht*) of another is bound to compensate him for any damages that thereby occurs.

The word "unlawfully" is used to make it clear that a person may intentionally or negligently harm another and still not be liable because he is not at fault: for example, if he harms another in self defense. Of course, in that case he is not liable in France either, but the point is not explicit in the French provisions.

Moreover, according to § 823(1), a person is not liable for any harm to another. He is liable for harm to life, body, health, freedom (meaning freedom of movement), property or a "similar right." One reason for the provision is that the drafters believed that there were certain harms for which the plaintiff should not recover. In particular, they believed that he should not recover for harm to privacy or dignity, or for an economic loss unaccompanied by harm to person or property. The drafters also wanted to say something definite about the harms for which the plaintiff could recover. Nevertheless, they realized that they could not make an exhaustive list of such harms. So they added the phrase "or a similar right." That phrase allows German courts to protect additional rights which they regard as "similar."

The drafters also extended liability in other ways. They added a second paragraph to § 823 to deal with the violation of rights created by particular statutes.

German Civil Code

§ 823(2)

The same obligation rests on a person who infringes a statute intended for the protection of others. If, according to the provisions of the statute, its infringement is possible even without fault, the duty to make compensation arises only in the event of fault.

The drafters also provided that in the case of intentional misconduct, the plaintiff could recover for "harm" he suffered even if the rights described in § 823 had not been violated.

German Civil Code

§ 826

A person who intentionally causes harm to another in a manner contrary to good morals (*gute Sitten*) is bound to compensate him for the harm.

From Roman law to the Modern Code Provisions

The French Civil Code was enacted in 1804. The German Civil Code came into force in 1900. Most other continental countries have enacted civil codes as well. Before the law was codified, the law in force in much of Germany and France and most of continental Europe was Roman law. Nevertheless, even where Roman law was in force, the law of delict or tort was understood rather differently by the 18th century than it had been by the Roman jurists.

The Roman jurists themselves had little to say about torts in general, or, for that matter, about contracts in general. They had a law of particular torts and particular contracts, each with its own rules. Gaius was the first Roman jurist to distinguish two general classes of obligations, *delictus* and *contractus*, tort and contract.[1] But he did not describe the general principles of tort or contract law. He discussed particular torts.

Two of these torts became the basis for later continental law. One was called an action for *iniuria*. It could be brought for many different kinds of offensive behavior such as insulting someone by striking him. The plaintiff could recover for a blow. He could also recover if he "be not in fact struck but hands are raised against him and he is frequently afraid of a beating, though not in fact struck. . . ." Dig. 47.10.15.1. He could recover if the defendant entered his house without permission. Dig. 47.2.21.7. He could also recover in a variety of instances in which he was insulted or his reputation was adversely affected.

For example, he could recover if someone composed or recited a song attacking him. Dig. 47.10.15.27. He could recover if someone attacked his reputation in a petition presented to the emperor. Dig. 47.10.15.29. He could recover if someone beat his slave. Dig. 47.10.15.34. He could recover if the defendant assembled people at his house to raise a loud and offensive clamor. Dig. 47.10.15.2.

The defendant was also liable for iniuria if he "accosted" a woman or abducted or removed her attendant—a companion every woman was supposed to have when she appeared in public. According to the jurist Ulpian, "To accost is with smooth words to make at attempt upon another's virtue." Dig. 47.10.15.20. Defendant was also liable for following a woman "assiduously." Dig. 47.10.15.22. Also, "one who uses base language does not make an attempt upon virtue, but he is liable to the action for iniuria." Dig. 47.10.15.21.

From the Middle Ages through the eighteenth century, the action was generalized so that it provided relief for almost any act wrongfully impairing another's dignity or reputation. Reinhard Zimmermann gives some examples from eighteenth century Germany:

> It could be injurious to taunt his person with his natural impediment by calling him a cripple, or a hunchback. To refer to someone, ironically, as a "bonus patiens vir" (and thus suggesting that he was a cuckold), to state emphatically "ego saltem scortator non sum" (and thus insinuate that a particular other person is a fornicator), to use obscene language, particularly in the presence of a virgo, to address a clergyman "du pfaff," or to use the familiar "du" when talking German to persona honorabilis. These are all cases of verbal injuries. Pulling faces, putting out one's tongue at another or kissing a woman against her will are examples of iniuriae reales." (*The Law of Obligations: Roman Foundations of the Civilian Tradition* (1990), 1065–66) [footnotes omitted].

Another Roman tort was an action under the *lex Aquilia*. It is the ancestor of provisions like arts. 1382–83 of the French Civil Code and

---

1. G. Inst. 3.88.

§ 823(1) of the German Civil Code. Today, French and German lawyers will sometimes say that these provisions create an "Aquilian" liability. There were two basic requirements for an action under the *lex Aquilia*. First, the defendant had to be at fault to be liable. That requirement will be described below when we deal with fault, but, in general, fault meant that he caused harm either intentionally or negligently, as it does in the modern codes.

Second, the plaintiff could recover only if he suffered certain types of harm. One Roman text said that the plaintiff had an action even if "the harm was not done physically nor an object physically injured." Inst. 4.3.16. But in almost all the Roman examples, the plaintiff has lost the use of a physical object even if it was not physically injured: for example, he could recover for the loss of a cup whether it was smashed or thrown into a river where he could not get it back. The plaintiff could not recover if he himself was physically injured.

The closest the Romans came to allowing such an action was to let him recover if his son was injured while still under his authority. Here are two (almost the only two) texts that indicate that he can. Both are from the jurist Ulpian.

> Julian also puts his case: A shoemaker, he says, struck with a last at the neck of a boy who was freeborn and whom he was teaching because he had done badly what he had been shown and so knocked out his eye. On these facts, Julian, says that the action for *iniuria* does not lie because he struck him not with the intent to insult but in order to correct and teach him. He wonders whether there is an action for breach of the contract for his services as a teacher, since a teacher is only permitted to punish lightly, but I have no doubt that an action can be brought against him under the *lex Aquilia*. Dig. 9.2.5.3.

> If a man kills another in wrestling or boxing, provided he kills him in a public match, the *lex Aquilia* does not apply because the harm appears to have been done in the cause of glory and virtue and not for the sake of injury. . . . This applies when a son under authority has been hurt. Dig. 9.2.7.4.

Beginning in the Middle Ages, the Roman texts were interpreted to allow recovery for many other types of harm although the jurists never arrived at a clear rule. The Glossators (the jurists who wrote from about 1100 under the mid-13th century) said that the plaintiff could recover if he was physically injured, citing the first of the two texts just quoted. Citing the second text, the jurist Azo (who died about 1210) said that there could be recovery if a person was killed, whether or not he was a son in authority. The plaintiffs in such an action would be his heirs and relatives. By the 17th century it was widely accepted that his wife and children could recover for loss of support. By that time, it has also become accepted that the plaintiff could recover for pain and suffering.[2] Whether he could recover for

---

2.   Reinhard Zimmermann, *The Law of Obligations: Roman Foundations of the Civilian Tradition* (1990), 1024–26.

economic harm that was not accompanied by physical loss was less clear, but jurists sometimes gave examples in which he did. For example, the medieval jurist Durandus said that the plaintiff could recover if the defendant put dung in the street in front of his house, and he therefore had to pay a fine imposed by statute.[3] One of the greatest medieval jurists, Baldus degli Ubaldi, said that the plaintiff could recover against his secretary who revealed his secrets.[4] In the 18th century, Lauterbach and Brunnemann said that a client could recover from an advocate who harmed him through lack of skill.[5] Thus, one change that had taken place by the time that modern civil codes were enacted is that a remedy was given under the *lex Aquilia* for many more kinds of harm than in Roman times.

Another change was that jurists had begun to theorize about the general principles of tort law. The medieval jurists were primarily interested in interpreting the Roman texts in a way that made sense to them. They were not trying to formulate a general principle or explain philosophically where it came from. Among jurists, that task began with the work of the so-called "natural law schools" which flourished from the 16th through the 18th centuries. The first of these schools (16th and early 17th century) was that of the "late scholastics" or "Spanish natural law school" whose leading members were Domenico Soto, Luis de Molina, and Leonard Lessius. The second was the northern natural law school founded by Hugo Grotius and Samuel Pufendorf in the 16th century. It influenced the French jurists Jean Domat and Robert Pothier who in turn influenced the drafters of the French Civil Code.

The late scholastics tried to explain Roman law with principles drawn from their intellectual heroes, the Greek philosopher Aristotle and the medieval philosopher and theologian Thomas Aquinas. They identified contract and tort with Aristotle's concepts of voluntary and involuntary commutative justice. For Aristotle, while distributive justice guarantees each citizen a fair share of whatever resources were to be distributed, commutative justice preserves the share of each citizen. When citizens exchange resources voluntarily, commutative justice requires that they do so at a just price, a price that preserves their share. If one citizen is involuntarily deprived of resources by another, commutative justice requires the person who did so to restore his victim's share of resources.[6] This distinction not only resembles the one we draw between contract and tort but may have been its lineal

3. G. Durandus, *Speculum iuris* (1574), lib. iv, par. iv, De iniuriis et damno dato, § 2 (sequitur) no. 15.

4. Baldus de Ubaldi, *Commentaria Corpus iuris civilis* (1577), to Dig. 9.2.41 (vulg.9.2.42) pr. in fine. In the 16th century, Zasius gave the same opinion in the case of the secretary, citing Baldus. Ulrich Zasius, *Commentaria seu Lecturas eiusdem in titulos primae Pandectarum* ad Dig. 9.2 no.l, in *Opera omnia* vol. 1 (1550) (repr. Scientia Verlag, 1966).

5. Wolfgang Lauterbach, *Collegium theorico-practici* (1793), to Dig. 9.2 no. xv; Johann Brunnemann, *Commentarius in quinquaginta libros Pandectarum* (1762), to Dig. 9.2.8 no. 5. Horst Kaufmann has found many other examples from the practice of early modern times. H. Kaufmann, *Rezeption und Usus Modernus der Actio Legis Aquiliae* (1958), 46–56.

6. *Nicomachean Ethics* V.ii 1130[b]–1131[a].

ancestor. Our distinction goes back to Gaius. Modern scholars think that he took it from Aristotle.[7]

Having taken that step, the late scholastics concluded that the distinctions between *iniuria*, the *lex Aquilia*, and the other particular Romans torts was a mere matter of Roman positive law. In principle (or as they put it, as a matter of natural law), the defendant should be liable whenever, through his own fault, he deprived the plaintiff of anything that belonged to him as a matter of justice.[8] They were not very specific about what belonged to a person as a matter of justice. Nevertheless, they thought that this principle explained not only recovery under the *lex Aquilia* but in the action for *iniuria* as well. In the action for *iniuria*, the plaintiff recovered for insult which deprived him of his reputation or his dignity.

Grotius borrowed many of his conclusions from the late scholastics, and this was an instance. In discussing tort law, he stated the same general principle but he also is not very specific about it:

> Enough has been said about contracts. We come to what is due by the law of nature because of a wrong.
>
> By a wrong, we mean every fault, whether of commission or of omission, which is in conflict with what men ought to do, either generally or because of some special characteristic. From such a fault, if damage is caused, an obligation arises by the law of nature, namely, that the damage should be made good.
>
> Damage, *damnum* (perhaps from *demo*) is when a man has less than what is his, whether it be his by mere nature or by some human act in addition such as ownership, pact, law. Things which a man may regard as his by nature are life, not indeed to throw away but to keep, his body, limbs, fame, honor, his own acts. The previous part of our treatise has shown how each man by property right and by agreements possesses his own not only with respect to property but also with respect to the acts of others. . . .[9]

This text had an enormous influence on the history of tort law. It was followed by many jurists including the 18th century French jurist Robert Pothier who influenced the drafters of the French Civil Code. Pothier said:

> A delict is an act by which a person through intent or malice causes a damage or injury to another.

7. Zimmermann, *Law of Obligations* 10–11; M. Kaser, *Das Römische Privatrecht* 1 (2d ed. 1971), 522; A. Honoré, *Gaius* (1962), 100; H. Coing, "Zum Einfluß der Philosophie des Aristoteles auf die Entwicklung des römischen Rechts," *Zeitschrift der Savigny-Stiftung für Rechtsgeschichte*, Rom. Abt 69 (1952), 24, 37–38.

8. For examples, Lessius said that by a "thing" (*res*) taken from the owner he understands not only an object such as a horse, clothes or money but "what is owed as a matter of justice . . . such as a legacy left another or something which has been sold but which I still have." Leonardus Lessius, *De iustitia et iure, ceterisque virtutibus cardinalis libri quatuor* (1628), lib. 2, cap. 7, dub. 5, no. 19.

9. Hugo Grotius, *De iure belli ac pacis libri tres* (1646), II.xvii.1–2.

A quasi-delict is an act by which a person without malice but by inexcusable imprudence causes an injury to another.[10]

Pothier, unlike Grotius, did not try to enumerate the different types of harm for which one could recover. When the French drafters wrote arts. 1382–83, they paraphrased Pothier. As a result, French courts today decide whether a plaintiff can recover without any guidance from the Code as to what constitutes a "harm."

The stage was then set for the German jurists to be concerned about the vagueness of the term harm, and to try to give it a more definite content in the ways we have seen.

b. Common law

A list of torts

Common lawyers do not decide whether the plaintiff can recover by asking whether he suffered "harm" or whether the defendant violated a right which is "similar" to certain enumerated rights. They ask whether the defendant committed a particular tort for which common law courts give relief.

One of these torts is "negligence." The defendant is liable if he negligently harmed the person or property of the plaintiff. "Negligence" was recognized as a distinct tort only in the 19th century. Before that, the defendant would sue in "trespass" if he had been injured in a straightforward manner: for example, if the defendant had struck him or carried off his goods. For injuries done in a less straightforward way (as some put it, for injuries done "indirectly" rather than "directly"), the plaintiff had to bring an action called "trespass on the case." Instead of just claiming that the defendant struck him or came on his land, he alleged particular facts that entitled him to relief.

Trespass was actually a family of actions which today are recognized as particular torts. Americans usually describe them as "intentional torts" and say that to be liable, the defendant must have acted intentionally. If he acted negligently, he should be sued in "negligence." In England, that view was taken by Lord Denning who said that the distinction between actions in trespass for direct injury and in trespass on the case for indirect injury has been superceded by one in trespass for intentional and negligent injury for negligence.[1] The House of Lords had not yet said whether it agrees, and English writers have different opinions. Some think that the defendant is liable in trespass if the contact was "direct" whether he acted intentionally or negligently.[2] The English do agree that

---

10. Robert Pothier, *Traité des obligations* (1761), nos. 116, 118.

1. [1965] 1 QB 232.

2. *Compare* W.V.H. Rogers, *Winfield and Jolowicz on Tort* (15th ed. 1998), 83–84

(favorable) *with* R.E.V. Heuston & R.A. Buckley, *Salmond and Heuston on the Law of Torts* (21st ed. 1996), 136-17 (critical).

the defendant is not liable for committing these torts if he acted neither intentionally nor negligently.[3]

Here is a brief list of some of the torts which the common law courts have traditionally recognized as actionable in trespass together with a description of when the plaintiff could recover in modern English and American law.

(1) *Trespass in assault and battery*: Today we speak of two torts, battery and assault. In either case, the defendant is liable even if he did no harm although then the damages may be nominal.

To be liable for battery, he must make contact with the body of the plaintiff or something closely associated with the body such as a cane or a glass the plaintiff is holding. The contact must not be one that would normally be presumed to be acceptable. Thus the defendant is liable if he bashes the defendant on the head, or if he merely tweaks his nose or spits on him, but not if he merely taps the plaintiff on the shoulder to ask him the time.

Americans generally agree that the defendant is liable for battery whether or not the contact was "direct." Thus the plaintiff can recover if the defendant poisons his drink or puts filth on a towel so that the plaintiff will rub it on himself.[4] Some English authors think that direct contact "may" still be required so that the defendant would not be liable for battery in these cases. He would be liable instead under the "principle in Wilkinson v. Downer" which will be described later (see p. xxx, below).[5]

To be liable for assault, the defendant must have done something that led the plaintiff to believe he may imminently be the victim of a battery. It is an assault to point a gun or throw a rock at someone. The plaintiff need not be put in fear but he must think that contact is about to occur. He cannot recover if his back was turned when the defendant shot at him, and he did not realize what was happening until the defendant was disarmed. He can recover if he sees the defendant is about to squirt him with a water pistol. The contact must be expected imminently: the plaintiff can recover if the defendant swings a fist at him but not if the defendant threatens to break his legs next week.

(2) *False imprisonment*: The defendant is liable if he confined the plaintiff. The confinement may be in any space, large or small, and it does not matter how it is effected, by force or threats or fraud. The defendant is

---

3. In Stanley v. Powell, [1891] 1 Q.B. 86, the plaintiff claimed that the defendant was negligent, and the jury found that he was not. The court said that the absence of negligence was a defense in an action of battery, and that the defendant should prevail since the jury verdict established that he was not negligent. In Fowler v. Lanning, [1959] 1 Q.B. 156, the plaintiff merely alleged that "the defendant shot the plaintiff." The court held that the defendant had the burden of proving either intention or negligence. It was decided even

earlier that the defendant is not liable for trespass to land if his entry was neither intentional nor negligent. River Wear Commissioners v. Adamson, [1877] 2 App. Cas. 743.

4. Dan B. Dobbs, *The Law of Torts* (2000), 53–54, 61 W. Page Keeton, Dan B. Dobbs, Robert E. Keeton & David G. Owen, *Prosser and Keeton on the Law of Torts* (5th ed. 1984), 40.

5. W.V.H. Rogers, *Winfield & Jolowicz on Tort* (15th ed. 1998), 64.

liable even if he mistakenly but reasonably thought he had the right to confine the plaintiff.

(3) *Trespass quare clausum fregit*: Today known as trespass to land. The defendant must enter, or cause something to enter, land in plaintiff's possession. He need not know that the land belongs to the plaintiff and he is liable even if he believes it belongs to himself. A trespasser is liable even if he did no harm although then only nominal damages may be awarded.

(4) *Trespass de bonis asportatis*: Today known as trespass to chattels. The defendant must physically interfere with plaintiff's goods, for example, by damaging them or carrying them off. Again, he is liable even if he thought they were his own.

As we will see, English and American courts have added to the list by recognizing new torts. But to recover, the plaintiff still has to identify a particular tort which the defendant committed.

From the forms of action to the modern torts

Traditionally, the common law was not organized into the categories of tort and contract. It was organized around particular actions like those just described. Originally, the English royal courts only heard cases when a "writ" was issued by the royal chancellor. At first, new writs were devised as the occasion demanded, but eventually the number became fixed. Consequently, to win, the plaintiff had to fit his case within one of the existing writs or "forms of action."

The forms of action were not meant be a list of rights or interests that the law ought to protect. They were merely the types of cases which, in the 12th and 13th centuries, it was thought proper for the royal courts to hear.

In the 19th century, legislation was enacted abolishing the forms of action. The plaintiff no longer had to identify which writ covered his case. Supposedly, the law did not change. The courts would give a remedy only in the types of cases that would previously fit within one of the traditional forms of action. Nevertheless, the law did change as treatise writers and courts tried to make sense of the traditional law. Indeed, part of the reason for the change may have been that, for the first time, the common lawyers were trying to think systematically about their law. The first university courses in the common law were taught by William Blackstone in the 18th century, who was also one of the first to write a common law treatise: *Commentaries on the Laws of England*. Before his time, there was little legal literature except for a few medieval tracts and the reports of decided cases. The first treatise on the common law of contracts was written by Powell in 1790.[6] The first treatise on the common law of torts was written by Hilliard in 1861.[7] In the process of trying to understand the common law, the treatise writers innovated.

---

6. John J. Powell, *Essay Upon the Law of Contracts and Agreements* (1790).

7. Francis Hilliard, *The Law of Torts or Private Wrongs* 1 (1861).

One innovation was to say, as Blackstone did, that certain of the traditional forms of action constituted a law of torts. These forms of action became the particular torts of the modern common law.

Another innovation was to say, as the civil lawyers had done for centuries, that the two principal grounds on which the defendant might be liable were intent and negligence. "Negligence" was recognized for the first time as a separate tort. There had never been a writ of "negligence," nor had the plaintiff ever had to allege that the defendant was negligent to bring any of the traditional actions.

Still another innovation, and the one that concerns us here, concerns the way that the particular torts were understood. Beginning with Blackstone, common law treatise writers identified the forms of action with different rights or interests which the law was attempting to protect. Blackstone distinguished actions that protected personal property (trespass de bonis asportatis and trover), those that protected real property (trespass quare clausum fregit), and those that protected the "personal security of individuals" against injuries to "their lives, their limbs, their bodies, their health or their reputations."[8] While the treatise writers of the 19th and early 20th century proposed different classifications, like Blackstone, they looked for a correspondence between forms of action and interests to be protected.[9] Hilliard and Addison, in two of the first treatises on tort law, explained that for the plaintiff to recover, he must have suffered some "injury"[10] or "damage."[11] Pollock and Salmond, in their more systematic works, said that he must have suffered some "harm."[12] Later writers such as Harper and Prosser spoke of the violation of "interests demanding protection"[13] or "legally recognized interests."[14] All of them, like Blackstone, tried to identify the traditional forms of action with the protection of distinct types of interests or the prevention of distinct types of harm, damage or injury.

At the same time, they tried to formulate a definition or list of the elements that the plaintiff must establish to recover under each of the forms of action. Judges traditionally had not decided cases by asking what type of harm the plaintiff had suffered or by formulating such lists. They decided them by looking for resemblances to clear cases in which an action would surely lie.

One problem for the treatise writers was to find a formula that could fit decisions that had not been made by a formula but by looking for

8. William Blackstone, *Commentaries on the Laws of England* 3 (1765–69), *119.

9. *Id.* 119–27.

10. Hilliard, *Torts* 1: 83–84.

11. C.G. Addison, *Wrongs and their Remedies. A Treatise on the Law of Torts* 1 (4th English ed., F.J.P. Wolferston ed., 1876), 2.

12. Sir Frederick Pollock, *The Law of Torts. A Treatise on the Principles of Obligations Arising from Civil Wrongs in the Common Law* 6 (8th ed. 1908), 6; John W. Salmond, *The Law of Torts. A Treatise on the English Law of Liability for Civil Injuries* (4th ed. 1916), 8.

13. Fowler Vincent Harper, *A Treatise on the Law of Torts A Preliminary Treatise on Civil Liability for Harms to Legally Protected Interests* (1933), 5.

14. William L. Prosser, *Handbook of the Law of Torts* (1941), 8–9. Similarly, Restatement of Torts § 1 cmt. d (1934) ("legally protected interests"); Restatement (Second) of Torts § 1 cmt. d (1965) (same).

such resemblances. A further problem was that the cases did not always correspond closely to a distinct interest worthy of protection. When they did, it was easy for the treatise writers could define a particular tort in terms of that interest. For example, false imprisonment could be defined in terms of confinement which deprived the plaintiff of his freedom of movement. Otherwise, unless the treatise writers were to challenge the cases, their choices were limited. They could devise a formula that fit the cases and then invent some reason why it corresponded only roughly to an interest worth protecting. They could redescribe the interest in question to make it fit their formula more closely. Or they could ignore the problem.

For example, the earliest treatise writers said that battery protected a person against bodily harm. Yet bodily harm was not all that mattered, as one can see from their definitions of battery, which still looked more like graphic images than boundary lines. Battery is "violence" inflicted on a person[15] or as "an angry, rude, insolent or revengeful touching." [16] Later definitions were less graphic. For example, according Bigelow and Salmond, battery is an "application of force" to "the person of another" that is "unpermitted" [17] or "without lawful justification." [18] But force did not mean harm. Even a person who had not been harmed could recover.[19] Some writers did not try to explain why. Some found a reason why legal protection extended beyond the interest supposedly in question. The reason, according to Clark, was "the very great importance attached by the law to the interest in physical security." [20] According to Seavy, a "very slight interference is sufficient" because the interest "in bodily integrity" is one of the "most highly protected." [21] Salmond redescribed the interest in question: it "not merely that of freedom from bodily harm, but also that of freedom from such forms of insult as may be due to interference with his person." [22] Harper, Prosser and the Restatements agreed,[23] and so were able to redefine battery in a way that fit the cases and also corresponded to the interests that Salmond had identified: plaintiff can recover for "unpermitted unprivileged contacts with [his] person" [24] for "harmful or offensive touching." [25]

15. Hilliard, *Torts* 1: 201; Francis M. Burdick, *The Law of Torts. A Concise Treatise on the Civil Liability at Common Law and Under Modern Statutes for Actionable Wrongs to Person and Property* (2d ed. 1908), 268.

16. Hilliard, *Torts* 1: 201. *See* Addison, *Wrongs* 2: 692 ("the person of a man is actually struck or touched in a violent, rude or insolent manner"); Burdick, *Torts* 268 ("touching of another in anger"); Thomas M. Cooley, *A Treatise on the Law of Torts or the Wrongs which arise Independent of Contract* (1880), 162 ("injury ... done ... in an angry or revengeful or rude or insolent matter").

17. Melville M. Bigelow, *Elements of the Law of Torts for the Use of Students* (3d ed. 1886), 101.

18. Salmond, *Torts* 382.

19. For example, Bigelow, *Torts* 101 ("any forcible contact may be sufficient"); Salmond, *Torts* 382 (force may be "trivial").

20. George L. Clark, *The Law of Torts* 10 (1926).

21. Warren Seavey, "Principles of Torts," *Harvard Law Review* 56 (1942), 72.

22. Salmond, *Torts* 383.

23. Prosser, *Torts* 44–45; Harper, *Torts* 38; Restatement of Torts ch. 2, titles of topics 1 & 2 (1934); Restatement (Second) of Torts ch. 2, titles, topics 1 & 2 (1965).

24. Prosser, *Torts* 43.

25. Harper, *Torts* 39. *See* Restatement of Torts §§ 13, 15, 18–19 (1934); Restatement (Second) of Torts §§ 13, 15, 18–19 (1965).

Similarly, according to the earlier treatise writers, an action of assault was supposed to protect a "right not to be put in fear of personal harm." [26] Yet, as one can see even from the graphic, image-like descriptions of the earliest treatise writers, this action did not protect against all reasonable fear of harm, or only against fear of harm. They described assault as " 'an unlawful setting upon one's person'; or a threat of violence exhibiting the intention to assault, and a present ability to carry the same into execution;" [27] an "attempt . . . to offer with force and violence to do hurt to another." [28] Later writers, somewhat more tamely, defined assault as "an attempt, real or apparent, to do hurt to another's person, within reaching distance;" [29] "an attempt with unlawful force to inflict bodily injury upon another, accompanied with the apparent present ability to give effect to the attempt if not prevented." [30] None of them claimed, however, that the plaintiff could recover always or only when he had been put in fear. As before, some like Seavy said that the reason was the importance of personal security as though that explained the matter. [31] Harper, Prosser and the Restatements, however, redefined the interest at stake as "the interest in freedom from apprehension of a harmful or offensive contact." [32] That interest corresponded to their more precise definition of assault: it required the "apprehension of a harmful or offensive contact" where apprehension simply means the awareness that such a contact may imminently occur. [33]

Similarly, the plaintiff's property was supposedly protected by an action by trespass to land, his reputation by actions for libel and slander. Yet the plaintiff could recover for trespass if the defendant entered his land even if he did no physical damage. This time, none of the treatise writers managed to redescribe the interest at stake to make it conform to the circumstances under which the plaintiff could recover. Some of them found reasons why the law would impose liability when no harm was done. Some said that the law "presumes" [34] or "implies" [35] damage. According to Salmond, "[t]he explanation [is] that certain acts are so likely to result in harm that the law prohibits them absolutely and irrespective of the actual issue." [36] According to Seavy, the reason was that like the interest in bodily integrity, the interests "in the possession and ownership of land, are [among] the most highly protected." [37] Some merely let the matter pass.

These explanations made it sound as though somebody—"the law"—had already decided what interests were worth protecting and how to protect them. Supposedly, for example, the law had decided to protect one's interest in not being offended but only against offence by physical contact;

---

26. Cooley, *Torts* 161. *See* Burdick, *Torts* 266 ("the right to live in society without being put in reasonable fear of unjustifiable personal harm").

27. Hilliard, *Torts* 1: 197.

28. Addison, *Wrongs* 2: 690.

29. Bigelow, *Torts* 98.

30. Cooley, *Torts* 160.

31. Seavey, "Principles of Torts."

32. Prosser, *Torts* 48; Harper, *Torts* 43 (same, but speaking of a "harmful or offensive

touching"); Restatement of Torts ch. 2, title of topic 3 (1934); Restatement (Second) of Torts ch. 2, title of topic 3 (1965).

33. Prosser, *Torts* 48; Harper, *Torts* 43; Restatement of Torts § 21 (1934); Restatement (Second) of Torts § 21 (1965).

34. Hilliard, *Torts* 1: 87.

35. Burdick, *Torts* 338.

36. Salmond, *Torts* 12.

37. Seavey, "Principles of Torts."

it had decided to protect one's freedom from the apprehension of imminent harmful or offensive physical contact whether one was put in fear or not; it had decided not only to protect one's interest in land or reputation but to allow recovery even when neither had suffered harm. The treatise writers suggested that the law had made all these decisions without saying that they themselves agreed on the merits. The matter is presented in much the same way in textbooks today. The common law torts are said to correspond to the legal interests that the law had decided to protect.

As an historical matter, however, such decisions had never been made. Trespass in assault and battery dates from a time when breaches of the peace often led to private vengeance, when the distinction between civil and criminal liability was not yet clear in everyone's mind, and when the very concept of tort as a distinct body of law was centuries off. The rules governing trespass in land were laid down before there were declaratory judgments. As Prosser himself observed, an action in trespass was used, not merely to redress an injury, but to vindicate "a legal right without which the defendant's conduct, if repeated, might in time ripen into prescription." [38] Historically, it would be hard to reconstruct what the common law judges had in mind when they set boundaries to the traditional forms of action. Surely, however, they were not considering what interests each form of action should protect and the best way to protect them.

However that may have been, common lawyers still determine whether the plaintiff can recover by asking what tort, if any, the defendant has committed. Since the traditional torts did not represent a list of rights or interests in which the defendant ought to be protected, inevitably, cases arise in which, although he should be protected, there is no appropriate tort. In those cases, the court must either deny relief, or stretch the boundaries of some existing tort, or invent a new tort.

2. Harm to dignity

a. Insult in general

Traditional common law

Before the enactment of a statute on "harassment" in England, and the recognition of a new tort of intentional infliction of mental distress in the United States, plaintiff had to bring his case within one of the traditional torts.

R.F.V. Heuston & R.A. Buckley, *Salmond and Heuston on the Law of Torts* (21st ed. 1996), 120

"[In English law], even to touch a person without his consent or some other lawful reason is actionable. Nor is anger or hostility essential to liability: an unwanted kiss may be a battery. For the interest that is protected by the law of assault and battery is not merely that of freedom from

---

38. Prosser, *Torts* 81.

bodily harm, but also that of freedom from such forms of insult as may be due to interference with his person. In respect of personal dignity, therefore, a man may recover substantial damages for a battery that has done him no physical harm whatever. . . ." [citations omitted].

Leichtman v. WLW Jacor Communications, Inc., 634 N.E. 2d 697 (Ohio App. 1994)

Plaintiff, an anti-smoking advocate, was invited to appear on a radio talk show to discuss the evils of smoking and breathing secondary smoke. He alleged that while he was in the studio, Furman, a talk show host with a different show who was an employee of the defendant, lit a cigar and repeatedly blew smoke in his face "for the purpose of causing physical discomfort, humiliation, and distress." The court held that Furman's act constituted a battery. The contact requirement was met because "tobacco smoke, as 'particulate matter,' has the physical properties capable of making contact."

Western Union Telegraph Co. v. Hill, 150 So. 709 (1933)

Sapp was in charge of a telegraph office. When the plaintiff's wife entered on business, he offered to "love and pet her" and reached for her with his hand. The court held that whether he committed an assault depended on the width of the counter. If, as some of the evidence indicated, it was so wide that he could not have touched her, there was no assault. If, as other evidence indicated, he could have reached from six to eighteen inches beyond the counter to where she was standing, then there was an assault. The court ruled that the trial court had rightly left this question to the jury.

Note: Although traditionally, in England as in the United States, a plaintiff could recover for insult if he could bring his case within one of the traditional torts, it is not clear that either of these cases would have come out the same way in England or in other American states. In England, it has never been decided whether "the infliction of such things as heat or light or blowing smoke upon a person" constitute a battery. W.V.H. Rogers, *Winfield & Jolowicz on Tort* (15th ed. 1998), 64. Moreover, in England, the requirement that the victim of an assault must apprehend imminent harm has been construed less strictly than in *Western Union Telegraph Co. v. Hill*. "[T]hreats on the telephone may be an assault provided that the plaintiff has reason to believe that they may be carried out in the sufficiently near future to qualify as 'immediate.'" *Id.* 67, citing the criminal case of *Regina v. Ireland*, [1997] 3 W.L.R. 534, which held that even a silent telephone call could be an assault.

Modern English law

W.V.H. Rogers, *Winfield & Jolowicz on Tort* (15th ed. 1998), 64

"Whether the infliction of such things as heat or light or blowing smoke upon a person would be held to be uncertain, but there is no doubt that if injury is thereby caused it would be actionable on the principle of *Wilkinson v. Downton*."

Wilkinson v. Downton, [1897] 2 Q.B. 57

"In this case, the defendant, in the execution of what he seems to have regarded as a practical joke, represented to the plaintiff that he was charged by her husband with a message to her to the effect that her husband was smashed up in an accident, and was lying at The Elms at Leytonstone with both legs broken, and that she was to go at once in a cab with two pillows to fetch him home. All this was false. The effect of the statement on the plaintiff was a violent shock to her nervous system, producing vomiting and other more serious and permanent physical consequences at one time threatening her reason, and entailing weeks of suffering and incapacity to her as well as expense to her husband for medical attendance. . . .

The defendant has, as I assume for the moment, wilfully done an act calculated to cause physical harm to the plaintiff—that is to say, to infringe her right to personal safety, and has in fact thereby caused physical harm to her. That proposition without more appears to me to state a good cause of action, there being no justification alleged for the act. This wilful injuria is in law malicious, although no malicious purpose to cause the harm which was caused nor any motive of spite is imputed to the defendant.

It remains to consider whether the assumptions involved in the proposition are made out. One question is whether the defendant's act was so plainly calculated to produce some effect of the kind which was produced that an intention to produce it ought to be imputed to the defendant, regard being had to the fact that the effect was produced on a person who proved to be in an ordinary state of health and mind. I think that it was. It is difficult to imagine that such a statement, made suddenly and with apparent seriousness, could fail to produce grave effects under the circumstances upon any but an exceptionally indifferent person, and therefore the intention to produce such an effect must be imputed, and it is no answer in law to say that more harm was done than was anticipated for that is commonly the case with all wrongs."

Tony Weir, *A Casebook on Tort* (8th ed. 1996), 340

"In this very illustrative case, a deliberate lie destroyed the plaintiff's peace of mind and caused her physical harm. These facts did not, however, quite fit the form of any established tort. Although the appropriate interest (peace of mind) was affected, it was not quite *assault*, since the defendant did nothing but speak, and trespass requires an act. It was not quite *deceit*, since the plaintiff took no detrimental action, except paying for her friends to take the train. Nor was *negligence* appropriate, since shock damage resulting from unreasonable behavior was not compensable in 1897. However, the defendant's behaviour was not just unreasonable, it was wilful; the harm was not just foreseeable, it was the calculated result; and there was a special relationship between the parties, who were face-to-face. So it was entirely correct of Wright, J., to infer and state a new principle of liability."

W.V.H. Rogers, *Winfield and Jolowicz on Tort*
(15th ed., 1998), 86–87

"The nature of the mental element required for this form of liability is not very clear, though so far we have spoken in terms of 'intention' (with which advertent recklessness is commonly equated). However, while Downton intended to tell lies, it is not at all clear that he intended to cause physical harm to Mrs. Wilkinson or even realised that it might occur—indeed, Wright, J.'s judgment implies that he did not. 'Calculated to cause harm' is ambiguous, for the phrase could refer to harm actually contemplated by the defendant or to harm which a reasonable person would foresee as a probable result. In practice in many cases the point may be of limited importance from a practical point of view, simply because there would be a clear liability in respect of the same damage caused by a negligent act. If putting out poison for the plaintiff (who dies by taking it) is an example of *Wilkinson v. Downton*, then the defendant will be liable whether he desired to kill, or foresaw death as a possibility but was indifferent to it, or thought there was no risk of death but making the plaintiff ill would be a good joke, or *merely left the poison out by complete inadvertence in circumstances where it might be consumed*. The point becomes significant, however, if there would be no liability for negligence in such a situation or if the harm complained of would not be remediable by an action for negligence, for then the limits of *Wilkinson v. Downton* cease to be a mere matter of classification and become the limits of liability. For example, suppose Downton had been a well-meaning bumbling neighbour who had misunderstood an accident report and had in error told Mrs. Wilkinson the same story, would he have been liable to her? It may be that in the modern law he would, but it is by no means certain. As to the harm suffered, Mrs. Wilkinson suffered shock, which is well-recognised in law as a variety of personal injury. However, in the United States liability under a similar theory for extreme and outrageous conduct has been extended to cover distress or humiliation without psychiatric trauma amounting to illness. Such 'harm' is plainly recoverable as part of the damages for trespass to the person or other torts, such as libel, which are actionable *per se*; equally plainly, it does not amount to sufficient damage to found an action for negligence and the liability under *Wilkinson v. Downton* is, in historical terms, like negligence, an action on the case requiring 'damage.' No Commonwealth court yet appears to have extended liability to other types of harm. . . ."

The Protection from Harassment Act 1997 c. 40

(1) Prohibition of harassment.

    1. A person must not pursue a course of conduct:

        (a) which amounts to harassment of another, and

        (b) which he knows or ought to know amounts to harassment of the other.

    2. For the purposes of this section, the person whose course of conduct is in question ought to know that it amounts to harassment of another if a reasonable person in possession of the

same information would think the course of conduct amounted to harassment of the other.

3. Subsection (1) does not apply to a course of conduct if the person who pursued it shows:

   (a) that it was pursued for the purpose of preventing or detecting crime,

   (b) that it was pursued under any enactment or rule of law or to comply with any condition or requirement imposed by any person under any enactment, or

   (c) that in the particular circumstances the pursuit of the course of conduct was reasonable.

(2) Offence of harassment.

1. A person who pursues a course of conduct in breach of section 1 is guilty of an offence.

2. A person guilty of an offence under this section is liable on summary conviction to imprisonment for a term not exceeding six months, or a fine not exceeding level 5 on the standard scale, or both.

   . . .

(3) Civil Remedy.

1. An actual or apprehended breach of section 1 may be the subject of a claim in civil proceedings by the person who is or may be the victim of the course of conduct in question.

2. On such a claim, damages may be awarded for (among other things) any anxiety caused by the harassment and any financial loss resulting from the harassment. . . .

(4) Putting people in fear of violence.

1. A person whose course of conduct causes another to fear, on at least two occasions, that violence will be used against him is guilty of an offence if he knows or ought to know that his course of conduct will cause the other so to fear on each of those occasions.

2. For the purposes of this section, the person whose course of conduct is in question ought to know that it will cause another to fear that violence will be used against him on any occasion if a reasonable person in possession of the same information would think the course of conduct would cause the other so to fear on that occasion.

   . . .

(7) Interpretation of this group of sections.

1. This section applies for the interpretation of sections 1 to 5.

2. References to harassing a person include alarming the person or causing the person distress.

3. A "course of conduct" must involve conduct on at least two occasions.

4. "Conduct" includes speech.

W.V.H. Rogers, *Winfield & Jolowicz on Tort* (15th ed. 1998), 88–89

"[H]arassment . . . is capable of embracing, for example persistent following, questioning or 'door stepping' by journalists, methods of debt collection which are humiliating or distressing, or conduct in the course of a neighborhood dispute which is designed to annoy, for example playing loud music or banging on walls. There is, therefore, a good deal of overlap with liability at common law.

Harassment in its ordinary sense seems to imply something sustained and intended to vex, annoy or distress. So if D quarrels with P in 1997 and makes an abusive telephone call to him on that occasion and this is repeated in 1998, but as a result of a wholly independent quarrel, that would not, it is submitted, fall within the Act. Nor would one describe the playing of loud music, caused not by spite but by selfish indifference to neighbours, as harassment, though it may amount to a common law nuisance and an offence under other legislation." [citations omitted]

Modern law in the United States

Restatement (Second) of Torts

§ 46: Outrageous Conduct Causing Severe Emotional Distress

(1) One who by extreme and outrageous conduct intentionally or recklessly causes severe emotional distress to another is subject to liability for such emotional distress, and if bodily harm to the other results from it, for such bodily harm.

(2) Where such conduct is directed at a third person, the actor is subject to liability if he intentionally or recklessly causes severe emotional distress:

   (a) to a member of such person's immediate family who is present at the time, whether or not such distress results in bodily harm, or

   (b) to any other person who is present at the time, if such distress results in bodily harm.

Halio v. Lurie, 222 N.Y.S.2d 759 (N.Y. A.D. 1961)

"[I]t is alleged that the plaintiff, a native of Turkey, and a citizen of this country, is an unmarried young woman; that plaintiff and defendant had been keeping company for about two years with a view to their ultimate marriage; that while they were still doing so, defendant married another woman without plaintiff's knowledge, and concealed the marriage from the plaintiff, who discovered it only by accident; that the relations between the parties then ceased, and that defendant thereafter composed and mailed to plaintiff, in an envelope addressed to Mrs. Vicky Halio, a communication in verse entitled 'An Ode to Vicky' in which he referred to her as 'the tortured Turk,' taunted her with her unsuccessful efforts to marry him, intimated that she had made a false claim that he was under an obligation to marry her, declared that he had avoided marriage to her because he was 'wise to her game,' and expressed the view that through the coming years she would be the object of derision and the subject of amusement, on the part of his wife and himself, by reason of her 'phone calls galore' (presumably to complain that she had not accomplished her purpose to marry him)."

The plaintiff recovered for infliction of emotional distress.

Flamm v. Van Nierop, 291 N.Y.S. 2d 189 (N.Y. A.D. 1968)

"Plaintiff alleges that defendant has maliciously caused him and is now causing him and will continue to cause him mental and emotional distress, sleeplessness, physical debilitation, and irreparable damage, by the following course of conduct: dashing at plaintiff with threatening gestures and malign looks accompanied by derisive laughter, walking closely behind or beside or in front of plaintiff on the public streets, telephoning plaintiff at his home and place of business and then either hanging up or remaining on the line in silence, and driving his automobile behind that of plaintiff at a dangerously close distance; wherefore plaintiff asks for damages and an injunction. This sufficiently states a cause of action for damages for the intentional infliction of emotional and physical harm, and for an injunction. Special damages need not be alleged. Probably this also states a cause of action for assault.

If a man finds himself perpetually haunted by an enemy; if he is greeted at every turn by baleful looks, sudden sorties which fall short of physical contact, and derisive laughter; if he cannot drive his car without the imminent threat of a collision from the rear; and if he is troubled at all hours by telephone calls followed only by silence, then it can hardly be doubted that he is being subjected to the extreme and outrageous conduct which gives rise to a cause of action in tort."

Note on racial insults: In a number of cases, plaintiffs have recovered for racial or ethnic insults; *e.g.*, Alcorn v. Anbro Engineering, Inc., 468 P.2d 216 (Cal. 1970) (plaintiff called a "god damn nigger" by his white foreman); Gomez v. Hug, 645 P.2d 916 (Kan. App. 1982) (plaintiff, a county employee, called a "fucking spic," a "fucking Mexican greaser" and "nothing but a pile of shit" by the county commissioner); Wiggs v. Courshon, 355 F.Supp. 206 (S.D. Fla. 1973) (plaintiff called a "black son of a bitch" by the waitress who brought him his food). In contrast, plaintiff did not recover in Patterson v. McLean Credit Union, 805 F.2d 1143 (4th Cir. 1986) (plaintiff's supervisor alleged to have harassed her for racial motives by assigning her too much work, assigning her sweeping and dusting that was not assigned to whites, telling her that blacks work slower than whites, and staring at her for minutes at a time).

Restatement (Second) of Torts

§ 46: SPECIAL LIABILITY OF PUBLIC UTILITY FOR INSULTS BY SERVANTS

A common carrier or public utility is subject to liability to patrons utilizing its facilities for gross insults which reasonably offend them, inflicted by the utility's servants while otherwise acting in the scope of their employment.

French law

In a criminal case, the victim can participate as a "civil party" (*partie civile*). If the defendant is convicted, he can be ordered to pay the victim damages. Thus typically in France, a party who has been offended will make a complaint so that a criminal action is brought against the person who offended him. That is why many of the cases that follow are criminal prosecutions.

The plaintiff is deemed to have suffered "harm" for which he can recover under arts. 1382–83 of the Civil Code when the defendant commits the crimes of defamation and insult. The defendant who has told a falsehood about the victim can be prosecuted for defamation (*diffimation*). According to art. 29(1) of the Law of 29 July 1881, art. 29(1), defamation includes "any allegation or imputation of a fact that harms the honor or respect of the person or body to whom the fact is imputed." The cases that follow do not deal with defamation but with *injure* which comes from the Latin *iniuria* and which we will translate as "insult." According to art. 29(2) of the law just cited, an insult is "any outrageous expression, words of contempt or invective that does not include the imputation of any fact." That provision applies to insults that are made "in public." Art. R-621-2 of the Criminal Code (*Code pénal*) prohibits "non-public insult of a person" without defining the word "insult" any further.

Cour de cassation, ch. crim., 3 December, 1970, pourvoi no. 69-92.381

The defendant was convicted of insult (*injure*) and ordered to pay damages to Regine Zylberberg who was a civil party (*partie civile*) to the criminal action. His magazine *Correfour* had printed an article condemning what it called a decline in morals. It was entitled, "Why are our children no longer safe? Too many fools at liberty." It was illustrated by a photograph of the complainant in the company of a third party (no other details are given) with the caption: "Snobism and hysteria. Regine Zylberberg (the mountain of money)—Regine for short—receives Sammy Davis, Jr. The talented American showman deserves better." The defendant argued that the term "hysteria" did not constitute a term of disdain or invective; that it indicates "a sickness or, at the most, a disorder of the nervous system." Rejecting that contention, the *Cour de cassation* said that "in the ensemble composed of the article, the photograph, and the caption, and taking account of the desire to which it indicates, the word 'hysteria' tends to represent Zylberberg as part of a corrupt circle of snobs and hysterics whose activities are condemned in the article ... [so that] in this association of ideas no medical significance should be given to this word which can only be understood in its common meaning as indicating a penchant to debauch."

Jean Larguier & Anne-Marie Larguier, *Droit pénale special* (8th ed. 1994)

"*Outrageous expressions*: examples taken from the case law: 'bandit, riffraff (*canaille*), traitor, pirate, little demagogue, filth, mountain of dung, dirty sewer stream, tart kosher pork butcher, *buse* (which means "buzzard" but can be used figuratively to mean blockhead), paranoid.' But it is not an insult to suggest that someone submit his resignation (Versailles, 1986)."

German law

The German Criminal Code (*Strafgesetzbuch*) also contains provisions on interference with reputation and dignity. It distinguishes "insult" (*Beleidigung*), "wrongful dissemination" (*üble Nachrede*) and "defamation" (*Verleumdung*). A statement is an "insult" if it affects a person's "good reputation" (*der gute Ruf in seiner realen Existenz*). StGB § 185(1). An "insult" need not be a statement of fact. In contrast, "wrongful dissemination" and "defamation" are committed by making a statement of fact which "brings [another] into contempt or lowers him in public opinion." Criminal Code §§ 186, 187. To constitute "wrongful dissemination" the statement must be one which is "not demonstrably true." Criminal Code § 186. To constitute defamation, the statement must be "demonstrably untrue" and made "against one's better knowledge" (*wider besseres Wissen*). Criminal Code § 187.

As we have seen, the drafters of the German Civil Code did not want people to be liable for the types of harm covered by the action for *iniuria*. Section 823(1) says that the plaintiff can only recover for injury to the "life, body, health, freedom, ownership or similar right (*sonstiges Recht*) of another." Originally, "similar right" was not supposed to include personal dignity. Section 823(2) said that the obligation to make compensation also rests "on a person who infringes a statute intended for the protection of others." As we have just seen, people are protected against defamation and insult by the German Criminal Code (*Strafgesetzbuch*). But to prevent them from recovering damages in tort, the drafters added the following provisions.

German Civil Code

§ 253 [Now § 253(1)]

In the case of harm that is not economic, compensation in money can be demanded only in the cases specified by statute.

§ 847(1) [As Originally Enacted]

In the case of injury to body or health or deprivation of liberty, the injured party may also demand fair compensation in money for non-economic harm.

§ 253(2) [Which Replaced § 847(1) According To Legislation Enacted in 2002]

In the case of injury to body, health, liberty or sexual self-determination, fair compensation in money can be required for non-economic harm.

Those provisions made it as clear as possible that, at the time the Code was enacted, the plaintiff was not supposed to recover for injuries to his dignity or privacy. But today German courts allow him recover anyway. In 1954, the Bundesgerichtshof declared that *Persönlichkeit*—"personality"— was a "similar right" within the meaning of § 823(1) of the German Civil

Code. It held that a newspaper had violated this right by publishing a letter written by a lawyer on his client's behalf as though it was written by him spontaneously and expressed his own views. BGHZ 13, 334. As we will see, since then it has awarded damages in many cases. The court's justification for disregarding the text of the German Civil Code is that arts. 1 and 2 of the German constitution (*Grundgesetz*) protect human dignity and personal freedom, and without a civil action, this protection would be incomplete.

Constitution of the Federal Republic of Germany (Grundgesetz)

ARTICLE 1: THE WORTH OF A HUMAN BEING

(1) The worth of a human being is unassailable. It is the duty of all state power to attend to it and protect it.

(2) The German people accordingly acknowledges that inviolable and inalienable human rights are the basis of every human community, of peace, and of justice in the world.

(3) The following basic rights are binding upon legislation, executive power, and judicial decisions as the law in force.

ARTICLE 2: FREEDOM OF THE PERSON, RIGHT TO LIFE AND PHYSICAL INTEGRITY

(1) Each person has the right to the free development of his personality (*Persönlichkeit*) insofar as he does not injure the rights of others and does not violate the constitutional order or moral law.

(2) Each person has the right to life and physical integrity. The freedom of a person is inviolable. Incursion on these rights can only occur on the basis of a statute.

* * *

ARTICLE 5: THE RIGHT TO FREE EXPRESSION OF OPINION

(1) Each person has the right freely to express and disseminate his opinion through word, writing, or image and to disseminate and to inform himself without hindrance through generally accessible sources.

(2) These rights are limited by the provisions of general statutes, statutory provisions in the protection of the young, and in the right to personal honor (*Ehre*).

(3) Art and science, research and teaching are free. The freedom of teaching does not release one from loyalty to the constitution.

Bundesgerichtshof, 16 January 1951, NJW 1951, 368

Little is reported of the facts except that the defendant put his hand under the skirt of Frau C. who was a stranger, and that she brought charges of rape and lewd behavior against him. The court dismissed these charges but held that the defendant was guilty of insult.

"What constitutes an insult is the manifestation of disrespect for the injured party. . . . He gave the impression that he expected that Frau C. would permit such an attack on her sexual honor. It is not a part of the external factual elements of insult that the defendant intended his behavior to be insulting, nor that the person concerned experienced and understood the act as an insult. It is decisive that the conduct of the defendant toward the woman in the circumstances of the case in general is to be understood as a manifestation of disrespect.

The manifestation of disrespect must, however, be unlawful to legally justify condemnation for insult. The insult is not unlawful if and so long as an adult woman consented to the lewd contact with her body."

Oberlandesgericht, Düsseldorf, 10 August 1989, JR 1990, 345

[To follow the next case, you have to know that German has two pronouns that mean "you": "du" ("dich" in the accusative case) and "sie." You are supposed to use the first with friends and the second in more formal relationships.]

"The *Amtsgericht* regarded the factual elements of insult as met by the use of the words 'du' and 'dich' according to the complaint of the witness Z, because in view of the tense relationship between the witness and the defendant, the use of 'du' could only have meant disrespect. The opinion of the Amstgericht cannot survive judicial scrutiny.

For the question of whether there has been an injury to honor, one must take into account not only the surrounding circumstances but also the views, the customs of life and the social circumstances of the parties, as well as the linguistic and social place where the expression occurred. (See Dreher/Tröndle, *StGB* 44th ed. § 185 St.GB no. 8 with further references; Schönke/Schröder/Lenckner 23rd ed. § 185 *StGB* no. 8 with further references.)

According to the findings of the *Amtsgericht*, there was a close relationship between the parties before their quarrel when they lived in the same house and usually called each other 'du.' By itself, consideration of the circumstance that the witness Z forbad the defendant to call her 'du' does not prove that by the use of the words 'du' and 'dich' on 5 September 1988 there was a manifestation of disrespect for the witness."

Oberlandesgericht, Düsseldorf, 7 July 1989, JR 1990, 126

When an acquaintance of the defendant, E.M., was on trial for fraud before the 10th criminal chamber of the *Landgericht* for Düsseldorf, the defendant sent a letter to the presiding judge of the chamber under the heading "circle of friends" of E.M. It said: "The circle of friends of E.M. attach importance to the conclusion that here the law has been massively bent and the health of a man has been trampled under foot by the legal authorities in a manner once known only in totalitarian states." He was protesting the removal of E.M. from a clinic to stand trial. Feeling offended, the judge had criminal changes brought before the *Amtsgericht* which convicted the defendant of insult. The defendant claimed that he merely wanted to call attention to the inappropriate treatment of E.M., and that he had not known the judge would be so sensitive. The *Oberlandesgericht* overturned his conviction. It said that the relevant question "is not how the sender understood the letter. In evaluating a possibly injurious statement attention must rather be paid to how the statement in its context would be read by a naive and unsophisticated reader, a reasonable third party." The lower court had made the mistake of looking only at its "literal sense."

"The statement considered in itself is not sufficient to deprecate the honor of the judge of the 10th criminal chamber. One cannot conclude from the defendant's statement that he wished to hold the judge of the criminal chamber responsible for the alleged bending of the law. By itself, his contention that, the law has been massively bent, on a reasonable evaluation does not show that this reproach was also directed against the judge of the civil chamber as addressee of the letter."

Oberlandesgericht, Oldenburg, 31 July 1989, JR 1990, 1217

The defendant, who was being held on other charges, told two state criminal system employees who were trying to escort her from her cell that they were "shit bulls" (*Scheissbullen*). When they asked her what she had against them, she said that she would kick them in a vulnerable part of their anatomy to which she indelicately referred, and that then they would see what she had against "bulls, state attorneys, and judges." She was convicted of insult along with other charges and sentenced to two years and three months in prison. On appeal, the *Landgericht* overturned the conviction for insult, sustained her conviction for the other charges, and reduced the sentence to one year and six months. The Oberlandesgericht reinstated the conviction for insult.

"This opinion [of the *Landgericht*] is based on the conception that there are no expressions which are simply insulting and that the judge has to examine the meaning of the specific expression under all of the surrounding circumstances to see if the expression in question constituted abuse of another (see Herdegen, LK, 10th ed. no. 18; Schönke/Schröder-Lenckner, *StGB*, 22nd ed. no. 8 to § 185 StrGB with further references). This conception is correct in principle even though with many kinds of expressions, their character as intentionally abusive can be seen more easily than with others. In principle, the observation of the *Landgericht* may also be correct that a general decline in the linguistic culture of people from the social group to which she belonged may have taken away the pejorative significance of the expression 'bull' even when used in conjunction with the word 'shit,' both in consciousness of this circle of people as well as in the use of language. Moreover, in principle, there is no legal objection when an expression which comes very close to carrying on insulting meaning is to be seen in a particular case as a simple expression of displeasure over, as the *Landgericht* put it, a most unlovable place and a protest against the treatment directed against the speaker and not as the abuse of an individual standing near her.

But these considerations cannot apply here in view of the circumstances in which the statement was made and which are to be used in its interpretation. The employees had gone to the cell of the defendant and explained the purpose for which they came. Thus they stand immediately opposite her. In such a situation, the use of abusive words directed at the class of persons to whom the listeners belong and which, according to their wording do not refer to a general condition or state of affairs, cannot be seen simply as an expression of dissatisfaction. . . .

Moreover, the *Landgericht* apparently left out of account that, in answering the question of what she had against them, she threatened a physical mistreatment of both employees which, aside from the feeling of pain attached to it, must normally be regarded as in a certain measure insulting. As to that point, it does not matter whether the defendant began to perform such an act or merely intended to."

b. Problems of free speech, group insult, and minority rights

Law in United States

Hustler Magazine v. Falwell, 485 U.S. 46 (1988)

"The inside front cover of the November 1983 issue of Hustler Magazine featured a 'parody' of an advertisement for Campari Liqueur that contained the name and picture of respondent and was entitled 'Jerry Falwell talks about his first time.' This parody was modeled after actual Campari ads that included interviews with various celebrities about their 'first times.' Although it was apparent by the end of each interview that this meant the first time they sampled Campari, the ads clearly played on the sexual double entendre of the general subject of 'first times.' Copying the form and layout of these Campari ads, Hustler's editors chose respondent as the featured celebrity and drafted an alleged 'interview' with him in which he states that his 'first time' was during a drunken incestuous rendezvous with his mother in an outhouse. The Hustler parody portrays respondent and his mother as drunk and immoral, and suggests that respondent is a hypocrite who preaches only when he is drunk. In small print at the bottom of the page, the ad contains the disclaimer, 'ad parody—not to be taken seriously.' . . .

Generally speaking the law does not regard the intent to inflict emotional distress as one which should receive much solicitude, and it is quite understandable that most if not all jurisdictions have chosen to make it civilly culpable where the conduct in question is sufficiently 'outrageous.' But in the world of debate about public affairs, many things done with motives that are less than admirable are protected by the First Amendment. . . .

Thus while such a bad motive may be deemed controlling for purposes of tort liability in other areas of the law, we think the First Amendment prohibits such a result in the area of public debate about public figures. Were we to hold otherwise, there can be little doubt that political cartoonists and satirists would be subjected to damages awards without any showing that their work falsely defamed its subject. Webster's defines a caricature as 'the deliberately distorted picturing or imitating of a person, literary style, etc. by exaggerating features or mannerisms for satirical effect.' Webster's New Unabridged Twentieth Century Dictionary of the English Language 275 (2d ed. 1979). The appeal of the political cartoon or caricature is often based on exploration of unfortunate physical traits or politically embarrassing events—an exploration often calculated to injure the feelings of the subject of the portrayal. The art of the cartoonist is often not reasoned or evenhanded, but slashing and one-sided. . . .

Several famous examples of this type of intentionally injurious speech were drawn by Thomas Nast, probably the greatest American cartoonist to date, who was associated for many years during the post-Civil War era with Harper's Weekly. In the pages of that publication Nast conducted a graphic vendetta against William M. 'Boss' Tweed and his corrupt associates in New York City's 'Tweed Ring.' . . .

Respondent contends, however, that the caricature in question here was so 'outrageous' as to distinguish it from more traditional political cartoons. There is no doubt that the caricature of respondent and his mother published in Hustler is at best a distant cousin of the political cartoons described above, and a rather poor relation at that. If it were possible by laying down a principled standard to separate the one from the other, public discourse would probably suffer little or no harm. But we doubt that there is any such standard, and we are quite sure that the pejorative description 'outrageous' does not supply one."

Note on group insult and group defamation: One question that will come up in the continental cases is to what extent can one be liable for insulting a group. So far as I know, that question has not arisen in American cases on intentional infliction of emotional distress. But it has in defamation cases. In Nieman-Marcus v. Lait, 13 F.R.D. 311 (S.D.N.Y. 1952), the defendants had published a book which charged that some models and saleswomen of the Nieman-Marcus store in Texas were "call girls" and that most of the male salesmen were homosexual. Suit was brought by all nine models who worked at the store, and by 30 out of the 382 saleswomen and by 15 out of the 25 salesmen who worked there. The defendants moved to dismiss the action as to the salesmen and saleswomen (not, apparently, as to the models). The court granted the motion as to the women but not as to the men, noting that the group of men was small and that the allegation concerned "most" of them. In contrast, American courts have consistently refused to allow an action to be brought for defaming a large group such as an ethnic or religious group. *See* Khalid Abdullah Tarig Al Mansour Faissal Fahd Al Talal v. Fanning, 506 F. Supp. 186 (N.D. Cal. 1980) (dismissing a class action on behalf of six hundred million Moslems alleging that a film, "Death of a Princess," was defamatory to all Moslems).

French law

Cour d'appel, Paris, 15 February 1988, JCP 1988.II.21115

Defendant Francois Brigneau, a journalist, published an article under a pseudonym in a newspaper *Présent* (also a defendant) which contained the following remark about Anne Sinclaire, a TV journalist: "As usual, at seven on the hour, sister Sinclair-Levaï, the tart kosher pork butcher received one of her co-religionists. If they wouldn't talk about anti-semitism, I would like to be transformed into a pillar of salt." Defendant argued to the *Tribunal de grande instance* that the expression "tart" could be taken as a compliment but in any case was merely banal and vulgar; that the expression "pork butcher" (*charcutière* which means butcher and is usually understood to mean pork butcher) "was in no way insulting, since it referred to the exercise of a profession perfectly worthy of esteem, evoking as well good health, a certain assurance of one's self"; and that the word "kosher" which "evokes the prohibition of the Jewish religion on eating the meat of pigs, is not incompatible with the trade of a *charautière* which is not limited to the use of this sort of meat, so that the juxtaposition of the words *charcutière* and kosher do not imply any contradiction and therefore cannot make the activity of the person referred to appear aberrational or hypocritical." The *Tribunal* agreed as to the word "tart" but held that the other expressions had a "regrettable anti-Semitic connotation" and exceeded the "rights recognized any critic." It found a violation of art. 29(2) of the Law of 29 July 1881, and instructed the defendants to pay the plaintiff 15,000 francs and to publish an extract from its opinion in its own journal and, again and at their own expense, in a national periodical to be chosen by the plaintiff.

While the case was on appeal, the defendants published another article referring to the plaintiff as a "Christian butcher," this time using the term *bouchère* which, unlike *charcutière*, does not connote pork. The plaintiff asked the *Cour d'appel* to affirm the judgment below in principle but to increase the damages to 50,000 francs. *The Cour d'appel* upheld the decision below and awarded 15,000 francs in damages. The court said the expression "kosher," in this context, had "racist resonance;" that the expression *charcutière* suggested that she sliced up reality like a "sausage"; and that the word "tart" associated with *charcutière* would "lead the reader to represent Mme. Sinclair, physically, as a caricature, and professionally . . . as a journalist triply mediocre: under the aspects of talent, ambition and intellectual honesty."

In a note on this case, Prof. Agostini said: "In fact, it would appear that the decision in question has condemned an expression for belonging to the category it discussed ['insult'] which should be called an outrage but is not punishable by the law on the press [the Law of 29 July 1881]. . . .

Now in a democratic society, it must be permitted to anyone to make an evaluation, even a severe one, of those who are makers of opinion and who do not refrain from erecting their own opinions into criteria for public morality. Austria was taken before the European Court of Human Rights because its courts had found that the jurist Lingens committed defamation by ascribing pro-Nazi sympathies to Chancellor Kreisky. The court of Strassburg deemed there had been a violation of article 10 of the Convention which states the principle of freedom of expression." Agostini, JCP 1988(2).II.21115.

Note: The case to which Prof. Agostini referred is Lingens v. Austria, European Court of Human Rights, 8 July 1986, Gaz. Pal. 1986(2).Chr. 525. Lingens used the expressions "the most detestable opportunism," "immoral," and "deprived of all dignity" to describe Chancellor Kreisky's tolerance of former Nazis in his government. He was convicted of "defamation." While truth is a defense to defamation under Austrian law, the defendant has the burden of proving it. The Austrian courts held that this burden had not been met. The European Court of Human Rights held that this decision deprived

Lingen of freedom of expression in violation of art. 10 of the European Convention on Human Rights. It said that the Austrian courts "deemed, in substance, that there are different ways of evaluating the conduct of Mr. Kreisky, and if one could not logically prove the justice of one's own interpretation to the exclusion of any other; as a result, they found the appellant guilty of defamation."

"In the eyes of the Court, one ought to distinguish between facts and value judgments. If the existence of the first can be proven, the second are not to be put to a proof of their exactitude. The Court observes that the facts on which Mr. Lingens based his value judgment are not in dispute any more than his good faith."

Cour de cassation, ch. crim., 28 June 1983, pourvoi no. 82-92.904

The defendant made this statement in a radio broadcast:

> The pretended Hitlerian gas chamber and the pretended genocide of the Jews constitute one and the same historical lie which has allowed a gigantic political–financial fraud of which the principal beneficiaries are the state of Israel and international Zionism and the principal victims are the German people, though not their leaders, and the entire people of Palestine.

He was convicted of defamation and sentenced to three months of imprisonment and a 5,000 franc fine. He was also ordered to pay civil damages to the *Ligue internationale contra le racisme et l'antisemitisme* (LICRA) (the International League Against Racism and Anti-semitism) which participated in the proceedings as a civil party (*partie civile*). The *Cour de cassation* upheld the conviction, citing with approval the *Cour d'appel's* observation that "the entire Jewish community had been represented as a participant in a gigantic fraud from which it was said to have the benefits."

German law

Bundesgerichtshof, 19 January 1989, JZ 1989, 644

This was a criminal case in which the defendant said had published an article which stated: "[T]here is hardly any other profession that can be compared to that of a soldier. At most, that of a torturer, concentration camp overseer or executioner. Where else is a person trained to kill as perfectly as possible? . . . A profession whose sole purpose is murder and the maintenance of a gigantic murder machine is, indeed, a morally reproachable profession." Below, the defendant was convicted of "insult" to past and present soldiers of the German army (*Bundeswehr*) and fined. The state prosecutor appealed on the ground that he had also committed "defamation." The *Bundesgerichtshof* held that he was not guilty of defamation, because he had not made any false statements of fact: he had not suggested that soldiers kill except on the battlefield. Then the court said:

"The comparative and evaluative statements of the defendant are in principle sufficient to constitute an injury to the honor of the soldiers of the German army (*Bundeswehr*). The *Landgericht* acted appropriately in determining that the undifferentiated comparison quoted expressed contempt for soldiers and that this effect was strengthened by use of the drastic description of the training to kill bound up with the activity of soldiers: for example, with the operation of a 'gigantic murder machine.'

The defendant cannot legally justify his expressions by invoking the basic right to freedom of opinion (Art. 5, par. 1, sent. 1 of the German Constitution (*Grundgesetz*)). Certainly, he is free to discuss critically the public celebration of the oath of the German army and in so doing he may use sharp and polemical expressions and overstated poster-like value judgments (see BVerfGE 24, 278, 286; BVerfGE 42, 163, 169; BGH(Z) NJW 1981, 2117, 2119; Bay ObLG N St.Z 1983, 265), but nevertheless that does not legally justify vituperation, abuse and defaming as is the case here. (See BGH(Z) NJW 1974, 1762, 1763; *id.* 1977, 626, 627; Bay ObLG NStZ 1983, 126; *id* 1983, 265; OLG Düsseldorf NJW 1986, 1262).

Nevertheless, the limits of culpability were pushed too far when the *Landgericht* held that all former soldiers are to be deemed to be insulted. . . .

Certainly, the case law has always recognized that it is possible to insult a number of individual people under a collective description in such a way that all the members of a distinct group of persons are injured by this description. Accordingly a collective insult has been found for the Prussian judiciary (RGR 1, 292), the great landowners except for those with social democratic opinions (RGSt 33, 46, 47), the German officers (RGLZ 1915, 60), the German physicians (RG JW, 1932, 31; *Id.* 13), the Jews living in Germany who were the victims of national socialist measures of persecution (BGHSt 11, 207, 208). The capacity to suffer a collective insult was denied for 'all who take part in de-nazification,' the Catholics, the Protestants, the academics (BGHSt 11, 207, 209), 'the robed men of Moab' (KG JR 1978, 422), the police taken as a whole (OLG Düsseldorf NJW 1981, 1522).

The prior case law recognized that because it must be established which individual persons are insulted, the essential criterion for the possibility of a collective insult is that the group of persons described must be set apart from people in general by specific characteristics so clearly that the circle of those injured is clearly bounded (see, for example, BGHSt 2, 38, 39; *Id.* 11, 207, 208; RGSt 33, 46, 47).

Nevertheless, the *Reichsgericht* [the predecessor of the *Bundesgerichtshof*] already recognized that the criterion of uncertainty as to the boundary is not sufficient to raise a doubt about injury to those people whose membership in the group is beyond doubt. Indeed, the criterion of a clear boundary is not enough to prevent the finding of a collective insult because in any event criminal penalties would be called for on account of those who undoubtedly did belong to the group of persons referred to (Androulakis, *Die Sammelbeleidigung* 1970, p. 46). But one can always determine who is or is not a Catholic or a member of the *Deutscher Gewerkschaftsbund*.

Accordingly, the absence of clear boundaries to the circle of those injured cannot be the true reason why large groups such as Catholics and Protestants and also women, unionized labor, and employers cannot be collectively insulted. Consequently, the literature has required a further criterion for the recognition of a collective insult: that the group of persons in question be numerically surveyable (*zahlenmässig überschaubar*) (Lenker in Schönke/Schröder, *StGB* 23rd ed., notes before §§ 185ff no. 7; Arzt, JuS 1982, 717, 719; also, in criticism, Androulekis, *op cit.* p. 63ff, p. 79 ff; Wagner JuS 1978, 674, 677). The starting point for further reflection is that collective insults exaggerate and stereotype. When a collective description concerns an unsurveyable mass of persons and consequently one cannot discover a concrete relationship between the actor's statement or value judgment and particular persons, then what is involved is a generalization which admits of individual exceptions by its very statement. For it is clear that whoever is insulted in general is not insulted. (Herdegen in LK 10th ed. before § 185 no. 22 with reference to BayObLGSt 1958, 34, 35; see Androvlakis, *op. cit.* p. 79 ff; Liepemann, *Die Beleidigung*, VDB vol. 4, 1906, p. 217; Wagner JuS 1978, 674, 678.)

The Senate is of the opinion that the size of the insulted group is not a sufficient criterion, together with the ability to find a boundary, to set a limit to collective insult as is required by the rule of law (*aus rechtstaatlichen Gründen*). It is not certain how to find the frontier where a mass that is no longer surveyable is supposed to start. On the contrary, it is correct that a collective insult often contains general value judgments that are not capable of injuring the honor of particular people. With statements such as 'all German doctors are quacks' or 'all German judges bend the law' it is clear that such assertions cannot be true, even in the eyes of the person who makes them. Thus no one can be considered to be injured absent a tie to some particular person.

Nevertheless, there are pejorative statements about a collectivity to which this objection does not apply. That is the case here. The defendant has bound his pejorative judgment to a criterion that unambiguously does apply to all soldiers because it describes an outer conduct and an objective attachment to the collectivity attacked. One who, as here, compares the profession of a soldier with the activity of concentration camp overseers, executioners and torturers encompasses all soldiers without limitation. The question of to whom the pejorative statement applies does not arise.

The Senate is therefore of the opinion that the defendant . . . has insulted all soldiers who, at the time of the publication of his article, were on active service. That is true of reservists only insofar as they found themselves engaged in defense service [citation omitted]. The circle of injured persons thereby identified is certainly large but clearly bounded and to that extent surveyable. Admittedly, one cannot rule out that some active soldiers of the German army—even with defense duties—share the value judgment of the defendant. To that extent there is a consent which excludes the elements necessary for liability.

It is otherwise with regard to former soldiers of the German army. The extent of culpability would then be too wide if only because the necessary charges (*Strafanträge*) have not been brought (StGB § 194 par. 1)....

Moreover, the circle of former soldiers is so large and unsurveyable that it no longer constitutes a group of persons susceptible of a collective insult. Aside from the fact that some individuals among the former soldiers may share the defendant's opinion, the former soldiers are less affected by his statements because they have no further tie to the army and many have not for decades. Only those former soldiers can be considered as injured parties who still feel themselves tied to the army and manifest this engagement by their conduct, for example, by regular participation in military exercises or participation or work in soldiers associations.

Nevertheless, there is also a legal objection to the considerations on which the *Landgericht* denied that there was an insult to the German army (*Bundeswehr*).

Under certain circumstances, associations of persons, like individual persons, are susceptible of insult (see, for example, BGHSt 6, 186 ff with references). For departments, political bodies, and similar positions who attend to the task of public administration that already follows from § 194, par. 3 of the Criminal Code (StGB). Accordingly, the German army is also as an institution capable of suffering an insult. (OLG Hamm NZWehrr 1977, 70 with a note in agreement by Hennings.)

The *Landgericht* made no mistake as to that matter but denied there was an insult because the intention was absent. Its considerations on this point are legally objectionable. Admittedly, interpretation of the publication of the defendant and therefore determining his motive is the task of the judge of the facts (BGHSt 21, 371, 372; *id*. 32, 310, 311). Considering the textual passages that conflict with it, however, the conclusion that the article was principally concerned with soldiers and not with their employer is unsatisfactory and cannot be reconciled with them. The occasion on which the article was written—the planned public celebration of the oath of the army in Brückmühl—shows that the direction in which the attack was aimed was at the institution of the army as much as individual soldiers. According, in the foreground were not insulting expressions about individual soldiers, or a number of them, or concrete activities which they had undertaken but abstract considerations about the profession of soldier: its primary purpose murder and the maintenance of a 'gigantic murder machine.' "

Note: In England, courts do not pass on the constitutionality of legislation. In the United States, any court may do so on the theory that the constitution is the highest law of the land. In France, questions of constitutionality may be considered only when legislation is submitted to a special constitutional court in advance by certain government authorities. It may not be considered in the course or ordinary legislation. In Germany, while constitutional questions may not be considered by the ordinary courts, when they arise in the course of litigation, they may be submitted to a special constitutional court, the *Bundesverfassungsgericht*. That is what happened in the following case.

Bundesverfassungsgericht, 28 August 1994, NJW 1994, 2943

During the 1991 Gulf war, a noted conscientious objector displayed a bumper sticker on his car which said, "Soldiers are Murderers." He was sentenced to pay a fine by two lower courts (an *Amtsgericht* and a *Landgericht*). This sentence was upheld by an intermediate appellate court (*Oberlandesgericht*). The German Constitutional Court (*Bundesverfassungsgericht*) struck it down as a violation of freedom of expression as protected by art. 5 I 1 of the German Constitution (*Grundgesetz*).

"The basic right of freedom of opinion guarantees everyone the right to express his opinion. Each person is allowed to say what he thinks even when he neither gives nor can give and demonstrable grounds for his opinion. (BVerfG 42, 163 [170 f.] = NJW 1976, 1680; BVerfGE 61, 1 [7] = NJW 1983, 1415.) Article 5 I 1 of the German Constitution protects freedom of opinion both in the interest of the development of the individual person, to which it is closely allied, and in the interest of the democratic process, in which it has a constitutive role. (See BVerfGE 7, 198 [208] = NJW 1983, 1145 . . .) Moreover, sharp and exaggerated criticism does not deprive an expression of the protection of the Constitution. Still more, value judgments are to be protected by art. 5 I 1 without regard to whether the expression is 'valuable' or 'valueless,' 'true' or 'false,' 'emotional' or 'rational.' (BVerfGE 33, 1 [14 f.] = NJW 1972, 811; BVerfGE 61, 1 [7] = NJW 1983, 1415.)

Nevertheless, the right to freedom of opinion is not protected without reservation. According to art. 5 II of the Constitution, its limits are set by the provisions of general laws which determine by statute the protection of youth and the right to personal honor. However, the provisions that limit the right itself are to be interpreted in the light of these underlying rights so that a significance reflecting its role can be assigned to the legal sphere of application of the right itself. (See BVerfGE 7, 198 [208] = NJW 1958, 257 . . .) Generally, that leads to a weighing in the individual case of freedom of opinion and the status of the legal interests injured by freedom of speech, the result of which in a given case cannot be determined generally and abstractly. . . .

The *Amtsgericht* and *Landgericht* unanimously presumed that the bumper sticker branded the soldiers of the federal army as the worst criminals and least worthy members of society. But the decisions under attack rest on an understanding of the concept of 'murder' that is oriented to the Criminal Code and conceives the actor as a murderer in the sense of § 211 of that Code, which imposes the highest penalties on such an act. The decisions under attack provide no justification why an intelligent reader of the sticker should understand it in such a specialized and technical sense. In ordinary speech, it is common to make an unspecific use of the terms 'murder' and 'murderer' which goes beyond legal limitations. Accordingly, 'murder' can be understood as any killing of a person which is unjustified and accordingly to be disapproved. . . .

Consequently, the *Landgericht* gave the expression in question a sense which objectively it did not have."

3. Invasion of privacy

Privacy can be invaded in many different ways. We will only consider the dissemination of pictures and of true information about the plaintiff.

a. Dissemination of pictures

English law

Kaye v. Robertson, [1991] F.S.R. 62 (C.A.)

Glidewell L.J. "The Plaintiff, Mr Gordon Kaye, is a well-known actor and the star of a popular television comedy series. . . . [After head injuries suffered in an accident], [h]e was then in intensive care until on February 2 he was moved into a private room, forming part of Ward G. at the hospital. . . .

The first Defendant is the editor and the second Defendant company is the publisher of *Sunday Sport*, a weekly publication which Mr Justice Potter, from whose decision this is an appeal, described as having 'a lurid and sensational style.' A copy of a recent edition of *Sunday Sport* which was put in evidence before us shows that many of the advertisements contained in it are for various forms of pornographic material. This indicates the readership it seeks to attract.

Until February 13, 1990, Mr Kaye had not been interviewed since his accident by any representative of a newspaper or television programme. On that day, acting on Mr Robertson's instructions, a journalist and photographer from *Sunday Sport* went to Charing Cross Hospital and gained access to the corridor outside Ward G. They were not intercepted by any of the hospital staff. Ignoring the notices on the door to the ward and on the Plaintiff's door [listing people who were permitted to visit Mr Kaye], they entered the Plaintiff's room. Mr Kaye apparently agreed to talk to them and according to a transcript that we have heard of a taped record they made of what transpired, did not object to them photographing various cards and flowers in his room. In fact, a number of photographs, both in colour and monochrome, were taken of the Plaintiff himself showing the substantial scars to his head amongst other matters. The taking of the photographs involved the use of a flashlight. . . .

Medical evidence . . . in this action says that Mr Kaye was in no fit condition to be interviewed or to give any informed consent to be interviewed. The accuracy of this opinion is confirmed by the fact that approximately a quarter-of-an-hour after the representatives of *Sunday Sport* had left his room, Mr Kaye had no recollection of the incident. . . .

It is well known that in English law there is no right to privacy, and accordingly there is no right of action for breach of a person's privacy. The facts of the present case are a graphic illustration of the desirability of Parliament considering whether and in what circumstances statutory provision can be made to protect the rights of individuals. In the absence of such a right, Plaintiff's advisers have sought to base their claim to injunctions upon other well-established rights of action."

Because the article the defendants proposed to publish implied that Mr Kaye had consented to give an interview and be photographed, when he was in no fit state to consent, Glidewell held that its publication would constitute libel and malicious falsehood; Bingham, L.J. agreed that it would constitute malicious falsehood. The court granted an injunction restraining the defendants from publishing anything that could be reasonably understood to mean "that the Plaintiff had voluntarily permitted photographs to be taken for publication in that newspaper or had voluntarily permitted representatives of the Defendants to interview him. . . ."

Law in the United States

Restatement (Second) of Torts

§ 652 D: Publicity Given to Private Life

One who gives publicity to a matter concerning the private life of another is subject to liability to the other for invasion of his privacy, if the matter published is of a kind that:

(a) would be highly offensive to a reasonable person, and

(b) is not of legitimate concern to the public.

Cape Publications, Inc. v. Bridges, 423 So. 2d 426 (Fla. App. 1982), review denied, 431 So. 2d 988 (Fla. 1983)

"Appellee Bridges brought suit against appellants on the theories of invasion of privacy, intentional infliction of emotional distress, and trespass, alleging that appellants' conduct in publishing a photograph of appellee was actionable. The news story reported the abduction of appellee by her estranged husband who came to her workplace and at gunpoint forced her to go with him to their former apartment. The police were alerted and after surrounding the apartment began efforts to free appellee. Her husband forced her to disrobe in an effort to prevent her escape. Her life was obviously in danger. This is a typical exciting emotion-packed drama to which newspeople, and others, are attracted. It is a newsworthy story. Upon hearing a gunshot, the police stormed the apartment and rushed appellee outside to safety. Appellee was clutching a dish towel to her body in order to conceal her nudity as she was escorted to the police car in full public view. The photograph revealed little more than could be seen had appellee been wearing a bikini and somewhat less than some bathing suits seen on the beaches. There were other more revealing photographs taken which were not published. The published photograph is more a depiction of grief, fright, emotional tension and flight than it is an appeal to other sensual appetites.

Although publication of the photograph, which won industry awards, could be considered by some to be in bad taste, the law in Florida seems settled that where one becomes an actor in an occurrence of public interest, it is not an invasion of her right to privacy to publish her photograph with an account of such occurrence.

Just because the story and the photograph may be embarrassing or distressful to the plaintiff does not mean the newspaper cannot publish what is otherwise newsworthy."

Howell v. New York Post, Inc., 612 N.E. 2d 699 (N.Y. 1993)

"In early September 1988, plaintiff Pamela J. Howell was a patient at Four Winds Hospital, a private psychiatric facility in Westchester County. Her complaint and affidavit (accepted as true on this appeal) allege that it was imperative to her recovery that the hospitalization remain a secret from all but her immediate family.

Hedda Nussbaum was also at that time a patient at Four Winds. Nussbaum was the 'adoptive' mother of six-year-old Lisa Steinberg, whose November 1987 death from child abuse generated intense public interest. . . .

On September 1, 1988, a New York Post photographer trespassed onto Four Winds' secluded grounds and, with a telephoto lens, took outdoor pictures of a group that included Nussbaum and plaintiff. That night, the hospital's medical director telephoned a Post editor requesting that the paper not publish any patient photographs. Nevertheless, on the front page of next day's edition two photographs appeared—one of Nussbaum taken in November 1987, shortly after her arrest in connection with Lisa's death, and another of Nussbaum walking with plaintiff, taken the previous day at Four Winds.

In the earlier photograph, Nussbaum's face is bruised and disfigured, her lips split and swollen, and her matted hair is covered with a scarf. By contrast, in the photograph taken at Four Winds, Nussbaum's facial wounds have visibly healed, her hair is coiffed, and she is neatly dressed in jeans, a sweater and earrings. Plaintiff, walking alongside her, smiling, is in tennis attire and sneakers. The caption reads: 'The battered face above belongs to the Hedda Nussbaum people remember—the former live-in lover of accused child-killer, Joel Steinberg. The serene woman in jeans at left is the same Hedda, strolling with a companion in the grounds of the upstate psychiatric center where her face and mind are healing from the terrible wounds Steinberg inflicted.' . . .

We have been reluctant to intrude upon reasonable editorial judgments in determining whether there is a real relationship between an article and photograph (Finger, 77 NY2d, at 143; see also, Gaeta v. New York News, 62 NY 2d 340, 349). In Finger, for example, a magazine without consent used a photograph of plaintiffs and their six children to illustrate a segment about caffeine-enhanced fertility. Although none of the children had been conceived in the manner suggested by the article, we concluded that the requisite nexus between the article and photograph was established because the article's theme—having a large family—was fairly reflected in the picture (See, Finger, 77 NY 2d, at 142–143).

In the present case, similarly, plaintiff has failed to meet her burden. The subject of the article was Hedda Nussbaum's physical and emotional recovery from the beatings allegedly inflicted by Joel Steinberg. The photograph of a visibly healed Nussbaum, interacting with her smiling, fashionably clad 'companion' offers a stark contrast to the adjacent photograph of

Nussbaum's disfigured face. The visual impact would not have been the same had the Post cropped plaintiff out of the photograph, as she suggests was required. Thus, there is a real relationship between the article and the photograph of plaintiff, and the civil rights cause of action was properly dismissed."

French law

French Civil Code

ARTICLE 9
Each person has the right to respect for his private life

Note: When art. 9 was added to the Civil Code, courts had already given an extensive protection to privacy by applying arts. 1382–83. Someone who violates another's privacy is still liable in tort under arts. 1382–83.

Cour de cassation, 1e ch. civ, 10 June 1987, pourvoi no. 86-16.185

Plaintiff was a well-known actress. Defendant was a newspaper that had published a photograph of the plaintiff, her eyes protected by glasses, and her face showing signs of suffering and of the effects of her illness. The photograph had been taken with a telephoto lens. The story said that she could not yet walk and must have long sessions of physical therapy. The defendant pointed out that the story showed good will toward the actress it said that it used the photograph "to establish the reality or an actual moment or to illustrate." The plaintiff prevailed before both the *Cour d'appel* and the *Cour de cassation*. The *Cour d'appel* said that use of the picture was unnecessary. The *Cour de cassation* said that it was taken "without the knowledge of the interested parties" and that it showed the actress marked by "suffering and wasting physically."

Cour de cassation, 2e ch. civ., 8 July 1981, arrêt no. 1.013, pourvoi nos. 80-12.286, 80-13.079

The defendant, the newspaper *Paris-Match*, published a picture of one of the plaintiffs, a famous singer, in a public place in Paris with a young woman (also a plaintiff) on his arm. The newspaper did not say or suggest anything about their relationship. The *Cour de cassation* held that the plaintiffs could recover. It noted that two of the five photographs in question had been taken in what it called a "private place" although it did not describe the location. It said that "if the publication of photographs of a public figure (*personne publique*) even without his express authorization does not constitute, in principle, an injury to his right to his image, that is only upon condition that the photographs in question concern exclusively his profession and not his private life . . . and, finally, if the reproduction of the image of a public figure in the conduct of his professional life is not, in principle, subject to obtaining his express permission nevertheless it is necessary that the interested party be considered as having tacitly authorized the reproduction of his image." Here, the court said, by his past conduct Jacques Brel "manifested an evident desire to be extremely discrete."

German law

Law Concerning the Right of Authors to Works of Pictoral Art and Photography (abbreviated KunstUrhG for Kunst Urheber Gesetz)

§ 22: RIGHT TO ONE'S OWN IMAGE

Images shall be disseminated or publicly displayed only with the consent of the person portrayed. In cases of doubt, consent is deemed to have been given when the person portrayed accepts payment to allow himself to be portrayed. For ten years after the death of the person portrayed, the consent of his relatives is necessary. Relatives in this sense include the surviving wife and children of the person portrayed, and, if neither the wife nor children are available, the parents of the person portrayed.

§ 23: EXCEPTIONS TO § 22

(1) It is permitted to disseminate or to publicly display without the consent required by § 22:

1. Images in the area of contemporary history;
2. Images in which the people appear only as an incident in a landscape or similar locale;
3. Images of gatherings, processions, and similar events in which the person in question was a participant;
4. Images that are not made upon order insofar as their dissemination or display serves an important artistic interest.

(2) Nevertheless, this authority does not extend to a dissemination and display by which a legitimate interest of the person portrayed is violated, or, in the event of his death, the interest of his relatives.

§ 24: EXCEPTIONS IN THE PUBLIC INTEREST

Public officials may duplicate, disseminate or publicly display images for purposes of the administration of justice and public security without the consent of the person entitled, that is, the person portrayed or his relatives.

Bundesgerichtshof, 15 January 1965, 1965 NJW 1374

"The appellate court saw a violation of the general right of personality of the plaintiff (Civil Code § 823(1)) and of his right to his own image (KunstUrhG § 22) in the publication of a picture of the plaintiff together with its caption and accompanying text. It found that the use of the picture along with the text was sufficient to lower the human dignity of the plaintiff in two ways. First, he was pointed out as the example and prototype of the 'satisfied German' by the caption. Second, the accompanying text created the possibility that the hasty reader would transfer to the plaintiff the enumeration of the outer characteristics of the former SS General Wolff which was to be found immediately next to the plaintiff's picture, and so get the impression that the person pictured was SS General Wolff. The unwary reader was particularly likely to do so because the nearby description of Wolff also fit the plaintiff. . . .

The appeal (*Revision*) erroneously contends that the result [below] cannot be reconciled with the claim proven by the defendant that the plaintiff consented to the taking and the publication of the picture. The appellate court found that he did give consent but that, nevertheless, according to the defendant's own statement, the consent was not to the manner and kind of the publication of the picture together with its demeaning caption and in proximity to an article about former SS General Wolff.

That decision is in harmony with the case law. According to it, the question of what kind of publication of an image is covered by the authorization of the person pictured that is not expressly limited is to be answered by interpreting what he said in giving permission, taking into consideration the circumstances of the particular case (BGHZ 20, 345 = NJW 56, 1554; BGH GRUR 1962, 211 f. = LM no. 5 to § 23 KunstUrhG). Where, as here, no payment was made for the picture, the burden of proving the consent and its *scope* falls on the person who is claimed to have violated the right to one's own image (BGHZ, op. cit. 348). . . .

The appeal claims . . . [that] internationally and generally, modern photo journalism maintains the position that is permissible, and not a violation to the right to one's own image, to take street pictures of people who are visible to the journalist in their everyday appearance. It answers to our experience of life, and corresponds to our convictions, that photo journalists are allowed to take and to use pictures of people for purposes of social criticism. . . .

We can leave aside the question of whether, as to appeal claims, there has been a change in the views held generally of the authority of photo journalists. . . . For the freedom to publish a picture without the consent of the person pictured under § 23(1) KunstUrhG does not extend, according to § 23(2), to the publication of pictures that violate a legitimate interest of the person pictured. In answering this question, the publication of the picture in its totality is to be evaluated, and not in isolation from its accompanying text (BGHZ 20, 346, 350f = NJW 565, 1554; BGHZ 24, 201, 209 = NJW 57, 1315 (late homecomer); BGH GRVR 1962, 212 no. 4 (wedding picture); id. 1962, 324 = NJW 62, 1004 (double murder)). As explained, the appellate court did not commit legal error in finding that the manner and kind of the publication of plaintiff's picture by defendant violated his legitimate interest."

Bundesgerichtshof, 19 December 1995, BGHZ 131, 332

[In this, and the two cases that follow, Princess Caroline of Monaco claimed that her right to privacy had been violated by the publication of three types of photographs by various German publishers: (1) photos show her with the actor Vincent Lindon at the far end of a restaurant courtyard in Saint-Rémy-de-Provence. The magazine referred to then as "the tenderest photos of her romance with Vincent"; photos bore the caption, "these photos are evidence of the tenderest romance of our time"; (2) photographs of

Princess Caroline in public with her children; and (3) photographs show-ing the applicant in public on horseback, shopping on her own, eating with Mr. Lindon in a restaurant, riding alone on a bicycle, and with her body-guard at a market, in public on a skiing holiday in Austria, accompanying Prince Ernst August von Hannover, alone leaving her Parisian residence, playing tennis with Prince Ernst August von Hannover and putting their bicycles down, and a photograph of Princess Caroline tripping over an obstacle at the Monte Carlo Beach Club.]

"Pictures that fall within the history of the times can be circulated and displayed without consent of the person affected unless the legitimate interest of the person depicted is thereby injured (§§ 23 (1)(2) of the Law Concerning the Right of Authors (*Urhebergesetz*)).

To history of the times belong all pictures of persons who belong to the history of the times, and in particular, all persons who are to be regarded as part of that history. The plaintiff belongs to this class of person. . . .

For a person to be classified as belonging to the history of the times, the criterion is that the picture made public is significant and the atten-tion paid to the person in question has value so that the public has a legit-imate interest in clear information and the pictorial presentation of it is to be approved [many citations omitted]. Those who clearly belong to this category include monarchs, leading state officials and politicians. [Citations omitted to cases involving Kaiser Wilhelm II, Reich President Ebert, Reichminister Noske, and the Chancellor of the Federal Republic.] . . .

Nevertheless, the use of pictures of persons belonging to the history of the times without their consent is not without its limits. . . . [I]t must be determined, by a weighing of values and interests in the individual case, whether the interest of the public in information, protected by the freedom of the press (art. 5 of the Constitution), to which the defendant can appeal should be placed above the interest in the right to personality for which the plaintiff can claim protection (art. 2 of the Constitution).

. . .

The appellate court recognized these principles. Only, it thought that legitimate public interest ends with the house door of the person affected. . . .

A person belonging to the history of our times can, as anyone else . . . reserve a place outside his own home for himself or at least from which the larger public is excluded.

. . .

That may, for example, be in an exclusive part of a restaurant or hotel, sports box, telephone booth, or under some circumstances even in open nature, so far as it does not appear to the person affected as a public place.

[On these grounds, the court ruled that the defendant could not pub-lish the photographs taken in the secluded portion of the restaurant. It held that the publication of the other photographs was legitimate.]

Photographs can be taken in places which are accessible to anyone. In such cases, the plaintiff has entered these public places and so become part of the public. . . .

Nor can she prohibit the publication of these pictures. She must as a person who belongs to the history of our times accept that the public has a legitimate interest in knowing how she behaves what she does in public place, whether it is buying in the market, or in a café, or in athletic activities, or in the ordinary activities of her own life.

. . .

It is common to all these pictures that they do not portray the plaintiff taking part in an official function but concern private life in the larger sense. The plaintiff would like the publication of such pictures to be prohibited in Germany as it is in France. In Germany, however, that is not possible.

In France the publication of such pictures is permissible in principle only with the permission of the person depicted according to art. 9 of the *Code civil* which concerns the protection of private life (*vie privée*). That provision applies to monarchs and other persons in public life unless the person concerned is engaged in the exercise of their official function. (See Cour de cassation, Bulletin des arrêts, Chambres civiles, April 1988, 1 ch. civ. No 98 p. 67. . . .)

German law is not applied in that way. . . ."

Note: On the role of the German Constitutional Court (*Bundesverfassungsgericht*), see p. 264 above. For Article 5 of the German Constitution, protecting freedom of expression, see p. 255 above.

Bundesverfassungsgericht, 15 December 1999, BVerfG 101, 361

[Translation of this portion of the opinion was taken from the decision of the European Court of Human Rights, below.]

[The facts of this case appear in the previous decision of the *Bundesgerichtshof.*

The court agreed that Princess Caroline was a "figure of contemporary society."]

"General personality rights do not require publications that are not subject to prior consent to be limited to pictures of figures of contemporary society in the exercise of their function in society. Very often the public interest aroused by such figures does not relate exclusively to the exercise of their function in the strict sense. It can, on the contrary, by virtue of the particular function and its impact, extend to information about the way in which these figures behave generally—that is, also outside their function—in public. The public has a legitimate interest in being allowed to judge whether the personal behaviour of the individuals in question, who are often regarded as idols or role models, convincingly tallies with their behaviour on their official engagements.

If, on the other hand, the right to publish pictures of people considered to be figures of contemporary society were to be limited to their official functions, insufficient account would be taken of the public interest properly aroused by such figures and this would, moreover, favour a selective presentation that would deprive the public of certain necessary judgmental possibilities in respect of figures of socio-political life, having regard to the function of role model of such figures and the influence they exert . . .

According to the decision being appealed, the privacy meriting protection that must also be afforded to figures of contemporary society *par excellence* presupposes that they have retired to a secluded place with the objectively perceptible aim of being alone and in which, confident of being alone, they behave differently from how they would behave in public. . . .

The criterion of a secluded place takes account of the aim, pursued by the general right to protection of personality rights, of allowing the individual a sphere, including outside the home, in which he does not feel himself to be the subject of permanent public attention—and relieves him of the obligation of behaving accordingly—and in which he can relax and enjoy some peace and quiet. This criterion does not excessively restrict press freedom because it does not impose a blanket ban on pictures of the daily or private life of figures of contemporary society, but allows them to be shown where they have appeared in public. In the event of an overriding public interest in being informed, the freedom of the press can even, in accordance with that case-law authority, be given priority over the protection of the private sphere. . . .

The *Bundesgerichtshof* properly held that it is legitimate to draw conclusions from the behaviour adopted in a given situation by an individual who is clearly in a secluded spot. However, the protection against dissemination of photos taken in that context does not only apply where the individual behaves in a manner in which he would not behave in public. On the contrary, the development of the personality cannot be properly protected unless, irrespective of their behaviour, the individual has a space in which he or she can relax without having to tolerate the presence of photographers or cameramen. That is not in issue here, however, since, according to the findings on which the *Bundesgerichtshof* based its decision, the first of the conditions to which protection of private life is subject has not been met.

Lastly, there is nothing unconstitutional, when balancing the public interest in being informed against the protection of private life, in attaching importance to the method used to obtain the information in question. . . . It is doubtful, however, that the mere fact of photographing the person secretly or catching them unawares can be deemed to infringe their privacy outside the home. Having regard to the function attributed to that privacy under constitutional law and to the fact that it is usually impossible to determine from a photo whether the person has been photographed secretly or caught unawares, the existence of unlawful interference with that privacy cannot in any case be made out merely because the photo was taken in those conditions. As, however, the *Bundesgerichtshof* has already established in respect of the photographs in question that the appellant was not in a secluded place, the doubts expressed above have no bearing on the review of its decision.

(cc) However, the constitutional requirements have not been satisfied insofar as the decisions of which the appellant complains did not take account of the fact that the right to protection of personality rights of a person in the appellant's situation is strengthened by section 6 of the Basic Law [i.e. the German Constitution] regarding that person's intimate relations with their children.

(dd) The following conclusions can be drawn from the foregoing considerations with regard to the photographs in question.

The decision of the *Bundesgerichtshof* cannot be criticised under constitutional law regarding the photos of the appellant at a market, doing her market shopping accompanied by her bodyguard or dining with a male companion at a well-attended restaurant. The first two cases concerned an open location frequented by the general public. The third case admittedly concerned a well circumscribed location, spatially speaking, but one in which the appellant was exposed to the other people present.

It is for this reason, moreover, that the *Bundesgerichtshof* deemed it legitimate to ban photos showing the applicant in a restaurant garden, which were the subject of the decision being appealed but are not the subject of the constitutional appeal. The presence of the applicant and her companion there presented all the features of seclusion. The fact that the photographs in question were evidently taken from a distance shows that the applicant could legitimately have assumed that she was not exposed to public view.

Nor can the decision being appealed be criticised regarding the photos of the applicant alone on horseback or riding a bicycle. In the *Bundesgerichtshof*'s view, the appellant had not been in a secluded place, but in a public one. That finding cannot attract criticism under constitutional law. The applicant herself describes the photos in question as belonging to the intimacy of her private sphere merely because they manifest her desire to be alone. In accordance with the criteria set out above, the mere desire of the person concerned is not relevant in any way.

The three photos of the applicant with her children require a fresh examination, however, in the light of the constitutional rules set out above. We cannot rule out the possibility that the review that needs to be carried out in the light of the relevant criteria will lead to a different result for one or other or all the photos. The decision must therefore be set aside in that respect and remitted to the *Bundesgerichtshof* for a fresh decision.

The European Convention on Human Rights

ARTICLE 8

(1) Everyone has the right to respect for his private and family life, his home and his correspondence.

(2) There shall be no interference by a public authority with the exercise of this right except such as is in accordance with the law and is necessary in a democratic society in the interests of national security, public safety or the economic well-being of the country, for the prevention of disorder or crime, for the protection of health or morals, or for the protection of the rights and freedoms of others.

* * *

ARTICLE 10

(1) Everyone has the right to freedom of expression. This right shall include freedom to hold opinions and to receive and impart information and ideas without interference by public authority and regardless of frontiers. This article shall not prevent States from requiring the licensing of broadcasting, television or cinema enterprises.

(2) The exercise of these freedoms, since it carries with it duties and responsibilities, may be subject to such formalities, conditions, restrictions or penalties as are prescribed by law and are necessary in a democratic society, in the interests of national security, territorial integrity or public safety, for the prevention of disorder or crime, for the protection of health or morals, for the protection of the reputation or rights of others, for preventing the disclosure of information received in confidence, or for maintaining the authority and impartiality of the judiciary.

Resolution 1165 (1998) of the Parliamentary Assembly of the Council of Europe on the Right to Privacy

(6) The Assembly is aware that personal privacy is often invaded, even in countries with specific legislation to protect it, as people's private lives have become a highly lucrative commodity for certain sectors of the media. The victims are essentially public figures, since details of their private lives serve as a stimulus to sales. At the same time, public figures must recognise that the special position they occupy in society—in many cases by choice—automatically entails increased pressure on their privacy.

(7) Public figures are persons holding public office and/or using public resources and, more broadly speaking, all those who play a role in public life, whether in politics, the economy, the arts, the social sphere, sport or in any other domain.

(8) It is often in the name of a one-sided interpretation of the right to freedom of expression, which is guaranteed in Article 10 of the European Convention on Human Rights, that the media invade people's privacy, claiming that their readers are entitled to know everything about public figures.

(9) Certain facts relating to the private lives of public figures, particularly politicians, may indeed be of interest to citizens, and it may therefore be legitimate for readers, who are also voters, to be informed of those facts.

(10) It is therefore necessary to find a way of balancing the exercise of two fundamental rights, both of which are guaranteed by the European Convention on Human Rights: the right to respect for one's private life and the right to freedom of expression.

(11) The Assembly reaffirms the importance of every person's right to privacy, and of the right to freedom of expression, as fundamental to a democratic society. These rights are neither absolute nor in any hierarchical order, since they are of equal value.

(12) However, the Assembly points out that the right to privacy afforded by Article 8 of the European Convention on Human Rights should

not only protect an individual against interference by public authorities, but also against interference by private persons or institutions, including the mass media.

* * *

(14) The Assembly calls upon the governments of the member states to pass legislation, if no such legislation yet exists, guaranteeing the right to privacy containing the following guidelines, or if such legislation already exists, to supplement it with these guidelines:

(i) the possibility of taking an action under civil law should be guaranteed, to enable a victim to claim possible damages for invasion of privacy;

(ii) editors and journalists should be rendered liable for invasions of privacy by their publications, as they are for libel;

(iii) when editors have published information that proves to be false, they should be required to publish equally prominent corrections at the request of those concerned;

(iv) economic penalties should be envisaged for publishing groups which systematically invade people's privacy;

(v) following or chasing persons to photograph, film or record them, in such a manner that they are prevented from enjoying the normal peace and quiet they expect in their private lives or even such that they are caused actual physical harm, should be prohibited;

(vi) a civil action (private lawsuit) by the victim should be allowed against a photographer or a person directly involved, where paparazzi have trespassed or used "visual or auditory enhancement devices" to capture recordings that they otherwise could not have captured without trespassing;

(vii) provision should be made for anyone who knows that information or images relating to his or her private life are about to be disseminated to initiate emergency judicial proceedings, such as summary applications for an interim order or an injunction postponing the dissemination of the information, subject to an assessment by the court as to the merits of the claim of an invasion of privacy;

(viii) the media should be encouraged to create their own guidelines for publication and to set up an institute with which an individual can lodge complaints of invasion of privacy and demand that a rectification be published.

Von Hannover v. Germany, European Court of Human Rights, 24 June 2004 (Application no. 59320/00)

[For the facts of these case, see the two preceding German decisions.]

"(48) The Court notes at the outset that the photos of the applicant with her children are no longer the subject of this application, as it stated in its admissibility decision of 8 July 2003.

The same applies to the photos published in *Freizeit Revue* magazine (edition no. 30 of 22 July 1993) showing the applicant with Vincent Lindon at the far end of a restaurant courtyard in Saint-Rémy-de-Provence (see paragraph 11 above). In its judgment of 19 December 1995 the *Bundesgerichtshof* prohibited any further publication of the photos on the ground that they infringed the applicant's right to respect for her private life (see paragraph 23 above).

. . .

(56) In the present case the applicant did not complain of an action by the State, but rather of the lack of adequate State protection of her private life and her image.

(57) The Court reiterates that although the object of Article 8 is essentially that of protecting the individual against arbitrary interference by the public authorities, it does not merely compel the State to abstain from such interference: in addition to this primarily negative undertaking, there may be positive obligations inherent in an effective respect for private or family life. These obligations may involve the adoption of measures designed to secure respect for private life even in the sphere of the relations of individuals between themselves (see, *mutatis mutandis*, *X and Y v. the Netherlands*, judgment of 26 March 1985, Series A no. 91, p. 11, § 23; *Stjerna v. Finland*, judgment of 25 November 1994, Series A no. 299-B, p. 61, § 38; and *Verliere v. Switzerland* (dec.), no. 41953/98, ECHR 2001-VII). That also applies to the protection of a person's picture against abuse by others (see *Schüssel*, cited above).

. . .

(60) In the cases in which the Court has had to balance the protection of private life against the freedom of expression it has always stressed the contribution made by photos or articles in the press to a debate of general interest (see, as a recent authority, *News Verlags GmbH & CoKG v. Austria*, no. 31457/96, § 52 et seq., ECHR 2000-I, and *Krone Verlag GmbH & Co. KG v. Austria*, no. 34315/96, § 33 et seq., 26 February 2002). The Court thus found, in one case, that the use of certain terms in relation to an individual's private life was not 'justified by considerations of public concern' and that those terms did not '[bear] on a matter of general importance' (see *Tammer*, cited above, § 68) and went on to hold that there had not been a violation of Article 10. In another case, however, the Court attached particular importance to the fact that the subject in question was a news item of 'major public concern' and that the published photographs 'did not disclose any details of [the] private life' of the person in question (see *Krone Verlag*, cited above, § 37) and held that there had been a violation of Article 10. Similarly, in a recent case concerning the publication by President Mitterand's former private doctor of a book containing revelations about the President's state of health, the Court held that 'the more time passed the more the public interest in President Mitterand's two seven-year presidential terms prevailed over the requirements of the protection of his rights with regard to medical confidentiality' (see *Plon (Société) v. France*, no. 58148/00, 18 May 2004) and held that there had been a breach of Article 10.

(61) The Court points out at the outset that in the present case the photos of the applicant in the various German magazines show her in scenes from her daily life, thus engaged in activities of a purely private nature such as practising sport, out walking, leaving a restaurant or on holiday. . . .

(62) The Court also notes that the applicant, as a member of the Prince of Monaco's family, represents the ruling family at certain cultural or charitable events. However, she does not exercise any function within or on behalf of the State of Monaco or one of its institutions.

(63) The Court considers that a fundamental distinction needs to be made between reporting facts—even controversial ones—capable of contributing to a debate in a democratic society relating to politicians in the exercise of their functions, for example, and reporting details of the private life of an individual who, moreover, as in this case, does not exercise official functions. While in the former case the press exercises its vital role of 'watchdog' in a democracy by contributing to 'impart[ing] information and ideas on matters of public interest' (*Observer and Guardian*, cited above, ibid.) it does not do so in the latter case.

(64) Similarly, although the public has a right to be informed, which is an essential right in a democratic society that, in certain special circumstances, can even extend to aspects of the private life of public figures, particularly where politicians are concerned (see *Plon (Société)*, cited above, ibid.), this is not the case here. The situation here does not come within the sphere of any political or public debate because the published photos and accompanying commentaries relate exclusively to details of the applicant's private life.

(65) As in other similar cases it has examined, the Court considers that the publication of the photos and articles in question, of which the sole purpose was to satisfy the curiosity of a particular readership regarding the details of the applicant's private life, cannot be deemed to contribute to any debate of general interest to society despite the applicant being known to the public (see, *mutatis mutandis, Jaime Campmany y Diez de Revenga and Juan Luís Lopez-Galiacho Perona v. Spain* (dec.), no. 54224/00, 12 December 2000; *Julio Bou Gibert and El Hogar Y La Moda J.A. v. Spain* (dec.), no. 14929/02, 13 May 2003; and *Prisma Presse*, cited above).

(66) In these conditions freedom of expression calls for a narrower interpretation (see *Prisma Presse*, cited above, and, by converse implication, *Krone Verlag*, cited above, § 37).

(67) In that connection the Court also takes account of the resolution of the Parliamentary Assembly of the Council of Europe on the right to privacy, which stresses the 'one-sided interpretation of the right to freedom of expression' by certain media which attempt to justify an infringement of the rights protected by Article 8 of the Convention by claiming that 'their readers are entitled to know everything about public figures' (see paragraph 42 above, and *Prisma Presse*, cited above).

. . .

(74) The Court therefore considers that the criteria on which the domestic courts based their decisions were not sufficient to protect the applicant's private life effectively. As a figure of contemporary society '*par excellence*' she cannot—in the name of freedom of the press and the public interest—rely on protection of her private life unless she is in a secluded place out of the public eye and, moreover, succeeds in proving it (which can be difficult). Where that is not the case, she has to accept that she might be photographed at almost any time, systematically, and that the photos are then very widely

disseminated even if, as was the case here, the photos and accompanying articles relate exclusively to details of her private life.

(75) In the Court's view, the criterion of spatial isolation, although apposite in theory, is in reality too vague and difficult for the person concerned to determine in advance. In the present case merely classifying the applicant as a figure of contemporary society '*par excellence*' does not suffice to justify such an intrusion into her private life.

(76) As the Court has stated above, it considers that the decisive factor in balancing the protection of private life against freedom of expression should lie in the contribution that the published photos and articles make to a debate of general interest. It is clear in the instant case that they made no such contribution since the applicant exercises no official function and the photos and articles related exclusively to details of her private life.

(77) Furthermore, the Court considers that the public does not have a legitimate interest in knowing where the applicant is and how she behaves generally in her private life even if she appears in places that cannot always be described as secluded and despite the fact that she is well known to the public.

Even if such a public interest exists, as does a commercial interest of the magazines in publishing these photos and these articles, in the instant case those interests must, in the Court's view, yield to the applicant's right to the effective protection of her private life.

(78) Lastly, in the Court's opinion the criteria established by the domestic courts were not sufficient to ensure the effective protection of the applicant's private life and she should, in the circumstances of the case, have had a "legitimate expectation" of protection of her private life.

(79) Having regard to all the foregoing factors, and despite the margin of appreciation afforded to the State in this area, the Court considers that the German courts did not strike a fair balance between the competing interests.

(80) There has therefore been a breach of Article 8 of the Convention.

Note: When Princess Caroline won before the *Bundesgerichtshof* and the *Bundesverfassungsgericht*, she could take it for granted that their decisions would be enforced in Germany. It is not so of the decision in her favor of the European Court of Human Rights which has only such force as German authorities choose to give it. If they give it no effect at all, however, Germany is subject to sanctions.

b. Dissemination of true information

About current events

English law

Stephens v. Avery, [1988] 1 Ch. 457

Sir Nicolas Browne-Wilkinson V.-C. "This is an application to strike out a statement of claim on the ground that it discloses no cause of action or, alternatively, on the ground that the claim is frivolous and vexatious. The action is brought by Mrs Stephens as plaintiff against three defendants. The first defendant is Mrs Avery to whom it is alleged she communicated certain information in confidence, the second defendant is the editor and the third defendant, Mail Newspapers plc, the publishers of the Mail on Sunday. Broadly, the ambit of the claim is that Mrs Stephens alleges that information communicated in confidence to Mrs Avery was communicated by Mrs Avery to the second and third defendants, and published in the Mail on Sunday in breach of the duty of confidence. The master refused to strike out the claim, and the defendants appeal to this court.

The background facts are lurid. The action is connected with the unlawful killing of a Mrs Telling by her husband. The trial of Mr Telling received much publicity in the press. It led to Mr Telling's conviction for manslaughter. . . .

The information disclosed by the plaintiff to Mrs Avery and alleged to have been disclosed by Mrs Avery to the newspaper and published by the newspaper related to the sexual conduct of the plaintiff. In particular, it related to a lesbian relationship between the plaintiff and Mrs Telling. For the first time it identified the plaintiff as the woman whom Mr Telling alleged at his trial he had discovered in a compromising position with his wife. The plaintiff was not called at the trial. . . .

Three requirements have to be satisfied before a court will protect information as being legally confidential. They were laid down by the Court of Appeal in Saltman Engineering Co Ltd v Campbell Engineering Co Ltd (1948) [1963] 3 All ER 413 and were summarised by Megarry J in Coco v A N Clark (Engineers) Ltd [1969] RPC 41 at 47 in this way:

> In my judgment, three elements are normally required if, apart from contract, a case of breach of confidence is to succeed. First, the information itself, in the words of Lord Greene, M.R. in the Saltman case (at 215), must 'have the necessary quality of confidence about it.' Secondly, that information must have been imparted in circumstances importing an obligation of confidence. Thirdly, there must be an unauthorised use of that information to the detriment of the party communicating it.

. . .

Counsel for the defendants submits that in the absence of either a legally enforceable contract or a pre-existing relationship, such as that of employer and employee, doctor and patient, or priest and penitent, it is not possible to impose a legal duty of confidence on the recipient of the information merely by saying that the information is given in confidence. In my judgment that is wrong in law. The basis of equitable intervention to protect confidentiality is that it is unconscionable for a person who has received information on the basis that it is confidential subsequently to reveal that information. Although the relationship between the parties is often important in cases where it is said there is an implied as opposed to express obligation of confidence, the relationship between the parties is not the determining factor. It is the acceptance of the information on the basis that it will be kept secret that affects the conscience of the recipient of the information. . . .

To my mind this case undoubtedly does raise fundamental difficulties as to the relationship between on the one hand the privacy which every individual is entitled to expect, and on the other hand freedom of information. To many, the aggressive intrusion of sectors of the press into the private lives of individuals is unpalatable. On the other hand, the ability of the press to obtain and publish for the public benefit information of genuine public interest, as opposed to general public titillation, may be impaired if information obtained in confidence is too widely protected by the law. Moreover, is the press to be liable in damages for printing what is true? I express no view as to where or how the borderline should be drawn in such a case. On any footing, such a point of law is in my judgment wholly unsuited for determination on a striking out application. The point requires the most accurate formulation and analysis. It is not the subject matter of existing decision directly in point and, therefore, it is in my view, a matter to be determined at trial."

Note: Reread the European Convention on Human Rights, arts. 8 & 10, above, pp. 275–76.

Human Rights Act 1998, ch. 42

6. - (1) It is unlawful for a public authority to act in a way which is incompatible with a Convention right.

(2) Subsection (1) does not apply to an act if-

(a) as the result of one or more provisions of primary legislation, the authority could not have acted differently; or

(b) in the case of one or more provisions of, or made under, primary legislation which cannot be read or given effect in a way which is compatible with the Convention rights, the authority was acting so as to give effect to or enforce those provisions.

(3) In this section "public authority" includes-

(a) a court or tribunal, and

(b) any person certain of whose functions are functions of a public nature,

but does not include either House of Parliament or a person exercising functions in connection with proceedings in Parliament.

Campbell v. MGN Ltd., [2004] UKHL 22

The plaintiff, Naomi Campell, was a celebrated fashion model. The defendant, the newspaper *Mirror*, ran an article describing her as a drug addict who "is attending Narcotics Anonymous meetings in a courageous attempt to beat her addiction to drink and drugs." The article was accompanied by a photograph of her attending a Narcotics Anonymous meeting. In a divided opinion, the House of Lords held the defendant liable. Both the majority and the minority agreed, however, that, in principle, she had a right of action if the newspaper revealed too much. Both the majority and minority also agreed that the newspaper did not violate this right by revealing that she was a drug addict since she had publicly stated she was not, and the newspaper had a right to set the record straight. The majority, however, believed that the newspaper had disclosed more than necessary to accomplish this purpose.

The reason she would otherwise have had an action is explained in this opinion by Lord Nicholls who held for the defendant.

Lord Nicholls of Birkenhead. *"Breach of confidence: misuse of private information*

11. In this country, unlike the United States of America, there is no over-arching, all-embracing cause of action for 'invasion of privacy': see *Wainwright v Home Office* [2003] 3 WLR 1137. But protection of various aspects of privacy is a fast developing area of the law, here and in some other common law jurisdictions. The recent decision of the Court of Appeal of New Zealand in *Hosking v Runting* (25 March 2004) is an example of this. In this country development of the law has been spurred by enactment of the Human Rights Act 1998.

12. The present case concerns one aspect of invasion of privacy: wrongful disclosure of private information. The case involves the familiar competition between freedom of expression and respect for an individual's privacy. Both are vitally important rights. Neither has precedence over the other. The importance of freedom of expression has been stressed often and eloquently, the importance of privacy less so. But it, too, lies at the heart of liberty in a modern state. A proper degree of privacy is essential for the well-being and development of an individual. And restraints imposed on government to pry into the lives of the citizen go to the essence of a democratic state: see La Forest J in *R v Dymont* [1988] 2 SCR 417, 426.

13. The common law or, more precisely, courts of equity have long afforded protection to the wrongful use of private information by means of the cause of action which became known as breach of confidence. A breach of confidence was restrained as a form of unconscionable conduct, akin to a breach of trust. Today this nomenclature is misleading. The breach of confidence label harks back to the time when the cause of action was based on improper use of information disclosed by one person to another in confidence. To attract protection the information had to be of a confidential nature. But the gist of the cause of action was that information of this character had been disclosed by one person to another in circumstances 'importing an obligation of confidence' even though no contract of non-disclosure existed: see the classic exposition by Megarry J in *Coco v A N Clark (Engineers) Ltd* [1969] RPC 41, 47–48. The confidence referred to in the phrase 'breach of confidence' was the confidence arising out of a confidential relationship.

14. This cause of action has now firmly shaken off the limiting constraint of the need for an initial confidential relationship. In doing so it has changed its nature. In this country this development was recognised clearly in the judgment of Lord Goff of Chieveley in *Attorney-General v Guardian Newspapers Ltd (No 2)* [1990] 1 AC 109, 281. Now the law imposes a 'duty of confidence' whenever a person receives information he knows or ought to

know is fairly and reasonably to be regarded as confidential. Even this formulation is awkward. The continuing use of the phrase ' duty of confidence' and the description of the information as 'confidential' is not altogether comfortable. Information about an individual's private life would not, in ordinary usage, be called 'confidential'. The more natural description today is that such information is private. The essence of the tort is better encapsulated now as misuse of private information.

15. In the case of individuals this tort, however labelled, affords respect for one aspect of an individual's privacy. That is the value underlying this cause of action. An individual's privacy can be invaded in ways not involving publication of information. Strip-searches are an example. The extent to which the common law as developed thus far in this country protects other forms of invasion of privacy is not a matter arising in the present case. It does not arise because, although pleaded more widely, Miss Campbell's common law claim was throughout presented in court exclusively on the basis of breach of confidence, that is, the wrongful *publication* by the 'Mirror' of private *information*.

16. The European Convention on Human Rights, and the Strasbourg jurisprudence, have undoubtedly had a significant influence in this area of the common law for some years. The provisions of article 8, concerning respect for private and family life, and article 10, concerning freedom of expression, and the interaction of these two articles, have prompted the courts of this country to identify more clearly the different factors involved in cases where one or other of these two interests is present. Where both are present the courts are increasingly explicit in evaluating the competing considerations involved. When identifying and evaluating these factors the courts, including your Lordships' House, have tested the common law against the values encapsulated in these two articles. The development of the common law has been in harmony with these articles of the Convention: see, for instance, *Reynolds v Times Newspapers Ltd* [2001] 2 AC 127, 203-204.

17. The time has come to recognise that the values enshrined in articles 8 and 10 are now part of the cause of action for breach of confidence. As Lord Woolf CJ has said, the courts have been able to achieve this result by absorbing the rights protected by articles 8 and 10 into this cause of action: *A v B plc* [2003] QB 195, 202, para 4. Further, it should now be recognised that for this purpose these values are of general application. The values embodied in articles 8 and 10 are as much applicable in disputes between individuals or between an individual and a non-governmental body such as a newspaper as they are in disputes between individuals and a public authority.

18. In reaching this conclusion it is not necessary to pursue the controversial question whether the European Convention itself has this wider effect. Nor is it necessary to decide whether the duty imposed on courts by section 6 of the Human Rights Act 1998 extends to questions of substantive law as distinct from questions of practice and procedure. It is sufficient to recognise that the values underlying articles 8 and 10 are not confined to disputes between individuals and public authorities. This approach has

been adopted by the courts in several recent decisions, reported and unreported, where individuals have complained of press intrusion. A convenient summary of these cases is to be found in Gavin Phillipson's valuable article 'Transforming Breach of Confidence? Towards a Common Law Right of Privacy under the Human Rights Act' (2003) 66 MLR 726, 726–728.

. . .

The present case

23. I turn to the present case and consider first whether the information whose disclosure is in dispute was private. Mr Caldecott QC placed the information published by the newspaper into five categories: (1) the fact of Miss Campbell's drug addiction; (2) the fact that she was receiving treatment; (3) the fact that she was receiving treatment at Narcotics Anonymous; (4) the details of the treatment – how long she had been attending meetings, how often she went, how she was treated within the sessions themselves, the extent of her commitment, and the nature of her entrance on the specific occasion; and (5) the visual portrayal of her leaving a specific meeting with other addicts.

24. It was common ground between the parties that in the ordinary course the information in all five categories would attract the protection of article 8. But Mr Caldecott recognised that, as he put it, Miss Campbell's 'public lies' precluded her from claiming protection for categories (1) and (2). When talking to the media Miss Campbell went out of her way to say that, unlike many fashion models, she did not take drugs. By repeatedly making these assertions in public Miss Campbell could no longer have a reasonable expectation that this aspect of her life should be private. Public disclosure that, contrary to her assertions, she did in fact take drugs and had a serious drug problem for which she was being treated was not disclosure of private information. As the Court of Appeal noted, where a public figure chooses to present a false image and make untrue pronouncements about his or her life, the press will normally be entitled to put the record straight: [2003] QB 633, 658. Thus the area of dispute at the trial concerned the other three categories of information.

25. Of these three categories I shall consider first the information in categories (3) and (4), concerning Miss Campbell's attendance at Narcotics Anonymous meetings. In this regard it is important to note this is a highly unusual case. On any view of the matter, this information related closely to the fact, which admittedly could be published, that Miss Campbell was receiving treatment for drug addiction. Thus when considering whether Miss Campbell had a reasonable expectation of privacy in respect of information relating to her attendance at Narcotics Anonymous meetings the relevant question can be framed along the following lines: Miss Campbell having put her addiction and treatment into the public domain, did the further information relating to her attendance at Narcotics Anonymous meetings retain its character of private information sufficiently to engage the protection afforded by article 8?

26. I doubt whether it did. Treatment by attendance at Narcotics Anonymous meetings is a form of therapy for drug addiction which is well

known, widely used and much respected. Disclosure that Miss Campbell had opted for this form of treatment was not a disclosure of any more significance than saying that a person who has fractured a limb has his limb in plaster or that a person suffering from cancer is undergoing a course of chemotherapy. Given the extent of the information, otherwise of a highly private character, which admittedly could properly be disclosed, the additional information was of such an unremarkable and consequential nature that to divide the one from the other would be to apply altogether too fine a toothcomb. Human rights are concerned with substance, not with such fine distinctions.

. . .

30. There remains category (5): the photographs taken covertly of Miss Campbell in the road outside the building she was attending for a meeting of Narcotics Anonymous. I say at once that I wholly understand why Miss Campbell felt she was being hounded by the 'Mirror'. I understand also that this could be deeply distressing, even damaging, to a person whose health was still fragile. But this is not the subject of complaint. Miss Campbell, expressly, makes no complaint about the taking of the photographs. She does not assert that the taking of the photographs was itself an invasion of privacy which attracts a legal remedy. The complaint regarding the photographs is of precisely the same character as the nature of the complaints regarding the text of the articles: the information conveyed by the photographs was private information. Thus the fact that the photographs were taken surreptitiously adds nothing to the only complaint being made.

31. In general photographs of people contain more information than textual description. That is why they are more vivid. That is why they are worth a thousand words. But the pictorial information in the photographs illustrating the offending article of 1 February 2001 added nothing of an essentially private nature. They showed nothing untoward. They conveyed no private information beyond that discussed in the article. The group photograph showed Miss Campbell in the street exchanging warm greetings with others on the doorstep of a building. There was nothing undignified or distrait about her appearance. The same is true of the smaller picture on the front page. Until spotted by counsel in the course of preparing the case for oral argument in your Lordships' House no one seems to have noticed that a sharp eye could just about make out the name of the café on the advertising board on the pavement.

32. For these reasons and those given by my noble and learned friend Lord Hoffmann, I agree with the Court of Appeal that Miss Campbell's claim fails."

Law in the United States

Reread Restatement (Second) of Torts, § 652D on p. 267, above.

Diaz v. Oakland Tribune, 139 Cal. App. 3d 118 (1983)

"Diaz is a transsexual. She was born in Puerto Rico in 1942 as Antonio Diaz, a male. . . . [She] scrupulously kept the surgery a secret from all but her immediate family and closest friends. She never sought to publicize the surgery. She changed her name to Toni Ann Diaz and made the necessary changes in her high school records, her social security records, and on her driver's license. She tried unsuccessfully to change her Puerto Rican birth certificate." . . .

"In spring 1977, she was elected student body president [of the College of Alameda] for the 1977–78 academic year, the first woman to hold that office. . . . In 1977 Diaz was also selected to be the student body representative to the Peralta Community College Board of Trustees. . . . Near the middle of her term as student body president, Diaz became embroiled in a controversy in which she charged the College administrators with misuse of student funds. The March 15, 1978, issue of the Tribune quoted Diaz's charge that her signature had improperly been 'rubber stamped' on checks drawn from the associated students' account. . . .

Shortly after the controversy arose, Jones was informed by several confidential sources that Diaz was a man. Jones considered the matter newsworthy if he could verify the information. Jones testified that he inspected the Tribune's own files and spoke with an unidentified number of persons at the College to confirm this information. It was not until Richard Paoli, the city editor of the Tribune, checked Oakland city police records that the information that Diaz was born a man was verified. . . .

On March 26, 1978, the following item appeared in Jones' newspaper column: 'More Education Stuff: The students at the College of Alameda will be surprised to learn that their student body president, Toni Diaz, is no lady, but is in fact a man whose real name is Antonio.'

'Now I realize, that in these times, such a matter is no big deal, but I suspect his female classmates in P.E. 97 may wish to make other showering arrangements.' . . .

The concept of a common law right to privacy was first developed in a landmark article by Warren and Brandeis, The Right to Privacy (1890) *4 Harv.L.Rev. 193*, and has been adopted in virtually every state [footnote omitted]. The specific privacy right with which we are concerned is the right to be free from public disclosure of private embarrassing facts, in short, 'the right to be let alone.' (*Melvin v. Reid (1931) 112 Cal. App. 285, 289 [297 P. 91].*) . . .

As discerned from the decisions of our courts, the public disclosure tort contains the following elements: (1) public disclosure (2) of a private fact (3) which would be offensive and objectionable to the reasonable person and (4) which is not of legitimate public concern [citing Forsher v. Bugliosi (1980) 26 Cal.3d 792, 808–09; Briscoe v. Reader's Digest Association, Inc. (1971) 4 Cal.3d 529, 541–44; Kapellas v. Kofman (1969) 1 Cal.3d 20, 34-329].

[W]hether the fact of Diaz's sexual identity was newsworthy is measured along a sliding scale of competing interests: the individual's right to keep private facts from the public's gaze versus the public's right to know. (See *Kapellas v. Kofman, supra, 1 Cal.3d at p. 36.*) In an effort to reconcile these competing interests, our courts have settled on a three-part test for determining whether matter published is newsworthy: [1] the social value of the facts published, [2] the depth of the article's intrusion into ostensibly private affairs, and [3] the extent to which the party voluntarily acceded to a position of public notoriety. (*Briscoe v. Reader's Digest Association, Inc., supra, 4 Cal.3d at p. 541.*)

[D]efendants urge that, as the first female student body president of the College, Diaz was a public figure, and the fact of her sexual identity was a newsworthy item as a matter of law. We disagree.

It is well settled that persons who voluntarily seek public office or willingly become involved in public affairs waive their right to privacy of matters connected with their public conduct. (*Kapellas v. Kofman, supra, 1 Cal.3d at pp. 36–38.*) The reason behind this rule is that the public should be afforded every opportunity of learning about any facet which may affect that person's fitness for office. (See *Briscoe v. Reader's Digest Association, Inc., supra, 4 Cal.3d at p. 535*; Rest.2d Torts, supra, § 652D, com. e.)

However, the extent to which Diaz voluntarily acceded to a position of public notoriety and the degree to which she opened her private life are questions of fact. (*Briscoe v. Reader's Digest Association, Inc., supra, 4 Cal.3d at p. 541.*) As student body president, Diaz was a public figure for some purposes. However, applying the three-part test enunciated in Briscoe, we cannot state that the fact of her gender was newsworthy per se.

Contrary to defendants' claim, we find little if any connection between the information disclosed and Diaz's fitness for office. The fact that she is a transsexual does not adversely reflect on her honesty or judgment. (Cf. *Kapellas v. Kofman, supra, 1 Cal.3d 20* [plaintiff, a mother and candidate for Alameda City Council, who repeatedly left her minor children unsupervised, could not maintain an action against a newspaper for publishing information taken from police records of her children's criminal behavior]; *Beruan v. French (1976) 56 Cal. App.3d 825* [candidate for secretary-treasurer of union local could not maintain action based on publication of a letter disclosing his six prior criminal convictions].)

Nor does the fact that she was the first woman student body president, in itself, warrant that her entire private life be open to public inspection. The public arena entered by Diaz is concededly small. Public figures more celebrated than she are entitled to keep some information of their domestic activities and sexual relations private. (See Rest.2d Torts, supra, § 652D, com. h.)

Nor is there merit to defendants' claim that the changing roles of women in society make this story newsworthy. This assertion rings hollow. The tenor of the article was by no means an attempt to enlighten the public on a contemporary social issue. Rather, as Jones himself admitted, the article was directed to the students at the College about their newly elected president. Moreover, Jones' attempt at humor at Diaz's expense removes all pretense that the article was meant to educate the reading public. The social utility of the information must be viewed in context, and not based upon some arguably meritorious and unintended purpose."

Florida Star v. B.J.F., 491 U.S. 524 (1989)

Marshall, J. "Florida Stat. § 794.03 (1987) makes it unlawful to 'print, publish, or broadcast . . . in any instrument of mass communication' the name of the victim of a sexual offense. Pursuant to this statute, appellant The Florida Star was found civilly liable for publishing the name of a rape victim which it had obtained from a publicly released police report. The issue presented here is whether this result comports with the First Amendment. We hold that it does not. . . .

On October 20, 1983, appellee B.J.F. reported to the Duval County, Florida, Sheriff's Department (Department) that she had been robbed and sexually assaulted by an unknown assailant. The Department prepared a report on the incident which identified B.J.F. by her full name. The Department then placed the report in its pressroom. The Department does not restrict access either to the pressroom or to the reports made available therein.

A Florida Star reporter-trainee sent to the pressroom copied the police report verbatim, including B.J.F.'s full name, on a blank duplicate of the Department's forms. A Florida Star reporter then prepared a one-paragraph article about the crime, derived entirely from the trainee's copy of the police report. The article included B.J.F.'s full name.

In printing B.J.F.'s full name, the Florida Star violated its internal policy of not publishing the names of sexual offense victims.

At the ensuing daylong trial, B.J.F. testified that she had suffered emotional distress from the publication of her name. She stated that she had heard about the article from fellow workers and acquaintances; that her mother had received several threatening phone calls from a man who stated that he would rape B.J.F. again; and that these events had forced B.J.F. to change her phone number and residence, to seek police protection, and to obtain mental health counseling. . . .

We conclude that imposing damages on appellant for publishing B.J.F.'s name violates the First Amendment, although not for either of the reasons appellant urges. Despite the strong resemblance this case bears to Cox Broadcasting, that case cannot fairly be read as controlling here. The name of the rape victim in that case was obtained from courthouse records that were open to public inspection, a fact which Justice White's opinion for the Court repeatedly noted. 420 U.S. at 492 (noting 'special protected nature of accurate reports of judicial proceedings') (emphasis added); see also id., at 493, 496. Significantly, one of the reasons we gave in Cox Broadcasting for invalidating the challenged damages award was the important role the press plays in subjecting trials to public scrutiny and thereby helping guarantee their fairness. Id., at 492–93. That role is not directly compromised where, as here, the information in question comes from a police report prepared and disseminated at a time at which not only had no adversarial criminal proceedings begun, but no suspect had been identified.

Nor need we accept appellant's invitation to hold broadly that truthful publication may never be punished consistent with the First Amendment. Our cases have carefully eschewed reaching this ultimate question, mindful that the future may bring scenarios which prudence counsels our not resolving anticipatorily. . . .

Our holding today is limited. . . . We hold only that where a newspaper publishes truthful information which it has lawfully obtained, punishment may lawfully be imposed, if at all, only when narrowly tailored to a state interest of the highest order, and that no such interest is satisfactorily served by imposing liability under § 794.03 to appellant under the facts of this case."

French law

Cour de cassation, 1e ch. civ., arrêt no. 1434, pourvoi no. 89-13-049

The magazine *l'Expansion* wrote an article about "the one hundred richest Frenchmen" which mentioned the amount of plaintiff's net worth, even though he had written a letter asking the magazine not to do so. He lost before the *Cour d'appel*. The *Cour de cassation* upheld its decision saying that a person's private life was not invaded by publishing "information of a purely financial order that excludes any allusion to the life or personality of the interested party."

Cour de cassation, 2e ch civ., 27 April 1988, pourvoi no. 86-13.303

Mr. Varin, the plaintiff, was a judge of a *Tribunal de grande instance* who was temporarily relieved of his functions. The defendant, the journal *La Haute-Marne Libérée*, published an article with his photograph describing his removal as a "serious sanction" for which the reasons were not clear, adding that "according to rumors," he had taken a vacation for nervous depression." The *Cour de cassation* held that while temporary removal was not a "grave sanction," any claim plaintiff had for defamation was barred by the statute of limitation to which such claims are subject; that use of the photograph was permissible because of the public character of his functions and the measures taken against him; but that "divulging information on the health of a person" without his consent "violated his right to a private life even if the information was presented decently and succinctly."

Cour de cassation, 2e ch. civ., 5 December 1979, arrêt no. 1.032, pourvoi no. 78-13.614

The defendant, the newspaper *Paris-Match*, published an article under the title "Violence" which described an alteration between Mrs. Dewi Sukarno, widow of the president of Indonesia, and Beatrice Chatelier, the former wife of Eddie Barclay, "for the handsome eyes of a Parisian playboy." The defendant argued that he was entitled, as a journalist, to describe the facts and give his interpretation. The *Cour de Cassation* held him liable for a violation of privacy because his article "discussed the emotional life (*vie sentimentale*) of Mrs. Sukarno in disclosing the personal and intimate motives of the parties said to be the origin of the altercation, here, 'the handsome eyes of a Parisian playboy.' "

Cour de cassation, 2e ch. civ., 14 November 1975, arrêt no. 729. pourvoi no. 74-11.278

The defendant, *Presse-Office Lui*, ran an article on Charles Chaplin, plaintiff here. Just what it said is described in the opinion rather imprecisely: "numerous details relative to the private life of Chaplin and his family." The *Cour d'appel* held the defendant liable on the grounds that even if disclosure of these details would not have violated Chaplin's right to privacy if published in an historical study, it does here because *Lui* is not an historical journal.

Without expressly accepting or rejecting that distinction, the *Cour de Cassation* upheld its decision, saying: "*Presse Office* has never claimed for the magazine *Lui* the character of a scientific and critical publication and did not present the article attacked as an historical study. [It follows that] the distinction which the *Cour d'appel* believed that it should draw in the interest of certain publications is of no application to the decision here."

The defendant also objected that the *Cour d'appel* had "recognized the discretionary right of a private person to object to the 'redisclosure' of facts already disclosed with his own consent. The *Cour de cassation* quoted with favor these words of the *Tribunal d'instance*: "everyone having the right to respect for his private life, it matters little that books and periodicals had already treated the same facts, and whoever, without a legitimate interest, publishes facts of this nature is liable if he cannot show he was specially authorized. . . ." It also quoted with favor these words from the *Cour d'appel*: "The person who himself discloses information about his private life so decides with full knowledge of the reason that it is made known to the public and the conditions on which it is made known." The *Cour de cassation* concluded that neither of the lower courts had recognized a "discretionary right" to object to "redisclosure."

German law

Oberlandesgericht, Hamburg, 26 March 1970, NJW 1970, 1325

"The claim of the plaintiff, the wife of Prince Friedrich William of Prussia, for culpable publication of her intention to divorce in a newspaper is valid under §§ 823(1) and 1004 of the Civil Code and arts. 1 and 2 of the Constitution.

It cannot be doubted that the private sphere of the person concerned is invaded by information given the reader by the press about an intention to divorce or discussions of divorce. The private or intimate sphere is protected in principle by arts. 1 and 2 of the Constitution. According to art. 6, par. 1 of the Constitution, marriage and the family are given special protection by the order of the state. In principle, the defendant is not entitled, without the permission of the person concerned, to report even true facts about her divorce and the discussions and actions relating to it. . . .

The defendant cannot invoke art. 5 of the Constitution in its defense. Certainly, freedom of the press does include freedom of information so that known facts can be reported. Nevertheless, in accord with art. 5(2) of the Constitution, this right is limited by the provisions of general statutes and by arts. 1 and 2 of the Constitution. By weighing the two fundamental rights, on the one hand, freedom of the press, and on the other, the right to personality, which interest to protect must depend upon the individual case. In principle, the private sphere must be given attention and has a preference over the right of the press to provide information. Every person is protected against all violation of his own sphere on the basis of the general right of personality. (BGHZ 24, 201 ff. = NJW 57, 1315). The protection of the personality must take second place to the right of the press to inform only when the public has a serious need for the information (BGH, LM no. 16 on art. 5 of the Constitution = MDR 65, 371 ff. with numerous references). One can recognise a legitimate public interest in information about events in the private or family sphere only by way of exception when the person involved has a particularly prominent position. The need for entertainment of the readership of a newspaper cannot justify such an attack. . . .

Certainly, through her marriage with Prince Friedrich William, the plaintiff became a member of the house of Hohenzollern as is the son born of this marriage. But that did not make her a figure of current history whose private life the press can report without her consent. Her husband is not a figure of contemporary history because he does not play a role in public life nor has he aroused general interest in art, science or sport. The mere fact that he is the oldest son of the head of the house of Hohenzollern does not make him a figure of contemporary history, and it is indeed questionable whether Prince Louis Ferdinand of Prussia is to be numbered among this circle of persons. In principle, current history is to be understood to include the events of the present of importance and interest generally. The members of the house of Hohenzollern are not figures of contemporary history in this sense since they do not occupy position either in political or in cultural life. If Prince Louis Ferdinand once did say that he was on hand if the German people should call him, that did not make him a figure of current history since it is not a matter of a person's subjective attitude. Since, with an interruption, Germany has been a republic for fifty years, the House of Hohenzollern has had only historical significance since the abdication of Kaiser Wilhelm II."

About historical events

Law in the United States

Haynes v. Alfred A. Knopf, Inc., 8 F.3d 1222 (7th Cir. 1993)

Posner, J. "Luther Haynes and his wife, Dorothy Haynes née Johnson, appeal from the dismissal on the defendants' motion for summary judgment of their suit against Nicholas Lemann, the author of a highly praised, best-selling book of social and political history called *The Promised Land: The Great Black Migration and How It Changed America* (1991), and Alfred A. Knopf, Inc., the book's publisher. The plaintiffs claim that the book libels Luther Haynes and invades both plaintiffs' right of privacy. . . .

Between 1940 and 1970, five million blacks moved from impoverished rural areas and, after sojourns of shorter or greater length in the poor black districts of the cities, moved to middle-class areas. Others, despite the ballyhooed efforts of the federal government, particularly between 1964 and 1972, to erase poverty and racial discrimination, remained mired in what has come to be called the 'urban ghetto.' *The Promised Land* is a history of the migration. It is not history as a professional historian, a demographer, or a social scientist would write it. Lemann is none of these. He is a journalist and has written a journalistic history, in which the focus is on individuals whether powerful or representative. In the former group are the politicians who invented, executed, or exploited the 'Great Society' programs. In the latter are a handful of the actual migrants. Foremost among these is Ruby Lee Daniels. Her story is the spine of the book. We are introduced to her on page 7; we take leave of her on page 346, within a few pages of the end of the text of the book.

The book describes how Daniel, who had been a sharecropper in Mississippi in the 1940s, moved to Chicago where she met and married Luther Haynes. The story describes his failures as a worker and a husband through drunkenness, bad temper, and adultery. They were divorced. Luther later married another woman, Dorothy, and lived a respectable life for twenty years. At the time the book was published, he had a home, a steady job, and was a deacon of his local church.]

The possibility of an involuntary loss of privacy is recognized in the modern formulations of this branch of the privacy tort, which require not only that the private facts publicized be such as would make a reasonable person deeply offended by such publicity but also that they be facts in which the public has no legitimate interest.

The two criteria, offensiveness and newsworthiness, are related. An individual, and more pertinently perhaps the community, is most offended by the publication of intimate personal facts when the community has no interest in them beyond the voyeuristic thrill of penetrating the wall of privacy that surrounds a stranger. The reader of a book about the black migration to the North would have no legitimate interest in the details of Luther Haynes' sex life; but no such details are disclosed. Such a reader does have a legitimate interest in the aspects of Luther's conduct that the book reveals. For one of Lemann's major themes is the transposition virtually intact of a sharecropper morality characterized by a family structure 'matriarchal and elastic' and by an 'extremely unstable' marriage bond to the slums of the northern cities, and the interaction, largely random and sometimes perverse, of that morality with governmental programs to alleviate poverty. Public aid policies discouraged Ruby and Luther from living together; public housing policies precipitated a marriage doomed to fail. No detail in the book claimed to invade the Hayneses' privacy is not germane to the story that the author wanted to tell, a story not only of legitimate but of transcendent public interest. . . .

Well, argue the Hayneses, at least Lemann could have changed their names. But the use of pseudonyms would not have gotten Lemann and Knopf off the legal hook. The details of the Hayneses' lives recounted in the book would identify them unmistakably to anyone who has known the Hayneses well for a long time (members of their families, for example), or who knew them before they got married; and no more is required for liability either in defamation law or in privacy law. Lemann would have had to change some, perhaps many, of the details. But then he would no longer have been writing history. He would have been writing fiction. The non-quantitative study of living persons would be abolished as a category of scholarship, to be replaced by the sociological novel. That is a genre with a distinguished history punctuated by famous names, such as Dickens, Zola, Stowe, Dreiser, Sinclair, Steinbeck, and Wolfe, but we do not think that the law of privacy makes it (or that the First Amendment would permit the law of privacy to make it) the exclusive format for a social history of living persons that tells their story rather than treating them as data points in a statistical study."

French law

Cour de cassation, 1e ch civ., 20 November 1990, arrêt no. 1432, pourvoi no. 89-12.580

Defendants were the writer (Paul Kern) and publisher of a book, "A Toboggan in the Torment of the France-Compte 1940–45," a study of the Nazi occupation of the Franche Compte, which, the author said, would describe "historical truth down to its smallest details." He mentioned a man who was tried and condemned as a traitor in 1946 "along with his mistress Mananges." She brought this action for infringement on her private life (*vie privée*). She won before the court of first instance and lost before the *Cour d'appel*. The *Cour d'appel* said: "it must be acknowledged that he had the right as an historian to present the evidence of facts, without the consent of the interested parties, even if they touch on one's private life, if they have a definite relation to the subject, are related with objectivity and without an intention to injure and if they were, as in this case, already brought to public awareness by the reports of judicial debates contained in the local press immediately after the war."

The *Cour de cassation* overturned this decision. It said that the *Cour d'appel* had erred by taking the author's assertion that he did not intend to injure at face value. It said that even an historian does not have the right to "bring up the private life of a person without necessity." The court concluded, however, that the author was entitled to mention her conviction for treason since it had once been reported in the local press. Nevertheless, he should also have mentioned that she was subsequently pardoned. He is liable because he failed to do so.

German law

Oberlandesgericht, Frankfurt, 6 September 1979, NJW 1980, 597

The defendant, the weekly magazine S., published a series on Nazi experiments on children in a concentration camp. One article in the series contained the following references to A., the plaintiff:

> One of the perpetrators lives among us. His name is A. On orders from Berlin, he let the children be killed.

> One of those responsible for the death of the children lives among us: the former Obersturmführer A.

The article accused him of responsibility for the deaths of twenty children in April, 1945.

The court held that the plaintiff could not recover for *üble Nachrede* because truth was a defense, and where, as here, constitutionally important interests were at stake, the usual burden of proof was reversed so that the plaintiff had the burden of proving that the statement was false. He had failed to do so.

"The starting point for the Senate must be that while the plaintiff's full guilt for these outrages has not been established, there is serious reason for suspicion. On those facts, the press has a legitimate interest in making the contentions to which the plaintiff objects public. In informing, instructing and supporting the shaping of public opinion, the press has a legitimate interest in reporting concretely the facts that are essential for evaluating a former period of time, in preserving the memory of the era of national socialist rule, in contributing to an impartial view by its readers of these horrible acts of power, and even to help toward a clarification of particular criminal acts through the publication of further details. It is not in dispute that the case law recognizes such an extensive right for the press in the public interest. (See OLG, München NJW 1970, 1745; OLG, Frankfurt, NJW 1971, 47; Thomas in Palandt, no. 15 D b to § 823.)

This interest must certainly in some cases conflict with the interest of the party affected, here the defendant, whom it would suit to remain undisturbed and to develop his personality (*Persönlichkeit*) without restriction according to his own wishes. It has not been overlooked that the defendant, now seventy years old, for whom the alleged wrongs lie over thirty years in the past, has a strong interest in not having to confront these horrible reproaches which must distress him and bring him into contempt in the eyes of his friends and acquaintances and the public. Since the defendant has not carried the burden which rests on him to prove falsity, and since many important indications are against him, his interest is outweighed for the reasons just given by the interest of the public in exposition and instruction concerning those events remote from the present.

The defendant has observed the limits commanded by the recognition of its legitimate interest. It confined its publication to the legally proper area. It carefully researched the alleged wrongs of the plaintiff."

Electronic collection and dissemination of information

Directive of the European Parliament and European Council on the Protection of Individuals with regard to the processing of personal data and on the free movement of such data [95/46/EC, 24 Oct. 1995, Official Journal of the European Communities L 281, 23/11/1995 p. 0031–0050]

THE EUROPEAN PARLIAMENT AND THE COUNCIL OF THE EUROPEAN UNION

Having regard to the Treaty establishing the European Community, and in particular Article 100a thereof, Having regard to the proposal from

the Commission (1), Having regard to the opinion of the Economic and
Social Committee (2), Acting in accordance with the procedure referred to
in Article 189b of the Treaty (3).

(1) Whereas the objectives of the Community, as laid down in the Treaty,
    as amended by the Treaty on European Union, include creating
    an ever closer union among the peoples of Europe, fostering closer
    relations between the States belonging to the Community, ensur-
    ing economic and social progress by common action to eliminate
    the barriers which divide Europe, encouraging the constant
    improvement of the living conditions of its peoples, preserving
    and strengthening peace and liberty and promoting democracy on
    the basis of the fundamental rights recognized in the constitution
    and laws of the Member States and in the European Convention
    for the Protection of Human Rights and Fundamental Freedoms;

(2) Whereas data-processing systems are designed to serve man;
    whereas they must, whatever the nationality or residence of nat-
    ural persons, respect their fundamental rights and freedoms,
    notably the right to privacy, and contribute to economic and social
    progress, trade expansion and the well-being of individuals;

(3) Whereas the establishment and functioning of an internal mar-
    ket in which, in accordance with Article 7a of the Treaty, the free
    movement of goods, persons, services and capital is ensured require
    not only that personal data should be able to flow freely from one
    Member State to another, but also that the fundamental rights of
    individuals should be safeguarded;

(4) Whereas increasingly frequent recourse is being had in the Com-
    munity to the processing of personal data in the various spheres
    of economic and social activity; whereas the progress made in
    information technology is making the processing and exchange of
    such data considerably easier;

(5) Whereas the economic and social integration resulting from
    the establishment and functioning of the internal market within
    the meaning of Article 7a of the Treaty will necessarily lead to
    a substantial increase in cross-border flows of personal data
    between all those involved in a private or public capacity in
    economic and social activity in the Member States; whereas the
    exchange of personal data between undertakings in different
    Member States is set to increase; whereas the national authori-
    ties in the various Member States are being called upon by virtue
    of Community law to collaborate and exchange personal data so
    as to be able to perform their duties or carry out tasks on behalf
    of an authority in another Member State within the context of the
    area without internal frontiers as constituted by the internal
    market;

["whereas" clauses 6 through 72 are omitted].

HAVE ADOPTED THIS DIRECTIVE:

CHAPTER I GENERAL PROVISIONS

ARTICLE 1: OBJECT OF THE DIRECTIVE

(1) In accordance with this Directive, Member States shall protect the fundamental rights and freedoms of natural persons, and in particular their right to privacy with respect to the processing of personal data.

(2) Member States shall neither restrict nor prohibit the free flow of personal data between Member States for reasons connected with the protection afforded under paragraph 1.

ARTICLE 2: DEFINITIONS

For the purposes of this Directive:

(a) "personal data" shall mean any information relating to an identified or identifiable natural person ("data subject"); an identifiable person is one who can be identified, directly or indirectly, in particular by reference to an identification number or to one or more factors specific to his physical, physiological, mental, economic, cultural or social identity;

(b) "processing of personal data" ("processing") shall mean any operation or set of operations which is performed upon personal data, whether or not by automatic means, such as collection, recording, organization, storage, adaptation or alteration, retrieval, consultation, use, disclosure by transmission, dissemination or otherwise making available, alignment or combination, blocking, erasure or destruction;

(c) "personal data filing system" ("filing system") shall mean any structured set of personal data which are accessible according to specific criteria, whether centralized, decentralized or dispersed on a functional or geographical basis;

(d) "controller" shall mean the natural or legal person, public authority, agency or any other body which alone or jointly with others determines the purposes and means of the processing of personal data; where the purposes and means of processing are determined by national or Community laws or regulations, the controller or the specific criteria for his nomination may be designated by national or Community law;

(e) "processor" shall mean a natural or legal person, public authority, agency or any other body which processes personal data on behalf of the controller;

(f) "third party" shall mean any natural or legal person, public authority, agency or any other body other than the data subject, the controller, the processor and the persons who, under the direct authority of the controller or the processor, are authorized to process the data;

(g) "recipient" shall mean a natural or legal person, public authority, agency or any other body to whom data are disclosed, whether a third party or not; however, authorities which may receive data in the framework of a particular inquiry shall not be regarded as recipients;

(h) "the data subject's consent" shall mean any freely given specific and informed indication of his wishes by which the data subject signifies his agreement to personal data relating to him being processed.

ARTICLE 3: SCOPE

(1) This Directive shall apply to the processing of personal data wholly or partly by automatic means, and to the processing otherwise than by automatic means of personal data which form part of a filing system or are intended to form part of a filing system.

(2) This Directive shall not apply to the processing of personal data:

– in the course of an activity which falls outside the scope of Community law, such as those provided for by Titles V and VI of the Treaty on European Union and in any case to processing operations concerning public security, defence, State security (including the economic well-being of the State when the processing operation relates to State security matters) and the activities of the State in areas of criminal law;

– by a natural person in the course of a purely personal or household activity.

ARTICLE 4: NATIONAL LAW APPLICABLE

(1) Each Member State shall apply the national provisions it adopts pursuant to this Directive to the processing of personal data where:

(a) the processing is carried out in the context of the activities of an establishment of the controller on the territory of the Member State; when the same controller is established on the territory of several Member States, he must take the necessary measures to ensure that each of these establishments complies with the obligations laid down by the national law applicable;

(b) the controller is not established on the Member State's territory, but in a place where its national law applies by virtue of international public law;

(c) the controller is not established on Community territory and, for purposes of processing personal data makes use of equipment, automated or otherwise, situated on the territory of the said Member State, unless such equipment is used only for purposes of transit through the territory of the Community.

(2) In the circumstances referred to in paragraph 1(c), the controller must designate a representative established in the territory of that Member State, without prejudice to legal actions which could be initiated against the controller himself.

CHAPTER II GENERAL RULES ON THE LAWFULNESS OF THE PROCESSING OF PERSONAL DATA

ARTICLE 5

Member States shall, within the limits of the provisions of this chapter, determine more precisely the conditions under which the processing of personal data is lawful.

SECTION I PRINCIPLES RELATING TO DATA QUALITY

ARTICLE 6

(1) Member States shall provide that personal data must be:

(a) processed fairly and lawfully;

(b) collected for specified, explicit and legitimate purposes and not further processed in a way incompatible with those purposes. Further processing of data for historical, statistical or scientific purposes shall not be considered as incompatible provided that Member States provide appropriate safeguards;

(c) adequate, relevant and not excessive in relation to the purposes for which they are collected and/or further processed;

(d) accurate and, where necessary, kept up to date; every reasonable step must be taken to ensure that data which are inaccurate or incomplete, having regard to the purposes for which they were collected or for which they are further processed, are erased or rectified;

(e) kept in a form which permits identification of data subjects for no longer than is necessary for the purposes for which the data were collected or for which they are further processed. Member States shall lay down appropriate safeguards for personal data stored for longer periods for historical, statistical or scientific use.

(2) It shall be for the controller to ensure that paragraph 1 is complied with.

SECTION II CRITERIA FOR MAKING DATA PROCESSING LEGITIMATE

ARTICLE 7

Member States shall provide that personal data may be processed only if:

(a) the data subject has unambiguously given his consent; or

(b) processing is necessary for the performance of a contract to which the data subject is party or in order to take steps at the request of the data subject prior to entering into a contract; or

(c) processing is necessary for compliance with a legal obligation to which the controller is subject; or

(d) processing is necessary in order to protect the vital interests of the data subject; or

(e) processing is necessary for the performance of a task carried out in the public interest or in the exercise of official authority vested in the controller or in a third party to whom the data are disclosed; or

(f) processing is necessary for the purposes of the legitimate interests pursued by the controller or by the third party or parties to whom the data are disclosed, except where such interests are overridden by the interests for fundamental rights and freedoms of the data subject which require protection under Article 1(1).

SECTION III SPECIAL CATEGORIES OF PROCESSING

ARTICLE 8: THE PROCESSING OF SPECIAL CATEGORIES OF DATA

(1) Member States shall prohibit the processing of personal data revealing racial or ethnic origin, political opinions, religious or philosophical beliefs, trade-union membership, and the processing of data concerning health or sex life.

(2) Paragraph 1 shall not apply where:

(a) the data subject has given his explicit consent to the processing of those data, except where the laws of the Member State provide that the prohibition referred to in paragraph 1 may not be lifted by the data subject's giving his consent; or

(b) processing is necessary for the purposes of carrying out the obligations and specific rights of the controller in the field of employment law insofar as it is authorized by national law providing for adequate safeguards; or

(c) processing is necessary to protect the vital interests of the data subject or of another person where the data subject is physically or legally incapable of giving his consent; or

(d) processing is carried out in the course of its legitimate activities with appropriate guarantees by a foundation, association or any other non-profit-seeking body with a political, philosophical, religious or trade-union aim and on condition that the processing relates solely to the members of the body or to persons who have regular contact with it in connection with its purposes and that the data are not disclosed to a third party without the consent of the data subjects; or

(e) the processing relates to data which are manifestly made public by the data subject or is necessary for the establishment, exercise or defence of legal claims.

(3) Paragraph 1 shall not apply where processing of the data is required for the purposes of preventive medicine, medical diagnosis, the provision of care or treatment or the management of health-care services, and where those data are processed by a health professional subject under national law or rules established by national competent bodies to the obligation of professional secrecy or by another person also subject to an equivalent obligation of secrecy.

(4) Subject to the provision of suitable safeguards, Member States may, for reasons of substantial public interest, lay down exemptions in addition to those laid down in paragraph 2 either by national law or by decision of the supervisory authority.

(5) Processing of data relating to offences, criminal convictions or security measures may be carried out only under the control of official authority, or if suitable specific safeguards are provided under national law, subject to derogations which may be granted by the Member State

under national provisions providing suitable specific safeguards. However, a complete register of criminal convictions may be kept only under the control of official authority. Member States may provide that data relating to administrative sanctions or judgements in civil cases shall also be processed under the control of official authority.

(6) Derogations from paragraph 1 provided for in paragraphs 4 and 5 shall be notified to the Commission.

(7) Member States shall determine the conditions under which a national identification number or any other identifier of general application may be processed.

ARTICLE 9: PROCESSING OF PERSONAL DATA AND FREEDOM OF EXPRESSION

Member States shall provide for exemptions or derogations from the provisions of this Chapter, Chapter IV and Chapter VI for the processing of personal data carried out solely for journalistic purposes or the purpose of artistic or literary expression only if they are necessary to reconcile the right to privacy with the rules governing freedom of expression.

SECTION IV INFORMATION TO BE GIVEN TO THE DATA SUBJECT

ARTICLE 10

Information in cases of collection of data from the data subject Member States shall provide that the controller or his representative must provide a data subject from whom data relating to himself are collected with at least the following information, except where he already has it:

(a) the identity of the controller and of his representative, if any;

(b) the purposes of the processing for which the data are intended;

(c) any further information such as:

- the recipients or categories of recipients of the data,

- whether replies to the questions are obligatory or voluntary, as well as the possible consequences of failure to reply,

- the existence of the right of access to and the right to rectify the data concerning him insofar as such further information is necessary, having regard to the specific circumstances in which the data are collected, to guarantee fair processing in respect of the data subject.

ARTICLE 11: INFORMATION WHERE THE DATA HAVE NOT BEEN OBTAINED FROM THE DATA SUBJECT

(1) [This provision is almost identical to Article 10. It leaves out the requirement that the data subject be told whether his replies are voluntary.]

(2) Paragraph 1 shall not apply where, in particular for processing for statistical purposes or for the purposes of historical or scientific research, the provision of such information proves impossible or would involve a disproportionate effort or if recording or disclosure is expressly laid down by law. In these cases Member States shall provide appropriate safeguards.

SECTION V THE DATA SUBJECT'S RIGHT OF ACCESS TO DATA

ARTICLE 12

Right of access Member States shall guarantee every data subject the right to obtain from the controller:

(a) without constraint at reasonable intervals and without excessive delay or expense:

- confirmation as to whether or not data relating to him are being processed and information at least as to the purposes of the processing, the categories of data concerned, and the recipients or categories of recipients to whom the data are disclosed,
- communication to him in an intelligible form of the data undergoing processing and of any available information as to their source,
- knowledge of the logic involved in any automatic processing of data concerning him at least in the case of the automated decisions referred to in Article 15(1);

(b) as appropriate the rectification, erasure or blocking of data the processing of which does not comply with the provisions of this Directive, in particular because of the incomplete or inaccurate nature of the data;

(c) notification to third parties to whom the data have been disclosed of any rectification, erasure or blocking carried out in compliance with (b), unless this proves impossible or involves a disproportionate effort. . . .

SECTION VII THE DATA SUBJECT'S RIGHT TO OBJECT

ARTICLE 14

The data subject's right to object Member States shall grant the data subject the right:

(a) at least in the cases referred to in Article 7(e) and (f), to object at any time on compelling legitimate grounds relating to his particular situation to the processing of data relating to him, save where otherwise provided by national legislation. Where there is a justified objection, the processing instigated by the controller may no longer involve those data;

(b) to object, on request and free of charge, to the processing of personal data relating to him which the controller anticipates being processed for the purposes of direct marketing, or to be informed before personal data are disclosed for the first time to third parties or used on their behalf for the purposes of direct marketing, and to be expressly offered the right to object free of charge to such disclosures or uses. Member States shall take the necessary measures to ensure that data subjects are aware of the existence of the right referred to in the first subparagraph of (b).

ARTICLE 15: AUTOMATED INDIVIDUAL DECISIONS

(1) Member States shall grant the right to every person not to be subject to a decision which produces legal effects concerning him or significantly affects him and which is based solely on automated processing of data intended to evaluate certain personal aspects relating to him, such as his performance at work, creditworthiness, reliability, conduct, etc.

(2) Subject to the other Articles of this Directive, Member States shall provide that a person may be subjected to a decision of the kind referred to in paragraph 1 if that decision:

(a) is taken in the course of the entering into or performance of a contract, provided the request for the entering into or the performance of the contract, lodged by the data subject, has been satisfied or that there are suitable measures to safeguard his legitimate interests, such as arrangements allowing him to put his point of view; or

(b) is authorized by a law which also lays down measures to safeguard the data subject's legitimate interests.

SECTION VIII CONFIDENTIALITY AND SECURITY OF PROCESSING

ARTICLE 16: CONFIDENTIALITY OF PROCESSING

Any person acting under the authority of the controller or of the processor, including the processor himself, who has access to personal data must not process them except on instructions from the controller, unless he is required to do so by law.

ARTICLE 17: SECURITY OF PROCESSING

(1) Member States shall provide that the controller must implement appropriate technical and organizational measures to protect personal data against accidental or unlawful destruction or accidental loss, alteration, unauthorized disclosure or access, in particular where the processing involves the transmission of data over a network, and against all other unlawful forms of processing. Having regard to the state of the art and the cost of their implementation, such measures shall ensure a level of security appropriate to the risks represented by the processing and the nature of the data to be protected.

(2) The Member States shall provide that the controller must, where processing is carried out on his behalf, choose a processor providing sufficient guarantees in respect of the technical security measures and organizational measures governing the processing to be carried out, and must ensure compliance with those measures.

(3) The carrying out of processing by way of a processor must be governed by a contract or legal act binding the processor to the controller and stipulating in particular that:

– the processor shall act only on instructions from the controller,

– the obligations set out in paragraph 1, as defined by the law of the Member State in which the processor is established, shall also be incumbent on the processor.

(4) For the purposes of keeping proof, the parts of the contract or the legal act relating to data protection and the requirements relating to the measures referred to in paragraph 1 shall be in writing or in another equivalent form. . . .

CHAPTER III JUDICIAL REMEDIES, LIABILITY AND SANCTIONS

ARTICLE 22: REMEDIES

Without prejudice to any administrative remedy for which provision may be made, inter alia before the supervisory authority referred to in Article 28, prior to referral to the judicial authority, Member States shall provide for the right of every person to a judicial remedy for any breach of the rights guaranteed him by the national law applicable to the processing in question.

ARTICLE 23: LIABILITY

(1) Member States shall provide that any person who has suffered damage as a result of an unlawful processing operation or of any act incompatible with the national provisions adopted pursuant to this Directive is entitled to receive compensation from the controller for the damage suffered.

(2) The controller may be exempted from this liability, in whole or in part, if he proves that he is not responsible for the event giving rise to the damage.

ARTICLE 24: SANCTIONS

The Member States shall adopt suitable measures to ensure the full implementation of the provisions of this Directive and shall in particular lay down the sanctions to be imposed in case of infringement of the provisions adopted pursuant to this Directive.

CHAPTER IV TRANSFER OF PERSONAL DATA TO THIRD COUNTRIES

ARTICLE 25: PRINCIPLES

(1) The Member States shall provide that the transfer to a third country of personal data which are undergoing processing or are intended for processing after transfer may take place only if, without prejudice to compliance with the national provisions adopted pursuant to the other provisions of this Directive, the third country in question ensures an adequate level of protection.

(2) The adequacy of the level of protection afforded by a third country shall be assessed in the light of all the circumstances surrounding a data transfer operation or set of data transfer operations; particular consideration shall be given to the nature of the data, the purpose and duration of the proposed processing operation or operations, the country of origin and country of final destination, the rules of law, both general and sectoral, in force in the third country in question and the professional rules and security measures which are complied with in that country.

(3) The Member States and the Commission shall inform each other of cases where they consider that a third country does not ensure an adequate level of protection within the meaning of paragraph 2.

(4) Where the Commission finds, under the procedure provided for in Article 31(2), that a third country does not ensure an adequate level of protection within the meaning of paragraph 2 of this Article, Member

States shall take the measures necessary to prevent any transfer of data of the same type to the third country in question.

(5) At the appropriate time, the Commission shall enter into negotiations with a view to remedying the situation resulting from the finding made pursuant to paragraph 4.

(6) The Commission may find, in accordance with the procedure referred to in Article 31(2), that a third country ensures an adequate level of protection within the meaning of paragraph 2 of this Article, by reason of its domestic law or of the international commitments it has entered into, particularly upon conclusion of the negotiations referred to in paragraph 5, for the protection of the private lives and basic freedoms and rights of individuals. Member States shall take the measures necessary to comply with the Commission's decision.

ARTICLE 26: DEROGATIONS

(1) By way of derogation from Article 25 and save where otherwise provided by domestic law governing particular cases, Member States shall provide that a transfer or a set of transfers of personal data to a third country which does not ensure an adequate level of protection within the meaning of Article 25(2) may take place on condition that:

(a) the data subject has given his consent unambiguously to the proposed transfer; or

(b) the transfer is necessary for the performance of a contract between the data subject and the controller or the implementation of precontractual measures taken in response to the data subject's request; or

(c) the transfer is necessary for the conclusion or performance of a contract concluded in the interest of the data subject between the controller and a third party; or

(d) the transfer is necessary or legally required on important public interest grounds, or for the establishment, exercise or defence of legal claims; or

(e) the transfer is necessary in order to protect the vital interests of the data subject; or

(f) the transfer is made from a register which according to laws or regulations is intended to provide information to the public and which is open to consultation either by the public in general or by any person who can demonstrate legitimate interest, to the extent that the conditions laid down in law for consultation are fulfilled in the particular case.

(2) Without prejudice to paragraph 1, a Member State may authorize a transfer or a set of transfers of personal data to a third country which does not ensure an adequate level of protection within the meaning of Article 25(2), where the controller adduces adequate safeguards with respect to the protection of the privacy and fundamental rights and freedoms of individuals and as regards the exercise of the corresponding rights; such safeguards may in particular result from appropriate contractual clauses.

(3) The Member State shall inform the Commission and the other Member States of the authorizations it grants pursuant to paragraph 2. If a Member State or the Commission objects on justified grounds involving the protection of the privacy and fundamental rights and freedoms of individuals, the Commission shall take appropriate measures in accordance with the procedure laid down in Article 31(2). Member States shall take the necessary measures to comply with the Commission's decision.

(4) Where the Commission decides, in accordance with the procedure referred to in Article 31(2), that certain standard contractual clauses offer sufficient safeguards as required by paragraph 2, Member States shall take the necessary measures to comply with the Commission's decision.

* * *

CHAPTER VI SUPERVISORY AUTHORITY AND WORKING PARTY ON THE PROTECTION OF INDIVIDUALS WITH REGARD TO THE PROCESSING OF PERSONAL DATA

ARTICLE 28: SUPERVISORY AUTHORITY

(1) Each Member State shall provide that one or more public authorities are responsible for monitoring the application within its territory of the provisions adopted by the Member States pursuant to this Directive. These authorities shall act with complete independence in exercising the functions entrusted to them.

* * *

FINAL PROVISIONS

ARTICLE 32

(1) Member States shall bring into force the laws, regulations and administrative provisions necessary to comply with this Directive at the latest at the end of a period of three years from the date of its adoption. . . .

(3) By way of derogation from paragraph 2, Member States may provide, subject to suitable safeguards, that data kept for the sole purpose of historical research need not be brought into conformity with Articles 6, 7 and 8 of this Directive.

* * *

4. Purely economic harm

a. Liability in principle for purely economic harm

French law

As we have seen, the French Civil Code, arts. 1382–83, simply say that the defendant is liable for harm (*dommage*) (p. 234, above). Supposedly, then, French law is equally simple. The defendant is liable for harm, whether it is economic or not.

Cour de cassation, 2e ch. civ., 8 May 1970, Bull. civ. 1970.II no. 160

"[A] gas pipe of the *Compagnie française du méthone* which supplied the factory of the *Allamignon Frères et Lacroix* company was broken by a bulldozer in the course of work done by the entrepreneur Lafarge." The court held Lafarge liable, noting with approval that the *Cour d'appel* had found "that the harm suffered by *Allamignon Frères et Lacroix* company appeared to be the direct consequence of the break in the pipe since this damage had caused the interruption of the activity of the factory."

Cour de cassation, ch. comm., 17 October 1984, JCP 1985.II.20458

Plaintiff company contributed capital to N. company after examining the financial statements prepared by defendants who were accountants. The financial statements were incorrect: company N. in fact had a deficit in assets of 480,000 francs. Company N. became insolvent. The court held plaintiff could recover from defendants.

Cour d'appel, Colmar, 20 April 1955, D. 1956.J.723

Kemp was under contract to play for "le Football Club de Metz." When he was killed in a traffic accident for which defendant was responsible, the Club sued to recover the financial losses it had incurred as a result. It claimed that the team had been put in disarray and that it had lost the fee it was entitled to charge to release Kemp from his contract and allow him to play for another club. While the contract was for the season, it was renewed every year and could only be canceled under strictly regulated conditions. The Club had already turned down offers from other clubs, one for 2,000,000 francs. To obtain a player of comparable standing the Club would have to pay a similar fee. Before Kemp's death the Club had been ranked 10th among 18 teams in the national division. The season following his death, it fell to 16th place. The year following it fell to 18th place and was expelled from the national division, so that it then had to play in the "second division." The court held that the Club could recover and remanded to determine the amount it had lost. The court noted: "every person, even an organization recognized by the law as a person (*même morale*) who is the victim of harm (*dommage*), whatever be its nature, has the right to obtain compensation from one who caused it by his fault or by the act of an object that he has in his custody (*garde*)." Here the Club could recover because the harm was "certain."

Cour de cassation, 2e ch. civ., 28 April 1965, D.S. 1965.J.777

Certain buses of the plaintiff, the Marseilles transit authority, were delayed by a traffic accident for which the defendant was responsible: his car hit a motorcycle blocking the street. The plaintiff sued to recover the fares it had lost because its potential customers grew tired of waiting and proceeded to their destinations on foot or by taxi. The *Cour d'appel* allowed the plaintiff to recover noting simply that the harm was "certain;" it was "neither hypothetical nor indirect." The damages awarded were 37.07 francs.

Note: Professor Paul Esmein observed that this was not the first time that the Marseilles transport authority had taken such a case all the way to the *Cour de cassation*. He cited two decisions of 11 July 1963 (Gaz. Pal 1963 2.389; D. 1964 Somm. 26).

Note: Consider whether the next two cases are consistent with the previous ones, and with the general principle that the plaintiff can recover for economic harm.

Cour de cassation, 2e ch. civ., 12 June 1987, JCP 1987. IV. 286

The plaintiff was a partnership whose "president-general director" was injured in an accident for which the defendant was responsible. The plaintiff sued to recover for the financial harm that it had suffered because the injured man was unable to consummate deals which were then under negotiation on behalf of the partnership. The plaintiff objected that the *Cour d'appel* had denied relief without considering whether the partnership had a serious chance to conclude these contracts. The *Cour de cassation* upheld the decision below on the ground that the harm was not "certain" since their conclusion was "hypothetical."

Cour de cassation, 2e ch. civ., 21 February 1979, JCP 1979.IV.145

The plaintiff had loaned money to a husband and wife who were both killed in an accident for which defendant was responsible. Plaintiff could not recover the debt from their estate because it was insufficient, nor from the heirs of the couple, as would otherwise be permitted under French law, since they had renounced the inheritance, as they had the right to do. The plaintiff sued to recover it from the defendant. The court held that they could not recover because the causal relationship between the accident and the loss was insufficiently direct. The loss was also due to the decision of the heirs to renounce the right to the inheritance. It was also due to the failure of the creditor to insist that the debtors buy a life insurance policy.

b. No liability in principle for purely economic harm

Origins

In the late 19th and early 20th century, a rule emerged, first in Germany, and then in England and the United States, that the defendant was not liable for "pure economic harm" caused to the plaintiff. "Pure economic harm" is harm unaccompanied by physical damage to the plaintiff's person or property.

In Germany, the idea that the plaintiff should not be able to recover for any sort of harm was suggested by the Roman texts which remained in force in much of Germany until 1900. As we have seen, in almost all the Roman examples, the plaintiff has lost the use of a physical object even if it was not physically injured: for example, he could recover for the loss of a cup whether it was smashed or thrown into a river where he could not get it back. In the universities, most jurists concluded that the defendant should be liable only for harm to defendant's person and property.[1] Some merely pointed to the texts. Others, such as Rudolf von Ihering, argued that liability would be too extensive unless limited in some way:

> Where would it lead if everyone could be sued, not only for intentional wrongdoing (*dolus*) but for gross negligence (*culpa lata*) absent a contractual relationship! A ill-advised statement, a rumor passed on, a false report, bad advice, a poor decision, a recommendation for an unfit serving maid by her former employer, information given at the request of a traveler about the way, the time, and so forth—in short, anything and everything would make one liable to compensate for the damage that ensued if their were gross negligence despite one's good faith. . . .[2]

Nevertheless, by the end of the century, it seemed as though this approach would be abandoned for a broader one more like the French. It had been challenged by jurists such as Otto von Gierke and Josef Kohler who argued that the defendant should be liable for violation of a panoply of rights that concerned plaintiff's freedom of action and personality.[3] In 1888, then the *Reichsgericht*—the highest German court for civil matters— allowed a plaintiff to recover whose person and property had not been injured. He had been temporarily unable to sell a product because the defendant had been "negligent at least" in raising a claim of patent infringement.[4] Indeed, in their first draft, the First Commission charged with drafting the German Civil Code proposed the following provision:

> One who has caused another harm (*Schaden*) by intention or by negligence by an unlawful (*widerrechtlich*) act or omission is obligated to make him compensation.[5]

The reason, according to the Commission, was that:

> Any act is not permitted in the sense of the civil law by which anyone impinges and violates the sphere of rights of another unlawfully in an unauthorized manner. For the sphere of rights of each person must be respected and left untouched by all other persons; whoever acts contrary to this general command of the law without there being any special grounds for justification has by that alone committed a tortious act.[6]

---

1. For example, B. Windscheid, *Lehrbuch des Pandektenrechts* 2 (7th ed. 1891), §§ 451, 455; K.A. von Vangerow, *Lehrbuch der Pandekten* 3 (6th ed. 1863), § 681 n. 1.I (3); Arndts, *Lehrbuch der Pandekten* (14th ed. 1889), § 324. *See* Reinhard Zimmermann, *The Law of Obligations: Roman Foundations of the Civilian Tradition* (1990), 1036–38

2. R. von Jhering, "Culpa in contrahendo oder Schadensersatz bei nichtigen oder nicht zur Perfektion gelangten Verträgen," *Jherings Jahrbücher* 4 (1861), 12–13.

3. O. von Gierke, *Der Entwurf eines bürgerlichen Gesetzbuches und das deutche Recht* (1889), 264; O. von Gierke, *Deutsches Privatrecht* 3 (1917), 885–87; J. Kohler, "Recht

und Prozen," *Zeitschrift für das privatöffentliche Recht der Gegenwart* 14 (1887), 1 at 4–5; J. Kohler, *Lehrbuch des bürgerlichen Rechts* 1 (1904), § 132; 2 (1906), § 190. *See* K.-H. Fezer, *Teilhabe und Verantwortung* (1986), 456–65.

4. Reichsgericht, 3 Dec. 1888, RGZ 22, 208 at 209.

5. *Teilentwurf des Vorentwurfs zu einem BGB, Recht der Schuldverhältnisse* no. 15, § 1.

6. W. Schubert, ed., *Die Vorlagen der Redaktoren für die erste Kommission zur Ausarbeitung des Entwurfs eines Bürgerlichen Gesetzbuches, Recht der Schuldverhältnisse, Teil 1, Allgemeiner Teil* 1 (1980), 657.

Why, then, did the German Civil Code allow the plaintiff to recover only for the types of harm enumerated in what is now § 823? At one of its early meetings, the First Commission discussed "what is to be understood as the 'violation of a right:' only the violation of a right which receives an absolute protection or any violation of the legal order by an act prohibited by law as contrary to the legal order for the sake of himself." [7] The Commission eventually chose the first of these alternatives. For the Commission, it seemed to follow that the violation of rights such as person and property is tortious because such rights are "absolute" in the sense that they could be asserted against anyone. In contrast, a "right of obligation" (*obligatorisches Recht*) such as a contract right was a right only against the other party to the contract. The Commission noted that a tort was not committed by the violation of such a right because it "cannot be violated by anyone except the debtor [i.e., the party who is bound]." [8] Consequently, the Commission added a final sentence to clarify the type of right that must be violated. It went without saying that the paradigm case of a violation of a right was an interference with property. The Commission added, "The violation of life, body, health, freedom and honor are also to be regarded as the violation of a right in the sense of the previous provision." This language had mixed fortunes before it passed into what is now § 823(1). At one point it was deleted as unnecessary. Later it was put back, with an explicit mention of the right of property and the subtraction of "honor." The phrase "or similar right" (*sonstiges Recht*) was added because it had proven impossible to enumerate all of the ownership-like "absolute rights" that a defendant could violate.

The drafters had not been discussing "pure economic harm." They were distinguishing between "absolute rights," good against all the world, and "relative rights," good against a particular party. But if one could not recover against a third party for interference with these relative rights (let alone mere economic opportunities), then it followed that one could not recover for what we now call pure economic harm. The German courts reached that conclusion soon after the Civil Code came into force. In 1901, it held that a defendant who interfered with the plaintiff's economic freedom of action had not violated his "freedom" within the meaning of § 823(1).[9] In 1904, it held that economic harm (*Vermögensschädigung*) was not in itself harm to a right protected by § 823(1).[10]

In Germany, then, the rule against recovery for pure economic harm originally rested on what today would seem a conceptualistic argument: if A interferes with B's performance of a duty that B owes to C, then C cannot recover against A because C was owed the duty by B, not by A. The same argument surfaced in England in several leading treatises on tort law written in the early 20th century. By that time, in some cases, English courts had denied recovery for what we today would call pure economic loss. In 1875, in *Cattle v. The Stockton Waterworks Co.*,[11] plaintiff did not recover his

---

7. *Protokolle* 1: 971–72.
8. *Protokolle* 1: 984, 986–87.
9. Reichsgericht, 11 Apr. 1901, RGZ 48, 114.

10. Reichsgericht, 27 Feb. 1904, RGZ 58, 24.
11. (1875) L.R. 10 Q.B. 453.

extra expenses building a tunnel when defendant's negligence made construction more difficult by flooding of a third party's land. In 1877, in *Simpson & Co. v. Thomson*,[12] an insurance company was denied recovery for the insurance money it had to pay for insured cargo that was lost when one of defendant's ships negligently struck one of his own ships containing the cargo. In 1908, in *Anglo-Algerian Steamship Co. Ltd. v. The Houlder Line, Ltd.*,[13] plaintiff could not recover for the loss he suffered when his ship could not use a third party's dock which the defendant had negligently damaged. But the courts did not say the plaintiff could not recover because the loss was economic.[14] They said that if he could recover, liability would extend to too many possible plaintiffs.[15] In *Cattle* and *Anglo-Algerian Steamship*, they also said that the damage was too "remote."[16]

But then some of the earliest systematic English treatises on torts reinterpreted these cases. They used the same conceptualistic argument that had appealed to the German drafters. According to J.F. Clerk and W.H.B. Lindsell, *Cattle* stood for the principle that "interference with rights of service or with rights of contract generally is not actionable."[17] According to William Gordon and Walter Griffiths, who edited the 8th edition of C.G. Addison's treatise on contracts, the principle was that the defendant is liable only "where there is an obligation toward the plaintiff."[18] According to Sir John Salmond, in *Cattle*, the principle was that "nuisance is actionable only at the suit of the occupier or owner of the land affected by it; not at the suit of strangers whatever pecuniary interest they may have in the non-existence of the nuisance."[19] In *Anglo-Algerian Steamship*, the principle was that "[n]egligent injury to property gives an action to the owner of that property, or to other persons having some proprietary interest therein, but not to mere strangers who are thereby subjected to pecuniary loss."[20] Both cases were instances of *damnum sine iniuria*.[21] In later editions, he generalized the principle: "He who does a wrongful act is liable only to the person whose rights are violated."[22]

This approach was then picked up by the courts. It was adopted by Justice Hamilton in 1911 in deciding the case of *La Société Anonyme de Remorquage à Hélice v. Bennets*.[23] The defendant had negligently rammed and sank a ship owned by a third party which the plaintiff had been towing under contract. The plaintiff was not allowed to recover the money he would have made under the contract. The plaintiff's attorney had argued that he should recover because the damage was not "too remote."[24]

12. [1877] 3 A.C. 279 (H.L.).

13. [1908] 1 K.B. 659.

14. As noted by R. Bernstein, *Economic Loss* (2nd ed. 1998), 11.

15. L.R. 10 Q.B. at 457; [1877] 3 A.C. at 289.; [1908] 1 K.B. at 668.

16. L.R. 10 Q.B. at 457; [1908] 1 K.B. at 665.

17. J.F. Clerk & W.H.B. Lindsell, *The Law of Torts* (W. Paine, ed., 3rd ed. 1904), 11. At another point they do suggest that the case turned on the remoteness of the damage. *Ibid.* 133.

18. C.G. Addison, *A Treatise on the Law of Torts or Wrongs and their Remedies* (W.E. Gordon & W.H. Griffith, eds., 8th ed. 1906), 701.

19. J.W. Salmond, *The Law of Torts A Treatise on the English Law of Liability for Civil Injuries* (2nd ed. 1910), 10.

20. *Id.* 10.

21. *Id.* 8, 11.

22. Salmond, *The Law of Torts* (W.T.S. Stallybrass, ed., 8th ed. 1934), 133.

23. [1911] 1 K.B. 243.

24. [1911] 1 K.B. at 245.

Instead of arguing whether it was or not, the defendant's attorney said, in the words of Salmon, that "[a]lthough there was a breach of duty followed by damage to the owner of the tow, there was only iniuria sine damno so far as the tug was concerned."[25] Justice Hamilton agreed. Although the headnote to the case said that the plaintiff' harm was not the "direct consequence of the negligence," Hamilton said that the plaintiffs must "shew not only an iniuria, namely, the breach of the defendant's obligation, but also damnum to themselves in the sense of damage recognized by law."[26] Like the treatise writers, he cited *Cattle* as authority. This same explanation was given in 1922, in *Elliott Steam Tug Co. Ltd. v. Shipping Controller*. Plaintiff was not allowed to recover in tort for profits he lost when the Admiralty requisitioned his tug "not because the loss of profits during repairs is not the direct consequence of the wrong, but because the common law rightly or wrongly does not recognise him as able to sue for such an injury to his merely contractual rights."[27]

In the United States, Oliver Wendell Holmes gave the same explanation of why plaintiff could not recover in his famous opinion *in Robins Dry Dock & Repair Co. v. Flint*, 275 U.S. 302 (1927). While the boat that plaintiff had chartered from a third party was moored at defendant's dock for maintenance, the defendant negligently damaged the propeller. Plaintiff's thus lost the use of the boat for two weeks while repairs were made. Holmes said:

> The injury to the propeller was no wrong to the respondents but only to those to whom it belonged. But suppose that the respondent's loss flowed directly from that source. Their loss arose only through their contract with the owners—and while intentionally to bring about a breach of contract may give rise to a cause of action [citation omitted], no authority need be cited to how that, as a general rule, at least, a tort to the person or property of one man does not make the tortfeasor liable to another merely because the injured person was under a contract with that other, unknown to the doer of the wrong [citation omitted]. The law does not spread its protection so far. A good statement, applicable here, will be found in Elliott Steam Tug Co., Ltd. v. The Shipping Controller [1922] 1 K.B. 127, 139, 140. . . .

Today, the argument that had influenced the German drafters, the English treatise writers, and the English and American courts seems conceptualistic. It draws a conclusion about who should be liable for what from abstract definitions of the persons to whom rights are owed. Judges and legal scholars today prefer to think functionally, about what the law should be trying to accomplish. Nevertheless, German, English and American courts still say that in many situations, one cannot recover for pure economic harm.

25. [1911] 1 K.B. at 246.

26. [1911] 1 K.B. at 248.

27. [1922] 1 K.B. 127, 140.

Physical harm to a third party's property

Anglo-American law

Spartan Steel & Alloys Ltd v. Martin & Co (Contractors) Ltd, [1973] 1 QB 27 (C.A.)

"The plaintiffs manufactured stainless steel alloys at a factory which was directly supplied with electricity by a cable from a power station. The factory worked 24 hours a day. Continuous power was required to maintain the temperature in a furnace in which metal was melted. The defendants' employees, who were working on a near-by road, damaged the cable whilst using an excavating shovel. The electricity board shut off the power supply to the factory for 14 1/2 hours until the cable was mended. There was a danger that a 'melt' in the furnace might solidify and damage the furnace's lining, so the plaintiffs poured oxygen on to the 'melt' and removed it, thus reducing its value by £368. If the supply had not been cut off, they would have made a profit of £400 on the 'melt', and £1,767 on another four 'melts', which would have been put into the furnace. They claimed damages from the defendants in respect of all three sums. The defendants admitted that their employees had been negligent, but disputed the amount of their liability."

Lord Denning M.R. "The more I think about these cases, the more difficult I find it to put each into its proper pigeon-hole. Sometimes I say: 'There was no duty.' In others I say: 'The damage was too remote.' So much so that I think the time has come to discard those tests which have proved so elusive. It seems to me better to consider the particular relationship in hand, and see whether or not, as a matter of policy, economic loss should be recoverable. . . .

So I turn to the relationship in the present case. It is of common occurrence. The parties concerned are the electricity board who are under a statutory duty to maintain supplies of electricity in their district; the inhabitants of the district, including this factory, who are entitled by statute to a continuous supply of electricity for their use; and the contractors who dig up the road. Similar relationships occur with other statutory bodies, such as gas and water undertakings. The cable may be damaged by the negligence of the statutory undertaker, or by the negligence of the contractor, or by accident without any negligence by anyone; and the power may have to be cut off whilst the cable is repaired. Or the power may be cut off owing to a short-circuit in the power house; and so forth. If the cutting off of the supply causes economic loss to the consumers, should it as matter of policy be recoverable? And against whom?

The first consideration is the position of the statutory undertakers. If the board do not keep up the voltage or pressure of electricity, gas or water—or, likewise, if they shut it off for repairs—and thereby cause economic loss to their consumers, they are not liable in damages, not even if the cause of it is due to their own negligence. The only remedy (which is hardly ever pursued) is to prosecute the board before the justices. Such is the result of many cases. . . .

The second consideration is the nature of the hazard, namely, the cutting of the supply of electricity. This is a hazard which we all run. It may

be due to a short circuit, to a flash of lightning, to a tree falling on the wires, to an accidental cutting of the cable, or even to the negligence of someone or other. And when it does happen, it affects a multitude of persons; not as a rule by way of physical damage to them or their property, but by putting them to inconvenience, and sometimes to economic loss. The supply is usually restored in a few hours, so the economic loss is not very large. Such a hazard is regarded by most people as a thing they must put up with—without seeking compensation from anyone. Some there are who install a stand-by system. Others seek refuge by taking out an insurance policy against breakdown in the supply. But most people are content to take the risk on themselves. When the supply is cut off, they do not go running round to their solicitor. They do not try to find out whether it was anyone's fault. They just put up with it. They try to make up the economic loss by doing more work next day. This is a healthy attitude which the law should encourage.

The third consideration is this. If claims for economic loss were permitted for this particular hazard, there would be no end of claims. Some might be genuine, but many might be inflated, or even false. A machine might not have been in use anyway, but it would be easy to put it down to the cut in supply. It would be well-nigh impossible to check the claims. If there was economic loss on one day, did the applicant do his best to mitigate it by working harder next day? And so forth. Rather than expose claimants to such temptation and defendants to such hard labour—on comparatively small claims–it is better to disallow economic loss altogether, at any rate when it stands alone, independent of any physical damage.

The fourth consideration is that, in such a hazard as this, the risk of economic loss should be suffered by the whole community who suffer the losses—usually many but comparatively small losses—rather than on the one pair of shoulders, that is, on the contractor on whom the total of them, all added together, might be very heavy.

The fifth consideration is that the law provides for deserving cases. If the defendant is guilty of negligence which cuts off the electricity supply and causes actual physical damage to person or property, that physical damage can be recovered [citation omitted] and also any economic loss truly consequential on the material damage [citation omitted]. Such cases will be comparatively few. They will be readily capable of proof and will be easily checked. They should be and are admitted.

These considerations lead me to the conclusion that the plaintiffs should recover for the physical damage to the one melt (£368), and the loss of profit on that melt consequent thereon (£400); but not for the loss of profit on the four melts (£1,767), because that was economic loss independent of the physical damage. I would, therefore, allow the appeal and reduce the damages to £768."

Note on law in the United States, Australia and Canada:
American courts have denied recovery in similar cases; *e.g., Byrd v. English*, 43 S.E. 419 (Ga. 1902). Defendant, by negligently excavating, severed the power lines that served plaintiff's factory. The power lines belonged to the

Georgia Electric Light Co. which was under contract to provide plaintiff with power. The court held that plaintiff could not recover for the profit he lost when his work was delayed.

These cases, and those cited in the historical introduction, represent the traditional position in England and the United States. Australian and Canadian courts have recently taken what seems to be a different approach. In *Canadian National Railway Co. v. Norsk Pacific Steamship Co. Ltd.*, [1992] 91 DLR 4th 289, the plaintiff's barge damaged a bridge over the Fraser River. Even though the bridge was owned by a third party, the railroad recovered the costs it incurred rerouting its traffic. In *Caltex Oil Ltd. v. The Dredge Willemstad* [1976–77] 136 CLR 529, a dredger broke the underwater pipeline that the plaintiff, an oil company, had been using to transport its oil underneath Botany Bay. Even though the pipeline had belonged to a third party, the plaintiff recovered the cost of transporting its oil around the bay.

German law

Bundesgerichtshof, 9 December 1958, BGHZ 29, 65

Defendant cut an underground electric cable in the course of excavating the property of a third party which cut off the power to plaintiff's factory. The court held that the plaintiff could not recover. The court said that the right to run its enterprise without such interference was not a "similar right" (*sonstiges Recht*) with the meaning of BGB § 823 par. 1. Therefore "a claim for damages . . . for violation of a duty of care by the defendant is not taken into consideration. A culpable omission to fulfill such a duty only gives rise to a claim for damages when the other party has been injured in the rights, and legal interests protected by BGB § 823 par. 1. Even if the defendant has violated a duty of care by which he was bound, which can be left aside, the plaintiff has not suffered harm to the legal interests and absolute rights protected by BGB 823 par. 1 but economic harm."

Bundesgerichtshof, 4 February 1964, BGHZ 41, 123

Defendants were felling trees along a public street. One of them fell against a power line owned by the *Rheinisch-Westfälischen Elektrizitätswerke*, cutting off the electricity to plaintiff's incubators for six hours. As a result, the 3,600 eggs that plaintiff was incubating produced only a few unsalable chickens instead of the 3,000 chickens which would otherwise have hatched.

The court held that the plaintiff could recover for the loss of the chickens. "It does not matter for the liability of the injurer whether the damage to property is immediate or the result of a 'chain reaction' and, as limited by the requirement of adequate causation, that is so also when a characteristic of a thing injured initially caused harm to other objects. One who is at fault for breaking a water pipe must answer for the harm that other property suffers from the escaping water. One has a similar liability if he injures a conduit and causes the escape of oil, gas or electric current. In this case, there would have been liability for damages for harm to property if the falling tree had broken the electric wires and brought them into contact with the plaintiff's property, thereby destroying it. . . .

The peculiarity of the present case is due merely to the fact that the plaintiff's property was harmed by breaking off the electric current rather than misdirecting it. That cannot legally justify a difference in result. If, to preserve its substance, a thing needs a continual supply of water, electricity, or the like, then a person causes its destruction in the legal sense by cutting off this supply. Whoever culpably causes a breakdown of the irrigation apparatus of a garden or the heating of a hot house is therefore liable for the harm done to the plants, regardless of who is the owner. . . .

It is otherwise when the failure of electricity does not cause the destruction of a thing but to the interruption of the accomplishment of certain results. In that event the case is one of pure economic loss (*reiner Vermögensschaden*)."

Plaintiff's property made unusable

Law in the United States

People Express Airlines v. Consolidated Rail Corp., 495 A.2d 107 (N.J. 1985)

"[T]he defendants' alleged negligence . . . caused a dangerous chemical to escape from a railway tank car, resulting in the evacuation from the surrounding area of persons whose safety and health were threatened. The plaintiff, a commercial airline, was forced to evacuate its premises and suffered and interruption of its business with resultant economic loss. . . .

The single characteristic that distinguishes parties in negligence suits whose claims for economic losses have been regularly denied by American and English courts from those who have recovered economic losses is, with respect to the successful claimants, the fortuitous occurrence of physical harm or property damage, however slight. It is well-accepted that a defendant who negligently injures a plaintiff or his property may be liable for all proximately caused harm, including economic losses. Nevertheless, a virtually per se rule barring recovery for economic loss unless the negligent conduct also caused physical harm has evolved throughout this century, based, in part, on Robins Dry Dock & Repair Co. v. Flint, 275 U.S. 303 (1927) and Cattle v. Stockton Waterworks Co., 10 Q.B. 453 (1875). This has occurred although neither case created a rule absolutely disallowing recovery in such circumstances. . . .

It is understandable that courts, fearing that if even one deserving plaintiff suffering purely economic loss were allowed to recover, all such plaintiffs could recover, have anchored their rulings to the physical harm requirement. While the rationale is understandable, it supports only a limitation on, not a denial of, liability. The physical harm requirement capriciously showers compensation along the path of physical destruction, regardless of the status or circumstances of individual claimants. Purely economic losses are borne by innocent victims who may not be able to absorb their losses. In the end, the challenge is to fashion a rule that limits liability but permits adjudication of meritorious claims. The asserted inability to fix crystalline formulae for recovery on the differing facts of future cases simply does not justify the wholesale rejection of recovery in all cases."

German law

Bundesgerichtshof, 21 December 1970, BGHZ 55, 153

The defendant, the Federal Republic of Germany, is the owner of a canal, which connected a mill with a harbor. The canal became blocked, for a considerable time due to defendant's failure to perform its duties of maintenance. The plaintiff was under contract to the mill. Because the canal was closed, plaintiff's ship, the Christobel, could not get out of the canal and remained moored by the mill. Moreover, three of plaintiff's barges that were outside the canal could not enter and reach the mill. The court allowed plaintiff to recover damages for the temporary loss of the ship but not damages suffered on account of the barges.

"The injury to property in a thing can result, not only from an impairment of its substance, but also through an impingement on the power of the owner. (Soergel/Zeuner, BGB, 10th ed. § 823 no. 24; see also BGB-RGRK, 11th ed., § 823 no. 15; Lorenz, Lehrbuch des Schuldrechts vol. 2, 9th ed. p. 407.) In the present case an injury to the property of the plaintiff in the MS Christobel occurred because the ship had to remain at the loading dock of the mill because of the blocking of the canal. It therefore lost any possibility of moving beyond the point of the canal between the loading dock and the tree trunks blocking the canal. It therefore could not be put to its characteristic use as a means of transport. . . .

In contrast, it is otherwise for the plaintiff's claim for damages for the barges on account of the canal being impassible. The defendant did not cause an injury to property because the blocking of the canal did not concern the barges as to the characteristic that they are means of transport and did not take away their normal use. This conclusion is not affected by the fact that the plaintiff could not sail the barges to the loading dock of the mill while the canal was blocked. That is not to be considered an encroachment on ownership but a hindering of the common use of the canal that belonged to all ships."

False information

Consider whether the following cases are consistent with the previous ones, with each other, and with the principle that the plaintiff cannot recover for purely economic harm.

English law

Hedley Byrne & Co., Ltd. V. Heller & Partners, Ltd., [1964] AC 465 (H.L.)

"A bank inquired by telephone of the respondent merchant bankers concerning the financial position of a customer for whom the respondents were bankers. The bank said that they wanted to know in confidence and without responsibility on the part of the respondents, the respectability and standing of E. Ltd., and whether E. Ltd. would be good for an advertising contract for £8,000 to £9,000. Some months later the bank wrote to the respondents asking in confidence the respondents' opinion of the respectability and standing of E. Ltd. by stating whether the respondents considered E. Ltd. trustworthy, in the way of business, to the extent of £100,000 per annum. The respondents' replies to the effect that E. Ltd. was respectably constituted and considered good for its normal business engagements were communicated to the bank's customers, the appellants. Relying on these replies the appellants, who were advertising agents, placed orders for advertising time and space for E. Ltd., on which orders the appellants assumed personal responsibility for payment to the television and newspaper companies concerned. E. Ltd. went into liquidation and the appellants lost over £17,000 on the advertising contracts. The appellants sued the respondents for the amount of the loss, alleging that the respondents' replies to the bank's inquiries were given negligently, in the sense of misjudgment, by making a statement which gave a false impression as to E. Ltd.'s credit."

Lord Reid. "Before coming to the main question of law it may be well to dispose of an argument that there was no sufficiently close relationship between these parties to give rise to any duty. It is said that the respondents did not know the precise purpose of the inquiries and did not even know whether National Provincial Bank, Ltd. wanted the information for its own use or for the use of a customer: they knew nothing of the appellants. I would reject that argument. They knew that the inquiry was in connexion with an advertising contract, and it was at least probable that the information was wanted by the advertising contractors. It seems to me quite immaterial that they did not know who these contractors were: there is no suggestion of any speciality which could have influenced them in deciding whether to give information or in what form to give it. I shall therefore treat this as if it were a case where a negligent misrepresentation is made directly to the person seeking information, opinion or advice, and I shall not attempt to decide what kind or degree of proximity is necessary before there can be a duty owed by the defendant to the plaintiff. . . .

A reasonable man, knowing that he was being trusted or that his skill and judgment were being relied on, would, I think, have three courses open to him. He could keep silent or decline to give the information or advice sought: or he could give an answer with a clear qualification that he accepted no responsibility for it or that it was given without that reflection or inquiry which a careful answer would require: or he could simply answer without any such qualification. If he chooses to adopt the last course he must, I think, be held to have accepted some responsibility for his answer being given carefully, or to have accepted a relationship with the inquirer which requires him to exercise such care as the circumstances require. . . .

[I]t must follow that Candler v. Crane, Christmas & Co.,[18] was wrongly decided. There the plaintiff wanted to see the accounts of a company before deciding to invest in it. The defendants were the company's accountants and

---

18. [1951] 1 All E.R. 426; [1951] 2 K.B. 164.

they were told by the company to complete the company's accounts as soon as possible because they were to be shown to the plaintiff who was a potential investor in the company. At the company's request the defendants showed the completed accounts to the plaintiff, discussed them with him, and allowed him to take a copy. The accounts had been carelessly prepared and gave a wholly misleading picture. It was obvious to the defendants that the plaintiff was relying on their skill and judgment and on their having exercised that care which by contract they owed to the company, and I think that any reasonable man in the plaintiff's shoes would have relied on that. This seems to me to be a typical case of agreeing to assume a responsibility: they knew why the plaintiff wanted to see the accounts and why their employers, the company, wanted them to be shown to him, and agreed to show them to him without even a suggestion that he should not rely on them. . . .

[B]efore leaving Candler's case, I must note that Cohen, L.J. (as he then was), attached considerable importance to a New York decision Ultramares Corporation v. Touche,[21] a decision of Cardozo, C.J. But I think that another decision of that great judge, Glanzer v. Shepard,[22] is more in point because in the latter case there was a direct relationship between the weigher who gave a certificate and the purchaser of the goods weighed, who the weigher knew was relying on his certificate: there the weigher was held to owe a duty to the purchaser with whom he had no contract. . . .

Here, however, the appellants' bank, who were their agents in making the enquiry, began by saying that 'they wanted to know in confidence and without responsibility on our part', i.e. on the part of the respondents. So I cannot see how the appellants can now be entitled to disregard that and maintain that the respondents did incur a responsibility to them."

Law in the United States

Ultramares Corporation v. Touch, 174 N.E. 441 (N.Y. 1934)

Defendants were a firm of public accountants hired to prepare and certify the balance sheet of Fred Stern & Co. They knew the balance sheet would be shown to banks, creditors, stockholders, purchasers and sellers. They did not know it would be shown to the plaintiff in particular. Through defendants' negligence, the balance sheet showed Fred Stern & Co. to have a net worth of over $1,000,000. In fact, it was insolvent. The plaintiff sued for money it lost by dealing with Fred Stern & Co. in reliance on the balance sheet. The court denied recovery.

Cardozo J. "The defendants owed to their employer a duty imposed by law to make their certificate without fraud, and a duty growing out of contract to make it with the care and caution proper to their calling. Fraud includes the pretense of knowledge when knowledge there is none. To creditors and investors to whom the employer exhibited the certificate, the defendants owed a like duty to make it without fraud, since there was notice in the circumstances of its making that the employer did not intend to keep it to himself. A different question develops when we ask whether

---

21. (1931), 255 N.Y. 170.   **22.** (1922), 233 N.Y. 236.

they owed a duty to these to make it without negligence. If liability for negligence exists, a thoughtless slip or blunder, the failure to detect a theft or forgery beneath the cover of deceptive entries, may expose accountants to a liability in an indeterminate amount for an indeterminate time to an indeterminate class. The hazards of a business conducted on these terms are so extreme as to enkindle doubt whether a flaw may not exist in the implication of a duty that exposes to these consequences."

Glanzer v. Shepard, 233 N.Y. 236 (1922)

Defendants, who were engaged in business as public weighers, were requested by sellers of beans to weigh them and certify the weight. The beans were accepted and paid for on the faith of the certificates. Plaintiffs then found that the actual weight was less than the weight certified in the return, and sued defendants for the amount they overpaid. The court held defendants liable.

Cardozo J. "The plaintiffs' use of the certificates was not an indirect or collateral consequence of the action of the weighers. It was a consequence which, to the weighers' knowledge, was the end and aim of the transaction. . . . The defendants held themselves out to the public as skilled and careful in their calling. They knew that the beans had been sold, and that on the faith of their certificate payment would be made. They sent a copy to the plaintiffs for the very purpose of inducing action. All this they admit. In such circumstances, assumption of the task of weighing was the assumption of a duty to weigh carefully for the benefit of all whose conduct was to be governed. We do not need to state the duty in terms of contract or of privity. Growing out of a contract, it has none the less an origin not exclusively contractual. Given the contract and the relation, the duty is imposed by law."

White v. Guarente, 372 N.E. 315 (N.Y. 1977)

Defendants did the accounting for a limited partnership. In a limited partnership, the limited partners contribute capital and have limited liability: that is, the amount they can lose is limited to the amount they have invested. The general partners manage the partnership and have liability that is not limited: creditors can go after their personal assets if those of the partnership are insufficient. In this case, defendants were alleged to have been negligent in failing to discover that the general partners had withdrawn their own funds from the partnership in violation of the partnership agreement. The court held that, if so, they were liable to the limited partners:

"*Ultramares* . . . presented a noticeably different picture than that here, since there involved was an 'indeterminate class of persons who, presently or in the future, might deal with the [firm] in reliance on the audit'. . . .

Here, the services of the accountant were not tied to a faceless or unresolved class of persons, but rather to a known group possessed of vested rights, marked by a definable limit and made up of certain components. The instant situation did not involve prospective limited partners unknown at the time and who might be induced to join, but rather actual limited partners, fixed and determined. Here, accountant Andersen was retained to perform an audit and prepare the tax returns of Associates, known to be a limited partnership, and the accountant must have been aware that a limited partner would necessarily rely on or make use of the audit and tax returns of the partnership, or at least constituents of them, in order to properly prepare his or her own tax returns. This was within the contemplation of the parties to the accounting retainer. In such circumstances, assumption of the task of auditing and preparing the returns was the assumption of a duty to audit and prepare carefully for the benefit of those in the fixed, definable and contemplated group whose conduct was to be governed, since, given the contract and the relation, the duty is imposed by law and it is not necessary to state the duty in terms of contract or privity."

Credit Alliance Corp. v. Andersen & Co., 483 N.E.2d 110 (N.Y. 1985)

The court decided two companion cases. In both, lenders sought to hold accountants liable for negligence in preparing financial statements on which they had relied. In the first case (Credit Alliance) the court dismissed the action because, although Smith, the lender, had relied on the statement, the accountants had not been "employed to prepare the reports with the Smith loan in mind." In the second (European American Bank & Trust v. Strauhs & Kaye), the court permitted the action because the accounting firm "was well aware that a primary if not the exclusive, end and aim of auditing its client, Majestic Electro, was to provide EAB [the lender] with the financial information it required."

German law

Oberlandesgericht, Munich, 13 July 1956, BB 1956, 866

An enterprise had the defendants, a credit report company, prepare a statement of its financial worth so that, as the defendant knew, it could obtain a loan from the plaintiff, a bank. The bank granted the loan and cannot now recover it from the borrower. The statement was false as to some essential points and gave an overly favorable picture of the borrower. The bank recovered from the defendant.

"In the eyes of an outsider and therefore of the bank, from the time it was given, the financial statement must have been a piece of information whose correctness was guaranteed by the corporate entity that was the credit information company. This peculiarity makes that information binding in the sense that in giving the information it must have understood that as a matter of good faith, it was assuming liability for its correctness to the bank; for no party could have taken the view that the credit report company prepared the information only as the exclusive representative of the interests of the party who commissioned the report. In such a case, the question is not whether the party receiving and giving information were then bound by a contract. It is also irrelevant whether the parties giving and receiving information intended to establish contractual relations. It is enough that the party giving information to the one receiving it has, by preparing and sending the information, entered into a relationship that ought to be regarded as contractual as a matter of good faith and therefore should be determined to be contractual. Here, the existence of a contractual relationship between the bank and the credit report company is beyond doubt because that company sent the report directly to the bank. But even if it had given it to the person who commissioned it, that would not lead to a basic doubt about the existence of a contractual relation between the bank and the credit report company."

Bundesgerichtshof, 12 February 1979, NJW 1979, 1595

U., a third party, built a hotel, Hotel P., financed by a 2.5 million DM loan from defendant bank. It decided to raise a further 3.5 million DM from private investors. The defendants prepared a description of the deal that was to be proposed to these investors. The description mentioned that the hotel had been opened in the presence of many dignitaries; that it had already made long-term arrangements with several international travel agencies; that it was owned by U. "whom we know as a client and a competent businessman; that U. also owned a hotel in Teneriffe and two sanatoria; and that U. needed to raise the loan; and that U.'s "liquidity position is strained." The court found that this statement gave a false impression. It did not mention that the hotel and sanatoria had not been paid for, and that U. was no longer in a position to pay their bills. The court held defendant liable.

"All of the factual presuppositions are present for the defendant to be liable in damages for culpably preparing false information. According to established case law, when information is supplied by a bank, contract or contract-like relations exist between the information seeker and the credit institution when the information the bank supplies is known to be important to the other party and to be the basis of substantial measures with regard to its assets. (See Senat, NJW 1970, 1737 = AGB der Banken 10 no. 4.) The state of affairs in this case is not essentially different. Here the bank addressed a quite clearly defined group of interested persons, namely, the private lenders who were interested in granting a loan for the project Hotel P. The information was directed at this group which defendant had an interest in attracting and which he knew would be making substantial financial decisions on the basis of this information. This was its aim. It cannot legally make a difference whether the party seeking information turned to the bank or it went to them. In view of the purpose of the information the bank must recognize that those who receive the information will understand it as a legally binding declaration."

5. Harm suffered because another is harmed

Traditional Anglo-American law

Note on actions for loss of consortium and wrongful death: Traditionally, to recover in tort the plaintiff himself had to be struck, his land invaded, and so forth, depending on the form of action. A traditional English exception was that a husband could recover for loss of his wife's services, and a parent for loss of a child's services, apparently because the plaintiff was thought to have a sort of proprietary interest in receiving them.[1] This was called an action for loss of "consortium." One traditional

---

1. John G. Fleming, *The Law of Torts* (8th ed. 1993), 180.

limitation on the action was that the action could not be brought if the wife or child died—only if she or he was injured. *Baker v. Bolton*, (1804) 170 E.R. 1033 (K.B., Lord Ellenborough). Another limitation was that only the husband or parent could recover. In 1952, the House of Lords refused to allow a wife to recover for loss of her husband's consortium. The action for loss of consortium came to be regarded as archaic and anomalous. It was abolished in England by the Administration of Justice Act 1982 s. 2.

The action survives in the United States. Since 1950, American courts have allowed a wife whose husband is injured to recover for "loss of consortium." *Hitaffer v. Argonne*, 183 F.2d 811 (1950). All American jurisdictions now agree. Loss of consortium includes the "loss of the society and services of the first spouse, including impairment of the capacity for sexual intercourse, and for reasonable expense incurred by the second spouse in providing medical treatment." Restatement (Second) of Torts § 693(1). American courts today are split on whether a child whose parent has been injured can recover for loss of consortium: *e.g. Borer v. American Airlines*, 563 P.2d 858 (Cal. 1977) (Tobriner, J.) (child cannot recover); *Berger v. Weber*, 303 N.W.2d 424 (Mich. 1981) (child can recover). By the end of the 20th century, sixteen jurisdictions had recognized the child's right to recover.[2] A few courts have held that parents can recover for the loss of companionship of an adult child, even one who is not supporting them. *Howard Frank, M.D. P.C. v. Superior Court*, 722 P.2d 955 (Ariz. 1986) (severe brain damage). Siblings and step-parents have been denied recovery. *Ford Motor Co. v. Miles*, 967 S.W.2d 377 (Tex. 1998). One California court allowed an unmarried cohabitant to recover for loss of consortium. *Butcher v. Superior Court*, 188 Cal Rptr. 503 (Cal. App. 1983). But that result was rejected in *Elden v. Sheldon*, 758 P.2d 582 (Cal. 1988).

The other traditional limitation on an action for loss of consortium was that the husband or parent could not recover after the wife or child had died. This limitation was overcome by enacting statutes. In England, a action for wrongful death was created by Lord Campbell's Act of 1846. Fatal Accidents Act, 9 & 10 Vict. c. 93. In its current amended form, the action gives a claim for pecuniary damages to a limited class of persons, and a claim for "bereavement" to a still more sharply limited group. Pecuniary damages can be recovered by a spouse, former spouse, or person who "was living ... as the husband or wife of the deceased" in his or her household for two years prior to the date of death. Pecuniary damages can also be recovered by those who are or were treated by the deceased as parents or other ascendants, or children or other descendants. They can also be recovered by a brother, sister, uncle or aunt of the deceased plus their "issue." Fatal Accidents Act 1976 s. 1(3). In contrast, claims for bereavement can be brought only by the spouse of the deceased or by the parents of a minor who never married. These people can recover only a fixed amount which is currently £7,500.

The question we will be asking in this next section is when, aside from the actions just mentioned, can one person recover for grief or shock over an injury to another.

---

2.   Dan B. Dobbs, *The Law of Torts* (2000), 842, n. 3.

Note on liability for intentional conduct: On English law, read *Wilkinson v. Downton*, p. 248, above. On American law, read *Restatement (Second) of Torts* § 46 on p. 252, above. In the United States, the English case of *Wilkinson v. Downton* is usually thought of an instance of this new tort described in *Restatement (Second) of Torts* § 46, sometimes called "intentional infliction of emotional distress." Before this new tort was recognized, courts sometimes gave relief without explaining the grounds for doing so. Consider the following cases.

Hill v. Kimball, 13 S.W. 59 (Tex. 1890)

Defendant entered plaintiff's land and severely beat two laborers in her presence, knowing she was pregnant. She suffered a miscarriage. She recovered although it is not clear for what tort.

Lambert v. Brewster, 125 S.E. 244 (W. Va. 1924)

Defendant struck plaintiff's father in her presence. She suffered a miscarriage. She recovered although it is not clear for what tort.

Note on liability for negligent conduct: England adopted a so-called "zone of danger" rule in *Dulieu v. White & Sons*, [1901] 2 K.B. 669. The plaintiff who becomes ill due to shock can recover as long as he was exposed to the danger of being injured physically. There, the plaintiff recovered when the defendant's servant drove a van into the public house where the plaintiff was seated behind the bar.[1] Under this rule, the plaintiff could recover for shock at seeing another person injured but only if the plaintiff might have been physically injured himself. Some American courts adopted such a "zone of danger" test, and it passed into the first Restatement of Torts § 313(2).

Today, English law, and the law of many American jurisdictions, take a more liberal approach. We will look first at the rule adopted in California in *Dillon v. Legg*, and then at the English rule, which goes a step beyond it.

Modern law in the United States

Dillon v. Legg, 441 P.2d 912 (Cal. 1968)

A child was struck and killed by an automobile in the presence of his mother and minor sister. The mother was outside of the zone of danger; the sister may have been within it. Tobriner, J., speaking for the court, rejected the zone of danger rule and allowed both to recover. He said:

"Normally the simple facts of plaintiff's complaint would establish a cause of action: the complaint alleges that defendant drove his car (1) negligently, as a (2) proximate result of which plaintiff suffered (3) physical injury. Proof of these facts to a jury leads to recovery in damages; indeed,

---

1. The House of Lords affirmed this rule in *Page v. Smith* [1996] 1 A.C. 211, where the plaintiff had suffered nervous shock, though he was not injured physically, because of a minor collision between his vehicle and the defendant's. The court said: "Since the defendant was admittedly under a duty of care not to cause plaintiff foreseeably physical injury, it was unnecessary to ask whether he was under a separate duty of care not to cause foreseeable psychiatric injury."

such a showing represents a classic example of the type of accident with which the law of negligence has been designed to deal. The assertion that liability must nevertheless be denied because defendant bears no 'duty' to plaintiff begs the essential question—whether the plaintiff's interests are entitled to legal protection against the defendant's conduct. . . .

Since the chief element in determining whether defendant owes a duty or an obligation to plaintiff is the foreseeability of the risk, that factor will be of prime concern in every case. Because it is inherently intertwined with foreseeability such duty or obligation must necessarily be adjudicated only upon a case-by-case basis. We cannot now predetermine defendant's obligation in every situation by a fixed category; no immutable rule can establish the extent of that obligation for every circumstance of the future. We can, however, define guidelines which will aid in the resolution of such an issue as the instant one.

We note, first, that we deal here with a case in which plaintiff suffered a shock which resulted in physical injury and we confine our ruling to that case. In determining, in such a case, whether defendant should reasonably foresee the injury to plaintiff, or, in other terminology, whether defendant owes plaintiff a duty of due care, the courts will take into account such factors as the following: (1) Whether plaintiff was located near the scene of the accident as contrasted with one who was a distance away from it. (2) Whether the shock resulted from a direct emotional impact upon plaintiff from the sensory and contemporaneous observance of the accident, as contrasted with learning of the accident from others after its occurrence. (3) Whether plaintiff and the victim were closely related, as contrasted with an absence of any relationship or the presence of only a distant relationship.

The evaluation of these factors indicate the degree of the defendant's foreseeability: obviously defendant is more likely to foresee that a mother who observes an accident affecting her child will suffer harm than to foretell that a stranger witness will do so. Similarly, the degree of foreseeability of the third person's injury is far greater in the case of his contemporaneous observance of the accident than that in which he subsequently learns of it. The defendant is more likely to foresee that shock to the nearby, witnessing mother will cause physical harm than to anticipate that someone distant from the accident will suffer more than a temporary emotional reaction. All these elements, of course, shade into each other; the fixing of obligation, intimately tied into the facts, depends upon each case.

In light of these factors the court will determine whether the accident and harm was reasonably foreseeable. Such reasonable foreseeability does not turn on whether the particular defendant as an individual would have in actuality foreseen the exact accident and loss; it contemplates that courts, on a case-to-case basis, analyzing all the circumstances, will decide what the ordinary man under such circumstances should reasonably have foreseen. The courts thus mark out the areas of liability, excluding the remote and unexpected."

Note: The California court has been strict about the requirement of close relationship. In *Elden v. Shedon*, 758 P.2d 582 (Cal. 1988), a plaintiff who had witnessed the death of his unmarried cohabitant and was injured himself was not allowed to recover for negligent infliction of emotional distress and loss of consortium. Compare *Dunphy v. Gregor*, 642 A.2d 372 (N.J. 1994) (unmarried cohabitant recovers).

California has also been strict about the other requirements as well. In *Thing v. La Chusa*, 771 P.2d 814 (Cal. 1989), a mother whose child had been killed was not allowed to recover because she did not witness the accident. In *Tobin v. Grossman*, 249 N.E.2d 419 (N.Y. 1969), the plaintiff was not allowed to recover for "physical injuries caused by shock and fear" when her two year old child was seriously injured because she had not seen the accident, though she had been a few feet away, had heard the screech of brakes, and arrived at the scene a moment later.

Modern English law

McLoughlin v. O'Brian, [1983] A.C. 410

"The plaintiff's husband and four children were involved in a road accident at about 4 p.m. on October 19, 1973, when their car was in collision with a lorry driven by the first defendant and owned by the second defendants that had itself just collided with an articulated lorry driven by the third defendant and owned by the fourth defendants. The plaintiff, who was at home two miles away at the time, was told of the accident at about 6 p.m. by a neighbour, who took her to hospital to see her family. There she learned that her youngest daughter had been killed and saw her husband and the other children and witnessed the nature and extent of their injuries. She alleged that the impact of what she heard and saw caused her severe shock resulting in psychiatric illness.

Lord Wilberforce. "Although in the only case which has reached this House (Bourhill v. Young [1943] A.C. 92) a claim for damages in respect of 'nervous shock' was rejected on its facts, the House gave clear recognition to the legitimacy, in principle, of claims of that character. As the result of that and other cases, assuming that they are accepted as correct, the following position has been reached:

1. While damages cannot, at common law, be awarded for grief and sorrow, a claim for damages for 'nervous shock' caused by negligence can be made without the necessity of showing direct impact or fear of immediate personal injuries for oneself. The reservation made by Kennedy J. in Dulieu v. White & Sons [1901] 2 K.B. 669, though taken up by Sargant. L.J. in Hambrook v. Stokes Brothers [1925] 1 K.B. 141, has not gained acceptance, and although the respondents, in the courts below, reserved their right to revive it, they did not do so in argument. I think that it is now too late to do so. The arguments on this issue were fully and admirably stated by the Supreme Court of California in Dillon v. Legg (1968) 29 A.L.R. 3d 1316.

2. A plaintiff may recover damages for 'nervous shock' brought on by injury caused not to him- or herself but to a near relative, or by the fear of such injury. So far (subject to 5 below), the cases do not extend beyond the spouse or children of the plaintiff (Hambrook v. Stokes Brothers [1925] 1

K.B. 141, Boardman v. Sanderson [1964] 1 W.L.R. 1317, Hinz v. Berry [1970] 2 Q.B. 40–including foster children—(where liability was assumed) and see King v. Phillips [1953] 1 Q.B. 429).

3. Subject to the next paragraph, there is no English case in which a plaintiff has been able to recover nervous shock damages where the injury to the near relative occurred out of sight and earshot of the plaintiff. In Hambrook v. Stokes Brothers an express distinction was made between shock caused by what the mother saw with her own eyes and what she might have been told by bystanders, liability being excluded in the latter case.

4. An exception from, or I would prefer to call it an extension of, the latter case, has been made where the plaintiff does not see or hear the incident but comes upon its immediate aftermath. In Boardman v. Sanderson the father was within earshot of the accident to his child and likely to come upon the scene: he did so and suffered damage from what he then saw. In Marshall v. Lionel Enterprises Inc. [1972] 2 O.R. 177, the wife came immediately upon the badly injured body of her husband. And in Benson v. Lee [1972] V.R. 879, a situation existed with some similarity to the present case. The mother was in her home 100 yards away, and, on communication by a third party, ran out to the scene of the accident and there suffered shock. Your Lordships have to decide whether or not to validate these extensions.

5. A remedy on account of nervous shock has been given to a man who came upon a serious accident involving numerous people immediately thereafter and acted as a rescuer of those involved (Chadwick v. British Railways Board [1967] 1 W.L.R. 912). 'Shock' was caused neither by fear for himself nor by fear or horror on account of a near relative. The principle of 'rescuer' cases was not challenged by the respondents and ought, in my opinion, to be accepted. But we have to consider whether, and how far, it can be applied to such cases as the present.

Throughout these developments, as can be seen, the courts have proceeded in the traditional manner of the common law from case to case, upon a basis of logical necessity. If a mother, with or without accompanying children, could recover on account of fear for herself, how can she be denied recovery on account of fear for her accompanying children? If a father could recover had he seen his child run over by a backing car, how can he be denied recovery if he is in the immediate vicinity and runs to the child's assistance? If a wife and mother could recover if she had witnessed a serious accident to her husband and children, does she fail because she was a short distance away and immediately rushes to the scene (cf. Benson v. Lee)? I think that unless the law is to draw an arbitrary line at the point of direct sight and sound, these arguments require acceptance of the extension mentioned above under 4 in the interests of justice.

If one continues to follow the process of logical progression, it is hard to see why the present plaintiff also should not succeed. She was not present at the accident, but she came very soon after upon its aftermath. If, from a distance of some 100 yards (cf. Benson v. Lee), she had found her family by the roadside, she would have come within principle 4 above. Can it make any difference that she comes upon them in an ambulance, or, as here in a nearby hospital, when, as the evidence shows, they were in the same condition, covered with oil and mud, and distraught with pain? . . .

As regards proximity to the accident, it is obvious that this must be close in both time and space. It is, after all, the fact and consequence of the defendant's negligence that must be proved to have caused the 'nervous shock.' Experience has shown that to insist on direct and immediate sight or hearing would be impractical and unjust and that under what may be called the 'aftermath' doctrine one who, from close proximity, comes very soon upon the scene should not be excluded. . . .

Finally, and by way of reinforcement of 'aftermath' cases, I would accept, by analogy with 'rescue' situations, that a person of whom it could be said that one could expect nothing else than that he or she would come immediately to the scene—normally a parent or a spouse—could be regarded as being within the scope of foresight and duty. Where there is not immediate presence, account must be taken of the possibility of alterations in the circumstances, for which the defendant should not be responsible.

Subject only to those qualifications, I think that a strict test of proximity by sight or hearing should be applied by the courts.

Lastly, as regards communication, there is no case in which the law has compensated shock brought about by communication by a third party. In Hambrook v. Stokes Brothers [1925] 1 K.B. 141, indeed, it was said that liability would not arise in such a case and this is surely right. It was so decided in Abramzik v. Brenner (1967) 65 D.L.R. (2d) 651. The shock must come through sight or hearing of the event or of its immediate aftermath. Whether some equivalent of sight or hearing, e.g. through simultaneous television, would suffice may have to be considered."

Alcock v. Chief Constable of South Yorkshire Police, [1992] 1 AC 310

Shortly before the commencement of a major football match at a football stadium the police responsible for crowd control at the match allowed an excessively large number of intending spectators into a section of the ground which was already full, with the result that 95 spectators were crushed to death and over 400 injured. Scenes from the ground were broadcast live on television from time to time during the course of the disaster and were broadcast later on television as news items. News of the disaster was also broadcast over the radio. However, in accordance with television broadcasting guidelines none of the television broadcasts depicted suffering or dying of recognisable individuals.

Lord Keith of Kinkel. "I would not seek to limit the class by reference to particular relationships such as husband and wife or parent and child. The kinds of relationship which may involve close ties of love and affection are numerous, and it is the existence of such ties which leads to mental disturbance when the loved one suffers a catastrophe. They may be present in family relationships or those of close friendship, and may be stronger in the case of engaged couples than in that of persons who have been married to each other for many years. It is common knowledge that such ties exist, and reasonably foreseeable that those bound by them may in certain circumstances be at real risk of psychiatric illness if the loved one is injured or put in peril. The closeness of the tie would, however, require to be proved by a plaintiff, though no doubt being capable of being presumed in appropriate cases. The case of a bystander unconnected with the victims of an accident is difficult. Psychiatric injury to him would not ordinarily, in my view, be within the range of reasonable foreseeability, but could not perhaps be entirely excluded from it if the circumstances of a catastrophe occurring very close to him were particularly horrific. . . .

Of the present appellants two, Brian Harrison and Robert Alcock, were present at the Hillsborough ground, both of them in the West Stand, from which they witnessed the scenes in pens 3 and 4. Brian Harrison lost two brothers, while Robert Alcock lost a brother-in-law and identified the body at the mortuary at midnight. In neither of these cases was there any evidence of particularly close ties of love or affection with the brothers or brother-in-law. In my opinion the mere fact of the particular relationship was insufficient to place the plaintiff within the class of persons to whom a duty of care could be owed by the defendant as being foreseeably at risk of psychiatric illness by reason of injury or peril to the individuals concerned. The same is true of other plaintiffs who were not present at the ground and who lost brothers, in one case a grandson. I would, however, place in the category of members to which risk of psychiatric illness was reasonably foreseeable Mr and Mrs Copoc, whose son was killed, and Alexandra Penk, who lost her fiance. In each of these cases the closest ties of love and affection fall to be presumed from the fact of the particular relationship, and there is no suggestion of anything which might tend to rebut that presumption. These three all watched scenes from Hillsborough on television, but none of these depicted suffering of recognisable individuals, such being excluded by the broadcasting code of ethnics, a position known to the defendant. In my opinion the viewing of these scenes cannot be equiparated with the viewer being within 'sight or hearing of the event or of its immediate aftermath', to use the words of Lord Wilberforce in McLoughlin v. O'Brian [1982] 2 All ER 298 at 305 [1983] 1 AC 410 at 423 . . . ."

French law

The French Civil Code in arts. 1382–83 merely speaks of "harm" (*dommage*). One sort of harm recognized by French law is "harm by ricochet" (*dommage par richochet*). This sort of harm occurs when an injury to one person causes harm to another. Thus when one spouse is killed or disabled, the other spouse or a child can sue for loss of support under arts. 1382–83. In principle, however, such a claim does not need to be made by a near relative or even a relative. Someone who was living with the injured person or having an affair with him can recover. When, exactly, is not clear. In allowing such an action, the *Chambre mixte* of the *Cour de cassation* insisted that the relationship had to be stable and that it could not be adulterous. Decision of 27 Feb. 1970, D. 1970.201. When suit was brought by two women over the death of a man who preferred to eat at home with one of them and spend the night with the other, recovery was denied them both on the grounds that such a relationship must have been unstable. Cour de cassation, ch. crim., 8 Jan. 1985, *Gaz. Pal.* 1985.2.480. Moreover, the Criminal Chamber of the *Cour de Cassation* has allowed recovery even if the relationship is adulterous. Cour de Cassation, ch. crim., 3 May 1977, Bull. crim. 1977.3.374. Accordingly, a lower court allowed two women to recover when a man died who was married to one of them. Cour d'appel, Riom, 9 Nov. 1978, *JCP* 79.II.19107.

The question examined in the following cases is when one can recover for grief or shock.

Boris Starck, Henri Roland & Laurent Boyer, *Obligations* 1. *Responsabilité délictuelle* §§ 155, 157–58, 160 (4th ed. 1991)

"The number of persons who can claim to have suffered physical or economic harm [*dommage matériel*] by richochet (*ricochet*) is necessarily limited. In contrast, the number who suffer or claim to suffer non-physical harm (*damage morale*) can be considerable. This harm can occur in the case of the death of a person dear to one, whose disappearance is the source of sorrow; it can occur also if the direct victim survives because it is painful for those around him to see him reduced or infirm; it can also occur absent any physical harm when, for example, it is a question of an injury to honor from which those near to him suffer. . . .

Throughout the 19th century, the case law proved liberal, referring only to the notion of harm without any other limitation. There were decisions allowing recovery to dozens of people, to two concubines at the same time as five brothers and sisters of the victim. . . .

After such excesses, the case law reacted and raised a double barrier (*barrage*) to recovery.

The first goes back to a decision made by the *Chambre des requêtes* [of the *Cour de cassation*] on 2 February 1931 . . . In that case, G., a woman who was the mother of the mistress of Mr. O., had raised his illegitimate child, born of a different liaison, Mrs. G., although she had no family tree or even a tie of blood with the girl, raised her and treated her as if she were her own child. There was no dispute as to the affection that united them. When the young girl was killed in an accident, Mrs. G claimed damages for injury to her feelings (*préjudice d'affection*) which no one denied that she had suffered. The judges of first instance granted them, but the *Cour d'appel* refused to do so. The *pourvoi* [to the *Cour de cassation*] was rejected. . . . [T]he *Chambre des requêtes* declared that "compensation for injury to feelings can be taken into consideration only if the claimant is bound to the victim by a tie of parenthood (*parenté*) or marriage 'which was not the case here.'". . .

[The second barrier was the requirement of the death of the victim.] Many decisions declared that only the death of the victim could support a claim for recovery. In case of his survival, only he could claim damages.] . . .

This double barrier was not going to be maintained: the case law had to take a more liberal position.

Note: The more liberal position will be seen emerging in the following cases.

Cour de cassation, 2e ch. civ., 16 February 1967, Bull. civ. 1967.II. no. 77

A child injured by the defendant was in danger of death for two weeks and remained 15% permanently disabled on account of headaches, difficulty sleeping, and "a little instability." The *Cour d'appel* denied his parents for compensation for their own suffering. The *Cour de cassation* upheld that decision on the grounds that the harm to the child did not have the "exceptional character" that would allow the parents to recover.

Cour de cassation, 2e ch. civ., 23 May 1977, Bull. civ. II, no. 139, p. 96

A son whose father had been totally incapacitated in an accident caused by the defendant sought recovery for the suffering he experienced seeing his father in such a state. The *Cour d'appel* rejected his claim on the ground that the harm was not of "exceptional gravity." Although totally incapacitated, the father was not bed-ridden and could give his son advice and show him affection. The *Cour de cassation* overturned that decision on the ground that "the only proof required is of personal harm suffered by the son that is certain and direct." Article 1382 "applies as much to non-physical harm (*damage morale*) as to physical harm (*dommage matériel*)."

In a note on this decision, Durry remarked: "One could not more clearly abandon the earlier position according to which harm to those near the victim was compensable only if it was of exceptional gravity, precisely the position on which the judges below had expected to avoid censure.

De lege lata, we can only approve this reaffirmation of the rule contained in the decision of 8 December 1971 which also seemed to us to be appropriate (this *Revue* 1974.601). Once one admits compensation for non-physical harm (*dommage morale*), one cannot see in the name of what legal argument one can reject the claim of those close to a surviving victim who can prove the pain that the state of this victim has caused them. Indeed, in addition one must be exacting as to this proof in order to avoid cascades of mythical claims. But to us personally it does not appear scandalous that a son claims to have suffered at the spectacle of his father disabled one hundred percent." G. Durry, RTDC 1977, 768 at 769.

Cour de cassation, 2e ch. civ., 20 January 1967, 1967 Bull. civ. II, no. 30

The *Cour d'appel* allowed a ward to recover for his suffering at the death of a guardian for whose death the defendant was responsible. The guardian was the father of the child's mother and raised him from the age of two months. The *Cour de cassation* upheld this decision.

In a note on these two cases, Durry said: "The second civil chamber as one knows has had reservations about actions to recover for non-physical harm (*préjudice morale*) brought by other persons than the initial victim of an accident. If the victim has survived, the *Cour de cassation* is especially reticent: it will only allow the action if the other party—in practice, the father or the mother—suffered non-physical harm of an exceptional nature. (Cass. civ. 22 Oct. 1946, JCP 1946.3.365, D. 1947, 59; Cass., 2d civ. ch., 15 Feb. 1956, D. 1956.350 . . .). In contrast, if the victim is deceased, the second civil chamber is less strict, while requiring, in conformity with the case law that began with a well-known decision of 2 February 1931 of the *Chambre des requêtes* [of the *Cour de cassation*] a bond of kinship or marriage between the victim of the injury and those who wish compensation for non-physical harm caused by his decease. . . .

[As to the decision of 16 February 1967, refusing to allow recovery when the child was disabled:] "If one admits the principle espoused by the court because it prevents too many claims, nevertheless, its application to this case seems overly hard. To our mind, it is not only a question of 15% permanent disability but of the danger of death which this child ran for fifteen days. If that is not a non-physical harm of exception of gravity for the parents, then these words do not have much meaning! No doubt, normally the parents will deem themselves only too happy that their child has escaped death and will not claim any compensation on this account. But if they do, on what ground can they be refused compensation? Or, indeed, should the very principle of recovery for non-physical harm be reconsidered (Cf. Ripert, *Le prix de douleur*, Chron. D. 1948.1), but that does not seem to be the position adopted by the case law."

[As to the decision of 20 January 1967 allowing the ward to recover:] "It is true that the case is one of the most favorable for recovery, the guardian having raised the child from the age of two months and being the father of the child's mother. . . . Evidently, given the very special character of the case, one cannot conclude that the second civil chamber has abandoned its earlier restrictive position. But it remains true that this decision is incompatible with that position . . . and that it can be considered a breach . . . in a bastion that can see no decisive reason for not dismantling entirely. If pain is real, there ought to be recovery." G. Durry, *Rev. trim. dr. civ.* 1967, 815 at 815–16.

Cour de cassation, 1e ch. civ., 16 January 1962, JCP 1962.II.12557

The plaintiff's race horse was accidentally electrocuted while in a stall provided by the defendant, *Société Hippique de Langdon*, on whose premises the horse had been brought for a race. Plaintiff sought recovery, not merely for the value of the horse, but for sorrow suffered at its death. Such damages were granted by the *Cour d'appel*, and the award was upheld by the *Cour de cassation*: "Independently of the material harm that it entails, the death of an animal can also cause harm to its owner that is subjective and to the feelings (*effectif*) which is subject to compensation; . . . in this case the *Cour d'appel* was able to determine that the harm suffered . . . was not limited to the sum necessary to buy another animal possessing the same qualities . . . it was equally appropriate in computing damages to include a sum to compensate for the harm caused by the loss of an animal to which he was attached."

Cour de cassation, ch. crim., 1 March 1973, JCP 1974.II.17615

Under French law, those who have been injured by the commission of a crime can be awarded compensation in the criminal proceeding brought against the defendant. Here, the wife and brother of a man killed by the defendant in a traffic accident sought damages for a psychological injury they had suffered as a result: depression. They asked the *Cour de cassation* to overturn a refusal by the appellate court to order that expert evidence be taken concerning this injury. The *Cour de Cassation* refused to do so. "[T]he *Cour d'appel* stated that if the commission of an involuntary homicide directly caused an injury to the feelings (*préjudice d'affection*) to those close to the victim, nevertheless the physical harms that the decease of the victim by repercussion on these near ones do not flow directly from the infraction and cannot be made the object of a demand for compensation. . . ."

Professor Viney, in her note on this case, said that the decision might be due to a desire to restrict liability "in response to a certain excess in the awarding of damages, notably for the sorrow experienced by the death or wounds inflicted on an animal . . . ." She concluded: "If we should think that such was the intention of the magistrates of the supreme court, we would not hesitate to criticize it. It would be singularly inequitable to refuse compensation for sorrow precisely at the moment when it goes beyond the threshold the psyche of the victim can bear, although compensation may always be obtained for 'reasonable' unhappiness. Moreover, on a juridical level, one may remark that when sorrow takes the form of physical troubles, granting compensation is not open to any of the objections traditionally addressed to compensation for non-physical harm (*dommage morale*): proof can be made by medical expertise, and while it's evaluation is not easy, it does not entail greater difficulties than those of evaluating physical harm."

German law

Note on actions for loss of support: Section 844(2) of the German Civil Code allows a plaintiff to recover for loss of support which the person killed was legally obligated to provide. The action only arises when the deceased person could have recovered against the defendant. The people who are under such a duty to provide support are identified in §§ 1360, 1570, 1601, 1615, 1736, 1739, 1754, and 1755. Section 845 allows a plaintiff to recover for loss of services which the person killed was legally obligated to perform. Again, the cases that follow deal with recovery for grief or shock at the death of another person.

Landgericht, Frankfurt am Main, 28 March 1969, NJW 1969, 2286

The defendant was a drunk driver who negligently drove onto the sidewalk and killed the plaintiff's companion, a member of the United States Air Force, who was walking with her hand in hand. She suffered minor physical injuries and a severe nervous shock for which she was treated for two months in a university nerve clinic. Thereafter, she remained nervous and fearful in traffic, she was often sleepless; she suffered nervous symptoms such as neck and back pains, and at the memory of the accident, she would break helplessly into tears. The court allowed her recovery for the shock and its after effects. She claimed that she and her companion had been engaged and planned to marry soon. The defendant denied that they were engaged.

"The shock of the accident . . . is to be considered an injury to health within the meaning of BGB § 823 par. 1. . . . That the psychic injury suffered by the plaintiff did not lead to organic harm does not contradict the conclusion that an injury to health occurred. Insofar as occasional divergent views appear in the case law (see, most recently, Landgericht Krefeld, VersR 69, 166), they fail to understand that limiting the concept of an injury to health to organic injury is irreconcilable with the modern scientific understanding of the nature of disease, and accordingly with the concept of an injury to health. . . .

It is true that the case law has previously recognized only an injury through the death of a nearest relative as a factual circumstance that will give rise to liability, but that is too narrow. . . . It is often forgotten in discussions of so-called 'damage by remote effect' (*Fernwirkungsschaden*), that it is a question of the immediate application of BGB § 823 par. 1, and when, as here, there is fault and causation, then there is a claim under BGB § 823 par. 1. Accordingly, in general, it does not matter whether the plaintiff was engaged to her companion or not. It may be that, as a rule, news of the death of a person is only sufficient to cause an injury to health to another when that person is a near relative. But this is not a case of nervous shock brought on by the news of a person's death but of a consequence produced by the immediate experience of the death of another person. That such a psychically mediated causation should be recognized is an obvious consequence of the wording of BGB § 823 par. 1."

Bundesgerichtshof, 11 May 1971, BGHZ 56, 163

The plaintiff's husband, a sixty-four year old man, was killed in a traffic accident for which defendant was responsible. The plaintiff, a fifty year old, suffered injury to her health upon learning that he had died. She was not present when the accident occurred. The court described the circumstances under which she could recover and then remanded the case for further findings.

"The decision of the appellate court is not to be sustained insofar as it affirms that in general, a pure injury to the plaintiff's health is caused by the news of an accident. (See BGH, Decision of 9 November 1965, Sixth Civil Senate 260/63 = VersR 1966, 283, 285ff. OLG Freiburg VZ 1953, 709, 705.)

The law in force deliberately rejects—aside from some particular cases that do not matter here—a claim for harm through mental pain insofar as the pain is not itself the result of an injury of one's own body or one's own health. It is consistent with this decision of the legislator that a person has an independent claim who has been caused a physical or mental/psychological injury to his health by the effect of experiencing an accident or receiving news of it. The recognition of a claim for compensation is not barred by the circumstance that in a particular case this unusual reaction to the experience occurred only on the basis of a preexisting organic or physical instability and that the experience of the accident therefore had only the effect of setting it off. The suggestion of Stoll to the contrary (*Gutachten fur den 45. Deuschen Juristentag*, 1964, p. 20) can therefore not be accepted. . . .

Otherwise, it must be noted that, according to general knowledge and experience, a strong negative experience that gives rise to such feelings as pain, sorrow and horror usually disturbs physiological processes and mental functions in noticeable ways. It would be inconsistent with the binding decision of the enacted law to recognize such disturbances as injuries to health within the meaning of BGB § 823 par. 1 (Stoll, op. cit., pp. 19ff.). Rather, in cases in which the psychologically mediated effect on health is not willed by the actor, then, independent of the issue of adequate causation, recovery must be limited to such harms which are considered to be injuries to body or health, not merely from a medical point of view, in the normal affairs of life (Stoll, op. cit., p. 21; see the numerous references to the inconsistent practice of the courts of first instance in Blick, *Haftung für psychisch verursachte Körperverletzungen*, Dissertation Freiburg, 1970, pp. 7 ff.).

Consequently, under some circumstances, injuries must go without compensation which, indeed, are medically verifiable, but do not have the character of 'shock-like' incursions on health so, as a rule, their can be no independent claim for compensation for disadvantages to one's state of health which are often not small ones that experience shows accompany a deeply experienced sorrowful event."

Landgericht, Hildesheim, 25 Oct. 1968, VersR 1970, 720

The plaintiff sought to recover for shock she experienced on learning that her husband had been in an accident, caused by the defendant, which had slightly damaged the car which he owned and was driving. The *Landgericht* denied recovery on the grounds that it is outside normal experience that such an event would cause an injury to the health of a person who had not even experienced the accident herself. Therefore, there was no "adequate causal relationship" between her injury and the accident for which the defendant was responsible.

II. THE CONDUCT FOR WHICH ONE IS LIABLE

1. Introduction

A fundamental idea in civil law and modern common law is that there are three distinct grounds holding a person liable in tort: he might have harmed someone intentionally, or negligently, or by engaging in an activity for which he is strictly liable. In civil law, this distinction is ancient. In Roman law, a plaintiff could recover under the *lex Aquilia* for harm the defendant caused by *culpa*, that is, by fault.[1] In the broad sense, fault

---

1. *See* Reinhard Zimmermann, *The Law of Obligations: Roman Foundations of the Civilian Tradition* (1990), 1007–09.

included *dolus* or intentionally causing harm.[2] Most often, however, the Romans had in mind what we call negligence. As we will see, if the defendant was not at fault, sometimes the plaintiff could still recover, though not under the *lex Aquilia*. The cases in which he could were heterogeneous. Eventually, the Romans lumped them together as "quasi torts" (*quasi ex delicto*).[3]

As we have already seen, like the *lex Aquilia*, the French and German Civil Codes impose liability for intentional or negligent misconduct. Neither code made provision for liability without fault, but, as we will see, French courts and the German legislature have recognized such liability. Thus in modern civil law, the grounds for liability are those recognized by the Romans: intent, negligence, and in certain situations, liability without fault.

Until the 19th century, the common law did not draw these distinctions. As we saw earlier, the plaintiff had to bring his case within one of the recognized forms of action. If the defendant had struck him, he could sue for trespass in assault and battery, if the plaintiff had entered his land he could sue for trespass quare clausum fregit, and so forth (see pp. 240–46, above). If the facts did not quite fit any of the trespass actions, he could bring an action called trespass on the special case or trespass on the case. He might do so, for example, if the plaintiff did not strike him but did something that caused him to be physically injured. In trespass on the case, he would have to plead the special facts that, in his view, entitled him to recover. Whether he could recover on these facts was up to the judges.

There is a long-standing debate over to whether the plaintiff was liable in either type of action absent fault. As Milsom and Fifoot have pointed out, the question is misleading because, traditionally, the common lawyers did not clearly distinguish fault-based and strict liability.[4]

If the plaintiff sued in one of the trespass actions, he did not need to allege fault. For example, he might simply allege that the defendant shot him or struck him. The defendant might then "plead the general issue" by answering with the set phrase "not guilty." Or he might set up a defense by making a special plea, in effect, admitting the trespass and offering some justification. It is hard to tell whether either course of action would allow a defendant to escape liability if he was not at fault in the sense in which civil lawyers or modern common lawyers understand fault. Suppose, for example, that the defendant struck the plaintiff because his horse bolted, either because the horse was high strung or because it was frightened by a flash of lightening or a third party or an animal. If the defendant pled, "not guilty," the jury was supposed to decide whether this allegation was true or false, originally, without instructions from the judge as to what to consider. It is hard to know what juries did.[5] They may have found for the defendant if they believed that the bolting of the horse that he was riding was really not something he did, that he was the passive instrument of forces

---

2. *Id.* 1005, 1027.
3. Inst. 4.5.
4. S.F.C. Milsom, *Historical Foundations of the Common Law* (1981), 392–98; C.H.S.

Fifoot, *History and Sources of the Common Law Tort and Contract* (1949), 189, 191.
5. Milsom, *Historical Foundations of the Common Law* 393.

of nature, a third party, or the animal he was riding. Possibly, they did so if they believed that he had not committed a trespass or wrong, whatever that might have meant to them. In the trespass actions, the common law did not really have a rule in such cases but a procedure: let the jury decide.

The defendant's other alternative was to plead, in justification, that he was not at fault. It was not clear what would happen then. Defendants did so in only a few cases, and the remarks of the judges are confusing and seem contradictory. Some judges said that the defendant was not liable if he had done his best,[6] some said that he was,[7] and some said he could escape liability if his conduct were the product of "unavoidable necessity."[8] It is hard to know what these statements meant to the judges who made them. They may not have been thinking in terms of a clear distinction between fault-based and strict liability. For example, in *Weaver v. Ward*, when a company of part-time soldiers were drilling with muskets, one soldier injured another because his musket accidentally went off. He pleaded that it was not his fault. The court said that he would be excused if he were "utterly without fault," if the accident were "inevitable," and if he "had committed no negligence to give occasion to the hurt."[9] As Fifoot said of this case, " '[f]ault,' 'inevitable accident,' 'negligence' are words used indiscriminately without reflection and almost without meaning."[10]

On account of these uncertainties, the plaintiff might sue, not in a trespass action, but in trespass on the case and allege that the defendant acted negligently in his statement of the facts that supposedly called for relief. Sometimes, the plaintiff did so.[11] But even then, it is not clear what the allegation meant.[12] It might or might not mean negligence in the modern (or ancient Roman) sense. Certainly, judges did not instruct the jury to ask themselves whether the defendant had behaved like a reasonable person. In any event, the defendants also brought actions of trespass on the case without alleging negligence.[13]

---

6.   *E.g.*, The Thorns Case, Y.B. Mich. 6 Ed. 4, f. 7, pl. 18 (1466) (Choke, C.J.: "As to what has been said that they [thorns] fell ipso invito [on another's land], this is not a good plea; but he should have said that he could not do it in any other manner or that he did all that was in his power to keep them out"); Millen v. Fandrye Popham 161 (1626) (defendant excused because he has "done his best endeavor"); Wakeman v. Robinson, 1 Bing. 213 (1823) (Dallas, C.J.: "If the accident happened entirely without default on the part of the defendant or blame imputable to him, the action does not lie").

7.   The Thorns Case, Y.B. Mich. 6 Ed. 4, f. 7, pl. 18 (1466) (Littleton, J.: "If a man suffers damage, it is right that he be recompensed."); Bessey v. Olliot, Sir T. Raym. 421, 467 (1682) (Sir Thomas Raymond: "in all civil acts the law doth not so much regard the intent of the actor as the loss and damage of the party

suffering"); Leame v. Bray, 3 East. 593 (1803) (Grose, J.: "if the injury be done by the act of the party himself at the time or he be the immediate cause of it, though it happen accidentally or by misfortune, yet he is answerable in trespass).

8.   Dickenson v. Watson, Sir T. Jones 205 (1682) (defendant who had shot the plaintiff and pleaded accident not excused "for in trespass the defendant shall not be excused without unavoidable necessity").

9.   Weaver v. Ward, Hobart 134 (1616).

10.   Fifoot, *History and Sources of the Common Law* 191.

11.   Milsom, *Historical Foundations of the Common Law* 394.

12.   *Id.* 399; A.I. Ogus, "Vagaries in Liability for the Escape of Fire," *Cambridge Law Journal* 27 (1969), 104, 105–06.

13.   *Id.* 394.

In the 19th century, the forms of action were abolished: the plaintiff could merely plead the facts that entitled him to recover without naming a certain form of action. Supposedly, the substantive law remained the same: the plaintiff could recover after the forms of action were abolished provided that he could have recovered under one of them before they were abolished. In fact, the law changed a good deal.

One of the changes was the rise of what we now call an action in negligence. A first step was to hold that the plaintiff could not recover for bodily injuries which the defendant caused accidentally and without negligence. In the United States, this step was taken in Massachusetts in 1851 by Chief Justice Shaw.[14] In England, it was not taken until 1891.[15] In the 1870s, some courts also held that a defendant would not be liable for trespass to land if he acted neither intentionally nor negligently.[16] As Prosser pointed out, it would be illogical not to take this step as well: it was "no great triumph of reason" to hold that if a streetcar jumped its track, its operator was liable for injuring a pedestrian if he was negligent, but that he was liable, negligent or not, for injuring the plate glass window behind the pedestrian.[17] In his first edition, written in 1941, Prosser could only say that "indications are" that the old rule for trespass to land "is undergoing modification." The indications he cited were the first Restatement of Torts and four cases, three of them decided in the 1870s.[18]

Having recognized a tort of "negligence," Americans concluded that the defendant must have acted intentionally to be liable in one of the trespass actions such as battery. As we have seen, in England, in 1965, Lord Denning took that position, although there is still a dispute over whether he was right.[19] English courts agree, however, that the defendant is not liable for committing these torts if he acted neither intentionally nor negligently.[20]

The common law courts also recognized that in certain cases the defendant was liable without fault. The first case was *Rylands v. Fletcher*[21] in which the owner of a reservoir was held liable without fault when the water escaped. The case was followed in the United States where eventually the principle was said to be that the defendant is liable for carrying on abnormally dangerous activities.

Thus by the 20th century, the common law had recognized the same three grounds for liability as that the civil law had recognized for centuries.

---

14. 60 Mass. 292 (1850).

15. Stanley v. Powell, 1 Q.B. 86 (1891).

16. *See* River Wear Commissioners v. Adamson [1877] 2 App. Cas. 743, 751 in which Lord Cairns said that one was liable at common law for "damage occasioned by wilful or negligent misconduct" as distinguished from "act of God."

17. William L. Prosser, *Handbook of the Law of Torts* (1941), 77–78.

18. *Id.*, citing Nitro-Glycerine Case, Parrott v. Wells Fargo & Co., 15 Wall 524 (U.S. Sup. Ct. 1872), 21 L. Ed. 206; Brown v. Collins, 53 N.H. 442 (1873); Losee v. Buchanon, 51 N.Y. 476 (1873); and "cf." Dobrowolski v. Penn. R. Co., 178 A. 488 (Pa. 1935).

19. [1965] 1 QB 232.

20. In Stanley v. Powell [1891] 1 Q.B. 86; Fowler v. Lanning [1959] 1 Q.B. 156.

21. [1826] L.R. 3 H.L. 330.

2. Intent

a. The intention to do harm or to do wrong

Civil law

Francois Terré, Philippe Simler & Yves Lequette, *Droit civil Les obligations* (7th ed. 1999), § 696

"*Intentional fault.* This fault, which is also called delictual, must be defined in the same way as intentionally wrongful fault (*faute dolosive*) in the area of contracts. It exists when the author of the harm acted intentionally in order to cause a prejudice to another and probably when he acted in a manner that he must have known would injure another."

Wolfgang Fikentscher, *Schuldrecht* (9th ed. 1997), no. 503

"In contrast to negligence, the concept of intent is not defined in the German Civil Code but left for legal scholarship and case law to clarify. According to the prevailing view, a person acts intentionally who mentally *envisions* the result of his action and receives it in his *will* even though he *knows* that it is a violation of duty. Intention is therefore the knowledge and will for an unlawful result, or more precisely, the knowledge and will for a result with the awareness that it is unlawful."

Common law

W.V.H. Rogers, *Winfield & Jolowicz on Tort* (15th ed. 1998), 66, 472

"For battery, there must be a voluntary act by the defendant intended to bring about contact with the plaintiff. I do not commit battery against you if X seizes my arm and uses it like a club—here X and X alone is liable. But the act need be intentional only as to the contact and intention to bring about the harmful consequence is not required. . . .

[I]t is clear law that an entry upon another's land is tortious whether or not the entrant knows that he is trespassing. Thus it is no defence that the only reason for his entry was that he had lost his way or even that he genuinely but erroneously believed that the land was his. It follows that the great majority of trespasses to land are, for legal purposes, self-evidently intentional—I intend to enter upon your land if I consciously place myself upon what proves to be your land even though I neither knew nor could reasonably have known that it was not mine. . . .

Trespass [to goods] . . . remains appropriate where one takes another's goods in the mistaken belief that he is entitled to do so, for the act is intentional towards the goods." [citations omitted]

Ellis v. D'Angelo, 253 P.2d 675 (Cal. App. 1953)

"According to the allegation the plaintiff was by the minor defendant 'pushed, impelled and knocked . . . violently to the floor' and suffered serious injuries including a fracturing of the bones of both her arms and wrists." At the time, the defendant was four years old.

"[A]n infant is liable for his torts even though he lacks the mental development and capacity to recognize the wrongfulness of his conduct so long as he has the mental capacity to have the state of mind necessary to the commission of the particular tort with which he is charged. Thus as between a battery and negligent injury an infant may have the capacity to intend the violent contact which is essential to the commission of battery when the same infant would be incapable of realizing that his heedless conduct might foreseeably lead to injury to another which is the essential capacity of mind to create liability for negligence."

Note on the "intention" required by the common law: In England and the United States, the standard view is that to be liable for intent, the defendant need not intend to do wrong. He merely needs to intend to do the act that defines the tort in question: the unauthorized contact, the entry on land, the carrying off of goods, and so forth. To call this the traditional position of the common law is misleading. As we have seen, before the 19th century, the common law did not distinguish between intention and negligence as a basis for liability. The question of what the defendant must have intended did not arise.

It did arise once it became accepted that the defendant was only liable for intentional and negligent conduct. But to two of the first to write systematic treatises on tort law—Sir Frederick Pollock and John Salmond—it seemed obvious that if the defendant were to be liable for acting intentionally, then the intention that mattered in principle must be the intention to cause harm or do wrong. Both writers were familiar with Roman law and the civil law of their own day. They thought the intent required must be the same in common law as in civil law. Pollock claimed that in the case of "personal wrongs" such as battery, assault, false imprisonment, slander and libel, liability is imposed where, "generally speaking, the wrong is wilful or wanton. Either the act is intended to do harm, or, being an act evidently likely to cause harm, it is done with reckless indifference to what may befall by reason of it."[1] He concluded that "the Roman conception of delict agrees very well with the conception that appears really to underlie the English law of tort."[2] According to Salmond, "[i]n general, though subject to important exceptions, a tort consists in some act done by the defendant whereby he has wilfully or negligently caused some form of harm to the plaintiff." There must be (a) damage and (b) "wrongful intent or culpable negligence".[3]

The problem was that under the common law forms of action, the defendant could be held liable even if he did not intend to do harm or wrong. Pollock addressed that problem when he discussed trespass to land and to chattels. He acknowledged that the defendant might be liable when he came on plaintiff's land even though he thought it was his own. In such cases, he

1. Sir Frederick Pollock, *The Law of Torts. A Treatise on the Principles of Obligations Arising from Civil Wrongs in the Common Law* (8th ed. 1908), 9.

2. *Id.* 17.

3. John W. Salmond, *The Law of Torts. A Treatise on the English Law of Liability for Civil injuries* (4th ed. 1916), 8.

said, there is an "absolute duty not to meddle . . . with land or goods that belong to another."[4] For a moment, he considered discarding this rule as an archaic feature of the forms of action that had no place in modern law. "We are now independent of the forms of action." "[A] rational exposition of tort law is free to get rid of extraneous matter brought in, as we have shown, by the practical exigency of conditions that no longer exist."[5] But he decided that the traditional rule was innocuous because it usually gave the right result. "A man can but seldom go by pure unwitting misadventure beyond the limits of his own dominion."[6] "If not wilfully or wantonly injurious, it is done with some want of due circumspection, or else it involves the conscious acceptance of a risk." Thus in all but "exceptional cases," strict liability would not result in "real hardship."[7] Thus for Pollock, in principle, intent-based liability required an intention to do harm wrongfully. Liability for trespass to land and chattels was not based on intent.

But the problem went beyond trespass to land and chattels. Traditionally, liability for battery, assault, false imprisonment and defamation had not turned on whether the defendant had acted intentionally any more than on whether he had acted negligently. Consequently, the defendant could not escape liability by proving that he had been mistaken as to the identity of the victim, or the existence of a privilege, or whether a statement was defamatory, any more than he could escape liability for trespass to land by proving he was mistaken as to privilege or ownership. One approach would have been to say, as Pollock did, that since we are now independent of the forms of action, we should reexamine whether such a defendant should be liable. But that was not the approach that of the treatise writers who were his near contemporaries. They took it for granted, as he did, that if liability were to be based on intent, the intent that mattered was an intent to do harm or wrong. But they invented reasons why the law imposed liability even absent that intent. According to Vold, the defendant was liable for mistakes in identity because "the risk . . . should be placed on the intentional wrongdoer rather than his innocent victim".[8] He did not explain why an actor who made a reasonable mistake should count as a wrongdoer. According to Smith, "an *intentional* entry standing alone and unexplained involves fault."[9] He did not ask why the law will not let such a person make an explanation. Salmond thought that the reason was "the evidential difficulties in which the law would find itself involved if it consented to make any inquiry into the honesty and reasonableness of a mistaken belief which a defendant set up as an excuse for his wrongful act."[10] He did not say why the defendant was held liable even if there were no evidential difficulties. These writers thus suggested that the law had already considered and answered a question which, in fact, no one had faced: whether, if liability were to depend on intent, the defendant should be held liable absent a intent to do wrong or harm.

4. Pollock, *The Law of Torts* 10.
5. *Id.* 15.
6. *Id.* 16.
7. *Id.* 11.
8. Lawrence Vold, 9 *Neb. L. Rev.* 17 (1938), 149.

9. Jeremiah Smith, "Tort and Absolute Liability—Suggested Changes in Classification—II," *Harv. L. Rev.* 30 (1917), 319.
10. Salmond, *The Law of Torts* 116.

This approach paved the way for the quite different one taken by the Seavy, Harper, Prosser, the Restatements, and English writers today.[11] They took it for granted that the defendant who did not intend harm or wrong could be held liable. According to them, however, the reason was that the kind of intention that mattered was different. According to Seavy, it was the intention "to deal with the things or with the interests of others." He claimed that "[t]he liability of one whose words unexpectedly prove to be defamatory can be based, in most instances, on his intent to deal with another's reputation." "[M]ost nuisance cases," he said, "involve a realization by the defendant that he is interfering with the factual interests of others."[12] Similarly, Harper claimed that the intention that matters is "to violate a legally protected interests of the plaintiff."[13] In the case of trespass to land or chattels the defendant need merely intend "the immediate effect of his act which constituted the interference with plaintiff's possession." Therefore a mistake as to ownership or privilege was no defense.[14] To be liable for defamation "the defendant must have intended to publish the defamatory matter, i.e., he must have voluntarily published the statement which harms the plaintiff's reputation and thus invades his legally protected interests." But he need not have intended that anyone's reputation be harmed.[15] Similarly, Prosser said that the intention that matters is not a desire to do harm but "an intent to bring about a result which will invade the interests of another in a way the law will not sanction."[16] He drew the same conclusions as Harper. So did the Restatements.[17] So do English writers such as W.V.H Rogers, R.F.V. Heuston and R.A. Buckley.[18] And in this way, Anglo-American jurists finally arrived at what is sometimes termed the traditional position of the common law.

b. The intent to cause a different harm or commit a different tort

Law in the United States

Talmage v. Smith, 59 N.W. 656 (Mich. 1894)

"On the evening of September 17, 1891, some limekilns were burning a short distance from defendant's premises, in Portland, Ionia county.

---

11. Beale had yet another explanation. He said that someone who enters land mistakenly thinking it is his own "acts on a mistake as to his own authority." The mistake cannot "give him an authority which in law or in fact he lacks Joseph H. Beale, "Justification for Injury," *Harv. L. Rev.* 41 (1928), 553. He did not explain why one who enters land without authority and without believing that he has authority is liable only if the entry is negligent but one who makes such a mistake is liable without negligence.

12. Warren Seavy, "Principles of Torts," *Harv. L. Rev.* 56 (1942), 72.

13. Fowler Vincent Harper, *A Treatise on the Law of Torts. A Preliminary Treatise on Civil Liability for Harms to Legally Protected Interests* (1933), 41.

14. *Id.* 55.

15. *Id.* 504.

16. Prosser, *Law of Torts* 40–41.

17. Restatement of Torts § 13, § 13 cmt. d, § 158, § 158 cmt. e, § 577, § 580 (1934); Restatement (Second) of Torts § 13, § 13 cmt. c, § 158, § 158 cmt. f (1965). In response to the constitutional challenges to no-fault liability, the second Restatement changed its rules to include a requirement of fault for liability in defamation. Restatement (Second) of Torts §§ 580, 581.

18. W.V.H. Rogers, *Winfield and Jolowicz on Tort* (15th ed. 1998), 66, 472–73; R.E.V. Heuston & R.A. Buckley, *Salmond and Heuston on the Law of Torts* (21st ed. 1996), 41, 121.

Defendant had on his premises certain sheds. He came up to the vicinity of the sheds, and saw six or eight boys on the roof of one of them. He claims that he ordered the boys to get down, and they at once did so. He then passed around to where he had a view of the roof of another shed, and saw two boys on the roof. The defendant claims that he did not see the plaintiff, and the proof is not very clear that he did, although there was some testimony from which it might have been found that plaintiff was within his view. Defendant ordered the boys in sight to get down, and there was testimony tending to show that the two boys in defendant's view started to get down at once. Before they succeeded in doing so, however, defendant took a stick, which is described as being two inches in width and of about the same thickness and about 16 inches long, and threw it in the direction of the boys; and there was testimony tending to show that it was thrown at one of the boys in view of the defendant." The stick missed him and struck the plaintiff.

"The right of the plaintiff to recover depend[s] upon an intention on the part of the defendant to hit somebody, and to inflict an unwarranted injury upon some one. Under these circumstances, the fact that the injury resulted to another than was intended does not relieve the defendant from responsibility. . . . The case is to be distinguished from a case of negligence on the part of defendant. The act is found by the jury to have been a willful act."

Wyant v. Crouse, 86 N.W. 527 (Mich. 1901)

"The plaintiffs commenced an action by declaration against the defendant to recover damages for the destruction of a blacksmith shop and other property by fire. The declaration stated that he wrongfully broke into the shop, and started a fire in the forge, and the undisputed proof shows that he did so. . . .

The testimony shows that the defendant was a blacksmith, who sometimes worked in the shop for plaintiffs' son, who occupied the shop as plaintiffs' tenant; that on this occasion he went to the shop to sharpen some shoes, built a fire in the forge, did his work, and went away. It is in evidence that the wind was blowing, and that, about 10 minutes after he went away, the shop was discovered to be on fire in the southwest corner of the building, the forge being in the northeast corner, and the flames coming out from the roof. . . .

We agree with the circuit judge that there is no proof tending to show an absence of ordinary care, but there certainly is proof tending to show that the only fire on the premises came from that started by the defendant. . . .

In the case before us, the defendant intended no such injury, nor did he any act which can be said to have given reason for expecting the consequences. It was a fortuitous consequence of his act, entirely unforeseen. . . .

The liability of the defendant is based upon a wrongful act, and the nature of the act, and not the consequences, determines his liability. He was engaged in an unlawful act, and therefore was liable for all of the consequences, indirect and consequential as well as direct, and there is no occasion to discuss the degree of his negligence in permitting the shop to burn, if the fire was caused by the fire he built."

[Normally, the plaintiff would have recovered in trespass. Since the statute of limitations had run for a trespass action, the court allowed him to recover in trespass on the case.

English law

In English criminal law, if A shoots at B and hits C, he would be guilty of intentionally shooting C under a doctrine called "transferred malice." English courts have not yet ruled on whether there is a similar doctrine in tort. The case below comes from Northern Ireland.

Livingstone v. Ministry of Defence, [1984] N.I. 356 (C.A.) (Northern Ireland)

"It was common case that on the afternoon of Sunday, 23 September 1979, the plaintiff was struck and injured by a baton round [a plastic bullet] fired by a soldier at a time when the security forces had cordoned off streets in the vicinity of Davis Street and Millfield in Belfast in order to prevent an unlawful procession reaching the centre of the city. . . . The defence did not plead any specific defence justifying the firing of the baton round, such as that the baton round was fired to disperse rioters, or constituted such force as was reasonable in the circumstances in the prevention of crime under section 3(1) of the Criminal Law Act (Northern Ireland) 1967, or that the baton round was fired in self-defence." The plaintiff sued for negligence and for "assault, battery and trespass." The court below dismissed the first claim on the ground that the plaintiff had not shown negligence. The plaintiff appealed from his failure to rule on the second claim.

"Mr. Kerr's principal submission in reply to this question was that the tort of battery was not committed unless the defendant, or the servants or agents of the defendant, deliberately fired a round with the intention of striking the plaintiff, and Mr. Kerr submitted that if, in dispersing a riot, a soldier fired a shot at one rioter in the riotous crowd but missed him and struck another rioter in the crowd, the soldier had not committed battery against the rioter who was struck (assuming that the force used was unjustified) because the soldier had not intended to hit that particular rioter. Therefore Mr. Kerr argued that the soldier who fired the baton round which struck the plaintiff was not guilty of the tort of battery towards him, because there was no evidence that the soldier had intended to hit the plaintiff and the soldier may well have intended to hit a rioter but struck the plaintiff by mistake." Kerr cited Lord Denning M.R. in Letang v. Cooper [1965] 1 Q.B. 232 at page 239D ["If one man intentionally applies force directly to another, the plaintiff has a cause of action in assault and battery, or, if you so please to describe it, in trespass to the person."] and Winfield & Jolowicz on Tort (12th ed.) at page 54 ["Battery is the intentional and direct application of force to another person."]

"However, I consider it to be clear that when Lord Denning and Winfield and Jolowicz refer to doing an injury 'intentionally' or to the 'intentional' application of force, they mean that the application of force towards some person is intended, even although the person directly struck may not be the person whom the assailant intended to strike. In my judgment when a soldier deliberately fires at one rioter intending to strike him and he misses him and hits another rioter nearby, the soldier has 'intentionally' applied force to the rioter who has been struck. Similarly if a soldier fires a rifle bullet at a rioter intending to strike him and the bullet strikes that rioter and passes through his body and wounds another rioter directly behind the first rioter, whom the soldier had not seen, both rioters have been 'intentionally' struck by the soldier and, assuming that the force used was not justified, the soldier has committed a battery against both." In support the court cited James v. Campbell (1832) 5 Car. & P 372, 172 E.R. 1015:

> "It appeared that, at a parish dinner, the plaintiff and defendant (who it seemed were not on good terms, in consequence of something which took place with respect to a leet jury), together with a Mr. Paxton and others were present. Mr. Paxton and the defendant quarreled, and had proceeded to blows, in the course of which the defendant struck the plaintiff, and gave him two black eyes, and otherwise injured him. . . .

> Mr. Justice Bosanquet (to the jury). If you think as I apprehend there can be no doubt, that the defendant struck the plaintiff, the plaintiff is entitled to your verdict, whether it was done intentionally or not."

German law

Bundesgerichtshof, 8 March 1951, NJW 1951, 596

In 1944, the defendant reported the plaintiff to the German authorities for listening to an allied radio broadcast. The plaintiff was arrested. On December 24, 1944, while he was still under arrest, the town was bombed by the allies, and the plaintiff's goods were destroyed. After the war, the plaintiff claimed compensation under §§ 823 and 826 of the Civil Code. The *Bundesgerichtshof* held that the incarceration of the plaintiff was the "adequate cause" of the destruction of the goods since the risk of an air attack was significant in 1944, and the plaintiff might have been able to save them if he had been at liberty. "Adequate cause" plays the same role in German law as "proximate cause" in American law. Then the court addressed the issue of intent.

"Intent is a will directed to the unlawful result. What is required is the awareness that the act or omission will have the harmful result, or that it could have this result and is willed even if it has although the intention to harm is not necessary. If a person has culpably willed an unlawful result, then in general he is liable for the harm that is caused, either in contract (§ 280 Civil Code) or in tort for the injury to a protected legal interest (§ 823(1)) even though the actor was not aware of the further harmful consequences of his unlawful conduct and even though his intention or negligence did not include these further consequences. (Enneccerus-Lehman, *Lehrbuch des Bürgerlichen Rechts Recht der Schuldverhältnisse* 13th ed., 61; Lehmann, *Allgemeiner Teil des BGB*, 5th ed., 263).

It would be a mistake, however, to accept this principle without a further distinction. In contrast to § 823(1), where the intention needs to extend only to the harm to particular protected legal interests, intention under § 826 must embrace the harmful consequences in their entirety. Although, in the former case, the actor who wills to harm a protected legal interest is liable for all of the consequences that follow even if he was unaware of them because the injury to a protected interest must be foreseen but not the harmful result (RGZ 57, 239; *id.* 58, 214), § 826 requires that the intention relates to bringing about the harm because the tort consists in bringing about harm (BGB *RGRK*, 9th ed., § 823 no. 2; RGZ 142, 122). [Thus under § 826] the defendant could have harmed the plaintiff intentionally only if he was aware that the plaintiff could lose his goods by being arrested and wanted him to be arrested so that he would, or when he was aware that the plaintiff could lose his goods and conditionally willed to accept this as a possible result which he envisioned and consented to it in the event that it occurred. (RGZ 56, 78; RG JW 29, 3149; BGB RGRK, 9th ed., § 826 no. 3; Palandt, *BGB*, 8th ed., § 826 no. 3; Enneccerus-Lehmann, 13th ed., 898). A conditional intention would be ruled out if the defendant had been convinced that no harm to plaintiff's things could occur. (RG Warn. Rspr. 1914 no. 109; RG JW 29, 3149). It would also be ruled out if the defendant considered the loss of them to be unlikely but, on the other hand, it is not required that he consider the loss to be likely. If he was not aware, the fact that he should have been aware of the possible loss of plaintiff's things is never enough since mere negligence of this kind is not a substitute for intent (RGZ 57, 238; *id.* 143, 52).

The proof that would be needed for the defendant when he reported the plaintiff to have the intent required by § 826 would only be unnecessary if the plaintiff sought compensation from another legal standpoint, namely, for deprivation of freedom under § 823(1). In contrast to § 826, this section requires unlawfulness. Making the report for listening to a foreign broadcast and interference with military potential (*Wehrkraftzersetzung*) cannot be accepted as unlawful unless more is shown. Proof must be made that the defendant was aware that he was acting unlawfully, and that issue must be investigated by the appellate court.

[The case was remanded for a finding on this issue and on whether the defendant might have been aware the plaintiff could lose his goods and, if so, whether he conditionally intended their loss.]

Note: In a comment to this decision (NJW 1951, 596 at 597) Prof. Helmut Coing said that the *Bundesgerichtshof* placed the appellate court in a dilemma: "either to say that reporting someone for listening to a foreign broadcast in 1944 was lawful and gives rise to no claim for compensation, or to bypass the requirement of unlawfulness of § 823(1) which, in my opinion, must be understood to refer to positive law."

Note: During the Nazi period, interference with military potential (*Wehrkraftzersetzung*) was an all-purpose crime that allowed the regime to prosecute anyone whom it deemed had done too little for the war effort or who had hindered it in any way.

Oberlandesgericht, Schleswig, 10 August 1976, VersR 1977, 718

"The plaintiff and the defendant (born 18 September 1960) were school fellows at a high school. On 18 December 1974, during class, the defendant threw a so-called geometry triangle made of plastic in the direction of student E. who was sitting in the next row diagonally to the right. The triangle flew by him and struck the plaintiff who was sitting diagonally behind him, striking his left eye which was seriously injured.

The plaintiff . . . claimed that the defendant had already had a quarrel with E. in the break before class and that this continued into the German lesson. She intentionally threw the triangle at him in order to hit him. It reached and struck the unsuspecting plaintiff only because E. ducked his head.

The defendant . . . claimed that the quarrel between her and E. had nothing to do with the throwing of the triangle. He had tapped her lightly, and she thought that he wanted to have the triangle back, and so she threw it with a gentle motion in his direction."

[Injuries in school are covered by a German social insurance statute which provides that a civil action can be brought against a person who harms another only if he did so intentionally. RVO §§ 539, 540, 636 ff.]

"It does not matter with what motivation the defendant threw the triangle in the direction of E. who was sitting diagonally behind her. It is irrelevant to the circumstances necessary for the exclusion of liability of the RVO whether it is determined that, as the plaintiff maintains though contradicted by the testimony of witnesses, she wished to give back the triangle she had borrowed from him or that, instead, she threw the triangle after a quarrel and to carry out a more or less serious prank or possibly also to cause pain. For if the defendant did act intentionally with regard to an injury to E., albeit an insignificant one, that does not have the least importance as regards the plaintiff who was completely disinterested. She certainly did not wish to injure him. The plaintiff can show nothing to the contrary. Her conception is unfounded that an intention must be ascribed to the defendant as regards plaintiff which is the same as the intention the defendant had as regards E. because of 'aberratio ictus' [which means 'a blow gone astray']. That legal expression describes an event that, on the contrary, is a typical case of negligence as regards the person struck to whom the conduct of the actor—here the throw—did not relate."

Note: In the last two cases, the courts held that a defendant who intended to cause the plaintiff one kind of harm is liable if he inadvertently causes the plaintiff one he did not intend, but he is not liable if he intended to cause harm to one plaintiff and caused the same kind of harm to another. Consider why and whether, if the defendant is liable in the one case, he should not be liable in the other.

French law

Cour de cassation, 1e ch. civ., 5 January 1970, D. S. 1970.J.155

One night the son of the insured party shot at some burglars to prevent them from escaping. He killed a neighbor who had been standing in the window of his own house and whom he did not see. The *Cour d'appel* held that the act was not intentional and therefore the defendant insurance company was liable despite art. 12(2) of the Law of 13 July 1930 of the Insurance Code. The defendant argued that the shooting of the neighbor was intentional whether the son had been trying to hit the burglars or trying to shoot out the tires of their car. The *Cour de cassation* upheld the decision below. It said:

> "There is no intentional fault within the meaning of art. 12(2) of the Law of 13 July 1930 unless the harm that occurred was wanted by its author."

Note: Nevertheless, French courts do not require that the author wanted to cause all of the harm that occurred. Cass, 1st Civ. Ch., 7 June 1974 Bull. civ. 1974.147 no. 168 (rugby player who kicked another player held to have intentionally caused more harm than he wanted to inflict).

Cour de cassation, 2e ch. civ., 14 December 1987, arrêt no. 1.307, pourvoi no. 86-17.537

Pierre Prebose, while hunting, came on Henry Escalette's property where there was a "no trespassing, no hunting" sign. For him to come there to hunt was a violation of arts. 365 and 374 of the Rural Code (*Code rural*). While he was standing a few meters from Escalette's house, Escalette in a "gesture of irritation," grabbed the rifle that Prebose was carrying and struck it against a block of cement in an effort to break it. The rifle went off twice and injured Escalette who sued for compensation. The *Cour d'appel* of Toulouse rejected his claim under art. 1382. The *Cour de cassation* said:

> "Whereas, in rejecting the claim of the victim, the decision [below] merely noted that the accident would not have happened if M. Escalette had not committed the 'folly' of taking away the weapon and striking it against a concrete block;
>
> Whereas in so determining, even though M. Prebose was hunting with a loaded rifle on the property of M. Escalette and a few meters from his house despite a sign prohibiting anyone from entering and hunting, the *Cour d'appel* did not give its decision a legal justification, the decision below is quashed and the case remanded to the *Cour d'appel* of Pau."

Note: In the previous case, the defendant did not intend to harm the plaintiff or his property. Nor does it seem he behaved negligently: would a careful hunter remove his cartridges before entering another's land because otherwise an incensed owner might grab his weapon, strike it against a cement block, and cause an injury? Consider why the court may have held the defendant liable anyway.

Note on the history of liability for the unforeseen consequences of unlawful activities: Notice that Anglo-American courts that hold the defendant liable for the unforeseen consequences of an intentional act phrase their rule in two different ways. Sometimes they say, as in

Talmage v. Smith, that "[t]he right of the plaintiff to recover depend[s] upon an intention on the part of the defendant to hit somebody" and that it doesn't matter who he hit.[1] That makes it sound as though there are two types of fault-based liability, intent and negligence, and that the defendant is liable because of his intent. But sometimes courts say, as in *Wyant v. Crouse,* that "[t]he liability of the defendant is based upon a wrongful act, and the nature of the act, and not the consequences, determines his liability. He was engaged in an unlawful act, and therefore was liable for all of the consequences. . . ." That makes it sound as though there are three types of fault-based liability: intending a harm, negligently causing a harm, and engaging in an unlawful activity which led to the harm.

Modern textbooks say there are two kinds of fault based liability: intent and negligence. Nevertheless, the second way of stating the doctrine is the older one. It appears in Blackstone who had been speaking about criminal liability. He did not apply it to civil liability: as already noted, the tort law of Blackstone's day (if we may call it that) did not distinguish intention and negligence. Blackstone had taken the doctrine from two 17th century English jurists, Matthew Hale[2] and Edward Coke.[3] They had taken it from the 13th century English jurist Bracton. Bracton took it from the 13th century canon lawyer Raymond of Penafort[4] who had been summarizing the canon law of his own time.[5]

Other canon law doctrines were adopted by civil lawyers, inherited by modern civil law, and borrowed by Anglo-American law. Examples are the doctrine of necessity which allows one person to use another's property in time of great need, and the doctrine of changed circumstances which allows a party to escape his contractual obligations when circumstances have changed enough. But in this case, the doctrine was borrowed from canon law by the English and applied to tort law in the United States although it died out in continental Europe.

The canon lawyers accepted this doctrine, not because it was found in the texts they regarded as authoritative, but because it seemed to give the right result in a number of hypothetical cases. The earlier canonists rested it on three texts in the *Decretum,* a collection of authorities made by Gratian about 1140. One was a vague statement by St. Augustine that no one can be blamed for doing what is "good and lawful."[6] Another was a ruling by the Council of

---

1. Similarly, the court said in Livingstone v. Ministry of Defence: "the application of force towards one person is intended, even although the person directly struck may not be the person whom the assailant intended to strike."

2. Matthew Hale, *Historia Placitorum Coronae* 1 (S. Emlyn & G. Wilson eds. 1800), *471–77. See also id.* 429–30, 431, 466.

3. Edward Coke, *The Third Part of the Institutes of the Laws of England* *56–57 (1817).

4. Raimundus de Penafort, *Summa de Poenitentia* (X. Ochoa & A. Diez, eds., 1976),

II.i.3. For his influence on Bracton, see F. Schulz, "Bracton on Raymond of Penafort," *L.Q. Rev.* 61 (1945), 286, 289–90.

5. Stephan Kuttner, *Kanonistische Schuldlehre von Gratian bis auf die Dekretalen Gregors IX* (1935), 201–07; James Gordley, "Responsibility in Crime, Tort and Contract for the Unforeseeable Consequences of an Intentional Wrong: A Once and Future Rule?" in *The Law of Obligations Essays in Celebration of John Fleming* (J. Stapleton & P. Kane, eds., 1998), 175, 184–86.

6. C. 23, q. 5, c. 8.

Worms in 868 that a person who cuts down a tree which crushes a passer-by "while carrying out some necessary work" need only do penance if acted "by will or by negligence."[7] The third was a decision by Pope Urban I that a priest who killed a boy by throwing a stone should do penance as a homicide but would not be suspended from his functions as those guilty of homicide usually were. The text said nothing about why the priest threw the stone.[8]

Just because their authorities said so little, the canonists found themselves improvising. The earliest canon lawyers to consider the problem said that the priest would not be guilty if he threw the stone for a "reason" (*causa*)[9] or "good reason" (*iusta causa*)[10] and did so with "diligence" in a place where people were not walking. Later canonists explained that the priest had a "reason" to throw the stone if he was engaged in a "lawful" activity rather than an "unlawful" one.[11] The priest would not have been guilty if he threw the stone to chase a wild boar or a pig out of a field of grain unless he had been careless.[12] He would be guilty if he engaged in an unlawful activity or failed to use the diligence he should.[13]

That meant that there were three grounds for holding that a person was responsible because he had been at fault: he might have caused harm intentionally, negligently, or while engaging in an unlawful activity. This three fold distinction was repeated by Thomas Aquinas.[14] Curiously enough, the jurists who rejected the category of "engaging in an unlawful activity" were the late scholastics of the 16th century for whom Aquinas was an intellectual hero.

The reason the late scholastics rejected it was, in part, that it did not seem to give a sensible result in other hypothetical cases. Suppose someone is prohibited for religious reasons from working on Sunday[15] or from

---

7. Dig. 50, c. 50.
8. Dig. 50, c. 37.
9. Paucapalea, *Summa über das Decretum Gratiani* (J.F. Schulte, ed., 1891; repr. Scientia Verlag, 1965), to D. 50 c. 37.
10. Stephanus Tornacensis, *Die Summa über das Decretum Gratiani* (J.F. Schulte, ed., repr. Scientia Verlag, 1965), to D. 50 c. 37.
11. Huguccio, *Summa*, Admont, Stiftsbibliothek, MS 7, to D. 50, c. 37, f. 71ra.
12. *Glossa Palatina*, Vatican City, Biblioteca Apostolica Vaticana, Cod. palatini latini MS. 658, to D. 50, c. 37, f. 13va; Huguccio, *Summa* to D. 50, c. 37, f. 71ra; Iohannes Teutonicus, *Glossa ordinaria*, Vatican City, Biblioteca Apostolica Vaticana, Cod. palatini latini MS 624, to D. 50 c. 37 to *Clerico*, f. 40rb.
13. *E.g., Glossa Palatina* to D. 50, c. 37, f. 13rb; Huguccio, *Summa* to D. 50, c. 37, f. 71ra; to D. 50, c. 44, f. 72va; to D. 50, c. 50, f. 73 ra; Iohannes Teutonicus, *Glossa ordinaria* to D. 50 c. 37 to *Clerico*, f. 40rb; Guido de Baisio (Archidiacanus), *Archidiaconus super Decretum* (1549), to D. 50, c. 37; to D. 50, c. 44 to *casu*. For other references, see Stephan Kuttner, *Kanonistische Schuldlehre*

von Gratian bis auf die Dekretalen Gregors IX (1935), 201 n. 1, 202 n. 1.

After the doctrine became generally accepted, popes referred to it in their own decisions which were in turn regarded as authoritative. Raymond of Penafort included two such decisions in his authoritative collection known as the *Decretales* of Pope Gregory IX. In one, the Pope exonerated a chaplain who had gone riding to restore his appetite after an illness and killed someone when the reins broke. *Decretales* 5.12.13. In the other, he exonerated a priest who was building a church and killed a coworker by dropping a load of wood on him. *Decretales* 5.12.25. In both decisions, the Pope noted that the activity was a lawful one. As a 16th century critic pointed out, these texts supported the doctrine only by negative inference: because a priest engaged in a lawful activity was exonerated, one was asked to infer that the priest engaged in an unlawful one would be held responsible. Domenicus Soto, *De iustitia et iure libri decem* (1553), lib. 5, q. 1, a. 9.
14. *Summa theologiae* II-II Q. 64, *a. 8*.
15. Soto, *De iustitia et iure* V.i.9.

hunting[16] and, while violating these rules, he accidentally kills somebody. It would be strange to hold him responsible. Suppose someone catches his spouse in adultery and tries to kill the adulterer. In the law of their time, as in modern law, the attempt to kill is unlawful, and the adulterer is allowed to defend himself, killing his attacker if that is the only way to preserve his own life. If the adulterer did kill his attacker, it would be odd to say he was responsible for the death because adultery was unlawful. That would be tantamount to saying he could not kill him.[17] Suppose someone steals a treasure and the owner dies of grief. Suppose someone kills Peter and malicious accusers see that Paul is punished for the crime.[18]

If the late scholastics had accepted the doctrine, it might not have died out. Grotius and Pufendorf, who borrowed many of their conclusions from the late scholastics, might have accepted it as well. It might have become part of modern civil law.

c. Intent and knowledge

English law

W.V.H. Rogers, *Winfield & Jolowicz on Tort* (15th ed. 1998), 49–50

"Everyone agrees that a person intends a consequence if it is his desire or motive to bring it about, but beyond that it is probably not possible to lay down any universal definition for the purposes of tort. In crime, the law now is that the jury is entitled (but not, it seems, required) to infer intention when the defendant was aware that the harm was 'virtually certain' to result from his act. There has been much less discussion of intention in tort and there are probably two reasons for this (apart from the relative infrequency of cases on intentional torts). First, since the abolition of the forms of action the plaintiff may sometimes be able to fall back upon a wider principle of liability for negligence: If I strike you, then provided I cause you hurt and that hurt could have been foreseen to a reasonable man then my conduct amounts to the tort of negligence even if the court is in doubt whether I acted intentionally. Secondly, while the criminal law may insist that the defendant's intention must extend to all the elements and consequences of his act making up the definition of the crime, the law of tort may separate the initial interference with the victim from the consequences of that interference (remoteness of damage) and while intention or foresight may be necessary as to the former it may not be as to the latter. Thus if A strikes B intending some slight harm but B suffers greater harm (because, for example, he falls as a result of the blow) A is responsible for the greater harm if it is a direct consequence of the blow; he need not even foresee the possibility of the greater harm, let alone intend it." [citations omitted]

---

16. Cajetan (Tomasso di Vio), *Commentaria* to Thomas Aquinas, *Summa theologica* (1698) to II-II, Q. 64, a. 8; Lessius, *De iustitia et iure, ceterisque virtutibus cardinalis libri quatuor* (1628), lib. 2, cap. 9, dub. 15, nos. 104–105.

17. Cajetan, *Commentaria* to II-II, Q. 64, a. 8; Lessius, *De iustitia et iure* lib. 2, cap. 9, dub. 15, nos. 104–105.

18. Lessius, *De iustitia et iure* lib. cap. 9, dub. 16, no. 113.

Law in the United States

Garratt v. Dailey, 279 P.2d 1091 (Wash. 1955)

"Brian Dailey (age five years, nine months) was visiting with Naomi Garratt, an adult and a sister of the plaintiff, Ruth Garratt, likewise an adult, in the backyard of the plaintiff's home, on July 16, 1951. It is plaintiff's contention that she came out into the backyard to talk with Naomi and that, as she started to sit down in a wood and canvas lawn chair, Brian deliberately pulled it out from under her. . . .

The trial court's finding that Brian was a visitor in the Garratt backyard is supported by the evidence and negatives appellant's assertion that Brian was a trespasser and had no right to touch, move, or sit in any chair in that yard, and that contention will not receive further consideration. . . .

We have here the conceded volitional act of Brian, i.e., the moving of a chair. Had the plaintiff proved to the satisfaction of the trial court that Brian moved the chair while she was in the act of sitting down, Brian's action would patently have been for the purpose or with the intent of causing the plaintiff's bodily contact with the ground, and she would be entitled to a judgment against him for the resulting damages. . . .

After the trial court determined that the plaintiff had not established her theory of a battery (i.e., that Brian had pulled the chair out from under the plaintiff while she was in the act of sitting down), it then became concerned with whether a battery was established under the facts as it found them to be. . . .

A battery would be established if, in addition to plaintiff's fall, it was proved that, when Brian moved the chair, he knew with substantial certainty that the plaintiff would attempt to sit down where the chair had been. If Brian had any of the intents which the trial court found, in the italicized portions of the findings of fact quoted above, that he did not have, he would of course have had the knowledge to which we have referred. The mere absence of any intent to injure the plaintiff or to play a prank on her or to embarrass her, or to commit an assault and battery on her would not absolve him from liability if in fact he had such knowledge. Mercer v. Corbin (1889), 117 Ind. 450, 20 N.E. 132, 3 L.R.A. 221. Without such knowledge, there would be nothing wrongful about Brian's act in moving the chair, and, there being no wrongful act, there would be no liability.

While a finding that Brian had no such knowledge can be inferred from the findings made, we believe that before the plaintiff's action in such a case should be dismissed there should be no question but that the trial court had passed upon that issue; hence, the case should be remanded for clarification of the findings to specifically cover the question of Brian's knowledge, because intent could be inferred therefrom. If the court finds that he had such knowledge, the necessary intent will be established and the plaintiff will be entitled to recover, even though there was no purpose to injure or embarrass the plaintiff. . . . If Brian did not have such knowledge, there was no wrongful act by him, and the basic premise of liability on the theory of a battery was not established."

French law

Reread François Terré, Philippe Simler & Yves Lequette, *Droit civil Les obligations* (7th ed. 1999), § 696, reproduced above at p. 339. The authors say that "intentional fault . . . exists when the author of the harm acted intentionally in order to cause a prejudice to another and probably when he acted in a manner that he must have known would injure another." In support of that statement, the authors cite § 12(2) of the Law of 13 July 1930 (L. 113-1 of the Insurance Code) and cross-cite to some cases decided under that provision and some commentators. The text of that law does not support their position. It says: "The insurer is never liable for loss or harm arising from a fault that is an intentional or fraudulent act despite any agreement to the contrary." Nor do the cases that they cite say that a person's act counts as intentional if he has knowledge of the consequences. Nevertheless, that is the position of some of the commentators on that the Law of 13 July 1930. *E.g.*, G. Brière de l'Isle, "La faute dolosive Tentative de clarification," D.S. 1980. Chron. 133, at 133; G. Durry, "Obligations et contrats spéciaux," *Rev. trim. dr. civ.* 1976, 352 at 362.

German law

Hein Kötz & Gerhard Wagner, *Deliktsrecht* (9th ed. 2001), 44.

"A person acts intentionally when he knows that his conduct will lead to an unlawful violation of another's body, property or 'similar right' (*sonstiges Recht*) and who attains this result wilfully and consciously. The party need not have done so with a 'direct intention'; he need not have the purpose of interfering with these rights of legal interests. Rather, it is enough if he recognized the possibility of such an interference, and proceeds to act despite this knowledge, taking into account that action may occur, although he may even hope that it does not (conditional intent). Thus, one who flees from an accident and runs over a policeman standing in his way has intentionally injured him even if he hopes the policeman can reach safety by a sudden leap. It is enough if the person fleeing took account of the injury to the policeman in the event that it should occur as a consequence of his act which is certainly regrettable but which is subordinated to his purpose of fleeing."

3. Negligence

a. The meaning of negligence

Introduction

There have been three ways of explaining negligence. One is by giving examples. The Romans gave dozens of them. For example, a person who cut off the branch of a tree over the public way without calling out was negligent.[1] So was someone who burnt stubble on a windy day when his fire

---

1. Dig. 9.2.31.

might get out of control,[2] or who shaved a customer near a sports field where a stray ball might strike the hand that held the razor.[3]

Another way is to describe negligence is the sort of conduct in which an idealized person, a "reasonable person," does not engage. In Roman law, this person was the *bonus paterfamilias*, the good head of a household.

A third way is to say that the negligent person has not properly weighed the pros and cons of his action. Many people now give this approach an economic interpretation. But a version of it was around before modern economics. When Aristotelian philosophy was in favor, the negligent person was said to lack the virtue of "prudence." "Prudence" was right reason about things to be done. The prudent person would balance the good against the evil that might arise from an action. Suppose a nurse put a child in bed with her at night to keep him from crying and rolled over on the child in the night, suffocating him. Here is a 16th century description of how to decide whether the nurse was negligent:

> [If] the bed is large and there is nothing else near it, the nurse is always accustomed to find herself in the same place and position in which she put herself to begin sleeping, and the implacability of the infant required it, she seems to be excused, because it is not rational when these things concur to fear the risk.[4]

The weighing of consequences

An English description

W.V.H. Rogers, *Winfield & Jolowicz on Tort* (15th ed. 1998), 180–83

"Theoretically at least, in every case where a duty of care exists the courts must consider whether the risk was sufficiently great to require of the defendant that he do more than he has actually done.

(1) *Magnitude of the risk*

Two elements go to make up the magnitude of the risk, the likelihood that injury will be incurred and the seriousness of the injury that is risked. In *Bolton v. Stone* [[1951] A.C. 850], the plaintiff was standing on the highway in a road adjoining a cricket ground when she was struck by a ball which a batsman had hit out of the ground. Such an event was foreseeable and, indeed, balls had to the defendant's knowledge occasionally been hit out of the ground before. Nevertheless, taking into account such factors as the distance from the itch to the edge of the ground, the presence of a seven foot fence and the upward slope of the ground in the direction in which the ball was struck, the House of Lords considered that the likelihood of injury to a person in the plaintiff's position was so slight that the cricket club was

---

2. Dig. 9.2.31.
3. Dig. 9.2.11.pr

4. Cajetan, *Commentaria* to Thomas Aquinas, *Summa theologica* (1698), post Q. 64, a. 8.

not negligent in allowing cricket to be played without taking additional precautions such as increasing the height of the fence. . . .

The relevance of the seriousness of the injury was recognised by the House of Lords in *Paris v. Stepney Borough Council* [[1951] A.C. 367] after having been denied by the Court of Appeal in the same case. In that case the plaintiff, a one-eyed man employed by the defendants, was working in conditions involving some risk of eye injury, but the likelihood of injury was not sufficient to call upon the defendants to provide goggles to a normal two-eyed workman. In the case of the plaintiff, however, goggles should have been provided for, whereas the risk to a two-eyed man was of the loss of one eye, the plaintiff risked the much greater injury of total blindness. . . .

(2) *The importance of the object to be attained*

Asquith L.J. summed it up by saying that it is necessary to balance the risk against the consequences of not taking it. 'As has often been pointed out, if all the trains in this country were restricted to a speed of five miles an hour, there would be fewer accidents but our national life would be intolerably slowed down. The purpose to be served, if sufficiently important, justifieds the assumption of abnormal risk.' [*Daborn Bath Tramways* [1946] 2 All. E.R. 333 at 336] . . .

(3) *The practicability of precautions*

The risk must be balanced against the measures necessary to eliminate it, and the practical measures which the defendant could have taken must be considered. In *Lattimer v. A.E.C.* [[1953] A.C. 643] a factory floor became slippery after a flood. The occupiers of the factory did everything possible to get rid of the effects of the flood, but nevertheless the plaintiff was injured and sought to say that the occupiers should have closed down the factory. The House of Lords held that the risk of injury created by the slippery floor was not so great as to justify, much less require, so onerous a precaution. The greater the risk, the less receptive a court is likely to be to a defence based simply on the cost, in terms of money, of the required precautions and there may be situations in which an activity must be abandoned altogether if adequate safeguards cannot be provided. The courts in England [citing part of the statement of McHugh JA in an Australian case reproduced below] have certainly not shown overt attachment to the theory that negligence is merely an economic cost/benefit equation [citing Learned Hand in *Carroll Towing* and Posner in *Economic Analysis of Law*], but at the end of the day the cost of a precaution and the ability of a socially useful activity to bear that cost have to be brought into account." [citations omitted]

Note: Here is the statement of McHugh JA in an Australian case, part of which was cited by Rogers in the passage just reproduced:

"When the cost of preventing a breach of duty does not exceed the likely quantum of consequential damage, discounted by the probability of its occurrence, it will generally be negligent for a person not to take precaution: United States v. Carroll Towing Co 159 F.2d 169 (1947) and Posner, *Economic Analysis of Law*, 2nd ed (1977) at 122–123. This does not mean that a defendant can escape liability by showing that his economic costs in eliminating the risk of injury exceed the likely damage to potential victims. Nor does liability automatically ensue from a finding that the costs of a precaution are outweighed by the costs of the consequences of a breach. Negligence is not an economic cost/benefit equation. Immeasurable 'soft' values such as community concepts of justice, health, life and freedom of conduct have to be taken into account. Nonetheless, it is generally a powerful indication of negligence that the cost of a precaution is small compared with the cost of the consequences of a breach even when the risk of the occurrence is small." Western Suburbs Hospital v. Currie, (1987) 9 N.S.W.R. 511, 523–24.

Some American descriptions

United States v. Carroll Towing Co., 159 F.2d 169 (2nd Cir. 1947)

The defendant's tug boat was moving a line of barges including the *Anna C*, owned by the Connors Company. The *Anna C* broke away from the line of barges being moved and was carried by the wind and tide into a tanker, whose propellor broke through the *Anna C*'s hull, after which the barge started to leak. Had a bargee been on board, the leak might have been discovered earlier, and the barge might have been saved. As to whether it was contributory negligence not to have a bargee on board, Learned Hand said:

"Since there are occasions when every vessel will break from her moorings, and since, if she does, she becomes a menace to those about her, the owner's duty, as in other similar situations, to provide against resulting injuries is a function of three variables: (1) The probability that she will break away; (2) the gravity of the resulting injury, if she does; (3) the burden of adequate precautions. Possibly it serves to bring this notion into relief to state it in algebraic terms: if the probability be called P; the injury L; and the burden, B; liability depends upon whether B is less than L multiplied by P: i.e., whether B [is less than] PL. Applied to the situation at bar, the likelihood that a barge will break from her fasts and the damage she will do, vary with the place and time; for example, if a storm threatens, the danger is greater; so it is, if she is in a crowded harbor where moored barges are constantly being shifted about. On the other hand, the barge must not be the bargee's prison, even though he lives aboard; he must go ashore at times. We need not say whether, even in such crowded waters as New York Harbor a bargee must be aboard at night at all; it may be that the custom is otherwise, as Ward, J., supposed in The Kathryn B. Guinan, 176 F.2d 301; and that, if so, the situation is one where custom should control. We leave that question open; but we hold that it is not in all cases a sufficient answer to a bargee's absence without excuse, during working hours, that he has properly made fast his barge to a pier, when he leaves her. In the case at bar the bargee left at five o'clock in the afternoon of January 3rd, and the flotilla broke away at about two o'clock in the afternoon of the following day, twenty-one hours afterwards. The bargee had been away all the time, and we hold that his fabricated story was affirmative evidence that he had no excuse for his absence. At the locus in quo—especially during the short January days and in the full tide of war activity—barges were being constantly 'drilled' in and out. Certainly it was not beyond reasonable expectation, that with the inevitable haste and bustle, the work might not be done with adequate care. In such circumstances we hold—and it is all that we do hold—that it was a fair requirement that the Connors Company should have a bargee aboard (unless he had some excuse for his absence), during the working hours of daylight."

Richard Posner, "A Theory of Negligence," *J. Legal Stud.* 1 (1972), 29, 32–33

"Hand was adumbrating, perhaps unwittingly, an economic meaning of negligence. Discounting (multiplying) the cost of an accident if it occurs by the probability of occurrence yields a measure of the economic benefit to be anticipated from incurring the costs necessary to prevent the accident. The cost of prevention is what Hand meant by the burden of taking precautions against the accident. It may be the cost of installing safety equipment or otherwise making the activity safer, or the benefit forgone by curtailing or eliminating the activity. If the cost of safety measures or of curtailment—whichever cost is lower—exceeds the benefit in accident avoidance to be gained by incurring that cost, society would be better off, in economic terms, to forgo accident prevention. A rule making the enterprise liable for the accidents that occur in such cases cannot be justified on the ground that it will induce the enterprise to increase the safety of its operations. When the cost of accidents is less than the cost of prevention, a rational profit-maximizing enterprise will pay tort judgments to the accident victims rather than incur the larger cost of avoiding liability. Furthermore, overall economic value or welfare would be diminished rather than increased by incurring a higher accident-prevention cost in order to avoid a lower accident cost. If, on the other hand, the benefits in accident avoidance exceed the costs of prevention, society is better off if those costs are incurred and the accident averted, and so in this case the enterprise is made liable, in the expectation that self-interest will lead it to adopt the precautions in order to avoid a greater cost in tort judgments."

Some French descriptions

Read pp. 224–26, above.

Some German descriptions

While the French rarely discuss the Hand formula, the Germans sometimes do. The passages that follow are excerpts from leading textbooks. The first is by a jurist who is more favorable to the formula; the second is by one who is less so.

Hein Kötz & Gerhard Wagner, *Deliktsrecht* (9th ed. 2001), 45.

"To determine if 'the care ordinarily required' has been used in a particular situation, what matters is what kind of harm is threatened in the situation, and with what probability its occurrence is to be feared; it also matters what action or omission could avoid the harm, and what disadvantages, costs and burdens were entailed for the person concerned in the taking of the measures to avoid the harm. The more serious the harm and the greater the probability of its occurrence the further one must go to answer the question, what conduct is expected of a 'careful person' in the interest of avoiding the harm.

Take the case in which someone's health is damages because a poisoned cutlet (*Schnitzel*) was put before him in an inn. If it is established here that the innkeeper kept rat poison in an unmarked jelly jar in the kitchen, and the cook, in a hurry, mistook it for curry powder and put it on the cutlet, the question of whether the innkeeper acted negligently comes down to the following considerations. The danger threatening the guests through accidental use of the rat poison was great. Taking into account the way and the place that the rat poison was stored, the danger of such a harm occurring was serious. Among the measures that could be considered to prevent the harm are taking the poison out of the kitchen, storing it in the kitchen in a locked container, and possibly marking the container in an appropriate way. It was possible for the innkeeper to take these measures and to do so would not have burdened him to an extent worth mentioning. Result: the innkeeper is to be blamed for negligence. . . ."

Karl Larenz & Claus-Wilhelm Canaris, *Lehrbuch des Schuldrechts* II/2 (13th ed., 1994), 413–14

"b) When a person has a responsibility [for preventing harm] it does not automatically follow that he has a duty to take measures to avoid the danger. Whether he does must be determined in the individual case on the basis of a number of criteria. The most important, even in the area of daily experience with risks, are the degree of *danger* and the extent and nature of the (possible) *harm* on the one hand, and the *burden* required to avoid its occurrence, on the other. The degree of danger depends essentially on the probability that it will occur. This in principle (only) gives rise to liability when 'the possibility arises which is foreseeable by a judgment based on experience, that the legal interests of another person may be injured,' supposing that the danger is concrete although it need not be great. As to the extent of the harm, not only material losses but also immaterial injuries such as occur with bodily harm and death are obviously of considerable significance. Also the level of the legal interest threatened plays a role so that essentially it matters to the importance of a harm whether injury to life and limb is to be feared or only injury to property. The burden of prevention includes not only financial costs but also loss of time and the engagement of one's ability to work of the (potential) violator of a duty. As these parameters and their *exact* correct weighing against each other virtually never permit an exact quantification (see h below) they do not permit one to arrive at a clear solution but only at comparative maxims . . .: the greater the danger, the worse the harm threatened, and the lower the burden of prevention, the sooner a duty to avoid the danger will arise. . . .

h) Finally, in this connection, a short word is in order about *'economic analysis of law'* even though only brief and superficial remarks can be made in the space available here. First, it must be stressed that the relevance of an economic standpoint to the development of duties of ordinary care is indisputable and for a long time has been recognized as obvious (see b, above). To have sharpened the awareness of the importance of this aspect is certainly a substantial service of the followers of this doctrine. Moreover, their arguments may be strong enough to influence the solution of a problem even as to its practical outcome.

On the whole, however, and in my opinion, one cannot succeed with the help of the teaching of 'economic analysis' in formulating the relevant criteria any more precisely than one could without using them, all the more because the extent of the burden of using difficult terminology is often out of proportion to the gain in cogent argumentation. Moreover, nearly always 'economic analysis' does not permit an accurate quantification of parameters such as the probability of harm, the size of the possible harm, and the extent of the burden of prevention (of both sides). On the contrary, in this respect, it can awaken considerations that are illusory. Finally, the instruments of economic analysis seem wholly inadequate insofar as non-material values are concerned, particularly in the area of protecting life and limb as these elude even a hypothetical model-like quantification. To that extent, one still cannot get around the famous saying of Kant that a person has a 'value' on account of which he is 'great beyond all price.' This sketch will show why no reference has been made to 'economic analysis' in this textbook. . . ."

The reasonable person

THE GENERAL PRINCIPLE

Blyth v. Birmingham Water Works [1856] 11 Exch. 781

Alderson, B. "Negligence is the omission to do something which a reasonable man, guided upon those considerations which ordinarily regulate the conduct of human affairs, would do, or doing something which a prudent and reasonable man would not do."

Restatement (Second) of Torts

§ 283 CONDUCT OF A REASONABLE MAN: THE STANDARD

Unless the actor is a child, the standard of conduct to which he must conform to avoid being negligent is that of a reasonable man under like circumstances.

Francois Terré, Philippe Simler & Yves Lequette, *Droit civil Les obligations* (7th ed. 1999), § 698

"Since the affirmation of responsibility implies a comparison between that which was and, ultimately, that which should have been, in matters regarding the faults of imprudence or negligence, the courts refer to an abstract model which represents the good family father (*bon père de famille*), that is to say, the reasonable man placed in the same situation."

German Civil Code

§ 276(1) SENTENCE 2

"A person acts negligently who fails to use the care ordinarily required."

Hein Kötz & Gerhard Wagner, *Deliktsrecht* (9th ed. 2001), 44.

"By the definition of § 276(1), 2nd sentence, a person acts negligently who fails to use 'the care ordinarily required.' That means chiefly that the person causing harm did not act as circumspectly, carefully and attentively in the concrete situation in which he found himself as was required by the state of the circumstances. Consequently, the actual conduct of the person whose liability is in question must be compared with that which would have been displayed by a careful person of ordinary circumspection and prudence to avoid an unreasonably large risk of harm to another. If there is a difference because the conduct of the defendant does not meet this standard of care, then there is negligence."

CHILDREN AND THE MENTALLY ILL

English law

Gough v. Thorne, [1966] 3 All E.R. 398 (C.A.)

"A 13½ year old girl (the plaintiff) was waiting on the pavement, with her two brothers, to cross a main road in London at a corner where there were bollards and a refuge in the middle of the road. An approaching lorry stopped between the plaintiff and the bollards, about five feet from the bollards, and the driver held out his right hand to warn traffic coming along to stop and with his left hand beckoned the plaintiff and her brothers to cross. They did so, but when they had just passed the front of the lorry the plaintiff was struck and injured by a bubble-car which was being driven at excessive speed, the driver of which failed to notice the lorry driver's outstretched hand and drove between the lorry and the bollards. In an action by the plaintiff for damages the trial judge found that the bubble-car driver, the defendant, was negligent, but also found that the plaintiff was negligent in advancing past the lorry into the open road without pausing to see whether there was any traffic coming from her right, and assessed the degree of her contributory negligence at one-third."

Lord Denning, M.R. "I am afraid that I cannot agree with the judge. A very young child cannot be guilty of contributory negligence. An older child may be; but it depends on the circumstances. A judge should only find a child guilty of contributory negligence if he or she is of such an age as reasonably to be expected to take precautions for his or her own safety: and then he or she is only to be found guilty if blame should be attached to him or her. A child has not the road sense or the experience of his or her elders. He or she is not to be found guilty unless he or she is blameworthy.

In this particular case I have no doubt that there was no blameworthiness to be attributed to the plaintiff at all. Here she was with her elder brother crossing a road. They had been beckoned on by the lorry driver. What more could you expect the child to do than to cross in pursuance of the beckoning? It is said by the judge that she ought to have leant forward and looked to see whether anything was coming. That indeed might be reasonably expected of a grown-up person with a fully developed road sense, but not of a child of 13½."

Note: No English court has yet decided whether the same rule applies to negligence rather than merely to contributory negligence. Nor has an English court passed on the liability of the insane for negligence. Here are two cases from Canada.

Buckley and Toronto Transportation Com'n V. Smith Transport Ltd., [1946] 4 D.L.R. 721 [1946] (British Columbia Supreme Court)

"The driver of a transport truck caused a collision with a street car by his operation of the truck. He suffered from a delusion that his vehicle was under the remote electrical control of his employer from its head office so that he could neither control its speed nor stop it. It was found that he was insane immediately after the collision and there was evidence indicating that the delusion was operative before the collision. He died in a mental hospital from general paresis within a month following the accident."

The court held that he was not negligent. "Having regard to all the evidence, I have reached the conclusion that at the time of the collision Taylor's mind was so ravaged by disease that it should be held, as a matter of reasonable inference, that he did not understand the duty which rested upon him to take care, and further that if it could be said that he did understand and appreciate that duty, the particular delusion prevented him from discharging it. Therefore, no liability for the damages which he caused could attach to him."

Attorney-General of Canada et al. v. Connolly, [1989] 64 D.L.R. 4th 84 (British Columbia Supreme Court)

"The defendant, who was suffering from a serious mental disorder, caused injury to a police officer, who had asked for his driver's licence, by pinning the officer's arm inside the defendant's car and driving away. The medical evidence was that the defendant knew that a person was standing by the car with his arm inside it, but that he did not know that what he was doing was wrong, or that it would cause harm."

Paris, J. "Actionable negligence involves foreseeability of harm of the kind, at least in general, that in fact results from the negligent act. Persons with severe mental illnesses of the kind from which the defendant in this case suffers, have their capacity for such foresight severely impaired. If an act entraining liability in negligence must be accompanied by foresight of harm in the above sense, then it is necessary to consider whether because of mental illness the person might be incapable of such foresight. If he is not capable of foreseeing that his act involves a significant risk of harm to others then one can say that there was not sufficient awareness or consciousness of the nature of his act to make it a true voluntarily negligent act.

This analysis respects the authority of the Buckley case and recognizes the psychological reality that an act of battery requires less mental capacity than an actionably negligent act. It does so, however, without importing into the law of tort the full criminal defence of insanity which one could misinterpret the Buckley case as having done.

Admittedly, it is a departure from the objective test usually applied in a claim for negligence. The foreseeability of the reasonable person is normally the measure of liability in an action in negligence. But negligence, perhaps more than most other torts, is about fault and mental state. This approach, I believe, is more in line with the evolution of the law away from the early strict common law rule which afforded no relief in tort to a defendant who suffered from severe mental illness." [The court held, however, that the defendant had committed battery even if he did not understand that his act was wrongful.]

Law in the United States

Restatement (Second) of Torts

§ 283A CHILDREN

If the actor is a child, the standard of conduct to which he must conform to avoid being negligent is that of a reasonable person of like age, intelligence, and experience under like circumstances.

Comment c. Child engaging in adult activity. An exception to the rule stated in this Section may arise where the child engages in an activity which is normally undertaken only by adults, and for which adult qualifications are required. As in the case of one entering upon a professional activity which requires special skill (see § 299 A), he may be held to the standard of adult skill, knowledge, and competence, and no allowance may be made for his immaturity. Thus, for example, if a boy of fourteen were to attempt to fly an airplane, his age and inexperience would not excuse him from liability for flying it in a negligent manner. The same may be true where the child drives an automobile. In this connection licensing statutes, and the examinations given to drivers, may be important in determining the qualifications required; but even if the child succeeds in obtaining a license he may thereafter be required to meet the standard established primarily for adults.

§ 283B MENTAL DEFICIENCY

Unless the actor is a child, his insanity or other mental deficiency does not relieve the actor from liability for conduct which does not conform to the standard of a reasonable man under like circumstances.

German law

German Civil Code

§ 827

A person who causes damage to another person when the former is unconscious or when he is suffering from a mental disturbance preventing the free exercise of his will, is not responsible for the damage. If he has brought himself into a temporary condition of this kind by alcoholic drinks or similar means, he is responsible for any damage which he in this condition unlawfully causes in the same manner as if negligence were imputable to him; the responsibility does not arise if he came into this condition without fault.

§ 828

A person who has not completed his seventh year of age is not responsible for any damage that he causes to another.

A person who has completed his seventh but not his eighteenth year of age is not responsible for any damage that he causes to another, if he, at the time of committing the damaging act, did not have the understanding required to realize his responsibility. The same applies to a deaf mute.

§ 829

A person who in one of the cases specified in §§ 823 to 826, is not responsible, by virtue of §§ 827, 828, for damage caused by him, shall, nevertheless, where compensation cannot be obtained from a third party charged with the duty of supervision, compensate for the damage to the extent reasonable under the circumstances, in particular where, in view of the circumstances of the parties, fairness requires that the damage be made good, and he is not deprived of the means that he needs for his own maintenance suitable to his station in life and for the fulfilment of the obligations imposed upon him by law to furnish maintenance to others.

French law

Law of 3 January 1968, now French Civil Code

ARTICLE 489-2

One who causes harm to another even if he is under the domination of a mental disturbance is nonetheless liable to make compensation.

Cour de cassation, Assemblée plénière, 9 May 1984 (4th case), D.S. 1984.J.529

Fatiha Derguini, then age five, was struck and fatally injured by a car driven by Tidu in an area where signs warned drivers to watch for pedestrians. The *Cour d'appel* of Nancy held him guilty of involuntary homicide and also divided the damages for the accident to reflect the partial responsibility of the victim. [France, like other continental legal systems, has a system of comparative negligence in which the victim's damages are reduced in proportion to the victim's own fault.] The victim's parents argued that the *Cour d'appel* should not have done so. They pointed out that the *Cour d'appel* of Metz, which had heard the case before it was remanded, to the *Cour d'appel* of Nancy, had found that "the victim, age five years and nine months . . . was much too young to appreciate the consequences of her acts." Her parents argued that "the absence of discernment excluded all responsibility on the part of the victim." The *Cour de cassation* upheld the decision below. It said that "after having found that

M. Tidu was at fault for a lapse of attention and also that the young Fatiha leaping into the street, had suddenly begun to cross it despite the imminent danger of M. Tidu's oncoming car and made a half turn to get back to the sidewalk, the decision declared that this untimely movement made any maneuver to rescue her impossible for the motorist." Consequently, "the *Cour d'appel* which was not bound to investigate whether the minor was capable of discerning the consequences of her actions, could, without contradicting itself, find on the basis of art. 1382 that the victim had committed a fault which in concurrence with that of M. Tidu had caused the harm in a proportion which it had the sovereign authority to determine. . . ."

Note: In a companion case, decided the same day, the *Assemblée plénière* of the *Cour de cassation* reached the same result when a thirteen year old boy was electrocuted as a result of defective work in an electrical installation in his parents' farm. The *Cour d'appel* had reduced the damages in proportion to the victim's fault in having screwed in a bulb without switching off the electric current. The *Cour de cassation* said that the *Cour d'appel* "was not bound to investigate whether the minor had the capacity to discern the consequences of the faulty act which he committed."

b. The duty to act

Civil and common lawyers agree that one has a duty to refrain from hurting others, and that a person who fails to use due care to discharge this duty is liable for negligence. But does one have a duty to help others when they are in danger?

The general principle

English law

Stovin v. Wise and Norfolk County Council, [1996] AC 923 (H.L)

"The plaintiff [Stovin] was riding a motor cycle along a road in December 1988 when he collided with a motor vehicle being driven by the defendant [Wise] out of a junction on the plaintiff's left across his path. The plaintiff was seriously injured in the collision. Although the particular junction was not a busy one, it was known by the county council, as the highway authority, to be dangerous because the view of road users turning out of the junction into the major road was restricted by a bank on adjoining land. Accidents in similar situation had occurred at the road junction on at least three previous occasions. In January 1988, after a site meeting at the junction, a divisional surveyor employed by the council accepted that a visibility problem existed and recommended removal of part of the bank. The council agreed that the work would be carried out providing the owner of the land, on which the bank was situated, agreed. No response to the council's proposal was forthcoming from the owner of the land before the time of the plaintiffs accident notwithstanding a further site meeting at which the representatives of the landowner and council were present."

Lord Hoffmann. "The judge [below] made no express mention of the fact that the complaint against the council was not about anything which it had done to make the highway dangerous but about its omission to make it safer. . . .

There are sound reasons why omissions require different treatment from positive conduct. It is one thing for the law to say that a person who undertakes some activity shall take reasonable care not to cause damage to others. It is another thing for the law to require that a person who is doing nothing in particular shall take steps to prevent another from suffering harm from the acts of third parties (like Mrs Wise) or natural causes. One can put the matter in political, moral or economic terms. In political terms it is less of an invasion of an individual's freedom for the law to require him to consider the safety of others in his actions than to impose upon him a duty to rescue or protect. A moral version of this point may be called the 'why pick on me?' argument. A duty to prevent harm to others or to render assistance to a person in danger or distress may apply to a large and indeterminate class of people who happen to be able to do something. Why should one be held liable rather than another? In economic terms, the efficient allocation of resources usually requires an activity should bear its own costs. If it benefits from being able to impose some of its costs on other people (what economists call 'externalities,') the market is distorted because the activity appears cheaper than it really is. So liability to pay compensation for loss caused by negligent conduct acts as a deterrent against increasing the cost of the activity to the community and reduces externalities. But there is no similar justification for requiring a person who is not doing anything to spend money on behalf of someone else. Except in special cases (such as marine salvage) English law does not reward someone who voluntarily confers a benefit on another. So there must be some special reason why he should have to put his hand in his pocket. . . .

To hold the defendant liable for an act, rather than an omission, it is therefore necessary to be able to say, according to common sense principles of causation, that the damage was caused by something which the defendant did. If I am driving at 50 miles an hour and fail to apply the brakes, the motorist with whom I collide can plausibly say that the damage was caused by my driving into him at 50 miles an hour. But Mr Stovin's injuries were not caused by the negotiations between the council and British Rail or anything else which the council did. So far as the council was held responsible, it was because it had done nothing to improve the visibility at the junction."

On the question of whether the council was under a statutory duty of care, Lord Hoffmann said, "It is clear, however, that this public law duty cannot in itself give rise to a duty of care. A public body almost always has a duty in public law to consider whether it should exercise its powers, but that does not mean that it necessarily owes a duty of care which may require that the power should actually be exercised. . . .

[Even if]it would be irrational (in the public law meaning of that word) for the public authority not to exercise its power, it does not follow that the law should superimpose a common law duty of care. This can be seen if one looks at cases in which a public authority has been under a statutory or common law duty to provide a service or other benefit for the public or a section of the public. In such cases there is no discretion but the courts have nevertheless not been willing to hold that a member of the public who has suffered loss because the service was not provided to him should necessarily have a cause of action, either for breach of statutory duty or for negligence at common law."

Law in the United States

W. Page Keeton, Dan B. Dobbs, Robert E. Keeton, David G. Owen, *Prosser and Keeton on Torts* (5th ed. 1984), 375

"[T]he law has persistently refused to impose on a stranger the moral obligation of common humanity to go to the aid of another human being who is in danger, even if the other is in danger of losing his life.[21] Some of the decisions are shocking in the extreme. The expert swimmer, with a boat and a rope at hand, who sees another drowning before his eyes, is not[22] required to do anything at all about it but may sit on the dock, smoke his cigarette, and watch the man drown."

Note: Here are the two cases cited in note 22, above. At the time they were decided, American states followed the doctrine of contributory negligence: a negligent plaintiff could recover nothing even if he could prove the defendant had been negligent. Today, an American court, like continental courts, will apply a rule of the comparative negligence. It will consider how gravely each party was at fault and apportion damages accordingly. Consider whether the plaintiff was at fault in the following two cases, and consequently, whether he could have recovered even if the court had recognized a duty to rescue him.

Yania v. Bigan, 155 A.2d 343 (Pa. 1959)

When Yania was visiting Bigan to discuss business Bigan jumped into a cut in a worked-out strip mine containing eight to ten feet of water and drowned. The complaint alleged that Bigan had caused him to jump "by urging, enticing, taunting and inveighing [him] to jump into the water, which [Bigan] knew or ought to have known . . . was dangerous to the life of anyone who would jump therein." It alleged Bigan was negligent for having done so, and also, inter alia, for "failing to go to Yania's rescue after he had jumped in the water." The court said:

"The mere fact that Bigan saw Yania in a position of peril in the water imposed upon him no legal, although a moral, obligation or duty to go to his rescue unless Bigan was legally responsible, in whole or in part, for placing Yania in the perilous position: Restatement, Torts, § 314. Cf: Restatement, Torts, § 322. The language of this Court in Brown v. French, 104 Pa. 604, 607, 608, is apt: 'If it appeared that the deceased, by his own

---

21. Three states (Vt., Minn. & R.I.) and several countries have statutes, generally criminal, which impose a duty, under certain limited conditions, to rescue another in peril. [references omitted]

22. Osterlind v. Hill, 1928, 263 Mass. 73, 160 N.E. 301; Yania v. Bigan, 1959, 397 Pa. 316, 155 A.2ds 343 [authors' descriptions of these cases omitted.]

carelessness, contributed in any degree to the accident which caused the loss of his life, the defendants ought not to have been held to answer for the consequences resulting from that accident.' "

Osterlind v. Hill, 160 N.E. 301 (Mass. 1928)

The complaint alleged that the defendant, who was in the business of renting canoes, rented one to the intestate and his companion "well knowing that they were intoxicated and manifestly unfit to go upon the lake in the canoe; that they went out in the canoe which shortly afterwards was overturned, and that the intestate, after hanging to it for approximately one-half hour making loud cries for assistance, which calls defendant heard and utterly ignored, was obliged to release his hold and was drowned."

The court held that the intestate was not in such a helpless condition that it was negligent to rent him a canoe. Then it said: "The failure of the defendant to respond to the intestate's outcries is immaterial. No legal right of the intestate was infringed."

Note: It is generally accepted that there is no duty to rescue at common law. Consider whether the following cases are consistent with that principle.

Rockhill v. Pollard, 485 P.2d 28 (Ore. 1971)

The plaintiffs, a mother-in-law and her 10 month old daughter, were seriously injured in an automobile accident. Both had cuts and bruises, and the daughter was pale and seemed lifeless. They were taken to the office of defendant, a medical doctor, by a passing motorist. He did not examine the women and only briefly examined the baby. When the baby vomited, he said it was due to overeating. He ordered the women to wait outside in the freezing rain until plaintiff's husband came for them. He took them to the hospital where the baby was operated on for a depressed skull fracture. Held: defendant is liable for intentional infliction of emotional distress.

Tarasoff v. Regents of the University of California, 551 P.2d 334 (Cal. 1970)

Prosenjit Poddar told Dr. Lawrence Moore, a psychologist employed at Cowell Memorial Hospital at the University of California at Berkeley, that he intended to kill Tatiana Tarasoff. At Moore's request, the campus police briefly detained Poddar, but Moore's superior, Dr. Harvey Powelson, ordered that he be released. Two months later, Poddar killed her. No one had tried to warn her. The court held that "plaintiffs can state a cause of action against defendant therapists for negligent failure to warn." It cited Dillon v. Legg (above p. 324) for the propositions that to say there is no duty "begs the essential question" and that duty is "only the expression of the sum total of those considerations of policy which lead the law to say that a particular plaintiff is entitled to protection."

Soldano v. O'Daniels, 190 Cal. Rptr. 310 (Cal. App. 1983)

Defendant owned the Circle Inn. The plaintiff alleged that a patron of Happy Jack's saloon across the street came in and told the bartender of the Circle Inn that a man had been threatened at Happy Jack's. He asked the bartender either to call the police or to let him use the telephone to call them. The bartender allegedly refused to do either. (It is not clear where the telephone was located.) The man threatened was the plaintiff's father who, soon afterward, was shot and killed.

After discussing the duty to rescue, the court held defendant liable:

"We conclude that the bartender owed a duty to plaintiff's decedent to permit the patron from Happy Jack's to call the police.

It bears emphasizing that the duty in this case does not require that one go to the aid of another. That is not the issue here. The employee was not the good Samaritan intent on aiding another. The patron was."

French law

French Criminal Code

ARTICLE 63(2)

One who voluntarily abstains from giving assistance to a person in peril when he can do so without risk to himself or a third party [is punishable by imprisonment of three months to five years and a fine of 360 to 20,000 francs.].

Note: French courts have held that one who violates this provision is civilly liable to the plaintiff under arts. 1382–83 of the French Civil Code for committing a fault. Cass., Crim. ch., 16 Mar. 1972, 1972 Bull. crim. 109.

German law

German Criminal Code

§ 323c

One who does not give help in the event of an accident, a common danger or need although it is necessary and demanded of him by the circumstances, and, in particular, is possible without serious danger to himself and without violation of other more important duties is punishable by imprisonment of up to one year or with a fine.

Oberlandesgericht, Frankfurt, 27 October 1988, NJW-RR 1989, 794

The plaintiff was accused of stealing a bottle of perfume at a store by one of the store detectives. This detective called another detective to his aid. An altercation ensued in which the first detective beat the plaintiff, causing him minor injuries. The plaintiff sued both of them. The *Oberlandesgericht* held that he could not recover against the second who had not struck him.

"Neither does the defendant have a valid claim for compensation for harm against [the detective who did not strike him] on the grounds of omission to give help (§ 823(2) Civil Code; § 323c Criminal Code). The purpose of the criminal provision on the failure to give help is the protection of the interest of the public in solidarity in avoiding danger in a situation of acute need. The protection of the interest of the person threatened is only a byproduct of a norm which was established in the general interest. The criminal provision is not a protective statute within the meaning of § 823(2) of the Civil Code because the person who fails to give help should not be left with the same liability as the injurer. (Staudinger-Schäfer, *BGB*, 12th ed. (1986), § 823 no. 591; Steffen in *RGRK*, 12th ed. (1981), § 823 no. 546; Dütz, NJW 1976, 1822)."

Note: This decision seems to be the only one to have considered whether the plaintiff can bring a civil action when the defendant has violated § 323c of the Criminal Code. The decisions reproduced below are all criminal cases. They have been included because they raise interesting questions about the duty to rescue and about what a civil action would look like if one could be brought.

Implications of recognizing a duty to rescue

It is clear how these French and German law would deal with cases like the shooting at Happy Jack's Saloon. As the following cases illustrate, other implications are less obvious. (Since the numbering of the provisions of the German Criminal Code has changed since these cases were decided, the new number has been substituted for the old to avoid confusion.)

RESCUING THOSE WHO ATTEMPT SUICIDE

French law

Cour de cassation, ch. crim., 13 May 1998, pourvoi no. 97-81.969, arrêt no. 2988

Valérie C. was charged with failure to come to the assistance of Emmanuel G. After telling her he would hang himself, he went into the bathroom and committed suicide. The lower court held C. not guilty; the *Cour d'appel* affirmed: "on the grounds that the civil parties (*parties civiles*) maintain that against Valérie C. are all the elements that constitute the crime of non-assistance to a person in peril; that nevertheless, the structure of this crime presupposes that there is an imminent and existing peril necessitating immediate assistance; that neither the threat of Emmanuel G. (whose personality would not make one fear that he would put his threat into execution) nor the fact that he entered the bathroom (a place a priori not propitious for the execution of such a threat), nor the unconfirmed declarations of the sister of Jean-Christolphe G. are circumstances sufficient to permit one to say that Emmanuel G. was seriously going to put an end to his life and that, effectively, there was an imminent and existing peril warranting immediate assistance. . . ."

[The *Cour de cassation* affirmed, saying that it was satisfied with the findings of the *Cour d'appel*.]

German law

Bundesgerichtshof, 12 February 1952, BGHSt 2, 150

"The defendant's husband killed himself by hanging because of marital and household quarrels. While he was already unconscious but still could be rescued, the defendant came, observed this, but nevertheless let him hang. She was 'in accord with the course of events that had come to pass without her doing anything' and 'did not wish to alter them by providing assistance.'

Section [323c] of the Criminal Code is certainly valid, but it is not applicable here. An 'accident' is a sudden outer event that causes serious harm to persons or things and threatens to cause further harm. RGSt 75, 68; *id.* 75, 162; *id.* 77,303. This outer event is independent of the will of the victim: he can only try to avoid it. Here, we can leave aside whether unexpectedly committing suicide can, under circumstances, be such an outer event. In any case, linguistically and conceptually, there cannot be an accident when person responsible for the suicide produced the danger to his life essentially as he conceived it, and as long as he truly had the will to kill himself."

[The court went on to say that the woman might still be guilty, not under § 323c, but because married people have a special duty to look out for each other. It remanded, however, for findings on her mental state and in particular on her awareness that she was violating this duty.]

Note: Later decisions make it clear (as this court implied) that suicide will count as an accident when the perpetrator is insane and therefore deemed not to "truly will" his own death.

Note: In American law, although there is no general duty to rescue, a case like this would be handled in a similar way. There is a duty to rescue a spouse, a child, or other person to whom one stands in a special relationship.

RESCUING ONE'S VICTIMS

French law

Cour de cassation, ch. crim., 3 December 1997, pourvoi no. 95-85.915, arrêt no. 6405

"The decision under appeal . . . declared A. responsible for 1/4 of the physical harm suffered by Serge G. and, as a result, held him liable *in solidum* with Nysor Z. to pay to this civil party (*partie civile*) the sum of 3,000 francs, the amount being provisional while awaiting the results of a medical report that the court ordered. . . .

[I]t is shown from the findings of the court below that after Serge G. was seriously injured and immobilized after hitting the stone marking the side of the road with his automobile, Somir A., A. and Nysor Z. arrived at the scene; that Samir A. took off his jacket and stole it along with several objects that it contained; that all three left without giving him help; that they were prosecuted and convicted, the first, a minor, by the *Tribunal pour enfants* for non-assistance to a person in peril and aggravated theft, and the others, by the *Tribunal correctionel*, for non-assistance to a person in peril and for complicity in theft."

The *Cour de Cassation* affirmed without discussion.

German law

Bundesgerichtshof, 6 May 1960, BGHSt 14, 282

"The lower court convicted the defendant of serious bodily injury leading to the death of the victim."

The prosecutor brought charges of wrongful omission of assistance under [§ 323c] of the Criminal Code. The accusation is that the defendant did not immediately seek medical care for F. on whom he had inflicted life threatening injuries from which he later died. . . .

On the night of 30 August 1958, defendant met F., an assistant, in a shop belonging to friends in H. He was unknown to F. and seriously drunk. [A fight ensued in which the defendant beat F. senseless and left him lying outside the shop on the street.]

[The court said that if the defendant had intended the death of F., he would be guilty of intentional homicide. That would be so even if his intent were conditional in the sense explained earlier: he envisioned it and was indifferent to it although he did not desire it. Here, however the defendant did not have that intent. Nevertheless, he is still liable under § 323c.]

"The established case law of this Senate holds that one whose negligence in traffic has placed another in danger of life or limb and does not provide him with the assistance he requires is culpable under § [323c]. This point of criminal law is also applicable when one person by an intentional criminal act has placed another in a condition which is an accident for the other person provided that the victim is threatened with greater harm than the actor intended."

DISTINGUISHING FAILURE TO RESCUE FROM MISDIAGNOSIS

French law

**Cour de cassation, ch. crim., 15 December 1999,
pourvoi no. 99-83.529, arrêt no. 8104**

Dr. C. was convicted of non-assistance to a person in peril fined 20,000 francs, and condemned to two months' imprisonment. The lower court also "ruled on the civil interests." The *Cour d'appel* upheld his conviction: "on the grounds that Dr. C., age 48, head of pediatrics at the hospital center, was informed on Sunday afternoon, December 3, of an aggravation in the condition of the infant by Miss A., age 30, medical attaché with the neonatology service for two years, and by Mr. Ab., age 35, neonatology intern for one year, who had neither his experience nor his competence; that when Dr. C. had taken over the visiting schedule of Dr. Y. on Friday and Saturday, August 1 and 2, he saw no confirmation of the slight improvement that was alleged to have taken place the preceding week; that new and alarming indications were perceptible and could not have escaped a normally attentive doctor, and, as a result, could not have escaped Dr. C. when he made the examinations he did Friday and Saturday; that it had been noted by hospital personnel on his medical charts that Valentin had lost weight again and had had new nocturnal vomitings and that his urination and bowel movements were infrequent, signals suggesting an organic origin; that Dr. C. said on September 3 that he had found all the signs to indicate 'something organic,' and they asked themselves about 'the origin of this illness of organic origin'; that in light of the information he had been given by telephone and the indications of aggravation of the state of health of the infant which were already apparent Friday and Saturday, when he was on duty at the hospital, and which were mentioned above, he must necessarily have been aware that Valentin—who had been put under light surveillance for mental anorexia and had not been given any other examination—was in a state of imminent peril."

The defendant had argued to the *Cour de cassation* that the art. 63(2) of the Criminal Code "was not intended to punish errors in medical diagnosis but only strictly intentional conduct consisting in the voluntarily and deliberate refusal to give help to a person in peril." The *Cour de cassation* upheld the decision of the *Cour d'appel* without comment.

German law

Bundesgerichtshof, 22 March 1966, BGHSt 21, 50

The defendant was a surgeon and the director of the hospital in L. He had begun to neglect his profession. He often went hunting and was sometimes hard to reach. Late one Saturday afternoon, a 59 year old woman suffering from polio fell in her house breaking her left leg. Her personal physician came, diagnosed her as having a *Oberschenkelhalsbruch* [a break in a small bone connecting the ball of the thigh with the pelvis]. He had her sent by ambulance to the hospital in L. The defendant was at home at the time but was on call by telephone. He was called and told of the other doctor's diagnosis. He said he would see the injured woman when he made his normal rounds on Sunday. He said she should be kept quiet and given an anti-pain medication. The hospital nurse did so, and also splinted her leg. The next day on his visit he lifted her covers, took a quick look at the injured leg, made no examination of his own, and said he would look at her the next day.

Only Monday morning did he authorize X-rays. Monday afternoon, he looked at her from the door of her room and told her she had a *Schenkelhalsbruch*. In the days that followed she was treated only with splints and pain medicine. She was released from the hospital three weeks later without ever having had the leg examined. Later, she saw another doctor who took X-rays and discovered she had a fracture of a quite different and more serious kind. Because she had been improperly treated, it took a longer time for her to recover. The defendant was held to be responsible.

"The [woman's own physician] satisfied his duty to give her help in time of need. [BGStZ, 296, 299f.) Instead, as a non-specialist he could not provide the necessary and appropriate medical help (BGHSt, 21 May 1963, 1 StR 93/63, pg. 5.). The duty of assistance fell instead upon the defendant as a specialist and the surgeon of the hospital on the basis of the notification he had received by telephone from the nurse. As the *Landgericht* correctly noted, he was obligated when informed of these facts to come immediately to the hospital and, if necessary by taking X-rays, to determine whether a surgical intervention or some other measures to avoid danger were called for."

FAILING TO BE IN A FIT STATE TO RESCUE

German law

Oberlandesgericht, Bavaria, 22 February 1974, NJW 1974, 1520

"The defendant, an innkeeper, through the use of alcohol fell into a state in which he was unable to discern the illegality of his action and to act accordingly. After 7:00 P.M., W. had a collision in front of the inn—presumably from failing to make a left turn—and suffered serious head injuries. Witness K. wanted to summon help quickly. She went into defendant's inn which was open since 7:00 to telephone from there. She called to the defendant, who was on the 1st floor [which Americans call the 2nd floor] that she needed an ambulance and police for a man who was lying in front of the building. The defendant, whose telephone was closest to the place of the accident, answered that what was in front of his building was of no concern to him."

[He was convicted under what is now § 323c of the German Criminal Code. The court observed that the Code makes it punishable for a person "negligently or intentionally" to get drunk if the person "commits an illegal act while in this state and cannot be punished for it because he was not capable of fault due to his drunkenness. . . ." The court said that it did not matter that his illegal act consisted in an omission—failure to give help as required by what is now § 323c. It also said:]

"[I]t is obvious that the 32 year old defendant, as an innkeeper, had sufficient experience of life to know that drunkenness can lead to criminally punishable acts or omissions. He could and should have foreseen that what can happen to one when one is drunk could happen to him as well. Besides, as the findings below establish, the defendant must have been aware that the inn he had closed in the afternoon would be open again at 7:00 P.M., and that he would then have to resume his duties to the public. . . ."

4. Strict liability

a. Liability for activities that cause physical harm

Liability for dangerous or "non-natural" activities

THE GENERAL PRINCIPLE

English law

Fletcher v. Rylands, (1866) L.R. 1 Ex. 265

The defendant built a reservoir on his land unaware that it had once been mined for coal and ancient shafts still lay under the ground. Because of the shafts, the water in the reservoir escaped and flooded the plaintiff's land.

Blackburn, J. "We think that the true rule of law is, that the person who for his own purposes brings on his lands and collects and keeps there anything likely to do mischief if it escapes, must keep it in at his peril, and, if he does not do so, is prima facie answerable for all the damage which is the natural consequence of its escape. He can excuse himself by shewing that the escape was owing to the plaintiff's default; or perhaps that the escape was the consequence of vis major, or the act of God; but as nothing of this sort exists here, it is unnecessary to inquire what excuse would be sufficient. The general rule, as above stated, seems on principle just. The person whose grass or corn is eaten down by the escaping cattle of his neighbour, or whose mine is flooded by the water from his neighbour's reservoir, or whose cellar is invaded by the filth of his neighbour's privy, or whose habitation is made unhealthy by the fumes and noisome vapours of his neighbour's alkali works, is damnified without any fault of his own; and it seems but reasonable and just that the neighbour, who has brought something on his own property which was not naturally there, harmless to others so long as it is confined to his own property, but which he knows to be mischievous if it gets on his neighbour's, should be obliged to make good the damage which ensues if he does not succeed in confining it to his own property. But for his act in bringing it there no mischief could have accrued, and it seems but just that he should at his peril keep it there so that no mischief may accrue, or answer for the natural and anticipated consequences. And upon authority, this we think is established to be the law whether the things so brought be beasts, or water, or filth, or stenches.

The case that has most commonly occurred, and which is most frequently to be found in the books, is as to the obligation of the owner of cattle which he has brought on his land, to prevent their escaping and doing mischief. The law as to them seems to be perfectly well settled from early times; the owner must keep them at his peril. . . ."

Rylands v. Fletcher, [1868] L.R. 3 H.L. 330

Cairns, L.C. "My Lords, the principles on which this case must be determined appear to me to be extremely simple. The Defendants, treating them as the owners or occupiers of the close on which the reservoir was constructed, might lawfully have used that close for any purpose for which it might in the ordinary course of the enjoyment of land be used, and if, in what I may term the natural use of that land, there had been any accumulation of water, either on the surface or underground, and if, by the operation of the laws of nature, that accumulation of water had passed off into the close occupied by the Plaintiff, the Plaintiff could not have complained that that result had taken place. If he had desired to guard himself against it, it would have lain upon him to have done so, by leaving, or by interposing, some barrier between his close and the close of the Defendants in order to have prevented the operation of the law of nature. . . .

On the other hand if the Defendants, not stopping at the natural use of their close, had desired to use it for any purpose which I may term a non-natural use, for the purpose of introducing into the close that which in its natural condition was not in or upon it, for the purpose of introducing water either above or below ground in quantities and in a manner not the result of any work or operation on or under the land, and if in consequence of their doing so, or in consequence of any imperfection in the mode of their doing so, the water came to escape and to pass off into the close of the Plaintiff, then it appears to me that that which the Defendants were doing they were doing at their own peril. . . ."

Read V. J. Lyons & Co., Ltd., [1947] A.C. 156 (H.L.)

"The respondents, under an agreement with the Ministry of Supply, undertook the operation, management and control of an ordnance factory as agents for the Ministry, and carried on in the factory the business of filling shell cases with high explosives. The appellant was an employee of the Ministry, with the duty of inspecting the filling of shell cases, and, while lawfully in the shell-filling shop in discharge of her duty, was injured by the explosion of a shell. In an action for damages for the injuries sustained no negligence was averred or proved against the respondents."

Viscount Simond. "Now, the strict liability recognised by this House to exist in Rylands v. Fletcher is conditioned by two elements which I may call the condition of 'escape' from the land of something likely to do mischief if it escapes, and the condition of 'non-natural use' of the land. This second condition has in some later cases, which did not reach this House, been otherwise expressed, e.g., as 'exceptional' user, when such user is not regarded as 'natural' and at the same time is likely to produce mischief if there is an 'escape.' . . . It is not necessary to analyse this second condition on the present occasion, for in the case now before us the first essential condition of 'escape' does not seem to me to be present at all. 'Escape,' for the purpose of applying the proposition in Rylands v. Fletcher means escape from a place which the defendant has occupation of, or control over, to a place which is outside his occupation or control. . . . Here there is no escape of the relevant kind at all and the appellant's action fails on that ground."

W.V.H. Rogers, *Winfield & Jolowicz on Tort* (15th ed. 1998), 546

"The rule is not confined to the case where the defendant is the freeholder of the land on which the dangerous thing is accumulated: the defendant in *Rylands v. Fletcher* itself appears to have had only a license from the land-owner to construct the reservoir. Similarly, the rule has been applied in cases where the defendant has a franchise or statutory right, for example to lay pipes to carry gas[55] or cables for electricity.[56] Indeed, there are statements to the effect that anyone who collects the dangerous thing and has control of it at the time of the escape would be liable,[57] even when it is being carried on the highway and escapes therefrom.[58]

---

55. *Northwestern Utilities Ltd v. London Guarantee Ltd* [1936] A.C. 108 at 118; *cf. Read v. Lyons* [1947] A.C. 156 at 183.

56. *Charing Cross Electricity Supply Co. v. Hydraulic Power Co.* [1914] 3 K.B. 772.

57. *Rainham Chemical Works v. Belvedere Fish Guano Co.* [1921] 2 A.C. 465 at 479.

58. *Powell v. Fall* (1880) 5 Q.B.D. 597; *Rigby v. Chief Constable of Northamptonshire* [1985] 1 Q.L.R. 1242. See also *Crown River Cruises v. Kimbolton Fireworks* [1995] 2 Lloyd's Rep. 533.

Cambridge Water Co Ltd v. Eastern Counties Leather plc., [1994] 2 AC 264 (H.L.)

"The defendant was an old-established leather manufacturer which used a chemical solvent in its tanning process. In the course of the process there were regular spillages of relatively small amounts of the solvent onto the concrete floor of the tannery prior to a change of method in 1971, the total spillage over a period of years being at least 1,000 gallons. The spilled solvent, which was not readily soluble in water, seeped through the tannery floor into the soil below until it reached an impermeable strata 50 metres below the surface from where it percolated along a plume at the rate of about 8 metres a day until it reached the strata from which the plaintiffs extracted water for domestic use via a borehole. The distance between the plaintiffs' borehole and the defendants' tannery was 173 miles and time taken for the solvent to seep from the tannery to the borehole was about 9 months."

The court held that the plaintiff could not recover either in nuisance or under the rule in *Rylands v. Fletcher* unless the defendant could have foreseen that its activity might cause the harm the plaintiff suffered. In reaching his conclusion, however, Lord Goff reconsidered the foundations and the scope of the rule in *Rylands v. Fletcher*.

Lord Goff of Chieveley. "In order to consider the question in the present case in its proper legal context, it is desirable to look at the nature of liability in a case such as the present in relation both to the law of nuisance and the rule in Rylands v. Fletcher, and for that purpose to consider the relationship between the two heads of liability.

I begin with the law of nuisance. Our modern understanding of the nature and scope of the law of nuisance was much enhanced by Professor Newark's seminal article 'The boundaries of nuisance' (1949) 65 LQR 480. . . . Professor Newark considered (at pp 487–488) [that there had been] a misappreciation of the decision in Rylands v. Fletcher:

'This case is generally regarded as an important landmark, indeed a turning point—in the law of tort; but an examination of the judgments shows that those who decided it were quite unconscious of any revolutionary or reactionary principles implicit in the decision. They thought of it as calling for no more than a restatement of settled principles, and Lord Cairns went so far as to describe those principles as "extremely simple". And in fact the main principle involved was extremely simple, being no more than the principle that negligence is not an element in the tort of nuisance. It is true that Blackburn J. in his great judgment in the Exchequer Chamber never once used the word "nuisance", but three times he cited the case of fumes escaping from an alkali works—a clear case of nuisance—as an instance of liability, under the rule which he was laying down. Equally it is true that in 1866 there were a number of cases in the reports suggesting that persons who controlled dangerous things were under a strict duty to take care, but as none of these cases had anything to do with nuisance Blackburn J. did not refer to them. But the profession as a whole, whose conceptions of the boundaries of nuisance were now becoming fogged, failed to see in Rylands v. Fletcher a simple case of nuisance. They regarded it as an exceptional case—and the rule in Rylands v. Fletcher as a generalisation of exceptional cases, where liability was to be strict on account of 'the magnitude of danger, coupled with the difficulty of proving negligence' [Pollock on Torts (14th edn, 1939) p 386] rather than on account of the nature of the plaintiff's interest which was invaded. They therefore jumped rashly to two conclusions: firstly, that the rule in Rylands v. Fletcher could be extended beyond the case of neighbouring occupiers; and secondly, that the rule could be used to afford a remedy in cases of personal injury. . . .'

We are not concerned in the present case with the problem of personal injuries, but we are concerned with the scope of liability in nuisance and in Rylands v. Fletcher. In my opinion it is right to take as our starting point the fact that, as Professor Newark considered, Rylands v. Fletcher was indeed not regarded by Blackburn J. as a revolutionary decision. . . . [T]he essential basis of liability was the collection by the defendant of such things upon his land; and the consequence was a strict liability in the event of damage caused by their escape, even if the escape was an isolated event. Seen in its context, there is no reason to suppose that Blackburn J. intended to create a liability any more strict than that created by the law of nuisance; but even so he must have intended that, in the circumstances specified by him, there should be liability for damage resulting from an isolated escape. . . .

It is against this background that it is necessary to consider the question whether foreseeability of harm of the relevant type is an essential element of liability either in nuisance or under the rule in Rylands v. Fletcher. I shall take first the case of nuisance."

[He concludes that foreseeability of the relevant type of harm is, indeed, required for liability in nuisance. He argues that "the historical connection with the law of nuisance must now be regarded as pointing towards the conclusion that foreseeability of damage is a prerequisite of the recovery of damages under the rule" in Rylands v. Fletcher.]

"Even so, the question cannot be considered solely as a matter of history. It can be argued that the rule in Rylands v. Fletcher should not be regarded simply as an extension of the law of nuisance, but should rather be treated as a developing principle of strict liability from which can be derived a general rule of strict liability for damage caused by ultra-hazardous operations, on the basis of which persons conducting such operations may properly be held strictly liable for the extraordinary risk to others involved in such operations. As is pointed out in Fleming on Torts (8th edn, 1992) pp 327–328, this would lead to the practical result that the cost of damage resulting from such operations would have to be absorbed as part of the overheads of the relevant business rather than be borne (where there is no negligence) by the injured person or his insurers, or even by the community at large. Such a development appears to have been taking place in the United States, as can be seen from § 519 of the Restatement of Torts (2d) vol 3 (1977). The extent to which it has done so is not altogether clear; and I infer from para 519, and the comment on that paragraph, that the abnormally dangerous activities there referred to are such that their ability to cause harm would be obvious to any reasonable person who carried them on.

I have to say, however, that there are serious obstacles in the way of the development of the rule in Rylands v. Fletcher in this way. First of all, if it was so to develop, it should logically apply to liability to all persons suffering injury by reason of the ultra-hazardous operations; but the decision of this House in Read v. J Lyons & Co Ltd [1946] 2 All ER 471 [1947] AC 156, which establishes that there can be no liability under the rule except in circumstances where the injury has been caused by an escape from land under the control of the defendant, has effectively precluded any such development. Professor Fleming has observed that 'the most damaging effect of the decision in Read v. Lyons is that it prematurely stunted the development of a general theory of strict liability for ultra-hazardous activities' (see Fleming on Torts (8th edn, 1992) p 341). Even so, there is much to be said for the view that the courts should not be proceeding down the path of developing such a general theory. In this connection, I refer in particular to the Report of the Law Commission on Civil Liability for Dangerous Things and Activities (Law Com no 32) 1970. In paras 14–16 of the report the Law Commission expressed serious misgivings about the adoption of any test for the application of strict liability involving a general concept of 'especially dangerous' or 'ultra-hazardous' activity, having regard to the uncertainties and practical difficulties of its application. If the Law Commission is unwilling to consider statutory reform on this basis, it must follow that judges should if anything be even more reluctant to proceed down that path.

Like the judge in the present case, I incline to the opinion that, as a general rule, it is more appropriate for strict liability in respect of operations of high risk to be imposed by Parliament, than by the courts. If such liability is imposed by statute, the relevant activities can be identified, and those concerned can know where they stand. Furthermore, statute can where appropriate lay down precise criteria establishing the incidence and scope of such liability."

W.V.H. Rogers, *Winfield & Jolowicz on Tort* (15th ed. 1998), 543–44

"Over the years *Rylands v. Fletcher* has been applied to a remarkable variety of things[31]: fire,[32] gas,[33] explosions,[34] electricity,[35] oil,[36] noxious fumes,[37] colliery spoil,[38] rusty wire from a decayed fence,[39] vibrations,[40]

---

31. See Stallybrass "Dangerous Things and the Non-Natural User of Land" (1929) 3 Camb. L.J. 382–85.

32. See pp. 559 *et seq.*, below.

33. *Batchellor v. Tunbridge Wells Gas Co.* (1901) 84 L.T. 765.

34. *Miles v. Forest Rock, etc. Co.* (1918) 34 T.L.R. 500; *Rainham Chemical Works Ltd. v. Belvedere Fish Guano Co. Ltd.* [1921] 2 A.C. 465.

35. *National Telephone Co. v. Baker* [1893] 2 Ch. 186; *Eastern and South African Telegraph Co., Ltd. v. Cape Town Tramways Companies Ltd* [1902] A.C. 381; *Hillier v. Air Ministry* [1962] C.L.Y. 2084 (cows electrocuted

by an escape of electricity from high-voltage cables laid under plaintiff's field).

36. *Smith v. G.W. Ry* (1926) 135 L.T. 112.

37. *West v. Bristol Tramways Co.* [1908] 2 K.B. 14 (insofar as the case applied the rule to a risk which was not foreseeable it cannot stand with the *Cambridge Water* case).

38. *Att.-Gen. V. Cory Bros Ltd* [1921] 1 A.C. 521.

39. *Firth v. Bowling Iron Co.* (1878) 3 C.P.D. 254.

40. *Hoare & Co. v. McAlpine* [1923] 1 Ch. 167; *cf. Dodd Properties Ltd v. Canterbury City Council* [1979] 2 All E.R. 118 at 122.

poisonous vegetation,[41] a flag pole,[42] a 'chair-o-plane' in a fair-ground,[43] and even (in a case of very questionable validity) noxious persons.[44] Given the emphasis in the *Cambridge Water* case on the close connection with the law of nuisance and the rejection of a broad rule governing ultra-hazardous activities there is probably now little point in seeking to identify the characteristics of a '*Rylands v. Fletcher* object' and it seems sufficient to rely on (1) the factual test stated by Blackburn J. of whether the thing is 'likely to do mischief if it escapes' and (2) the requirement of non-natural user."

W.V.H. Rogers, *Winfield & Jolowicz on Tort* (15th ed. 1998), 548–49

"Notwithstanding the refusal to develop *Rylands v. Fletcher* into a general principle of strict liability for ultra-hazardous activities, the *effect* of the case law seems to go some way along this road by excluding from the scope of the rule minor or common or domestic uses of things which have some potential for danger. So the following have been regarded as natural uses of land: water installations in a house or office[78]; a fire in a domestic grate[79]; electric wiring[80]; gas pipes in a house or shop[81]; erecting or pulling down houses or walls[82]; burning stubble in the normal course of agriculture[83]; the ordinary working of mines or minerals[84]; the possession of trees whether planted or self-sown[85]; or generating steam on a ship.[86] There has, however, been a greater willingness to apply the rule to the bulk storage or transmission of water[87] or gas or electricity,[88] or to the bulk

41. *Crowhurst v. Amersham Burial Board* (1878) 4 Ex. D. 5; *Ponting v. Noakes* [1894] 2 Q.B. 281.

42. *Shiffman v. Order of St. John* [1936] 1 All E.R. 557 (*obiter*, it was decided on the ground of negligence).

43. *Hale v. Jennings Bros* [1938] 1 All E.R. 579.

44. *Att.-Gen. V. Corke* [1933] Ch. 89; but *cf. Smith v. Scott* [1973] Ch. 314, where it is suggested that this case could at least equally well have been decided on the basis that the landowner was in possession of the property and was himself liable for nuisances created by his licensees. A New Zealand court refused to follow *Corke's* case in *Matheson v. Board of Governors of Northcote College* [1975] 2 N.Z.L.R. 106 but accepted that the occupier could be liable for creating a nuisance. Liability in nuisance was imposed in similar circumstances in *Dunton v. Dover District Council* (1977) 76 L.G.R. 87.

78. *Rickards v. Lothian* [1913] A.C. 263; *cf. Wei's Western Wear Ltd v. Yui Holdings Ltd* (1984) 5 D.L.R. (4th).

79. *Sochacki v. Sas* [1947] 1 All E.R. 344.

80. *Collingwood v. Home and Colonial Stores Ltd* [1936] 3 All E.R. 200.

81. *Miller v. Addie & Sons (Collieries) Ltd*, 1934 S.C. 150.

82. *Thomas and Evans Ltd v. Mid-Rhondda Co-operative Society* [1941] 1 K.B.

381; *cf. Gertsen v. Municipality of Metropolitan Toronto* (1973) 41 D L.R. (3d) 646 (landfill project using household waste which generated methane gas, not a natural user).

83. *Perkins v. Glyn* [1976] R.T.R. ix (note); *cf.* in the somewhat different climatic conditions of New Zealand, *New Zealand Forest Products Ltd v. O'Sullivan* [1974] 2 N.Z.L.R. 80, where, however, negligence was clearly established. In *Metson v. De Wolfe* (1980) 117 D.L.R. (3d) 278 at 283, it was said that there was no case in Nova Scotia: "Where the application of the rule in *Rylands v. Fletcher* has been in any way modified or eroded for considerations of normal agricultural husbandry."

84. *Rouse v. Gravelworks Ltd* [1940] 1 K.B. 489.

85. *Noble v. Harrison* [1926] 2 K.B. 332; *cf. Crowhurst v. Amersham Burial Board* (1878) 4 Ex.D. 5 (poisonous yew tree).

86. *Howard v. Furness etc. Ltd* [1936] 2 All E.R. 781; *Eastern Asia Navigation Co. Ltd v. Freemantle* (1951) 83 C.L.R. 353 (fuel oil store a natural user); *Miller Steamship Co. Pty. Ltd v. Overseas Tankship (U.K.) Ltd* [1963] 1 Lloyd's Rep. 402 at 426.

87. *Rylands v. Fletcher* itself.

88. *Charing Cross Electricity Supply Co. v. Hydraulic Power Co.* [1914] 3 K.B. 772; *Northwestern Utilities v. London Guarantee and Accident Co.* [1936] A.C. 108.

storage of chemicals,[89] though the defence of statutory authority has in many cases prevented a decision in the plaintiff's favour."

Law in the United States

Restatement (Third) of Torts (tentative draft on traditional strict liability)

§ 21 ABNORMALLY DANGEROUS ACTIVITIES

(A) A defendant who carries on an abnormally dangerous activity is subject to strict liability for physical harm resulting from the activity.

    (B) An activity is abnormally dangerous if:

        (1) the activity creates a foreseeable and highly significant risk of physical harm even when reasonable care is exercised by all actors; and

        (2) the activity is not a matter of common usage.

W. Page Keeton, Dan B. Dobbs, Robert E. Keeton & David G. Owen, *Prosser and Keeton on Torts* (5th ed. 1984), 549–51

"The conditions and activities to which the rule has been applied have followed the English pattern. They include water collected in quantity in a dangerous place,[65] or allowed to percolate;[66] explosives[67] or inflammable liquids[68] stored in quantity in the midst of a city; blasting;[69] pile driving;[70] crop dusting;[71] Contra: S.A. Gerrard Co. v. Fricker, 1933, 42 Ariz. 503, 27 P.2d 678; Miles v. A. Arena & Co., 1937, 23 Cal. App.2d 680, 73 P.2d 1260; Lawler v. Skelton, 1961, 241 Miss. 274, 130 So.2d 56. See Notes, 1968, 19 Hast. L.J.

89. *Cambridge Water co. v. Eastern Counties Leather plc* [1994] 2 A.C. 264.

65. Wilson v. City of New Bedford, 1871, 108 Mass. 261; Defiance Water Co. v. Olinger, 1896, 54 Ohio St. 532, 44 N.E. 238; Bridgeman-Russell Co. v. City of Duluth, 1924, 158 Minn. 509, 197 N.W. 971; Weaver Mercantile Co. v. Thurmond, 1911, 68 W. Va. 530, 70 S.E. 126; Smith v. Board of County Road Commissioners of Chippewa County, 1966, 5 Mich.App. 370, 146 N.W.2d 702, affirmed 381 Mich. 363, 161 N.W.2d 561. Cf. Kennecott Coopper Corp. v. McDowell, 1966, 100 Ariz. 276, 413 P.2d 749 (water in stream diverted against bridge).

66. Ball v. Nye, 1868, 99 Mass. 582; Kall v. Carruthers, 1922, 59 Cal.App. 555, 211 P. 43; Healey v. Citizens Gas & Electric Co., 1924, 199 Iowa 82, 201 N.W. 118; Norfolk & Western Railway Co. v. Amicon Fruit Co., 4th Cir. 1920, 269 F. 559.

67. Exner v. Sherman Power Construction Co., 2d Cir. 1931, 54 F.2d 510; Bradford Glycerine Co. v. St. Mary's Woolen Manufacturing Co., 1899, 60 Ohio St. 560, 54 N.E. 528; French v. Center Creek Powder Manufacturing Co., 1913, 173 Mo.App. 220, 158 S.W. 723; cf. Koster & Wythe v. Massey, 9th Cir. 1961, 293 F.2d 922, certiorari denied 368 U.S. 927,

82 S.Ct. 362, 7 L.Ed.2d 191 (incendiary bomb). See Notes, 1932, 17 Corn. L.Q. 703; 1966, 39 U.Colo. L. Rev. 161.

68. Brennan Construction Co. v. Cumberland, 1907, 29 U.S.App.D.C. 554; Berger v. Minneapolis Gaslight Co., 1895, 60 Minn. 296, 62 N.W. 336; Yommer v. McKenzie, 1969, 255 Md. 220, 257 A.2d 138. Cf. MacKenzie v. Fitchburg Paper Co., 1966, 351 Mass. 292, 218 N.E.2d 579 (dumping inflammable ink at city dump).

69. Caporale v. C.W. Blakeslee & Sons, Inc., 1961, 149 Conn. 79, 175 A.2d 561; Sachs v. Chiat, 1968, 281 Minn. 540, 162 N.W.2d 243.

70. Colton v. Onderdonk, 1886, 69 Cal. 155, 10 P. 395; Britton v. Harrison Construction Co., S.D.W.Va. 1948, 87 F.Supp. 405; Central Exploration Co. v. Gray, 1954, 219 Miss. 757, 70 So.2d 33; Brown v. L.S. Lunder Construction Co., 1942, 240 Wis. 122, 2 N.W.2d 859; Davis v. L. & W. Construction Co., Iowa 1970, 176 N.W.2d 223; see McNeal, Use of Explosives and Liability Questions Involved, 1956, 23 Ins.Counsel J. 125.

71. Young v. Darter, Ok. 1961, 363 P.2d 829; Loe v. Lenhardt, 1961, 227 Or. 242, 362 P.2d 312; Gotreaux v. Gary, La.App., 1957, 232 La. 373, 94 So.2d 293, appeal transferred 80 So.2d 578.

476; 1962, 40 Tex.L.Rev. 527; 1963, 49 Iowa L.Rev. 135. the fumigation of part of a building with cyanide gas;[72] drilling oil wells or operating refineries in thickly settled communities;[73] an excavation letting in the sea;[74] factories emitting smoke, dust or noxious gases in the midst of a town;[75] roofs so constructed as to shed snow into a highway;[76] and a dangerous party wall.[77]

On the other hand the conditions and activities to which the American courts have refused to apply Rylands v. Fletcher, whether they purport to accept or reject the case in principle, have been with few exceptions what the English courts would regard as a 'natural' use of land, and not within the rule at all. They include water in household pipes,[78] the tank of a humidity system,[79] or authorized utility mains;[80] gas in a meter,[81] electric wiring in a machine shop,[82] and gasoline in a filling station;[83] a dam in the natural bed of a stream;[84] ordinary steam boilers;[85] an ordinary fire in a factory;[86] an automobile;[87] Bermuda grass on a railroad

72. Luthringer v. Moore, 1948, 31 Cal.2d 489, 190 P.2d 1.

73. Green v. General Petroleum Corp., 1928, 205 Cal.328, 270 P. 952; Niagara Oil Co. v. Jackson, 1910, 48 Ind.App. 238, 91 N.E. 825; Helms v. Eastern Kansas Oil Co., 1917, 102 Kan. 164, 169 P. 208; Berry v. Shell Petroleum Co., 1934, 140 Kan. 94, 33 P.2d 953, rehearing denied, 1935, 141 Kan. 6, 40 P.2d 359. Cf. State Highway Commission v. Empire Oil & Refiing Co., 1935, 141 Kan. 161, 40 P.2d 355. See Green, Hazardous Oil and Gas Operations: Tort Liability, 1955, 33 Tex.L. Rev. 574.

74. Mears v. Dole, 1883, 135 Mass. 508.

75. Susquehanna Fertilizer Co. v. Malone, 1890, 73 Md. 268, 20 A. 900; Frost v. Berkeley Phosphate Co., 1894, 42 S.C. 402, 20 S.E. 280; Holman v. Athens Empire Laundry Co., 1919, 149 Ga. 345, 100 S.E. 207.

76. Shipley v. Fifty Associates, 1869, 101 Mass. 251, affirmed 1870, 106 Mass. 194; Hannem v. Pence, 1889, 40 Minn. 127, 41 N.W. 657.

77. Gorham v. Gross, 1878, 125 Mass. 232.

78. McCord Rubber Co. v. St. Joseph Water Co., 1904, 181 Mo. 678, 81 S.W. 189; Stevens-Salt Lake City, Inc. v. Wong, 1953, 123 Utah 309, 259 P.2d 586; Shanander v. Western Loan & Building Co., 1951, 103 Cal.App.2d 507, 229 P.2d 864.

79. Fibre Leather Manufacturing Corp. v. Ramsay Mills, Inc., 1952, 329 Mass. 575, 109 N.E.2d 910.

80. Midwest Oil Co. v. City of Aberdeen, 1943, 69 S.D. 343, 10 N.W.2d 701; Interstate Sash & Door Co. v. City of Cleveland, 1947, 148 Ohio St. 325, 74 N.E.2d 239; Grace & Co. v. City of Los Angeles, S.D.Cal. 1958, 168 F.Supp. 344, affirmed 9th Cir.1960, 278 F.2d 771. But a city which deliberately adopted a policy of

burying cast iron pipe six feet underground and leaving it there until leaks developed, was held to strict liability in Lubin v. Iowa City, 1964, 257 Iowa 383, 131 N.W.2d 765.

81. Triple-State Natural Gas & Oil Co. v. Wellman, 1902, 114 Ky. 79, 70 S.W. 49. Cf. St. Mary's Gas Co. v. Brodbeck, 1926, 114 Ohio St. 423, 151 N.E. 323.

82. Mangan's Administrator v. Louisville Electric Light Co., 1906, 122 Ky. 476, 91 S.W. 703. Cf. McKenzie v. Pacific Gas & Electric Co., 1962, 200 Cal.App.2d 731, 19 Cal.Rptr. 628 (power line).

83. Greene v. Spinning, Mo.App.1932, 48 S.W.2d 51. Cf. Collins v. Liquid Transporters, Inc., Ky.1953, 262 S.W.2d 382 (tank trucks on highway).

84. City Water Power Co. v. City of Fergus Falls, 1910, 113 Minn. 33, 128 N.W. 817; Barnum v. Handschiegel, 1919, 103 Neb. 594, 173 N.W. 593; McHenry v. Ford Motro Co., E.D. Mich.1956, 146 F.Supp. 896, affirmed, 6th Cir.1959, 261 F.2d 833, rehearing 269 F.2d 18; New Brantner Extension Ditch Co. v. Derguson, 1957, 134 Colo. 502, 307 P.2d 479, Cf. Esson v. Wattier, 18993, 25 Or. 7, 34 P. 756; Clark v. United States, D.Or.1952, 109 F.Supp. 213, affirmed 9th Cir.1955, 218 F.2d 446.

85. Huff v. Austin, 1889, 46 Ohio St. 386, 21 N.E. 864; Losee v. Buchanan, 1873, 51 N.Y. 476; Marshall v. Welwood, 1876, 38 N.J.L. 339. Cf. Fitz v. E. I. De Pont De Nemours & Co., 1950, 45 Del. (6 Terry) 427, 75 A.2d 256 (chlorine gas in industrial plant where specific use not shown).

86. O'Day v. Shouvlin, 1922, 17 Ohio App. 62, affirmed 104 Ohio St. 519, 136 N.E. 289. Steffen v. McNaughton, 1910, 142 Wis. 49, 124 N.W. 1016.

87. See footnote 115 supra.

right of way;[88] a small quantity of dynamite kept for sale in a Texas hardware store;[89] barnyard spray in a farmhouse;[90] a division fence;[91] the wall of a house left standing after a fire;[92] coal mining operations regarded as usual and normal;[93] vibrations from ordinary building construction;[94] earth moving operations in grading a hillside;[95] the construction of a railroad tunnel;[96] and even a runaway horse.[97]"

German law

Note on the origins of strict liability in Germany: Roman law recognized instances of strict liability. Nevertheless, the German Civil Code does not provide for strict liability in tort. The reason is that for centuries before it was drafted, legal scholars had been sceptical about whether there could be any reason in principle for strict liability.

As we have seen, Roman law gave an action under the *lex Aquilia*, for damage done by fault (*culpa*). It also recognized certain cases of strict liability. A number of them look like the kind American law treats with the doctrine of *res ipsa loquitur*. The defendant is likely to have been at fault though there is no direct evidence. For example, the plaintiff is struck by an object thrown from the defendant's window or hung by the defendant over the street, or he is robbed while staying in the defendant's inn.[1] In American law, if the plaintiff were struck by an object that fell from defendant's building, and if it is likely that this event occurred because the defendant or his employee was negligent, then the plaintiff does not have to make any other proof of negligence: the thing speaks for itself, which is what *res ipsa loquitur* means. The defendant then has the burden of proving that he was not negligent. Roman law was different. The defendant was liable without any proof of fault in the situations just described, and he was not allowed to prove he had not been negligent. But perhaps the underlying problem is the same: what to do when the defendant is likely to have been negligent, and the plaintiff has no way of proving that he was other than by pointing to the situation.

Two Roman actions were available in situations with a closer resemblance to those in which some modern systems impose strict liability. Plaintiff could recover using the action *de pauperie* against the owner of

---

88. Gulf, Colorado & Santa Fe Railway Co. v. Oakes, 1900, 94 Tex. 155, 58 S.W. 999.

89. Barnes v. Zettlemoyer, 1901, 25 Tex.Civ.App. 468, 62 S.W. 111. Cf. Henn v. Universal Atlas Cement Co., Ohio Com. P. 1957, 144 N.E.2d 917 (blasting in a rural area, causing vibration).

90. Branstetter v. Robbins, 1955, 178 Kan. 8, 283 P.2d 455.

91. Quinn v. Crimmings, 1898, 171 Mass. 255, 50 N.E. 624.

92. Ainsworth v. Lakin, 1902, 180 Mass. 397, 62 N.E. 746.

93. Pennsylvania Coal Co. v. Sanderson, 1886, 113 Pa. 126, 6 A. 453; Kentucky lock Fuel Co. v. Roberts, 1925, 207 Ky. 137, 268 S.W. 802; Venzel v. Valley Camp Coal o., 1931, 304 Pa. 583, 156 A. 240; Jones v. Robertson, 1886, 116 Ill. 543, 6 N.E. 890.

94. Gallin v. Poulou, 1956, 140 Cal. App.2d 638, 295 P.2d 958.

95. Beck v. Bel Air Properties, 1955, 134 Cal.App.2d 834, 286 P.2d 503.

96. Marin Municipal Water District v. Northwestern Pacific Railroad Co., 1967, 253 Cal.App.2d 83, 61 Cal.Rptr. 520.

97. Brown v. Collins, 1873, 53 N.H. 442.

1. G. Inst. 4.5.

domestic animals for harm that they caused.[2] The action was "noxal": the owner could escape further liability by surrendering the animal to the plaintiff. The plaintiff could recover for harm caused by wild animals under the *edictum de feris*.[3] This action could be brought against anyone who had custody of the animal, whether or not he owned it. Also, a Roman family head (*paterfamilias*) was liable for torts committed by his child or his slave.[4] Again, liability was "noxal": he could escape liability by surrendering the child or the slave. By post classical times, he was no longer permitted to surrender the child.[5]

Medieval and early modern jurists preserved the Roman rules, although, as slavery had largely disappeared, there was an on-going debate over whether a master was liable for torts committed by his servants.[6] They did not suggest why there should be strict liability in such cases.

Most of the late scholastics and northern natural lawyers found the matter puzzling. Again, late scholastics were drawing on Aristotle and Thomas Aquinas. As we have seen, Aristotle had distinguished voluntary from involuntary commutative justice. In the former case, the parties exchanged equivalents; in the latter, one party had wrongfully deprived the other of something and had to restore equality by giving him an equivalent.[7] Aquinas put the two ideas together: a party who injured another through his fault was obliged as a matter of commutative justice to compensate him.[8] If the party was not at fault, he was not obliged to compensate because, according to Aquinas, *qua* human being, he had not caused the harm.[9] Here, he was drawing on Aristotle's idea that man was a rational animal: he acts by understanding his end and choosing accordingly. Therefore, a person was not responsible if he did not choose, for example, if he did harm because his body was moved by irresistible force.[10] Late scholastics such as Luis de Molina and Leonard Lessius concluded that, in principle, a person should only be liable for fault.[11] Hugo Grotius agreed.[12]

Samuel Pufendorf was one of the few who thought that one could find a principled explanation for strict liability. The owner of an animal should be liable for the harm it does because "the owner gets the profit from his animal while [the victim] suffered loss from it."[13] As we will see, this suggestion was picked up by Jean Domat and may have influenced the drafters of the French Civil Code. But no one made a systematic attempt to turn this insight into a theory of liability without fault.

---

2. *See generally*, Reinhard Zimmermann, *The Law of Obligations: Roman Foundations of the Civilian Tradition* (1990), 1096–1104.

3. *See generally id.* 1104–07.

4. *See generally id.* 1118–20.

5. *Id.* 1118–19.

6. *Id.* 1119.

7. Nicomachean Ethics V.ii.

8. *Summa theologiae* Q. 61, a. 3; Q. 64, a. 8.

9. *Id.* I-II, Q. 6, aa. 1, 5–8; II-II, Q. 64, a. 8.

10. *Nicomachean Ethics* III.i.

11. Ludovicus Molina, *De iustitia et iure tractatus* (1614), disp. 698; Leonardus Lessius, *De iustitia et iure ceterisque virtutibus cardinalis libri quatuor* (1628), lib. 2, cap. 7, dubs. 2 & 6.

12. Hugo Grotius, *De iure belli ac pacis libri tres* (1646), II.xvii.21.

13. Samuel Pufendorf, *De iure nature ac gentium libri octo* (1688), III.i.6.

Nineteenth century German jurists took the same position as most of the natural lawyers. In principle or in theory, one could not explain strict liability. The German jurist Puchta argued that liability that went beyond fault was liability for chance.[14] The implied premise was that such a liability would extend indefinitely. There would be no way in principle to limit it.

Nevertheless, while the German Civil Code contains no provisions on strict liability, since the 19th century, the German legislature has been enacting special statutes holding a person strictly liable who engages in certain activities. The German courts have refused to extend the scope of strict liability by drawing analogies to these activities. And so, today, the defendant is strictly liable only if he engaged in an activity covered by a special statute.

Konrad Zweigert & Hein Kötz, *An Introduction to Comparative Law* (3rd ed. trans. by Tony Weir, 1998), 653–59

"In *German* law, apart from liability for 'luxury animals',[1] strict liability has been introduced exclusively by the legislator in a long series of special statutes not incorporated in the BGB. The reason for this is presumably that the German legislator still regards the principle of fault as the essence of the law of delict, and considers strict liability as anomalous and exceptional, meriting the less exalted status of enactment in special detailed statutes. There is also a long tradition behind this tendency to use special statutes: in 1838 § 25 of the Prussian Law of Railway Undertakings imposed strict liability on railways for all harm to persons or property occurring 'through carriage on the railway' unless the defendant could prove 'that the harm was caused by the fault of the victim or by an external and unavoidable event'. This statute was adopted in similar form by other states in Germany and in 1869 by Austria as well. 1871 saw the enactment of the Imperial Law of Liability, which is still in force today, though it has been amended frequently and is now called simply the Law of Liability. It lays down strict liability for harm to persons arising 'through the operation' of railways.

Harm is caused 'through the operation' of the railway if it is caused or contributed to by sudden braking, collapse of the track, sparks from the trains, signal failure, or other incidents of the technical operation of running a railway. Accidents to persons mounting or dismounting from trains or using railway stations are also included if they are due to the specific dangers of railway travel such as the height of the running-boards, the haste of

---

14. G.F. Puchta, *Pandekten* (7th ed. 1853), § 266. Similarly, see B. Windscheid, *Lehrbuch des Pandektenrechts* (7th ed. 1891), § 101.

1. Editor's note: The authors are referring to § 833 of the Civil Code: "If a person is killed or a person's body or health is injured or an object is harmed by an animal, the one who keeps [*hält*] the animal is obligated to compensate the injured person for the harm that results. The duty to compensate does not arise when the harm is caused by a tame

animal [*Haustier*] which is kept on account of the occupation, livelihood or maintenance of its keeper, and either the keeper has used the care ordinarily required to look after the animal, or the harm would have been done even if this care had been used." The original version contained only the first sentence. The second was added at the urging of agricultural interests. The animals to which the exemption of the second sentence does not apply are the so-called "luxury animals."

passengers, or the crowd on the platform, but a person who falls on a stairway in a station simply because the steps are defective can claim damages only under § 823 par. 1 BGB. The railway is not liable for accidents caused by *force majeure (höhere Gewalt)*. This is understood by the courts to mean external and elemental forces of nature or the conduct of third parties whose effects could not have been prevented even by the most extreme precautions. The railways will even be liable for flash floods, heavy snowstorms, or avalanches unless no conceivable precautions, such as a warning system or a reduction of speed, could have forestalled the accident. Nor is it a case of *force majeure if* the event which caused the harm is of such frequent occurrence that the railway should take account of it even if it can do nothing about it.

A passenger injured by sudden braking may sue the railway even if it is due to the quite unforeseeable appearance on the track of children or cattle which have broken through the protective fence. See RGZ 54,404; BGH VersR 1955,346.

If a victim contributes to the accident by his own fault, the courts weigh up the extent to which the dangerousness of the railway and the fault of the victim contributed to the harm and apportion that damages accordingly (see BGHZ 2,355).

In 1943 and 1977 the Law of Liability was extended by special statutes to cover cases in which death or personal injury is caused 'by the effects of electricity, gases, vapours, or liquids' coming from 'an installation for their transmission or supply by cable, pipe, or otherwise'. Included in particular are high tension cables, gasholders, steam conduits, and waterpipes. Once again liability is in principle excluded only in cases of *force majeure*. In a case where an 11-year-old child was injured when his kite, attached by wire rather than thread, came in contact with a high tension cable the Bundesgerichtshof held the defendant liable (BGHZ 7,338); such an accident was very unusual but it did not have that extraordinary, 'almost elemental quality' required before one could speak of *force majeure*. In such a case, however, the damages may be reduced on the ground of the plaintiff's contributory fault.

The liability of the custodian of a *motor vehicle* is less strict. It was introduced in 1908 and is now contained in the Road Traffic Act of 1952 (StVG). § 7 StVG makes the custodian of a motor vehicle ('Halter'—normally, but not necessarily, the owner) liable for damage to person or property which arises 'through the operation' of the vehicle. Liability is excluded:

> 'if the accident is caused by an unavoidable event attributable neither to a defect in the construction of the vehicle nor to a failure of any of its functional parts. In particular an event is unavoidable when it is attributable to the behaviour of the victim or of a third party not involved in the operation or of an animal, and both the custodian and the driver of the vehicle have taken all the care called for in the circumstances of the case.'

This means that even unforeseeable and unavoidable failure of the components of vehicle—such as a tyre defect, axle fracture through metal fatigue, brake failure, or the steering seizing up—makes the custodian liable, but if the accident is due to an 'external' event such as the occurrence of black ice or an animal running in front of the vehicle or faulty driving on the part of other motorists, the custodian is not liable if he can prove that both the driver and he himself observed 'all the care called for in the circumstances'. Such case is defined by the courts as 'care going beyond what is usually required, extreme and thoughtful concentration and circumspection' (BGH VersR 1962, p. 164 and repeatedly thereafter). In practice such proof is hardly ever forthcoming, and only in very few cases—such as when a car leaves the road because of entirely unpredictable black ice or a small child darts out on to the street from between two parked cars and is run over—has it been accepted that the accident was one which an 'ideally careful' driver could not have avoided. If any fault on the part of the victim contributed to the occurrence of the harm, damages are reduced as under the Law of Liability. Passengers in a vehicle can only sue the custodian under the Road Traffic Act if they were being carried by way of business and for reward, as in a taxi or bus; injured passengers in other cases must use the general provisions of the law of delict (§§ 823 ff. BGB).

The Air Traffic Law of 1922 lays down an especially strict liability for harm caused to persons and things other than those being carried in the airplane pursuant to contract. In practice this means harm caused on the surface of the earth, whether by flight noise or by crashing or crash-landing: the custodian of an airplane is liable even if he can show that the harm was caused by *force majeure* (see §§ 33 ff. Air Traffic Law).

A characteristic feature of all the statutes mentioned so far is that they strictly limit the amount of damages payable. Claims in respect of immaterial harm are wholly excluded, and an upper monetary limit is also fixed for the liability of the defendant. In the case of death or personal injury the custodian of a motor vehicle is liable only up to 500,000 DM, and if damages are payable in the form of an annuity, it may not exceed 30,000 DM per year. These limits are increased by statutory amendment from time to time in order to take inflation and other factors into account. If several people are injured or killed in the same accident, the applicable limits are 750,000 DM and 45,000 DM; if the total damage exceeds these limits, the victims' claims are scaled down. This is why almost all damages suits for personal injuries sustained in traffic accidents are based on §§ 823 ff. BGB as well as the Road Traffic Act. Indeed, only so can one obtain damages for pain and suffering. This means that even if liability under the Road Traffic Act is clear there is often a long and tiresome dispute about the proof of fault.

Since 1939 the custodian of a motor vehicle has been required by law to have insurance covering his own liability and that of the driver for the harm caused by the use of the vehicle. A licence to use the vehicle will only be issued if a certificate of insurance is produced. An analogous duty to insure is imposed on the custodian of an airplane but not on the enterprises rendered liable by the Law of Liability.

Strict liability also arises under the Atomic Energy Act of 1959. A distinction is drawn between the liability of the operator of an *installation* for the production or fission of nuclear materials and the liability of any other possessor or radioactive *materials*. The first is liable for personal injury and property damage caused by the effects of nuclear operations within the installation, even if those effects are due to *force majeure*. The possessor of radioactive materials is less strictly liable: like the custodian of a motor vehicle, he may escape liability by proving that he observed 'all the care called for in the circumstances', but this does not apply if the harm is due to a failure of safety devices, even if this could not have been known or avoided by the defendant. Here also there is a duty to take out insurance, but in view of the enormous risks appertaining to the operation of nuclear installations, further cover is mandatorily provided by the state.

Also important is the liability laid down by the Water Maintenance Act of 1957 (§ 22) for *pollution of water*. Water for this purpose includes all ponds, lakes, rivers, and streams as well as the water-table, and anyone who introduces into such water substances which alter its composition is liable to pay damages for the harm thereby caused to others, including pure economic loss. The same liability, with the exception of *force majeure*, attaches to the operator of an installation for the manufacture, storage, or carriage of materials: if any materials are introduced into water as defined, the operator of the installation is liable in damages. 'Installation' for the purpose of the statute includes not only storage-tanks for oil and paraffin, tanker vessels, and oil pipelines, but also the sort of petrol tankers which supply gas-stations (so BGH VersR 1967, 374). Considering that the pollution of a river or the water-table itself may cause enormous harm, especially of the pure economic variety, it is all the more surprising to find that the Water Maintenance Act diverges from the usual practice of imposing an upper monetary limit to the strict liability of the defendant. The statute does not introduce any obligation to insure, although one may be confident that practically all the operators of installations which carry a risk of water pollution will have taken out suitable insurance policies. All such policies, however, will contain an upper limit and beyond that limit the risk must be borne by the operator himself.

In 1990 a statute made those involved in genetic research strictly liable for personal injury or property damage due to organisms genetically altered.—The Law on Liability for Damages to the Environment (*Unwelthaftungsgesetz*) *of* the same year makes those operating certain large industrial installations liable for personal injury or property damage due to the effects of emissions. On this see Hager NJW 1991, 134. . . .

Given this variety in the grounds of statutory liability, it is not surprising that the German courts have always held that the imposition of strict liability is a matter for the legislature and not for the judiciary. This view may already be found in a judgment of the Reichsgericht in 1912. Graf Zeppelin, whose airship had had to make a forced landing, was sued by a spectator who was struck and injured by the anchor chain when a sudden gust of wind tore the airship loose from its anchors. The question for the Reichsgericht was whether it were possible to apply by analogy the texts which laid down strict liability, such as § 833 BGB, the Imperial Law of Liability, and the very recent statute which imposed liability on the custodian of a motor car. The Reichsgericht held that no such application by analogy was possible, even although the operation of an airship was an act of bravado entailing risks much less under control than those of railways or motor cars; the provisions laying down strict liability were 'by reason of their exceptional character not applicable even to the unusual circumstances of travel by airship' (RGZ 78,172). In a case in which a person was killed by a high tension cable the Reichsgericht decided likewise before the enactment of the special liability for electricity installations. It held that liability without fault could only be imposed by the legislator: 'if the legislator has not done so, it must be concluded that the legislator rejects such far-reaching liability'. Fortunately the court was able to help the widow in the case by reversing the burden of proof and by holding that the duty of care called for very remarkable precautions (see RGZ 147,353). . . .

A glance at the patchwork of special instances of strict liability imposed by statutes in Germany . . . makes it clear that they leave uncovered many businesses, installations, and activities which pose at least as great a risk of harm. It is far from obvious why a person should be strictly liable if he decides to move earth by means of a light railway while he is liable only for negligence if he uses heavy bulldozers for the job. And why should an injured person's right to damages depend on whether the accident took place on board a steamer or a train? And if a motorized conveyance causes injury, why should liability turn on whether it is a chairlift, a motor car, a motorboat, a light railway, a hoist, a funicular, or an escalator? It may be said that the legislator can always deal with novel needs by introducing new instances of strict liability . . . but even so the law will inevitably limp along behind technology; in any case, is it not perhaps unreasonable to take up the time and energy of the legislative machinery, already very stretched, on the amendment of the law on matters which, even in the context of the law of tort, are fairly interstitial?"

LIABILITY TO THE ABNORMALLY OR UNEXPECTEDLY VULNERABLE

English law

Note: There seems to be no case in point applying English law. But here are cases in which the principle of *Rylands v. Fletcher* was applied under Capetown law and Scots law.

Eastern and South African Telegraph Co., Ltd. v. Cape Town Tramways Cos., Ltd., [1902] A.C. 381 (P.C.) (applying the law of Capetown)

Some of the electricity defendant used to power its tramway found its way into plaintiff's telegraph cable, garbling transmissions while the tramway was running. The court found for defendant.

"Was there such a resulting injury as to found a claim on the principle of *Rylands* v. *Fletcher*? Now in the present case, neither person nor property was injured. . . . Certainly there is here no injury of the same genus or species with the tangible and sensible injuries which have hitherto founded liability on the principle in question, and which have always constituted some interference with the ordinary use of property. . . .

The true comparison is with things used in the ordinary enjoyment of property, and this instrument differs from such things in its peculiar liability to be affected by even minute currents of electricity. Now, having regard to the assumptions of the appellants' argument, it seems necessary to point out that the appellants, as licensees to lay their cable in the sea and as owners of the premises in Capetown where the signals are received, cannot claim higher privileges than other owners of land, and cannot create for themselves, by reason of the peculiarity of their trade apparatus, a higher right to limit the operations of their neighbours than belongs to ordinary owners of land who do not trade with telegraphic cables. . . . A man cannot increase the liabilities of his neighbour by applying his own property to special uses, whether for business or pleasure. The principle of *Rylands* v. *Fletcher*, which subjects to a high liability the owner who uses his property for purposes other than those which are natural, would become doubly penal if it implied a liability created and measured by the non-natural uses of his neighbour's property."

The Western Silver Fox Ranch, Ltd. v. The County Council of Ross and Cromart, [1940] S.C. 601 (applying Scots law)

"Contractors, employed by a county council to construct a road bridge, adopted the method of blasting when excavating for foundations. Vixens in the breeding pens of a neighbouring silver fox ranch, terrified by the noise of the explosions, aborted or destroyed their cubs." Held, for plaintiffs. The court said:

"The 'special use' of land by a neighbour to which the doctrine of *Rylands* v. Fletcher will not apply must be a non-natural use, and I do not regard the breeding of foxes as a non-natural use of the land. It is true that the silver fox is not indigenous to this country, but that, in my opinion, cannot make the use of land for breeding it an unnatural use. Neither Frisian cattle nor Jersey cattle are indigenous to this country, yet I do not think it would occur to anyone that the use of land in Scotland for the breeding of these animals is a non-natural use of property. It is also true that silver foxes in the breeding season are more nervous than our domestic animals, and may more readily abort or eat their young when subject to unusual disturbance, such as blasting in the neighbourhood. This, however, does not alter the quality of the risk to which he who blasts subjects his neighbour, but only the quantity of the damage the neighbour will suffer. Thus, upon the uncontradicted evidence of the witness Dallas, who has been connected with the breeding of animals all his life, some of the sows in a pig-breeding farm would have been affected by the blasting in this case, just as the silver fox vixens were, and with similar results."

Law in the United States

Madsen v. East Jordan Irrigation Co., 125 P.2d 794 (Utah 1942)

"The facts, as alleged in the amended complaint, are as follows: Appellant owns the Madsen Mink Farm in Sandy, Utah, using said farm to breed and raise mink for sale. The farm is located 100 yards north of respondent's irrigation canal and, on May 5, 1941, respondent, in repairing its canal, blasted with explosives, causing vibrations and noises which frightened the mother mink and caused 108 of them to kill 230 of their 'kittens' (offspring). The appellant further alleges that, by nature, habit and disposition all mink, when with and attending their young, are highly excitable and, when disturbed, will become terrified and kill their young." . . .

"[H]e who fires explosives is not liable for every occurrence following the explosion which has a semblance of connection to it. Jake's horse might become so excited that he would run next door and kick a few ribs out of Cy's jersey cow, but is such a thing to be anticipated from an explosion? Whether the cases are concussion or nonconcussion, the results chargeable to the nonnegligent user of explosives are those things ordinarily resulting from an explosion. Shock, air, vibrations, thrown missiles are all illustrative of the anticipated result of the explosives; they are physical as distinguished from mental in character."

German law

Reichsgericht, 4 July 1938, RGZ 158, 34

Plaintiff owned a farm on which he raised silver foxes. Defendant was an airline whose planes flew over the farm flying from Cologne to Saarbrücken and back. On several occasions when they did so, the mother foxes became excited and bit their cubs to death. Such behavior is common among excited mother silver foxes. The lower court allowed the plaintiffs to recover under the *Luftverkehrsgesetz* which imposes strict liability when an object is harmed by accident by air traffic. The *Reichsgericht* reversed.

"According to the case law of the *Reichsgericht*, an adequate causal relationship [between the defendant's conduct and the plaintiff's harm] exists when an act or omission is sufficient to produce the result that occurred in general and not under circumstances which are wholly particular, wholly improbable, and to be left out of account in the ordinary course of events. (RGZ 133, 126; *id.* 135, 149 at 154; *id.* 141, 169 at 172.) In the case law, an adequate causal relation is denied for psychological consequences when the harm occurs because of an unusual condition of that which was affected by the accident despite the non-dangerous character of the event which it is considered objectively. (RG, JW 1908, 41 no. 16.) Given the development that aviation has undergone by 1935, the sight or sound of an airplane flying peacefully by at a great height must be regarded as non-dangerous, when objectively considered, to normal people and normally constituted animals. If it has been shown that the reaction of silver foxes is different, it is only because this type of animal, which is not native here, is particularly sensitive to the sight and sound of airplanes because of their origin in regions that are removed from modern traffic and because of the particular circumstances of their breeding."

Liability for harm caused by objects in one's custody: French law

INTRODUCTION

Today, strict liability in France is based on articles 1384–86 of the Civil Code.

French Civil Code

ARTICLE 1384

A person is liable not only for the damage he causes by his own act, but also for that caused by the acts of persons for whom he is responsible or of things that he has under his guard.

. . .

ARTICLE 1385

The owner of an animal, or the person using it during the period of usage, is liable for the damage the animal has caused, whether it was under his guard or whether it had strayed or escaped.

ARTICLE 1386

The owner of a building is responsible for the damage caused by its collapse when this has taken place because the building was not maintained properly or because it was poorly constructed.

During the 19th century, the plaintiff has to prove that the defendant was at fault to recover under these articles. They were thought to be special cases of the liability for fault established by arts 1382–83. Maybe that is what the drafters had in mind. But it is hard to say. Neither Domat and Pothier, from whom these provisions were taken, nor the drafters of the Code seem to have been clear in their minds about what they were doing.

As described earlier, the Roman *edictum de feris* imposed strict liability for the keeping of animals. Domat explained the *edictum* by suggesting that a person who had custody or guard (*garde*) of a fierce animal was liable because he was at fault. But he also made an argument like the one which, as we have seen, Pufendorf made to defend strict liability: "As he profits from the use he can make from this animal, being its owner, and as he can obtain possession of it again, having acquired it for money or by his own efforts, and having expended time and trouble to acquire some profit, he should answer".[1] Although Pothier did not make this argument, he may not have regarded fault as the only basis for liability.[2]

---

[1] Jean Domat, *Les Loix civiles dans leur ordre naturel* (2nd ed. 1713), liv. 2, tit. 8.

[2] Other paragraphs of article 1384 modeled on Pothier impose liability on parents, teachers and guardians for harm done by those under their care and by masters for harm done by their servants. Pothier said that parents, guardians and teachers were not liable for a torts they could not prevent committed by those under their authority. In contrast, masters were liable vicariously for torts of their servants even when they could not prevent them. They, apparently, were liable without fault, although Pothier threw this conclusion in doubt by adding: "This has been established to render masters careful to employ only good servants." Robert Pothier, *Traité des Obligations* (1761), § 121.

Articles 1384 and 1385 were based on the passages from Domat and Pothier just described. The ambiguities which we have just seen passed into the Code. One can see them in the legislative history of these provisions. Bertrand-de-Greuille explained the liability of the owner of animals by stating the "general thesis" that "nothing that belongs to a person can injure another with impunity."[3] In contrast, Tarrible explained it by the principle that "damage, to be subject to reparation, must be the effect of a fault or imprudence on the part of someone" since otherwise "it is only the work of chance."[4]

THE RISE OF STRICT LIABILITY

The following cases played a critical role in the development of strict liability under Article 1384. Note that in many of these cases, the legislature later enacted a statute to deal with the problem which had concerned the court. Consider whether strict liability might have developed differently in France if these statutes had already been in place.

Cour de cassation, ch. civ., 16 June 1896, D. 1897.1.433

On June 4, 1891 there was an explosion aboard the steam-tug Marie. Teffaine, a member of the crew, was fatally injured in the explosion. His widow brought an action for damages in her own name and as guardian of his minor children against the owners of the tug, Guissez and Cousin. She claimed that the accident was caused by a defect in the welding of the pipe that exploded. Guissez and Cousion joined Oriolle who manufactured the engine. The plaintiff lost in the court of first instance because she could not prove that any of the defendants had been at fault.

She won before the *Cour d'appel* on the grounds that "Guissez and Cousin, in contracting with Teffaine, assumed as to him the obligation to provide a machine fit for the purposes for which it was to be used." "[I]f, in the instant case, a special clause, guaranteeing the engineer against an explosion of the engine or the escape of steam was not inserted in the contract, it is appropriate to apply Article 1160 of the Civil Code and to supply in the contract a clause that is customary and is entirely necessary here; . . ."

The *Cour de cassation* upheld this decision but on different grounds:

"Whereas the challenged decision found finally as a matter of fact that the explosion of the act that the explosion of the engine on the steam-tug Marie, which caused Teffaine's death, was due to a defect in construction; whereas under Article 1384 of the Civil Code this finding, which excludes the *cas fortuit* and *force majeure*, established the responsibility of the owner of the tug to the victim of the accident, and the owner of the tug cannot avoid

3. "Rapport fait par Bertrand-de-Greuille, Communication officielle au Tribunat," 10 pluviose an XII (31 Jan. 1804), in P.A. Fenet *Recueil complet des travaux préparatoires du Code Civil* 13 (1827), 477.

4. According to Tarrible, vicarious liability and liability for animals are based on the principle that "damage, to be subject to reparation, must be the effect of a fault or imprudence on the part of someone" since otherwise "it is only the work of chance." "Discours prononcé par le Tribun Tarrible, Discussion devant le Corps Législatif," 18 pluviose, an XII (8 Feb. 1804), in Fenet 13: 488.

this responsibility by proving either the fault of the builder of the engine or the hidden character of the fault in question . . ." the decision is affirmed.

Note: *Cas fortuit* might be translated as "utter accident" and *force majeure* as "irresistible force" or "act of God." They both describe an event that is unforeseen and completely beyond the plaintiff's power to prevent or avoid. As we will see, they provide a defense to an action under art. 1384.

Two years after this decision, compensation of workers for job-related accidents was dealt with by the Law of 9 April 1898, the "Law Concerning Liability for Accidents of which Workers are the Victims in Their Work." Art. 1 provides:

> "The victim has the right to demand an indemnity from his employer when his work has ceased for more than four days because of accidents that occur because of the performance of work or at work to workers and employees employed in the building trade, in plants, factories, yards, transportation by land or water, loading and unloading, public store-houses, mines, pits, quarries, and also in any employment in which explosives are manufactured or used or in which a machine driven by a force other than human or animal force is customarily used."

Art. 2 provides that the victim and his family can only recover under the provisions of this law. Art. 3 establishes a scale of indemnities. For example, a worker who is completely incapacitated has the right to a yearly annuity equal to two-thirds of his annual wages.

Cour de cassation, ch. civ., 21 January 1919, D. 1922.I.25

"[O]n July 4, 1904 a locomotive . . . exploded and caused damage to movable property belonging to Marcault . . . [T]he decision [below] found that the cause of the explosion was unknown. . . . [I]n all events, the hypothesis that some explosive substance was present in the locomotive must be eliminated and . . . the explosion is probably to be explained by the fragility of the metal in the locomotive's fire box . . . [T]his fragility was not, however, due to the company's fault as the locomotive had after construction and subsequent periodic repairs stood up under the regular pressure tests. . . . [A]fter having passed over articles 1382 and 1383 of the Civil Code on the ground that a fault on the part of the company was not proved, the decision awarded damages to the plaintiff, holding the company liable, under paragraph 1 of article 1384, for the damages caused by the explosion. . . . [I]n so holding, the decision correctly applies this article and does not violate any articles cited in the appeal (*pourvoi*) . . . [I]n sum, the presumption of fault, established by paragraph 1 of article 1384, on the part of the person who has under his guard the inanimate object causing the damage, can be rebutted only by the proof of a *cas fortuit*, a *force majeure* or a *cause étrangère* that cannot be imputed to him . . . [I]t is not sufficient to prove that he did not commit any fault or that the cause of the damage has not been determined. . . ."

Note: *Cause étrangère* might be translated an "extraneous cause." It is a close cousin to *cas fortuit* and *force majeure*. Again, the defendant escapes liability if he shows that an unforeseen event has placed matters completely out his control.

Cour de cassation, ch. civ., 16 November 1920, D. 1920.I.169

On July 2, 1906, a fire broke out in Bordeaux at the Brienne railroad station of which the defendant, a railroad company, was the lessee. It was fed by casks of rosin stored on the premises. It spread and destroyed the rails, poles, and transmission installation of the plaintiff, another railroad company. The *Cour d'appel* held that the casks were under the "guard" of the defendant but that the defendant was not liable because "the cause of damage must reside in the thing that one has under his guard, must be intrinsic to that thing, that the rosin could not ignite because of an inherent defect. . . ." The *Cour de cassation* quashed this decision on the ground that "the presumption of fault that arises [under art. 1384] against a person who has an inanimate thing that caused harm under his guard can only be rebutted by proof of *cas fortuit* or *force majeure* or a *cause étrangère* that cannot be imputed to him," that "it is not sufficient to prove that he did not commit any fault or that the cause of the damage has remained unknown" and that "it is not necessary that the object have an inherent defect capable of causing the damage."

Note: This decision led, due to pressure from the insurance companies, to the insertion by the Law of 7 November 1922 of the following two paragraphs in art. 1384 immediately after the first paragraph:

> "However, a person who is in possession of immovable or movable property in which a fire has started, regardless of the legal basis for his possession, shall not be liable toward third parties unless it is proved that the fire was due to his fault or to the fault of persons for whom he is responsible.

> This provision does not apply to the landlord and tenant relation, which remains governed by articles 1733 and 1734 of the Civil Code."

Cour de cassation, ch. civ., 29 July 1925, D. 1925.1.5

On July 11, 1918, Mrs. Bessières was in her store. Suddenly a passing automobile owned by the defendant company jumped the curb, crashed into the store, and injured her. The *Cour d'appel* held that the defendant was not liable because it was not at fault. It had been determined in a separate action that the driver was not at fault and consequently not liable for the accident.

The *Cour de cassation* quashed the decision, saying that "the presumption of fault, established by that [art. 1384] as to one who has an inanimate object that has caused damage under his guard cannot be overcome except by proving a cas fortuit, a force majeure, or a cause étrangère not imputable to him." "[I]t does not suffice to prove that he did not commit any fault or that the cause of the damage has not been ascertained."

Cour de cassation, Chambres réunies, 13 February 1930, D. 1930.1.57

On April 22, 1925, a truck belonging to the Compagnie Les Galeries Belfortaises knocked down and injured a child, Lise Jand'heur. The *Cour d'appel* refused to allow her to recover under art. 1384 "on the ground that an accident caused by an automobile in movement, under the impulsion and direction of an individual, does not constitute the act of an object that one has under one's guard within the meaning of art. 1384 as long as it has not been shown that the accident was due to a defect in the automobile."

Judge Le Marc'hadour made a long report to the *Chambres réunies* of the *Cour de cassation*. He said, in part:

"In reality, the defendant argued in conclusion, the system of the decision of the Civil Chamber tends to make the liability almost irrebuttable, to launch in our law the conception of [responsibility for] the risk created, while the courts have always been able to avoid this. Such a system is shocking because it places the careless driver and the careful driver in the same situation; it is unjust because the driver who has not committed any fault will be responsible merely because he cannot show the fault of the victim, and this even when the accident will really have been caused by the victim's fault.

In taking the place of the legislature and in creating a legal system of responsibility for drivers of automobiles, the case law resulting from the decision of 1927 led to consequences that have not been adopted in the laws of various countries which have regulated this question. Thus the German Law of 3 May 1909 and the Austrian Law of 9 August 1908 excluded from their scope automobiles whose speed did not exceed 20 to 25 kilometers an hour while permitting the possessor to prove that the accident was not due to a defect in the vehicle and that they had taken every precaution necessary to prevent the accident. This last formula is that of the Italian Law of 30 June 1912. The English Law of 14 August 1903 makes only those liable who drive with recklessness or lack of care considering the nature of the road and the traffic normally present at the time of the accident.

It is for the reasons which have just been stated that the defendant asks you to reject the appeal (*pourvoi*).

It is not concealed that you are thus requested to depart from a well-established case law; you are asked to say that, if paragraph 1 of article 1384 of the Civil Code is applicable to inanimate objects, the presumption that it establishes contemplates only the act of the object, these words extending to damage resulting from a defect in the object independent of any human intervention or any human act. You have held since your decisions of 1919 and 1920 that article 1384 attaches the responsibility to the guard of the object, not to the object itself. You are now asked to hold, in consequence, that the accident is not the act of the object where the automobile is put in motion by, and is under the direction of, man. You have held the contrary constantly since 1927. This case law does not bind the *Chambres réunies*. From the opposing theses that divide the legal writers and the case law of the courts of appeal you will have to choose the solution to be followed in the future."

The *Procureur général* Paul Matter also made a long statement to the court. He argued for quashing of the decision below:

"[T]he *Chambres réunies* is not at all, so far as I know, a jurisdiction of great changes. It follows—this is the greatest of our traditions—the totality of the general movement, recognizing and accepting the advances and thus completing the whole case law. . . .

Does this case law exceed the terms of the written law? Not at all. This case law has sought its principle and its basis in an article of the law. In addition, it can be said that this case law adapted to new needs an article of which the preceding decisions had not seen the full scope, and this is also in our tradition. Perhaps it would be appropriate to recall here the thought of a great judge on this matter when he said that the case law performs a creative function; that faced by all the changes in ideas, in mores, in institutions, in the economic situation of France, it is necessary to adapt in a liberal, humane spirit the text to the realities and requirements of modern life. Have you ever failed to perform this task? . . .

The first paragraph of article 1384 was enacted in a much earlier era, in a period of stagecoaches and one-horse chaises, but at a time when they knew how to draft a statute not only for that time, not only for the needs of the moment, but for the future. These provisions, some taken from our ancient law, some from Roman law, others from the customary law, others from the written law, have the immense advantage of stating general principles. Whenever one talks with a foreign lawyer, and discusses with him the scope of an article of our Civil Code, especially in its title "On Obligations," he always expresses his profound admiration for those articles which contain formulae so supple and yet at the same time so precise, so large and so comprehensive that, formulated at the time of the horse-drawn carriage, they are equally applicable to the automobile and even to the airplane."

The *Chambres réunies* quashed the decision below. It said that "the presumption of responsibility established by that article as to one who has an inanimate object that has caused harm to another under his guard can be rebutted only by proving a *cas fortuit*, a *force majeure*, or a *cause étrangère* that cannot be imputed to him." "[T]he law does not distinguish, whether the object that caused the harm was or was not put in motion by man for purposes of applying the presumption that it has established."

Note: Liability for motor vehicle accidents is now covered by special legislation. The Law of 31 December 1951 (Law no. 51-1508) established a "guarantee fund" from which the plaintiff could recover for physical injury, though not pain and suffering, when the person liable to them is unknown or has insufficient assets. Its funds are contributed by member insurance companies, by motorists who buy liability insurance, and by uninsured motorists held liable for traffic accidents. By 1957, the fund was running a deficit of six million francs. To limit charges, a mandatory insurance program was enacted in 1958 (Law no. 58-208 of 27 February 1958). With certain exceptions, all those who might be liable for damages caused by a motor vehicle are required to buy liability insurance from a private company. Then, in a decision that was widely regarded as a piece of judicial legislation, the *Cour de cassation* held that a defense of contributory negligence was never available to a motorist, not even if the victim's negligence made the accident so unforeseeable or avoidable that would otherwise constitute *cas fortuit, force majeure,* or *cause étrangère.* (Cass., 2nd Civ. Ch., 21 July 1982, D. 1982.449) The French legislature responded by enacting the Law of 5 July 1985. It provides that when a traffic accident has resulted in personal injury or death, *force majeure* and kindred defenses are not available. The defense of contributory negligence is available against other motorists (who can protect themselves by a special and very popular type of insurance) but, with certain exceptions, not against victims who are not motorists unless their fault was "inexcusable" and the "exclusive cause" of the accident. Many believe it is "a law about indemnification and not responsibility." F. Terré, P. Simler & Y. Lequette, *Droit civil Les obligations* (7th ed. 1999), § 893.

THE REQUIREMENT OF AN "ACT OF AN OBJECT"

In reading this section and the section follows, which deals with *cas fortuit,* and *force majeure,* consider to what extent the court's decisions really have nothing to do with fault, or whether they concern the sort of actions for which a person is usually at fault.

Cour de cassation, ch. req., 16 April 1945, S. 1945. I. 73

Birraux sought to recover damages from Christin, alleging that the latter had hit him on the head with an iron bar. In order to avoid the three-year period of prescription that applies to claims based on article 1382, Birraux sought unsuccessfully to rest the action on article 1384(1). The court held that article 1384(1) is not applicable because the damage was "caused by a personal act of the defendant," the iron bar being "only a simple instrument obedient to his hands."

Cour de cassation, 2e ch. civ., 15 July 1962, Gaz. Pal. 1965.II.330

A bicyclist hit Mrs. Pellerin, who, having gotten out of her husband's car, was closing the door. The bicyclist was thrown to the ground and died. In the court below, Mr. Pellerin, as the guardian of the car, was held liable for a portion of the resulting damage. The *Cour de cassation* quashed the judgment "because, it having been found that the collision which brought about Bahurel's fall was between the bicycle and Mrs. Pellerin who, standing on the street, did not form a whole (*ensemble*) with the automobile, the judge below could not conclude that the car was the instrument of the damage and that its guardian was liable for damages on the basis of article 1384(1)."

Note: A note to the decision points out that, if the person closing the door had been in the car, article 1384(1) would presumably have been applied. In a case in which the body of one motorcyclist struck the body of another in passing, causing an accident, the *Cour de cassation* held article 1384(1) applicable. Cass., ch. civ., 2d sect., Gaz. Pal. 1963.I.25.

Tribunal de grand instance, Lyon, 24 February 1971, J.C.P. II. 16822

The defendant skier passed, at a high speed, very close to the plaintiff skier, who fell either because of fear and surprise or due to an actual physical contact. The defendant was held liable, the court reasoning, in part, that since "nothing turns on whether Mrs. Briday's fall was caused by the sight of the skier coming very close rather than by the sight of his skis, one must treat the skier and his skis as forming an ensemble, a whole with its own dynamism. The movement of the skier depends so closely on his skis that, even if his body alone caused the emotion that brought about the fall, his skis were certainly the instrument of the damage. . . ."

Cour de cassation, 2e ch. civ., 13 March 1967, [1967] Bull. civ. no. 120

After being passed by the defendant's automobile, the plaintiff's car left the road and the driver and car were injured. An action for damages based on article 1384(1) was rejected below. The appeal (*pourvoi*) urged that "as the cause of the accident was unknown, the [defendant] must be held entirely responsible." The *Cour de cassation* upheld the decision below. "[E]very person driving on a road must expect to be passed by another vehicle and a wrong maneuver on his part has no relation with the passing unless it is established that this takes place under irregular conditions." Accordingly, the plaintiff "has not furnished proof—the burden of which, in the absence of contact between the two vehicles, rests upon him—of the participation of the [defendant's] vehicle in bringing about the damage."

Cour de cassation, ch. civ., 24 February 1941, D.C. 1941. J.85

The plaintiff alleged that her minor son fell over a folding chair when crossing the terrace of the Pialet Café one evening in order to enter the establishment. She claimed that the café was liable under art. 1384. The *Cour de cassation* upheld her recovery below. It said: "in establishing a presumption of responsibility against the guardian of an object whose act has caused damages, a presumption which is not rebutted unless the guardian proves that the act could neither have been foreseen nor prevented by him, article 1384 does not make a distinction depending upon whether the object is inert or moving." "[I]t is sufficient, for the guardian's liability to arise, that it be proven that the object is, in some measure, the cause of the damage which, without it, would not have occurred. . . ."

Cour de cassation, 2e ch. civ., 19 November 1964, J.C.P. 11. 1965. 14022

A shopper slipped on the floor of a store, injuring herself. She brought an action against the store relying on art. 1384. The *Cour de cassation* held that the defendant was not liable because the plaintiff "had not shown that the covering of the floor of the Monoprix department store was the generating cause (*cause génératrice*) of the harm."

Note on burden of proof: The court placed the burden of proof on the plaintiff in the last case, the decision of 19 Nov. 1964, while in the one before, the decision of 24 Feb. 1941, it placed this burden on the defendant. The last decision illustrates the current practice: if the object was not in motion (like the floor) or if it was in motion but did not make contact with the plaintiff or his property (like the other car in the decision of 13 March 1967), then the plaintiff has the burden of proving that the harm was caused by the "act of an object." Otherwise, the defendant has the burden of proving that it was not. F. Terré, P.Simler & Y. Lequette, *Droit civil Les obligations* (7th ed. 1999), § 745.

Cour de cassation, 2e ch. civ., 20 March 1968, [1968] Bull. civ. 1968.II. no. 89

The victim was injured by walking into a glass door. Having lost before the *Cour d'appel*, the plaintiff argued that that court should have considered whether, so far as the store was concerned, the accident was "unforeseeable and irresistible." The *Cour de cassation* found for the defendant. It noted that the *Cour d'appel* had "found that the door was marked by two metal edges and by a handle of gilded metal, that it was closed and that Mrs. Serignan had opened it in order to enter the store. . . ." "[F]rom these findings the *Cour d'appel* could conclude that the door had only submitted to an alien action of the victim, a conclusion which made it unnecessary to investigate whether the victim's act had the character of *force majeure*."

Cour de cassation, ch. civ., 5 March 1947, D. 1947.J.296

At 3:00 A.M., Biro drove his car into Taupin's truck which was parked by the curb. The court found that the truck required lighting. The lighting had been checked by the police forty minutes before the accident. Nevertheless, the court found that it was impossible to know if the lighting was functioning at the time of the accident. The court held that the *Cour d'appel* was correct to conclude that "'the cause of the accident was unknown' [and therefore] the presumption of responsibility established by article 1384(1) of the Civil Code operated as to each of the two guardians and that each was liable for the damage caused to the other by the collision." "[O]f course, the guardian of an object that has intervened in the realization of damage can avoid the presumption of responsibility that rests upon him by proving that his object, inert or not, only played a passive role and only suffered a separate force which produced the damage; but . . . a vehicle parked at night on a public road, even though it is placed at the curb, cannot be considered as in a normal situation unless it is provided with the required lighting capable of revealing to others the obstacle that its presence represents; . . . if the guardian does not prove this circumstance, the legal presumption continues, since there is no basis for affirming that the vehicle struck suffered the shock that caused the damage without having caused or facilitated it and that, in consequence, its role was entirely passive. . . ."

Cour de cassation, 2e ch. civ., 29 March 1971, J.C.P. 1972, II. 17086

The plaintiff was sitting on a branch of a tree, picking the tree's fruit with the owner's permission, when the branch broke. The *Cour d'appel* held for the plaintiff because the defendant could not show that he was "an unforeseeable and irresistible fault." The decision was quashed by the *Cour de cassation* on the ground that "in deducing from the sole finding of the branch's breaking that the tree was the instrument of the damage, the *Cour d'appel* failed to give a legal basis to its decision." In a note to the decision, Boré remarked that "with respect to the burden of proof, the decision seems to accept a judicial tendency, which has discretely manifested itself on several occasions, to require the victim to prove the abnormal use of the object which is inert at the moment of damage and was simply subject to an alien action."

CAS FORTUIT AND *FORCE MAJEURE*

Cour de cassation, 2e ch. civ., 19 March 1956, D. & S. 1956.J.349

The plaintiff was injured by a ricocheting bullet fired by a fellow hunter. The *Cour d'appel* held for the defendant on the ground that the character of the ground thus relied upon was "general and absolute." In the view of the *Cour de cassation*, "the ricochet of a bullet during a hunting expedition does not constitute a cas fortuit or force majeure, unless the circumstances of the case indicate the contrary."

Cour de cassation, ch. civ., 9 December 1940, D. A. 1941. J. 33

During a hunting expedition, Guilbert's right eye was injured by a richocheting bullet that Neveu fired at a rabbit climbing up on an embankment two feet in height. The *Cour d'appel* held that Neveu was not liable under art. 1384 because the event was a *cas fortuit*. The *Cour de cassation* upheld this decision on the ground that, as the *Cour d'appel* had found, Neveu "had done an act normal in hunting" and Guilbert "was not in his direct line of fire, but at least 25 meters to his left." Neveu therefore was unable to "foresee that the bullet would ricochet in the direction of his hunting companion" and consequently, the accident was "unforeseeable and unpreventable."

Trib. Civil of Chartres, 18 June 1941, D.A. 1942. J. 13

"Fillon . . . must be held responsible as guardian of his gun as he does not prove that this accident was either a *cas fortuit* or a case of *force majeure*. Even if it is admitted that the bullet hit Mauté after ricocheting, the ricochet cannot be considered a *cas fortuit* as Fillon committed an imprudence in firing close to a road, where the ground was hard, and where there were a pole and apple trees that could have caused the ricochet."

Cour d'appel, Paris, 28 October 1943, Gaz. Pal. 1943. II.269

"The icy condition of a road can, in certain circumstances, constitute a *cas fortuit* when, the condition arising suddenly, the roads are very quickly rendered dangerous. However, it is not shown that the icy condition that caused this accident arose unexpectedly and could not have been foreseen. . . . [T]he report of the accident prepared by the police of Gaguy states that the ground was covered with frozen snow. . . . Therefore, there is no question of an icy condition that developed suddenly and could not have been foreseen. Instead, . . . the icy condition was already of the law present, that is to say, had existed for some time in the area traversed by the road. Indeed, the melting of the ice was prevented by a wall that shaded the road from the sun. Hence, a prudent driver could have foreseen the icy condition."

Cour de cassation, 2e ch. civ., 29 June 1966, D. & S. 1966.J.645

A car skidded on a patch of ice, the driver lost control, and a pedestrian was killed. The victim's widow sought to recover damages under article 1384(1). The court held for the defendant on the ground that the formation of a patch of ice on a highway when the temperature is just below freezing is normally unforeseeable.

"GUARD"

F. Terré, P. Simler & Y. Lequette, *Droit civil Les obligations* (7th ed. 1999), § 690

"[T]he owner of an object can *lose his status as its guardian without losing that of owner.* That is the case, notably, in all instances where there is a *transfer of guard* of an inanimate thing, as in contracts of rental, loan, deposit, transport of goods, and so forth: the guard belongs to the renter, borrower, depositary or transporter. . . . Still it should be noted that both subjective and objective facts affect the transfer of guard so that even when it occurs by agreement it does not invariably create obligations for a third party, and the situation arising as to him may be the opposite under certain conditions. Here, the *Cour de cassation* has said that the owner of an object only ceases to be responsible for it when the third party has received correlatively every possibility of himself preventing the harm that the object may cause which means that an enterprise that wishes to transfer its guard has an obligation to inform the other contracting party in an adequate manner."

Cour de cassation, 1e ch. civ., 11 June 1953, J.C.P. 1953.II.7825

"[T]he presumption of responsibility that rests upon the guardian of an object that has caused damage is based on the obligation of guard, the corollary of the powers of use, direction, and control that characterize the guardian . . . [A] person who has rented an object, and who has thus become its new guardian, assumes as to third parties from then on the risks of damage even if the damage is caused by an inherent defect in the object, subject only to such recourse as he may have against the person from whom the object is rented . . . [T]herefore, the driver to whom an automobile is turned over under a contract of hire is legally the guardian during the existence of the contract, without his being able to object that the guard of the car remained with the owner because the accident was caused by a defect in the car . . . [H]olding that Bouchaid must be presumed to be liable for an accident suffered by Schneider while he was being transported in a car owned by Bouchaid, and which had been rented to Lugassy, on the ground that, as the accident was due to defects in the car. Bouchaid had retained the guard, the *Cour d'appel* gave a judgment for Schneider of 336,350 francs damages. . . . But . . . as a consequence of the contract of hire, the guard of the car was transferred to Lugassy who had the use, direction, and control, and the defect in the object cannot create a presumption of responsibility against Bouchaid, as this presumption rests upon Lugassy alone as the guardian. . . ."

Note on who has "guard": Normally, then, if the someone other than the owner has control over an object, that person has "guard" of it rather than the owner. A parking lot attendant has "guard" of the owner's automobile while his is parking it. Cass, 2nd Civ. Ch., 13 Oct. 1965, J.C.P. 1966.II.14503. A thief has "guard" of a car he has stolen. Cass., Ch. réunies, 2 Dec. 1941, D. 1941.J.369. Nevertheless, an employer does not transfer the "guard" of an object by allowing his employee to use it for business purposes; the employee does have "guard" of it if he uses it for purposes of his own. Cass., ch. req., 8 Oct. 1940, Gaz Pal. 1940.2.65.

Some commentators have argued that the courts should distinguish guard of the object's structure from guard of its conduct. If a person rents an object, the owner should be liable if an accident occurs because the object is defective; the renter should be liable if the object is not but goes out of control. B. Goldman, *De la détermination du gardien responsable du fait des choses inanimées* (1947), 208. In the last case, the decision of 11 June 1953, this distinction was squarely rejected by the *Cour de cassation*. As the cases that follow show, while the courts have not accepted such a distinction, they have sometimes managed to hold that guard did not pass despite physical delivery.

Cour de cassation, 1e ch. civ., 9 June 1993, J.C.P. 1994.II.22202

After a grain silo exploded, the company owning the silo, *Société La Malterie de la Moselle*, hired other companies, the *Sociétés Cardem et Somafer*, to demolish the structure and haul off the rubble. They did so, dumping the rubble in a ravine near the reservoir that supplied water to the town of Montigny-les-Metz. Some time later, the town officials discovered traces of fermented barley were mixed in with the debris, creating a risk of pollution. They stopped using the reservoir and bought water for the town from another source. They now seek to recover their expenses from whichever companies are liable to them.

"[T]he responsibility for harm caused by the act of a thing is tied to the exercise of the powers of surveillance and control which characterize having guard of it . . . [A]side from the effect of valid provisions to the contrary between the parties, the owner of a thing, even after entrusting it to a third party, does not cease to be responsible unless it is established that the third party received correlatively every possibility of himself preventing the harm that the object may cause. . . .

"[T]o maintain that the *Société La Malterie de la Moselle* no longer had guard of the debris containing the barley and that the *Société Cardem* became the guardian, the opinion [of the lower court] stated that the latter had assumed responsibility for the removal of the rubble by the terms of the agreement with the *Société La Malterie de la Moselle*, and that the grains of barley suffered from no particular defect except that arising from their nature . . . [G]iven that the *Société La Malterie de la Moselle*, owner of the rubble and of the barley, could not, being professionals, be ignorant of the risk presented by the barley, a substance subject to a dangerous fermentation, and yet failed to draw the attention of *Société Cardem* to this risk, which was one it would not normally contemplate, the *Société La Malterie de la Moselle* therefore retained its guard of the thing which was the instrument of damage, and, in ruling as it did, the *Cour d'appel* failed to draw the proper legal consequences from these fact and violated the text [of art. 1384]. . . ."

Cour de cassation, ch. comm., 30 June 1953. J.C.P. 1953. II. 7811

A railroad was held not to be liable under article 1384 for the damage caused by the explosion of bottles of compressed gas that it was transporting. The cause of the explosion had been established as a defect in the bottles of which the railroad had no knowledge.

Cour de cassation, 2e ch. civ., 15 June 1972, Bull. civ. 1982 no. 186

"[T]he responsibility for damage caused by an inanimate object is linked to the use that is made of the object, as well as to the power of supervision and control exercised over it, which characterize having guard of it . . . [I]t appears from the decision [below] that Mrs. Jonquières, who had been injured in her eye by the explosion of a phial of medicine manufactured by the *Société des Laboratoires Novalis* and contained in a box which had been given to her by an employee of Dr. Vitel, sought to recover damages from that company and from its insurer . . . and, on appeal, also from Dr. Vitel, who had been brought into the action by the defendants. . . . [A]ccording to the findings of the judgment [below], the product in question was delivered by the *Société* to Dr. Vitel no later than December, 1955 . . . [T]he accident occurred in January 1967 . . . [T]he informational material accompanying the product specified its great instability, indicated by the solution turning more or less markedly yellow . . . [N]either the doctor nor the nurse opened the box in order to determine the medicine's condition, the improper state of which would have been revealed by inspecting the appearance of the contents of the phial and by reading the notice . . . [I]t follows that in declaring that, at the moment when occurred, the *Société des Laboratoires Novalis* had the power which characterizes the guard of this sample, the *Cour d'appel* did not draw the legal consequences that are appropriate. . . ."

THE EXTENT OF LIABILITY

If both parties have "guard" of an object, and the object of each party harms the other, some French jurists believe that neither should be able to rely on article 1384, and that each should bear his own harm unless he can prove that the other was at fault. But that is not how French courts see the matter. They hold each party liable for the damage he does to another. F. Terré, P. Simler & Y. Lequette, *Droit civil Les obligations* (7th ed. 1999), § 824.

The defendant's liability is not affected by the fact that he was not at fault. For example, he is still liable if the harm was due to the fact that he had an epileptic fit and so lost control of the object under his guard. Cass., 2e ch. civ., 18 Dec. 1964, D. &. S. 1965.J.191. Similarly, even before the law of 3 January 1968 imposed liability on the insane, the *Cour de cassation* had held that an insane person is liable under art. 1384. Cass., 2e ch. civ., 18 Dec. 1964, D.S. 1965.J.191. The same day that it held that children are liable under arts. 1382–83 for acts they could not help on account of their age, it held that they are also liable under art. 1384. Cass., ass. plén., 9 May 1984 (3rd case), D.S. 1984.J.529 (three year old child has "guard" of a stick with which he struck a playmate in the eye).

As we have seen, however, the defendant escapes liability if the court decides the harm was done by *force majeure* or *cas fortuit*. The defendant may be completely exonerated. Or he may be exonerated only partially so that he pays for only a portion of the harm that the plaintiff suffered. Cass., Ch. Civ., 19 June 1951, D. 1951.J.717.

If the plaintiff's conduct is sufficiently unforeseeable, it may itself count as *force majeure* or *cas fortuit* and hence serve to exonerate the defendant wholly or partially. That is particularly likely to be the case if the victim was at fault. In 1982, in a celebrated decision, the *Cour de cassation* took the opposite view. Cass., 2e ch. civ., 21 July 1982, D. 1982.449. The court was concerned about traffic accidents. It believed that a driver should be fully liable even if the party injured was at fault. Partly in response to this decision, the legislature enacted the Law of 5 July 1985 which made traffic accidents the subject of a special regime so that the driver would not longer be liable under art. 1384. Art. 3 of this law provided that the driver is liable even if the injured party is not at fault as long as his fault is not "inexcusable." With that problem solved, the returned to its traditional position: that the fault of the plaintiff can wholly or partially exonerate the guardian. Cass., 2e ch. civ., 6 Apr. 1987, D.S. 1988.32.

b. Liability for defective products

Law in the United States

Escola v. Coca-Cola Bottling Co. of Fresno, 150 P.2d 436 (Cal. 1944)

A bottle of Coca-Cola exploded in the plaintiff's hand as she was placing it in a refrigerator as part of her job as a waitress. The majority of the California Supreme Court held that the jury could properly find the defendant had been negligent in manufacturing the bottle. Judge Traynor concurred on a different ground:

"I concur in the judgment, but I believe the manufacturer's negligence should no longer be singled out as the basis of a plaintiff's right to recover in cases like the present one. In my opinion it should now be recognized that a manufacturer incurs an absolute liability when an article that he has placed on the market, knowing that it is to be used without inspection, proves to have a defect that causes injury to human beings. MacPherson v. Buick Motor Co. established the principle, recognized by this court, that irrespective of privity of contract, the manufacturer is responsible for an injury caused by such an article to any person who comes in lawful contact with it. In these cases the source of the manufacturer's liability was his negligence in the manufacturing process or in the inspection of component parts supplied by others. Even if there is no negligence, however, public policy demands that responsibility be fixed wherever it will most effectively reduce the hazards to life and health inherent in defective products that reach the market. It is evident that the manufacturer can anticipate some hazards and guard against the recurrence of others, as the public cannot. Those who suffer injury from defective products are unprepared to meet its consequences. The cost of an injury and the loss of time or health may be an overwhelming misfortune to the person injured, and a needless one, for the risk of injury can be insured by the manufacturer and distributed among the public as a cost of doing business. It is to the public interest to discourage the marketing of products having defects that are a menace to the public. If such products nevertheless find their way into the market it is to the public interest to place the responsibility for whatever injury they may cause upon the manufacturer, who, even if he is not negligent in the manufacture of the product, is responsible for its reaching the market. However intermittently such injuries may occur and however haphazardly they may strike, the risk of their occurrence is a constant risk and a general one. Against such a risk there should be general and constant protection and the manufacturer is best situated to afford such protection.

The injury from a defective product doers not become a matter of indifference because the defect arises from causes other than the negligence of the manufacturer, such as negligence of a sub-manufacturer of a component part whose defects could not be revealed by inspection, or unknown causes that even by the device of res ipsa loquitur cannot be classified as negligence of the manufacturer. The inference of negligence may be dispelled by an affirmative showing of proper care. If the evidence against the fact inferred is "clear, positive, uncontradicted, and of such a nature that it cannot rationally be disbelieved, the court must instruct the jury that the nonexistence of the fact has been established as a matter of law." An injured person, however, is not ordinarily in a position to refute such evidence or identify the cause of the defect, for he can hardly be familiar with the manufacturing process as the manufacturer himself is. In leaving it to the jury to decide whether the inference has been dispelled, regardless of the evidence against it, the negligence rule approaches the rule of strict liability. It is needlessly circuitous to make negligence the basis of recovery and impose what is in reality liability without negligence. If public policy demands that a manufacturer of goods be responsible for their quality regardless of negligence there is no reason not to fix that responsibility openly."

Restatement (Second) of Torts

§ 402A SPECIAL LIABILITY OF SELLER OF PRODUCT FOR
PHYSICAL HARM TO USER OR CONSUMER

(1) One who sells any product in a defective condition unreasonably dangerous to the user or consumer or to his property is subject to liability for physical harm thereby caused to the ultimate user or consumer, or to his property, if

   (a) the seller is engaged in the business of selling such a product, and

   (b) it is expected to and does reach the user or consumer without substantial change in the condition in which it is sold.

(2) The rule stated in Subsection (1) applies although

    (a) the seller has exercised all possible care in the preparation and sale of his product, and

    (b) the user or consumer has not bought the product from or entered into any contractual relation with the seller.

Caveat: The Institute expresses no opinion as to whether the rules stated in this Section may not apply (1) to harm to persons other than users or consumers; (2) to the seller of a product expected to be processed or otherwise substantially changed before it reaches the user or consumer; or (3) to the seller of a component part of a product to be assembled.

Note: Despite the first of these "caveats," virtually all American states now impose liability for harm to persons who were neither users or consumers of the product.

Restatement (Second) of Torts

Official comments to § 402A.

f. Business of selling. The rule stated in this Section applies to any person engaged in the business of selling products for use or consumption. It therefore applies to any manufacturer of such a product, to any wholesale or retail dealer or distributor, and to the operator of a restaurant. It is not necessary that the seller be engaged solely in the business of selling such products. Thus the rule applies to the owner of a motion picture theater who sells popcorn or ice cream, either for consumption on the premises or in packages to be taken home.

The rule does not, however, apply to the occasional seller of food or other such products who is not engaged in that activity as a part of his business. Thus it does not apply to the housewife who, on one occasion, sells to her neighbor a jar of jam or a pound of sugar. Nor does it apply to the owner of an automobile who, on one occasion, sells it to his neighbor, or even sells it to a dealer in used cars, and this even though he is fully aware that the dealer plans to resell it. The basis for the rule is the ancient one of the special responsibility for the safety of the public undertaken by one who enters into the business of supplying human beings with products which may endanger the safety of their persons and property, and the forced reliance upon that undertaking on the part of those who purchase such goods. This basis is lacking in the case of the ordinary individual who makes the isolated sale, and he is not liable to a third person, or even to his buyer, in the absence of his negligence. . . .

g. Defective condition. The rule stated in this Section applies only where the product is, at the time it leaves the seller's hands, in a condition not contemplated by the ultimate consumer, which will be unreasonably dangerous to him. The seller is not liable when he delivers the product in a safe condition, and subsequent mishandling or other causes make it harmful by the time it is consumed. The burden of proof that the product was in a defective condition at the time that it left the hands of the particular seller is upon the injured plaintiff; and unless evidence can be produced which will support the conclusion that it was then defective, the burden is not sustained.

Safe condition at the time of delivery by the seller will, however, include proper packaging, necessary sterilization, and other precautions required to permit the product to remain safe for a normal length of time when handled in a normal manner.

h. A product is not in a defective condition when it is safe for normal handling and consumption. If the injury results from abnormal handling, as where a bottled beverage is knocked against a radiator to remove the cap, or from abnormal preparation for use, as where too much salt is added to food, or from abnormal consumption, as where a child eats too much candy and is made ill, the seller is not liable. Where, however, he has reason to anticipate that danger may result from a particular use as where a drug is sold which is safe only in limited doses, he may be required to give adequate warning of the danger (see Comment j), and a product sold without such warning is in a defective condition.

i. Unreasonably dangerous. The rule stated in this Section applies only where the defective condition of the product makes it unreasonably dangerous to the user or consumer. Many products cannot possibly be made entirely safe for all consumption, and any food or drug necessarily involves some risk of harm, if only from over-consumption. Ordinary sugar is a deadly poison to diabetics, and castor oil found use under Mussolini as an instrument of torture. That is not what is meant by "unreasonably dangerous" in this Section. The article sold must be dangerous to an extent beyond that which would be contemplated by the ordinary consumer who purchases it, with the ordinary knowledge common to the community as to its characteristics. Good whiskey is not unreasonably dangerous merely because it will make some people drunk, and is especially dangerous to alcoholics; but bad whiskey, containing a dangerous amount of fusel oil, is unreasonably dangerous. Good tobacco is not unreasonably dangerous merely because the effects of smoking may be harmful; but tobacco containing something like marijuana may be unreasonably dangerous. Good butter is not unreasonably dangerous merely because, if such be the case, it deposits cholesterol in the arteries and leads to heart attacks; but bad butter, contaminated with poisonous fish oil, is unreasonably dangerous.

k. Unavoidably unsafe products. There are some products which, in the present state of human knowledge, are quite incapable of being made safe for their intended and ordinary use. These are specially common in the field of drugs. An outstanding example is the vaccine for the Pasteur treatment of rabies, which not uncommonly leads to very serious and damaging consequences when it is injected. Since the disease itself invariably leads to a dreadful death, both the marketing and the use of the vaccine are fully justified, notwithstanding the unavoidable high degree of risk which they involve. Such a product, properly prepared, and accompanied by proper directions and warning, is not defective, not is it *unreasonably* dangerous. The same is true of many other drugs, vaccines, and the like, many of which for this very reason cannot legally be sold except to physicians, or under the prescription of a physician. It is also true in particular of many new or experimental drugs as to which, because of lack of time and opportunity for sufficient medical experience, there can be no assurance of safety, or perhaps even of purity of ingredients, but such experience as there is justifies the marketing and use of the drug notwithstanding a medically recognizable risk. The seller of such products, again, with the qualification that they are properly prepared and marketed, and proper warning is given, where the situation calls for it, is not to be held to strict liability for unfortunate consequences attending their use, merely because he has undertaken to supply the public with an apparently useful and desirable product, attended with a known but apparently reasonable risk.

Note: Suppose a product met state of the art safety standards at the time it was designed and manufactured but, because technology has advanced, would not do so at the time of trial. The dominant view is that what matters is the state of the art when the product was designed and manufactured. *See Bruce v. Martin Marietta Corp.*, 544 F.2d 442 (10th Cir. 1976).

Brown v. Superior Court (Abbott Laboratories), 751 P.2d 470 (Cal. 1988)

Plaintiffs sued the defendant drug manufacturers who had produced DES, a drug which they claimed had been taken by their mothers to prevent miscarriage. They alleged that the drug was defective and had injured them before birth. The court denied their claim.

"Comment k [of Restatement § 402A] has been analyzed and criticized by numerous commentators. While there is some disagreement as to its scope and meaning, there is a general consensus that, although it purports to explain the strict liability doctrine, in fact the principle it states is based on negligence. That is, comment k would impose liability on a drug manufacturer only if it failed to warn of a defect of which it either knew or should have known. This concept focuses not on a deficiency in the product—the hallmark of strict liability—but on the fault of the producer in failing to warn of dangers inherent in the use of its product that were either known or knowable—an idea which 'rings of negligence,' in the words of Cronin [v. J.B.E. Olson Corp.], 501 P.2d 1153 (1972).

Comment *k* has been adopted in the overwhelming majority of jurisdictions that have considered the matter. . . .

We shall conclude that (1) a drug manufacturer's liability for a defectively designed drug should not be measured by the standards of strict liability; [and] (2) because of the public interest in the development, availability, and reasonable price of drugs, the appropriate test for determining responsibility is the test stated in comment k; . . .

Perhaps a drug might be made safer if it was withheld from the market until scientific skill and knowledge advanced to the point at which additional dangerous side effects would be revealed. But in most cases such a delay in marketing new drugs—added to the delay required to obtain approval for release of the product from the Food and Drug Administration—would not serve the public welfare. Public policy favors the development and marketing of beneficial new drugs, even though some risks, perhaps serious ones, might accompany their introduction, because drugs can save lives and reduce pain and suffering.

If drug manufacturers were subject to strict liability, they might be reluctant to undertake research programs to develop some pharmaceuticals that would prove beneficial or to distribute others that are available to be marketed, because of the fear of large adverse monetary judgments. Further, the additional expense of insuring against such liability—assuming insurance would be available—and of research programs to reveal possible dangers not detectable by available scientific methods could place the cost of medication beyond the reach of those who need it most."

Law in Europe

European Community Council Directive on the Approximation of the Laws, Regulations and Administrative Provisions of the Member States Concerning Liability for Defective Products

[32 I.L.M. 1347, Official Journal of the European Communities, L 210/29–33, August 7, 1985]

Whereas approximation of the laws of the Member States concerning the liability of the producer for damage caused by the defectiveness of his products is necessary because the existing divergences may distort competition and affect the movement of goods within the common market and entail a differing degree of protection of the consumer against damage caused by a defective product to his health or property;

Whereas liability without fault on the part of the producer is the sole means of adequately solving the problem, peculiar to our age of increasing technicality, of a fair apportionment of the risks inherent in modern technological production;

. . .

Whereas protection of the consumer requires that all producers involved in the production process should be made liable, in so far as their finished product, component part or any raw material supplied by them was defective; whereas, for the same reason, liability should extend to importers of products into the Community and to persons who present themselves as producers by affixing their name, trade mark or other distinguishing feature or who supply a product the producer of which cannot be identified;

. . .

Whereas, to protect the physical well-being and property of the consumer, the defectiveness of the product should be determined by reference not to its fitness for use but to the lack of the safety which the public at large is entitled to expect; whereas the safety is assessed by excluding any misuse of the product not reasonable under the circumstances;

Whereas a fair apportionment of risk between the injured person and the producer implies that the producer should be able to free himself from liability if he furnishes proof as to the existence of certain exonerating circumstances;

Whereas the fair protection of the consumer requires that the liability of the producer remains unaffected by acts or omissions of other persons having contributed to cause the damage; whereas, however, the contributory negligence of the injured person may be taken into account to reduce or disallow such liability;

Whereas the protection of the consumer requires compensation for death and personal injury as well as compensation for damage to property; whereas the latter should nevertheless be limited to goods for private use or consumption and be subject to a deduction of a lower threshold of a fixed amount in order to avoid litigation in an excessive number of cases; whereas this Directive should not prejudice compensation for pain and suffering and other non-material damages payable, where appropriate, under the law applicable to the case;

. . . .

Whereas products age in the course of time, higher safety standards are developed and the state of science and technology progresses; whereas, therefore, it would be reasonable to make the producer liable for an unlimited period for the defectiveness of his product; whereas, therefore, liability should expire after a reasonable length of time, without prejudice to claims pending at law;

. . .

ARTICLE 1

The producer shall be liable for damage caused by a defect in his product.

ARTICLE 2

For the purpose of this Directive "product" means all movables, with the exception of primary agricultural products and game, even though incorporated into another movable or into an immovable. "Primary agricultural products", means the products of the soil, of stock-farming and of fisheries, excluding products which have undergone initial processing. "Product" includes electricity.

ARTICLE 3

(1) "Producer" means the manufacturer of a finished product, the producer of any raw material or the manufacturer of a component part and any person who, by putting his name, trade mark or other distinguishing feature on the product presents himself as its producer.

(2) Without prejudice to the liability of the producer, any person who imports into the Community a product for sale, hire, leasing or any form of distribution in the course of his business shall be deemed to be a producer within the meaning of this Directive and shall be responsible as a producer.

(3) Where the producer of the product cannot be identified, each supplier of the product shall be treated as its producer unless he informs the

injured person, within a reasonable time, of the identity of the producer or of the person who supplied him with the product. The same shall apply, in the case of an imported product, if this product does not indicate the identity of the importer referred to in paragraph 2, even if the name of the producer is indicated.

ARTICLE 4

The injured person shall be required to prove the damage, the defect and the causal relationship between defect and damage.

ARTICLE 5

Where, as a result of the provisions of this Directive, two or more persons are liable for the same damage, they shall be liable jointly and severally, without prejudice to the provisions of national law concerning the rights of contribution or recourse.

ARTICLE 6

(1) A product is defective when it does not provide the safety which a person is entitled to expect, taking all circumstances into account, including:

(a) the presentation of the product;

(b) the use to which it could reasonably be expected that the product would be put;

(c) the time when the product was put into circulation.

(2) A product shall not be considered defective for the sole reason that a better product is subsequently put into circulation.

ARTICLE 7

The producer shall not be liable as a result of this Directive if he proves:

(a) that he did not put the product into circulation; or

(b) that, having regard to the circumstances, it is probable that the defect which caused the damage did not exist at the time when the product was put into circulation by him or that this defect came into being afterwards; or

(c) that the product was neither manufactured by him for sale or any form of distribution for economic purpose nor manufactured or distributed by him in the course of his business; or

(d) that the defect is due to compliance of the product with mandatory regulations issued by the public authorities; or

(e) that the state of scientific and technical knowledge at the time when he put the product into circulation was not such as to enable the existence of the defect to be discovered; or

(f) in the case of a manufacturer of a component, that the defect is attributable to the design of the product in which the component has been fitted or to the instructions given by the manufacturer of the product.

ARTICLE 8

(1) Without prejudice to the provisions of national law concerning the right of contribution or recourse, the liability of the producer shall not be reduced when the damage is caused both by a defect in product and by the act or omission of a third party.

(2) The liability of the producer may be reduced or disallowed when, having regard to all the circumstances, the damage is caused both by a defect in the product and by the fault of the injured person or any person for whom the injured person is responsible.

ARTICLE 9

For the purpose of Article 1, "damage" means:

(a) damage caused by death or by personal injuries;

(b) damage to, or destruction of, any item of property other than the defective product itself, with a lower threshold of 500 ECU, provided that the item of property:

> (i) is of a type ordinarily intended for private use or consumption, and
> (ii) was used by the injured person mainly for his own private use or consumption.

This Article shall be without prejudice to national provisions relating to non-material damage.

ARTICLE 15

(1) Each Member State may:

. . .

> (b) by way of derogation from Article 7 (e), maintain or, subject to the procedure set out in paragraph 2 of this Article, provide in this legislation that the producer shall be liable even if he proves that the state of scientific and technical knowledge at the time when he put the product into circulation was not such as to enable the existence of a defect to be discovered.

. . .

ARTICLE 16

(1) Any Member State may provide that a producer's total liability for damage resulting from a death or personal injury and caused by identical items with the same defect shall be limited to an amount which may not be less than 70 million ECU.

. . .

ARTICLE 19

(1) Member States shall bring into force, not later than three years from the date of this Directive, the laws, regulations and administrative provisions necessary to comply with this Directive. They shall forthwith inform the Commission thereof.

PART THREE:

CONTRACT LAW

I. THE STRUCTURE OF CONTRACT LAW

1. Civil law

The Romans did not explain contract formation by abstract principles. As has often been said, they had a law of particular contracts, not a general law of contract.[1] The rules that governed when a contract was formed depended on the kind of contract the parties had made.

Some contracts were formed by the consent of the parties alone. They came to be called contracts *consensu* or consensual contracts. They included sale, lease, partnership, and mandate (*mandatum*) which was a gratuitous agency.[2]

Others became binding on delivery of the object with which the contract is concerned. They came to be called contracts *re* which literally means "thing contracts." (Since that sounds odd, they are sometimes called "real contracts" even though that sounds odd, too.) They included a gratuitous loan of an object for use (*commodatum*) or consumption (*mutuum*). In a gratuitous loan for use, the borrower had to return the same object he was lent: for example, he borrowed a horse and had to return the very same horse. In a gratuitous loan for consumption, the borrower had to return as much of the same kind and quality as he had borrowed but not the very same objects: for example, he borrowed money or wine and had to give the same amount back. The contracts *re* also included pledge (*pignus*) and the deposit of an object (*depositum*) with someone who would look after it gratuitously.[3]

Still other contracts became binding by completing a formality. The most general formality was *stipulatio*. Originally, the parties completed the formality by having the promisee formally ask the promisor a question which the promisor would formally answer. The promisee would say, "*Spondesne* such-and-such?" and the promisor would answer, "*Spondeo* such-and-such" ("Do you promise . . .?" answered by "I do promise . . .?"). In time, it became customary to state in a document that a *stipulatio* had been made. According to Justinian's legislation, such a document raised a presumption that could only be overcome by showing the parties had not

---

1. W.W. Buckland, Arnold McNair & F.H. Lawson, *Civil Law and Common Law* (1952), 265; Helmut Coing, *Europäisches Privatrecht* 1 (1985), 398; Alan Watson, *The Law of the Ancient Romans* (1970), 58.

2. Inst. 3.13.22–26.
3. Inst. 3.14.

been in the same town the day of its execution. The oral formality was thus replaced for practical purposes by a written formality. In medieval and early modern times, the accepted way to complete the formality, and the only safe way, was to go before a notary, who was not a person like the American notary public but a member of the legal profession.[4]

A gift above a certain amount required a special formality called *insinuatio*. The gift had to be registered with a court.

Contracts outside these recognized types came to be called "innominate" (nameless). Suppose the parties trade a horse for a mule. The contract is not a sale since money is not given in return. It is not a *stipulatio* since the parties did not make a formal question and answer. Originally, such a contract was unenforceable although, if one party performed, he could demand his performance back if the other party refused to perform. Later, provided that he had performed, he was given a choice: to demand back his own performance or to require the other party to perform. But he could not enforce the agreement if he had not performed. This rule was summarized by saying "ex nudo pacto actio non oritur": no action arises on a bare agreement or "naked pact."[5]

This system was preserved by the medieval jurists. It sounds complicated, but actually it may have functioned reasonably well. Parties to a sale or lease usually wish to lock in the advantage of a certain price or rent. A partner or an agent needs to know an agreement is binding so he can conduct business on the basis of it. But in other transactions, the parties' need to bind themselves in advance is less clear. In any event, in Roman times, if they wished to be bound, they could easily make a *stipulatio*. The notarial formality in the Middle Ages was more cumbrous than the original oral question and answer.[6] But according to the 14th century jurist Bartolus, the unenforceability of innominate contracts had few practical consequences.[7] In the 16th century, Luis de Molina repeated Bartolus' remark.[8] Presumably they meant that important transactions such as an exchange of parcels of land would be notarized anyway.

Nevertheless, the medieval jurists found the Roman distinctions among contracts puzzling. The medieval canon lawyers recognized that breaking a promise was wrongful. They allowed the promisee an action on a broken promise before a canon law court.[9] The civil lawyers did not disagree in principle. By conflating a Roman text that said all contracts require consent[10] with others that spoke of a *ius gentium* (a law "established among all men by natural reason"),[11] they concluded that consent

---

4. Reinhard Zimmermann, *The Law of Obligations Roman Foundations of the Civilian Tradition* (1990), 547.

5. See generally W.W. Buckland, *Manual of Roman Private Law* (1953), 247–71; Max Kaser, *Das Römische Privatrecht* (1971), 534–27.

6. Zimmermann argues that because of its technical requirements, even the written formality of Justinian required the help of professionals: the tabelliones. Hence the need to extend the range of enforceable

contracts. Zimmermann, *Law of Obligations* 547–48.

7. Bartolus de Saxoferrato, *Commentaria Corpus Iuris Civilis* in *Omnia quae extant opera* (1577), to C. 4.6.2.

8. Ludovicus Molina, *De iustitia et iure tractatus* (1614) disp. 255.

9. Jules Roussier, *Le Fondement de l'obligation contractuelle dans le droit classique de l'église* (Paris 1933), 20–94, 177–216.

10. Dig. 2.14.1.3.

11. Inst. 1.2.1; Dig. 1.1.9.

to any contract creates an obligation under the *ius gentium* although not one that the civil law would enforce.[12] Thus, the medieval civilians found themselves denying that all promises were legally enforceable while agreeing with the canonists that promises should be kept,[13] just as the ancient Romans themselves refused to enforce all promises even though they placed a high moral value on promise-keeping.

Still, it seemed odd to them that not all promises were legally enforceable. In the late 13th century, Hostiensis quipped that the point of the Roman distinctions among contracts was to fill law books until scholars grew tired of spending money uselessly.[14] His contemporary Jacobus de Ravanis said:

> If I agree that you give me ten for my horse there is an action on the agreement. But if I agree that you give me your ass for my horse there is no action on the agreement. If a layman were to ask the reason for the difference it could not be given for it is merely positive law. And if you ask why the law was so established, the reason can be said to be that the contract of sale is more frequent than that of barter.[15]

Bartolus and Baldus tried to find a better reason although the one they found would not seem persuasive to us. They said that the contracts such as sale which are binding by consent take their "name" from an act the party performs by agreeing. I can sell you my house today by so agreeing even if I do not put you in possession until next month. Contracts such as deposit are not binding on consent because they take their name from an act a party performs by delivering. I cannot say I am depositing an object with you unless I am actually depositing it right now.[16] Baldus not only accepted this explanation and concluded that innominate contracts were unenforceable even in canon law.[17] This strange explanation may have seemed persuasive to Bartolus and Baldus because it was coaxed out of the word "name" which appeared in their Roman texts. Their usual method was to explain Roman texts in terms of other Roman texts rather than to look for theoretical or philosophical explanations.

From the 16th to the 18th century, as jurists took a more philosophical approach to law, the Roman system ceased to command respect and was eventually abolished. As with torts, the starting point for the late scholastics of the 16th and early 17th century was the philosophy of

12. E.g., Accursius, *Glossa Ordinaria* (1581), to I. 3.14 pr. to necessitate; Iacobus de Ravanis, Super Institutionibus Commentaria (published under the name of Bartolus de Saxoferrato in Omnia quae extant opera (1615), to I. 3.14.1 nos. 3, 9 (on the authorship see Eduard Meijers, *Etudes d'histoire du droit*, III, *Le droit romain au moyen âge* (1959), 68–69); Petrus de Bellapertica, *Lectura Institutionum* (1536), to I. 1.2.1 nos. 30–31.

13. Guido Astuti, "I principii fondamentali die contratti nella storia del diritto italiano," *Annali di storia del diritto* 1 (1957), 13–42, 34–37.

14. Hostiensis, *Summa* to X. 1.25 no. 3 (1537), ("Quae sunt divisiones pactorum ut quid mebranes occupabit: nisi ut scholares expensis inutilis fatigent.").

15. Iacobus de Ravanis, *Lectura Super Codice* (published under the name of Petrus de Bellapertica, 1519), to C. 4.64.3 (photographic reproduction, *Opera Iuridica Rariora* 1, 1967) (on the authorship, see Meijers, *Etudes* 72–77).

16. Bartolus, *Commentaria* to Dig. 2.14.7 no. 2.

17. Baldus de Ubalis, *Commentaria Corpus Iuris Civilis* to C. 2.3.27.

Aristotle. He had described transactions such as sale and lease as acts of "voluntary commutative justice." The parties exchanged resources voluntarily. Commutative justice required that the value of what each party gave equaled that of what he received. In contrast, in acts of "involuntary commutative justice" one party took or injured another's resources. Equality was restored by requiring him to pay their value.[18] In another passage in the *Ethics*, Aristotle discussed the virtue of "liberality": the liberal person disposed of his money wisely, giving "to the right people the right amounts and at the right time."[19] Thomas Aquinas put these ideas together: when one person transferred a thing to another, either it was an act of commutative justice that required an equivalent or it was an act of liberality. The late scholastics concluded that a party might enter voluntarily into either of two basic types of arrangements, a gratuitous contract in which he enriched the other party at his own expense, or an onerous contract in which he exchanged his own performance for one of equivalent value. Following them, Grotius and Pufendorf, the 17th century founders of the northern natural law school, developed elaborate schemes of classification to show how the contracts familiar in Roman law can be fitted into these two grand categories.[20] The French jurists Domat and Pothier explained that these are the two *causes* or reasons for making a binding promise.[21]

For these jurists, this classification meant more than the tautology that a party either does or does not receive back something in return for what he gives. In a gratuitous contract, the donor must actually intend to benefit the other party, and if he does not, the contract is not a gratuitous contract whatever the document to which the parties subscribed may say.[22] In an onerous contract, a party must receive, not simply a counter-performance, but one of equivalent value. These jurists thought that the rules that govern the parties' obligations should depend on which sort of agreement they had entered into. The rules should ensure, so far as practicable, that in the case of an exchange, each party receives an equivalent, and in the case of a gratuitous contract, that the donor behaves sensibly.[23]

---

18. Aristotle, *Nicomachean Ethics* V.iv 1130ᵇ.

19. Thomas Aquinas, *Summa theologiae* at II–II, Q. 61, a. 3.

20. Hugo Grotius, *De iure belli ac pacis libri tres* (1646), II, xii, 1–7; Samuel Pufendorf, *De iure naturae ac gentium libri octo* (1688), V.ii.8–10.

21. Jean Domat, *Les Loix civiles dans leur ordre naturel* (2d ed. 1713), liv. 1, tit. 1, § 1, nos. 5–6; § 5, no. 13; Robert Pothier, *Traité des obligations*, in *Oeuvres de Pothier* 2 (Bugnet, ed., 2d ed. 1861), § 42. Actually, the first jurist to describe these two *causes* or *causae* was Baldus. It can be shown that he was drawing on Aristotle. James Gordley,

The Philosophical Origins of Modern Contract Doctrine (1991), 49–57.

22. Thus according to Grotius: "Nor is it enough for anyone to say that what the other party has promised more than equality is to be regarded as a gift. For such is not the intention of the contracting parties, and is not to be presumed so, except it appear." Grotius, *De iure belli ac pacis* II.xii.11.1.

23. For an argument that these considerations can explain the way American courts apply such doctrines as consideration, promissory reliance, waiver, and offer and acceptance, see James Gordley, "Enforcing Promises," *California Law Review* 83 (1995), 547.

This classification cut across the Roman categories. Sale, lease and mandate were all contracts *consensu* but the first two were onerous and the third was gratuitous. Mandate and gratuitous loan for use and for consumption are all gratuitous but the first is a contract *consensu* and the others are contracts *re*. Sale, lease and barter are all onerous contracts but the first two are nominate contracts *consensu* and the third is innominate. Once the new classification was accepted, it seemed that the Roman categories were mere matters of Roman positive law.

The late scholastics consequently asked when, in principle a contract should be enforceable. Aristotle and Aquinas had described promise-keeping as similar to truth-telling. One who keeps promises is faithful in deed as one who tells the truth is faithful in word.[24] But did it follow that, as a matter of justice, all promises should be enforced? In the case of a gratuitous promise, however faithless the promisor may have been, the disappointed promisee may be no poorer. Therefore, according to the 16th century theologian and philosopher Cajetan, when the promise was gratuitous, the promisee could not demand that it be enforced as a matter of commutative justice. Nevertheless, if he had suffered damages by changing his position, then he could recover the amount of his damage.[25] A similar position was defended by the French jurist Connanus.[26]

Had this view prevailed, continental civil law might have anticipated the American doctrine of promissory reliance. It was rejected, however, by Soto, Molina and Lessius in the 16th century and by Grotius and Pufendorf in the 17th.[27] They pointed out that executory promises to exchange were binding even though no one had become poorer. Gifts were acts of liberality, but they could not be revoked after delivery. They concluded that, in principle, promises of gifts should be binding as long as the promisor intended to transfer a right to the object to the promisee.

They did not object, however, to the Roman requirement that one who promised to give away property must complete a formality. That was to ensure deliberation so that the promisor would behave sensibly. This requirement survived during the natural law era as did certain traditional exceptions to it: for example, even without the formality, courts would enforce promises to charitable causes (*ad causas pias*),[28] to people on account of their marriage (*ad nuptias vel propter nuptias*),[29] or to someone who had conferred a benefit on the promisor, for example, by rescuing him from robbers (*donatio remuneratoria*).[30]

---

24. Aristotle, *Nicomachean Ethics* IV.vii 1127ᵃ–1127ᵇ; Thomas Aquinas, *Summa theologiae* II–II, Q. 88, a. 3; Q. 110, a. 3, ad. 5.

25. Cajetan (Tomasso de Vio), *Commentaria* to Thomas Aquinas, *Summa theologiae* (1698), to II–II, Q. 88, a. 1; Q. 113, a. 1.

26. Connanus, *Commentariorum iuris civilis libri 10* (1724), I.6.v.1.

27. Domenicus Soto, *De iustitia et iure libri decem* (1553), lib. 8, q. 2, a. 1; Ludovicus Molina, *De iustitia et iure tractatus* (1614),

disp. 262; Leonardus Lessius, *De iustitia et iure, ceterisque virtutibus cardinalis* (1628), lib. 2, cap. 18, dub. 2; Grotius, *De iure belli ac pacis* II.xi.1.5; Pufendorf, *De iure naturae ac gentium* II.v.9.

28. Molina, *De iustitia et iure* disp. 279 no. 2; Lessius, *De iustitia et iure*, lib. 2, cap. 18, dub. 13, no. 102.

29. Molina, *De iustitia et iure*, disp. 279 no. 7.

30. Molina, *De iustitia et iure* disp. 279 no. 6.

When the promisor made a gratuitous promise but not one to give away property, the late scholastics could not see why the promise should not be binding right away, without any need for delivery. The promisor might be able to perform without making himself any poorer, and so there wasn't the same need to ensure deliberation. In a gratuitous loan for use or consumption, he might be loaning something that he did not need for a while. In a deposit, he might be able to look after the other party's goods without any cost to himself. In any event, the late scholastics thought that in principle, these gratuitous contracts were binding on consent if the promisor intended to be bound. But they said that he should be able to demand his goods back if he found that he needed them himself even if he had promised that the promisee could keep them for a longer time.[31] The Roman rule seems to have been that he had to let the promisee keep them for as long as he had promised.[32]

The late scholastics and the northern natural lawyers had been discussing when promises were binding in principle, or as they put it, as a matter of natural law. They acknowledged that the Roman law was different. Often, they invented pragmatic justifications for these deviations: for example, the Romans wished to avoid a flood of litigation. Nevertheless, their work undermined the Roman system by providing a coherent, philosophically grounded account of which promises should be enforced. Eventually, the Roman distinctions ceased to be part of continental positive law. They were abolished by statute in a few places such as Castile.[33] Elsewhere, beginning in the 16th century, jurists simply declared that the custom of courts was not to follow this rule.[34] By the 18th century this view had become universal.[35] The Roman system had disappeared.

Nanz has shown that the first jurist to mention this custom was Wesenbeck who miscited earlier jurists who had not mentioned it.[36] Later jurists cited Wesenbeck. To start a major legal reform by a miscitation is a bit like starting a landslide with a pebble. It only works if something is almost ready to fall by its own weight. Wesenbeck and his successors would not have been so seemingly careless had they wished to reach a different

---

31. Molina, *De iustitia et iure* disp. 294, nos. 8–10; Lessius, *De iustitia et iure* lib. 2, cap. 27, dub. 5.

32. Dig. 13.6.17.3 ("[A]fter he has made the loan, not only decency but the obligation undertaken between lender and borrower prevent his fixing time limits and claiming the object back in disregard of the times agreed. . . .").

33. Molina, *De iustitia et iure* disps. 257–58.

34. Johannes Voet, *Commentarius ad pandectas* (1698), to Dig. 2.14 no. 9; Wolfgang Lauterbach, *Collegii theoretico-pratici* (1744), to Dig. 2.14 no. 68; Johannes Wissenbach, *Exercitationum ad l. pandectarum libros* (1661), lib. 2, disp. 9 no. 35; Arnoldus Vinnius, *In quatuor libros institutionum imperialium commentariius academicus et forensis* (1726),

to I. 3.14 no. 11. See Burkhard Struvius, *Syntagma iurisprudentiae secundum ordinem pandectarium coccinatum* (1692), to Dig. 2.14 no. 32 (arguing that some agreements still would not be enforced when the parties did not so intend).

35. Zimmermann, *Law of Obligations* 539–40.

36. Matthaeus Wesenbeck, *In pandectas iuris civilis et codicis iustinianei libros viii commentaria* (1597), col. 189 to Dig. 2.14. Klaus-Peter Nanz, *Die Entstehung des allgemeinen Vertragsbegriff im 16. bis 18. Jahrhundert* (1985), 85. See Italo Birocchi, "La questione dei patti nella dottrina tedesca dell'Usus modernus," in John Barton, ed., *Toward a General Law of Contract* (1990), 197–213, 146–55.

conclusion. Wesenbeck explained why he favored the conclusion he did reach: by the natural law, all promises should be enforced.[37]

Nevertheless, even though naked pacts were now enforceable, the rule that promises of gifts required a formality was preserved. Jurists continued to give the same explanation as Molina and Lessius: the rule encouraged deliberation.[38] Eventually, such a requirement passed into the modern French and German Civil Codes, although the formality became subscribing to the promise before a notary.

French Civil Code

ARTICLE 893

One can only dispose of one's goods gratuitously by an inter vivos gift or a testament made in the forms hereafter prescribed.

ARTICLE 931

All gifts inter vivos must be made before notaries in the ordinary form of a contract and an original copy shall remain with the notary; otherwise the gift is void.

German Civil Code

§ 516 [CONCEPT (OF A GIFT)]

A gift is a disposition by which one person enriches another out of his own property if both parties agree that the disposition is made gratuitously.

§ 518 FORM

Notarial authentication is required for the validity of a contract by which a performance is promised as a gift. . . .

By and large, however, the Codes did not preserve traditional exceptions to the requirement for gifts to charities, to people about to marry, and to someone who had previously done a service for the promisor. One exception is a German provision.

§ 1624 [ENDOWMENT (*AUSSTATTUNG*) FROM THE PARENTS' ASSETS]

(1) What a child is to be given by the father or mother on account of marriage or obtaining an independent position in life, for founding or preserving the establishment of the position in life (endowment), even when there is no obligation to do so, only counts as a gift to the extent that the endowment exceeds the amount that is appropriate under the circumstances, and in particular, the financial situation of the father or mother.

In any event, when the required formality is completed, a promise of gift is enforceable although in France and Germany, gifts can be revoked

---

37. Wesenbeck, *Commentaria* col. 189 to Dig. 2.14.

38. Molina, *De iustitia et iure* disp. 278 no. 5; Lessius, *De iustitia et iure* lib. 2, cap. 18, nos. 2, 8.

for gross ingratitude,[39] and in Germany, if the donor becomes unable to support himself or to fulfill his legal duty to support others.[40]

Similarly, in France and Germany, the parties can bind themselves in advance of delivery to make a gratuitous loan, to care for another's goods, or to give a pledge. But in the case of gratuitous loans, even if the lender agreed the borrower can keep the object until a certain date, he can demand it back earlier if he needs it.

French Civil Code

ARTICLE 1888

The lender [in a loan for use] cannot take back the object loaned before the date agreed, or, if there was no agreement, before the object has served the use for which it was borrowed.

ARTICLE 1889

Nevertheless, if during this period or before the need of the borrower is at an end, the judge can require the borrower to return the object if the lender has a pressing and unforeseen need for it.

German Civil Code

§ 605 [RIGHT TO ABROGATE]

The lender can abrogate [a loan for use]:

(1) when he needs the object loaned because of circumstances that were unforeseeable. . . .

Thus the structure of modern civil law looks much as it did in the natural law era even though, by the 19th century, the Aristotelian ideas that originally inspired it no longer seemed to make sense. Jurists were developing "will theories" of contract: contract was expression of the will of the parties,

---

39. French Civil Code art. 955: An inter vivos gift may be revoked for ingratitude only in the following cases:

1. If the donee attempts to take the life of the donor;

2. If the donee is been cruel to him, wrongs him unlawfully, or seriously harms him;

3. If the donee has refused him support [in case of need].

German Civil Code § 530 Revocation of gift: A gift may be revoked if the donee is guilty of gross ingratitude on account of serious misconduct toward the donor or a near relative of his. . . .

40. German Civil Code § 519 Defense of need: The donor is entitled to refuse to perform a promise of gift insofar as he is not in position to fulfill his promise when, taking into account his other obligations, he cannot do so without endangering his own maintenance or his legal duties to maintain others.

§ 528 Requiring return because of need: After the gift has been bestowed, the donor can require that the donee return the gift in accordance with the provisions that govern restitution of unjust enrichment if the donor is not in a position to maintain himself reasonably or to fulfill his legal duty to maintain his relatives, his spouse or his former spouse. The donee may avoid returning it by payment of the amount required for maintenance. . . .

§ 529 Barring of the claim for return: The claim for return of the gift is barred if the donee has brought about his poverty intentionally or by gross negligence or if ten years have elapsed since the gift was bestowed.

The same rule applies if the donee is not in a position to return the gift, having regard to his other obligations, without endangering the maintenance appropriate to his own status in life or his legal duty to maintain others.

and the job of contract law was simply to enforce their will. The requirement that a contract must have a *causa* or *cause* had passed into the French Civil Code. But in the 19th century, it seemed to be a tautology: the party's motive for contracting was either to get something or not to get something. Thus the 19th century French found it hard to see how a contract could fail to have a *cause*.[41] Sometimes they explained a contract without a *cause* as one without a "legally sufficient motive,"[42] one made by mistake,[43] one concerning an object that was non-existent[44] or which the buyer already owned.[45] But if that was all the doctrine of *cause* meant, it was hard to see why there should be such a doctrine rather than simply a doctrine of mistake. Similarly, the 19th century German jurists had no use for the doctrine as traditionally understood. It did not appear in the German Civil Code.

2. Common law

As mentioned earlier, before the 19th century, the common lawyers organized their thinking, not in terms of tort and contract, but in terms of the traditional forms of action. By the 18th century, a disappointed promisee could sue in one of two forms of action: covenant or assumpsit. He could recover in covenant only if the promise had been made under seal, a formality originally performed by making an impression in wax on the document containing the promise. He could recover in assumpsit if the promise had "consideration."

There is famous and inconclusive controversy about whether the common law courts originally borrowed the idea that a promise needs consideration from the civil law idea of a *causa* of an onerous contract.[1] However that may have been, the common law courts found consideration, not only for promises to exchange, but for other promises that were not exchanges or bargains in the normal sense: for example, promises to give money to prospective sons-in-law and a variety of gratuitous loans and bailments.[2] In *Coggs v. Bernard*, defendant had negligently broken open and spilled the contents of some of plaintiff's casks of brandy while moving them from one place to another. The court held that there was consideration for his promise to look after them even though he had not been paid: "the owner's trusting him with the goods is a sufficient consideration."[3] Actually, it is misleading to compare *causa* and consideration since the doctrines were devised for different purposes. The continental doctrine identified the reasons why, in principle or theory, a promise should be enforced. The common law doctrine was a pragmatic tool for limiting the enforceability of promises.

---

41. Charles Aubry & Charles Rau, *Cours de droit civil français* 4 (4th ed. 1869–71), § 345 n. 7; A.M. Demante & E. Colmet de Santerre, *Cours analytique de Code Civil* 5 (2d ed. 1883), § 47; Charles Demolombe, *Cours de Code Napoléon* 24 (1854–82), § 357; Charles Toullier, *Le Droit civil français suivant l'order du Code* 5 (4th ed. 1824–37), § 166. See François Laurent, *Principles de droit civil français* 15 (3d ed. 1869–78), § 110–11.

42. Aubry & Rau, *Cours* 4: § 345.
43. Toullier, *Droit civil* 6: § 168.
44. Demolombe, *Cours* 24: § 357.
45. Léobon Larombière, *Théorie et pratique des obligations* 1 (1857), 273–75.
1. A.W.B. Simpson, *A History of the Common Law of Contract* (1975), 316–405.
2. *Id.* 416–52.
3. (1703) 92 Eng. Rep. 107 (K.B.)

In the common law, for centuries, "consideration" was not a term one could define. Promises were enforceable in those cases in which courts had said there was "consideration" because it seemed sensible to enforce them.

The search for a definition of "contract" and "consideration" began in the late 18th and early 19th centuries when common lawyers began to write treatises. Following continental authors, the treatise writers defined "contract" in terms of promise, engagement, agreement or assent.[4] And, often citing continental authors, they identified "consideration" with the *causa* of an onerous contract.[5] As Simpson has said, the early 19th century treatise writers regarded consideration as a local version of the doctrine of *causa*.[6] At first, the treatise writers did not explain the cases in which promises had been held to have consideration although they were not exchanges in any normal sense.

The common lawyers thus gave their contract law a shape like that of the civil law. Promises to make gifts were enforceable only with a formality although in common law the formality required was a seal. Promises to bargain or exchange were enforceable without a formality.

At first, the 19th century common lawyers explained consideration as the natural lawyers had explained the *causa* of a contract of exchange. They said the reason or sole motive of each party was to receive an equivalent. Christopher Columbus Langdell even claimed that "[a]s every consideration is in theory equal to the promise in value, so it is in theory the promisor's sole inducement to make the promise."[7] He acknowledged that this definition did not fit the common law cases, but the reason, he said, was that the law shut its eyes to certain discrepancies.

As on the continent, in the 19th century, these expressions no longer seemed to make sense. Oliver Wendell Holmes pointed out that a party might have many motives for contracting: "A man may promise to paint a picture for five hundred dollars, while his chief motive may be a desire for fame."[8] Sir Frederick Pollock quoted Thomas Hobbes: "[T]he value of all things contracted for, is measured by the appetite of the contractors, and therefore the just value, is that which they be contented to give."[9]

4. William Blackstone, *Commentaries on the Laws of England* 2 (14th ed. 1803), *442; Samuel Comyn, *A Treatise on the Law Relative to Contracts and Agreements Not Under Seal* (1809) I *2; John Newland , *A Treatise on Contracts Within the Jurisdiction of Courts of Equity* (1821), 1; Joseph D. Chitty, *A Practical Treatise on the Law of Contracts Not Under Seal* (1826), 3; James Kent, *Commentaries on American Law* 2 (13th ed. 1884), *450; William Wentworth Story, *A Treatise on the Law of Contracts Not Under Seal* (3d ed. 1851), 1; Theophilus Parsons, *The Law of Contracts* 1 (4th ed. 1860), *6; S. Martin Leake, *The Elements of the Law of Contracts* (1867), 7–8.

5. Blackstone, *Commentaries* 2, *444–46; John J. Powell, *Essay Upon the Law of Contracts and Agreements* 1 (1790), 331; William Taylor, *A Treatise on the Differences Between the Laws of England and Scotland Relating to Contracts* (1849) 16; W.W. Story, *Law of Contracts* 431, 431 n. 1; Comyn, *Contracts and Agreements* 1: *8; Kent, *Commentaries* 2: *630.

6. A.W.B. Simpson, "Innovation in Nineteenth Century Contract Law," *Law Quarterly Review* 91 (1975), 247 at 262.

7. Christopher Columbus Langdell, *A Summary of the Law of Contracts* (1880), 78–79.

8. Oliver Wendell Holmes Jr., *The Common Law* (1881), 293.

9. Sir Frederick Pollock, *Principles of Contract* (4th ed. 1888), 172.

Consequently, just as, on the continent, the doctrine of *causa* either disappeared or was no longer understood in the same way, so, in England and the United States, the requirement of consideration was reformulated. Pollock managed to define bargain so as to accommodate the common law cases without using concepts like equivalence that had become mysterious. At the same time, he managed to fit most of the cases in which English courts had said there was consideration. According to Pollock, whatever "a man chooses to bargain for must be conclusively taken to be of some value to him."[10] That was so even if the man himself had received nothing, consideration having moved to a thirdparty. The rule that a court will not "enter into an inquiry as to the adequacy of consideration" is reached "by a deduction" from this principle.[11] Therefore, to say the promisor entered into a bargain simply means he was induced to give his promise by some change in the position of the promisee.[12] A variation of Pollock's formula was adopted in the United State by Holmes.[13]

Modern authorities still explain consideration in terms of "bargain"[14] or "reciprocity."[15] Like Pollock, however, they define bargain in terms of something, of whatever value, sought by the promisor which induces him to promise.[16] But that does not mean that the only promises that lack consideration are those to give gifts or do favors in any ordinary sense. Suppose, for example, that someone promises to hold an offer open (as in *Dickenson v. Dodds*, below). If he receives nothing in return for this commitment, there is no consideration. Suppose, that after the parties contract, one agrees to pay the other more or to accept less. If the other party gives nothing in return beyond what he already under contract to give, again, there is no consideration.

Today, Anglo-American jurists are less inclined to apply the doctrine formalistically and more inclined to ask whether any useful purpose is served by refusing to enforce a promise. When the promise is a gift or

10. Pollock, *Principles of Contract* (10th ed. 1936), 172.

11. *Id.* 172.

12. *Id.* 164.

13. Holmes, *Common Law* 293–94; Letter from Holmes to Pollock, June 17, 1880 in Mark de Wolfe Howe (ed.), *The Holmes-Pollock Letters* 1 (2nd ed. 1961), 14–15. Holmes had received a manuscript of the first edition of Pollock's treatise (Letter from Pollock to Holmes, Dec. 16, 1875, in *id* 276) which contained the core of Pollock's theory. Pollock, *Principles of Contract* (1st ed. 1876), 150–51.

14. Restatement (Second) of Contracts §§ 17, 71 (1981).

15. G.H. Treitel, *The Law of Contract* (9th ed. 1995), 63.

16. Restatement (Second) of Contracts § 71 (1981) ("A performance or return promise is bargained for if it is sought by the promisor in exchange for his promise. . ."); Treitel, *Law of Contract* 68 ("The consideration for a promise (unless it is nominal or invented) is always a motive for promising. . . .). But while Pollock had said that the promise must be made to the promisee in order to induce him to change his legal position, the Second Restatement provides that "[t]he performance or return promise may be given to the promisor or to some other person. It may be given by the promisee or by some other person." According to Treitel, consideration can be either a benefit to the promisor or a detriment to the promisee, although he requires that consideration move from the promisee. *Law of Contract* 77–78. The number of cases in which these variants would produce a different result is rather small, and, indeed, the precise meaning of them is not very clear.

favor, the purpose may be the same that civil law systems achieve by other means: to encourage a person to act deliberately. When a promise is made in a business context, the purpose presumably is a different one. In the case of a promise to hold an offer open or to pay more or accept less than originally agreed, the purpose seems to be to prevent one party from taking unfair advantage of another. But if that is so, the doctrine of consideration is a blunt instrument since not all such promises are unfair.

Melvin Eisenberg has concluded that in such cases we no longer need a doctrine of consideration. American courts now can review the fairness of a contract directly by applying a doctrine called "unconscionability."

Others have tried to modify the traditional doctrine of consideration. In the United States, the Uniform Commercial Code, which governs the sale of goods and has been adopted in virtually every state, provides that among merchants, a written promise to hold an offer to sell goods open for a reasonable time does not require consideration.[17] The British Law Commission has recommended providing by statute that a firm offer is to be binding if it is made in the course of business and is expressed to be irrevocable for a definite period which is not to exceed six years.[18]

Similarly, under the Uniform Commercial Code, consideration is no longer required for promises to take less or give more than initially agreed in a sale of goods.[19] The Second Restatement of Contracts recommends a different approach: consideration is not required if the modification is fair because of a change of circumstances or enforcing the promise is fair because the promisee changed his position in reliance on it.[20] In England, the traditional doctrine was changed in *Williams v. Roffey Bros. & Nicholls (Contractors) Ltd*.[21] A contractor promised extra money to a subcontractor for completing the performance to which he had already agreed. He did so because his own surveyor recognized that the amount originally promised was too low, and because he was afraid that if the subcontractor had financial difficulties, he would not be able to complete the work on time. The subcontractor had not threatened that unless paid more he would not perform. Traditionally, the promise of extra payments would have been unenforceable. But the court held that the "practical benefit" that the contractor received would count as consideration.

Another escape route from the rigidities of the doctrine of consideration has been to hold that a promise without consideration can still have legal effects if the promisee changes his position in reliance on it. This doctrine, called promissory estoppel or promissory reliance, has been taken further in the United States than in England. In the United States, the promisor is liable to the promisee who relies.

---

17. U.C.C. § 2–205.
18. Working Paper 60 (1975).
19. U.C.C. § 2–209.

20. Restatement (Second) of Contracts § 89 (1981).
    21. [1991] 1 Q.B. 1.

Restatement (Second) of Contracts

§ 90 PROMISE REASONABLY INDUCING ACTION OR FORBEARANCE

(1) A promise which the promisor should reasonably expect to induce action or forbearance on the part of the promisee or a third person and which does induce such action or forbearance is binding if injustice can be avoided only by enforcement of the promise. The remedy granted for breach may be limited as justice requires.

(2) A charitable subscription or a marriage settlement is binding under Subsection (1) without proof that the promise induced action or forbearance.

The last sentence of Subsection (1) was added in the Second Restatement to allow courts to award a promisee his reliance damages—compensation for the amount that he had been by relying on the promise—rather than his expectation damages the amount necessary to put him—where he would have been had the promise been kept.

Subsection (2) was added in the Second Restatement to reflect the way in which courts had actually been applying the doctrine of promissory estoppel. Before the rise of the doctrine of promissory estoppel, courts in the United States (though not in England) had continued to say there is consideration for promises to prospective children-in-law and had sometimes found consideration for promises to a charity: for example, in naming a fund after the donor. Finding consideration in such cases seemed a bit fictitious. After the First Restatement, courts began applying the doctrine of promissory reliance instead. But they did not demand proof of reliance: proof that the couple would not have married otherwise, or that the charity really changed its position because of the promise. Subsection (2) makes it clear that the promisee does not have to provide such proof.

A doctrine of promissory reliance has also been accepted in England, but there it is much more limited. There, the doctrine protects a person who relies on a promise so as to excuse his performance of a prior obligation. But it does not create a new obligation to perform. As it is sometimes said, the doctrine can be used as a shield but not as a sword. For example, in *Central London Property Trust Ltd. v. High Trees House Ltd*, the landlords had rented a block of flats on a 99 year lease. In 1940, they agreed to take a lower rent because war-time conditions made it harder to find tenants. According to Lord Denning, they would not be able to recover the full rent originally agreed because of the reliance of the defendants. In a case like this, the doctrine is a shield which prevents the plaintiff from successfully suing on the defendant's original promise. In contrast, in *Combe v. Combe*,[22] during divorce proceedings, a husband promised to pay his wife £100 year, and she relied on that promise by not asking the court for maintenance. She was not able to use the doctrine of promissory reliance as a sword, to enforce the promise.

---

22. [1951] 2 K.B. 215.

II. VOLUNTARY COMMITMENT

1. The moment at which a commitment is binding

In comparing the rules described in this section, consider whether the offeree who mails an acceptance before receiving a revocation of an offer can hold the offeror to the contract (a) if the offeror receives his acceptance and (b) if he does not, for example, because it is lost in the mail. Consider whether the offeror who has sent a revocation should be bound in these situations.

Common law

Adams v. Lindsell, (1818) 1Barn. & Ald. 681 (K.B.)

"The defendants, who were wool dealers in St. Ives, wrote to the plaintiffs, who were wool manufacturers in Bromsgrove, Worcester: 'We now offer you eight hundred tods of wether fleeces, of a good fair quality of our country wool, at 35s. 6d. per tod, to be delivered at Leicester, and to be paid for by two months' bill in two months, and to be weighed up by your agent within fourteen days, receiving your answer in course of post.'

This letter was misdirected by the defendants, to Bromsgrove, Leicestershire, in consequence of which it was not received by the plaintiffs in Worcestershire till 7 p.m. on Friday, September 5th. On that evening the plaintiffs wrote an answer, agreeing to accept the wool on the terms proposed. The course of the post between St. Ives and Bromsgrove is through London, and consequently this answer was not received by the defendants till Tuesday, September 9th. On Monday, September 8th, the defendants not having, as they expected, received an answer on Sunday, September 7th (which in case their letter had not been misdirected would have been in the usual course of the post), sold the wool in question to another person." . . .

The defendants argued: "Till the plaintiffs' answer was actually received there could be no binding contract between the parties; and before then the defendants had retracted their offer by selling the wool to other persons." But the court said that "if that were so, no contract could ever be completed by the post. For if the defendants were not bound by their offer when accepted by the plaintiffs till the answer was received, then the plaintiffs ought not to be bound till after they had received the notification that the defendants had received their answer and assented to it. And so it might go on ad infinitum. The defendants must be considered in law as making, during every instant of the time their letter was traveling, the same identical offer to the plaintiffs, and then the contract is completed by the acceptance of it by the latter. Then as to the delay in notifying the acceptance, that arises entirely from the mistake of the defendants, and it therefore must be taken as against them that the plaintiffs' answer was received in course of post."

Restatement (Second) of Contracts

§ 63 TIME WHEN ACCEPTANCE TAKES EFFECT

Unless the offer provides otherwise,

(a) an acceptance made in a manner and by a medium invited by an offer is operative and completes the manifestation of mutual assent as soon as put out of the offeree's possession, without regard to whether it ever reaches the offeror. . . .

Dickinson v. Dobbs, [1876] 2 Ch. Div. 463 (C. A.)

"On Wednesday, the 10th of June, 1874, the defendant John Dodds signed and delivered to the plaintiff, George Dickinson, a memorandum, of which the material part was as follows:

I hereby agree to sell to Mr. George Dickinson the whole of the dwellinghouses, garden ground, stabling, and outbuildings thereto belonging, situate at Croft, belonging to me, for the sum of £800. As witness my hand this tenth day of June, 1874.

[Signed] J. Dodds.

* * *

In the afternoon of the Thursday [June 11], the plaintiff was informed by a Mr. Berry that Dodds had been offering or agreeing to sell the property to Thomas Allan, the other defendant. Thereupon the plaintiff, at about half past seven in the evening, went to the house of Mrs. Burgess, the mother-in-law of Dodds, where he was then staying, and left with her a formal acceptance in writing of the offer to sell the property. According to the evidence of Mrs. Burgess this document never in fact reached Dodds, she having forgotten to give it to him.

On the following (Friday) morning, at about seven o'clock, Berry, who was acting as agent for Dickinson, found Dodds at the Darlington railway station, and handed to him a duplicate of the acceptance by Dickinson, and explained to Dodds its purport. He replied that it was too late, as he had sold the property. A few minutes later Dickinson himself found Dodds entering a railway carriage, and handed him another duplicate of the notice of acceptance, but Dodds declined to receive it, saying: 'You are too late. I have sold the property.'" . . .

The court said: "The document, though beginning 'I hereby agree to sell,' was nothing but an offer, and was only intended to be an offer, for the plaintiff himself tells us that he required time to consider whether he would enter into an agreement or not. Unless both parties had then agreed, there was no concluded agreement then made; it was in effect and substance only an offer to sell. The plaintiff, being minded not to complete the bargain at that time, added this memorandum: 'This offer to be left over until Friday, 9 o'clock a.m. 12th June, 1874.' That shows it was only an offer. There was no consideration given for the undertaking or promise, to whatever extent it may be considered binding, to keep the property unsold until 9 o'clock on Friday morning; but apparently Dickinson was of opinion, and probably Dodds was of the same opinion, that he (Dodds) was bound by that promise, and could not in any way withdraw from it, or retract it, until 9 o'clock on Friday morning, and this probably explains a good deal of what afterwards took place. But it is clear settled law, on one of the clearest principles of law, that this promise, being a mere nudum pactum, was not binding, and that at any moment before a complete acceptance by Dickinson of the offer, Dodds was as free as Dickinson himself.

Well, that being the state of things, it is said that the only mode in which Dodds could assert that freedom was by actually and distinctly saying to Dickinson, 'Now I withdraw my offer.' It appears to me that there is neither principle nor authority for the proposition that there must be an express and actual withdrawal of the offer, or what is called a retraction. It must, to constitute a contract, appear that the two minds were at one, at the same moment of time, that is, that there was an offer continuing up to the time of the acceptance. If there was not such a continuing offer, then the acceptance comes to nothing. Of course it may well be that the one man is bound in some way or other to let the other man know that his mind with regard to the offer has been changed; but in this case, beyond all question, the plaintiff knew that Dodds was no longer minded to sell the property to him as plainly and clearly as if Dodds had told him in so many words, 'I withdraw the offer.' This is evident from the plaintiff's own statements in the bill."

Restatement (Second) of Contracts

§ 25 OPTION CONTRACTS

An option contract is a promise which meets the requirements for the formation of a contract and limits the promisor's power to revoke an offer.

§ 87 OPTION CONTRACT

(1) An offer is binding as an option contract if it

    (a) is in writing and signed by the offeror, recites a purported consideration for the making of the offer, and proposes an exchange on fair terms within a reasonable time; or

    (b) is made irrevocable by statute.

(2) An offer which the offeror should reasonably expect to induce action or forbearance of a substantial character on the part of the offeree before acceptance and which does induce such action or such forbearance is binding as an option contract to the extent necessary to prevent injustice.

Uniform Commercial Code

§ 2.205 FIRM OFFERS

An offer by a merchant to buy or sell goods in a signed writing which by its terms gives assurance that it will be held open is not revocable, for lack of consideration, during the time stated or if no time is stated for a reasonable time, but in no event may such period of revocability exceed three months; but any such term of assurance on a form supplied by the offeree must be separately signed by the offeror.

Note: As mentioned earlier, the Uniform Commercial Code has been enacted in virtually all American states. Article 2 governs the sale of goods.

German law

German Civil Code

§ 145 [BINDING FORCE OF AN OFFER]

One who has offered to conclude a contract with another is bound by that offer unless he states that he is not bound.

§ 146 [THE LAPSE OF THE OFFER]

The offer lapses if the offeror is refused or if he is not given an acceptance within due time according to §§ 147–49.

§ 147 [TIME TO ACCEPT]

An offer made to a person who is present can only be accepted immediately. That is so as well when an offer is made by one person to another by telephone.

An offer made to a person who is absent can be accepted only within the time that an answer would be expected under ordinary circumstances.

French law

Cour de cassation, ch. soc., 22 March 1972, D.S. 1972.468

"In response to an offer of employment published by the *Société salaissonnière du Centre* and at its request, Vandendriesche went from Brest to Saint-Mathieu in Haute-Vienne to the main office of the company to discuss the eventual conclusion of a contract of employment as factory manager." "[B]y a letter dated 3 March 1970, the company 'confirmed' its 'decision' to hire him on specified terms and requested him, if he found this proposal acceptable, to inform the company of the date on which he planned to assume his duties." He claimed to have written a letter of acceptance to the company on March 11. "[O]n March 14, it wrote to him to cancel its 'offer of employment' on the grounds that it had not received his acceptance as of that date and that its administrative council had just decided not to create such a position in the immediate future."

The court found for Vandendriesche. "[I]f Vandendriesche could not prove that he had, as he claimed, sent a simple letter to his future employer on March 11, 1970, informing him that he would assume his duties on the 23rd, nevertheless a delay of only nine days occurred between the receipt by the employee of his offer of employment and its revocation by the employer." The lower court was correct "in finding, on the one hand, that this delay did not exceed the time for reflection and response which—in the absence of a fixed time period—the company was required to give Vandendriesche, and, on the other hand, that the decision taken during this period of time by its administrative council not to create a position for economic reasons and to retract its offer cannot be invoked against an employee who had been induced to resign his previous job and incur traveling expenses. . . ."

The "Lando Principles"

Two "Commissions on European Contract Law," sponsored by funds from the Commission of the European Union, and under the direction of Ole Lando, drafted a set of "Principles of European Contract Law." The Second Commission, which met from 1992–96, continued the work of the First, which met from 1980–1990. Their "Principles" have not been enacted as law. They are intended to serve the following purposes: "to serve as a foundation for European legislation," to govern a contract in the event of "express adoption by the parties," to provide "a modern formulation of the *lex mercatoria* or law merchant," and to serve as "a model for the judicial and legislative development of contract law" and "a basis for harmonization." Ole Lando & Hugh Beale, eds., *Principles of European Contract Law* (2000), xxiii–xxiv. These purposes are reflected in Article 1.101, quoted below.

The Principles of European Contract Law of the Commission on European Contract Law

ARTICLE 1.101 APPLICATION OF THE PRINCIPLES

(1) These Principles are intended to be applied as general rules of contract law in the European Community.

(2) These Principles will apply when the parties have agreed that their contract is to be governed by them.

(3) These Principles may be applied

(a) when the parties have agreed that their contract is to be governed by "general principles of law", the "lex mercatoria" or the like; or

(b) when the parties have not chosen any system or rules of law to govern their contract.

(4) These Principles may provide a solution to the issue raised where the system or rules of law applicable do not do so.

ARTICLE 2.202: REVOCATION OF AN OFFER

(1) An offer may be revoked if the revocation reaches the offeree before it has dispatched its acceptance. . . .

* * *

(3) However, a revocation of an offer is ineffective if:

(a) it states that it is irrevocable, or

(b) it states a fixed time for acceptance, or

(c) it was reasonable for the offeree to rely on the offer as being irrevocable and the offeree acted in reliance on the offer.

ARTICLE 2.203: REJECTION

When a rejection of an offer reaches the offeree, the offer lapses.

ARTICLE 2.205: THE TIME OF CONCLUSION OF THE CONTRACT

(1) If an acceptance has been dispatched by the offeree the contract is concluded when the acceptance reaches the offeror.

The Unidroit Principles

UNIDROIT is an acronym for the International Institute for the Unification of Private Law. It is a an independent intergovernmental organization founded in 1926. At the time of the drafting of the Unidroit Principles of International Commercial Law, the organization was composed of twenty-six member states. While approved by the member states, the Principles are not binding either as legislation or as a treaty. They have been described by Michael Joachim Bonnell, under whose leadership they were drafted, as "an international restatement of contract law." The purposes to be served by the Principles are described in the provisions of the Preamble quoted below.

The Unidroit Principles of International Commercial Contracts

PREAMBLE (PURPOSE OF THE PRINCIPLES)

These Principles set forth general rules for international commercial contracts.

They shall be applied when the parties have agreed that their contract be governed by them.

They may be applied when the parties have agreed that their contract be governed by general principles of law, the *lex mercatoria* or the like.

They may provide a solution to an issue raised when it proves impossible to establish the relevant rule of the applicable law.

They may be used to interpret or supplement international uniform law instruments.

They may serve as a model for national and international legislators.

ARTICLE 2.1 MANNER OF FORMATION

A contract may be concluded either by the acceptance of an offer or by conduct of the parties that is sufficient to show agreement.

ARTICLE 2.3 WITHDRAWAL OF OFFER

(1) An offer becomes effective when it reaches the offeree.

(2) An offer, even if it is irrevocable, may be withdrawn if the withdrawal reaches the offeree before or at the same time as the offer.

ARTICLE 2.4 REVOCATION OF OFFER

(1) Until a contract is concluded an offer may be revoked if the revocation reaches the offeree before it has dispatched an acceptance.

(2) However, an offer cannot be revoked

    (a) if it indicates, whether by stating a fixed time for acceptance or otherwise, that it is irrevocable; or

    (b) if it was reasonable for the offeree to rely on the offer as being irrevocable and the offeree has acted in reliance on the offer.

ARTICLE 2.5 REJECTION OF OFFER

An offer is terminated when a rejection reaches the offeror.

(1) A statement or other conduct of the offeree indicating assent to an offer is an acceptance. Silence or inactivity does not in itself amount to acceptance.

(2) An acceptance of an offer becomes effective when the indication of assent reaches the offeror.

(3) However, if, by virtue of the offer or as a result of practices which the parties have established between themselves or of usage, the offeree may indicate assent by performing an act without notice to the offeror, the acceptance is effective when the act is performed.

2. Liability before a final commitment is made

English law

Walford v. Miles, [1992] 2 A.C. 128 (H.L.)

Lord Ackner. "The respondents owned a company, together with premises which were let to the company where it carried on a photographic processing business. In 1986 the respondents decided to sell the business and the premises and received an offer of £1.9m from a third party. In the meantime the appellants entered into negotiations with the respondents and on 12 March 1987 the respondents agreed in principle to sell the business and the premises to them for £2m and warranted that the trading profits in the 12 months following completion would be not less than £300,000. On 7 March it was further agreed in a telephone conversation between the parties that if the appellants provided a comfort letter from their bank by a specified date confirming that the bank had offered them loan facilities to enable them to make the purchase for £2m the respondents 'would terminate negotiations with any third party or consideration of any alternative with a view to concluding agreements' with the appellants and that even if the respondents received a satisfactory proposal from any third party before the close of business on 20 March 1987 they 'would not deal with that third party and nor would [they] give further consideration to any alternative.' The appellants duly provided the comfort letter from their bank in the time specified and on 25 March the respondents confirmed that, subject to contract, they agreed to the sale of the property and the shares in the company at a total price of £2m. On 30 March the respondents withdrew from the negotiations and decided to sell to the third party because they were concerned that their staff would not get on with the appellants and that a loss of staff would put the warranted £300,000 profit in jeopardy.

Although the cases in the United States did not speak with one voice your Lordships' attention was drawn to the decision of the United States Court of Appeals, Third Circuit in Channel Home Centers Division of Grace Retail Corp v Grossman (1986) 795 F 2d 291 as being 'the clearest example' of the American cases in the appellants' favour. That case raised the issue whether an agreement to negotiate in good faith, if supported by consideration, is an enforceable contract. I do not find the decision of any assistance. While accepting that an agreement to agree is not an enforceable contract, the United States Court of Appeals appears to have proceeded on the basis that an agreement to negotiate in good faith is synonymous with an agreement to use best endeavours and, as the latter is enforceable, so is the former. This appears to me, with respect, to be an unsustainable proposition. The reason why an agreement to negotiate, like an agreement to agree, is unenforceable is simply because it lacks the necessary certainty. The same does not apply to an agreement to use best endeavours. This uncertainty is demonstrated in the instant case by the provision which it is said has to be implied in the agreement for the determination of the negotiations. How can a court be expected to decide whether, subjectively, a proper reason existed for the termination of negotiations? The answer suggested depends upon whether the negotiations have been determined 'in good faith.' However, the concept of a duty to carry on negotiations in good faith is inherently repugnant to the adversarial position of the parties when involved in negotiations. Each party to the negotiations is entitled to pursue his (or her) own interest, so long as he avoids making misrepresentations. To advance that interest he must be entitled, if he thinks it appropriate, to threaten to withdraw from further negotiations or to withdraw in fact in the hope that the opposite party may seek to reopen the negotiations by offering him improved terms. Mr Naughton [the plaintiff's attorney] of course, accepts that the agreement upon which he relies does not contain a duty to complete the negotiations. But that still leaves the vital question: how is a vendor ever to know that he is entitled to withdraw from further negotiations? How is the court to police such an 'agreement'? A duty to negotiate in good faith is as unworkable in practice as it is inherently inconsistent with the position of a negotiating party. It is here that the uncertainty lies. In my judgment, while negotiations are in existence either party is entitled to withdraw from these negotiations, at any time and for any reason. There can be thus no obligation to continue to negotiate until there is a 'proper reason' to withdraw. Accordingly, a bare agreement to negotiate has no legal content."

William Lacey (Hounslow), Ltd. v. Davis, [1957] 2 All E.R. 712 (Q.B.)

"D., the owner of certain premises, which had suffered war damage, obtained tenders [i.e., bids] from three builders, including the plaintiffs, for the rebuilding of the premises as a shop with residential flats above. The plaintiffs' tender, which was received in January, 1951, was the lowest and the plaintiffs were led to believe that they would receive the contract. At the request of D.'s agents, they then calculated the timber and steel required for the proposed building for the purpose of obtaining the necessary licences, and they also submitted their estimate for the notional reconstruction of the building as it was before the war damage and a schedule of the basic prices on which their original tender was based, in order to enable D. to negotiate with the War Damage Commission the amount payable to him under the War Damage Act, 1943. A licence in respect of the original plans having been refused by the Ministry of Works, the plaintiffs were asked to submit a revised estimate in respect of new plans, although D. did not intend to decide on the type of house which he proposed to erect until the amount of his war damage claim had been agreed. The plaintiffs undertook a considerable amount of work in preparing their revised estimate, which was submitted in December, 1951, and they also provided further particulars required by D. for the War Damage Commission. As a result of the estimates and the other information provided by the plaintiffs, the amount receivable by D. from the War Damage Commission was substantially increased. After the commission's decision had been given in April, 1952, the plaintiffs were asked to submit another estimate in regard to revised plans and, later, to make still further amendments to the new estimate. After they had complied with these requests they were informed that D. intended to employ another builder to rebuild the premises. Subsequently D. sold the premises instead of having them rebuilt."

Barry, J. "On this evidence, I am quite satisfied that the whole of the work covered by the schedule fell right outside the work which a builder, by custom and usage, normally performs gratuitously, when invited to tender for the erection of a building. . . . The earlier estimates, as the correspondence shows, were in fact used, and used for some purpose, in Mr. Davis' negotiations with the War Damage Commission and, an apparent result of the plaintiffs' efforts, not only were the reconstruction plans approved, but a much higher 'permissible amount' was also agreed with the War Damage Commission. It is perhaps justifiable to surmise that these facts, especially the reconstruction plans and the increase in the permissible amount, had at least some influence on the price of the damaged building which Mr. Davis obtained when it was ultimately sold by him.

The work itemised in the schedule which does not relate to estimation, as I think, falls even more clearly outside the type of work which any builder would be expected to do without charge when tendering for a building contract. The plaintiffs are carrying on a business and, in normal circumstances, if asked to render services of this kind, the obvious inference would be that they ought to be paid for so doing. No one could expect a business firm to do this sort of work for nothing, and again, in normal circumstances, the law would imply a promise to pay on the part of the person who requested the services to be performed. Counsel for the defendants, however, submits that no such promise can be implied, in the circumstances of the present case. The existence, he submits, of a common expectation that a contract would ultimately come into being, and that the plaintiffs' services would be rewarded by the profits of that contract, leaves no room for—and, indeed, wholly negatives—any suggestion that the parties impliedly agreed that these services would be paid for in any other way.

This, at first sight, is a somewhat formidable argument which, if well founded, would wholly defeat the plaintiffs' alternative claim. If such were the law, it would, I think, amount to a denial of justice to the plaintiffs in the present case, and legal propositions which have that apparent effect must always be scrutinised with some care. In truth, I think that counsel's proposition is founded on too narrow a view of the modern action for quantum meruit. . . . In these quasi-contractual cases the court will look at the true facts and ascertain from them whether or not a promise to pay should be implied, irrespective of the actual views of intentions of the parties at the time when the work was done or the services rendered. . . .

I am unable to see any valid distinction between work done which was to be paid for under the terms of a contract erroneously believed to be in existence, and work done which was to be paid for out of the proceeds of a contract which both parties erroneously believed was about to be made. In neither case was the work to be done gratuitously, and in both cases the party from whom payment was sought requested the work and obtained the benefit of it. In neither case did the parties actually intend to pay for the work otherwise than under the supposed contract, or as part of the total price which would become payable when the expected contract was made. In both cases, when the beliefs of the parties were falsified, the law implied an obligation—and in this case I think the law should imply an obligation—to pay a reasonable price for the services which had been obtained. I am, of course, fully aware that in different circumstances it might be held that work was done gratuitously merely in the hope that the building scheme would be carried out and that the person who did the work would obtain the contract. That, I am satisfied, is not the position here."

Law in the United States

Channel Home Centers v. Grossman, 795 F.2d 291 (3rd Cir. 1986)

"This diversity case presents the question whether, under Pennsylvania law, a property owner's promise to a prospective tenant, pursuant to a detailed letter of intent, to negotiate in good faith with the prospective tenant and to withdraw the lease premises from the marketplace during the negotiation, can bind the owner for a reasonable period of time where the prospective tenant has expended significant sums of money in connection with the lease negotiations and preparation and where there was evidence that the letter of intent was of significant value to the property owner. We hold that it may. . . .

In the third week of November, 1984, Tri-Star wrote to Richard Perkowski, Director of Real Estate for Channel, informing him of the availability of store location in Cedarbrook Mall which Tri-Star believed Channel would be interested in leasing. Perkowski expressed some interest, and met the Grossmans on November 28, 1984. After Perkowski was given a tour of the premises, the terms of a lease were discussed. App. at 457a, 498a. Frank Grossman testified that 'we discussed various terms, and these terms were, some were loose, some were more or less terms.' App. at 364a, 496a–497a. . . .

Frank Grossman [part owner of Tri-Star] then requested that Channel execute a letter of intent that, as Grossman put it, could be shown to 'other people, banks or whatever.' App. at 366a–367a. . . . Apparently, Frank Grossman was anxious to get Channel's signature on a letter of intent so that it could be used to help Grossman secure financing for his purchase of the mall. App. at 366a–367a, 497a.

On December 11, 1984, in response to Grossman's request, Channel prepared, executed, and submitted a detailed letter of intent setting forth a plethora of lease terms which provided, *inter alia*, that:

> '[t]o induce the Tenant [Channel] to proceed with the leasing of the Store, you [Grossman] will withdraw the Store from the rental market, and only negotiate the above described leasing transaction to completion.'

> 'Please acknowledge your intent to proceed with the leasing of the store under the above terms, conditions and understanding by signing the enclosed copy of the letter and returning it to the undersigned within ten (10) days from the date hereof.'

Frank Grossman promptly signed the letter of intent and returned it to Channel.

On February 6, 1985, Frank Grossman notified Channel that 'negotiations terminated as of this date' due to Channel's failure to submit a signed and mutually acceptable lease for the mall site within thirty days of the December 11, 1984 letter of intent. App. at 42a. (This was the first and only written evidence of the purported thirty-day time limit. The letter of intent contained no such term. . . .) On February 7, 1985, Mr. Good Buys and Frank Grossman executed a lease for the Cedarbrook Mall. App. at 147a–196a. Mr. Good Buys agreed to make base-level annual rental payments which were substantially greater than those agreed to by Channel in the December 11, 1984 letter of intent. App. at 147a. Channel's corporate parent, Grace, approved the terms of Channel's proposed lease on February 13, 1985. App. at 443a–444a. . . .

It is hornbook law that evidence of preliminary negotiations or an agreement to enter into a binding contract in the future does not alone constitute a contract. *See Goldman v. McShain*, 432 Pa. 61, 68, 247 A.2d 455, 458 (j1968); *Lombardo v. Gasparini Excavating Co.*, 385 Pa. 388, 392, 123 A.2d 663, 666 (1956); *Kazanjian v. New England Petroleum Corp.*, 332 Pa.Super. 1, 7, 480 A.2d 1153, 1157 (1984); *see* Restatement (Second) of Contracts § 26 (1979). Appellees believe that this doctrine settles this case, but, in so arguing, appellees misconstrue Channel's contract claim. Channel does not contend that the letter of intent is binding as a lease or an agreement to enter into a lease. Rather, it is Channel's position that this document is enforceable as a mutually binding obligation to negotiate in good faith. By unilaterally terminating negotiations with Channel and precipitously entering into a lease agreement with Mr. Good Buys, Channel argues, Grossman acted in bad faith and breached his promise to 'withdraw the Store from the rental market and only negotiate the above-described leasing transaction to completion.' See *supra* note 2.

Under Pennsylvania law, the test for enforceability of an agreement is whether both parties have manifested an intention to be bound by its terms and whether the terms are sufficiently definite to be specifically enforced. . . .

Applying Pennsylvania law, then, we must ask (1) whether both parties manifested an intention to be bound by the agreement; (2) whether the terms of the agreement are sufficiently definite to be enforced; and (3) whether there was consideration. . . .

The letter of intent, signed by both parties, provides that '[t]o induce the Tenant [Channel] to proceed with the leasing of the Store, you [Grossman] will withdraw the Store from the rental market, and only negotiate the proposed leasing transaction with Channel to completion.'

Evidence of record supports the proposition that the parties intended this promise to be binding. After the letter of intent was executed, both Channel and the Grossmans initiated procedures directed toward satisfaction of lease contingencies. Channel directed its parent corporation to prepare a draft lease; Channel planning representatives visited the lease premises to obtain measurements for architectural alterations, renovations, and related construction. Channel developed extensive marketing plans; delivery schedules were prepared and material and equipment deemed necessary for the store were purchased. The Grossmans applied to the township zoning committee for permission to erect Channel signs at various locations on the mall property. Channel submitted a draft lease on January 11, 1985, and the parties, through correspondence and telephone conversations and on-site visits, exhibited an intent to move toward a lease as late as January 23, 1985. . . . Accordingly, the letter of intent and the circumstances surrounding its adoption both support a finding that the parties intended to be bound by an agreement to negotiate in good faith.

We also believe that Grossman's promise to 'withdraw the Store from the rental market and only negotiate the above described leasing transaction to completion,' viewed in the context of the detailed letter of intent (which covers most significant lease terms, *see supra* n. 2), is sufficiently definite to be specifically enforced, provided that Channel submitted sufficient legal consideration in return."

Hoffman v. Red Owl Stores, Inc., 133 N.W. 2d 267 (Wis. 1965)

"The complaint alleged that Lukowitz, as agent for Red Owl Stores, represented to and agreed with plaintiffs that Red Owl would build a store building in Chilton and stock it with merchandise for Hoffman to operate in return for which plaintiffs were to put up and invest a total sum of $18,000; that in reliance upon the above mentioned agreement and representations plaintiffs sold their bakery building and business and their grocery store and business; also in reliance on the agreement and representations Hoffman purchased the building site in Chilton and rented a residence for himself and his family in Chilton; plaintiffs' actions in reliance on the representations and agreement disrupted their personal and business life; plaintiffs lost substantial amounts of income and expended large sums of money as expenses. Plaintiffs demanded recovery of damages for the breach of defendants' representations and agreements. . . .

The action was tried to a court and jury. The facts hereafter stated are taken from the evidence adduced at the trial. Where there was a conflict in the evidence the version favorable to plaintiffs has been accepted since the verdict rendered was in favor of plaintiffs.

Hoffman assisted by his wife operated a bakery at Wautoma from 1956 until sale of the building late in 1961. . . . Red Owl is a Minnesota corporation having its home office at Hopkins, Minnesota. It owns and operates a number of grocery supermarket stores and also extends franchises to agency stores which are owned by individuals, partnerships and corporations. . . .

In November, 1959, Hoffman was desirous of expanding his operations by establishing a grocery store and contacted a Red Owl representative by the name of Jansen, now deceased. Numerous conversations were had in 1960 with the idea of establishing a Red Owl franchise store in Wautoma. In September, 1960, Lukowitz succeeded Jansen as Red Owl's representative in the negotiations. Hoffman mentioned that $18,000 was all the capital he had available to invest and he was repeatedly assured that this would be sufficient to set him up in business as a Red Owl Store. About Christmastime, 1960, Hoffman thought it would be a good idea if he bought a small grocery store in Wautoma and operated it in order that he gain experience in the grocery business prior to operating a Red Owl store in some larger community. On February 6, 1961, on the advice of Lukowitz and Sykes, who had succeeded Lukowitz as Red Owl's district manager, Hoffman bought the inventory and fixtures of a small grocery store in Wautoma and leased the building in which it was operated.

After three months of operating this Wautoma store, the Red Owl representatives came in and took inventory and checked the operations and found the store was operating at a profit. Lukowitz advised Hoffman to sell the store to his manager, and assured him that Red Owl would find a larger store for him elsewhere. Acting on this advice and assurance, Hoffman sold the fixtures and inventory to his manager on June 6, 1961. Hoffman was reluctant to sell at that time because it meant losing the summer tourist business, but he sold on the assurance that he would be operating in a new location by fall and that he must sell this store if he wanted a bigger one. Before selling, Hoffman told the Red Owl representatives that he had $18,000 for 'getting set up in business' and they assured him that there would be no problems in establishing him in a bigger operation. The makeup of the $18,000 was not discussed; it was understood plaintiff's father-in-law would furnish part of it. By June 1961, the towns for the new grocery store had been narrowed down to two, Kewaunee and Chilton. In Kewaunee, Red Owl had an option on a building site. In Chilton, Red Owl had nothing under option, but it did select a site to which plaintiff obtained an option at Red Owl's suggestion. The option stipulated a purchase price of $5,000 with $1,000 to be paid on election to purchase and the balance to be paid within 30 days. On Lukowitz's assurance that everything was all set plaintiff paid $1,000 down on the lot on September 15th.

On September 27, 1961, plaintiff met at Chilton with Lukowitz and Mr. Reymund and Mr. Carlson from the home office who prepared a projected financial statement. Part of the funds plaintiffs were to supply as their investment in the venture were to be obtained by sale of their Wautoma bakery building.

On the basis of this meeting Lukowitz assured Hoffman: '[E]verything is ready to go. Get your money together and we are set.' Shortly after this meeting Lukowitz told plaintiffs that they would have to sell their bakery business and bakery building, and that their retaining this property was the only 'hitch' in the entire plan. On November 6, 1961, plaintiffs sold their bakery building for $10,000. Hoffman was to retain the bakery equipment as he contemplated using it to operate a bakery in connection with his Red Owl store. After sale of the bakery Hoffman obtained employment on the night shift at an Appleton bakery. . . .

[Eventually, Red Owl presented Hoffmann with a statement which he interpreted to require] 'a total of $34,000 cash made up of $13,000 gift from his father-in-law, $2,000 on mortgage, $8,000 on Chilton bank loan, $5,000 in cash from plaintiff, and $6,000 on the resale of the Chilton lot.' . . . Hoffman informed Red Owl he could not go along with this proposal, and particularly objected to the requirement that his father-in-law sign an agreement that his $13,000 advancement was an absolute gift. This terminated the negotiations between the parties. . . .

Originally the doctrine of promissory estoppel was invoked as a substitute for consideration rendering a gratuitous promise enforceable as a contract. See Williston, Contracts (1st ed.), p. 307, sec. 139. In other words, the acts of reliance by the promisee to his detriment provided a substitute for consideration. If promissory estoppel were to be limited to only those situations where the promise giving rise to the cause of action must be a definite with respect to all details that a contract would result were the promise supported by consideration, then the defendants' instant promises to Hoffman would not meet this test. However, sec. 90 of Restatement, 1 Contracts, does not impose the requirement that the promise giving rise to the cause of action must be so comprehensive in scope as to meet the requirements of an offer that would ripen into a contract if accepted by the promisee. Rather the conditions imposed are:

(1) Was the promise one which the promisor should reasonably expect to induce action or forbearance of a definite and substantial character on the part of the promisee?

(2) Did the promise induce such action or forbearance?

(3) Can injustice be avoided only by enforcement of the promise?

We deem it would be a mistake to regard an action grounded on promissory estoppel as the equivalent of a breach of contract action. As Dean Boyer points out, it is desirable that fluidity in the application of the concept be maintained. 98 University of Pennsylvania Law Review (1950), 459, at page 497. While the first two of the above listed three requirements of promissory estoppel present issues of fact which ordinarily will be resolved by a jury, the third requirement, that the remedy can only be invoked where necessary to avoid injustice, is one that involves a policy decision by the court. Such a policy decision necessarily embraces an element of discretion.

We conclude that injustice would result here if plaintiffs were not granted some relief because of the failure of defendants to keep their promises which induced plaintiffs to act to their detriment."

Note: Courts in the United States have recognized a duty to perform a contract in good faith once it has been made. But they have not recognized a duty to negotiate in good faith absent an agreement to do so or, as in *Red Owl*, a promise on which the plaintiff has relied. Alan Farnsworth claimed that American law does not need to recognize such a duty because the plaintiff should recover only if the defendant has deceived him during negotiations, broken an express or implied promise made during negotiations, or enriched himself unjustly by receiving something from the plaintiff before a contract was made.[1] In all of these cases, American courts would give relief because of deceit, the breaking of a promise, or unjust enrichment. Ewould Hondius, a leading continental jurist, has said that, aside from some caveats that do not matter here, "I would underwrite [Farnsworth's] opinion"[2] as to when relief should be given. Farnsworth also claimed that with rare exceptions, continental courts that recognize a duty to negotiate in good faith actually give relief in the same circumstances as American courts, although he acknowledged there have been exceptions. One of them, he said, is the first case in the next section, the decision of the *Cour de cassation* of 20 March 1972. Consider whether, with this exception, the decisions of French and German courts in the following sections would be decided the same way in the United States, as Farnsworth claims. If so, consider why that case is an exception.

French law

Cour de cassation, ch. comm. et finan., 20 March 1972,
Bull. civ. 1972.IV. no. 93

The court below found that the *Société des éstablissements Gerteis* entered into negotiations in April 1966 with the *Société établissements Vilber-Lourmat*, the sole distributor in France of machines, used for the manufacture of cement pipes made by the American firm Hydrotile Co. After Robert Gerteis made a trip to the United States from May 13 to 23, 1966 in order to observe the operation of these machines, the *Société Gerteis* requested from the *Société Vilber-Lourmat* further information

---

1. E. Allan Farnsworth, "Precontractual Liability and Preliminary Agreements: Fair Dealing and Failed Negotiations," *Colum. L. Rev.* 87 (1987), 217.

2. Ewoud Hondius, "General Report," in E. Hondius, ed., *Precontractual Liability Reports to the XIIIth Congress International Academy of Comparative Law Montreal, Canada, 18–24 August 1990* (1991), 3, 27.

before making its choice among several types of machines manufactured by the Hydrotile company. The *Société Vilber-Lourmat* did not reply to this letter. The *Société Gerteis* learned later that on June 4, 1966, the American manufacturer had sent an estimate to *Vilber-Lourmat* which it had not transmitted the estimate to *Gerteis*. On June 16, 1966, *Vilber-Lourmat* signed a contract with the company *Les Tuyaux Centrifugés du Rhin*, a competitor of *Gerteis*, for the sale for a Hydrotile machine. The contract contained a clause obligating *Vilber-Lourmat* not to sell a similar machine in an area including the east of France for twenty-four months from the delivery of the machine ordered by the company *Les Tuyaux Centrifugés*.

The court below "found that *Vilber-Lourmat* had deliberately withheld the final estimate of the American firm intended for *Gertais* and had broken off the negotiations it had entered into with *Gervais* brutally (*brutalement*), unilaterally and without a legitimate reason when they were far advanced when *Gerais*, as *Vilber-Lourmat* knew, had made large expenditures, and *Vilbert-Lourmat* had kept *Gerteis* for a long time in a state of uncertainty . . . *Vilber-Lourmat* therefore did not live up to the rules of good faith in commercial relations." It was accordingly "liable for a delict." The *Cour de cassation* held that the court below had correctly found that there had been "an abusive breaking off of negotiations." noting that although *Vilber-Lourmat* "had inquired one last time to learn *Gerteis's* intentions [it] did not furnish the slightest justification for breaking off negotiations and . . . , in any event, such extended negotiations could not be terminated by a simple telephone call whose occurrence was more than problematic."

Note: As mentioned earlier, Alan Farnsworth claimed that relief should only be given when the defendant deceived the plaintiff, made and broke a promise, or unjustly enriched himself during negotiations. He claimed those are the circumstances in which continental courts normally give relief although he acknowledged that this French case was an exception. Another case he regarded as an exception is Dutch: the decision *Plas v. Valburg, Hoge Raad*, 18 June 1982, NJ 1983, 723, in which the plaintiff construction firm submitted a proposal to the municipal authorities of a small town to build a swimming pool. Although there was no official bidding, its proposal was judged the best and was agreed to by the mayor and alderman. Their decision required approval from the city council. It was not approved because, at the initiative of one member of the city council, a rival bid was submitted at a lower price and accepted instead. The highest Dutch court (*Hoge Raad*) ruled in favor of the plaintiff, holding that the process of negotiation is divisible into three stages: an initial one, in which either party can break off negotiations; a middle stage, in which he can do so only if he compensates the other party for expenses incurred; and a final stage in which to break off negotiations at all would be a violation of good faith, and a party who does so is responsible for what a common lawyer would call expectation damages. He is liable, that is, to the same extent that he would be had a final contract been signed. Rarely, if ever, however, has a Dutch court held that negotiations had reached this final stage.

Cour d'appel, Pau, January 14, 1969, D.S. 1969.J.716

Muroiterie Fraisse was a firm that sold and installed mirrors. The defendant invited *Fraisse* to the site to discuss the installation of some mirrors in its apartment building. *Muroiterie Fraisse* installed mirrors in a model apartment and was paid for doing so. After being invited back to the site and receiving exact measurements, *Fraisse* submitted an estimate for the entire job of 30,800 francs. The defendants rejected it without informing him of the offers of competing firms or giving him a chance to bid a lower price for the job.

The *Cour d'appel* noted that "the *Société Muroiterie Fraisse* has clearly stated . . . that it does not make a claim . . . for failure to perform a supply contract definitively concluded between the parties but for a fault in the negotiation stage anterior to agreement, in other words, for a fault in contrahendo." The court rejected this claim, observing that while "it must be recognized, in actual fact, that in the preliminary phase of negotiations, during which the conditions of the contemplated contract are studied and discussed, certain obligations of rectitude and good faith rest on the parties, these obligations clearly relate not to the conclusion of the eventual contract but to the conduct of the negotiators themselves. . . . [H]owever, the negotiation phase is designed to permit the eventual contracting parties to study and understand the risks and advantages of the future contract taking into account elements which can be, at times, imponderable and depend more upon intuition than on formal logic. . . . [C]onsequently, without seriously compromising individual liberty and commercial security, it could not be easily admitted that a merchant could be liable for not having dealt with a competitor; in other words, any fault in contrahendo must be patent, beyond discussion." In this case, the court said, the fact that *Muroiterie Fraisse* had installed mirrors in a model apartment "was irrelevant . . . [as] another, entirely separate, contract was involved, which had been performed, for which the *Muroiterie Fraisse* had received normal compensation and which did not, in itself, imply any obligation for the building as a whole." The initial visit to the worksite "clearly had no object other than to permit the firm to see the job to be done and to enable the owner and his architect to establish relations with the dealer in mirrors." "[A] businessman as experienced as *Fraisse* could not help but know that no reciprocal engagement would be entered into before presentation and acceptance of an estimate." The defendant "had no obligation to accept that estimate if he found it too high; nor can one see any obligation on his part to communicate to *Fraisse* the offers of competitive firms with a view to entering into discussion with *Fraisse* the offers of competitive firms with a view to entering into discussion with *Fraisse* and of causing *Fraisse* to give a lower price in order to obtain the job."

Cour d'appel, Paris, 13 December 1984, Rev. trim. dr. civ. 1986. 97

In 1980, the *Société Sofracima* decided to make a film based on the novels of Isaac Bebel, brought together under the title "King Benya." On

June 11, 1981, Mlle Isabel Adjani signed a contract hiring her as the female lead. This contract was ultimately rescinded by the company which paid her an indemnity. Sometime later, the company took up the project again with a new director and some new male actors. It sent Mlle Adjani a new proposal for a contract which indicated that the filming would start between August 15 and September 30, 1984. The provisions that concerned her compensation were left blank. In response, she sent them another proposal which indicated the amount of her remuneration but not when the filing was to start. In May, 1984, the company returned this proposal, signed by its legal agent, along with a check for 140,000 francs as a first payment which was to be made on signing the contract. She did not cash the check but returned it to the company. The company sued her for 18 million francs in damages claiming breach of contract and a wrongful breaking off of negotiations. The court held that no contract had been formed because of the "absence of essential provisions": "in the document drafted by the *Société Sofracima*, articles 3 and 4, which would normally govern the compensation of Mlle Adjani, were left blank; in the document drafted by Mme Israel (agent of the artist) the date of filming was not indicated. . . ." The court also found that there had been no wrongful breaking off of negotiations: "nothing permits one to say that Mlle Adjani led the *Société Sofracima* to believe with certainly that she would give her consent and sign the contract, and it is shown by the correspondence sent her by the directoress of the company that the directoress had written to her several times to obtain a definitive response—which, shows the reticence of Mlle Adjani, her refusal to commit herself, and the absence of all the things necessary for her to agree to the proposal."

German law

Reichsgericht, 19 January 1934, RGZ 143, 219

"The plaintiff claimed 64711.40 Reichsmarks for the delivery of newsprint to the H.B. Corporation in H. ("the Corporation" for short) in April, 1931. On April 21, 1933, it sought security and payment from the defendant, who was the sole shareholder and manager of the Corporation. Thereafter, it delivered more newsprint to the Corporation for 47,878.45 Reichsmarks.

The plaintiff, who has sued the defendant because it is unable to get satisfaction from the Corporation, claims [that] on April 21, 1931, the defendant told its agent M. that he would provide adequate security for the Corporation's debt out of his own assets. This statement also concerned the future delivery of newsprint to the Corporation. . . . [But adequate security was never provided.]

The appellate court judge found:

(a) the defendant's declaration of April 21, 1931 to the plaintiff's agent M. that he would provide security was too indefinite, and therefore did not legally bind the defendant. . . .

(b) It cannot be shown that in promising to provide security, the defendant . . . acted with the intention of harming the plaintiff. Accordingly the defendant is not liable in tort.

(c) Nevertheless, the defendant negligently harmed the plaintiff by giving him an indication which outwardly considered meant that he agreed to provide security, thereby causing him to make a further delivery. For in April 1931, he had among his personal assets nothing of value that the plaintiff could have considered sufficient security. The defendant was therefore liable to the plaintiff . . . for fault in the conclusion of a contract for payment for the second delivery, not, however, for the earlier one. . . .

The statements made [by defendant] on appeal presuppose that liability for fault in the conclusion of a contract can only arise when the fault of the defendant prevented a contract from arising [whereas here, the contract did not arise because of indefiniteness]. That view is not correct. The appeal cites the Kommentar von Reichsgerichtsräten, 6th ed. to BGB § 155 no. 2 where it is said: 'A party is liable for *culpa in contrahendo* for the negative interest [that is, for the harm the other party suffered in reliance] when he was at fault that agreement was not reached because of a concealed disagreement. . . .' [But] it is never said [in this commentary] that this is the only case in which liability can arise for fault in the conclusion of a contract. . . . The following pertinent example is given in Staudinger-Werner 9th ed., vol. II(1) to BGB § 276 no. I 2, par. 2: 'During contractual negotiations, one person negligently awakens in the other an objectively unfounded hope that a transaction will be concluded and thereby causes him in a discernable manner to incur expenses which would be of use had the transaction been concluded but are useless otherwise.' The explanation means that in such cases the needs of commerce require that the negligent party be held liable for the harm caused: here, for the useless expense. This liability can be traced neither to contract nor tort since a contract did not come to exist and liability in tort could arise only under § 826 of the Civil Code whose requirements (intention) are not met here."

Bundesgerichtshof, 22 February 1989, JZ 1991, 199

"The first defendant published two newspapers. It was a . . . partnership in which the second and third defendants were partners.

In September 1985, negotiations began between the plaintiff and the third defendant, acting on behalf of the first defendant over plaintiff's participation [as an investor] in the first defendant. Afterward, after a number of conversations had been held and the plaintiff had been allowed to study the commercial position of the first defendant, plaintiff's manager and the third defendant agreed, on February 3, 1986, that negotiations would take place on the transfer to the plaintiff of both newspapers instead of the participation of the plaintiff in the first defendant. The plaintiff needed the agreement of the administrative board of its Swiss parent corporation. To make this decision possible, the first defendant prepared a 'detailed offer.'

On February 7, 1986, the plaintiff allowed the defendant to send a draft text of the offer to be given. On March 3, 1986, after further negotiations the defendant offered the plaintiff in writing the acquisition of the rights to both newspapers for 3 million DM, sending along with it alterations in the draft text.

The plaintiff's parent corporation agreed in principle to the acquisition of the newspapers on April 7, 1986. This was communicated to the third defendant on April 10, 1986. On the same day, the plaintiff's legal representative sent a written notification of the intended acquisition to the *Bundeskartellamt* (Federal Cartell Office). On April 11, 1986, after further negotiation between the plaintiff's manager and the third defendant, the plaintiff sent the first defendant the draft of a purchase agreement prepared by its legal representative which was sent back with comments and alterations to the plaintiff on April 15, 1986, by the legal representative and accountant of the first defendant.

On April 17, 1986, the plaintiff's legal representative produced a second draft of the contract. On April 18, 1986, negotiations took place between plaintiff's manager and accountant, on the one hand, and the defendant on the other, in which agreement was reached on the most important points concerning the conclusion of the contract. The plaintiff's legal representative then prepared a third draft of the contract and sent an altered and supplemented notification to the *Bundeskartellamt*.

On 28 April 1986, the plaintiff informed the defendant in writing that it accepted its offer of 3 March 1986. Nevertheless, the same day the third defendant notified the plaintiff by telephone that a transfer of the two newspapers could no longer be considered."

The plaintiff brought suit for 105 773.61 DM which it claimed were the expenses it had incurred in the course of negotiations. Included were the expense of its economic study, accounting and legal fees, secretarial expenses, fees for the *Bundeskartellamt*, office renovations and travel expenses.

"The appellate court said of the basis for this claim that there was no contract between the plaintiff and the first defendant. The offer of March 3, 1986 became ineffective because of later further offers of contract and consequently could no longer be accepted by the plaintiff's statement of 28 April 1986. Moreover, it had been intended that the contract be concluded in writing, and this never occurred (§ 154(2) of the Civil Code).

Neither was a preliminary contract concluded. The plaintiff and the first defendant did not wish to bind themselves before all the points of the contract had been definitely settled and a final written contract had been drafted and signed. Nevertheless, the appellate court found that the defendants were liable for fault in the contractual negotiations having awakened on expectation that a contract would be concluded and then breaking off negotiations without a sufficient ground." The Bundesgerichtshof disagreed with this last point and overturned the decision.

"In principle, each party must bear the costs incurred in the expectation that a contract will be concluded. The risk that a contract will not come to be later on and that the expenses will be useless falls on each party to the negotiations himself.

Even when the parties find themselves in long and seriously conducted contractual negotiations, either side can object to the conclusion of a contract without for that reason being liable to make compensation for fault in contractual negotiations (BGH WM 1962, 936, 937 = BB 1962, 816 no. 1335 and WM 1977, 618, 620; Staudinger/Löwisch, *BGB* 12th ed., 1979, to §§ 275–83 no. 54). A duty to pay compensation only exists when a partner to the negotiations is accountable for awakening in the other party the trust—justifiable from his point of view—that a contract will certainly come to be, and then breaks off contractual negotiations without a sufficient reason. (BGH WM 1962, 936; *id.* 1967, 1010, 1011 = NJW 1967, 2199; *id.* WM, 1967, 798, 799; *id.* NJW 1975, 1774 = BB 1975, 1128; id. WM 1977, 618; Staudinger/Löwisch *op. cit.*)

· · ·

The 'offer' of March 3, 1986, when objectively evaluated, was not sufficient to arouse this kind of trust by the plaintiff. It may be sufficient as a rule that an offer for a fixed period of time is made (§ 148 of the Civil Code). But the written communication to the first defendant was not an offer within the meaning of § 145 ff. of the Civil Code which would become a contract upon mere acceptance by the plaintiff.

The purpose of the offer as agreed in the conversation of February 3, 1986, was only to make it possible for the administrative board of the plaintiff's parent corporation to make a decision about whether to agree to the intended acquisition. Accordingly, the 'detailed offer' contained only those written provisions for the conclusion of the transaction on which the defendant was willing to agree. The 'offer' did not deal with all the questions on which, according to the will of the parties, provision had to be made. It was left open who was to be the contract partner of the defendant, the plaintiff itself or a corporation that it was to organize. (draft contract no. 1) Further, negotiations were to concern the question of which publishing employees were to be taken on by the plaintiff. (*Id.* no. 5) Also the content of a new agreement on competition was not settled. (*Id.* no. 6) The 'offer' contained no specification of in what way the third defendant would work for the plaintiff and how the required payments to customers of the newspaper would be taken care of." The court concluded that the plaintiff could not recover for expenses incurred before the conversation of April 18, 1986. As to whether it could recover for those incurred thereafter, the court said:

"It cannot be decided as yet whether the appellate court was correct to award the plaintiff compensation for the expenses incurred for the expenses of notification of the *Bundeskartellamt* [incurred after April 18].

The appellate court maintained that, according to the credible testimony of witness G., in the conversation on April 18, 1986, agreement was reached on all essential points and consequently, because of defendant's conduct, the plaintiff could rely on the conclusion of a contract.

But this finding is not enough to justify a claim for compensation for fault in contractual negotiations. It is not sufficient that the plaintiff could have the impression, because all the essential points were agreed upon, that a contract would ultimately be concluded. In addition, it must be shown that the first defendant went beyond the mere fact of agreement and presented the conclusion of a contract as certain. An express declaration is not required. But the defendant must at least have made its firm will to conclude a contract to appear clearly. That could be accepted, for example, if the third defendant had encouraged the plaintiff to take measures that would only be of use if a contract should arise. . . ."

Note: In 2002, the Civil Code was amended in light of the case law. Section 311 (2) of the code now provides that duties may arise from "1. entering into contractual negotiations; 2. preparation of a contract in which one party, in light of the transactional relation (*rechtsgeschäftliche Beziehung*) to the other party, has allowed his rights, legally protected benefits (*Rechtsgüter*) or interests to be affected, or entrusted them to the other party, or 3. Similar transactional relations." What duties arise is not clear.

The "Lando Principles"

The Principles of European Contract Law, Prepared by the Commission on European Contract Law

ARTICLE 2.301: NEGOTIATIONS CONTRARY TO GOOD FAITH

(1) A party is free to negotiate and is not liable for failure to reach an agreement.

(2) However, a party which has negotiated or broken off negotiations contrary to good faith and fair dealing is liable for the losses caused to the other party.

(3) It is contrary to good faith and fair dealing, in particular, for a party to enter into or continue negotiations with no real intention of reaching an agreement with the other party.

ARTICLE 2.302: BREACH OF CONFIDENTIALITY

If confidential information is given by one party in the course of negotiations, the other party is under a duty not to disclose that information or use it for its own purposes whether or not a contract is subsequently concluded. The remedy for breach of this duty may include compensation for loss suffered and restitution of the benefit received by the other party.

The Unidroit Principles

The Unidroit Principles of International Commercial Contracts

ARTICLE 2.15 NEGOTIATIONS IN BAD FAITH

(1) A party is free to negotiate and is not liable for failure to reach an agreement.

(2) However, a party who negotiates or breaks off negotiations in bad faith is liable for the losses caused to the other party.

(3) It is bad faith, in particular, for a party to enter into or continue negotiations when intending not to reach an agreement with the other party.

ARTICLE 2.16 DUTY OF CONFIDENTIALITY

Where information is given as confidential by one party in the course of negotiations, the other party is under a duty not to disclose that information or to use it improperly for its own purposes, whether or not a contract is subsequently concluded. Where appropriate, the remedy for breach of this duty may include compensation based on the benefit received by the other party.

3. Mistake

In modern legal systems, the problem of when a contract is void for mistake is often thought to involve a basic question of contract law. A contract is formed by the consent of the parties. Can the parties truly consent even if one or both of them is mistaken, and if so, when? The question of the effect of mistake on consent was raised by the Roman jurists. Nevertheless, they were not trying to discover general principles underlying contract law. They were concerned with particular problems. The most important passage discussing the problem—written by Ulpian—was buried in a title of the *Digest* that dealt with the law of sales. It uses some high powered philosophical terms in what seems to be a hopelessly vague way, and resolves a number of hypothetical cases:

> In contracts of sale there must be consent; the sale is invalid if there is disagreement either as to the fact of sale (*in ipsa emptione*) or the price or any other matter. If therefore I thought I was buying the Cornelian estate and you that you were selling the Sempronian, the sale is void on the ground that we were not at one as to the thing sold (*in corpore*). . . . Then next comes the question whether there is a good sale if there is no mistake as to the identity of the thing (*in corpore*), but there is in regard to its substance (*in substantia*), for example where vinegar is sold for wine, or copper for gold, or lead or something else resembling silver for silver. Marcellus . . . writes that there is a good contract, because there has been agreement as to the specific thing, though mistake as to the material (*in materia*). I take the same view in the wine case, because the *ousia* [a Greek word meaning essence] is pretty much the same, if the wine has just gone sour; but if it is not wine gone sour, but was in origin a specially prepared vinegar, then it appears that one thing has been sold for another. In the remaining cases, however, I hold that whenever there is a mistake as to material, there is no sale. Dig. 18.1.9.

Accursius, the 13th century jurist who wrote the standard commentary or Ordinary Gloss on the Digest, simply enumerated the types of mistakes that Ulpian mentioned: errors in (1) whether there was a sale, (2) price, (3) *corpore*, (4) *substantia* or *ousia*; and (5) *materia*.[1]

In early modern times, the late scholastics and northern natural lawyers tried to develop a theory and systematic doctrine of contract law. As noted earlier, following Aristotle, the late scholastics thought that through contract a party voluntarily entered into either of two basic kinds of arrangements: a gratuitous contract in which he enriched the other party at his own expense, or an onerous contract in which he exchanged his own performance for one of equivalent value. Since either of them had to be voluntary, they asked when a decision truly was voluntary. Aristotle had said in the *Nicomachean Ethics* that an action would be involuntary if a person was mistaken as to what he was doing.[2] That conclusion fit in with his view that a human being was an animal who acts by understanding. If he acts without understanding what he is doing, the action cannot be one he has chosen. For Aristotle, moreover, a thing is what it is because it has a certain "substance," "substantial form" or "essence." A human being has one essence, a lion has another. When it loses its substantial form or essence it is no longer what it was before—as when a tree is burned to ashes—but it can change its "accidental form" or "accidents" while remaining the same thing—as when a tree grows taller. The late scholastics concluded that there was one sort of mistake that made a contract involuntary: a mistake as to the substance or substantial form or essence of what one was doing. By and large, the natural lawyers agreed. It became a commonplace that error in substance voids a contract.

It was easier for the late scholastics and the natural lawyers to read this conclusion into Roman law because mistake in substance (*substantia*) and essence (*ousia*) were mentioned in the Roman text quoted earlier. Indeed, medieval jurists who admired Aristotle such as Bartolus of Saxoferrato and Baldus de Ubaldis had already read an Aristotelian meaning into the Roman text quoted earlier. For Bartolus, error in *substantia* meant error in substance as Aristotle had understood it. Baldus regarded this as the basic type of error.

Of course, it was one thing to say that contract was void for an error in substance and another to explain what this phrase might mean. The problem was not so hard in the case of "artifacts": man-made things. In Aristotelian philosophy, the essence of a thing was captured by its definition, and an artifact was defined in terms of the purpose for which it was made. But what about natural things? In the following passage, Bartolus seems to suggest that what matters is not necessarily what a biologist or a geologist would take to be their essence:

> One and the same thing is taken in different ways according to a difference in the way it is considered, as will now be seen. A field may be

---

1. Accursius, *Glossa ordinaria* (1581), to Dig. 18.1.9 to *aliquo alio*. Actually, he had a sixth category as well: error in "sex." That category was based on D. 18.1.11.1 which said that the buyer of a slave could void the sale if he mistakenly thought that the slave was male but not if he knew she was female but mistakenly thought she was a virgin.

2. *Nicomachean Ethics* III.i 1110^a–1111^b.

considered with regard to its matter, which is earth, and then if a river makes a channel through it, it does not cease to be earth, and so the earth remains something of the same kind. It can also be considered as earth suitable for the driving (*agi*) of animals, that is, earth on which animals are led and can labor, and it is from this use that "field" (*ager*) receives the name which is proper to it. . . . Taken in this way, it loses its proper form [if the river makes channels through it]. . . . It is much the same with the wine. If it is made vinegar, it is still of the same substance insofar as its matter is considered. Properly considered, however, it is not wine but another kind of thing, and it does not come under the name "wine."[3]

Centuries later, Pufendorf was to express a similar idea: what mattered was the "substance" of a thing as it would be considered from the standpoint of the parties.

Explaining the Roman cases proved considerably harder. For example, why should it matter whether the vinegar bought for wine was wine that had accidentally soured or wine that was deliberately soured in order to make vinegar? But Ulpian said the sale was valid in the first case but not the second.

In any event, the phrase "error in substance" outlasted the popularity of Aristotelian philosophy. It found its way into the French and German Civil Codes.

French Civil Code

ART. 1109

There is no valid consent if the consent was only given because of error or was extorted by duress or induced by fraud.

ART. 1110

Error is only a cause of the invalidity of an agreement when it concerns the substance itself of the thing which is its object.

It is not a cause of invalidity when it only concerns the person with whom one intends to contract unless the consideration of this person was the principal cause of the contract.

German Civil Code

§ 119 [Voidability due to Error]

(1) One who was in error as to the content of his declaration of will or did not wish to make a declaration of will with this content can void the declaration when it is established that he would not have made it with knowledge of the state of affairs and intelligent appreciation of the case.

---

3. Bartolus, *Tractatus de alveo*, in *Omnia quae extant opera* (1615), *§ Stricta ratione*, nos. 6–7 The derivation of *ager* (field) from *ago* (drive) is given by Varro, *De lingua latina* 34 (Cambridge ed., 1977), 32.

(2) A mistake over any characteristics of the person or thing that are regarded as essential in ordinary dealings counts as an error in the content of the declaration.

Similar expressions found their way into Anglo-American treatises and cases. See *Sherwood v. Walker*, below ("A barren cow is substantially a different creature than a breeding one"). Few if any French, German or American jurists have a clear idea of what an error in "substance" or in an "essential" characteristic really means. In the United States, the Restatement (Second) of Contracts tried to add clarity by speaking not of a mistake in "substance" but of one in "basic assumption."

Restatement (Second) of Contracts

§ 152

(1) Where a mistake of both parties at the time the contract was made as to a basic assumption on which the contract was made has a material effect on the agreed exchange of performances, the contract is voidable by the adversely affected party [unless that party bears the risk, as described in a later section.]

Whether the expression "basic assumption" adds clarity may be judged by the official comments to this section:

"*b. Basic assumption*. A mistake of both parties does not make the contract voidable unless it is a basic assumption on which both parties made the contract. . . . [M]arket conditions and the financial situation of the parties are ordinarily not such assumptions. . . . The parties may have had such a 'basic assumption', even if they were not conscious of alternatives. . . . Where, for example, a party purchases an annuity on the life of another person, it can be said that it was a basic assumption that the other person was alive at the time, even though the parties never consciously addressed themselves to the possibility that he was dead."

Thus we arrive at the curious rule that an assumption must be basic, although it need not be basic even if it is of great importance to the parties, and that the parties must have made an assumption, even if they never did so consciously.

a. When relief is granted

English law

Griffith v. Brymer, (1903) 19 T.L.R. 434 (K.B.)

At 11:00 A.M., June 24, 1902, plaintiff agreed to rent a flat from defendant for one day to view the coronation procession of King Edward VII, and paid £ 100. The parties were unaware that an hour earlier a decision had been made to operate on the king, which made the procession impossible. Held: the contract was void, and plaintiff is entitled to rescission: "The agreement was made on the supposition by both parties that nothing had happened which made performance impossible. This was a missupposition of the state of facts which went to the whole root of the matter."

Law in the United States

Sherwood v. Walker, 33 N.W. 919 (Mich. 1887)

"The main controversy depends upon the construction of a contract for the sale of a cow.

The defendants . . . introduced evidence tending to show that at the time of the alleged sale it was believed by both the plaintiff and themselves that the cow was barren and would not breed; that she cost $850, and if not barren would be worth from $750 to $1,000; that after the date of the letter, and the order to Graham, the defendants were informed by said Graham that in his judgment the cow was with calf, and therefore they instructed him not to deliver her to plaintiff. . . .

It appears from the record that both parties supposed this cow was barren and would not breed, and she was sold by the pound for an insignificant sum as compared with her real value if a breeder. . . .

If there is a difference or misapprehension as to the substance of the thing bargained for; if the thing actually delivered or received is different in substance from the thing bargained for, and intended to be sold, then there is no contract; but if it be only a difference in some quality or accident, even though the mistake may have been the actuating motive to the purchaser or seller, or both of them, yet the contract remains binding. . . .

It seems to me . . . in the case made by this record, that the mistake or misapprehension of the parties went to the whole substance of the agreement. If the cow was a breeder, she was worth at least $750; if barren, she was worth not over $80. The parties would not have made the contract of sale except upon the understanding and belief that she was incapable of breeding, and of no use as a cow. It is true she is now the identical animal that they thought her to be when the contract was made; there is no mistake as to the identity of the creature. Yet the mistake was not of the mere quality of the animal, but went to the very nature of the thing. A barren cow is substantially a different creature than a breeding one. There is as much difference between them for all purposes of use as there is between an ox and a cow that is capable of breeding and giving milk. If the mutual mistake had simply related to the fact whether she was with calf or not for one season, then it might have been a good sale, but the mistake affected the substance of the whole consideration, and it must be considered that there was no contract to sell or sale of the cow as she actually was. The thing sold and bought had in fact no existence. She was sold as a beef creature would be sold; she is in fact a breeding cow, and a valuable one."

Sherwood, J. dissenting: "I do not concur in the opinion given by my brethren in this case. . . .

[T]he buyer purchased her believing her to be of the breed represented by the sellers, and possessing all the qualities stated, and even more. He believed she would breed. There is no pretense that the plaintiff bought the cow for beef, and there is nothing in the record indicating that he would have bought her at all only that he thought she might be made to breed. Under the foregoing facts,—and these are all that are contained in the record material to the contract,—it is held that because it turned out that the plaintiff was more correct in his judgment as to one quality of the cow than the defendants, and a quality, too, which could not by any possibility be positively known at the time by either party to exist, the contract may be annulled by the defendants at their pleasure. I know of no law, and have not been referred to any, which will justify any such holding, and I think the circuit judge was right in his construction of the contract between parties."

Smith v. Zimbalist, 38 P.2d 170 (Cal. App. 1934)

Zimbalist, an internationally known violinist, agreed to pay $8000 for two violins from Smith, a collector, calling one a "Stradivarius" and the other a "Guanerius." I turned out that the violins were not made by Antonius Stradivarius or Josef Guanerius but were cheap imitations worth not more than $300. Zimbalist sued successfully to avoid the contract on the grounds of both mutual mistake and breach of express warranty.

French law

Cour d'appel, Versailles, 30 March 1989, Rev. trim. dr. civ. 1989. 739

The couple D. contracted to buy real estate belonging to the couple B for a price of 645,000 francs. They claimed that they later learned that a highway was to be built fifty meters away. The court granted their request that the sale be avoided for error "considering the discovery by the buyers, after their commitment, of the construction project already mentioned and the potential for noise and which manifestly changed the possibility of normal enjoyment of a habitation given that the sale included a wooded park."

Cour de cassation, 1e ch. civ., 23 February 1970, J.C.P. 1970. J.16347

Chalom bought two chairs described as "marquises" of the Louis XV period at a public auction from the couple *Lièvre-Aubin de la Messuzière*. After they were dismantled and scraped, they proved to be chairs of another type—"bergères"—which had been "adroitly reconstructed with pieces from the period of Louis XV and of the period following." The *Cour de cassation* held that the lower court was correct to annul the sale for mistake, noting that "the sale can be declared invalid although the object has preserved its individuality and its specific qualities."

German law

Reichsgericht, 22 February 1929, RGZ 124, 115

"In the spring of 1925, Frau F. had her husband deliver two Chinese vases to store W. to be sold on commission. This firm with the owner's agreement placed the vases on sale in its department for modern Chinese and Japanese goods. On August 1, 1925, the defendant bought them there for the price requested which was 390 Reichsmarks. He immediately sold them in Holland at a large profit (the plaintiff claims for 1500 Dutch guilders). At an auction organized by the Dutch purchaser, they were sold to the Kensington Museum in London in return for 200,000 Reichsmarks. The lawyer Dr. T. served written notice on November 19, 1925, on behalf of the interested parties—the former owner and the commission broker—that the contract was void on account of error since these parties were of the opinion at the time the contract was concluded that the pieces were from the beginning of the 19th century when, in fact, the vases were from the time of the Ming dynasty (1380–1644) in which the Chinese empire saw its greatest flowering of art. In his notice he also declared that the defendant was obligated to redeliver the vases or, if that were impossible, to make compensation for their value or at least to pay the net proceeds just described to the interested parties. . . ."

The rarity which is due to the age of a thing is to be considered a characteristic of the thing. There is no doubt that both vases had a value on account of their rarity in this sense. Firm W. was in error concerning this value. . . .

The decision under appeal is reversed and the matter is remanded to the lower court. In the future proceedings, the following point is to be given attention. As the appellate court correctly observed, . . . Frau F. cannot make a claim on the basis of an error of the commission broker if she herself was not in error. A finding must be made on whether at the time the contract was concluded, she or her husband, who carried on the transaction with Firm W., took into account the possibility that the object originated centuries ago and had a particular value because of its rarity, and whether, had they been aware of this possibility, the contract for sale by commission at the price in question would not have been concluded.

The "Lando Principles"

The Principles of European Contract Law, Prepared by the Commission on European Contract Law

ARTICLE 4.103: FUNDAMENTAL MISTAKE AS TO FACTS OR LAW

(1) A party may avoid a contract for mistake of fact or law existing when the contract was concluded if:

    (a) (i) the mistake was caused by information given by the other party; or

         (ii) the other party knew or ought to have known of the mistake and it was contrary to good faith and fair dealing to leave the mistaken party in error; or

(iii) the other party made the same mistake, and

    (b) the other party knew or ought to have known that the mistaken party, had he known the truth, would not have entered the contract or would have done so only on fundamentally different terms.

(2) However a party may not avoid a contract if:

    (a) in the circumstances the mistake was inexcusable, or

    (b) the risk of the mistake was assumed, or in the circumstances, should be borne by it.

The Unidroit Principles

The Unidroit Principles of International Commercial Contracts

ARTICLE 3.4 DEFINITION OF MISTAKE

Mistake is an erroneous assumption relating to facts or to law existing when the contract was concluded.

ARTICLE 3.5 RELEVANT MISTAKE

(1) A party may only avoid the contract for mistake if, when the contract was concluded, the mistake was of such importance that a reasonable person in the same situation as the party in error would only have concluded the contract on materially different terms or would not have concluded it at all if the true state of affairs had been known, and

    (a) the other party made the same mistake, or caused the mistake, or knew or ought to have known of the mistake and it was contrary to reasonable commercial standards of fair dealing to leave the mistaken party in error; or

    (b) the other party had not at the time of avoidance acted in reliance on the contract.

(2) However, a party may not avoid the contract if

    (a) it was grossly negligent in committing the mistake; or

    (b) the mistake relates to a matter in regard to which the risk of mistake was assumed or, having regard to the circumstances, should be borne by the mistaken party.

b. When relief is denied

Consider whether there is any way to distinguish the following cases, in which relief was denied despite a mistake, from the ones in the previous section, in which relief was granted.

English law

Kennedy v. The Panama, New Zealand, and Australian Royal Mail Co., [1867] 2 Q.B. 580

Plaintiff was induced to buy shares of stock from defendant in defendant company by a statement in its prospectus that it had a contract with the government of New Zealand to carry mail. While the company believed it had such contract, in fact it did not, since the agent that had signed on behalf of the government had no authority to do so, and the government refused to ratify the contract, although it eventually agreed to a contract on somewhat different terms. Plaintiff sued for rescission.

Blackburn, J. "[W]here there has been an innocent misrepresentation or misapprehension, it does not authorize a rescission unless it is such as to shew that there is a complete difference in substance between what was supposed to be and what was taken, so as to constitute a failure of consideration. For example, where a horse is bought under a belief that it is sound, if the purchaser was induced to buy by a fraudulent misrepresentation as the horse's soundness, the contract may be rescinded. If it was induced by an honest misrepresentation as to its soundness, though it may be clear that both vendor and purchaser thought that they were dealing about a sound horse and were in error, yet the purchaser must pay the whole price, unless there was a warranty....

The principle is well illustrated in the civil law [quoting at length from Digest 18.1.9, reproduced above], and the answers given by the great jurists are to the effect that if there be misapprehension as to the substance of the thing there is no contract; but if it be only a difference in some quality or accident, even though the misapprehension may have been the actuating motive to the purchaser, yet the contract remains binding....

[W]e do not think that [the misstatement in this case] affected the substance of the matter, for the applicant actually got shares in the very company for shares in which he had applied; and that company has, by means of the invalid contract, got the benefit, and is now carrying the mails on terms, not the same as those they supposed, but still on profitable terms...."

Bell v. Lever Brothers, Ltd., [1932] A.C. 161 (1932)(H.L.)

Lever Brothers hired the defendants to be chairman and vice chairman of a subsidiary for a period of years. When the subsidiary merged with another company, and it became necessary to terminate them, Lever Brothers agreed to pay them £20,000 and £30,000 respectively, in compensation. It then discovered that they had violated their duties by secretly speculating in cocoa, and that it would have had the right to terminate their contracts without compensation because of this breach of duty. Held (by a narrow margin) that the contracts for compensation are valid.

Lord Atkin. "[A] mistake [as to quality of the thing contracted for] will not affect assent unless it is the mistake of both parties, and is as to the existence of some quality which makes the thing without the quality essentially different from the thing as it was believed to be....

[Here,] [t]he contract released is the identical contract in both cases, and the party paying for release gets exactly what he bargains for. It seems immaterial that he could have got the same result in another way, or that if he had known the true facts he would not have entered into the bargain.

A. buy's B.'s horse; he thinks the horse is sound and he pays the price of a sound horse. . . . A. is bound and cannot recover back the price. A. buys a picture from B.; both A. and B. believe it to be the work of an old master, and a high price is paid. It turns out to be a modern copy. A. has no remedy in the absence of representation or warranty. A. agrees to take on lease or to buy from B. an unfurnished dwelling-house. The house is in fact uninhabitable. A. would never have entered into the bargain if he had known the fact. A. has no remedy. . . . A. buys a roadside garage business from B. abutting on a public thoroughfare: unknown to A., but known to B., it has already been decided to construct a bypass road which will divert substantially the whole of the traffic from passing A.'s garage. Again, A. has no remedy."

Amalgamated Investment & Property Co. Ltd. v. John Walker & Sons, Ltd., [1977] 1 W.L.R. 164 (C.A.)

"In July 1973, the plaintiff purchasers agreed to purchase the freehold of a warehouse from the defendant vendors for £ 1,700,000 subject to contract. The warehouse had been advertised as being suitable for redevelopment and during the negotiations, the purchasers inquire whether the property had been designated as a building of 'special architectural or historic interest' and the vendors replied in the negative. On September 25, the parties signed the contract. . . . The following day, September 26, the Department of Environment wrote to the vendors informing them that the property had been selected for inclusion in the statutory list of buildings of 'special architectural or historic interest' and, on September 27, the list was signed on behalf of the Secretary of State." Held: the contract is not void for mistake.

Buckley, L.J. "For the application of the doctrine of mutual mistake as a ground for setting the contract aside, it is of course necessary to show that the mistake existed at the date of the contract; and so Mr. Balcombe [attorney for the buyers] relies in that respect not upon the signing of the list by the officer who alone was authorized to sign it on behalf of the Secretary of State, but upon the decision of Miss Price that the list should contain the particular property with which we are concerned. That decision, although in fact it led to the signature of the list in the form in which it was eventually signed, was merely an administrative step in the carrying out of the operations of the branch of the ministry. It was a personal decision on the part of Miss Price that the list should contain the particular property with which we are concerned. But there was still the possibility that something else might arise before the list was signed. . . . The crucial date, in my judgment, is the date when the list was signed."

Leaf v. International Galleries, [1950] 2 K.B. 86

"In 1944 the defendants sold to the plaintiff for £ 85 a picture which they represented to have been painted by J. Constable. In 1949 the plaintiff tried to sell it at Christies and was then informed that it had not been painted by Constable." It was found at trial that the painting was not by Constable, but that the defendant had believed that it was.

Denning, L.J. "There was a mistake about the quality of the subject-matter because both parties believed the picture to be a Constable; and that mistake was in one sense essential or fundamental. But such a mistake does not avoid the contract: there was no mistake at all about the subject-matter of the sale. It was a specific picture, 'Salisbury Cathedral.' The parties were agreed in the same terms on the same subject-matter, and that is sufficient to make a contract [citation omitted].

There was a term in the contract as to the quality of the subject-matter: namely as to the person by whom the picture was painted—that it was by Constable. . . . I think it is right to assume in the buyer's favor that this term was a condition, and that, if he had come in proper time he could have rejected the picture; but the right to reject for breach of condition has always been limited by the rule that, once the buyer has accepted the goods in performance of the contract, then he cannot thereafter reject but is relegated to his claim for damages. [citations omitted].

The circumstances in which a buyer is deemed to have accepted goods in performance of the contract are set out in s. 35 of the [Sale of Goods Act, 1893], which says that the buyer is deemed to have accepted the goods, amongst other things, 'when, after the lapse of a reasonable time, he retains the goods without intimating to the seller that he has rejected them.' In this case, the buyer took the picture into his house and, apparently, hung it there, and five years passed before he intimated any rejection at all. . . . His remedy . . . is for damages only, a claim which he has not brought before the court.

Is it to be said that the buyer is in any better position by relying on the representation, not as a condition, but as an innocent misrepresentation. I agree that on a contract for the sale of goods an innocent material misrepresentation may, in a proper case, be a ground for rescission even after the contract has been executed [citing, inter alia, Bell v. Lever Bros. Ltd.] . . .

Although rescission may in some cases be a proper remedy, it is to be remembered that an innocent misrepresentation is much less potent than a breach of condition; and a claim to rescission for innocent misrepresentation must at any rate be barred when a right to reject for breach of condition is barred."

Law in the United States

Firestone & Parson, Inc. v. Union League of Philadelphia, 672 F. Supp. 819 (E.D. Pa. 1987)

In 1981, the Union League Club sold Firestone and Parson an oil painting for $500,000 which was generally believed in art circles to be by Albert Bierstadt, an American landscape painter. In 1985, some art historians began to doubt its authenticity. In 1986, an article published in *Antiques* magazine ascribed it to another artist, John Ross Key. That view became generally accepted among experts. If it had been painted by Key, it was worth only about $50,000. In 1988, the Firestone and Parsons company brought suit to rescind the contract. The court held that it could not. "[I]n the arcane world of high-priced art, market value is affected by market perceptions; the market value of a painting is determined by the prevailing views of the marketplace concerning its attribution. Post-sale fluctuations in generally accepted attributions do not necessarily establish that there was a mutual mistake of fact at the time of the sale."

Lenawee County Board of Health v. Messerly, 331 N.W.2d 203 (Mich. 1982)

Carl and Nancy Pickles bought a 600 square foot tract of land from William and Martha Messerly on which was a three unit apartment building. Shortly after, the Lenawee County Board of Health condemned the property and obtained a permanent injunction prohibiting human habitation on the grounds that the sewage system violated the sanitation code. The sanitation system has been installed by Messerly's predecessor in title, and they were unaware of its condition. The Pickles agreed to pay $25,500 for the land. Because of its condition, the land had no value at all. The contract contained a clause which said, "Purchaser has examined the property and agrees to accept it in its present condition."

"We find that the inexact and confusing distinction between mistakes running to value and those touching the substance of the consideration serves only as an impediment to a clear and helpful analysis for the equitable resolution of cases in which mistake is alleged and proven. Accordingly, the holdings of *A & M Land Development Co.* and *Sherwood* with respect to the material or collateral nature of a mistake are limited to the facts of those cases.

Instead, we think the better-reasoned approach is a case-by-case analysis whereby rescission is indicated when the mistaken belief relates to a basic assumption of the parties upon which the contract is made, and which materially affects the agreed performances of the parties [citations omitted].

All of the parties to this contract erroneously assumed that the property transferred by the vendors to the vendees was suitable for human habitation and could be utilized to generate rental income. The fundamental nature of these assumptions is indicated by the fact that their invalidity changed the character of the property transferred, thereby frustrating, indeed, precluding, Mr. and Mrs. Pickles's intended use of the real estate. . . .

Despite the significance of the mistake made by the parties, we reverse the Court of Appeals because we conclude that equity does not justify the remedy sought by Mr. and Mrs. Pickles. . . .

Equity suggests that, in this case, the risk should be allocated to the purchasers. . . . While there is no express assumption in the contract by either party of the risk of the property becoming uninhabitable, there was indeed some agreed allocation of the risk to the vendees by the incorporation of an 'as is' clause into the contract. . . ."

French law

Cour de cassation, 1e ch. civ., 24 March 1987, J.C.P. 1989.J.21300

In 1933, before his death, Sean-André Vincent sold a painting at a public auction entitled Le Verrou as being "attributed to Fragonard." After it had been recognized that the painting truly was by Fragonard, the heirs of Vincent sued to have the sale annulled on the ground that Vincent had been in error as to its authenticity. The *Cour de cassation* refused to annul the sale. It said that the court below had found "that in 1933, in buying or in selling a work attributed to Fragonard the contracting parties had accepted the risk as to the authenticity of the work."

Cour d'appel, Riom, 10 May 1988, Rev. trim. dr. civ. 1989.740

The *Société d'équipement d'Auvergne* sold land for which a building permit had been obtained to the *Société H.L.M. Carpi*. During construction work, a shifting of the earth was observed. After a geological study was made, it appeared that only twenty-two individual houses could be built instead of the thirty-two which the *Société Carpi* had intended. The court refused to annul the contract for mistake. It noted that "the sale was concluded among companies which were professionals quite aware of problems of land and of construction," and "the parties stipulated [in their contract] that the buyer 'will take the land sold in its state as of the day he enters into enjoyment of it without power to have any recourse or recission against the seller for any reason whatever, and in particular, on account of the bad state of the soil or sub-soil, digging, or excavation.'

Cour d'appel, Paris, 23 September 1988, Rev. trim. dr. civ. 1989.741

The buyer of a used car discovered that it was first sold in 1955 although the sales catalog described it as a "Rolls Royce, 26 CV, 1954 Silver Wraith model." The court refused to annul the sale for error. It said that "supposing that one has been established, an error as to the year of fabrication would not justify annulling the contract unless the buyer proved that it concerned a substantial characteristic of the object." "[S]ince the matter concerns a vehicle which is a collectors' item, its age, attested by the year it was made, certainly does constitute a determining criterion for the sale, [but], nevertheless, the authenticity of a collectors' item is subject to nuances [and] the exactness of a date close to the date of fabrication of an old car would not constitute a sine qua non condition of its acquisition in the opinion of collectors as long as no change had been made that really differentiated the vehicles of one year form those of the next, as is the case here. . . ."

German law

Reichsgericht, 11 March 1932, RGZ 135, 339

"On 18 January 1928, the plaintiff bought an oil painting from the defendant, 'Ice on Water,' which was indicated to him as an original painting of Jacob I. (Isaakson) van Ruysdael and accompanied by an opinion by the late museum director B. attesting, as the parties understood, that the work originated with this painter. The picture was immediately delivered and the purchase price of 15,000 Reichsmarks was paid. The plaintiff claims that the work was done not by 'the famous master' Jacob I. van Ruysdael but by his 'much less famous cousin and imitator' Jacob S. (Solomonsson) van Ruysdael. Accordingly, on 18 October 1929, he claimed that the contract of sale was void for mistake and demanded the return of the purchase price with interest. Both lower courts rejected his claim. The plaintiff's appeal (*Revision*) is to be rejected on the following grounds. . . . Naturally, one cannot speak of a defect in the painting and warranty, nor of an error and voidability in a speculative acquisition where the seller does not give any guarantee (and it is not found that he did here) but perhaps expressly refused to do so, and the buyer himself takes into account that the picture can be by someone other than the designated master, for example, a pupil, and buys it only in hopes that the opinion of the parties will prove to be correct. In such a case it is even true that the characteristic of the thing— its production by a certain master—is contractually presumed, be it known in commerce with a greater or lesser degree of certainty."

III. FAIRNESS

1. Fairness of the price term

a. Origins

Civil law

Classical Roman law did not require that a price be fair.[1] As one text said, in a sale: "it is permitted by nature for one party to buy for less and other to sell for more, and thus each is allowed to outwit the other."[2] In the late empire, however, a text attributed to Diocletian, but possibly added by Justinian, gave a remedy to one who sold land for less than half the "just price." The buyer had either to rescind the transaction or to make up the difference between the price paid and the "just price."[3]

---

1. Reinhard Zimmermann, *The Law of Obligations Roman Foundations of the Civilian Tradition* (1990), 255–56.

2. Dig. 19.2.22.3. See also Dig. 4.4.16.4.

3. C. 4.44.2; C. 4.44.8. See Zimmermann, *Law of Obligations* 259–61; Hackl, "Zu dem Wurzeln der Anfechtung wegen laesio enormis," *Zeitschrift der Savigny-Stiftung für Rechtsgeschichte*, Rom. Abt. 98 (1981), 147–61.

At a very early date, the medieval jurists interpreted this text to apply to buyers as well as sellers and to parties to analogous contracts.[4] So they created a generalized remedy for a very unfair price—for what came to be called *laesio enormis*, literally, a very large hurt.

They identified the just price with the price for which goods were sold commonly, a price that differed from day to day and region to region.[5] As Accursius noted, one who sold an object for less than half the amount he paid for it might not be entitled to relief since "it could be . . . that when the sale of the object to him occurred, it was worth more than when he now sells."[6] They had no theory to explain why the market price was fair.

Again, an explanation was developed by the late scholastics in the 16th century based on the ideas of Aristotle and Thomas Aquinas. Commutative justice preserved the distribution of wealth among citizens. In the case of "voluntary commutative justice," the parties exchanged resources of equal value so that neither was enriched.[7] According to Thomas Aquinas, this principle explained the remedy for *laesio enormis*. While in principle, every deviation from the just price was wrong, relief was given only for large deviations because the law cannot remedy every evil.[8]

The late scholastics adopted this explanation. For the most part, the northern natural lawyers of the 17th and 18th century followed them. At least, they usually explained the remedy by saying that exchange required equality, even those who felt little or no allegiance to Aristotelian philosophy.

Like the medieval jurists, they identified the just price that preserved equality with the market price.[9] Soto, Molina, and Lessius explained in the 16th century, and Grotius and Pufendorf in the 17th, that if no price is set by public authority, the just price is the price for which goods are commonly traded as long as there are no monopolies. Therefore the just price varies from day to day and region to region. It depends, not only on the cost of production, but also on the need for the goods and on their scarcity.[10] As Odd Langholm has noted, the late scholastics were hardly being original since all three factors had been mentioned continually in

---

4. The *Brachylogus*, written at the beginning of the 12th century, does not speak of land but of objects sold. *Brachylogus* (1743) III.xiii.8. *Dissensiones dominorum* of the early 13th century reports a dispute in which all participants take it for granted that the buyer as well as the seller has a remedy. The dispute is over whether to be entitled to the remedy the buyer must have paid twice or one and a half times the just price. The participants are said to be Placentinus and Albericus, who wrote in the 12th century, and Martinus, a student of Irnerius. Hugolinus de Presbyteris, *Diversitates sive dissensiones dominorum super toto corpore iure civilis* (ed. Haenel 1834), § 253.

5. Accursius, *Glossa ordinaria* (1581), to Dig. 13.4.3 to varia.

6. Accursius, *Glossa ordinaria* to C. 4.44.4 to *autoritate iudicis*.

7. Aristotle, *Nichomachean Ethics* V.iii 1131[a]; Thomas Aquinas, *Summa theologiae* II-II, Q. 61, a. 2–3.

8. *Id.* a. 3.

9. John Noonan, *The Scholastic Analysis of Usury* (1957), 82–88; Raymond de Roover, "The Concept of the Just Price Theory and Economic Policy," *J. Economic History* 18 (1958), 418–434; Ambrosetti, "Diritto privato ed economia nella seconda scolastica," in Paolo Grossi (ed.), *La seconda scolastica nella formazione del diritto privato moderno* (1973), 23–52, 28.

10. Domenicus Soto, *De iustitia et iure libri decem* (1553), lib. 6, q. 2, a. 3; Ludovicus Molina, *De iustitia et iure tractatus* (1614), disp. 348; Leonardus Lessius, *De iustitia et iure, ceterisque virtutibus cardinalis* (1628), lib. 2, cap. 21, dub. 4; Hugo Grotius, *De iure belli ac pacis libri tres* (1646), II.xii.14;

medieval commentaries to Aristotle's *Ethics*.[11] For that matter, all three had been mentioned, albeit cryptically, by Aquinas.[12] The writers in this tradition did not, as some scholars once imagined, identify the just price with the cost of production.[13]

They thought, then, that an exchange at the market price preserved equality even though they knew that the seller would sometimes recover more or less than his costs. They may have thought such a price was as equal as possible given that prices must fluctuate to take account of need and scarcity. Any inequalities caused by the market price had to be tolerated. In contrast, one did not need to tolerate inequalities which arose when, as Lessius put it, one party took advantage of another's "ignorance" or "necessity" to sell to him for more than the market price or to buy from him for less.[14] Also, the seller who lost if market prices had fallen could just as easily have gained if they had risen. Thus that transaction would be equal in the sense that a bet is fair when each party has an equal risk of gain and loss. As Soto said, a merchant must suffer a loss if "bad fortune buffets him, for example, because an unexpected abundance of goods mounts up," and conversely, if "fortune smiles on him" he may keep the gain "for as the business of buying and selling is subject to fortuitous events of many kinds, merchants ought to bear risks at their own expense, and on the other hand, they may wait for good fortune."[15]

In the 17th and 18th centuries, the French, Dutch and German jurists who wrote about positive law explained the remedy available in their countries by saying, like the natural lawyers, that a contract must be made at a just price. They did not change positive law. German and Dutch jurists said, like the medieval jurists, that buyer as well as the seller could receive a remedy, as could the parties to similar types of contracts.[16] French jurists preserved a traditional French rule which, like the original Roman text, limited relief to the seller of land.[17]

Samuel Pufendorf, *De iustitia naturae ac gentium* (1688), V.i.6. See Paulo Cappellini, *Schemi contrattuali e cultura teologico-giuridico nella seconda scolastica: verso una teoria generale* (thesis, Univ. Firenze, 1978/79), 184–96.

11. Odd Langholm, *Price and Value in the Aristotelian Tradition* (1979), 61–143.

12. Thomas Aquinas, *In decem libros Ethicorum Aristotelis ad Nicomachum Expositio* (A. Pirotta, ed., 1934), lib. 5, lec. 9 (mentioning labor and expenses and *indigentia* or need); *Summa theologiae* II-II, q. 77 a. 3 ad 4 (permitting a sale at famine prices).

13. E.g., Hagenauer, *Das "justum pretium" bei Thomas Aquinas* (1931). Hagenauer was following still earlier scholars who distinguished the "subjective" factors of need and scarcity from the "objective" factors of labor and expenses, and believed that Thomas had emphasized the latter. E.g., Kaulla, *Die geschichtliche Entwicklung der modernen Werttheorien* (1906), 53; Schreiber, *Die volkswirtschaftlichen Anschauungen der Scholastik seit Thomas von Aquin* (1913), 120.

14. Lessius, *De iustitia et iure* lib. 2, cap. 21, dub. 4; Soto, *De iustitia et iure* lib. 6, q. 3, a. 1.

15. Soto, *De iustitia et iure* lib. 6, q. 2, a. 3.

16. Heinrich Coccejus, *Ius civile controversum* (1766), to Dig. 18.5, q. 7, 16; Wolfgang Lauterbach, *Collegii theoretico-pratici* (1744), to Dig. 18.5 § 23–24; Burkhard Struvius, *Syntagma academicus et forensis* (1692), Exerc. XXIII ad lib. 18, tit. 1, § 85, 92; Johannes Voet, *Commentarius ad pandectas* (1698), to Dig. 18.1 § 7, 13; Iohannes Westenberg, *Principia iuris secundum ordinem digestorum seu pandectorum* (4th ed. 1764), to Dig. 18.1 § 12–13.

17. Robert Pothier, *Traité des obligations*, in *Oeuvres de Pothier* 2 (Bugnet ed., 2d ed. 1861), § 38–39; Claude de Ferrière,

Nevertheless, though they continued to repeat the natural law principle, it is not clear how much of the natural law theory most French, Dutch and German jurists understood. Usually, they did not explain the remedy except to say that a price should be just. Occasionally, they said that exchange requires equality.[18]

In the late 18th and early 19th century, some jurists were becoming sceptical about whether one could ever say that a price was unjust. It seemed to them to involve mystical notions about economic value. The 18th century jurist Christian Thomasius argued that to speak of a just price was to imagine that value is an intrinsic property of things, like their color. But value depends "on the mere judgment of men."[19] This argument impressed Suarez[20] who drafted a code for Prussian law, the Allgemeines Landrecht which was enacted in 1794. This Code eliminated relief for an unjust price "in and of itself"[21] although it said that error would be "presumed" when a buyer paid twice the normal price.[22]

In France, when the Civil Code was drafted, this argument persuaded Berlier that the traditional remedy should be abolished.[23] But he was in the minority. Article 1674 gave a remedy only to seller of land, as had the original Roman text and traditional French law. The article required, however, that the seller receive less than five-twelfths its value rather than less than half.

The reason relief was limited to the seller of land was not scepticism about the principle of equality in exchange. Portalis, Cambacérès, and Tronchet all said that an exchange or commutative contract requires equality.[24] Napoleon acknowledged that "[t]here is not a contract of sale when one does not receive the equivalent of what one gives."[25] The limitation on relief was explained pragmatically: land was more important than other things sold;[26] its price is more stable;[27] the buyer is less likely than the seller to be the victim of necessity[28] or mistake[29] and more likely to seek to avoid the transaction because his plans had changed.[30]

Dictionnaire de droit et de pratique (nouv. ed. 1769), II, v. "lézion d'outre moité de juste prix," 135, 137; Honoré Lacombe de Prezel, *Dictionnaire portatif de jurisprudence et de pratique* (1763), II, v. "lézion," 430.

18. E.g., Pothier, *Traité des obligations* § 33; Lauterbach, *Collegii* to Dig. 18.1, § 37; Struvius, *Synallagma* Exerc. XXIII to Dig. 18, tit. 1 § 19 (citing Aristotle).

19. Christian Thomasius, "De aequitate cerebrina legis II. Cod. de rescind. vendit. et eius usu practico" cap. II, § 14, printed as Dissertatio LXXIII in Thomasius, *Dissertationum Academicarum varii inprimis iuridici argumenti* (1777), III, 43. See Klaus Luig, *Der gerechte Preis in der Rechtstheorie und Rechtspraxis von Christian Thomasius (1655–1728)*," in *Diritto e potere nella storia europea: Scritti in onore di Bruno Paradisi* 2 (1982), 775.

20. Koch, ed., *Allgemeines Landrecht für die Preussischen Staaten* 1 (7th ed. 1978), § 58 n. 8.

21. Hottenhauer, ed., *Allgemeines Landrecht für die Preussischen Staaten von 1794* 1 (1970), § 58.

22. *Id.* § 59.

23. P. A. Fenet, ed., *Recueil complet des travaux préparatoires du Code Civil* 14 (1836), 36.

24. *Id.* 43, 46–47, 130–31 (Portalis); Ibid. 43 (Cambacérès); Ibid. 63 (Tronchet).

25. *Id.* 58.

26. *Id.* 57–58 (Bonaparte).

27. *Id.* 49, 140–41 (Portalis).

28. *Id.* 145 (Portalis), 75 (Tronchet), 177 (Faure). Portalis had originally wished to give the buyer a remedy but was outvoted. *Ibid.* 76.

29. *Id.* 75 (Ségur).

30. *Id.* 77 (Bonaparte).

With the rise of the will theories of contract, however, arguments like those of Thomasius and Berlier seemed unanswerable. The terms of a contract could have no other source than the will of the parties. Most 19th century French treatise writers doubted that a remedy should be given at all. Demolombe argued that value was "subjective," "variable and relative."[31] Laurent observed that things worth one amount "from a commercial point of view" might be worth quite a different amount to the parties because of their "needs, tastes and passions."[32] Jurists more sympathetic to the remedy defended it without invoking a principle of equality in exchange. Duranton, Colmet de Santerre and Marcadé claimed that disparity in the price constituted evidence of fraud, mistake, duress or a sort of moral constraint.[33] Glasson thought that, although relief violated the "principle of freedom of contract," it was justified for reasons of "humanity."[34]

Nineteenth century German jurists were also sceptical. In Germany, relief for an unjust price was abolished by statute in Bavaria in 1861,[35] in Saxony in 1863,[36] and in commercial matters by the Allgemeines Handelsgesetzbuch of 1861.[37] Defending this step, Endemann argued, like Thomasius, that value was relative.[38]

The Roman text remained in force where it had not been replaced by statute. But German jurists regarded the remedy as an exception to the normal rules of contract law. The basic principle—"rooted in the law of sale" according to Windscheid,[39] "lying in the nature of things" according to Vangerow,[40] was to be found in the other Roman text that said each party could outwit the other.[41] Relief for unfairness was an exception to the principle that contracts are binding.[42]

German jurists usually explained that relief was an exception based upon equity[43] and argued how large the exception was. Some wished to limit relief to sellers of land on the ground that relief was given by way of exception;[44] others wished to extend relief to buyers of land and parties to

31.   Charles Demolombe, *Cours de Code Napoléon* 24 (1854–82), § 194.

32.   François Laurent, *Principes de droit civil français* 15 (3d ed. 1867–78), § 485.

33.   Alexandre Duranton, *Cours de droit civil français suivant le Code civil* 10 (3d ed. 1834–37), § 200–01; A.M. Demante & E. Colmet de Santerre, *Cours analytique du Code civil* 5 (2d ed. 1883), § 28 bis. (by Colmet de Santerre); Victor Marcadé, *Explication théorique et pratique du Code Napoléon* (5th ed. 1859), 357–58.

34.   Glasson, *Eléments du droit français considéré dans ses rapports avec le droit naturel et l'economie politique* (2d ed. 1884), 550, 553.

35.   Landtagsabschiedes of Nov. 10, 1861 § 282.4 [1861–62] *Gesetzblatt*, quoted in Danzer, *Das Bayerische Landrecht (Codex Maximilianeus Bavaricus Civilis) vom Jahre 1756 in seiner heutigen Geltung* (1894), 229–30. Until then, the remedy for an unjust price had been preserved in the Codex

Maximilianeus Bavaricus Civilis IV iii §§ 19–22 (enacted in 1756).

36.   Bürgerliches Gesetzbuch für des Königreich Sachsen § 864.

37.   Allgemeines deutsches Handelsgesetzbuch art. 286.

38.   Endemann, *Handbuch des deutschen Handels . . . , See . . . , und Wechselrechts* 2 (1882), § 261.III.

39.   Bernhard Windscheid, *Lehrbuch des Pandektenrechts* 2 (7th ed. 1891), § 396 n. 2.

40.   Karl Vangerow, *Leitfaden für Pandekten-Vorlesungen* 3 (Marburg 1847), § 611 n. 1.

41.   Dig. 19.2.22.3.

42.   Rudolph Holzschuher, *Theorie und Casuistik des gemeinen Civilrechts* 3 (1864), 729–30.

43.   Vangerow, *Leitfaden* 3: § 611 n. 1; Wächter, *Pandekten* 2 (Leipzig 1881) § 207; Windscheid Lehrbuch 2: § 396 n. 2

44.   Holzschuher, *Theorie* 3: 729–30; Vangerow, *Leitfaden* 3, § 611; Wächter, *Pandekten* 2, § 207. Some said the exception

other kinds of contracts because to do so would be equally equitable.[45] Everyone agreed, however, that they were dealing with an exceptional kind of relief that departed from the normal principles of contract law. The initial drafts of the German Civil Code abolished the traditional remedy. In the final draft, however, § 138(2) was added which, as we will see, voids a transaction in which one person exploits certain enumerated weakness of another to obtain a "striking disproportion" in the value of the performances exchanged.[46] The rule seemed to be a fair one even though no one had a theory of why a "striking disproportion" should matter.

Common law

Traditionally, a promise was enforceable in assumpsit whether the consideration given in return was adequate or not. Courts of equity, however, could give relief if a bargain was so harsh as to be "unconscionable." Nevertheless, the common law courts had not rejected the principle of equality in exchange. Nor had the courts of equity accepted it.

As A.W.B. Simpson observed,[1] the judges who fashioned the rule against examining the adequacy of consideration were not facing the problem of what to do about hard bargains. They were deciding what promises to enforce. As we have seen, they found consideration for certain gratuitous arrangements such as gifts to prospective sons-in-law and gratuitous loans and bailments.[2] To demand that consideration be equal would have prevented the judges from achieving the goal of enforcing certain promises for which the consideration was not a recompense. For example, in *Sturlyn v. Albany*,[3] the court said that "when a thing is done, be it never so small, this is a sufficient consideration to ground an action." These words were often quoted in later cases. As Simpson has pointed out, however, *Sturlyn* had nothing to do with enforcing a hard bargain.[4] The plaintiff had leased to a third party who then granted his estate to the defendant. The plaintiff demanded rent from the defendant who promised to pay if the plaintiff would show him a deed proving the rent was due. The showing of the deed was said to be consideration.

Conversely, the courts of equity gave relief from hard bargains without espousing the principle that each party to an exchange should receive something equal in value to what he gave. It is hard to find even a passing reference to such a principle in the 17th and 18th century court opinions

---

should be limited to sellers because it was meant to protect those in need, and sellers who accepted a low price would be more likely to be needy than buyers who paid a high one. Georg Friedrich Puchta, *Pandekten* (2d ed. 1844), § 364; F. von Keller, *Pandekten* (1861), 333.

45. E.g., J. Seuffert, *Praktisches Pandektenrecht* 2 (3rd ed. 1852), § 272.

46. The weaknesses were originally "necessity, indiscretion or inexperience." In 1976, to make them harmonize with Criminal Code (*Strafgesetzbuch*) § 302(a), the phrase was changed to "distressed situation, inexperience, lack of judgmental ability, or grave weakness of will." Law of July 29, 1976, *BGBl* 1976 I 2034, 2038 (art. 3).

1. A.W.B. Simpson, *A History of the Common Law of Contract: The Rise of the Action of Assumpsit* (1975), 445–49.

2. *Id.* 416–52.

3. Sturlyn v. Albany, Cro. Eliz. 67, 78 Eng. Rep. 327 (Q.B. 1587).

4. Simpson, *History* 447.

or the arguments of counsel. Instead, there is general talk about whether a bargain is "unreasonable,"[5] "unjust,"[6] "unequitable and unconscientious,"[7] "hard and unequal,"[8] or entered into for "inadequate" or "grossly inadequate" consideration[9] or through "imposition."[10] Moreover, before 1750, nearly all the cases in which courts of equity gave relief concerned either necessitous heirs who sold their inheritance at a low price or else the repercussions of the South Sea Bubble.[11] In helping heirs, they seem to have been concerned, not about equality in exchange, but about the squandering of family estates.[12] In assisting victims of the South Sea Bubble, they were not helping those who paid more than the market price but those who bought when the market price of land was high due to the high price of South Sea company stock.[13] Thus giving relief may thus actually have contradicted the natural lawyers' position that the just price is the market price.

In the 19th century, however, Anglo-American jurists, like their continental brethren, claimed that, in principle, there could be no relief for an unfair price. They said that the reason the common law courts would not examine the adequacy of consideration was because, in principle, the fairness of an exchange did not matter. Their arguments were like those made on the continent. According to Joseph and W.W. Story, Chitty, Metcalf, and Addison to give relief would raise imponderable questions about value.[14] Pollock, as noted earlier, addressed the subject by quoting part of Hobbes' remark that "the value of all things contracted for is measured by the

---

5. Earl of Arglasse v. Muschamp, 1 Vern. 237, 238–39; 23 Eng. Rep. 438, 439 (1684); Earl of Chesterfield v. Jannsen, 2 Ves. Sen. 125, 130, 28 Eng. Rep. 82, 85 (1750–51) (argument for plaintiff).

6. Earl of Chesterfield v. Jannsen, 2 Ves. Sen. 125, 130, 28 Eng. Rep. 82, 85 (1750–51) (argument for plaintiff).

7. Chesterfield v. Jannsen, 2 Ves. Sen. 125, 155, 28 Eng. Rep. 82, 100 (1750–51).

8. Kien v. Stukeley, 1 Bro. 191, 192, 1 Eng. Rep. 506, 507 (H.L. 1722) (argument for defendant).

9. Gwynne v. Heaton, 1 Bro. C.C. 1, 6, 28 Eng. Rep. 949, 951 (1778).

10. Earl of Chesterfield v. Jannsen, 2 Ves. Sen. 125, 145, 152, 156, 28 Eng. Rep. 82, 94, 98, 100 (1750–51); Nichols v. Gould, 2 Ves. Sen. 422, 423, 28 Eng. Rep. 270, 270 (1752).

11. See A.W.B. Simpson, "The Horwitz Thesis and the History of Contracts," *U. Chi. L. Rev.* 46 (1979), 533–601, 562–66. A few cases involved neither necessitous heirs nor the South Sea Bubble. Even in these cases, however, the courts did not endorse a principle of equality in exchange. Osmond v. Fitzroy & Duke of Cleveland, 3 P. Wms. 129, 24 Eng. Rep. 997 (1731)(bond given servant by lord during his minority set aside for

breach of trust); Willis v. Jernegan, 2 Atk. 251, 26 Eng. Rep. 555 (1741)(relief denied when plaintiff bought lottery tickets from defendant); How v. Waldon & Edwards, 2 Ves. Sen. 516, 28 Eng. Rep. 330 (1754)(relief given to sailor who sold in advance and for a small sum the right to the prize money where "inadequateness of value" was combined with a risk of obtaining the money that had been so "greatly misrepresented" as to constitute "gross fraud").

12. As the court mentions in Johnson, Ex'r of Hill v. Nott, 1 Vern. 271, 272, 23 Eng. Rep. 464, 465 (1684); Twistleton v. Griffith, 1 P. Wms. 310, 311, 24 Eng. Rep. 403, 404 (1716); Earl of Chesterfield v. Janssen, 2 Ves. Sen. 125, 144–45, 28 Eng. Rep. 82, 93–94 (1750–51).

13. As mentioned in Kien v. Stukeley, 1 Bro. 191, 192, 11 Eng. Rep. 506, 507 (H.L. 1722); Savile v. Savile, 1 P. Wms. 745, 746–47, 24 Eng. Rep. 596 (1721).

14. Joseph Story, *Commentaries on Equity, Jurisprudence as Administered in England and America* 1 (14th ed. 1918), 437–38; William Wentworth Story, *A Treatise on the Law of Contracts Not Under Seal* (3rd ed. 1851), 437–38; Theoron Metcalf, *Principles of the Law of Contracts as Applied by the Courts of New York* (1878), 163.

appetite of the contractors . . ."[15] Moreover, to give relief would be to interfere with the decision of the parties themselves.[16]

The jurists then explained away the doctrine of unconscionability by giving it a new rationale. As Simpson notes, a disparity in price came to be considered as "evidence of fraud, not as an independent substantive ground, and not as constituting hardship."[17] While the fraud theory never swept the field,[18] it found its way into many treatises beginning with the early one by Powell in 1790.[19] Indeed, Joseph Story, William Whetmore Story, and Metcalf[20] argued that the fraud theory must be correct since questions of value are imponderable. Courts of equity nevertheless continued to give relief, perhaps as generously as they would have if the theory had not changed.[21]

The jurists also claimed that the reason the common law courts would not examine the adequacy of consideration was because, in principle, the fairness of an exchange did not matter. Their arguments were like those made on the continent. According to Joseph and W.W. Story, Chitty, Metcalf, and Addison to give relief would raise imponderable questions about value.[22] Pollock, as noted earlier, addressed the subject by quoting part of Hobbes' remark that "the value of all things contracted for is measured by the appetite of the contractors . . ."[23] Moreover, to give relief would be to interfere with the decision of the parties themselves.[24]

As we will see, however, in the last half of the 20th century, the doctrine of unconscionability has seen a renaissance. Section 2-302 of the Uniform Commercial Code allows a judge to remedy "unconscionable" contracts without any distinction between law and equity. Section 208 of the Second Restatement of Contracts contains a similar provision applicable to contracts in general.

---

15. Sir Frederick Pollock, *Principles of Contract* (4th ed. 1888), 172.

16. J. Story, *Commentaries* 1: 337; W.W. Story, *Law of Contracts* 435; Joseph Chitty, *A Practical Treatise on the Law of Contracts Not Under Seal* (1826), 7; Metcalf, *Law of Contracts* 163; Charles Addison, *A Treatise on the Law of Contracts* (11th ed. 1911), 12; S. Martin Leake, *The Elements of the Law of Contracts* (London 1867), 311–12; Bishop, *Law of Contracts* 18; John Newland, *A Treatise on Contracts Within the Jurisdiction of Courts of Equity* (1821), 357; Louis Hammon, *The General Principles of the Law of Contract* (1912), 692.

17. Simpson, "Horwitz Thesis" 569.

18. See, e.g., Theophilus Parsons, *The Law of Contracts* 1 (4th ed. 1860), *362–63; John Norton Pomeroy, *A Treatise on the Specific Performance of Contracts as it is Enforced by Courts of Equitable Jurisdiction in the United States of America* (2nd ed. 1897), 274–75.

19. John J. Powell, *Essay Upon the Law of Contracts and Agreements* 2 (1790), 157–58; Bishop, *Law of Contracts* 18–19; Hammon, *Law of Contract* 694–695; Metcalf, *Law of Contract* 163; Newland, *Treatise on Contracts* 358–59; J. Story, *Commentaries* 1: 341; W. W. Story, *Law of Contracts* 437–38.

20. J. Story, *Commentaries* 1: 399; W.W. Story, *Law of Contracts* 437–38; Metcalf, *Law of Contracts* 163.

21. James Gordley, "Equality in Exchange," *Calif. L. Rev.* 69 (1981), 1587 at 1650–55.

22. J. Story, *Commentaries* 1: 339; W.W. Story, *Law of Contracts* 435; Chitty, *Law of Contracts*, 12.

23. Sir Frederick Pollock, *Principles of Contract* (4th ed. London 1888), 172.

24. J. Story, *Commentaries* 1: 337; W.W. Story, *Law of Contracts* 435; Chitty, *Law of Contracts* 7; Metcalf, *Law of Contracts* 163; Addison, *Law of Contracts* 12; Leake, *Law of Contracts* 311–12; Bishop, *Law of Contracts* 18; Newland, *Treatise on Contracts* 357; Hammon, *Law of Contract* 692.

b. Modern law

English law

Cresswell v. Potter, [1978] 1 WLR 255 (Ch.)

While plaintiff and defendant were married, plaintiff had a half interest in the house in which they lived. She had contributed, indirectly at least £65 and perhaps £200 toward its purchase price. It was bought for £1,500 of which £1,200 was raised by a mortgage. The plaintiff left the defendant after admitting to adultery. The defendant obtained an uncontested divorce, evidence of plaintiff's adultery having been obtained by Thomas Olyott, an "inquiry agent." The plaintiff signed a "release" of her rights in the house presented to her by Olyott. She claimed that she did not read it but thought it would enable the defendant to sell the house without affecting her rights in it. Later, he sold it for £3350. Plaintiff sued to set aside the release. Held, for plaintiff.

Megarry J. "I think I can go straight to the well-known case of Fry v. Lane (1888) 40 Ch.D. 312. . . . The judge[in that case] laid down three requirements. What has to be considered is, first, whether the plaintiff is poor and ignorant; second, whether the sale was at a considerable undervalue; and third, whether the vendor had independent advice. I am not, of course, suggesting that these are the only circumstances which will suffice; thus there may be circumstances of oppression or abuse of confidence which will invoke the aid of equity. But in the present case only these three requirements are in point. . . .

I think that the plaintiff may fairly be described as falling within whatever is the modern equivalent of 'poor and ignorant.' Eighty years ago, when Fry v. Lane was decided, social conditions were very different from those which exist today. I do not, however, think that the principle has changed, even though the euphemisms of the 20th century may require the word 'poor' to be replaced by 'a member of the lower income group' or the like, and the word 'ignorant' by 'less highly educated.' The plaintiff has been a van driver for a tobacconist, and is a Post Office telephonist. The evidence of her means is slender. The defendant told me that the plaintiff probably had a little saved, but not much; and there was evidence that her earnings were about the same as the defendant's, and that these were those of a carpenter. The plaintiff also has a legal aid certificate.

In those circumstances I think the plaintiff may properly be described as 'poor' in the sense used in Fry v. Lane, where it was applied to a laundryman who, in 1888, was earning £1 a week. In this context, as in others, I do not think that 'poverty' is confined to destitution. Further, although no doubt it requires considerable alertness and skill to be a good telephonist, I think that a telephonist can properly be described as 'ignorant' in the context of property transactions in general and the execution of conveyancing documents in particular. I have seen and heard the plaintiff giving evidence, and I have reached the conclusion that she satisfies the requirements of the first head.

The second question is whether the sale was at a 'considerable under-value.' Slate Hall cost £1,500, £1,200 of the price being provided by the mortgage. . . . If Slate Hall was worth no more than it cost, she was giving up her half share in an equity worth £30. . . . In fact, as is now known, within a little over two years the property fetched £ 3,350, so that at the time in question the plaintiff's share of the equity may have been worth appreciably more than £150. . . .

As for independent advice, from first to last there is no suggestion that the plaintiff had any."

Note: Notice that relief in this case was given in Chancery, the court which developed the doctrine of "unconscionability" in England and was traditionally the only one to concern itself with the fairness of a bargain.

Law in the United States

Uniform Commercial Code

§ 2-302 UNCONSCIONABLE CONTRACT OR CLAUSE

(1) If the court as a matter of law finds the contract or any clause of the contract to have been unconscionable at the time it was made the court may refuse to enforce the contract, or it may enforce the remainder of the contract without the unconscionable clause, or it may so limit the application of any unconscionable clause to avoid any unconscionable result.

(2) When it is claimed or appears to the court that the contract or any clause thereof may be unconscionable the parties shall be afforded a reasonable opportunity to present evidence as to its commercial setting, purpose and effect to aid the court in making the determination.

Restatement (Second) of Contracts

§ 208

If a contract or term thereof is unconscionable at the time the contract is made a court may refuse to enforce the contract, or may enforce the remainder of the contract without the unconscionable term, or may so limit the application of any unconscionable term as to avoid any unconscionable result.

Toker v. Westerman, 274 A.2d 78 (N.J. Super. 1970)

"On November 7, 1966 plaintiff's assignor, People's Foods of New Jersey, sold a refrigerator-freezer to defendant under a retail installment contract. The cash price for the unit was $899.98. With sales tax, group life insurance and time price differential the total amount was $1,229.76, to be paid in 36 monthly installments of $34.16 each.

Defendants made payments over a period of time, but resist payment of the balance in the sum of $573.89, claiming that the unlit was so greatly over-priced as to make the contract unenforceable under N.J.S. 12A:2-302. . . .

At the trial defendant presented an appliance dealer who had inspected the refrigerator-freezer in question. He stated that the same had a capacity of approximately 18 cubic feet, was not frost-free, and, with no special features, was known in the trade as a stripped unit. He estimated the reasonable retail price at the time of sale as between $350 and $400. He testified that the most expensive refrigerator-freezer of comparable size, with such additional features as butter temperature control and frost-free operation, at that time sold for $500. . . .

It is apparent that the court should not allow the statutory provision in question [U.C.C. 2-302] to be used as a manipulative tool to allow a purchaser to avoid the consequences of a bargain which he later finds to be unfavorable. Suffice it to say that in the instant case the court finds as shocking, and therefore unconscionable, the sale of goods for approximately 2½ times their reasonable retail value. This is particularly so where, as here, the sale was made by a door-to-door salesman for a dealer who therefore would have less overhead expense than a dealer maintaining a store or showroom. In addition, it appeared that defendants during the course of the payments they made to plaintiff were obliged to seek welfare assistance."

Carboni v. Arrospide, 2 Cal. App. 4th 76 (1991)

"In this case we consider whether a secured note providing for interest at a rate of 200 percent per annum is unconscionable. In the circumstances presented here, we conclude that it is. . . .

The evidence at trial established that on July 27, 1988, George Arrospide, Jr., signed a $4,000 note and deed of trust on behalf of his father, Jorge Arrospide, Sr., as his attorney in fact. The note was made in favor of Michael Carboni, a licensed real estate broker. It carried an interest rate of 200 percent per annum, was due in three months. . . . The parties originally intended the note would be paid off in a single lump sum payment of $6,000 after three months. However, over the next four months, Carboni continued to make cash advances to Jorge Sr. which were secured by the original note and deed of trust. By November 25, 1988, the principal amount of the note had ballooned to $99,346, all of which was carried at an interest rate of 200 percent per annum. At the time of trial in March of 1990, the principal and accumulated interest amounted to nearly $390,000.

The testimony was sharply divided concerning the purpose for the loan. Carboni testified that the money was advanced directly to George Jr. to be used to refurbish residential property which he intended to resell at a profit. The Arrospides, on the other hand, claimed the money was used for Jorge Sr.'s 'personal obligations'—primarily to pay medical expenses for his ailing parents who lived in Peru. George Jr. testified that his father was under 'emotional duress' because of these personal obligations, and that he obtained the loan at his father's specific instruction. . . .

The leading California case on unconscionability generally follows Professor Williston's analysis of the issue. In A & M Produce Co. v. FMC Corp. [(1982) 135 Cal.App.3d 473, 476 (1982)] the court recognized that unconscionability has both a 'procedural' and a 'substantive' aspect. The procedural aspect is manifested by (1) 'oppression,' which refers to an inequality of bargaining power resulting in no meaningful choice for the weaker party, or (2) 'surprise,' which occurs when the supposedly agreed-upon terms are hidden in a prolix document.

'Substantive' unconscionability, on the other hand, refers to an overly harsh allocation of risks or costs which is not justified by the circumstances under which the contract was made. [citation omitted] Presumably, both procedural and substantive unconscionability must be present before a contract or clause will be held unenforceable. However, there is a sliding scale relationship between the two concepts: the greater the degree of substantive unconscionability, the less the degree of procedural unconscionability that is required to annul the contract or clause. [citations omitted]. . . .

We have little trouble concluding that an interest rate of 200 percent on a secured $99,000 loan is substantively unconscionable; i.e., that it imposes a cost on the borrower which is overly harsh and was not justified by the circumstances in which the contract was made. . . .

[A]ccording to Carboni's own testimony, the interest rate (200 percent) was approximately 10 times the rate then prevailing in the credit market for similar loans. . . . Carboni contends the high interest rate was justified because no other charges were made for the loan (such as points and documentation fees) and, if it had been paid off as scheduled, the loan would have actually been cheaper than the alternatives available to the Arrospides. Carboni's own testimony again undermines his argument. Carboni claimed the Arrospides could have obtained a $4,000 loan secured by a third deed of trust for 10 points ($400) at 18 to 21 percent interest (approximately $200 for 3 months) plus costs for document preparation, title insurance and 'so forth.' Thus the entire cost for a three-month 'conventional' loan would have been $600 plus unspecified costs for document fees and title insurance. As it was, at 200 percent interest, Jorge Sr. would have paid $2,000 to borrow $4,000 for three months. In these circumstances, we doubt whether the loan obtained was cheaper than more conventional financing.

In any event, Carboni's argument ignores the fact that the principal amount of the note ballooned over the next four months to more than $99,000, and that the due date was extended (at least implicitly) beyond three months. Carboni voluntarily transformed a $4,000 note into a $99,000 line of credit. His argument simply cannot justify a 200 percent rate on the amount ultimately borrowed ($99,000) for an unspecified term. . . .

[T]he procedural aspect of unconscionability refers to an absence of meaningful choice on the part of one of the parties. . . . [W]e believe there was an inequality of bargaining power which effectively robbed Jorge Sr. of any meaningful choice.

Viewing the evidence in the light most favorable to the judgment, we must presume Jorge Sr. was acting under emotional distress when he borrowed the funds to pay his parents' medical expenses. Most important, it appears Jorge Sr. had attempted unsuccessfully to secure a loan from other sources. The 'Agreement' signed by the parties in connection with the loan states that 'Owner acknowledges and agrees that Lender's charges for the loan are costly, but Owner has tried unsuccessfully to obtain a loan from other sources and now feels that making this loan is the best way for Owner to make the payments on his bills and obligations.' Thus, it appears that Jorge Sr. had unequal bargaining power because he was unable to obtain a loan from other sources. Consequently, Carboni was able to offer him credit on a 'take it or leave it' basis. This effectively deprived Jorge Sr. and his son of any meaningful choice, since they had no alternative for obtaining credit."

***Note*:** The court seems to be saying that the contract is 'substantively' unconscionable because the borrower could have obtained credit at a lower rate and 'procedurally' unconscionable because he could not. Consider whether this decision is correct if, given his credit status, the borrower could not have obtained credit at a lower rate.

The "Lando Principles"

The Principles of European Contract Law, Prepared by the Commission on European Contract Law

ARTICLE 4.109: EXCESSIVE BENEFIT OR UNFAIR ADVANTAGE

(1) A party may avoid a contract if, at the time of the conclusion of the contract:

  (a) it was dependent upon or had a relationship of trust with the other party, was in economic distress or had urgent needs, was improvident, ignorant, inexperienced, or lacking in bargaining skill, and

  (b) the other party knew or ought to have known this and, given the circumstances and purpose of the contract, took advantage of the first party's situation in a way which was grossly unfair or took an excessive benefit.

(2) Upon the request of the party entitled to avoidance, a court may if it is appropriate adapt the contract in order to bring it into accordance with what might have been agreed had the requirements of good faith been followed.

(3) A court may similarly adapt the contract upon the request of a party receiving notice of avoidance for excessive benefit or unfair advantage, provided that this party informs the party which gave the notice promptly after receiving it and before that party has acted in reliance on it.

The Unidroit Principles

The Unidroit Principles of International Commercial Contracts

ARTICLE 1.1 FREEDOM OF CONTRACT

The parties are free to enter into a contract and to determine its content.

ARTICLE 3.10 GROSS DISPARITY

(1) A party may avoid the contract or an individual term of it if, at the time of the conclusion of the contract, the contract or term unjustifiably gave the other party an excessive advantage. Regard is to be had, among other factors, to

> (a) the fact that the other party has taken unfair advantage of the first party's dependence, economic distress or urgent needs, or of its improvidence, ignorance, inexperience or lack of bargaining skill; and
>
> (b) the nature and purpose of the contract.

(2) Upon the request of the party entitled to avoidance, a court may adapt the contract or term in order to make it accord with reasonable commercial standards of fair dealing.

(3) A court may also adapt the contract or term upon the request of the party receiving notice of avoidance, provided that the party informs the other party of its request promptly after receiving such notice and before the other party has acted in reliance on it.

German law

German Civil Code

§ 138 TRANSACTION CONTRARY TO GOOD MORALS

(1) A legal transaction that violates good morals (*gute Sitten*) is void.

(2) A legal transaction is also void when a person takes advantage of the distressed situation, inexperience, lack of judgmental ability, or grave weakness of will of another to obtain the grant or promise of financial advantages for himself or a third party that are obviously disproportionate to the performance given in return.

Note on the term "usury": In the Middle Ages, "usury" meant taking any interest on a loan. In modern English, it means taking excessive interest. In modern German, "usury" (*Wucher*) means taking excessive advantage. So § 138(b) is said to be a remedy for "usury" even though that sounds a bit odd in English.

Note on door to door sales: Section 312 of the German Civil Code now provides that if a consumer enters into a contract of exchange with someone who has come to his home or his place of work he has the right to cancel it. According to § 355, he must do so within two weeks. He can cancel or any reason or no reason, not simply if the price is unfair.

Reichsgericht, 14 October 1921, RGZ 103, 35

"The defendant leased certain property from the plaintiff in March 1918. In April 1918 the defendant sought to withdraw from the contract and to have it set aside for error and for fraud, and also argued that it was void under § 138 of the Civil Code. The plaintiff brought an action to establish that the lease was valid. Judgments below and on appeal were for the plaintiff. The defendant's appeal [*Revision*] was successful. . . .

The court of appeal . . . was in error in holding that § 138 of the Civil Code was not applicable. The court only concerned itself with the objection of usury under the second paragraph of § 138. In view of the factual situation, as it was established, and the claims of the defendant, which are backed by evidence, even this result is legally doubtful. The lease, which generally puts the burdens predominantly on the lessee (see §§ 1, 4, 6) contains especially oppressive provisions in §§ 5, 7, and 8. Under § 5 the lessor has the right to restrict the lessee's use to one-half of the leased property. In this event the yearly payment is to be reduced from 650 to 350 Reichsmarks, but no refund is to be made on the lump-sum payment of 8,000 Reichsmarks made at the commencement of the lease regardless of the year of the lease in which this occurs. The court of appeal recognized that this provision was particularly oppressive for the defendant but considered that it should refuse, even for the situation thus envisaged, to recognize a gross disproportion in the rent and the other obligations assumed by the defendant. The court of appeal relied here upon its own evaluation, but did not even say what it would consider to be the normal rent. The defendant asserted, relying upon experts, that the normal rent would be 500 Reichsmarks, thus without regard to § 5, only one-third of the yearly rent paid under the lease that the court of appeal set at 1594 Reichsmarks. Although the court of appeal is free to call its own experts or to decide on the basis of its own knowledge, it must make a finding on this point. Under § 7 the lessor is given the right to require the lessee to give up the premises at once in the event that the rent is not paid on time or other duties under the lease are not properly performed by the lessee. The lessee, however, remains liable for the future rent and the lump-sum payment of 8,000 Reichsmarks is lost, also without any distinction as to when this took place. Under § 8, the lessor's heirs, in the event of her death, have the right to terminate the lease. If this termination occurs within the first three years of the lease, half of the 81,000 Reichsmark payment will be returned. The disproportion that emerges from all of these provisions taken together cannot be justified by the interests of the lessee upon which the court of appeal relied. There is no evidence that the lessee was in special difficulties at the time the lease was concluded, but the fact that the lessee entered so easily upon such an unusually burdensome contract indicates indiscretion, that is to say, a failure to understand the consequences of acts due to indifference or to a lack of sufficient reflection. The defendant has offered proof that she was, in general, inexperienced in business matters and that the plaintiff knew this. Therefore, it is not necessary to have further evidence taken as to the factual situation nor to consider the case again under § 138(2) of the Civil Code as the lease is void under the facts as found under § 138(1), which the court of appeal did not consider. The courts, to be sure, have usually drawn the conclusion as to § 138(2) that standing alone, a disproportion between performance and counter-performance, even if very large, cannot justify the applying the general principle of § 138(1). Nevertheless, other circumstances, either alone or in combination with such a disproportion, may cause a transaction to appear as immoral and, therefore, void under § 138(1). That is so with § 7 of the contract which provides that every defect in performance not only made the lessee lose the right to continued use of the property, while the rent still had to be paid, but also results in the loss of the entire 8,000 Reichsmark payment. Particularly objectionable is the intention, which finds expression in various provisions of the contract, including § 7, to retain the 8000 Reichsmark down payment, if at all possible, without giving any performance in return. . . . The contract is therefore void under § 138(1). The complaint is rejected and the plaintiff ordered to repay the 8,000 Reichsmarks with interest."

Reichsgericht, 31 March 1936, RGZ 150, 1

"The Fifth Civil Senate of the Reichsgericht . . . brought the following question before the Great Senate for Civil Matters of the Reichsgericht:

According to the judicial decisions interpreting § 138 of the Civil Code . . . , is it to be maintained that:

A transaction in which performance and counterperformance are strikingly disproportionate is invalid when either all of the elements of usury (§ 138, par. 2) are present, or some additional circumstance is added to the disproportion which, taken together with the disproportion, makes the contract contrary to good mores given the entire form of the contract as shown by the combination of its content, motive, and purpose, and hence as shown by the combination of objective and subjective criteria (§ 138, par. 1) or, in the alternative, can a transaction be held invalid under § 138, par. 1 of the Civil Code when the mere presence of a striking disproportion is proven without the addition of an additional circumstance and without consideration of the character of the party interested in the transaction, and thus when the transaction is considered in a purely objective manner . . . ?

The Great Senate for Civil Matters of the Reichsgericht answered the question in the following manner:

A juristic act (*Rechtsgeschäft*) in which performance and counterperformance are strikingly disproportionate but in which the remaining elements of usury (§ 138, par. 2) are not present is invalid under § 138, par. 1 when, in addition to the disproportion, the party claiming the disproportionate advantage exhibits such a character that the juristic act, given its content, motive, and purpose, offends healthy national and popular feeling (*gesunde Volksempfindungen*). Under some circumstances, such a character may be inferred from the disproportion. When one party, through malice or gross negligence, ignores the fact that the other has consented to hard terms to escape a difficult situation, this consideration can, in conjunction with the disproportion, make the juristic act invalid. . . .

[T]he judicial decisions of the *Reichsgericht* indicate that when all the elements of usury are not present, the transaction is to be declared invalid if, in addition to the magnitude of what is promised, some other circumstance is also present which, taken in conjunction with the disproportion, makes the juristic act appear contrary to good morals, given the entire form of the juristic act as shown by the combination of its content, motive, and purpose. As a rule, the party who will be harmed if the transaction is declared to be invalid must have been aware of the factual circumstances which make his action appear offensive to proper conduct, although he need not have been aware that his action offended good morals. The *Reichsgericht* has abandoned the narrower view . . . that transactions in which a disproportion is present between performance and counterperformance . . . is sufficient of itself to prove the invalidity of the transaction on the basis of § 138, par. 1, without the conjunction of any additional circumstances, and in particular without consideration of the character of the party interested in the transaction, and thus by a purely objective evaluation. . . .

The Great Senate for Civil Matters . . . considers a legal transaction in which performance is strikingly disproportionate to counterperformance, but in which the remaining characteristics of usury are absent, to be invalid under § 138, par 1 of the Civil Code if, in addition to the disproportion, the party claiming the disproportionate advantage exhibits such a character that the juristic act, given its content, motive, and purpose, offends the healthy national and popular feeling (*gesunde Volksempfindungen*).

The following considerations lead it to this conclusion.

The concept of an 'offense to good morals,' as contained in §§ 138 and 826 of the Civil Code must, by its nature, receive its content from the feelings of the people dominant since the revolution: from the National Socialist world view (*Weltanschauung*). Section 138, with its content completed in this way, is also applicable to juristic acts of the earlier period in which all matters have not yet been finally settled. If a contract is offensive to good morals, according to the viewpoint that is now determinative, then no legal protection can be granted to it by a German court.

The whole of the content of § 138 shows that a disproportion alone does not lead to the invalidity of a legal transaction. For, if the presence of a disproportion were a sufficient factual circumstance for invalidity, it would be pointless for paragraph 2 to add particular requirements for invalidity which look to the external and internal factual situation of the parties. The mention of additional elements necessary for invalidity demonstrates that the factual circumstance of a disproportion, taken alone, cannot lead to invalidity. For the provisions of paragraph 1 to be applied, more ought to be present than simply the disproportion which is one of the elements of usury of paragraph 2. For paragraph 1 to apply, some other circumstance must be added in the place of the elements of exploitation which are not present, a circumstance which, together with the disproportion, gives the transaction the mark of an offense to good morals.

Such an interpretation of the statute is internally correct because it corresponds to the general concept of an 'offense to good morals.' A proper view of the morality of an action requires that the total form of the action be examined, and not that single factual circumstances be treated in isolation and separation from each other. When the question arises of whether a transaction is to be countenanced or not, all circumstances must be taken into account which constitute the transaction and give it color. Otherwise an incomplete picture would be created. Now it is precisely the character of the interested party and his motive and purpose that contribute to giving an individuality to each individual transaction. Participation in a legal transaction which offends good morals stigmatizes the party who seeks a profit from it in a manner consistent with healthy national and popular feelings and exposes him to the contempt of honest national comrades. The judge must take these legitimate feelings into account. He can only take the responsibility for exposing a party to contempt by rendering a decision when that party has truly deserved it, when the party himself is to blame. This is only the case when the character which the party has displayed is reprehensible and worthy of reproach. Moreover, in evaluating a contract, proceeding form these considerations of a general nature, one must look beyond the content of the contract which indicates a disproportion to the motives of the interested party and the purpose he pursued; one must accordingly ask the question whether the legal transaction, given its entire form as determined in this way, offends healthy national and popular feeling, or, to use the expression of the *Motive* [the drafter's explanation] of the Civil Code (vol. 2, p. 727), whether it offends the sense of decency of all fair and right-thinking persons.

A transaction which leaves the channels of lawful fair exchange in which both parties' interests are correctly reflected will only come into being where wholly particular and irregular circumstances are present which trick the weaker party into entering such an unfair contract. Whoever in commercial life knowingly uses the weaker position of another to obtain an excessive profit displays impermissible self-interestedness and thereby acts reprehensibly. However, one also offends healthy national and popular feeling when he maliciously or through grossly negligent indiscretion ignores the fact that the other party is consenting to harsh conditions only because of the difficulties of his situation. One who will not see and who obtains advantages in this way which are not justified by the state of affairs must resign himself to being treated as one who acts knowingly.

The judge initially has to decide, in adjudicating such a disputed case, whether a striking disproportion between performance and counterperformance is present and to what extent this is the case. The degree of this disproportion is an important source of knowledge about the character of the party accepting the advantage. It can be so large that it forcefully suggests the conclusion of the contract through knowing or grossly negligent use of some factual circumstance impinging on the other contracting party.

The contemporary conception of social and commercial life moves in a particularly sharp manner against a self-interest of an individual national comrade which is disadvantageous to the whole; it prosecutes the struggle against such a mental attitude with all means at its command, in the area of criminal law as in that of civil law. This conception provides correct interpretation and application of the statutes, even as they are set forth. For in this way all cases of this type are to be understood, cases which in their entire form conflict with healthy national and popular feeling and with the interests of the national popular community. Moreover, a proof limited to the objective content of the contract, which did not consider the character of the interested parties and particularly that of the party seeking the advantage, would not only contradict the existing law of § 138, but would also be incorrect by reason of its incompleteness and a false application of the general concept of proper conduct.

For commercial life, the careful and prudent conduct which is an essential condition for the welfare of the national whole, and the security of commercial legal transactions is imperatively required. Pertaining to this security is, in the first place, fidelity to contracts. Accordingly, the invalidity of a contract which has been concluded ought to be declared only with care and circumspection. Thus, judicial decisions concerning the application of § 138 have with good reason been disposed to grant such requests only after careful proof of the totality of circumstances of the individual transaction, circumstances pertaining both to persons and to things. The decisions have been wary of following the path of "laesio enormis" (rescission of sale for disproportion of more than half) of Roman general law, a path expressly abandoned by the legislator of the Civil Code as well (*Motive*, vol. 2, p. 321). Moreover, an effective device in the struggle against reprehensible self-interestedness is indicated by the consideration that not only knowing exploitation of the other contracting party, but also malicious or grossly negligent ignorance of the existence of a critical situation by the contracting party who enjoys the advantage may, in conjunction with the disproportion, lead to the invalidity of the legal transaction.

Note: As mentioned earlier, judges during the Third Reich would sometimes use terms drawn from Nazi ideology which showed their allegiance to the regime and which may or may not have had anything to do with their decision. One of them was *gesunde Volksempfindungen* translated here as "healthy national and popular feeling." According to § 2 of the Criminal Code of 1935 (*Strafgesetzbuch*), a person was punishable if he "commits an act which either the statute declares to be punishable or which deserves punishment according to the basic principles of a criminal statute or according to healthy national and popular feeling." In his commentary on this section, Schönke explained that "[h]ealthy national and popular feeling means the natural feeling for law of all fair and right thinking national comrades (*Volksgenossen*)." Adolf Schönke, *Strafgesetzbuch für das deutsche Reich Kommentar* (1944), p. 23, to § 2. After the allied victory, the Control Council of the Allies which administered Germany promulgated a law prohibiting punishment of acts on the grounds that they violated *gesunde Volksempfindungen*. Military Government-Germany, United States Zone, Law no. 1, Ordinance No. 7, art. 4, Oct. 18, 1946, in Leon Friedman, *The Law of War, A Documentary History* 1 (1972), 913.

Today, however, the Nazi terminology appears superfluous to the principle at stake. German courts continue to give relief under § 138 (1) of the Civil Code when a party not only took a disproportionate advantage but exhibited a "reprehensible character" by so doing as in the next case. Consider what, if anything the requirement of immoral behavior adds to the requirement that he must have taken a disproportionate advantage.

Bundesgerichtshof, 9 November 1961, BB 1962, 156

"The conclusion of a contract of loan for over 20,000 DM provided the lender with an 'agreed profit' of 750 DM per month. This profit was, in reality, an interest rate on the loan of 45 percent annually. Because of the amount of the agreed interest rate, a striking disproportion did exist between performance and counterperformance. However, an offense to good morals and hence the invalidity of the contract under § 138 par. 1 of the Civil Code can only be found where, in addition to the objective disproportion of the two performances, the reprehensible character of the lender at the conclusion of the contract can be established. . . .

A high rate of interest going beyond all reasonable measure itself clearly indicates that the defendant has a character that merits disapproval. An interest charge of 45 percent should be condemned . . . because an acceptance of it has an unhealthy influence on the capital market and also creates the danger of causing the financial collapse of the debtor, which actually occurred in this case soon after the conclusion of the contract. The question of whether an interest rate of 45 percent can accordingly make a contract of loan invalid by itself need not be answered. In this contract, the parties agreed not only to the high interest charge, but also to security for the loan which was high to an entirely uncustomary degree: in addition to a note for the entire sum borrowed, payment of which was guaranteed by his wife, it included the conveyance for security of the debt of a small store and six oil paintings. One who offers security of this amount can always obtain credit at the normal bank rate of interest and does not need to pay a 45 percent interest charge. Thus it was forcibly brought to the attention of the defendant that only wholly particular circumstances could have induced the general debtor (the borrower) to conclude a contract of loan on such terms. Either the general debtor must have been in a difficult position which prevented him from obtaining credit on normal terms, or the transaction for which he needed credit must have been so dubious that a credit institution would not finance it. . . .

If these considerations—whether relating to the entire economic position of the general debtor (the borrower) or to the nature of his transaction—which come forcibly to one's attention, were unknown to the defendant, then they were carelessly ignored, his sole concern was to procure himself a wholly uncustomary profit on his money. The contract of loan must be held to offend good morals because of this heedless struggle for profit. That the general debtor himself offered this interest rate and security does not affect this result. Neither can the defendant make the objection that it was necessary for the general debtor, because of his difficult economic position or the type of transaction he intended, to accept a loan on such harsh terms." [citations omitted]

Note: According to the court, the borrower could have received normal credit terms elsewhere because he could offer as security a small
store and six oil paintings. It does not discuss the value of the store, or the
borrower's equity in it, or the value of the paintings. It does not explain
why a person who could have obtained credit on normal terms and seems
to have had none of the weaknesses mentioned in § 138(2) would have
agreed to the terms so onerous if he could get normal terms elsewhere.
Consider what a court should do if he could not have received normal
terms because of his poor credit status. See *Carboni v. Arrospide*, above.

French law

As mentioned earlier, the medieval remedy for an extreme disparity
in value was said to be a remedy for *laesio enormis*: extreme harm. The
French still refer to a disparity in the values exchanged as a *lésion*
(French for *laesio*). For lack of anything better it is translated here
"lesion." "Disparity in the values exchanged" would be a better translation
but it would hide the fact that a technical legal expression is being used.

French Civil Code

ARTICLE 1118

Lesion invalidates some but not all contracts, and these only as to certain persons, and in the manner explained [subsequently].

ARTICLE 1305 [ADDED BY LAW NO. 68-5 OF 3 JANUARY 1968]

Simple lesion is a basis for recission by an unemancipated minor in
all agreements.

ARTICLE 1313

Persons who have attained their majority cannot recover on the basis of
lesion except in the cases and under the conditions provided for in this Code.

ARTICLE 1674

If the seller receives less than five-twelfths of the value of immovable
property, he can have the sale set aside even if he has expressly renounced
this right in the contract and stated that he was making a gift of the
excess value.

ARTICLE 1675

In order to determine whether there has been a lesion of more than
seven-twelfths, it is necessary to evaluate the immovable property according to its condition and value at the time of sale.

[added by the Law of 28 November 1949]: In the case of a unilateral
promise of sale, the lesion is evaluated as of the day the sale is completed.

Note: A "unilateral promise of sale" (see art. 1675(2)) is a promise in
which one party agrees to sell for a certain price and the other neither
promises to buy nor promises anything in return for the option to buy
which he is receiving.

In addition to the provision of the Civil Code, special statutes have given a remedy to buyers of fertilizer, seeds, and fodder who pay a quarter more than their value;[1] victims of sea[2] or aviation accidents[3] who pay an unfair amount for rescue or salvage; and those who sell artistic or literary property for less than five-twelfths its value.[4]

The decisions that follow apply arts. 1109 (on error, fraud and duress) and 1110 (on error) translated earlier. They also apply the following articles:

French Civil Code

ARTICLE 1113

There is duress when it is of such a nature as to make an impression on a reasonable person and to cause him to fear that his body or fortune is exposed to a considerable and present harm.

ARTICLE 1116

Fraud is a ground for setting an agreement aside when one party employs an artifice such that the other party clearly would not have entered into the contract had it not been employed.

Fraud cannot be presumed; it must be proved.

Note: In reading the following decisions, consider whether the courts were giving relief because of error, fraud or duress, or because the price was unfair.

Cour de cassation, ch. req., 27 April 1887, D. 1888. I. 263

On September 22, 1886, Fleischer, captain of the steamship *Rolf* whose ship was stuck in the sands of the Bay of the Seine and was about lose both his ship and cargo. He agreed to pay 18,000 francs for the services of a tug boat which was the amount that the captain of the tug fixed as the value of salvage. He only escaped a total loss by agreeing to this amount. The *Tribunal de commerce* of Rouen held that Fleischer only had to pay 4,190 francs for the services he had received. The *Cour de cassation* upheld that decision. It said that according to "article 1108 of the Civil Code the consent of the person who obligates himself is an essential condition for the validity of an agreement; as, when the consent is not free, when it is only given because of fear inspired by a considerable and present evil to which the promisor's person or fortune is exposed, the contract concluded in these circumstances is infected with a defect that renders it voidable. . . .' The decision under appeal finds that the captain of the *Rolf* only agreed to the contract now in litigation in order to save his ship, which otherwise would have very shortly foundered and have been lost. . . .

---

1. Law of July 8, 1907, D.P. 1908.IV.173, as amended by Law of July 8, 1937, D.P. 1938.IV.168.

2. Law of April 29, 1916, art. 7, D.P. 1919.IV.IV. 285, current version Law of July 7, 1967, art. 15, D.S.L. 1967.258.

3. Law of May 31, 1925, art. 57, 1925 D.P.IV.41, 45, current version in Civil Aviation Code (Code de l'aviation civile) art. L. 142–1, Decree of March 31, 1967, D.S.L. 1967.184.

4. Law of March 11, 1957, art. 33, D.L. 1957.102, 104.

[He] was compelled to enter into the agreement forced upon him by the abuse of his desperate situation only after having vainly argued with the captain of the *Arbeillei.* . . ."

Cour de cassation, ch. req., 27 January 1919, S. 1920. I. 198

"Whereas gratuitous payments made between living persons or by testament must be the free expression of the donor's own independent will; as it is the task of the courts to invalidate such gratuities when the donor's consent was extorted by force; whereas in the judgment under appeal it was found as a fact that Antoine Duvoisin, a paralyzed old man, weakened by illness, confined to bed, and abandoned by the members of his family, was at the mercy of Mr. and Mrs. Vigneron, his *métayers* [tenants of a farm who pay rent in kind], and that the threat they made not to continue their services to him unless he consented to give them his goods was of a kind to inspire such a fear in him that he found it impossible to resist their demand; as proof of constraint can also be found in the fact that, according to the decision under review, Antoine Fuvoisin answered the notary who was drawing up the contract and had asked if he consented, by saying 'I must' (*Il le faut bien*); as the decision under review also found that the pressure applied by the Vignerons was made more apparent by a series of later actions in which Antoine Duvoisin made gifts to his *métayers* to assure himself of their services" the decision of the lower court invalidating the gratuitous payments is upheld.

Cour d'appel of Douai, 2 June 1930, Jurisprudence de la Cour d'Appel de Douai 82, 183

"Lawniezak has taken an appeal from the decision of the court of d'Avesnes . . . which ordered him to pay the sum of 60,000 francs to Hautmont for damages on account of an accident for which Lawniezak was adjudged liable. . . . He demands this decision be modified, claiming that Hautmont, in a contract dated July 3, 1930 and signed by the parties, declared him to be discharged from the consequences of the accident, this being pursuant to a settlement which set 1,500 francs as the amount receivable by the said Hautmont for all damages. . . .

[J]udicial decisions have consistently affirmed that fraud can be established by all methods of proof including presumptions. . . . [I]n this case, this proof has been made by clear, weighty, and consistent presumptions. . . . [T]he contract itself contains the proof of the fraudulent maneuvers by means of which it was obtained by the *Caisse d'Assurances Mutuelles*. . . . [I]t is certain that Hautmont, without taking leave of his senses, would not have given up for 1,500 francs the benefits of a judgment which entitle him to 60,000 francs in damages when Lamy, in a contract which appears in his files, had bound himself to advance all his expenses and to claim nothing in return if the case were lost. . . . [I]t is evident that the insurer took advantage of the state of depression of Hautmont—a state established by experts appointed by the court without the need even arising to turn to the even more conclusive opinion of Dr. Rouges de Fursac, whose authority is incontestable—in order to extort a waiver of rights by inspiring the spurious fear in him of fees which in any event he would not have had to pay. . . ."

Cour d'appel, Paris, 22 January 1953, J.C.P. 1953.II. 7435

S. sold three 17th century paintings of the Dutch and Flemish schools to S. for 250,000 francs each. At trial, experts valued the paintings at 40,000 francs, 45,000 francs, and 55,000 francs The *Tribunal civil de la Seine* declared the sale void and ordered Delvaux to restore the amount he had been paid by S. (400,000 francs) and to pay him 100,000 francs as damages. The *Cour d'appel* upheld this decision, saying "that Delvaux thus committed a considerable error in the value of the oil paintings which were offered him, and that fraud is a basis for invalidating a contract when it has produced an error in value. . . . [T]he facts of the case show that S., who knew Delvaux to be lacking in experience, as he recognized in a letter of November 7, 1946, deceived the buyer in the value of the three oil paintings offered. . . . [T]his deceit has clearly surpassed the exaggeration and hedging permitted to every seller. . . . [T]he buyer of old paintings, unless he possesses special knowledge himself, finds himself forced to leave much to the affirmations of the merchant, particularly when the merchant presents himself as one with a reputation guaranteeing honesty and a special technical ability. . . . [I]n this case, by publicizing his reputation as an 'art critic, expert on old paintings, arbitrator at the *Tribunal de commerce de la Seine*, member of the French Society of Literature, Officer of Public Education,' S. obligated himself to demonstrate competence and probability and, in any event, renounced the use of any deceit as to Delvaux, an uninstructed buyer who placed a particular confidence in him because of his reputation. . . . [T]he circumstances show that S. only used this reputation, and particularly his title as arbitrator at the *Tribunal de commerce*, which he held at the time, for the purpose of capturing Delvaux's confidence. . . . [T]he letter of S. cited above, written several days after the sale, is indicative of the procedures he used with regard to Delvaux. . . . [T]o hold on to Delvaux, who was disturbed by the valuations of experts, S. did not hesitate to boast of his 'long experience as an expert recognized by the government, an art critic, and a correspondent with all the journals of the fine arts both in France and abroad,' and of his large fortune, nor did he hesitate to present himself as 'often called to act as judge of the false opinion of ignorant experts who give themselves titles which they do not really possess,' and to affirm that the paintings sold 'have an international value'. . . ."

Cour d'appel, Paris, 14 October 1931, D. 1934. II. 128

In a contract with *Ciment Verre*, *Marchand et fils* agreed to demolish reinforced concrete tanks at a price of 100 francs per cubic meter. The trial court held *Marchand et fils* liable, finding that *"Ciment Verre* was able to believe that *Marchand et fils* possessed all the means of demolition appropriate for any concrete of this type, which in this case turned out to be of a special kind of particular hardness, a fact which *Marchand and fils* should have taken into account before entering into the agreement." The *Cour d'appel* overturned this decision. It said: "[T]here is no indication that *Marchand et fils*, who by profession were suppliers of sand, gravel and cement and not owners of a demolition business, were aware when they bound themselves to the agreement of the special difficulties inherent in the relationship of *Ciment Verre* to the *Brasseries Karcher*, even though at the time of construction they had furnished some of the materials in which they deal. . . . [O]n its part, *Ciment Verre*, having done the construction, was aware of the special nature of the building and the very particular hardness of the cement which they had mixed and the particularly high percentage of steel added to the cement because of the purpose for which the tanks were intended. . . . [T]he expert report shows that it is improbable that a specialist in reinforced concrete and in tanks such as *Ciment Verre* would not have known of the flagrant and absolute impossibility of performing this demolition at a price of 100 francs per cubic meter. . . . [T]his substantial difference indicates sufficiently that *Marchand et fils*, in setting the price of 100 francs, perhaps hastily, only had in view the demolition of normal reinforced concrete and that, given the silence intentionally preserved by *Ciment Verre*, the common intention of the parties only covered concrete of such a nature. . . . [O]ne must see in this case an error in substance in a quality of the thing which was the object of the contract, an error which a party committed or was induced to commit, and which is sufficient to vitiate the consent of *Marchand et fils*, *Ciment Verre* having only itself to blame both for its silence over the nature of the work and for the fact that it had accepted performance of the work to which it was obligated before ever having contracted with *Marchand et fils*. . . ."

Cour de Cassation, ch. soc., 4 May 1956, J.C.P. 1957. II. 9762

The lower court invalided a lease between Sanchez-Boxa and Vidal Associates on the ground of an error in substance. The *Cour de cassation* affirmed. It noted that the court below had found that "the rented property is in a dilapidated state, having vast amounts of uncultivated land not mentioned in the contract and important deficiencies in the vineyards and orchards . . . but also that the lessee could not have understood the difficulty and the importance of the efforts necessary to put the property in order, and this situation is due to the initial failure of the lessor to give an objective initial presentation of the circumstances," and the decision adds that "the silence or maneuvers of the lessor to conceal the importance and difficulty of putting the property in order led the lessee into error, and if the lessee had known the true situation, the contract would never have been accepted in its current form and perhaps would never have been accepted at all. . . . [T]he result of these findings is that

Sanchez-Boxa took the lease to the knowledge of the lessor with the view of rapidly putting the property in order, and consequently the decision below could hold, without violating the relevant texts, that there was an error in the substantial qualities of the thing leased, which the judge called its 'agricultural value'. . . ."

Cour de cassation, ch. civ., 29 November 1968, Gaz. Pal. 1969.J.63

Vanden-Borre leased a villa on the Côte d'Azur for the month of July from its owner, Berthon. The lower court held that the lease was void for an error in substance. It ordered the lessor to return the rent paid in advance and to pay damages. The *Cour de cassation* upheld this decision. It noted that "the decision under review states that, standing alone, the lease, taken for the month of July, 1964, at a price of 6,000 francs with additional charges would permit Vanden-Borre to assume that the premises were correspondingly desirable given that the bureau which was Berthon's agent had told him specifically that this was a comfortably equipped villa. . . . [H]owever, both the interior and exterior of this villa gave the incontrovertible impression of a general lack of maintenance, the bedding, doors and walls being manifestly in a filthy condition, the furniture being clearly inadequate, and major construction work, undertaken by the *Société Caliqua* in the immediate area of the villa, would disturb the peace and independence of the occupant. . . ."

2. Fairness of the auxiliary terms
Law in the United States

Weaver v. American Oil Co., 276 N.E.2d 144 (Ind. 1971)

"In this case the appellee oil company presented to the appellant-defendant lessee, a filling station operator, a printed form contract as a lease to be signed, by the defendant, which contained, in addition to the normal leasing provisions, a 'hold harmless' clause which provided in substance that the lessee operator would hold harmless and also indemnify the oil company for any negligence of the oil company occurring on the leased premises. The litigation arises as a result of the oil company's own employee spraying gasoline over Weaver and his assistant and causing them to be burned and injured on the leased premises. This action was initiated by American Oil and Hoffer (Appellees) for a declaratory judgment to determine the liability of appellant Weaver, under the clause in the lease.

It will be noted that this lease clause not only exculpated the lessor oil company from its liability for its negligence, but also compelled Weaver to indemnify them for any damages or loss incurred as a result of its negligence. . . .

This is a contract, which was submitted (already in printed form) to a party with lesser bargaining power. As in this case, it may contain unconscionable or unknown provisions which are in fine print. Such is the case now before this court.

The facts reveal that Weaver had left high school after one and a half years and spent his time, prior to leasing the service station, working at various skilled and unskilled labor oriented jobs. He was not one who should be expected to know the law or understand the meaning of technical terms. The ceremonious activity of signing the lease consisted of nothing more than the agent of American Oil placing the lease in front of Mr. Weaver and saying 'sign,' which Mr. Weaver did. There is nothing in the record to indicate that Weaver read the lease; that the agent asked Weaver to read it; or that the agent, in any manner, attempted to call Weaver's attention to the 'hold harmless' clause in the lease. Each year following, the procedure was the same. A salesman, from American Oil, would bring the lease to Weaver, at the station, and Weaver would sign it. The evidence showed that Weaver had never read the lease prior to signing and that the clauses in the lease were never explained to him in a manner from which he could grasp their legal significance. The leases were prepared by the attorneys of American Oil Company, for the American Oil Company, and the agents of the American Oil Company never attempted to explain the conditions of the lease nor did they advise Weaver that he should consult legal counsel, before signing the lease. The superior bargaining power of American Oil is patently obvious and the significance of Weaver's signature upon the legal document amounted to nothing more than a mere formality to Weaver for the substantial protection of American Oil.

Had this case involved the sale of goods it would have been termed an 'unconscionable contract' under sec. 2-302 of the Uniform Commercial Code. . . .

The facts of this case reveal that in exchange for a contract which, if the clause in question is enforceable, may cost Mr. Weaver potentially thousands of dollars in damages for negligence of which he was not the cause[.] Weaver must operate the service station seven days a week for long hours, at a total yearly income of $5,000–$6,000. The evidence also reveals that *the clause was in fine print and contained no title heading* which would have identified it as an indemnity clause. It seems a deplorable abuse of justice to hold a man of poor education, to a contract prepared by the attorneys of American Oil, for the benefit of American Oil which was presented to Weaver on a 'take it or leave it basis' . . .

We do not mean to say or infer that parties may not make contracts exculpating one of his negligence and providing for indemnification, but it must be done *knowingly* and *willingly* as in insurance contracts made for that very purpose."

Law in Europe

Directive of the European Council on Unfair Terms in Consumer Contracts

[93/13/EEC, 5 April 1993]

ARTICLE 1

(1) The purpose of this Directive is to approximate the laws, regulations and administrative provisions of the Member States relating to unfair terms in contracts concluded between a seller or supplier and a consumer.

(2) The contractual terms which reflect mandatory statutory or regulatory provisions and the provisions or principles of international conventions to which the Member States or the Community are party, particularly in the transport area, shall not be subject to the provisions of this Directive.

ARTICLE 2

For the purposes of this Directive:

(a) "unfair terms" means the contractual terms defined in Article 3;

(b) "consumer" means any natural person who, in contracts covered by this Directive, is acting for purposes which are outside his trade, business or profession;

(c) "seller or supplier" means any natural or legal person who, in contracts, covered by this Directive, is acting for purposes relating to his trade, business or profession, whether publicly owned or privately owned.

ARTICLE 3

(1) A contractual term which has not been individually negotiated shall be regarded as unfair if, contrary to the requirement of good faith, it causes a significant imbalance to the parties' right and obligations arising under the contract, to the detriment of the consumer.

(2) A term shall always be regarded as not individually negotiated where it has been drafted in advance and the consumer has therefore not been able to influence the substance of the term, particularly in the context of a preformulated standard contract.

The fact that certain aspects of a term or one specific term have been individually negotiated shall not exclude the application of this Article to the rest of a contract if an overall assessment of the contract indicates that it is nevertheless a pre-formulated standard contract.

Where any seller or supplier claims that a standard term has been individually negotiated, the burden of proof in this respect shall be incumbent on him.

(3) The Annex shall contain an indicative and non-exhaustive list of the terms which may be regarded as unfair.

ARTICLE 4

(1) Without prejudice to Article 7, the unfairness of a contractual term shall be assessed, taking into account the nature of the goods or

services for which the contract was concluded and by referring, at the time of conclusion of the contract, to all the circumstances attending the conclusion of the contract and to all the other terms of the contract or of another contract on which it is dependent.

(2) Assessment of the unfair nature of the terms shall relate neither to the definition of the main subject matter of the contract nor to the adequacy of the price and remuneration, on the one hand, as against the services or goods supplied in exchange, on the other, insofar as these terms are in plain intelligible language.

ARTICLE 5

In case of contracts where all or certain terms offered to the consumer are in writing, these terms must always be drafted in plain, intelligible language. Where there is doubt about the meaning of a term, the interpretation most favourable to the consumer shall prevail. This rule on interpretation shall not apply in the context of the procedures laid down in Article 7(2).

ARTICLE 6

(1) Member States shall lay down that unfair terms used in a contract concluded with a consumer by a seller or supplier shall, as provided for under their national law, not be binding on the consumer and that the contract shall continue to bind the parties upon those terms if it is capable of continuing in existence without the unfair terms.

(2) Member States shall take the necessary measures to ensure that the consumer does not lose the protection granted by this Directive by virtue of the choice of the law of a non-Member country as the law applicable to the contract if the latter has a close connection with the territory of the Member States.

ARTICLE 7

(1) Member States shall ensure that, in the interests of consumers and of competitors, adequate and effective means exist to prevent the continued use of unfair terms in contracts concluded with consumers by sellers or suppliers.

(2) The means referred to in paragraph 1 shall include provisions whereby persons or organizations, having a legitimate interest under national law in protecting consumers, may take action according to the national law concerned before the courts or before competent administrative bodies for a decision as to whether contractual terms drawn up for general use are unfair, so that they can apply appropriate and effective means to prevent the continued use of such terms.

(3) With due regard for national laws, the legal remedies referred to in paragraph 2 may be directed separately or jointly against a number of sellers or suppliers from the same economic sector or their associations which use or recommend the use of the same general contractual terms or similar terms.

ARTICLE 8

Member States may adopt or retain the most stringent provisions compatible with the treaty in the area covered by this Directive, to ensure a maximum degree of protection for the consumer.

ARTICLE 9

The Commission shall present a report to the European Parliament and to the Council concerning the application of this Directive five years at the latest after the date in Article 10(1).

ARTICLE 10

(1) Member States shall bring into force the laws, regulations and administrative provisions necessary to comply with this Directive no later than 31 December 1994. They shall forthwith inform the Commission thereof.

These provisions shall be applicable to all contracts concluded after 31 December 1994.

(2) When Member States adopt these measures, they shall contain a reference to this Directive or shall be accompanied by such reference on the occasion of their official publication. The methods of making such a reference shall be laid down by the Member States.

(3) Member States shall communicate the main provisions of national law which they adopt in the field covered by this Directive to the Commission.

ARTICLE 11

This Directive is addressed to the Member States. . . .

Annex

Terms Referred to in Article 3(3)

(1) Terms which have the object or effect of:

    (a) excluding or limiting the legal liability of a seller or supplier in the event of the death of a consumer or personal injury to the latter resulting from an act or omission of that seller or supplier;

    (b) inappropriately excluding or limiting the legal rights of the consumer *vis-à-vis* the seller or supplier or another party in the event of total or partial non-performance or inadequate performance by the seller or supplier of any of the contractual obligations, including the option of offsetting a debt owed to the seller or supplier against any claim which the consumer may have against him;

    (c) making an agreement binding on the consumer whereas provision of services by seller or supplier is subject to a condition whose realization depends on his own will alone;

    (d) permitting the seller or supplier to retain sums paid by the consumer where the latter decides not to conclude or perform the contract, without providing for the consumer to receive compensation of an equivalent amount from the seller or supplier where the latter is the party cancelling the contract;

    (e) requiring any consumer who fails to fulfill his obligation to pay a disproportionately high sum in compensation;

(f) authorizing the seller or supplier to dissolve the contract on a discretionary basis where the same facility is not granted to the consumer, or permitting the seller or supplier to retain the sums paid for services not yet supplied by him where it is the seller or supplier himself who dissolves the contract;

(g) enabling the seller or supplier to terminate a contract of indeterminate length without reasonable notice except where there are serious grounds for doing so;

(h) automatically extending a contract of fixed duration where the consumer does not indicate otherwise, when the deadline fixed for the consumer to express this desire not to extend the contract is unreasonably early;

(i) irrevocably binding the consumer to terms with which he had no real opportunity of becoming acquainted before the conclusion of the contract;

(j) enabling the seller or supplier to alter the terms of the contract unilaterally without a valid reason which is specified in the contract;

(k) enabling the seller or supplier to alter unilaterally without a valid reason any characteristics of the product or service to be provided;

(l) providing for the price of goods to be determined at the time of delivery or allowing a seller of goods or supplier of services to increase their price without in both cases giving the consumer the corresponding right to cancel the contract if the final price is too high in relation to the price agreed when the contract was concluded;

(m) giving the seller or supplier the right to determine whether the goods or services supplied are in conformity with the contract, or giving him the exclusive right to interpret any term of the contract;

(n) limiting the seller's or supplier's obligation to respect commitments undertaken by agents or making his commitments subject to compliance with a particular formality;

(o) obliging the consumer to fulfill all his obligations where the seller or supplier does not perform his;

(p) giving the seller or supplier the possibility of transferring his rights and obligations under the contract, where this may serve to reduce the guarantees for the consumer, without the latter's agreement;

(q) excluding or hindering the consumer's right to take legal action or exercise any other legal remedy, particularly by requiring the consumer to take disputes exclusively arbitration not covered by legal provisions, unduly restricting the evidence available to him or imposing on him a burden of proof which, according to the applicable law, should lie with another party to the contract.

(2) Scope of subparagraphs (g), (j), and (l)

    (a) Subparagraph (g) is without hindrance to terms by which a supplier of financial services reserves the right to terminate unilaterally a contract of indeterminate duration without notice where there is a valid reason, provided that the supplier is required to inform the other contracting party or parties thereof immediately.

    (b) Subparagraph (j) is without hindrance to terms under which a supplier of financial services reserves the right to alter the rate of interest payable by the consumer or due to the latter, or the amount of other charges for financial services without notice where there is a valid reason, provided that the supplier is required to inform the other contracting party or parties thereof at the earliest opportunity and that the latter are free to dissolve the contract immediately.

        Subparagraph (j) is also without hindrance to terms under which a seller or supplier reserves the right to alter unilaterally the conditions of a contract of indeterminate duration, provided that he is required to inform the consumer with reasonable notice and that the consumer is free to dissolve the contract.

    (c) Subparagraphs (g), (j) and (l) do not apply to:

      – transactions in transferable securities, financial instruments and other products or services where the price is linked to fluctuations in a stock exchange quotation or index or a financial market rate that the seller or supplier does not control;

      – contracts for the purchase or sale of foreign currency, traveller's cheques or international money orders denominated in foreign currency;

    (d) Subparagraph (l) is without hindrance to price-indexation clauses, where lawful, provided that the method by which prices vary is explicitly described.

Note on the law in England, France and Germany. All three countries have enacted legislation giving effect to the provisions of this Directive.[1] In each case, this legislation supplements laws that were previously enacted that govern unfair terms.

In France, art. 35 of Law no. 78-23 of 10 January 1978 (Code de la consommation art. L. 132-1) provides:

In contracts concluded between professionals (*professionnels*) and non-professionals, decrees of the *Conseil d'Etat* issued after hearing

1. Unfair Terms in Consumer Contracts Regulations 1994, S.I. 1994/3159 (England); Law 95–96 of 1 Feb. 1995, Code de la consommation art. L. 132–1 (France); Gesetz zur Änderung des AGB-Gesetzes, BGBl I 1996, 1013 (Germany).

the opinion of the commission established in by art. 36, may prohibit, limit or regulate clauses dealing with the way the price is determined or to be determined as well as with its payment, the integrity (*consistance*) or delivery of the object paid for, the placement of risks, the extent of liabilities and warranties, the conditions of performance, rescission, dissolution or renewal of agreements, as well as those clauses which seem to be imposed on non-professionals or consumers by an abuse of the other party's economic power and confer on him an excessive advantage.

The *Conseil d'Etat*, which is to issue these decrees, is the highest administrative court in France. The commission established by art. 36 to give it advice consists of three judges, two experts on law and contracts, four consumer representatives, and four representatives of "professionals." While this law did not authorize courts to police contract terms in the absence of a decree, courts nevertheless began to do so on a case by case basis. Cass., 1e ch. civ., 14 May 1991, Bull. civ. I, no. 153, p. 101.

Legislation in France, England and Germany has brought the law of these countries into compliance with the Directive. In England and Germany, even before the Directive, statutes were already in place enumerating certain terms which could be struck down as unfair: in England, the Unfair Contract Terms Act 1977, c. 50, and in Germany, the Standardized Contract Terms Act (*Gesetz zur Regelung des Rechts der Allgemeinen Geschäftsbedingungen*) BGBl. 1976, I 3317, much of which is now incorporated in §§ 305–10 German Civil Code. Even before the Standard Contract Terms Act was enacted, German courts had refused to enforce unfair terms on the grounds that they violated the very general language to § 242 of their civil code which requires a party to perform in accordance with "good faith" (*Treu und Glauben*). The Standard Contract Terms Act was largely a codification of their experience.

The French statute introduced the distinction between "professionals" and "non-professionals" which is reflected in the EU Directive. English and French law, however, do not confine relief to "non-professionals." According to § 3(1) of the English Unfair Contract Terms Act: "This section applies as between contracting parties where one of them deals as consumer or on the other's written standard terms of business." According to the German Standard Contract Terms Act, § 1(2), the Act applies to "standard contract terms" which are "drafted to apply to a multitude or contacts and set by one contracting party for the other at the time of contracting." That provision has now been incorporated in § 305 of the German Civil Code. Thus while English and German law are similar in structure to the Directive, they apply to "non-professionals" as well.

The Directive, and the French, English, and German legislation, contain a list of specific terms that could be deemed unfair. A different approach would have been to have a "general clause" but not to try to enumerate particular contract terms that might be unfair. This is the approach of the American Uniform Commercial Code and also of the Unidroit Principles.

The "Lando Principles"

The Principles of European Contract Law, Prepared by the Commission on European Contract Law

ARTICLE 4.110 UNFAIR TERMS NOT INDIVIDUALLY NEGOTIATED

(1) A party may avoid a term which has not been individually negotiated if, contrary to the requirements of good faith and fair dealing, it causes a significant imbalance in the parties' rights and obligations arising under the contract to the detriment of that party, taking into account the nature of the performance to be rendered under the contract, all the other terms of the contract and the circumstances at the time the contract was concluded.

(2) This Article does not apply to:

- (a) a term which defines the main subject matter of the contract provided the term is in plain and intelligible language; or to
- (b) the adequacy in value of one party's obligations compared to the value of the obligations of the other party.

The Unidroit Principles

The Unidroit Principles of International Commercial Contracts

ARTICLE 1.1 FREEDOM OF CONTRACT

The parties are free to enter into a contract and to determine its content.

ARTICLE 2.20 SURPRISING TERMS

(1) No term contained in standard terms which is of such a character that the other party could not reasonably have expected it, is effective unless it has been expressly accepted by that party.

(2) In determining whether a term is of such a character regard is to be had to its content, language and presentation.

IV. EXCUSES FOR NON-PERFORMANCE

1. Impossibility and *force majeure*

Suppose you hire a doctor or a lawyer. In the United States, France, and Germany, he is normally liable only if he is negligent. If he is not negligent, he is not liable even if he fails to cure you or win your lawsuit. On the other hand, suppose that you hire someone to transport your goods to a certain destination by a certain date. If he fails to perform, sometimes he is liable even if it was not his fault: for example, if his financial resources are insufficient to hire his crew, or if the crew strikes. But he would not be liable, for example, if war is declared and no ships are allowed to sail. That is so in common law, French law, and German law. And yet jurists in these countries express these conclusions by using very different language.

The language they use traces back to Roman law. It is different because of the different ways in which they altered or deformed Roman law in the process of borrowing from it.

Roman law denied enforcement to some but not all contracts in which performance is impossible. A famous Roman text contained the maxim, "there is no obligation to the impossible."[1] A number of texts excuse a party when performance was impossible at the time the contract was made. Nevertheless, if his performance was initially impossible, a party cannot escape if performance is merely beyond his own power. It must be beyond anyone's power.[2] As later commentators put it, impossibility must be "objective" or "absolute," not "subjective" or "personal." Other texts excused a party's performance if it became impossible after the time it was made. To escape liability, a party then had to prove that he was not at fault. Nevertheless, he could not escape merely because he was not at fault in the ordinary sense of the word. One who borrowed property gratuitously for his own use is liable if he failed to exercise the most scrupulous diligence (*exactissima diligentia*).[3] He was not liable if the property is destroyed by invading enemies or bands of robbers.[4] He was not liable for *vis maior*, that is, for accidents that no one could have prevented.[5] The medieval jurists classified this kind of "fault" as *culpa levissima*—most light fault. From there, one ascended through *culpa levis*, *culpa lata*, and *culpa latior* to *dolus* or intentional wrongdoing, the correct definition of each degree remaining a matter of continual argument.[6] The type of fault for which one was liable was said to depend on for whose benefit the contract was made.

The medieval canon lawyers, however, turned impossibility and fault into basic principles of moral responsibility which the late scholastics then defended on Aristotelian principles. The canonists concluded, after some initial hesitation, that one could not be morally obligated to do the impossible.[7] Such a person was not at fault. In the 13th century, Thomas Aquinas used Aristotle's theory of human responsibility to explain the conclusions of the canonists. Choice was an act of will, and one could only choose what was possible.[8] A promise to do the impossible was not binding.[9] Once impossibility and fault had been interpreted as principles of moral responsibility, it was difficult to harmonize them with the Roman rules. A struggle now began in which the Roman rules were never displaced by Aristotelian principles—as were the rules governing contract formation—nor explained by them—as were the rules governing relief for mistake and unfairness. The late scholastics borrowed the conclusion that one cannot be obligated to keep an impossible promise.[10] They never

1. Dig. 50.17.185.
2. Dig. 45.1.137.
3. Dig. 44.7.1.4.
4. Dig. 13.6.18.pr.
5. Reinhard Zimmermann, *The Law of Obligations Roman Foundations of the Civilian Tradition* (1990), 192–97.
6. *E.g.*, Bartolus de Saxoferrato, *Commentaria Corpus Iuris Civilis* to D. 16.3.32 nos. 13, 16, 26, 27, in *Omnia quae extant opera* (1615).

7. *Glossa ordinaria* to Gratian, *Decretum* (1595), to *dicta Gratiani ante* D. 13, c. 1.
8. Thomas Aquinas, *Summa theologiae* I-II, Q. 13 a. 5 ad 1.
9. *Id.* II-II, Q. 88 a. 2 (vow to do the impossible not binding); Q. 89, a. 7 (oath to do the impossible not binding).
10. Cajetan (Tomasso di Vio), *Commentaria* to Thomas Aquinas, *Summa theologica* (1698), to II-II, q. 113, a. 1; Domenicus Soto, *De iustitia et iure libri decem* (1551), lib. 8,

explained how to reconcile this maxim with the Roman rules. The confusion lasted throughout the natural law era. Pufendorf claimed that the seller was never liable for failing to do the impossible but, if he were at fault in making the promise, the buyer could recover any loss suffered.[11] He had achieved consistency but only by sacrificing the Roman texts.

The 19th century jurists thus inherited a body of law in disarray. The principled explanations of the natural lawyers did not seem to explain the Roman law, which was very hard to explain in any case. As we will see, they borrowed their rules from Roman law, but borrowed selectively.

Common law

Taylor v. Caldwell, (1863) 3 Best & S. 826 (Q.B.)

Blackburn, J. "In this case the plaintiffs and defendants had, on May 27th, 1861, entered into a contract by which the defendants agreed to let the plaintiffs have the use of The Surrey Gardens and Music Hall on four days then to come, viz., June 17th, July 15th, August 5th, and August 19th, for the purpose of giving a series of four grand concerts, and day and night fêtes, at the Gardens and Hall on those days respectively; and the plaintiffs agreed to take the Gardens and Hall on those days, and pay £100 for each day. . . .

After the making of the agreement, and before the first day on which a concert was to be given, the Hall was destroyed by fire. This destruction, we must take it on the evidence, was without the fault of either party, and was so complete that in consequence the concerts could not be given as intended. And the question we have to decide is whether, under these circumstances, the loss which the plaintiffs have sustained is to fall upon the defendants. . . .

There seems no doubt that where there is a positive contract to do a thing, not in itself unlawful, the contractor must perform it or pay damages for not doing it, although in consequence of unforeseen accidents the performance of his contract has become unexpectedly burdensome or even impossible. The law is so laid down in 1 Roll.Abr. 450, Condition (G), and in the note (2) to Walton v. Waterhouse (2 Wms.Saund. 421a, 6th Ed.) And is recognized as the general rule by all the judges in the much discussed case of Hall v. Wright (E.B. & E. 746). But this rule is only applicable when the contract is positive and absolute, and not subject to any condition either express or implied; and there are authorities which, as we think, establish the principle that where, from the nature of the contract, it appears that the parties must from the beginning have known that it could not be fulfilled unless when the time for the fulfilment of the contract arrived some particular specified thing continued to exist, so that, when entering into the contract, they must have contemplated such continuing

q. 2, a. 1; Ludovicus Molina, *De iustitia et iure tractatus* (1614), disp. 271. no. 1; Leonardus Lessius, *De iustitia et iure, ceterisque virtutibus cardinalis libri quartuor* (1628), lib. 2, cap. 10, dub. 10 no. 70.

11. Samuel Pufendorf, *De iure naturae et gentium libri octo* (1688), III.vii.2–3.

existence as the foundation of what was to be done; there, in the absence of any express or implied warranty that the thing shall exist, the contract is not to be construed as a positive contract, but as subject to an implied condition that the parties shall be excused in case, before breach, performance becomes impossible from the perishing of the thing without default of the contractor.

There seems little doubt that this implication tends to further the great object of making the legal construction such as to fulfill the intention of those who entered into the contract. For in the course of affairs men in making such contracts in general would, if it were brought to their minds, say that there should be such a condition. . . .

There is a class of contracts in which a person binds himself to do something which requires to be performed by him in person; and such promises, e.g. promises to marry, or promises to serve for a certain time, are never in practice qualified by an express exception of the death of the party; and therefore in such cases the contract is in terms broken if the promisor dies before fulfilment. Yet it was very early determined that, if the performance is personal, the executors are not liable; Hyde v. The Dean of Windsor (Cro.Eliz. 552, 553). See 2 Wms.Exors. 1560 (5th Ed.), where a very apt illustration is given. 'Thus,' says the learned author, 'if an author undertakes to compose a work, and dies before completing it, his executors are discharged from this contract; for the undertaking is merely personal in its nature, and by the intervention of the contractor's death, has become impossible to be performed.' For this he cites a dictum of Lord Lyndhurst in Marshall v. Broadhurst (1 Tyr. 348, 349) and a case mentioned by Patteson, J., in Wentworth v. Cock (10 A. & E. 42, 45–46). In Hall v. Wright (E.B. & E. 746, 749), Crompton, J., in his judgment, puts another case. 'Where a contract depends upon personal skill, and the act of God renders it impossible, as, for instance, in the case of a painter employed to paint a picture who is struck blind, it may be that the performance might be excused.' . . .

These are instances where the implied condition is of the life of a human being, but there are others in which the same implication is made as to the continued existence of a thing. For example, where a contract of sale is made amounting to a bargain and sale, transferring presently the property in specific chattels, which are to be delivered by the vendor at a future day; there, if the chattels, without the fault of the vendor, perish in the interval, the purchaser must pay the price, and the vendor is excused from performing his contract to deliver, which has thus become impossible. . . .

We think, therefore, that the Music Hall having ceased to exist, without fault of either party, both parties are excused, the plaintiffs from taking the gardens and paying the money, the defendants from performing their promise to give the use of the Hall and Gardens and other things. Consequently the rule must be absolute to enter the verdict for the defendants."

Note on Taylor v. Caldwell: It is hard to speak of a common law rule before the 19th century. Sometimes, English courts sometimes excused a party who could not perform. They did so, for example, when the performance was illegal,[1] or the party obligated to perform had died,[2] or the object bailed had been destroyed by an "act of God,"[3] or a plague suspended construction work.[4] On the other hand, in the case of *Paradine v. Jane*,[5] a lessee was not excused from paying rent when soldiers in the English Civil War made it impossible for him to occupy the property.

Blackburn seems to have been drawing on two different lines of continental authority. One is the doctrine of changed circumstances which we will meet later on. For centuries, continental lawyers had said that every contract is subject to an implied condition that "matters remain in their present state," the so called *clausula rebus sic stantibus*. As we will see, that doctrine can excuse a party even when performance has not become impossible.

As Samuel Williston, Max Rheinstein, and others have noted, Blackburn was also drawing on a Roman rule about impossibility.[6] A contract was void if it was impossible to perform although, again, the defendant could not escape liability by simply proving the performance was impossible for him personally. He had to show that the performance was beyond the power of people generally.[7] Blackburn not only borrowed this rule but extended it. As we saw, the Romans distinguished between whether performance was impossible initially or whether it became so subsequently. In the latter case, liability depended on whether the party who failed to perform was at "fault" but they did not mean fault in the ordinary sense of the term. They meant a party was liable unless he could prove *vis maior*. Here, although Blackburn was borrowing from Roman law, he did not distinguish between initial and subsequent impossibility nor of did he speak of *vis maior*.

French law

French Civil Code

ARTICLE 1137

(1) Whether the agreement is for the benefit of one of the parties or for their common benefit, the obligation to take care so that a thing will be preserved, requires the person obligated to use the care of a reasonable person [literally, of a good father of a family (*bon père de famille*)].

(2) This obligation is more or less extensive for certain contracts whose effects in this regard are explained under the titles that concern them.

ARTICLE 1147

The person who owes a performance shall be ordered to pay damages for non-performance of the obligation or for delay in performing it whenever he fails to establish that non-performance is due to an external cause

---

1. Abbott of Westminster v. Clerke, 1 Dy. 26b, 28b, 73 Eng. Rep. 59, 63 (K.B. 1536).

2. Hyde v. Dean of Windsor, Cro. Eliz. 552, 78 Eng. Rep. 798 (K.B. 1597).

3. Williams v. Hide, Palm. 548 (1624).

4. H. Rolle, Abridgment 450, Cond. (G), p. 10 (London 1668).

5. Aleyn 26, 82 Eng. Rep. 897 (K.B. 1647).

6. Samuel Williston, *The Law of Contracts* (1920), § 1931; Max Rheinstein, *Die Struktur des vertraglichen Schuldverhältnisses im anglo-amerikanischen Recht* (1932), 175.

7. Dig. 45.1.137.

(*cause étrangère*) that cannot be imputed to him provided, moreover, that there is no bad faith on his part.

ARTICLE 1148

No damages are due when the person who owes a performance was prevented from giving or doing what he had bound himself to do, or was caused to do what he was obligated not to do, by an irresistible force (*force majeure*) or an utter accident (*cas fortuit*).

Note: The Code does not speak of "impossibility" as an excuse for failing to perform. Instead, it contains the provisions just quoted.

They are not very clear. Article 1137 suggests that in some contracts at least, a party who fails to perform is liable only if he is at fault in the ordinary sense of the word. Articles 1147–48 say that he is liable unless he proves *cause étrangère*, *force majeure* or *cas fortuit*. *Force majeure* means that performance has been prevented by an irresistible force; *cas fortuit* that it has been prevented by an utter accident; and *cause étrangère* that it has been prevented by an external cause. Nevertheless, it does not matter which of these expressions a party uses to describe the situation since, whatever the expression, he must prove the same thing: that non-performance was due to some event that is external (not simply his own personal lack of skill, judgment or resources) and irresistible (completely outside his control). So at least sometimes a party is liable even if he is not at fault in the ordinary sense.

With variations, the leading 19th century French jurists agreed that the standard of care required by art. 1137(1) is ordinary negligence.[1] Nevertheless, they also agreed that under Articles 1147–48, a party escapes only if he proves that he couldn't perform because of an external irresistible event: tempest, earthquake, war, and so forth.[2] They then sloughed over the contradiction, usually, by asserting or implying that these standards are always or nearly always the same: there is fault when there is no *force majeure*, *cas fortuit* or *cause étrangère*.[3]

A modern French jurist would explain the Code more clearly by using terminology first developed by René Demogue. He said that some contracts entail a duty to use best efforts (*obligation de moyens*) and others entail a duty actually to achieve a specific result (*obligation de résultat*).

---

1. Charles Aubry & Charles Rau, *Cours de droit civil français* 4 (4th ed. 1869–71), § 308 n. 28 (art. 1137 par. 1 sets the general standard; other articles create exceptions that can be extended by analogy to like cases); Charles Demolombe, *Cours de Code Napoléon* 24 (1854–82), § 1137 (art. 1137 par. 1 sets the general standard; par. 2 allows the judge to apply it flexibly); François Laurent, *Principes de droit civil français* 16 (3d ed. 1869–78), § 219, 231 (art. 1137 par. 1 sets the general standard; other articles create exceptions); Leobon Larombière, *Théorie et pratique des obligations* 1 (1857), 400–01 (art. 1137 par. 1 sets a maximum standard of care; other articles reduce it).

2. Aubry & Rau, *Cours* 4: § 308; Demolombe, *Cours* 24: 549–52; Laurent, *Principes* 16: § 256–7; Larombière, *Théorie et pratique* 1: 541–42.

3. See Aubry & Rau *Cours* 4: § 308; Laurent, *Principes* 16: § 256; Larombière, *Théorie et pratique* 1: 541–42. Demolombe did observe that sometimes a party might not be at fault even though no such event had occurred, but he simply noted that the security of transactions requires that the party be held liable. Demolombe, *Cours* 24: § 550.

In the former case, a party was liable only if he was at fault in the ordinary sense. In the latter case he was liable unless he could prove *force majeure, cas fortuit* or *cause étrangère*.[4] Articles 1147 and 1148 apply only in the latter case. French courts decide on a case by case basis which obligations fall into each category.[5]

The reason the Code provisions themselves are not clear is that the drafters did not have a clear idea of what they were doing. They were borrowing scraps of Roman law which came to them through Robert Pothier and Jean Domat. As mentioned earlier, in Roman law, if performance became impossible after a contract was formed, the party who failed to perform was liable only if he was at "fault." But "fault" was not used in the ordinary sense of the word. In certain contracts, a party could not escape merely because he used reasonable efforts to perform. He had to prove the sort of event which the Romans called *vis maior* which, translated into French, is *force majeure*. For example he was not liable if the property is destroyed by invading enemies or bands of robbers.[6]

As we have seen, in Roman law, the kind of "fault" that would excuse a party from a contract depended on the kind of contract he had made, and, in particular, on whether each party or only one of them benefitted from the contract. That view had been adopted by Domat and Pothier, whose opinions usually influenced the drafting committee. This time they did not. Speaking for the committee, Bigot-Préameneu denounced the old view as useless and overly subtle.[7] So Article 1137(1) declared that when a person is charged with looking after an object, there would be one standard of care, that of ordinary negligence, "whether the agreement is for the benefit of one of the parties or for their common benefit." But the drafters did not consistently root out the older view.[8] According to Article 1137(2), the standard "is more or less extensive" for certain contracts. And the standard prescribed by articles 1147–48 is, in effect, liability unless one could prove *vis maior*—which is not liability for fault in any normal sense. The drafters had thus preserved two of the traditional Roman standards for determining whether a contracting party was liable without explaining that they were really different standards and without explaining when to apply one and when to apply the other.

We can now see why the results are much the same in France as in common law jurisdictions even though the rules sound so different. As we saw, the Romans said that a contract was void for impossibility if it was impossible to perform at the time it was made. The performance must be impossible for people generally, however, not just for the debtor. In England, Blackburn borrowed this rule and applied it to contracts that

---

4. René Demogue, *Traité des obligations en général* 5 (1921–33), § 1237.

5. Alex Weill & François Terré, *Droit civil Les Obligations* (1986), § 399–402.

6. Dig. 13.6.18.pr.

7. Bigot-Préameneu, Exposé des motifs, in P. A. Fenet, ed., *Recueil complet des travaux préparatoires du Code Civil* 13 (1836), 230.

8. In addition to the provisions cited in the text, art. 1992 provided that if an agent (*mandataire*) acted gratuitously, his liability for fault would be less "rigorous" then if he received a salary. Art. 804 provided that a person administering an estate would be liable only for "serious faults" (*fautes graves*).

become impossible after they are formed: for example, the music hall burns down. The drafters of the French Civil Code ignored the rule about impossibility. They borrowed from the other Roman rule that if performance becomes impossible after the contract is made, a party is excused for *vis maior* and sometimes if he merely were not at fault. Since this was the only rule they borrowed, in effect, the French drafters extended it to performances that were impossible when the contract was made. The practical results are much the same in common law and French law because almost any time a performance is impossible for people generally, and not just the party who was supposed to perform, some irresistible external event has made the performance impossible. One wonders why the Romans thought they needed two rules instead of one. Anyway, they had two rules, and the common lawyers adopted one, and the French the other.

The "Lando Principles"

The Principles of European Contract Law, Prepared by the Commission on European Contract Law

ARTICLE 4.102 INITIAL IMPOSSIBILITY

A contract is not invalid merely because at the time it was concluded performance of the obligation assumed was impossible, or because a party was not entitled to dispose of the assets to which the contract relates.

ARTICLE 8.108 EXCUSE DUE TO AN IMPEDIMENT

(1) A party's non-performance is excused if it proves that it is due to an impediment beyond its control and that too could not reasonably have been expected to take the impediment into account at the time of the conclusion of the contract, or to have avoided or overcome the impediment or its consequences.

(2) Where the impediment is only temporary the excuse provided by this Article has effect for the period during which the impediment exists. However, if the delay amounts to a fundamental non-performance, the creditor may treat it as such.

The Unidroit Principles

The Unidroit Principles of International Commercial Contracts

ARTICLE 3.3 INITIAL IMPOSSIBILITY

(1) The mere fact that at the time of the conclusion of the contract the performance of the obligation assumed was impossible does not affect the validity of the contract.

(2) The mere fact that at the time of the conclusion of the contract a party was not entitled to dispose of the assets to which the contract relates does not affect the validity of the contract.

ARTICLE 5.4 DUTY TO ACHIEVE A SPECIFIC RESULT; DUTY OF BEST EFFORTS

(1) To the extent that an obligation of a party involves a duty to achieve a specific result, that party is bound to achieve that result.

(2) To the extent that an obligation of a party involves a duty of best efforts in the performance of an activity, that party is bound to make such efforts as would be made by a reasonable person of the same kind in the same circumstances.

ARTICLE 5.5 DETERMINATION OF THE KIND OF DUTY INVOLVED

In determining the extent to which an obligation of a party involves a duty of best efforts in the performance of an activity or a duty to achieve a specific result, regard shall be had, among other factors, to

(a) the way in which the obligation is expressed in the contract;

(b) the contractual price and other terms of the contract;

(c) the degree of risk normally involved in achieving the expected result;

(d) the ability of the other party to influence the performance of the obligation.

ARTICLE 7.1.7 FORCE MAJEURE

(1) Non-performance by a party is excused if that party proves that the non-performance was due to an impediment beyond its control and that it could not reasonably be expected to have taken the impediment into account at the time of the conclusion of the contract or to have avoided or overcome it or its consequences.

(2) When the impediment is only temporary, the excuse shall have effect for such period as is reasonable having regard to the effect of the impediment on the performance of the contract.

German law

Until 2002, the German Civil Code followed Roman law by distinguishing initial from subsequent liability. The Code was then amended so that it did not matter when the impossibility. Retained from the past, however was the principle that liability for an impossible performance depended on whether a party was responsible for the fact that performance became impossible, and he is responsible. According to § 276 of the Code, he was "responsible" only for "willful default and negligence."

The drafters had meant what they said. If a performance was impossible, and it was not the fault of the person who was supposed to perform, why should he be held liable? For several hundred years, many jurists had been insisting that a party who did not perform a contract should only be liable for fault in the ordinary sense. The late scholastics[1] and the natural lawyers[2] did not understand strict liability in contract for much the

---

[1]. Ludovicus Molina, *De iustitia et iure libri decem* (1614), disp. 293 no. 23; Leonardus Lessius, *De iustitia et iure, ceterisque virtutibus cardinalis* (1628), lib. 2 cap. 7 dubs. 6–8.

[2]. Hugo Grotius, *De iure belli ac pacis libri tres* (1646), II.xvii.1; Samuel Pufendorf, *De iure naturae et gentium libri octo* (1688), III.i.2, III.i.6; Jean Barbeyrac, *Le droit de la* *nature et des gens ... par le baron de Pufendorf, traduit du latin* (5th ed. 1734), n. 1 to III.i.2, n. 4 to III.i.6. See generally Reinhard Zimmermann, *The Law of Obligations Roman Foundations of the Civilian Tradition* (1990), 692–93, 1032–34. The natural lawyers generally applied the same principles to liability in both contract and tort. See Grotius, *supra*, II.xvii.1–2;

same reason that they did not understand it in tort. Neither did the 19th century German jurists.[3] If a party had behaved like a reasonable person should, any event that made performance impossible for him was an accident. As Puchta said, liability that went beyond fault was liability for chance.[4] What could be the point of distinguishing between an accident and an utter accident? The drafters of the German Civil Code agreed although they made an exception when "what is owed is designated only by species."

But even before the reforms of 2002, the German courts were unable to live with that position. As a result, cases in Germany come out in much the same way as in France, England and the United States.[5] In some contracts, a party can escape liability if he was not at fault. But in others—the sort that the French would call contracts to achieve a particular result—he is liable even if he was not at fault if the performance became impossible because of an event that is normally within a person's control: if he failed to perform because he lacked the financial resources to do so,[6] or materials were delivered to him late,[7] or his suppliers failed him.[8] Moreover, the event that prevents performance must be one that the parties would not foresee or take into account at the time the contract was formed.[9]

And so, by implication, this idea of when a party was excused was accepted by the drafters of the 2002 reforms.

2. Changed circumstances

a. Origins

The Romans did not have a doctrine of changed circumstances. This doctrine was an invention of the medieval Canon lawyers. Gratian's *Decretum* contained a passage in which St. Augustine, following Cicero, said that one need not keep a promise to return a sword to a person who has become insane.[1] A gloss to the *Decretum* explained that "this condition is always understood: if matters remain in the same state."[2] Baldus

Pufendorf, *supra*, III.i.2–3; Barbeyrac, *supra*, n. 1 to III.i.3.

3. Karl Ludwig Arndts, *Lehrbuch der Pandekten* (14th ed. 1889), § 86 n. 3; Aloys Brinz & Philipp Lotmar, *Lehrbuch der Pandekten* 2 (2nd ed. 1892), § 267 n. 26; Georg Friedrich Puchta, *Pandekten* (2nd ed. 1844), § 266; Bernhard Windscheid, *Lehrbuch des Pandektenrechts* 1 (7th ed. 1891), § 101; Karl Vangerow, *Leitfaden für Pandekten-Vorlesungen* 1 (1847), § 107.

4. Puchta, *Pandekten* § 266. Similarly, see Windscheid, *Lehrbuch* 1: § 101.

5. Manfred Löwisch in Staudinger, *Kommentar zum Bürgerlichen Gesetzbuch* (13th ed. 1994) no. 11 to § 282; Peter Schlechtriem, "Rechtvereinheitlichung in Europa und Schuldrechtreform in Deutschland," *Zeitschrift für Europäisches Privatrecht* 1 (1993), 228–29.

6. Emmerich in *Münchener Kommentar zum Bürgerlichen Gesetzbuch* (3rd ed. 1995), no. 3 to § 285; Löwisch in Staudinger, *Kommentar* no. 12 to § 285; Frank Peters in Staudinger, *Kommentar* no. 13 to § 635.

7. Battes in Erman, *Handkommentar zum Bürgerlichen Gesetzbuch* (9th ed., 1993), no. 2 to § 285.

8. Emmerich in *Münchener Kommentar* no. 3 to § 285.

9. Emmerich *Münchener Kommentar* no. 3 to § 285; Peters in Staudinger, *Kommentar* no. 10 to § 635; Herbert Wiedemann, in Soergel, *Kommentar zum Bürgerlichen Gesetzbuch* (12th ed., 1990), no. 6 to § 285.

1. Gratian, *Decretum* C. 22, q. 2, c. 14.

2. *Glossa ordinaria* to Gratian, *Decretum* to "furens" to C. 22, q. 2, c. 14.

then read the doctrine into civil law. All promises were subject to such a condition.[3]

The canon lawyers did not have a theoretical explanation for the doctrine. It just seemed reasonable to them. An explanation was proposed by Thomas Aquinas on the basis of an idea he took from Aristotle and was eventually adopted by the late scholastics in the 16th century.

The idea was Aristotle's theory of "equity." According to Aristotle, since laws are made to serve purposes, circumstances can always arise in which obeying the law will no longer serve the purpose for which it was made. Under these circumstances, the law maker would not want it to be obeyed. Therefore, as a matter of "equity" it should not be obeyed. Aquinas said that a promise is like a law that a person makes for himself. Therefore, like a law, a promise is not binding not binding in circumstances where the promisor would not have intended to be bound.[4]

Aquinas' explanation was adopted by late scholastics such as Lessius.[5] Again, the principle was preserved by the northern natural lawyers of the 17th and 18th century. The promisor is not bound if the change of circumstances concerns the "unique reason" or "unique cause" for his promise[6] or the "presumption of some fact" on which his consent was conditioned.[7] Grotius used this doctrine to explain relief for mistake as well.[8]

Again, with the rise of the will theories of contract in the 19th century, this doctrine went into eclipse. To most jurists, enforcing the will of the parties meant enforcing what the parties had consciously and expressly willed. Nevertheless, a few defenders of the doctrine explained relief by saying the existence of certain circumstances was a tacit or implied condition of the contract. According to the French jurist Larombière, an "error in motive" affected the validity of a contract only if the parties so wished, but a judge would determine whether they so wished by examining "according to the circumstances, if the fact alleged as a motive was taken to be the determining reason (*raison déterminante*) and if the consent depended on its reality."[9] The German jurist Windscheid said that the continuation of certain circumstances could be an "undeveloped condition" of the contract, "undeveloped" in the sense that it was not expressly willed by the parties.

The doctrine forced itself on the attention of Anglo-American jurists when the Coronation Cases were decided in the early 20th century. Rooms had been rented along the route of the coronation procession of Edward VII for a single day and at a suitably enhanced price. When Edward became ill, the procession was postponed. In *Krell v. Henry*, relief was granted on

---

3. Baldus de Ubaldis, *Commentaria Corpus Iuris Civilis* (1577), to Dig. 12.4.8.

4. Thomas Aquinas, *Summa theologiae* II-II, q, 88, a. 10; q. 89, a. 9.

5. Lessius, *De iustitia et iure,* lib. 2, cap. 17, dub. 10; cap. 18, dub. 10.

6. Grotius, *De iure belli ac pacis*, II.xvi.25.2; Barbeyrac, *Le droit de la nature*, to

n. 3 to III.vi.6; Christian Wolff, *Ius naturae methodo scientifica pertractatum* 3 (1764), § 504.

7. Pufendorf, *De iure naturae ac gentium* III.vi.6.

8. Grotius, *De iure belli ac pacis* II.xi.6.

9. Leobon Larombière, *Théorie et pratique des obligations* 1 (1857), 282–83.

the grounds, again, that an implied condition of the contract had not been fulfilled.[10] Anglo-American jurists repeated this explanation.

For most 19th century jurists, the obvious objection to the doctrine was that a tacit or undeveloped condition was one that the parties never consciously willed. They had never thought about the change in circumstances, let alone agreed on what should happen if the change occurred. The judge said the contract was subject to such a condition in order to obtain what he thought was a sensible and fair result. As Williston said, "any qualification of the promise is based on the unfairness or unreasonableness of giving it the absolute force which its words clearly state."[11] French courts in the 19th century refused to give relief for change of circumstances, and, except in administrative courts where claims are brought against the government, they still refuse to do so. The drafters of the German Civil Code did not include such a doctrine. And yet, as we will see, in Germany and the United States, the doctrine of changed circumstances, like relief for unfairness, has seen a renaissance.

b. Modern law

English law

Krell v. Henry, [1903] 2 K.B. 740

"The plaintiff, Paul Krell, sued the defendant, C.S. Henry, for £ 50, being the balance of a sum of £ 75, for which the defendant had agreed to hire a flat at 56A, Pall Mall on the days of June 26 and 27, for the purpose of viewing the processions to be held in connection with the coronation of His Majesty [King Edward VII]. The defendant denied his liability, and counterclaimed for the return of the sum of £ 25, which had been paid as a deposit, on the ground that, the processions not having taken place owing to the serious illness of the King, there had been a total failure of consideration for the contract entered into by him."

Vaughn Williams, L.J. "The real question in this case is the extent of the application in English law of the principle of the Roman law which has been adopted and acted on in many English decisions, and notably in the case of Taylor v. Caldwell. . . . I do not think that the principle of the civil law as introduced into the English law is limited to cases in which the event causing the impossibility of performance is the destruction or nonexistence of some thing which is the subject matter of the contract, or of some condition or state of things expressly specified as a condition of it. I think that you first have to ascertain, not necessarily from the terms

---

10. [1903] 2 K.B. 740.

11. Samuel Williston, *The Law of Contracts* (1920), § 1937. Instead of speaking of implied conditions, Williston said that relief was given because of a "presumed assumption by the parties of some vital supposed fact." He acknowledged that "[t]he only evidence . . . of such mutual assumption is, generally, that the court thinks a reasonable person, that is, the court itself, would not have contemplated taking the risk of the existence of the fact in question." *Id.* Thus although Williston did not talk about "implied conditions," he asked the same question: what was sensible for the parties to have done.

of the contract, but, if required, from necessary inferences, drawn from surrounding circumstances recognized by both contracting parties, what is the substance of the contract, and then to ask the question whether that substantial contract needs for its foundation the assumption of the existence of a particular state of things. If it does, this will limit the operation of the general words, and in such a case, if the contract becomes impossible of performance by reason of the nonexistence of the state of things assumed by both contracting parties as the foundation of the contract, there will be no breach of the contract thus limited. . . .

In my judgment the use of the rooms was let and taken for the purpose of seeing the Royal procession. . . . And in my judgment the taking place of those processions along the proclaimed route, which passed 56A, Pall Mall, was regarded by both contracting parties as the foundation of the contract. . . .

Tsakiroglou & Co., Ltd. v. Noblee & Thorl G.m.b.h., [1962] A.C. 93 (H.L.)

"By a contract dated Oct. 4, 1956, the appellants agreed to sell to the respondents three hundred tons of Sudanese groundnuts c.i.f. Hamburg, shipment during November/December, 1956. . . . [A]t the date of the contract, the usual and normal route for the shipment of Sudanese groundnuts from Port Sudan to Hamburg was via the Suez Canal. Sufficient groundnuts were held at Port Sudan to the appellants' order to fulfil the contract, and space was booked on ships for them. Following the military operations against Egypt by British and French armed forces, the Suez Canal was blocked to shipping on Nov. 2, 1956, and it remained blocked until April, 1957, but the appellants could have transported the groundnuts via the Cape of Good Hope during November/December, 1956. The appellants did not ship any groundnuts. . . ."

Lord Reid. "My Lords, the appellants agreed to sell to the respondents three hundred tons of Sudan groundnuts at £ 50 per ton c.i.f. Hamburg. Admittedly the groundnuts had to be shipped from Port Sudan. The usual and normal route at the date of the contract was via Suez Canal. Shipment was to be November/December, 1956, but, on Nov. 2, 1956, the canal was closed to traffic and it was not reopened until the following April. . . . The freight via Suez would have been about £7 10s. per ton. The freight via the Cape was increased by stages. It was £15 per ton after Dec. 13. I shall assume in favour of the appellants that the proper comparison is between £7 10s. and £15 per ton. . . . The question now is whether, by reason of the closing of the Suez route, the contract had been ended by frustration. . . .

There might be cases where damage to the goods was a likely result of the longer voyage which twice crossed the Equator, or, perhaps, the buyer could be prejudiced by the fact that the normal duration of the voyage via Suez was about three weeks, whereas the normal duration via the Cape was about seven weeks. But there is no suggestion in the case that the longer voyage could damage the groundnuts or that the delay could have caused loss to these buyers of which they could complain. Counsel for the appellants rightly did not argue that this increase in the freight payable by the appellants was sufficient to frustrate the contract, and I need not, therefore, consider what the result might be if the increase had reached an astronomical figure. The route by the Cape was certainly practicable. There could be, on the findings in the case, no objection to it by the buyers, and the only objection to it from the point of view of the sellers was that it cost them more. And it was not excluded by the contract. Where, then, is there any basis for frustration? It appears to me that the only possible way of reaching a conclusion that this contract was frustrated would be to concentrate on the altered nature of the voyage. I have no means of judging whether, looking at the matter from the point of view of a ship whose route from Port Sudan was altered from via Suez to via the Cape, the difference would be so radical as to involve frustration, and I express no opinion about that. As I understood the argument, it was based on the assumption that the voyage was the manner of performing the sellers' obligations and that, therefore, its nature was material. I do not think so. What the sellers had to do was simply to find a ship proceeding by what was a practicable and now a reasonable route—if, perhaps, not yet a usual route—to pay the freight and obtain a proper bill of lading, and to furnish the necessary documents to the buyer. That was their manner of performing their obligations, and, for the reasons which I have given, I think that such changes in these matters as were made necessary fell far short of justifying a finding of frustration."

Lord Hodson. "Nothing was proved or found as to the nature of the goods or other circumstances which would render the route round the Cape unreasonable or impracticable, and this route was at all times available. Unless shipment by the Cape route was so onerous to the sellers as to make the performance of the contract fundamentally different in kind from any performance they had promised, the contract of Oct. 4, 1956, remained binding between the parties."

Viscount Simonds. "[T]he seller may be put to greater cost; his profit may be reduced or even disappear. But it hardly needs reasserting that an increase of expense is not a ground of frustration. . . ."

Law in the United States

Mineral Park Land Co. v. Howard, 172 Cal., 289, 156 P. 458 (1916)

Defendants made a contract with public authorities to build a concrete bridge across a ravine on land owned by the plaintiff. They made a contract with the plaintiff in which he granted them the right to haul gravel and earth from his land, and the defendants agreed to take from the land all the gravel and earth necessary for the fill and cement work on the bridge. Defendants used 101,000 cubic yards for this work but obtained 50,869 cubic yards from persons other than plaintiff. The trial court found that the plaintiff's land contained over 101,000 cubic yards of earth and gravel but that only the 50,131 cubic yards taken by defendants were above water. To take more, the defendants would have to have used a steam dredger, and the earth and gravel taken could not have been used before drying it. According to the trial court, the defendants took all the earth and gravel from plaintiff's land "that was practical to take and remove from a financial standpoint." To take more would have cost ten or twelve times the usual cost per yard which would have been possible but not "advantageous or practical." The trial court held that the defendant was excused. In affirming the decision, the California Supreme Court said:

"When [the parties] stipulated that all of the earth and gravel needed for this purpose should be taken from plaintiff's land, they contemplated and assumed that the land contained the requisite quantity, available for use. The defendants were not binding themselves to take what was not there. And, in determining whether the earth and gravel were 'available,' we must view the conditions in a practical and reasonable way. Although there was gravel on the land, it was so situated that the defendants could not take it by ordinary means, not except at a prohibitive cost. To all fair intents then, it was impossible for defendants to take it. . . .

A thing is impossible in legal contemplation when it is not practicable; and a thing is impracticable when it can only be done at an excessive and unreasonable cost. 1 Beach on Cont. § 216. We do not mean to intimate that the defendants could excuse themselves by showing the existence of conditions which would make the performance of their obligation more expensive than they had anticipated, or which would entail a loss upon them. But, where the difference in cost is so great as here, and has the effect, as found, of making performance impracticable, the situation is not different from that of a total absence of earth and gravel."

Transatlantic Financing Corp. v. United States, 363 F.2D 312 (D.C. Cir. 1966)

On October 2, 1956, Transatlantic Financing Corp. contracted with the United States to carry a full cargo of wheat from a United States Gulf port to a port in Iran. On July 26, the government of Egypt had nationalized the Suez Canal. On October 27, the ship operated by Transatlantic Financing left Galvaston on a course that would have taken her through Gibraltar and the Suez Canal. Israel invaded Egypt on October 29, Britain and France did so on October 31. On November 2, the Egyptian government closed the canal. On or about November 7, a Transatlantic employee asked an employee of the United States to agree to additional compensation for a voyage around the Cape of Good Hope. This request was refused. The ship changed course and reached Iran by sailing around the Cape.

Skelly Wright, J. "When the issue [of impossibility] is raised, the court is asked to construct a condition of performance based on the changed circumstances, a process which involves at least three reasonably definable steps. First, a contingency—something unexpected—must have occurred. Second, the risk of the unexpected occurrence must not have been allocated either by agreement or by custom. Finally, occurrence of the contingency must have rendered performance commercially impracticable. Unless the court finds these three requirements satisfied, the plea of impossibility must fail.

The first requirement was met here. It seems reasonable, where no route is mentioned in a contract, to assume the parties expected performance by the usual and customary route at the time of contract. . . .

Proof that the risk of a contingency's occurrence has been allocated may be expressed in or implied from the agreement. . . . If anything, the circumstances surrounding this contract indicate that the risk of the Canal's closure may be deemed to have been allocated to Transatlantic. We know or may safely assume that the parties were aware, as were most commercial men with interests affected by the Suez situation [citation omitted], that the Canal might become a dangerous area. No doubt the tension affected freight rates, and it is arguable that the risk of closure became part of the dickered terms. Uniform Commercial Code § 2-615, comment 8. We do not deem the risk of closure so allocated, however. Foreseeability or even recognition of a risk does not necessarily prove its allocation. Compare Uniform Commercial Code § 2-615, Comment 1; Restatement, Contracts § 457 (1932). Parties to a contract are not always able to provide for all the possibilities of which they are aware, sometimes because they cannot agree, often simply because they are too busy. Moreover, that some abnormal risk was contemplated is probative but does not necessarily establish an allocation of the risk of the contingency which actually occurs. In this case, for example, nationalization by Egypt of the Canal Corporation and formation of the Suez Users Group did not necessarily indicate that the Canal would be blocked even if a confrontation resulted. The surrounding circumstances do indicate, however, a willingness by Transatlantic to assume abnormal risks, and this fact should legitimately cause us to judge the impracticability of performance by an alternative route in stricter terms than we would were the contingency unforeseen.

We turn then to the question whether occurrence of the contingency rendered performance commercially impracticable under the circumstances of this case. The goods shipped were not subject to harm from the longer, less temperate Southern route. The vessel and crew were fit to proceed around the Cape. Transatlantic was no less able than the United States to purchase insurance to cover the contingency's occurrence. If anything, it is more reasonable to expect owner–operators of vessels to insure against the hazards of war. They are in the best position to calculate the cost of performance by alternative routes (and therefore to estimate the amount of insurance required), and are undoubtedly sensitive to international troubles which uniquely affect the demand for and cost of their services. The only factor operating here in appellant's favor is the added expense, allegedly $43,972.00 above and beyond the contract price of $305,842.92, of extending a 10,000 mile voyage by approximately 3,000 miles. While it may be an overstatement to say that increased cost and difficulty of performance never constitute impracticability, to justify relief there must be more of a variation between expected cost and the cost of performing by an available alternative than is present in this case, where the promisor can legitimately be presumed to have accepted some degree of abnormal risk, and where impracticability is urged on the basis of added expense alone."

The "Lando Principles"

The Principles of European Contract Law, prepared by the Commission on European Contract Law

ARTICLE 2.117 CHANGE OF CIRCUMSTANCES

(1) A party is bound to fulfill his obligations even if performance has become more onerous, whether because the cost of performance has increased or because the value of the performance he receives has diminished.

(2) If, however, performance of the contract becomes excessively onerous because of a change in circumstances, the parties are bound to enter into negotiations with a view to adapting the contract or terminating it, provided that:

(a) If a change of circumstances occurred after the time of conclusion of the contract, or had already occurred at that time but was not and could not reasonably have been known to the parties; and

(b) the possibility of a change of circumstances was not one which could reasonably have been taken into account at the time of conclusion of the contract; and

(c) the risk of the change of circumstances is not one which, according to the contract, the party affected should be required to bear.

(3) If the parties fail to reach agreement within a reasonable period, the court may:

(a) terminate the contract at a date and on terms to be determined by the court; or

(b) adapt the contract in order to distribute between the parties in a just and equitable manner the losses and gains resulting from the change of circumstances; and

(c) in either case, award damages for the loss suffered through the other party refusing to negotiate or breaking off negotiations in bad faith.

The Unidroit Principles

The Unidroit Principles of International Commercial Contracts

ARTICLE 6.2.1 CONTRACT TO BE OBSERVED

Where the performance of a contract becomes more onerous for one of the parties, that party is nevertheless bound to perform its obligations subject to the following provisions on hardship.

ARTICLE 6.2.2 DEFINITION OF HARDSHIP

There is hardship where the occurrence of events fundamentally alters the equilibrium of the contract either because the cost of a party's performance has increased or because the value of the performance a party receives has diminished, and

(a) the events occur or become known to the disadvantaged party after the conclusion of the contract;

(b) the events could not reasonably have been taken into account by the disadvantaged party at the time of the conclusion of the contract;

(c) the events are beyond the control of the disadvantaged party; and

(d) the risk of events was not assumed by the disadvantaged party.

ARTICLE 6.2.3 EFFECTS OF HARDSHIP

(1) In case of hardship the disadvantaged party is entitled to request renegotiations. The request shall be made without undue delay and shall indicate the grounds on which it is based.

(2) The request for renegotiation does not in itself entitle the disadvantaged party to withhold performance.

(3) Upon failure to reach agreement within a reasonable time either party may resort to the court.

(4) If the court finds hardship it may, if reasonable,

(a) terminate the contract at a date and on terms to be fixed; or

(b) adapt the contract with a view to restoring its equilibrium.

German law

German Civil Code

§ 242 [PERFORMANCE IN GOOD FAITH]

The party owing a performance is bound to perform in the way which is required by good faith (*Treu und Glauben*) having regard to the ordinary usage.

Note: The following provision was enacted in 2002 to amend the German Civil Code codifying, as we will see, a doctrine the courts had already developed by applying § 242.

German Civil Code

§ 313 [DESTRUCTION OF THE BASIS OF THE TRANSACTION (*GESCHÄFTSGRUNDLAGE*)]

(1) If circumstances that formed the basis of the transaction have seriously changed thereafter and the parties would not have entered into the contract or one with the same content had they foreseen the change, then the adaptation of the contract can be required insofar as for one of the parties, taking into account all of the circumstances of the particular case, and especially the division or risks provided for by the contract or by statute, adherence to the contract no longer can be expected.

(2) It is equivalent to a change of circumstances when essential conceptions which formed the basis of the contract have proven false.

(3) If an adaptation of the contract is not possible or unreasonable in part, then the disadvantaged party can withdraw from the contract. . . .

Reichsgericht, 21 September 1920, RGZ 100, 129

"In 1912, the plaintiff rented the defendant business space in its Berlin property for a period ending on April 1, 1915. The contract continued to run until the end of March, 1920 because the defendant availed itself of the right [contained in the lease] to renew for five years. Under article 20 of the contract, the defendant could require that steam be furnished for industrial purposes. The plaintiff considers that it is justified, because of the basically changed conditions since the time when the contract was concluded, in demanding additional compensation, besides the compensation paid under article 20, for the steam provided between September 1, 1917, through the end of July, 1919. The plaintiff also seeks to establish either that the contract for the delivery of steam was invalid or that in the future there was no obligation to deliver steam unless a reasonable price was paid. Both the *Landgericht* and the court of appeal gave judgment for the defendant, but the plaintiff's appeal [*Revision*] has been successful. . . .

The court of appeal properly refused to accept the plaintiff's argument, according to which, under a proper interpretation, article 20, number 6, of the contract . . . 'the price for industrial steam is determined as follows,' as well as other contractual language, requires a change in the price of steam when a fundamental change in conditions occurs. The discussion of the court of appeal on this point is basically directed to factual matters and does not reveal any error as to the law. Nor can any objections be raised to the discussion of the court of appeal in which it rejected the attempt of the plaintiff to find a basis for its claim by seeing in the defendant's hardheaded insistence upon the contract price a violation of good morals under § 138 of the Civil Code, from which would follow, according to the plaintiff's further argument, the present invalidity of the contractual stipulations as to the price of steam so that the possibility of establishing a fair price for steam under the provisions of § 632 or § 812 of the Civil Code would be open.

However, the request of the plaintiff appears to be justified from the point of view of the so-called *clausula rebus sic stantibus*.

The Civil Code recognizes this principle only as applied to a few special cases and, as this Senate said recently in a decision of 8 July 1920, RGZ 99, 259, the *Reichsgericht* has not recognized this as a general principle.

However, the *Reichsgericht* has recognized, in a series of decisions of this and other Senates in the last few years, in exceptional cases, the effect upon existing contracts of the collapse of, and changes in, all economic relations brought about by the unexpected course and conclusion of the war. The court has held the request of one party for the dissolution of a contractual relationship to be justified when it could no longer be expected, from the economic point of view, that the party to the contract carry it out under the new, completely changed conditions. This rule found and finds support in the positive written law in §§ 242 (157) and 325 of the Civil Code. If, under the first of these provisions, good faith (*Treu und Glauben*) regulates the debtor's duty to perform as well as the creditor's right of performance—his right to the performance—then, under this provision, the performance of a contract can no longer be owed or demanded when, as a result of a complete change in conditions, the performance has become completely different from the performance originally contemplated and desired by both parties. And if, in § 325 of the Civil Code, under impossibility not only factual but also economic impossibility is to be understood, the *clausula rebus sic stantibus* is, to this extent, clearly contained in the code.

In the cases decided earlier, the situation was such that one party to the contract demanded a complete dissolution of the contractual bond on the ground of completely changed conditions. In the present case both parties desire to continue the contract or have continued it. One of them, here the plaintiff, demands in connection with the continuation of the contract an increase in the contract price. This demand is based upon the assertion that its own performance, as a result of the complete change in all the important relationships, has, economically speaking, become so entirely different from that created upon the conclusion of the contract, that, if the other performance is not changed, there would be a completely unsupportable disproportion, economically speaking, between the two performances, so that good faith requires that the other performance be changed. The Senate could not, assuming the correctness of the plaintiff's assertion, refuse to recognize the propriety of his request. In the decision of July 8 of this year, discussed above (RGZ 99, 260), this Senate accepted the point of view that in such a case fairness requires a corresponding change in the contractual performance of the other party, and the Senate holds to this point of view now and for the instant case. To be sure this Senate in a decision of 4 May 1915 (RGZ 86, 398) and again in a later decision of 3 July 1917 (RGZ 90, 375) stated that the judge cannot adjust relations between the parties in order to relieve the hardships of war. But the first and highest task of the judge is to recognize in his decisions the imperative demands of life and in this matter to let himself be led by his experience. It is now the Senate's conviction that the statement of this Senate [that contractual relations could not be modified to relieve the hardships of war] can no longer be supported as a strict, general proposition. The statement has become outmoded due to the experience that the Senate has had during the subsequent course of war and especially due to the unexpected outcome of the war and the subsequent, and also unexpected, overturning of all economic relations. These conditions clearly require an interference by the judge with existing contractual relations if an unbearable condition in which good faith and every requirement of justice and fairness are ignored is not to be created. The point of contact with positive law, which is considered desirable or necessary, is found in the above-discussed provisions of the Civil Code. If the dissolution of the whole contractual relationship is justified upon the demand of one of the parties, then it seems to us still more justifiable to change a single contractual stipulation in a contractual relationship that the parties desire to continue when good faith, fairness, and justice require this. Moreover, the thought is also warranted that when a contractual performance has become economically impossible due to changes in conditions, a gap in the contact arises that the judge must fill as in the case of other contractual gaps.

But in order to prevent from the very beginning every misuse of this principle three things must be required for its application:

First, as has already been repeatedly noted, both parties must desire the continuation of the contract. The case of compulsory continuation cannot be considered here. Second, only very special and very exceptional changes in circumstances, such as have now been brought about by the war, can bring about the result described. The mere circumstance that a later change in conditions was not foreseen and could not have been foreseen does not suffice. Third, in a case of this sort an adjustment of the interests on each side must take place. A change cannot take place only in favor of the person who suffers under the new conditions suffers because of the continuation of the contract, but one must also consider the interests of the other party who in the future must give more or something else in performing. The whole disadvantage cannot be placed on him, so that the condition now becomes unsupportable for him and fairness and justice are not observed. Instead the damages must be fairly apportioned between both parties. Proper finding of this adjustment depends upon the experience of the judge and his understanding judgment of the reciprocal relations.

If one considers the instant case from this point of view the decision below is at least supportable. The plaintiff showed that because of the enormous increase in coal and other prices, it had added the amount of 89,000 Reichsmarks to the payment made by the defendant under the contract for the steam delivered in the period between September 1, 1917 and the end of July 1919, and thus had a clear loss in this amount. In this connection it should be noted that the yearly rental for the space rented to the defendant amounted to only 9,362 Reichsmarks. The condition in question will be most clearly seen, however, in the fact that the Rent Office in Berlin raised by more than ten times the contract price the price for the steam to be delivered by the plaintiff to the defendant in the period from March 31, 1920, the end of the contract, to March 31, 1921, the time to which the Rent Office extended the lease the plaintiff had terminated. In view of this fact and the other clearly apparent relations, the argument of the judge on appeal, that the plaintiff merely miscalculated when the contract was concluded by not considering the consequences of a war, cannot be accepted. Faulty calculations when a contract is concluded do not, of course, constitute a basis for a change in prices that were agreed upon. But even if one wished to agree with the argument of the judge on appeal that the plaintiff should perhaps have taken the consequences of a possible war into consideration, one cannot claim that when the contract was concluded in 1912, the plaintiff should have given any consideration, in view of the situation of the German Reich at that time, to the possibility of such a war with such a size, such an outcome, and such effects, or that it could have taken such a war into consideration. No one in Germany had, or could have had, any notion of such a thing; the events were beyond human prognostication. The judge on appeal thus did a clear wrong to the plaintiff, when, because the plaintiff did not consider the consequences of a possible war, he put the consequences of the present war in the plaintiff's relationship with the defendant upon the plaintiff alone. That the failure to have a war clause in the contract cannot prejudice the plaintiff needs no further explanation. . . ."

Reichsgericht, 29 November 1921, RGZ 103, 177

"In October, 1918, the plaintiff bought ten tons of iron wire for immediate delivery from the defendant. When the defendant failed to make delivery, the plaintiff brought . . . an action for damages for nonperformance. The defendant based his defense on changed conditions. A judgment in the court of first instance for the defendant was reversed on appeal and judgment entered for the plaintiff. This decision has been overturned on appeal [*Revision*].

The defendant argues that because of changes that arose since the contract was concluded, it cannot now be expected to perform the contract. The court of appeal had the following to say on this point: 'The defendant's position, that the contract was terminated due to subsequent impossibility, is not acceptable. It would be acceptable only if the collapse [of Germany] had brought about a complete change in economic conditions and such a considerable increase in prices that the performance of the contract would entail economic ruin for the defendant.' This, the court of appeal said, was not claimed. The appeal quite properly challenges this analysis. That analysis shows a position that is too narrow from every point of view. The court of appeal should have considered the question not only from the point of view of impossibility, but, above all, should have determined whether the performance could have been expected in good faith (*Treu und Glauben*) taking into account ordinary usage. The court of appeal's analysis is also too narrow in that it makes the decision turn upon whether performance would have resulted in economic ruin for the obligee. It was not claimed that this would result, nor, apparently, could it have been claimed. Where this can be shown it is, of course, quite decisive. But such a showing is not indispensable. For such a requirement clearly does not correspond to the idea that lies behind the *clausula rebus sic stantibus* doctrine and justifies its results. In the first place the requirement of economic ruin leads to a difference in treatment depending upon a party's wealth. . . . The *clausula rebus sic stantibus* doctrine is rather justified by the reciprocal nature of bilateral contracts of exchange. . . . In such a contract it must be assumed that the parties concluding the contract intended to enter into a fair contract of exchange, one in which each side is ready to give the other a performance that this latter considers as a full equivalent for his own performance. In general, it is true that each party has to look out for his own interests and that the contract remains effective even though one or both parties are mistaken relative to past or future events. But the case is otherwise if the events so change values, especially the value of money, that the obligee would receive for his performance a counter-performance that no longer comes even near to containing the equivalent that the contract had contemplated. The obligor violates the requirement of good faith when he insists upon the performance under such circumstances.

The decisions of the *Reichsgericht* that emphasize that the performance will cause the obligee's economic ruin are not contrary to what has been said. In these cases, the defendant actually claimed that performance would result in his economic ruin and it is quite understandable, in view of the difficulty of drawing the proper line in these cases, why decisive importance was placed on this consideration. This was the case in the decision of the Third Senate reported in RGZ 100, 135. It is true that a decision of the same Senate, reported in RGZ 102, 273, stated as a general proposition that the *clausula rebus sic stantibus* doctrine was applicable when the performance was commercially impossible only when the performance alone, or together with other obligations, would cause the commercial ruin of the obligee or bring him to the brink of such ruin. . . . But in this case the Third Senate also went on to consider closely the particular facts of the case. It reached the conclusion that the increase in prices, and the losses connected with performance, were not sufficient to justify the defense. That the Third Senate was adopting the general proposition that commercial ruin was a prerequisite for the application of the *clausula rebus sic stantibus* is even more doubtful when it is remembered that such a decision would have placed the Third Senate in clear disagreement with previous decisions of the *Reichsgericht* and could, therefore, not have been rendered without calling upon the Combined Senate to decide the case (RGZ 93, 341; RGZ 94, 68; RGZ 100, 264; cf. also RGZ 99, 258)."

Reichsgericht, 28 November 1923, RGZ 107, 78

"The plaintiff is the owner of real property entered on the land register of the former German court in Lüderitzbucht [in Africa]. The defendant has been, since 1913, the holder of a mortgage for 13,000 Reichsmarks, which was noted on the land register. The mortgage debt fell due on April 1, 1920. The plaintiff, in payment of the principal obligation and of overdue interest, paid the defendant 18,980 Reichsmarks through a bank. The plaintiff seeks a judgment ordering the defendant to turn over the mortgage papers and to agree to the extinguishing of the mortgage. The defendant refused to do this on the ground that the debt must either be paid in the hard currency of the former German protectorate in Southwest Africa or in money of corresponding value. The *Landgericht* gave judgment for the plaintiff and was upheld by the *Kammergericht* on appeal. The defendant's appeal [*Revision*] is successful. . . .

B. *If Berlin were the place of performance*:

In this case . . . it is necessary to answer the question of whether, under German law, the defendant, as mortgage-creditor, can demand a revalorization of the claim secured by the mortgage in view of the heavy inflation in German paper money. . . .

It cannot be assumed that the extent of the inflation was not great enough when the mortgage fell due (April 1, 1920) so that the legal possibility of a revalorization was excluded from the very beginning. The cost-of-living index had at that time already risen by about ten times; judging from a quotation for April 1920, the gold Reichsmark was about 60 (paper) Reichsmarks to the dollar; in February and March, 1920, the Reichsmark had stood still higher at 270 (paper) Reichsmarks to the pound sterling, quoted at 15 (paper) Reichsmarks. The purchasing power of the paper Reichsmark had thus already fallen considerably on April 1, 1920. Nonetheless, initially, it is the job of the court of appeal to decide whether the factual requirements for a revalorization of mortgage debts . . . were present at this time. . . .

If the court of appeal concludes that the factual requirements for a revalorization of the debt were not present in the spring of 1920 and that the defendant was in default due to his failure to accept payment in the proffered paper money, it will then be necessary to investigate whether the defendant as a result lost the right, in view of the later, heavy inflation of the German currency, to demand a revalorization of his debt (cf. on this point RGZ 106, 422).

The legal possibility of a revalorization of mortgage debts is to be recognized under the German law now in force, especially under § 242 of the Civil Code. In the case of mortgage debts, as a rule—at least when paper money is taken as a basis—the debtor has received a corresponding increase in value due to the considerably increased value of the land. Whether this increase in value has occurred with reference to the property located in Lüderitzbucht that is involved in the instant case must be determined by the *Kammergericht*.

It is not important whether—as the plaintiff argues—the admissibility of revalorization of mortgage debts was legally recognized in 1920 or whether revalorization was accepted later, under the influence of continuing inflation. Incorrect legal conceptions of the year 1920 are not decisive today.

Under § 242 of the Civil Code, the requirements of good faith (*Treu und Glauben*), taking into account commercial practice, must be considered in the individual case. A fair consideration of the interests of both sides is required. It follows from this that a general principle requiring the revalorization of every mortgage debt cannot be established. Nor will the extent of the revalorization . . . be the same in each case. It will be necessary to take into account, besides the increase in terms of paper Reichsmarks of the value of the real property, which will have the principal weight, also the other circumstances of the cases: for example, the economic ability of the debtor to perform under the circumstances, whether agricultural, industrial, or city property is involved. There must also be taken into account the public charges that the property must pay. In the case of rental property the reduction of income resulting from the measures taken to protect renters deserves consideration.

The provisions of the German currency law do not stand in the way of a revalorization. It is true that under the *Gesetz über die Abänderung des Bankgesetzes* of 1 June 1909 (RGB 515) the notes of the Reichsbank are legal tender. [References to other statutory provisions omitted.] But all these provisions rested, at the time of their promulgation, on the . . . assumption that the notes . . . had a value equal to hard money. . . . The legislator had not considered the possibility of a considerable paper money inflation, let alone one of the extent that has occurred . . ., when these provisions were enacted. . . .

The permissibility of revalorization can also be shown by way of an interpretation of the contract in which the court considers what the parties would have wanted, in view of the whole purpose of the contract, if they had foreseen the possibility of a considerable degree of inflation. . . .

The provisions of the currency legislation do not stand in the way of an agreement by which a provision for revalorization in included in the contract nor does this legislation make it impossible to find that such a contract provision is implied in face of the parties' silence.

Therefore, the legal possibility of a revalorization must, in view of the considerable inflation of German paper money, be recognized as legally permissible."

Note: In this decision, the court dealt with the problem of hyperinflation which the legislature had refused to confront. The mortgage indebtedness in Germany in 1913 was approximately 40,000,000,000 Reichsmarks, or about one-sixth of the total German wealth. In 1923, this amount of Reichsmarks was worth less than one American cent. F. Graham, *Exchange, Prices, and Production in Hyper-Inflation: Germany*, 1920–1923 (1930), 241 n. 1. The consequence of the court's decision was that the terms of hundreds of thousands of contracts were open to revision, and hundreds of new judges were hired to decide on a case by case basis how they should be revised.

Bundesgerichtshof, 14 October 1959, NJW 1959, 2203[1]

"A claim for an increase in the amount of the dead rent fixed in a contract for the extraction of saltpetre at the turn of the century cannot be upheld on the ground that the intervening decline in the purchasing power of money has caused the collapse of the basis of the transaction.

. . . 3. The court below held that the landowners had no claim for any increase in the amount of the dead rent, and did so on the ground that the 'equivalence' between performance and counter-performance had not really been disturbed by intervening events. The court held that although the contract of 1898 for the extraction of saltpetre was a reciprocal contract,

1. Excerpt from translation by Kurt Lipstein in B.S. Markesinis, W. Lorenz & G. Dannemann, *The German Law of*   *Obligations* vol. 1 *The Law of Contracts and Restitution: A Comparative Introduction* (1997).

and the agreed dead rent was the mining company's counter-performance for the right of extraction granted to it by the landowner and the agreement of the latter not to dispose otherwise of the minerals during the period of the contract, it was impossible to say why the dead rent was set at 1,200 Reichsmark per annum: that sum was not related to the current price of saltpetre, since the parties in 1898 did not refer to it, and indeed did not know, because there was technically no means of finding out, whether there were any extractable saltpetre at all in the area covered by the contract or if so, how much of it there might be. Nor could the landowners' claim for an increase in the amount of the dead rent be based on the view that revaluation was justified because the original basis of the transaction had collapsed owing to general changes in the economy. According to the jurisprudence of the [*Bundesgerichtshof*], it was only in very exceptional cases that there was any scope for adapting a long-term contract to altered circumstances, i.e. when the relationship between performance and counter-performance had shifted so fundamentally that it would be inconsistent with the requirements of good faith and fair dealing and the principle of fidelity to contracts to maintain the original allocation of rights and duties. That was not the situation in the present case. The dead rent was not part of a direct exchange, and cannot be seen as a sufficient counterpart for the landowners' contractual duty. To grant the requested increase in the agreed amount would be to make an impermissible revaluation of a debt in Reichsmarks; the Reichsmark was set at par by the *Aufwertungsgesetz* (Revalorization Act) of 1925 and again at par for DM by UmstG § 18 I no. I, and the official indexes and other publications show that there has been no revolutionary change in the general economy since that currency reform.

The appellant claims that these views are wrong in law.

(a) To a certain extent the appellant is right. We cannot agree with the court below on all the points related to collapse of the basis of the transaction on which it rejected the landowners' claim for an increase in the dead rent. It is indeed possible that in the course of a long-term contractual relationship the balance between performance and counter-performance may become so upset that it would no longer be fair to keep the disadvantaged party to what was originally agreed. If that be so, then the principle of good faith and fair dealing which dominates the whole of our law. § 242 BGB requires either that the reciprocal obligations be adapted to the changed situation, supposing that the maintenance of the contract is in the interests of the parties as properly conceived, or that the contract be completely canceled. Actually, this was the position from which the court below started. It first asked whether there was a relationship of equivalence between the obligation the landowners undertook in the contract of 1898 and the agreed dead rent. They held that there was. This was correct, since the question is not whether performance and counter-performance were objectively equivalent in value, but whether the parties treated them as being so. But the court went on to say that no disturbance of this relationship of equivalence could be found because the agreed annual sum of 1,200 Reichsmark was an 'arbitrary figure' which bore no relation to the current price of saltpetre or the amount extractable from the land in question. This is very dubious, and the appellant is right to argue that even an arbitrary sum may in the minds of the contractors have been geared to the general condition of the economy and the current purchasing power of money. If such circumstances have changed very materially in the intervening period one could no more exclude the possibility of a shift in the relationship of equivalence in the case of an 'arbitrary' sum than in the case of a sum fixed in relation to concrete factors in the situation.

Again, the lower court's reasoning is dubious in that it first asked whether the plaintiff had a claim for the 'reinstatement of the relationship of equivalence' as such, that is, as an independent ground of claim, and only then asked as a subsidiary question whether 'the change in the basis of the transaction' entitled the landowners to demand an increase in the dead rent under § 242 BGB on the ground of the alteration in the economic situation. In reality, though the court below does not seem to have seen this, these are one and the same question: the shift in the balance between performance and counter-performance ('disturbance of the relationship of equivalence') is simply an instance of the destruction or collapse of the basis of the transaction, that is, of a situation which may lead to a cancellation of the contract or its adaptation to the new situation, under the very narrowly defined conditions laid down in the jurisprudence of the *Reichsgericht* and *Bundesgerichtshof.*

(b) Despite these defects in the decision of the court below, the outcome is correct. One of the stated requirements for the application of the theory of the collapse of the basis of the transaction, and one which is especially important in cases of this kind, is that the intervening change be of a critical nature and affect the interests of the parties to a significant degree. Not every adverse modification of the prior relationship of equivalence, unforeseen by the parties at the time of the contract, justifies a departure from the principle that contracts must be adhered to ('pacta sunt servanda').

What is really required is such a fundamental and radical change in the relevant circumstances that it would be an intolerable result quite inconsistent with law and justice to hold the party to the contract [references omitted]. This test is crucial in this case. The court below recognized this and was right to apply this test. In doing so it went thoroughly into the facts and after considering the interests of both parties came to the conclusion that the stated pre-conditions for breaking with the principle that contracts must be kept were not satisfied.

This court is in entire agreement. The imbalance between the duties of the parties which is in issue in this case is the result of the fall in the purchasing power of money since the contract was formed. According to the calculations in the expert opinion of Larenz, which we can unhesitatingly accept, the value of money diminished by two-thirds during the period in question; thus the sum agreed as dead rent in the contract has only about one third of the purchasing power today it had in 1898. But the plaintiff is quite wrong to say that the landowners are now entitled to claim three times the original sum, namely 3,600 DM. Simple arithmetic does not answer the question whether a reduction in purchasing power produces a situation which is intolerable by the test of good faith and fair dealing. The expert opinion just mentioned, which itself proposes a rise of only 75% rather than 200%, pays too much attention to the figures in stating that if in 1898 1,200 Reichsmarks was fair compensation to the owners for their performance (i.e. agreeing not to exploit the minerals), the fall in the value of money in the ensuing sixty years was so great that it would be inequitable not to increase that sum.

The very writer of the opinion in his book *Geschäftsgrundlage und Vertragserfüllung* (2nd edn., 1957) is right to emphasize the basic principle that contracts must be adhered to, and states that the law should only intervene under § 242 BGB in cases where holding the party to his contract would be manifestly and grossly contrary to its spirit (p. 165), and that a rigorous standard should be applied: it is not every serious shift in equivalence that justifies departing from the contract, but only such a shift as a reasonable person would see as going far beyond the risk assumed and as negating nearly the entire interest which the affected party had in the transaction [references omitted]. We agree with these principles, and if one keeps them in mind it is clear that the claim in the instant case is unjustified. The court below rightly saw the critical question as being whether the dead rent as originally fixed 'must now be regarded as a wholly inadequate return,' and did not fall into any legal error in concluding that it could not. This finding alone justified the court in dismissing the claim."

Bundesgerichtshof, 28 May 1973, BGHZ 61, 31[1]

"The plaintiff became a director of the defendant company in 1926. By a contract of employment dated 18 February 1935, he received a fixed salary of 50,000 Reichsmarks and a percentage of the profits. The contract provided further that his pension was to be calculated as follows: after ten years' service 25% of 40,000 Reichsmarks with an annual increase of 1% up to a maximum of 60% after 35 years. After 20 years' service the basic standard was to be increased to 50,000 Reichsmarks.

The plaintiff retired in 1951 and received from then onwards an annual pension of 15,000 DM equal to monthly payments of 3,083.33 DM. In 1969, plaintiff asked for an increase, which was refused. He claimed an additional pension at the monthly rate of 804.17 DM on the ground that wages and salaries and the general cost of living had increased considerably.

[The *Bundesgerichtshof* dismissed the defendant's appeal.]

I. The court of appeal regards the claim as justified because § 252 BGB requires the adjustment of the pension to the changed condition, especially because the cost of living rose by 45.2 points between 1950 and 1970 [references omitted]. This division agrees as to the result.

---

1. Excerpt from translation by Kurt Lipstein in B.S. Markesenis, W. Lorenz & G. Dannemann, *The German Law of* *Obligations* vol. 1. *The Law of Contracts and Restitution: A Comparative Introduction* (1997), 595.

II. It is true that in its previous practice this Division has refused to increase a pension on the grounds of the depreciation of money in the absence of a contractual adaptation clause, at least in cases in which the agreed pension could still be regarded as a performance in accordance with the contract [references omitted]. This practice was identical with that of the Federal Supreme Labour Court which held on 12 March 1965 [reference omitted] that, while contrary to earlier decisions [references omitted] the adjustment of contractual pension payments to the increased cost of living was no longer excluded in principle, it could only be considered if, as a result of the rise in prices, the agreed payments can no longer be regarded as a performance which provides a living in accordance with the purpose of the contract [reference omitted].

III. Meanwhile the development has continued. The constant increase in the cost of living in the Federal Republic which . . . up to 1960 amounted on average to little more than 1% per year, has since gained momentum . . . All in all the cost of living has increased between 1958 . . . and 1971 . . . by approximately 53.6%. This corresponds to an internal devaluation of approximately 34.9%.

IV. In the light of this recent development, the Federal Supreme Labour Court in two decisions of 30 March 1973 [references omitted] abandoned the practice of restricting the adjustment of pensions to cases in which, as a result of increased prices, the purpose of the agreed performance to provide a living has been frustrated altogether. The Federal Supreme Labour Court now holds that, at least when the cost of living has risen by more than 40%, the value of a pension no longer corresponds to what was promised originally to such an extent that the limit has been reached where the pensioner can be expected according to good faith to observe a standstill and where to deny any adjustment would offend the sense of justice intolerably. In so holding the Federal Supreme Labour Court distinguished between other contractual obligations and promises of maintenance, the special characteristic of which are to assure the livelihood of the beneficiary, or at least to make a contribution thereto. The payments are made out of the profits of the enterprise, the foundations of which the pensioner has helped to create during his activity on behalf of the enterprise. The Federal Supreme Labour Court takes into account, in addition, that the provision of maintenance by the enterprise is also a remuneration for the pensioner's loyalty towards it and for the sum total of his services. These services had been rendered by the pensioner in advance, trusting that he could plan the later stages of his life on the basis of a maintenance promised to him. If this expectation should be disappointed as a result of the depreciation of the currency, a pensioner would have no longer the means of bargaining for an adjustment, contrary to other sections of the population whose income would have kept up with the increase in prices.

The [Bundesgerichtshof] observes that in these circumstances it was first of all a matter for the enterprise to examine the question of such a compensation by adjusting the maintenance payments to the economic development, and to offer an equitable and legal settlement, having regard to the existing situation. Many enterprises had done so already and were doing so continuously. In the case of provision for old age by enterprises, considerable differences existed in the size of the payments, in the gradations among the individual groups of employees and in the conditions for payment as well as in the ability of enterprises to afford payments. Moreover, the reflex effect upon other duties of support owed by the enterprise and the total cost arising from each of these could not be established easily. Consequently, the courts could not prescribe in advance the measure and the form of any adjustment. No automatic increase of pension payments without a contractual promise to this effect could be based on § 242 BGB.

If the party owing the pension had not yet met the creeping inflation by an adequate increase of the pension, he should first of all negotiate with the pensioner or pensioners. If no agreement could be reached, the debtor would have to decide on his own in his reasonable discretion in accordance with § 315 BGB. If he failed to do so, or if his decision was not reasonable, the courts would have to determine the performance due in accordance with § 315 III BGB. In this connection the facts put forward by the parties for and against an adjustment of a retirement pension were particularly relevant. The extent of the rise in prices must be the standard for fixing the extent of the adjustment. No attention should be given in principle to any other aspects of the pensioner's assets or income, except possibly any increase in income arising form any statutory insurance. Equally, the question of need should not be taken into account as a rule. On the other hand, the profitability of the enterprise and the principle of equality of treatment might be relevant.

V. This Division agrees in all matters of principle. Insofar as the special circumstances of cases coming before it should make it necessary to deviate in certain respects, each individual case will have to be decided on its own.

1. The fact that this Division is not concerned with pension claims by employees in the meaning of labour law, but only by organs of enterprises—namely directors and managers—does not in principle call for a different decision from that of the Federal Supreme Labour Court. Normally both contracting parties envisage that the pension provided to a director or manager will serve, either alone or with other revenues, to assure for the beneficiary a standard of living commensurate to his position hitherto in case of old age, premature incapacity to work or of dismissal without any expectation of an equivalent means of livelihood of another kind. Here, too, the pension can be regarded as part of the remuneration for services which the beneficiary has given before he retired and which contributes to the prosperity of the enterprise, the profits of which now feed the pension. This balance, assumed to exist when the obligation to pay a pension is incurred, is seriously disturbed if, as a result of a fall in the purchasing power as compared with that outlined previously, the pension can no longer fulfill by its agreed amount its intended function which is to guarantee the previous standard of living completely or in part. The enterprise, on the other had, is not affected in the result by the depreciation of money, for generally the revenues have at least kept up with the increase in prices or they have even overtaken it as a result of economic growth. It is true that costs, especially wages and salaries, have

increased as well. The proportion of the individual pension obligations, however, the nominal value of which has remained the same, has decreased correspondingly.

The special features set out here preclude a comparison with other obligations of long duration which are not concerned with maintenance (e.g. for the production of potash) as the practice of this court cited by the appellant has underlined expressly [references omitted]."

French law

The French name for the defense of changed circumstances is *imprévision*. While French administrative courts have recognized that defense in contracts between private people and the government, French civil courts have refused to do so. The first two of the following cases reflect the accepted doctrine.

Cour de cassation, ch. civ., 6 March 1876, D. 1876.1.193

"By a contract of June 22, 1567, Adam de Craponne agreed to construct an irrigation canal, to maintain the canal, and to irrigate the lands of the Commune of Pélissane. It was further agreed that certain persons were to pay to Adam de Craponne, within a period of three years, the sum of 20 florins. The same persons and the commune agreed to stand as surety for Adam de Craponne on a loan of 1,000 écus to be used for the construction of the canal. It was further agreed that for each irrigation of a carteirade (equivalent to about 190 ares, an are being equivalent to 100 square meters) of land 3 sols (worth 15 centimes at the time of the instant case) were to be paid to Adam de Craponne or his heirs and the Commune was not to levy any taxes upon the revenues from the canal. Adam de Craponne agreed to maintain the canal and certain bridges over it in perpetuity.

An action was brought by the present owner of the canal before the Civil Court of Aix, which rendered its judgment on March 18, 1841. The court found . . . that the cost of water and of maintaining the canal had so risen since the time when the contract was concluded that the payment made for the irrigation of each cateirade was insufficient and out of all relation to the costs of maintaining the canal and furnishing the water. The disproportion was such that the enterprise would have to be abandoned, the court found, unless the charge for the irrigation of each carteirade was raised.

The court ordered that the charge for the irrigation of each carteirade should be raised to 60 centimes. This result was justified on the ground that, where a contract contemplates successive performances over a long period, the court may, under equitable principles, when changed conditions have rendered the contract unjust, revise the contract in the light of the changed situation.

On December 31, 1873, the *Cour d'appel* of Aix . . . affirmed the decision below, stating: 'It is recognized, in law, that contracts that rest upon a periodic performance may be modified by the court when an equilibrium no longer exists between the performance of the one party and the obligation of the other. . . .' "

The *Cour de cassation* overturned this decision. It said: "Whereas the provision [art. 1134 of the Civil Code] only reproduces ancient principles continually followed in the law of obligations, the fact that the contracts, whose execution gives rise to the instant action, were concluded before the promulgation of the Civil code is not, in the instant case, an obstacle to the application of this article. . . . [T]he rule that it sets forth is general, absolute, and regulates those contracts whose performance extends into successive periods as well as contracts of an entirely different nature: . . . any case, it is not for the courts, however equitable their decisions may appear, to take time and circumstances into consideration in order to modify the parties' agreement and to substitute new clauses for those freely accepted by the contracting parties; . . . [I]n deciding to the contrary and in raising the irrigation charge, fixed at 3 sols by the agreements of 1560 and 1567, to 30 centimes, for the period 1834 to 1874, and 60 centimes, for the period after 1874, under the pretext that that charge was no longer in balance with the costs of maintaining the Craponne canal, the decision challenged violated article 1134."

Cour de cassation, ch. soc., 8 March 1972, D. & S. 1972. J. 340

In 1968, there was massive political unrest in Paris. The *Théâtre du Gymnase-Marie Bell* cancelled its performances and then refused to pay its employees for work that they did not do as a result. It claimed that the cancellation was a case of *force majeure*. The *Cour d'appel* of Paris held for the employees. It said that "the management of the theater simply gave way, in the condition of fear that existed at the time, to the pressure of the striking union and to the threats it made which were not certain to be carried into effect." Moreover, "the management could not justify its position by arguing that the public would not come and that the actors would play before an empty hall, because this was a mere hypothesis." The theater argued "there was a clear contradiction in recognizing the state of fear that existed in Paris at the time as well as the threats made against the theater, which constituted a constraint that amounted to *force majeure*, and to deny, nonetheless," that it constituted *force majeure*. Also, "the *Cour d'appel* could decide that the risk of playing to an empty house was a mere hypothesis only by a flagrant distortion of the report of the *conseiller prud'homme* since it was established that the performance of May 20 took place in a hall deserted by most of the public."

The *Cour de cassation* upheld this decision. It said that "the *Conseil de prud'hommes* concluded that the closing of the theater . . . was caused by the social disorders that were then more in evidence in Paris than in the provinces. . . . [S]ome establishments were occupied and sacked by political demonstrators. . . . [I]f it concluded that the violence and insecurity created at the time of a true case of *force majeure*, the *Cour d'appel* nevertheless found that the theater technicians had not struck, that two of the three actors in the play, the third being Marie Bell, had expressly stated their willingness to perform and that most movie theaters had continued to present their programs to audiences. . . . [A]fter having observed in addition that, although the union of actors that launched the strike had exercised pressure on Marie Bell and had even threatened her, the *Cour d'appel* could conclude, without contradicting itself, that if the management had given in to fear, it did not find itself facing an insurmountable obstacle, nor in a position where it was absolutely impossible for it to pursue its activity. . . . "[T]he appeal vainly objects that the judges of the merits rejected the argument that the performance would take place in an empty theater, an assumption justified by the experience of the May 20 performance. . . . [T]he absence of an audience would merely render the performance of the contract more onerous without constituting a case of *force majeure.* . . ."

Note: In the following cases, however, French courts managed to give relief by invoking a special rule that governs leases, by finding that the parties committed a mistake, or by holding that one party would be acting in bad faith if he insisted on enforcing the contract literally.

French Civil Code

ARTICLE 1721

If during the term of the lease, the thing leased is totally destroyed by an utter accident (*cas fortuit*) the lease is discharged as a matter of law; if it is only destroyed in part, then, according to the circumstances, the lessee can demand either a diminution in the rent or the discharge of the lease. In neither case is there an action for damages.

Cour d'appel of Paris, 1 May 1875, D. 1875. II. 204

"[T]he Decree of September 15, 1870 forbade hunting for a period of one year. . . . [T]he exercise of the right to hunt was the essential object of the lease entered into between the Vicomte Aguado and the Marquise de Calvière, and constituted for them the thing that was leased. . . . [D]ue to the decree cited above, the appellant has been deprived of part of what was rented. . . . [A]s a result, he is entitled under article 1722 of the Civil Code to demand a reduction in the rent equivalent to the time during which hunting was forbidden. . . ."

Cour de cassation, 3e ch. civ., 11 Jan. 1995, pourvoi 92-16729[1]

A construction company agreed to excavate rock at a fixed price per cubic meter. The rock proved harder, and excavation more expensive, than

1. www.legifrance.gouv.fr/WAspad/
Visu?cid=81099&indice=166&table=
CASS& ligneDeb=161.

it could have expected from the report furnished by the architect. The court gave relief because "the person in charge of the work was given an assurance by the architect and would never have signed the agreement except for the completion of a study which only concealed the extent of hard features. Nothing would have enabled a party to foresee a removal of rocks that was so difficult and important. The *Cour d'appel* was justified in recognizing that the importance of the rocks which existed and were present at the moment of the execution of the warranted the voiding of the agreement for error in substance."

Cour de cassation, ch. soc., 9 May 1990, Bull. Civ. 1990.IV no. 219, p. 160

A company reassigned an employee on short notice from Paris to Tourcoing. He was fired when he refused to go. His contract contained a clause providing that he could be moved by the company to any location in France. His wife, however, was then seven months pregnant. The court held the *Cour d'appel* was correct in determining that "the employer, held to execute the labor contract in good faith, had used abusively this clause by which the employee was bound as he found himself in a critical family situation and a change in location could have been effected by using other employees."

V. REMEDIES

1. Specific performance

a. Origins

In England, law was administered by two sets of courts: the common law courts and the court of equity which was presided over by the Chancellor. The role of the court of equity was to help parties whose cause was deemed to be just but who could not get relief from a court of common law. One such case was the person who could not receive an adequate remedy in an action of assumpsit. The common law courts could award damages when a promise was broken but they could not order the promise breaker to perform. A court of equity could do so: the court of equity "acts on the conscience" which meant that the court could order a party to be imprisoned until he was prepared to do as the court ordered. But since the role of the court of equity was only to provide a remedy when the remedy at common law was inadequate, that court would only order specific performance of an obligation when an award of damages from a common law court would not be an adequate remedy.

In countries which had adopted Roman law, a crucial role was played by two Roman texts. According to one: "If an object sold is not delivered, there is an action for damages (*id quod interest*), that is, for the damages suffered by the buyer by not having the object (*hoc est quod rem habere interest emptoris.*).”[1] According to the other: “[A]s he did not do as he promised, he is to be adjudged to pay a sum of money, as is the case in all obligations to do something.”[2] It is not clear what these statements meant to the Romans. Their meaning was controversial throughout the Middle Ages and early modern times, some jurists claiming that a court could never order specific performance in such cases, and others claiming that it could.[3] Pothier took the position that when a party defaulted on an obligation to do or not to do something, the only remedy available against him was an action for damages. As we will see, this rule passed into art. 1142 of the French Civil Code, only to be subverted by the courts.

The late scholastics and the natural lawyers took the position that, whatever the Roman law might be, as a matter of “natural law,” the party owing a performance should have to do so. According to Molina: “But surely if the Roman law or any other means that when a person is obligated to do something, he then has the option not to perform but only to pay damages, that would plainly be irrational. . . .”[4] He cited the Canon law which was to the contrary.[5] Grotius agreed that “as a matter of natural law, whoever promises to do something is obligated to do it if he can” although he thought that only damages could be recovered in civil law.[6] As Reinhard Zimmermann pointed out, this was the position that triumphed in 19th century Germany after the natural law era was over. As we will see, it was incorporated in § 241 of the German Civil Code.

b. Modern law

English law

G. Treitel, *The Law of Contract* (10th ed. 1999), 950–60

“(1) *Granted where damages not ‘adequate’*
The traditional view is that specific performance will not be ordered where damages are an ‘adequate’ remedy.[58] After illustrating this requirement, we shall see that it now requires some reformulation.

(a) *Availability of satisfactory equivalent.* Damages are most obviously an adequate remedy where the claimant can get a satisfactory equivalent of what he contracted for from some other source. For this reason specific performance is not generally ordered of contracts for the sale of commodities, or of shares, which are readily available in the market.[57] In such cases the claimant can buy in the market and is adequately

---

1. Dig. 19.1.1.pr. *but see* 2.7.2.
2. Dig. 42.1.13.1.
3. Reinhard Zimmermann, *The Law of Obligations Roman Foundations of the Civilian Tradition* (1990), 773–76.
4. Ludovicus de Molina, *De iustitia et iure tractatus* (1614), II, disp. 562, no. 5.
5. *Id.*

6. Hugo Grotius, *Institutiones iuris Hollandici* (trans. J. van der Linden, ed. H.F.W.D. Fischer, 1962), III.iii.41.
58. *Co-operative Insurance Society Ltd v. Argyll Stores (Holdings) Ltd.* [1998] A.C. 1 at 11.
57. *Cud v. Rutter* (1719) 1 P.Wms. 570; *Re Schwabacher* (1908) 98 L.T. 127 at 128; *cf.*

compensated by recovering the difference between the contract and the market price by way of damages. Indeed, he is required to make the substitute purchase in performance of the duty to mitigate his loss.[59] If he fails to do so, he cannot recover damages for extra loss suffered because the market has risen after the date when the substitute contract should have been made. To award him specific performance in such a case would, in substance, conflict with the principles of mitigation[60] as well as being oppressive to the defendant.[61] Similar reasoning seems to underlie the rule that a contract to lend money cannot be specifically enforced by either party:[62] it is assumed that damages can easily be assessed by reference to current rates of interest.

Damages will, on the other hand, not be regarded as an adequate remedy where the claimant cannot obtain a satisfactory substitute. The law takes the view that a buyer of land or of a house[63] (however ordinary) is not adequately compensated by damages, and that he can therefore get an order of specific performance.[64] Even a contractual license to occupy land, though creating no interest in the land,[65] may be specifically enforced.[66] ...

(b) *Damages hard to quantify.* A second factor which is relevant (though not decisive[71]) in considering the adequacy of damages is the difficulty of assessing and recovering them. This is one reason why specific

Fothergill v. Rowland (1873) L.R. 17 Eq. 137; *Garden Cottage Foods Ltd v. Milk Marketing Board* [1984] A.C. 130; *aliter* if the shares are not readily available: *Duncuft v. Albrecht* (1841) 12 Sim. 189; *Langen & Wind Ltd v. BellI* *[1972] Ch. 685; Jobson v. JohnsonI [1989] 1 W.L.R. 1026;* Grant v. Cigman [1996] 2 B.C.L.C. 24; or if the contract is for the sale of shares giving a controlling interest in the company; *Harvela Investments Ltd. v. Royal Trust Co. of Canada* (C.I.) *Ltd* [1986] A.C. 207.

59. *Ante*, p. 910.

60. See *Buxton v. Lister* (1746) 3 Ark. 383 at 384.

61. See *Re Schwabacher* (1908) 98 L.T. 127, where shares rose in value after breach. In such a case the defendant could be given the option of transferring the shares or paying the difference between contract and market price on the day fixed for performance, as in *Colt v. Nettervill* (1725) 2 P.Wms. 301. See also *Whiteley Ltd. v. Hilt* [1918] 2 K.B. 808; *M.E.P.C. v. Christian Edwards* [1978] Ch. 281 at 293 (affirmed on other grounds [1981] A.C. 205); *Chinn v. Hochstrasser* [1979] Ch. 447 (reversed on other grounds [1981] A.C. 533).

62. *Rogers v. Challis* (1859) 27 Beav. 175 (suit by lender); *Sichel v. Mosenthal* (1862) 30 Beav. 371 (suit by borrower: decision based on lack of mutuality (*post*, p. 965) rather than adequacy of damages); *cf. Larios v.*

Bonnany y Gurety (1873) L.R. 5 C.P. 346. By statute the court can specifically enforce a contract to take debentures in a company, that is, to make a secured loan to the company: Companies Act 1985, s.195 reversing *South African Territories Ltd v. Wallington* [1898] A.C. 109. A contract to subscribe for shares in a company is also specifically enforceable: *Odessa Tramways Co. v. Mendel* (1878) 8 Ch.D. 235; *Sri Lanka Omnibus Co. v. Perera* [1952] A.C. 76.

63. Fry, *Specific Performance* (6th ed.), § 62. Damages are, however, an adequate remedy for breach of a "lockout" agreement relating to land (*ante*, p. 51) since such an agreement is intended merely to protect the prospective purchaser from wasting costs and does not give him any right to insist on conveyance of the land: *Tye v. House* [1997] 2 E.G.L.R. 171.

64. Unless he elects to claim damages, as in *Meng Leong Developments Pte. Ltd v. Tip Hong Trading Co. Pte. Ltd.* [1985] A.C. 511.

65. See *Ashburn Anstalt v. Arnold* [1989] Ch. 1, overruled on another point in *Prudential Assurance Co. Ltd v. London Residuary Body* [1992] 2 A.C. 386.

66. *Verrall v. Great Yarmouth B.C.* [1981] Q.B. 202.

71. *Soc. des Industries Metallurgiques S.A. v. Bronx Engineering Co. Ltd* [1975] 1 Lloyd's Rep. 465.

performance has been ordered of contracts to sell (or to pay) annuities,[72] and of a sale of debts proved in bankruptcy,[73] the value of such rights being uncertain. . . .

(c) *Appropriateness of the remedy.* The more satisfactory approach found in the cases just discussed is also expressed in dicta to the effect that the availability of specific performance depends on 'the *appropriateness* of that remedy in the circumstances of each case.' The question is not whether damages are an 'adequate' remedy, but whether specific performance will 'do more perfect and complete justice than an award of damages.'[10] The point was well put in a case concerned with the analogous question whether an injunction should be granted: 'The standard question . . ., Are damages adequate remedy? Might perhaps, in the light of the authorities in recent years, be rewritten: Is it just in all circumstances that the plaintiff should be confined to his remedy in damages. . .?'[11] . . .

(2) *Discretionary*

Specific performance is a discretionary remedy: the court is not bound to grant it merely because the contract is valid at law and cannot be impeached on some specific equitable ground such as misrepresentation or undue influence.[14] The discretion is, however, 'not an arbitrary . . . discretion, but one to be governed as far as possible by fixed rules and principles.'[15] . . .

(3) *Contracts not specifically enforceable*

(a) *Contracts involving personal service.* It has long been settled that equity will not, as a general rule, enforce a contract of personal service.[50] Specific enforcement against the employee was thought to interfere unduly with his personal liberty. . . .

The equitable principle applies to all contracts involving personal service even though they are not strictly contracts of service. Thus an agreement to allow an auctioneer to sell a collection of works of art cannot be specifically enforced[68] by either party, though specific enforcement

---

72. *Ball v. Coggs* (1710) 1 Bro. P.C. 140; *Kenney v. Wexham* (1822) 6 Madd. 355; *Adderley v. Dixon* (1824) 1 C. & S. 607 at 611; *Clifford v. Turrell* (1841) 1 Y. & C.C.C. 138; *Beswick v. Beswick* [1968] A.C. 58; see however Fry, *Specific Performance* (6th ed.), pp. 30, 111, 112; *Crampton v. Varna Ry.* (1872) L.R. 7 Ch. App. 562.

73. *Adderly v. Dixon* (1824) 1 C. & S. 607.

10. *Tito v. Waddell* (No. 2) [1977] Ch. 106 at 322. *Rainbow Estates Ltd v. Tokenhold* [1998] 2 All E.R. 860 et 868.

11. *Evans Marshall & Co. Ltd. v. Bertola S.A.* [1973] 1 W.L.R. 349 et 179.

14. *Stickney v. Keeble* [1915] A.C. 386 et 419.

15. *Lamare v. Dixon (1873) L.R. 6 H.IL. 414 et 423; Co-operative Insurance Society*

Ltd v. Argyll Stores (Holdings) Ltd. [1998] A.C. 1 at 16.

50. *Johnson v. Shrewsbury and Birmingham Ry.* (1853) 3 D.M. & G. 358; *Brett v. East India and London Shipping Co. Ltd* (1864) 2 H. & M. 404; *Britain v. Rossiter* (1883) 11 Q.B.D. 123 at 127; *Rigby v. Connol* (1880) 14 Ch.D. 482 at 487. *Cf. Taylor v. N.U.S.* [1967] 1 W.L.R. 532; *Chappell v. Times Newspapers Ltd* [1975] 1 Ch.D. 482 (injunction); *The Scaptrade* [1983] 2 A.C. 694 et 700–701 (*post*, p. 960); *Wishart v. National Association of Citizens Advice Bureaux* [1990] I.C.R. 794; *Wilson v. St. Hellen's B.C.* [1998] 3 W.L.R. 1070 at 1081.

68. *Chinnock v. Sainsbury* (1861) 30 L.J.Ch. 409; *cf. Mortimer v. Beckett* [1920] 1 Ch. 571.

would hardly be an undue interference with personal liberty, even in a suit against the auctioneer. Again, an agreement to enter into a partnership will not be specifically enforced as "it is impossible to make persons who will not concur carry on a business jointly, for their common advantage."[69] The court can, however, order the execution of a formal partnership agreement, and leave the parties to their remedies on the agreement.[70] Similarly, the court can order the execution of a service contract even though that contract, when made, may not be specifically enforceable.[71]

The equitable principle here under discussion applies only where the services are of a personal nature. There is no general rule against the specific enforcement of a contract merely because one party undertakes to provide services[72] under it. Thus specific performance can be ordered of a contract to publish a piece of music[73] and sometimes of contracts to build.[74] It has, indeed, been suggested that a time charterparty cannot be specifically enforced against the shipowner because it is a contract for services[75]; but the services that the shipowner undertakes under such a contract will often be no more personal than those to be rendered by a builder under a building contract. Denial of specific performance in the case of time charters is best explained on other grounds.[76]

Law in the United States

Restatement (Second) of Contracts

§ 359. Effect of Adequacy of Damages

(1) Specific performance or an injunction will not be ordered if damages would be adequate to protect the expectation interest of the injured party. . . .

§ 369. Factors Affecting Adequacy of Damages

In determining whether the remedy in damages would be adequate, the following circumstances are significant:

(a) the difficulty of proving damages with reasonable certainty,

---

69. *England v. Curling* (1844) 8 Beav. 129 at 137. On the same principle, specific performance has been refused of a house-sharing arrangement which had been made between members of a family who later quarreled: *Burrows and Burrows v. Sharp* (1991) 23 H.L.R. 82, where the basis of liability was not contract but proprietary estoppel.

70. As in *England v. Curling (supra)*, where the object of obtaining such a decree was to ascertain the exact terms that had been agreed, and then to prevent one of the contracting parties from competing in business with the other.

71. *C. H. Giles & Co. Ltd v. Morris* [1972] 1 W.L.R. 307; *cf. Posner v. Scott-Lewis* [1987] Ch. 25.

72. *E.g. Regent International Hotels v. Pageguide, The Times*, May 13, 1985 (injunction against preventing claimant company from managing a hotel); *Posner v. Scott-Lewis* [1987] Ch. 25 (*post*, p. 961 at n. 90).

73. *Barrow v. Chappel & Co.* (1951), now reported in [1976] R.P.C. 355, and cited in *Joseph v. National Magazine Co. Ltd* [1959] Ch. 14; contrast *Malcolm v. Chancellor Masters and Scholars of the University of Oxford, The Times*, December 19, 1990, where specific performance of a contract to publish a book was refused on the ground that continued co-operation between author and publishers would have been required.

74. *Post*, p. 963.

75. *The Scaptrade* [1983] 2 A.C. 94 at 700–701.

76. See *infra* at n. 86.

(b) the difficulty of procuring a suitable substitute performance by means of money awarded as damages, and

(c) the likelihood that an award of damages could not be collected.

E. Allan Farnsworth, *Contracts* (3d ed. 1999), 781

"A court will not grant specific performance of a contract to provide a service that is personal in nature. This refusal is based in part on the difficulty of passing judgment on the quality of performance. . . . It is also based on the undesirability of compelling the continuance of personal relations after disputes have arisen confidence and loyalty have been shaken and the undesirability, in some instances, of imposing what might seem like involuntary servitude."

French law

French Civil Code

ARTICLE 1142

Every obligation to do or not to do resolves itself in damages in the event that the party who owes performance fails to perform.

Law of 9 July 1991

ARTICLE 33

Any judge may, even on his own initiative, order an *astreinte* to ensure that his decision is carried out.

F. Terré, P. Simler & Y. Lequette, *Droit civil Les obligations* (7th ed. 1999), § 1023

"Lacking a power to directly compel a person to perform his obligation specifically . . . or to deprive him of liberty as a sanction, it is possible to attain that end through his assets by imposing a penalty which exposes him to considerable loss if he remains obstinate in his refusal to perform his obligation. The *astreinte* is the technique used to accomplish this goal. It consists in a judgment that the person owing performance must pay the other party as a private fine an amount set by the judge either as a total amount or, more frequently, as so much for each day (or week or month) of delay in the case of an obligation to do something, or, in the case of an obligation not to do something, for each infraction.

The major feature of the *astreinte* is its power to compel. What is involved is a legitimate means of intimidation exerted to obtain a performance voluntarily. Its effectiveness is consequently a function of the choice of the amount which is freely determined by the judge. The amount must clearly be higher than the advantage that the person owing performance derives from failing to perform without being disproportionate to his means of paying. . . .

A purely praetorian creation [meaning, created by the judges] just after the Civil Code was promulgated, the *astreinte* never ceased to gain ground despite a lively scholarly debate and a few hesitations in the case law.

The permanent problem concerns the distinction between the *astreinte* and damages. The *astreinte* is a private fine that the party owing performance must pay to the other party without taking into account the damages compensating him for harm. This idea of a private fine is extravagant, and, in certain respects, shocking, because it can result in an enrichment of the party owed performance which is both substantial and unjustified. It is not astonishing, then, that scholars hesitated to recognize that courts have a power which is extravagant and discretionary absent any legislative text. The case law and even the legislature have had moments of doubt.

Legislative approval—late in coming, but clear—was given with the Law of 5 July 1972 concerning the reform of civil procedure. Its provisions have themselves been abrogated and replaced by the more substantial ones of the Law of 9 July 1991, arts. 33–37. . . .

The *astreinte* can be used in order to obtain the performance of any type of obligation. If its favored use is with obligations to do or not to do because of the rule of article 1142, there is no reason it could not be used even for an obligation to pay a sum of money. It can be used in the field of contracts or outside the field of contracts, for matters civil or commercial, and also in administrative matters including those in which the party owing performance is the state or a public body.

However, certain limits must be observed. The first comes from simple good sense: when specific performance (*exécution en nature*) has become impossible, one cannot make use of the *astreinte* because it cannot fulfil its function. The procedure must also not be used in the case of obligations which are of a very personal nature in which at stake is individual liberty, liberty of conscience, or the moral rights of an artist or author." [footnotes omitted]

German law

German Civil Code

§ 241

The effect of an obligation is that the person owed performance is entitled to claim performance from the person who owes it.

Konrad Zweigert & Hein Kötz, *An Introduction to Comparative Law* (3rd ed. trans. by Tony Weir, 1998), 505–09

"In German law and in related systems it is axiomatic that a creditor has the right to bring a claim for performance of a contract and to obtain a judgment ordering the debtor to fulfil it. For this purpose it is immaterial whether the debtor's obligation is to deliver goods pursuant to a sale, to vacate a dwelling house, or to produce a work of art. The view that it is of the very essence of an obligation that it be actionable in this sense is so fundamental that it is not expressly stated in any legislative text, but the words of § 241 of the Civil Code, the creditor is entitled, on the grounds of the creditor-debtor relationship, 'to demand performance from the debtor', imply that actual performance may be demanded before a court and that a judgment ordering performance in kind may be issued by it.

A judgment ordering the debtor to perform his contract in kind can be issued only if performance by the debtor is still *possible*. As the Reichsgericht once said, it would be 'nonsensical to order a person to perform when it has been established that performance is objectively impossible' (RGZ 107, 15, 17). Accordingly a judgment for performance cannot be issued if, for instance, a picture has been destroyed after sale, or if a ship has been requisitioned while under charter, or if, just before the première, an opera-singer is rendered so hoarse by a bad cold that for the duration she cannot sing; in such cases the creditor can bring only a claim for damages. . . .

It is clear from the Civil Code and the Code of Civil Procedure that their draftsmen believed that a disappointed contractor who decided to sue would always choose to claim performance. This is not what happens in practice, but their belief explains the fact that several texts concern themselves in loving detail with the creditor who, having brought a claim for performance, then finds that this is not the right step and that a claim for damages makes better sense. Thus, according to § 268 Code of Civil Procedure, it is not a change of claim (*Klageänderung*) of which the defendant can complain as being an unfair surprise or procedural trick if a plaintiff in the course of a suit abandons his claim for performance in kind and prosecutes his claim for damages instead. A plaintiff who has actually obtained a judgment for performance may, instead of executing it, wish to proceed immediately to a judgment for damages; this case also has been foreseen and carefully regulated. By § 283 Civil Code the creditor who has obtained a judgment for performance may, instead of executing it, wish to proceed immediately to a judgment for damages; this case also has been foreseen and carefully regulated. By § 283 Civil Code the creditor who has obtained judgment for performance can fix a time within which performance from the debtor must be forthcoming. On the expiry of this period the plaintiff can forthwith institute a claim for damages, against which the only admissible defence is that performance has been rendered impossible by circumstances not entailing the defendant's responsibility and arising after the judgment for performance was handed down (see RGZ 107, 15, 19). These well-intentioned provisions are rarely used today. They stem from the legislator's belief that the creditor who did not know or could not prove that performance by the debtor was impossible would always bring a claim for performance. Today commercial men resolve this uncertainty differently: they grant the debtor an additional period for performance in accordance with § 326 Civil Code and, if this period elapses without result, they forthwith institute a claim for damages. . . .

Claims for performance may not be very frequent in practice, since creditors bring them only when their interest in performance cannot easily be reckoned in money, but it remains the theory that, in a case where performance is still possible and the creditor so elects, the courts are bound to deliver judgment ordering the debtor to perform. . . . If the claim on which the creditor has obtained judgment is that the debtor should take some positive action other than handing over property, a distinction is made. If the act in question is one which could be equally well performed by someone else, that is, it need not be performed by the debtor personally but is, as the Code of Civil Procedure puts it, *vertretbar*, then the method of execution—the only method—is for the creditor, on the authority of the court granted at his request, to have the act performed by a third party at the expense of the debtor (*Ersatzvornahme*, § 887 Code of Civil Procedure).

As examples of acts which are *vertretbar*, or capable of substitute performance, one may cite manual tasks which call for no especial talent and can therefore be carried out by third parties—the execution of building operations (LG Hagen JR 1948, 314), the installation of a lift in an apartment block (KG JW 1927, 1945), the printing of a manuscript (OLG Munich MDR 1955, 682). The making of an extract from the books of a business or the production of its accounts may also be *vertretbar* if an expert could do it after inspecting the debtor's records (OLG Hamburg MDR 1955, 43).

If the act to which the creditor lays claim is one which can be performed only by the debtor himself, it is said to be *unvertretbar*. In such a case the method of execution provided by the Code of Civil Procedure (§ 888) is to threaten the unwilling debtor with a fine or imprisonment. Should the debtor still not perform, he may be imprisoned for up to six months in all; fines, unlimited in amount, are collected like judgment debts, and go to the Treasury. . . .

[These means of execution cannot] be used against a debtor whose obligation is to do something which calls for special artistic or scientific talent, for here also the performance of the act does not depend exclusively on the debtor's will. However good his intentions may be, a composer cannot compose his sonata nor a law professor write his commentary without the right inspiration, mood, energy, and other preconditions of great spiritual creativity (see OLG Frankfurt OLGE 29, 251).

Note: Consider the relief that each legal system would give (1) when the contract is obtain some unique performance, such as the purchase of a painting, and (2) when the contract is to obtain fungible goods, such as steel, which are readily available on the market at the prevailing market price. In the first case, could the plaintiff obtain the picture? In the second case, is the plaintiff any better or worse off whether the defendant is ordered to perform or the plaintiff receives damages equal to the difference between the contract and market price? Consider then whether it matters that the common law, French law, and German law adhere to different rules.

2. Damages

a. The general principle

G. Treitel, *The Law of Contract* (10th ed. 1999), 873

"The object of damages for breach of contract is to put the victim 'so far as money can do it . . . in the same situation . . . as if the contract had been performed' [citing Robinson v. Harman, (1848) 1 Ex. 850, 855]. In other words, the victim is to be compensated for the loss of his bargain, so that his expectations arising out of or created by the contract are protected."

Restatement (Second) of Contracts

§ 347

Subject to the limitations stated in §§ 350–51, the injured party has a right to damages based on his expectation interest as measured by

  (a) the loss in the value to him of the other party's performance caused by its failure or deficiency, plus

  (b) any other loss, including incidental or consequential loss, caused by the breach, less

  (c) any cost or other loss that he has avoided by not having to perform.

Note: § 344 defines the "expectation interest as a party's interest in having the benefit of his bargain by being put in as good a position as he would have been in had the contract been performed."

French Civil Code

ARTICLE 1149

The damages due to the person owed the performance are, in general, the loss which he has incurred plus the gain of which he was deprived with the exceptions and qualifications to be described.

German Civil Code

§ 249 [NATURE AND EXTENT OF COMPENSATION]

One who is obligated to make compensation must bring about the condition that would have existed if the circumstance which gave rise to his duty to compensate had not arisen.

b. Limitations on recovery

Recovery for non-economic harm

English law

Jarvis v. Swans Tours Ltd., [1973] 1 QB 233

"The defendants, a firm of travel agents, issued a brochure of winter sports holidays for 1969–70 in which one of the holidays was described as a 'Houseparty in Morlialp', Switzerland, with 'special resident host'. The brochure stated that the price of the holiday included the following house-party arrangements: 'Welcome party on arrival. Afternoon tea and cake. . . Swiss Dinner by candlelight. Fondue-party. Yodler evening. . . farewell party.' It also stated that there was a wide variety of ski runs at Morlialp; that ski-packs, i.e. skis, sticks and boots, could be hired there; that the houseparty hotel was chosen by the defendants because of the 'Gemut-lichkeit', i.e. geniality, comfort and cosiness, that the hotel owner spoke

English, and that the hotel bar would be open several evenings a week. The brochure added, '. . . you will be in for a great time, when you book this houseparty holiday.' The plaintiff, a solicitor aged about 35, who was employed by a local authority, preferred to take his annual fortnight's holiday in the winter. He looked forward to his holidays and booked them far ahead. In August 1969, on the faith of the representations in the defendants' brochure, he booked with the defendants a 15 day houseparty holiday at Morlialp, with ski-pack, from 20th December 1969 to 3rd January 1970. The total cost of the holiday was £63.45. The plaintiff went on the holiday but he was very disappointed. In the first week the houseparty consisted of only 13 people, and for the whole of the second week the plaintiff was the only person there. There was no welcome party. The ski-runs were some distance away and no full length skis were available except on two days in the second week. The hotel owner did not speak English and in the second week there was no one to whom the plaintiff could talk. The cake for tea was only potato crisps and dry nutcake. There was not much entertainment at night; the yodler evening consisted of a local man in his working clothes singing a few songs very quickly, and the hotel bar was an unoccupied annexe open only on one evening."

Lord Denning. "What is the right way of assessing damages? It has often been said that on a breach of contract damages cannot be given for mental distress. Thus in Hamlin v Great Northern Railway Co[2] Pollock CB said that damages cannot be given 'for the disappointment of mind occasioned by the breach of contract.' And in Hobbs v London & South Western Railway Co[3] Mellor J said that '. . . for the mere inconvenience, such as annoyance and loss of temper, or vexation, or for being disappointed in a particular thing which you have set your mind upon, without real physical inconvenience resulting, you cannot recover damages.' The courts in those days only allowed the plaintiff to recover damages if he suffered physical inconvenience, such as, having to walk five miles home, as in Hobbs's case[4]; or to live in an overcrowded house: see Bailey v Bullock.[5]

I think that those limitations are out of date. In a proper case damages for mental distress can be recovered in contract, just as damages for shock can be recovered in tort. One such case is a contract for a holiday, or any other contract to provide entertainment and enjoyment. If the contracting party breaks his contract, damages can be given for the disappointment, the distress, the upset and frustration caused by the breach. I know that it is difficult to assess in terms of money, but it is no more difficult than the assessment which the courts have to make every day in personal injury cases for loss of amenities. Take the present case. Mr Jarvis has only a fortnight's holiday in the year. He books it far ahead, and looks forward to it all that time. He ought to be compensated for the loss of it."

---

2. (1856) 1 H & N 408 at 411.
3. (1875) LR 10 QB 111 at 122, [1874–80] All ER Rep 458 at 463.

4. (1875) LR 10 QB 111, [1874–80] All ER Rep 458.
5. [1950] 2 All ER 1167.

Law in the United States

Restatement (Second) of Contracts

§ 353

Recovery for emotional disturbance will be excluded unless the breach also caused bodily harm or the contract or the breach is of such a kind that serious emotional disturbance was a particularly likely result.

Deitsch v. The Music Company, 6 Ohio Misc. 2d 6 (Mun. Ct. 1983)

"This is an action for breach of contract. Plaintiffs and defendant entered into a contract on March 27, 1980, whereby defendant was to provide a four-piece band at plaintiffs' wedding [reception on November 8, 1980]. The reception was to be from 8:00 p.m. to midnight. The contract stated 'wage agreed upon $295.00,' with a deposit of $65, which plaintiffs paid upon the signing of the contract.

Plaintiffs proceeded with their wedding, and arrived at the reception hall on the night of November 8, 1980, having employed a caterer, a photographer and a soloist to sing with the band. However, the four-piece band failed to arrive at the wedding reception. Plaintiffs made several attempts to contact defendant but were not successful. After much wailing and gnashing of teeth, plaintiffs were able to send a friend to obtain some stereo equipment to provide music, which equipment was set up at about 9:00 p.m. . . .

The court holds that in a case of this type, the out-of-pocket loss, which would be the security deposit, or even perhaps the value of the band's services, where another band could not readily be obtained at the last minute, would not be sufficient to compensate plaintiffs. Plaintiffs are entitled to compensation for their distress, inconvenience, and the diminution in value of their reception. For said damages, the court finds that the compensation should be $750."

French law

Boris Starck, Henri Roland & Laurent Boyer, *Obligations 1. Responsabilité délictuelle* (4th ed., 1991), § 1437

The elements of damage which are recoverable are the same in the area of contracts as in the area of torts: material damage (*dommage matériel*), that is to say, the loss that was suffered and the gain that was missed under art. 1149 of the Civil Code; injury to physical integrity and life in contracts that carry with them an obligation of safety; non-economic harm (*dommage moral*, a category which includes pain and suffering) in the different senses of this term; loss of a chance; harm that occurs because of harm to another (*dommage par ricochet*)." [footnotes omitted]

Tribunal de commerce de la Seine, 20 February 1932, Gaz. Pal. 1932.1.895

"[P]ursuant to agreements dated in Paris, April 9, 1930, the *Etablissements [J.] Haïck* engaged Mlle. Devillers to shoot a film, 'The

Sweetness of Love,' with Victor Boucher as a partner—this, in accordance with certain clauses and conditions which were contained in the said agreements;

[R]esisting the claim for the payment of the sum of 15,000 francs and an *astreinte* of 1,000 francs per day of delay until the wall posters and placards are modified to conform to the contract, the *Etablissements J. Haïck* claims that this demand is unjustified;

[I]t is appropriate to recall that according to the complaint and facts brought forward by Mlle. Devillers that one of the clauses of the agreements already mentioned provides that this artist would have the female lead and that, in all publications in which Victor Boucher was mentioned, she would have letters two-thirds the size of those with his name;

[I]t appears from the argument and from the documents submitted that from the beginning of the publicity campaign undertaken for 'The Sweetness of Love,' the *Etablissements J. Haïck* violated the provision just described. . . . [I]ndeed, numerous omissions occurred in the announcements, in the placards, in the programs, and in the posters. . . [W]ith the help of documents, the *Tribunal* was able to determine either that the name of Mlle Devillers did not appear alongside that of Victor Boucher or that it did not appear in letters of the size contractually specified. . . .

[B]ecause of the failure of *Etablissements J. Haïck* to perform its obligations, Mlle Devillers suffered commercial disturbance and a certain non-economic harm (*préjudice moral*) for which the *Etablissements J. Haïck* must be held to make compensation. . . .

The *Etablissements cinématographiques Jacques Haïck* is adjudged to pay the sum of 15,000 francs definitively and not provisionally as damages, and an *astreinte* in imposed of 100 francs per day of delay for a month so long as the wall posters and placards are not modified as provided in the contract. . . ."

German law

Read §§ 847 and 253 of the German Civil Code on p. 254 above.

Oberlandesgericht, Saarbrücken, 20 July 1998, NJW 1998, 2913

The plaintiff sought assistance with the costs of her action against the defendant for damages for pain and suffering. She had contracted for a room with a fireplace in defendant's hotel that could accommodate twelve people for the evening of her marriage which was to take place on June 27, 1997. Due to a mistake of the defendant, that room had already been reserved for that night by another party. Because an appropriate alternative was not available, the evening celebration of her marriage did not take place. Because of this "disaster" she "cried for days on end," "her nerves reached their utter limit," and she suffered "psychological shock." She claimed damages for pain and suffering of 3000 DM. The trial court dismissed her request for assistance on the grounds that her action could not succeed as she had suffered no physical harm and could not recover damages for pain and suffering for breach of contract. The *Oberlandesgericht* agreed.

"In the present case, the plaintiff's claim against the defendant for damages for pain and suffering could not be taken into account according to § 847 of the Civil Code unless the defendant, together with the breach of contract for which he is responsible – the failure to reserve the room – also caused a result that falls within § 823(1) of the Civil Code in the form of an injury to her body or health. But the allegations of the plaintiff do not go far enough to raise such a claim.

We need not consider here whether and to what extent an interference with the psychological state of contracting party through a breach of contract is included within the protective purpose of § 823. Even if that question were to be answered in the affirmative, which would contradict the trial court's opinion, the plaintiff still would not have sufficiently alleged the factual basis for a claim for damages for pain and suffering.

At the outset, the plaintiff has failed to make a sound claim that the defendant's breach of contract caused an injury to her body or health. It is true that a person who harms another must answer for the psychological effects of the conduct for which he is responsible, and also that a mere interference caused by this conduct with the psychological state of the party who is affected can constitute an injury to body or health (BGH, NJW 1991, 2337. . .). In a case like the present, however, for the interference with the psychological state of the injured party caused by the conduct of the party responsible for the harm to give rise to liability, the type, intensity and duration of the psychological interference must so clearly surpass the reactions normally present in life to disagreeable events that one can at least compare them to the effects of an illness. (see Palandt/Heinrichs, BGB, before § 249 no.71. . . .) That this happened to the plaintiff as a consequence of the defendant's breach of contract is shown neither by her contention that she 'cried day after day after this disaster' and 'was not able to speak about this event for weeks without crying fits,' nor by her opinion that her nerves reached their 'utter limit,' and she suffered 'psychological shock,' an opinion which cannot be understood without more commentary on the facts.

Nevertheless, even if, according to these allegations, the interference with plaintiff's psychological state had reached the requisite degree of severity, her claim would be defective insofar as the fault of the defendant is concerned, for it must be considered that this fault must encompass, not only the breach of contract constituted by his failure to reserve the room, but also the psychological interference with the plaintiff caused by this failure which would be the basis for liability. Certainly, in using the appropriate degree of care, the hotel keeper must consider that the result of neglecting to reserve the room requested by the bride for an evening wedding dinner will be a negative psychological reaction, perhaps a serious one. But absent contrary indications, he could not foresee that, under normal circumstances, the type, intensity and duration of this reaction would be so severe as to constitute an injury to body or health."

Bundesgerichtshof, 10 October 1974, BGHZ 63, 98.

The plaintiff, the owner of a clothing factory, contracted with the defendant, a travel agent, for a package tour for himself, his wife, and their two children for a fixed price of 2322 DM which would take them to the coast of the Black Sea in Romania for two weeks. He had many complaints about the hotel accommodations, the food, and the opportunities for swimming at the beach. He sued the defendant for damages for 60% of the amount he had paid for the package tour as well as a further 1500 DM as compensation for wasted vacation time.

"The damages sought by the plaintiff for 'wasted vacation time' were refused by the appellate court. In its opinion, the loss of vacation time did not as such constitute a diminution in the value of plaintiff's assets which could be the object of a claim for damages.

. . .

Here the question is whether the free time spent on vacation, and therefore the *vacation as such* does have an asset value (*Vermögenswert*) so that its loss can constitute material harm when it is spent uselessly ('wasted').

. . .

The prevailing, and, indeed, the dominant opinion answers that question in the affirmative taking into account that by current commercial views a vacation is a large extent 'commercialized.' [many citations omitted]

Those who oppose this opinion see in the useless expenditure of vacation time only non-material harm for which compensation could be due only under the particular provisions of § 847 of the Civil Code [many citations omitted].

The *Bundesgerichtshof* has not yet determined whether a vacation has an asset value. Yet a decision pointing in this direction is found in the 'sea trip' case (BGH NJW 1956, 1234, 1235) in which damages for the interference with the enjoyment of a trip were granted because a traveller's luggage was not made available to him. In this opinion, it was considered decisive that the 'purchased enjoyment of a vacation' could not be fully realized without the luggage.

. . .

The Senate follows the dominant opinion, according to which the vacation as such possesses as asset value. . . ."

Note: Results in cases like this one eventually received legislative sanction in what is now § 651f(2) of the German Civil Code: "If a trip is frustrated or seriously disrupted, the traveller can also recover an appropriate compensation in money for uselessly expended vacation time."

Recovery for unforeseeable harm

ORIGINS

One change that the Emperor Justinian made in his compilation of Roman law was to place a limit on the damages that a party could recover in contract:

"In all cases which have a certain quantity or nature . . . damages are not to exceed twice the quantity; however, in other cases which appear to be uncertain judges are to require that the damages which was truly incurred be paid for."[1]

This rule was followed where Roman law was adopted in medieval and early modern Europe. There was much dispute about what it meant to speak of "cases which have a certain quantity or nature" or "cases which appear to be uncertain." As Reinhard Zimmermann notes, "[g]enerations of lawyers have been mystified by the terms of this poorly drafted enactment."[2]

In the 16th century, the French jurist Molinaeus (or, in French, du Moulin) thought he had discovered the rationale behind the rule:

"The rationale on which all the law is based is the dislike of enormity and so the particular rationale of the limitation in the cases of what is certain is that most likely it was not foreseen or thought that greater damage would be suffered or that there was a risk beyond the principal object than the principal object itself."[3]

He noted that it would be equally equitable to limit the damages recoverable in the cases that concern what is uncertain.

As Zimmermann has noted, in the 18th century "Pothier generalized this idea and detached it from the specific provisions" of the Roman text. He said that "the person who owes a performance is only liable for the damages that one could have foreseen at the time of the contract that the party owed a performance would suffer." [4]

"For instance, suppose I sell a person a horse which I am obliged to deliver in a certain time, and I cannot deliver it accordingly: if in the meantime horses have increased in price, whatever the purchaser is obliged to pay more than he would have given for mine, in order to procure another of the like quality, is a damage for which I am obliged to indemnify him, because it is a damage ... which only relates to the thing that was the object of the contract, and which I might have foreseen; the price of horses like that of all other things being subject to variation. But if this purchaser was a canon, who for want of having the horse that I had engaged to deliver to him, and not having been enabled to get another, was prevented from arriving at the place of his benefice in time to be entitled to his revenue, I should not be liable for the loss which he sustained thereby, although it was occasioned by the nonperformance of my obligation; for this is a damage which is foreign to the obligation, which was not contemplated at the time of the contract, and to which it cannot be supposed that I had any intention to submit. . . ."[5]

He recognized one exception: full damages could be recovered if the performance was due to wilful misconduct (*dol*).

1. C. 7.47.1.
2. Reinhard Zimmermann, *The Law of Obligations Roman Foundations of the Civilian Tradition* (1990), 828.
3. Carolus Molinaeus, *Tractatus de eo quod interest* (1574), no. 60.

4. Robert Pothier, *Traité des obligations* no. 160, in *Oeuvres de Pothier* 2 (Bugnet ed., 2d ed. 1861) 497.
5. *Id.* no. 159 (W. Evans trans., 1806.)

MODERN LAW

In reading the following cases, consider when the courts are chiefly concerned with whether a loss is foreseeable or when they are concerned instead or in addition, as in Roman law, with the disproportion between the loss suffered and the contract price.

French law

French Civil Code

ARTICLE 1150

One who owes a performance is only liable for damages which were foreseen or could have been foreseen at the time of the contract unless the failure to perform his obligation was due to wilful misconduct (*dol*).

Cour de cassation, 1e ch. civ., 11 May 1982, Gaz. Pal. 1982.2.612

"[A]ccording to this text [art. 1150] one who owes a contractual obligation is only liable for the damages which were foreseen or could have been foreseen at the time of the contract as long as his nonperformance was not due to wilful misconduct. . . .

[B]y a decision of 21 April 1978 . . . M. Roche, a roofing and plumbing contractor, was held contractually responsible on account of his negligence for a fire caused by the use of a blowtorch which partially destroyed a chateau belonging to the married couple Galliaud whose roof Roche was engaged in repairing. . . .

[T]he decision challenged here, rendered on 1 October 1980 . . . required M. Roche to pay various indemnities including an amount of 60,000 francs representing the interest on a loan that the proprietor contracted to undertake the initial expenses of putting the building that burned into shape and a sum of 70,000 francs for loss of rent of the premises on the first floor of the chateau. . . .

[I]n requiring M. Roche to pay damages of these two kinds, even though no wilful misconduct or gross negligence had been imputed to him, on the grounds that his failure to perform a contractual obligation coincided with a fault in tort in that it constituted culpable negligence, and that therefore he was obligated to repair even the harm that was not foreseen at the time of the contract, the *Cour d'appel* misunderstood the principle that the victim of a harm for which the perpetrator is contractually responsible cannot hold the perpetrator to the rules of delictual liability. . . ."

Cour de cassation, ch. civ., 29 December 1913, D.P. 1916.1.117

"[I]n conformity with art. 1150, and except in case of wilful misconduct, a carrier is only liable for damages which were foreseen or which could have been foreseen at the time of the contract . . . [N]o provision in the list of changes and fees imposes an obligation on passengers to declare the content of the baggage which accompanies them, and as a result, railroad companies must foresee that certain travelers will be carrying objects of a more or less considerable value in their baggage. . . . [I]n any event, in case of loss and of argument over the amount of damages, it pertains to the courts to limit the liability of these companies by the principles just mentioned according to the circumstances of each case, taking into account the quantity and the value of the objects a traveler would normally bring with him, having regard to his profession, his financial condition, the object of the trip and the price of a ticket. . . .

[According to the decision under appeal, on May 23, 1908, at the railway station at Cannes, Rouquier checked, as baggage to accompany him to his destination at Courthézon (Vauclussse), a box weighing 30 kg [66 pounds] containing three cans of essence of neroli worth 725 francs per kilogram . . . [T]his box, left in the station where the train arrived, was stolen on the night of May 29–30 . . . [I]t was discovered the next day but it was missing 5 kg 650 g. of the essence it had contained. . . [A]s compensation for the damage he suffered, Rouquier demanded from the Paris-Lyon-Mediterranean Railroad Co. a payment of 4096 francs 25 centimes, reflecting the price of the essence, and 2000 francs of [other] damages . . . [T]he Company responded with an offer of compensation of 100 francs, maintaining that there was no way it could foresee that merchandise worth 16,000 francs was contained in a box checked as ordinary baggage which bore no indication of the sort that would enlighten the transporter as to the value of its contents, and which had been abandoned in the baggage claim of a tiny railway station for six days without any notice given to the employees. . . .

[N]evertheless, the *Cour d'appel* of Nîmes, affirming the decision of the *Tribunal de commerce* of Avignon, held that compensation must be made for the entire sum demanded for the value of the essence that was lost and 100 francs additional damages, declaring that, as *force majeure* was not present in this case, the Company could not invoke any legal limitation to its harm, 'art. 1150 of the Civil Code having in view only the damages due in the event that delivery is delayed, but not dealing with compensation for a box for which the traveler has established the value'. . . [I]n ruling in this way, according to a distinction which does not belong to the article . . . the decision violated [the Civil Code]. . . ."

Cour de cassation, ch. civ., 7 July 192, D.P. 1927.1.119

When plaintiff's merchandise was shipped, its value was declared to be 475 francs. It was lost. Plaintiffs sued for 16,685 francs which, they claimed, was 70% of its true value. The court below awarded 475 francs. The *Cour de cassation* affirmed. "[A]ccording to the appeal (*pourvoi*), in all cases, the compensation must be in accord with the real value, and not the presumed value of the merchandise . . . [I]n effect, within the meaning of art. 1150, the party who does not fulfil his obligation is held, if he was in good faith, to the integral reparation of the harm as long as the cause of the harm could have been foreseen . . . [B]ut . . . this text does not make any reference to the foreseeability of the cause of the harm, and, far from charging a party who acted in good faith with damages which surpass in amount what he could have foreseen, it explicitly declares that except in cases of wilful misconduct, that party is liable only for the damages which could have been foreseen at the time of the contract."

English law

Hadley v. Baxendale, (1854) 9 Exch. 341

"At the trial before Crompton, J., at the last Gloucester Assizes, it appeared that the plaintiffs carried on an extensive business as millers at Gloucester; and that, on the 11th of May, their mill was stopped by a break-age of the crank shaft by which the mill was worked. The steam-engine was manufactured by Messrs. Joyce & Co., the engineers, at Greenwich, and it became necessary to send the shaft as a pattern for a new one to Greenwich. The fracture was discovered on the 12th, and on the 13th the plaintiffs sent one of their servants to the office of the defendants, who are the well-known carriers trading under the name of Pickford & Co., for the purpose of having the shaft carried to Greenwich. The plaintiffs' servant told the clerk that the mill was stopped, and that the shaft must be sent immediately; and in answer to the inquiry when the shaft would be taken, the answer was, that if it was sent up by twelve o'clock any day, it would be delivered at Greenwich on the following day. On the following day the shaft was taken by the defendants before noon, for the purpose of being conveyed to Greenwich, and the sum of £2, 4s. was paid for its carriage for the whole distance; at the same time the defendants' clerk was told that a special entry, if required, should be made to hasten its delivery. The delivery of the shaft at Greenwich was delayed by some neglect; and the consequence was, that the plaintiffs did not receive the new shaft for several days after they would otherwise have done and the working of their mill was thereby delayed, and they thereby lost the profits they would otherwise have received. . . ." In a divided opinion, the court held that the plaintiff could not recover lost profits.

Parke B. [speaking to counsel]. "The sensible rule appears to be that which has been laid down in France, and which is declared in their Code Civil, liv, iii, tit. iii. ss. 1149, 1150, 1151, and which is thus translated in Sedgwick [on Damages, p. 67]: 'The damages due to the creditor consist in general of the loss that he has sustained, and the profit which he has been prevented from acquiring, subject to the modifications hereinafter contained. The debtor is only liable for the damages foreseen, or which might have been foreseen, at the time of the execution of the contract, when it is not owing to his fraud that the agreement has been violated. Even in the case of non-performance of the contract, resulting from the fraud of the debtor, the damages only comprise so much of the loss sustained by the creditor, and so much of the profit which he has been prevented from acquiring, as directly and immediately results from the non-performance of the contract.' If that rule is to be adopted, there was ample evidence in the present case of the defendants' knowledge of such a state of things as would necessarily result in the damage the plaintiffs suffered through the defendants' default. . . ."

Alderson, B. "Now we think the proper rule in such a case as the present is this: Where two parties have made a contract which one of them has broken, the damages which the other party ought to receive in respect of such breach of contract should be such as may fairly and reasonably be considered either arising naturally, i.e., according to the usual course of things, from such breach of contract itself, or such as may reasonably be supposed to have been in the contemplation of both parties at the time they made the contract, as the probable result of the breach of it. Now, if the special circumstances under which the contract was actually made were communicated by the plaintiffs to the defendants, and thus known to both parties, the damages resulting from the breach of such a contract, which they would reasonably contemplate, would be the amount of injury which would ordinarily follow from a breach of contract under these special circumstances so known and communicated. But, on the other hand, if these special circumstances were wholly unknown to the party breaking the contract, he, at the most, could only be supposed to have had in his contemplation the amount of injury which would arise generally, and in the great multitude of cases not affected by any special circumstances, from such a breach of contract. For, had the special circumstances been known, the parties might have specially provided for the breach of contract by special terms as to the damages in that case; and of this advantage it would be very unjust to deprive them. Now the above principles are those by which we think the jury ought to be guided in estimating the damages arising out of any breach of contract. It is said, that other cases such as breaches of contract in the non-payment of money, or in the not making a good title to land, are to be treated as exceptions from this, and as governed by a conventional rule. But as, in such cases, both parties must be supposed to be cognizant of that well-known rule, these cases may, we think, be more properly classed under the rule above enunciated as to cases under known special circumstances, because there both parties may reasonably be presumed to contemplate the estimation of the amount of damages according to the conventional rule. Now, in the present case, if we are to apply the principles above laid down, we find that the only circumstances here communicated by the plaintiffs to the defendants at the time the contract was made, were, that the article to be carried was the broken shaft of a mill, and that the plaintiffs were the millers of that mill. But how do these circumstances shew reasonably that the profits of the mill must be stopped by an unreasonable delay in the delivery of the broken shaft by the carrier to the third person? Suppose the plaintiffs had another shaft in their possession put up or putting up at the time, and that they only wished to send back the broken shaft to the engineer who made it; it is clear that this would be quite consistent with the above circumstances, and yet the unreasonable delay in the delivery would have no effect upon the intermediate profits of the mill. Or, again, suppose that, at the time of the delivery to the carrier, the machinery of the mill had been in other respects defective, then, also, the same results would follow."

Koufos v. C. Czarnikow, Ltd., [The Heron II] [1969] A.C. 350 (H.L.1967)

Lord Reid. "By charter party of Oct. 15, 1960, the respondents chartered the appellant's vessel, Heron II, to proceed to Constanza, there to load a cargo of three thousand tons of sugar; and to carry it to Basrah, or, in the charterers' option, to Jeddah. The vessel left Constanza on Nov. 1. The option was not exercised and the vessel arrived at Basrah on Dec. 2. The umpire has found that 'a reasonably accurate prediction of the length of the voyage was twenty days.' But the vessel had in breach of contract made deviations which caused a delay of nine days.

It was the intention of the respondent charterers to sell the sugar 'promptly after arrival at Basrah and after inspection by merchants.' The appellant shipowner did not know this, but he was aware of the fact that there was a market for sugar at Basrah. The sugar was in fact sold at Basrah in lots between Dec. 12 and 22 but shortly before that time the market price had fallen partly by reason of the arrival of another cargo of sugar. It was found by the umpire that if there had not been this delay of nine days the sugar would have fetched £32 10s. per ton. The actual price realized was only £31 2s.9d. per ton. The charterers claim that they are entitled to recover the difference as damage for breach of contract. The shipowner admits that he is liable to pay interest for nine days on the value of the sugar and [plaintiff's cable] expenses but denies that fall in market value can be taken into account in assessing damages in this case. . . .

There is no finding that the charterers had in mind any particular date as to the likely date of arrival at Basrah or that they had any knowledge or expectation that in late November or December there would be a rising or a falling market. The shipowner was given no information about these matters by the charterers. He did not know what the charterers intended to do with the sugar. But he knew there was a market in sugar at Basrah, and it appears to me that, if he had thought about the matter, he must have realized that at least it was not unlikely that the sugar would be sold in the market at market price on arrival. And he must be held to have known that in any ordinary market prices are apt to fluctuate from day to day: but he had no reason to suppose it more probable that during the relevant period such fluctuation would be downwards rather than upwards—it was an even chance that the fluctuation would be downwards." [Held: that the charterers can recover damages for the fall in market value.]

Law in the United States

Restatement (Second) of Contracts

§ 351. UNFORESEEABILITY AND RELATED LIMITATIONS ON DAMAGES

(1) Damages are not recoverable for loss that the party in breach did not have reason to foresee as a probable result of the breach when the contract was made.

(2) Loss may be foreseeable as a probable result of a breach because it follows from the breach.

    (a) in the ordinary course of events, or

    (b) as a result of special circumstances, beyond the ordinary course of events, that the party in breach had reason to now.

(3) A court may limit damages for foreseeable loss by excluding recovery for loss of profits, by allowing recovery only for loss incurred in reliance, or otherwise if it concludes that in the circumstances justice so requires in order to avoid disproportionate compensation.

* * *

Illustrations

* * *

17. A, a private trucker, contracts with B to deliver to B's factory a machine that has just been repaired and without which B's factory, as A knows, cannot reopen. Delivery is delayed because A's truck breaks down. In an action by B against A for breach of contract the court may, after taking into consideration such factors as the absence of an elaborate written contract and the extreme disproportion between B's loss of profits during the delay and the price of the trucker's services, exclude recovery for loss of profits.

18. A, a retail hardware dealer, contracts to sell B an inexpensive lighting attachment, which, as A knows, B needs in order to use his tractor at night on his farm. A is delayed in obtaining the attachment and, since no substitute is available, B is unable to use the tractor at night during the delay. In an action by B against A for breach of contract, the court may, after taking into consideration such factors as the absence of an elaborate written contract and the extreme disproportion between B's loss of profits during the delay and the price of the attachment, exclude recovery for loss of profits.

The "Lando Principles"

The Principles of European Contract Law, prepared by the Commission on European Contract Law

ARTICLE 9.503: FORESEEABILITY

The non-performing party is liable only for loss which it foresaw or could reasonably have foreseen at the time of the conclusion of the contract which is a likely result of its non-performance unless the non-performance was intentional or grossly negligent.

The Unidroit Principles

The Unidroit Principles of International Commercial Contracts

ARTICLE 7.4.4 (FORESEEABILITY OF HARM)

The non-performing party is liable only for harm which it foresaw or could reasonably have foreseen at the time of the conclusion of the contract as being likely to result from its non-performance.

Comment

* * *

The concept of foreseeability must be clarified since the solution contained in the Principles does not correspond to certain national systems which allow compensation even for harm which is unforeseeable when the non-performance is due to wilful misconduct or gross negligence. Since the present rule does not provide for such an exception, a narrow interpretation of the concept of foreseeability is called for. Foreseeability relates to the nature or type of the harm but not to its extent unless the extent is such as to transform the harm into one of a different kind. In any event, foreseeability is a flexible concept which leaves a wide measure of discretion to the judge.

What was foreseeable is to be determined by reference to the time of the conclusion of the contract and to the non-performing party itself (including its servants or agents), and the test is what a normally diligent person could reasonably have foreseen as the consequences of non-performance in the ordinary course of things and the particular circumstances of the contract, such as the information supplied by the parties of their previous transactions.

Illustrations

1. A cleaning company orders a machine which is delivered five months late. The manufacturer is obliged to compensate the company for lost profit caused by the delay in delivery as it could have foreseen that the machine was intended for immediate use. On the other hand the harm does not include the loss of a valuable government contract that could have been concluded if the machine had been delivered on time since that kind of harm was not foreseeable.

2. A, a bank, usually employs the services of a security firm for the conveyance of bags containing coins to its branches. Without informing the security firm, A sends a consignment of bags containing new coins for collectors worth fifty times the value of previous consignments. The bags are stolen in a hold-up. A can only recover compensation corresponding to the value of the normal consignments as this was the only kind of harm that could have been foreseen and the value of the items lost was such as to transform the harm into one of another kind.

German law

German Civil Code

§ 254 [CONTRIBUTORY FAULT]

If the fault of the injured party contributed to causing the injury, the obligation to compensate the injured party and the extent of the obligation depend upon the circumstances, and especially on the extent to which the injury was caused by one party or the other.

This provision also applies if the fault of the injured party consisted of an omission to call the attention of the party owing performance to the danger of an unusually serious injury of which that party neither knew nor should have known, or of an omission to avert or mitigate the injury.

Note: Paragraph 2 of § 254 was added, so to speak, at the last minute when the draft was before the legislature. Previous drafts had contained provisions like the following:

> "The liability for failure to perform of the person owing performance does not extend to compensation for harm the occurrence of which lay beyond the realm of probability given the awareness of the circumstances which that person had or must have had."[1]

The change was made because this provision appeared to be too restrictive, and yet it was felt that some limitation was necessary.[2]

Oberlandesgericht, Hamm 28 February 1989, NJW 1989, 2066

"The plaintiff entrusted the defendant with the task of translating a brochure concerning parts that would improve the suspension of motorcycles into the Dutch, French, English, Spanish and Italian languages. Claiming that the printed brochures were unusable due to faulty translation, the plaintiff seeks damages in the amount of 21,398.15 DM. . . .

There was fault on the part of the plaintiff . . . within the meaning of § 254(2) sentence 1 of the Civil Code because, in violation of its duty, the plaintiff failed to inform the defendant of the danger of an unusually severe harm as a consequence of the error in translation. After all, the damage that threatened, and which occurred, was forty times as large as the fee for translation. Such a relationship between the payment for translation on the one hand and the consequences of mistakes on the other lies outside the normal course of experience in commercial translations.

According to the evidence presented . . . the defendant neither actually knew nor should have known of the possibility that these unusually high damages would occur. Such a state of knowledge does not follow from the use of the word 'brochure' in their contract. Certainly, the defendant must have inferred that use would be made of its translation. But, on the other hand, it need not have expected that the plaintiff would have the translation immediately printed in full for its customers in the Netherlands without any proofreading."

Bundesgerichtshof, 29 January 1969, NJW 1969, 789

Plaintiff was a jewellery salesman who stayed in defendant's hotel. He gave his car key to the night porter so that his car could be left in a

---

1. § 218 in *Protokolle der Kommission für die zweite Lesung des Entwurfs des Bürgerlichen Gesetzbuchs* (1897), 292.
2. "Antrag von Enneccerus in der XII. Kommission" no. 134 in *Die Beratung des*

Bürgerlichen Gesetzbuchs Recht der Schuldverhältnisse 1 (H.H. Jakobs & W. Schubert, eds., 1978), 117–18.

garage, not owned by the hotel, but which, by arrangement with its owner, the defendant used to provide parking for his guests. A valuable collection of jewellery, which plaintiff had left locked in his trunk, was stolen during the night. The trunk showed no signs of damage. Plaintiff sued for the value of jewellery.

"The decision of the present case . . . depends on whether the defendant can assist himself by pointing to a fault [the plaintiff] within the meaning of § 254 BGB and so avoid, in whole or in part, liability for damages. . . .

It must be considered, in the first place, that [the plaintiff] left his collection in the trunk of his car without informing the porter or any other personnel of relevance to the defendant of its value and hence the danger of an abnormally high loss (§ 254 BGB par. 2 sentence 1)."

[The court remanded for a finding on contributory fault.]

Wolfgang Grunsky, *Münchener Kommentar zum Bürgerlichen Gesetzbuch* (H. Heinrichs, ed., 3rd ed. 1994), § 254 nos. 40–41.

"The duty to warn of the injured party presupposes that the injurer neither knew nor must have known about the danger. If the injurer and the injured had equally good possibilities of knowing, then a warning need not be given (BGH VersR 1963, 14). If through negligence neither the injurer nor the injured party know of the danger, then the injurer bears the risk. The harm is not to be divided as in § 254. . . .

The duty to warn is supposed to give the injured party the opportunity to take counter measures. If such measures are no longer possible, then the duty to warn disappears."

PART FOUR:

UNJUST ENRICHMENT

I. THE PRINCIPLE

Roman law

Dig. 50.17.206

By nature, it is equitable that no one should be wrongfully enriched at another's expense.

English law

Moses v. Mcferlan, (1760) 2 Burr. 1005, 97 Eng. Rep. 676 (K.B.)

[The plaintiff had endorsed a negotiable instrument but the defendant had agreed in writing not to take any action against him. The plaintiff, having been compelled by another court to pay the note notwithstanding the collateral agreement, prevailed.]

Lord Mansfield: "If the defendant be under an obligation from the ties of natural justice, to refund, the law implies a debt, and gives this action, founded in the equity of the plaintiff's case, as it were upon a contract (quasi ex contractu, as the Roman law expresses it) . . . the gist of this kind of action is that the defendant, on the circumstances of the case, is obliged by the ties of natural justice and equity to refund the money."

Orakpo v. Manson Investments Ltd., [1978] AC 95, 104 (HL)

Lord Diplock. "My Lords, there is no general doctrine of unjust enrichment recognised in English law. What it does is to provide specific remedies in particular cases of what might be classified as unjust enrichment in a legal system that is based on the civil law. There are some circumstances in which the remedy takes the form of 'subrogation', but this expression embraces more than a single concept in English law. It is a convenient way of describing a transfer of rights from one person to another, without assignment or assent of the person from whom the rights are transferred and which takes place by operation of law in a whole variety of widely different circumstances. Some rights by subrogation are contractual in their origin, as in the case of contracts of insurance. Others, such as the right of an innocent lender to recover from a company moneys borrowed ultra vires to the extent that these have been expended on discharging the company's

552

lawful debts, are in no way based on contract and appear to defeat classification except as an empirical remedy to prevent a particular kind of unjust enrichment.

This makes particularly perilous any attempt to rely on analogy to justify applying to one set of circumstances which would otherwise result in unjust enrichment a remedy of subrogation which has been held to be available for that purpose in another and different set of circumstances.

One of the sets of circumstances in which a right of subrogation arises is when a liability of a borrower B to an existing creditor C secured on the property of B is discharged out of moneys provided by the lender L and paid to C either by L himself at B's request and on B's behalf or directly by B pursuant to his agreement with L. In these circumstances L is prima facie entitled to be treated as if he were the transferee of the benefit of C's security on the property to the extent that the moneys lent by L to B were applied to the discharge of B's liability to C. This subrogation of L to the security on the property of B is based on the presumed mutual intentions of L and B; in other words where a contract of loan provides that moneys lent by L to B are to be applied in discharging a liability of B to C secured on property, it is an implied term of that contract that L is to be subrogated to C's security. The mere fact that money lent has been expended on discharging a secured liability of the borrower does not give rise to any implication of subrogation unless the contract under which the money was borrowed provides that the money is to be applied for this purpose."

Note: It was once thought, as Lord Diplock said, that there was no general claim for unjust enrichment in English law. That opinion has since been rejected, beginning with the following case.

Lipkin Gorman v. Karpnale. Ltd., [1991] 2 AC 548 (H.L.)

[Cass was a partner in the plaintiff firm of solicitors and had authority to operate the firm's client account at the bank. He was a compulsive gambler and without their knowledge he withdrew cash from that account. Cass used that money to fund his gambling at the defendant club. There the cash was exchanged for chips which were used for gambling at the casino and also for payment for refreshments. Although they were used as currency within the club they were worthless and remained the property of the club. Having discovered the truth, the firm sued the club for the amount by which it had profited.]

Lord Bridge of Harwich. "With respect to the view that prevailed in the Court of Appeal I cannot see that the respondents ('the club') are in any better position to resist the solicitors' claim to recover the money which Cass stole from them and gambled away in the casino by reason of the fact that cash was exchanged for gaming chips before being wagered at the gaming tables. The club was nevertheless a mere volunteer who gave no consideration for the stolen money. This was the common sense view expressed in the dissenting judgment of Nicholls L.J. Both my noble and learned friends have thoroughly analysed this issue and I agree with the reasoning in both their speeches.

I agree with my noble and learned friend, Lord Goff of Chieveley, that it is right for English law to recognise that a claim to restitution, based on the unjust enrichment of the defendant, may be met by the defence that the defendant has changed his position in good faith. I equally agree that in expressly acknowledging the availability of this defence for the first time it would be unwise to attempt to define its scope in abstract terms, but better to allow the law on the subject to develop on a case by case basis. In the circumstances of this case. I would adopt the reasoning of my noble and learned friend, Lord Templeman for the conclusion that the club can only rely on the defence to the extent that it limits the club's liability to the solicitors to the amount of their net winnings from Cass which must have been derived from the stolen money."

Law in the United States

Restatement of the Law of Restitution, Quasi-Contracts and Constructive Trusts (1937)

§ 1 UNJUST ENRICHMENT

A person who has been unjustly enriched at the expense of another is required to make restitution to the other.

§ 2 OFFICIOUS CONFERRING OF A BENEFIT

A person who officiously confers a benefit upon another is not entitled to restitution therefore.

§ 3 TORTIOUS AQUISITION OF A BENEFIT

A person is not permitted to profit by his own wrong at the expense of another.

French law

French Civil Code

ARTICLE 1372

A person who voluntarily takes charge of another's business, whether or not the other person is aware that he does, the one who takes charge tacitly contracts the obligation to continue the care which he has begun and to do so until the owner is in a position to do so himself. Correspondingly, he may charge for all the expenses he has incurred in the business.

He is subject to all the obligations that follow from an express commission given him by the owner.

ARTICLE 1375

The master whose business has been well discharged must fulfil the engagements which the person conducting it has contracted in his name, compensate him for all the personal obligations which he has undertaken, and reimburse him for all the useful or necessary expenses which he has incurred.

ARTICLE 1376

One who has, with knowledge or in ignorance, received what is not due to him is obligated to make restitution to the person from whom he has received what is not due.

Cour de cassation, ch. req., 15 June 1892, DP 1892.1.596, S. 1893.1.283

Boudier, the plaintiff, had supplied fertilizer to the tenant of a farm who used it on his field. The lease was then terminated. The landlord and tenant agreed that the landlord would have the unharvested crop at a price fixed by experts which would be deducted from the outstanding rent. The plaintiff sued the landlord for the value of the fertilizer. The court allowed this claim.

"[G]iven that there are no fixed conditions for the exercise of this action [the Roman *actio in rem verso*] which derives from the principle of equity that no one should be enriched at another's expense, and which is not covered by any text in our laws, . . . it is enough for the claim to be admissible that the plaintiff alleges and offers to prove that a benefit has accrued to the defendant as his expense or by his own act. . . ."

German law

German Civil Code

§ 683 [COMPENSATION FOR EXPENDITURES]

If the undertaking of the affairs of another correspond to the interests or the actual probable will of that person, then the person undertaking these affairs can require compensation for his expenses. . . .

§ 684 [RESTITUTION OF ENRICHMENT]

If the requirements of section 683 are not met, then the person whose business is conducted is still obligated to pay for the expenses of the person who conducted them in accordance with the provisions on unjust enrichment. . . .

§ 812 [BASIC PRINCIPLE]

(1) One who by transfer from another person or in some other way obtains something at that person's expense without legal justification is required to give it up. He is also under this obligation when the legal justification later ceases to exist or when, according to the content of the legal transaction, the purpose of the transfer is not achieved.

(2) A transfer includes the contractual recognition of the existence or non-existence of an obligation with regard to another.

Note: While the principle against unjust enrichment seems to universally recognized, despite the recalcitrance of the English and the absence of any express text in France, many jurists doubt whether it means anything definite. Even the Romans recognized a few limited cases in which a plaintiff would be entitled to relief. As we have seen, they recognized the maxim that no one should be enriched at another's expense. But they did not use it to explain why relief should be given in some cases, which they had traditionally recognized, but not in others. The maxim was an afterthought.

The late scholastics and natural lawyers thought it was the key to understanding why relief should be given. Thomas Aquinas had said that a person might violate commutative justice either by interfering with another's property in a wrongful manner (*acceptio rei*) or simply by having what belonged to another (*ipsa res accepta*).[1] The late scholastics examined this last possibility more closely. Suppose he no longer had another's property. He was liable, they said, if he had thereby become richer. They thus recognized unjust enrichment as a distinct ground for relief,[2] and the northern natural lawyers followed them.[3] As Robert Feenstra has pointed out, the late scholastics were the first to recognize this principle as the foundation of a law of unjustified enrichment coeval with contract and tort. The northern natural lawyers borrowed their conclusions.[4] We should note the context in which they spoke of unjust enrichment. Resources, from which one party had the exclusive right to benefit, had been used to confer on someone else the very benefit to which the first party had the exclusive right. Commutative justice forbad the second party to keep the benefit.

Many modern jurists who doubt that the principle is meaningful take it in a different sense. They take it to mean that no one should benefit as the result of a loss or cost suffered or incurred by somebody else. Of course, that isn't true. Ernst von Caemmerer agreed pointed out that a person might lose his rights to another by prescription. Or he might renounce a right which is consequently acquired by someone else. Or he might open a tourist hotel in a hitherto unknown village or build a dam, thereby enhancing the value of neighboring properties.[5] Other jurists have pointed out that "enrichment may be due to the display of particular skills in (lawful) competition."[6] Von Caemmerer concluded that in many cases, "third parties are advantaged without a contractual or statutory claim to be. But they are not unjustifiably enriched, and there is no action in unjustified enrichment against them."[7] That is certainly true, although in none of these cases has the defendant benefitted by using resources to which the plaintiff had the exclusive right to draw a benefit.

In any event, whether the general principle is valid or not, one can best see what it means in modern law by seeing how modern legal systems have applied it.

1. *Summa theologiae* II-II, Q. 62, a. 6.

2. Ludovicus Molina, *De iustitia et iure tractatus* (1614), disp. 718, no. 2; Leonardus Lessius, *De iustitia et iure, ceterisque virtutibus cardinalis libri quatuor* (1628), lib. 2, cap. 14, dub. 1, no. 3. *See* Halleback, *Unjust Enrichment* 47–58.

3. Hugo Grotius, *De iure bellis ac pacis libri tres* (1646), II.x.5; Samuel Pufendorf, *De iure naturae et gentium libri octo* (1688), II.viii.9.

4. Robert Feenstra, "Grotius' Doctrine of Unjust Enrichment as a Source of

Obligation: its Origin and its Influence on Roman-Dutch Law," in *Unjust Enrichment* (E.J.H. Schrage, ed., 1995), 197.

5. Ernst von Caemmerer, "Grundprobleme des Bereicherungsrechts," *Gesammelte Schriften*, (Hans G. Leser, ed., 1968), 370 at 374–75.

6. Reinhard Zimmermann, *The Law of Obligations Roman Foundations of the Civilian Tradition* (1990), 889.

7. Von Caemmerer, "Grundprobleme" 375.

II. UNJUST ENRICHMENT WHEN THE PLAINTIFF DID NOT LOSE

1. The use or violation of another's property rights

English law

Phillips v. Homfray, (1883) 24 Law Reports 439 (Ch. Div.)

[The defendants took coal and ironstone from their own land but conveyed it away through tunnels and passages beneath the land of another person. He died, and those who inherited his estate brought suit.]

Baggallay L.J. "That it is in form an action form a claim in the nature of a claim for trespass, the damages for which were to be measured by the amount of wayleave which the Defendants would have had to pay for the use of Plaintiff's ways and passages, cannot be disputed. But [the judge below] was of the opinion that this was one of the class of cases in which a deceased man's estate remains liable for a profit derived out of his wrongful acts during his lifetime. . . .

The only cases in which, apart from questions of breach of contract, express or implied, a remedy for a wrongful act can be pursued against the estate of a deceased person who has done the act, appear to us to be those in which property, or the proceeds or value of property, belonging to another, have been appropriated by the deceased person and added to his estate or moneys." [The court denied recovery because it held that was not the case here.]

Swordheath Properties Ltd v. Tabet, [1979] 1 WLR 285

A landlord let a flat to a tenant for a fixed term. His tenancy came to an end before this term expired. The defendants then lived in the flat. The lower court held that while the landlord could recover any damages he suffered from them, he could not recover rent without showing that he otherwise would have rented the flat to someone else.

Megarry J. "[C]ounsel for the plaintiffs has referred us to a decision of Lord Denning MR (sitting as an additional judge of the Queen's Bench Division) in Penarth Dock Engineering Co Ltd v Pounds [[1963] 1 Lloyd's Rep 359]. In his decision in the case, so far as the question of damages arose, Lord Denning MR had no hesitation in saying that the plaintiffs, even though they would not themselves have made use, bringing in financial return, of the dock in respect of which the trespass was committed, were nevertheless entitled to damages for that trespass, calculated by reference to the proper value to the trespassers of the use of the property on which they had trespassed, for the period during which they had trespassed.

It appears to me to be clear, both as a matter of principle and of authority, that in a case of this sort the plaintiff, when he has established that the defendant has remained on as a trespasser in residential property, is entitled, without bringing evidence that he could or would have let the property to someone else in the absence of the trespassing defendant, to have as damages for the trespass the value of the property as it would fairly be calculated; and, in the absence of anything special in the particular case it would be the ordinary letting value of the property that would determine the amount of damages."

Law in the United States

Raven Red Ash Coal Co. v. Ball, 39 S.E. 2d 231 (Va. 1946)

The defendant, a coal company, built a small railway across plaintiff's land and, for years, hauled coal across it.

"The illegal transportation of the coal in question across plaintiff's land was intentional, deliberate and repeated from time to time for a period of years. Defendant had no moral or legal right to enrich itself by this illegal use of plaintiff's property. To limit plaintiff to the recovery of nominal damages for the repeated trespasses will enable the defendant, as a trespasser, to obtain a more favorable position than a party contracting for the same right. Natural justice plainly requires the law to imply a promise to pay a fair value for the benefits received. Defendant's estate has been enhanced by just this much."

Olwell v. Nye & Nissen Co., 173 P. 2d 652 (Wash. 1946)

"It appears that the plaintiff arranged for and had [an egg washing machine] stored in a space adjacent to the premises of the defendant but not covered by its lease. Due to the scarcity of labor immediately after the outbreak of the war, the defendant's treasurer, without the knowledge or consent of the plaintiff, ordered the egg washer to be taken out of storage. The machine was put into operation by defendant on May 31, 1941, and thereafter, for a period of three years, was used approximately one day a week in the regular course of the defendant's business. . . .

It is argued by the plaintiff that, since the machine was put into storage by respondent, who had no present use for it, and for a period of almost three years did not know that appellant was operating it, and since it was not injured by its operation . . . the respondent was not damaged since he is as well off as if the machine had not been used by the appellant.

The very essence of the nature of property is the right to its exclusive use. Without it, no beneficial right remains. However, plausible, the appellant cannot be heard to say that its wrongful invasion of the respondent's property right to exclusive use is not a loss compensable in law. To hold otherwise would be subversive of all property rights, since its use was admittedly wrongful and without claim of right. The theory of unjust enrichment is applicable in such a case."

French law

Cour de cassation, ch. req., 11 December 1928, D.H. 1929.18

A water company utilized a pipe belonging to the plaintiff to distribute water to its other customers. The plaintiff sought compensation for the use of its pipe.

"As to the violation of the principle of unjust enrichment . . .

[T]he decision under attack declares that the Water Company from Ms. Matitia by using her pipe to distribute water to other users who paid a price for it . . . [I]n deciding that the company owed compensation to Ms. Matitia for the use it made of her pipe, the decision merely applied the principle that no one can be enriched at another's expense." Therefore, the water company is liable.

German law

Reichsgericht, 20 Dec. 1919, RGZ 97, 310

The defendant built a small railroad across plaintiff's property which it used to haul its goods. The plaintiff sued for unjust enrichment.

"The findings of the appellate court as to the plaintiff's right to recover for unjust enrichment are justified. . . . It is clear from the letters of the plaintiff of 27 July 1911 that the plaintiff need only suffer this use if he were paid an appropriate compensation. . . . If the defendant is enriched at the expense of the plaintiff insofar as it must in the ordinary course of affairs pay an appropriate compensation for it unlawful use, it has saved this sum, and the plaintiff has therefore lost it."

2. The question of what the defendant should pay

Suppose, as in some of the cases just described, the defendant would have had no alternative but to deal with the plaintiff. Is the plaintiff then entitled to any amount he could have forced the defendant to pay? The problem is illustrated by the following English case.

Wrotham Park Estate Company v. Parkside Homes Ltd, [1974] 1 WLR 798 (Ch. div.)

Land was sold subject to a covenant that any buyer would develop the land only in accord with a development plan approved by the seller.

"On 14th February the plaintiffs issued a writ against Parkside. The relief sought was an injunction to restrain Parkside from building on the allotment site other than in accordance with a layout plan approved by the plaintiffs and a mandatory injunction for the demolition of any buildings erected in breach of the stipulation. The issue of the writ and the service of the statement of claim a fortnight later did not deter Parkside. Holding deposits had been accepted in respect of all 14 houses (although no contracts had been signed) and building works proceeded. . . .

I turn first to the nature, scope and purpose of the layout covenant. In terms it is an absolute prohibition against development for building purposes except in strict accordance with a layout plan approved by the vendor, the sixth earl, or his surveyors. No point was taken before me that the stipulation was personal to the sixth earl and died with him. Counsel on both sides accepted that the word 'vendor' in the stipulation must, as a matter of construction, be capable of including successors in title. Counsel for the plaintiffs submitted that a layout plan was one which indicated the position of houses, that is to say density and arrangement of buildings and the position of roads, and also in the context of this particular stipulation, the line of sewers and drains. He conceded that the covenantee would have no right under such a stipulation to refuse approval unreasonably, and in particular, that the stipulation could not lawfully have been used as a bargaining counter in order to demand money from Mr Blake as the price for allowing him to develop. The plaintiffs were not able to produce any application by Mr Blake for approval of a layout plan or any copy of an approval granted to him. . . .

I turn to the consideration of the quantum of damages. I was asked by the parties to assess the damages myself, should the question arise, rather than to direct an enquiry. The basis rule in contract is to measure damages by that sum of money which will put the plaintiff in the same position as he would have been in if the contract had not been broken. From that basis, the defendants argue that the damages are nil or purely nominal, because the value of the Wrotham Park estate (as the plaintiffs concede) is not diminished by one farthing in consequence of the construction of a road and the erection of 14 houses on the allotment site. If, therefore (the defendants submit), I refuse an injunction I ought to award no damages in lieu. That would seem, on the face of it, a result of questionable fairness on the facts of this case. Had the offending development been the erection of an advertisement hoarding in defiance of protests and writs, I apprehend (assuming my conclusions on other point to be correct) that the court would not have hesitated to grant a mandatory injunction for its removal. If, for social and economic reasons, the court does not see fit in the exercise of its discretion, to order demolition of the 14 houses, is it just that the plaintiffs should receive no compensation and that the defendants should be left in undisturbed possession of the fruits of their wrongdoing? Common sense would seem to demand a negative answer to this question. A comparable problem arose in wayleave cases where the defendant had trespassed by making use of the plaintiff's underground ways to the defendant's profit but without diminishing the value of the plaintiff's property. The plaintiff in such cases received damages assessed by reference to a reasonable wayleave rent. This principle was considered and extended in Whitwham v Westminster Brymbo Coal and Coke Co [[1896] 2 Ch 538.] For six years the defendants wrongfully tipped colliery waste on to the plaintiff's land. At the trial the defendants were directed to cease tipping and to give up possession. The question then arose what damages should be awarded for the wrongful act done to the plaintiff during the period of the defendant's unauthorised user of the land. The official referee found that the diminution in the value of the plaintiff's land was only £200, but that the value of the plaintiff's land to the defendants in 1888 for tipping purposes for six years was some £900. It was held that the proper scale of damages was the higher sum on the ground that a trespasser should not be allowed to make use of another person's land without in some way compensating that other person for that user.

In my judgment a just substitute for a mandatory injunction would be such a sum of money as might reasonably have been demanded by the plaintiffs from Parkside as a quid pro quo for relaxing the covenant. The plaintiffs submitted that that sum should be a substantial proportion of the development value of the land. This is currently put at no less than £10,000 per plot, i.e. £140,000 on the assumption that the plots are undeveloped. Mr Parker gave evidence that a half or a third of the development value was commonly demanded by a landowner whose property stood in the way of a development. I do not agree with that approach to damages in this type of case. I bear in mind the following factors: (1) The layout covenant is not an asset which the estate owner ever contemplated he would have either the opportunity or the desire to turn to account. It has no commercial or even nuisance value. For it cannot be turned to account except to the detriment of the existing residents who are people the estate owner professes to protect. (2) The breach of covenant which has actually taken place is over a very small area and the impact of this particular breach on the Wrotham Park estate is insignificant. The validity of the covenant over the rest of area 14 is unaffected. I think that in a case such as the present a landowner faced with a request from a developer which, it must be assumed, he feels reluctantly obliged to grant, would have first asked the developer what profit he expected to make from his operations. With the benefit of foresight the developer would, in the present case, have said about £50,000, for that is the profit which Parkside concedes it made from the development. I think that the landowner would then reasonably have required a certain percentage of that anticipated profit as a price for the relaxation of the covenant, assuming, as I must, that he feels obliged to relax it. In assessing what would be a fair percentage I think that the court ought, on the particular facts of this case, to act with great moderation. For it is to be borne in mind that the plaintiffs were aware, before the auction took place, that the land was being offered for sale as freehold building land for 13 houses, and the plaintiffs knew that they were not going to consent to any such development. The plaintiffs could have informed the urban district council of their attitude in advance of the auction or could have given the like information to Parkside prior to completion of the contract for sale. In either event it seems highly unlikely that Parkside would have parted with its £90,000, at any rate unconditionally. I think that damages must be assessed in such a case on a basis which is fair and, in all the circumstances, in my judgment a sum equal to 5 per cent of Parkside's anticipated profit is the most that is fair. I accordingly award the sum of £2,500 in substitution for mandatory injunctions. I think that this amount should be treated as apportioned between the 14 respective owners or joint owners of the plots and Parkside (as the owner of the road) in 1/15th shares, so that the damages awarded will be £166 odd in each case. In fact, I apprehend that by virtue of the arrangement between Parkside and the insurance office the entirety of the £2,500 will ultimately be recoverable from Parkside, so that the apportionment does not have any real significance. I will also grant a declaration in appropriate terms after I have heard submissions from counsel as to such terms."

III. UNJUST ENRICHMENT WHEN IT IS DOUBTFUL WHAT THE DEFENDANT GAINED

1. The problem of improvements

Anglo-American law

Ramsden v. Dyson, [1866] L.R. 1 HL 129

A tenant spent over £1,800 on land that he had leased. His lease was short term but he believed that by building he became entitled to a sixty year lease. He was wrong, and his landlord evicted him. The House of Lords denied the tenant compensation on the grounds that the landlord had not known or encouraged the tenant to make the improvements. Lord Cransworth did note that the result would have been different if he had.

"If a stranger begin to build on my land supposing it to be his own, and I, perceiving his mistake, abstain from setting him right, and leave him to persevere in his error, a court of equity will not allow me afterwards to assert my title to the land on which he had expended money on the supposition that the land was his own. It considers that, when I saw the mistake into which he had fallen, it was my duty to be active and to state my adverse title; and that it would be dishonest in me to remain wilfully passive on such an occasion, in order afterwards to profit by the mistake that I could have prevented."

Greenwood v. Bennett, [1973] 1 QB 195 (CA)

Harper spent £226 repairing a car which he bought in good faith but which in fact had been stolen.

Lord Denning. "I should have thought that the county court judge here should have imposed a condition on Mr Bennett's company [the owner of the car]. He should have required them to pay Mr Harper the £226 as a condition of being given delivery of the car. But the judge did not impose such a condition. They have regained the car, and sold it. What then is to be done? It seems to me that we must order them to pay Mr Harper the £226 for that is the only way of putting the position right.

On what principle is this to be done? Counsel for Mr Bennett has referred us to the familiar cases which say that a man is not entitled to compensation for work done on the goods or property of another unless there is a contract express or implied to pay for it. We all remember the saying of Pollock CB: 'One cleans another's shoes. What can the other do but put them on?' [citation omitted] That is undoubtedly the law when the person who does the work knows, or ought to know, that the property does not belong to him. He takes the risk of not being paid for his work on it. But it is very different when he honestly believes himself to be the owner of the property and does the work in that belief. (That distinction is drawn in the mining cases such as Wood v Morewood and Livingstone v Rawyards Coal Co [citations omitted].) Here we have an innocent purchaser who bought the car in good faith and without notice of any defect in the title to it. He did work on it to the value of £226. The law is hard enough on him when it makes him give up the car itself. It would be most unjust if Mr Bennett's company could not only take the car from him, but also the value of the improvements he has done to it—without paying for them. There is a principle at hand to meet the case. It derives from the law of restitution. Mr Bennett's company should not be allowed unjustly to enrich themselves at his expense. The court will order them, if they recover the car, or its improved value, to recompense the innocent purchaser for the work he has done on it. No matter whether they recover it with the aid of the courts, or without it, the innocent purchaser will recover the value of the improvements he has done to it."

Torts (Interference with Goods Act) 1977

§ 6 (1)

In proceedings for wrongful interference against a person (the "improver") who has improved the goods, if it is shown that the improver acted in the mistaken but honest belief that he had good title to them, an allowance shall be made to the extent to which, at the time as at which the goods fall to be valued in assessing damages, the value of the goods is attributable to the improvement.

Jensen v. Probert, 148 P.2d 248 (Ore. 1944)

"The plaintiff Jensen was owner in fee of the Probert tract. The plaintiffs were neither guilty of negligence, fraud or bad faith nor did they take any affirmative action tending to mislead Probert or his purported predecessors in title. Probert, acting in good faith and without negligence and reasonably believing himself to be the owner of the Probert tract, built thereon a small house. Did the court [below] err in imposing a lien on the plaintiff's land for the sum of $1,500? . . .

By the early American and English common law, the true owner might recover his land in ejectment without incurring any liability to pay for improvements by an occupier, even though the latter acted in good faith believing himself to be the owner. . . .

On the other hand, it is firmly established by the weight of authority that where the occupant in good faith believes himself to be the owner and makes improvements which enhance the value of the property, and where the true owner seeks relief in a court of equity, the equitable maxim will apply and the court will grant relief only upon condition that the appropriate restitution is made to the occupier."

[Here, however, the plaintiff's claim was denied because the owner of the property did not want the small house. He wanted it to be removed.]

German law

German Civil Code

§ 994

(1) The possessor can require compensation from the owner for the expenses necessary for the upkeep of the object. . . .

§ 996

The possessor can claim compensation for other expenses that were not necessary . . . only insofar as they have increased the value of the object at the time the owner receives it.

Bundesgerichtshof, 31 Oct. 1963, BGHZ 40, 272[1]

[The plaintiff built several buildings on defendant's land and hired a firm to install electrical fixtures in them. The appellate court concluded that the defendant acquired title to the appliances when they were installed, independent of any contractual obligation.]

The appellate court must be followed in its view that the plaintiff was the owner of the appliances until the moment when they were installed in defendant's building, so that the plaintiff lost title by this installation. . . .

[T]he reference to unjust enrichment implies that a restitutionary claim does arise only under the requirements set forth in § 812 I BGB (BGHZ 35, 356, 359 [other citations omitted]). This position is also shared by the Appeal Court. What matters therefore is whether the defendant received the enrichment, which consists of the installed appliances, by performance of the plaintiff, or in any other way, without legal ground (§ 812 I 1 BGB).

The installation of the appliances cannot be considered as performance by the plaintiff. It was carried out by the B. firm, and this firm owed both installation and appliances to the defendant on the basis of the contract which this firm had concluded with the defendant, the Appeal Court states. . . .

By judgment of 5 October 1961 (VII ZR 207/60, BGHZ 36, 30), this present Senate denied a claim in unjust enrichment to a client who was similar to the present one. In this case, an owner of real property had instructed a company to construct a building for a certain price. The company had, in turn, instructed a building contractor to erect the building. The present Senate decided that the building contractor had no claim in unjust enrichment against the owner of the real property even if the building contractor's contract with the company were void. . . .

On this point, the Senate stated that the direct shift of wealth from the building contractor onto the owner of the real property, which was necessary for a restitutionary claim, was lacking. For the owner, the increased value of the property was not a transfer of value by the building contractor, but by his contractual partner, the company.

2. Situations in which the defendant would not have paid the amount he is judged to have been enriched

Bundesgerichtshof, 7 Jan. 1971, NJW 1971, 609[1]

[The defendant flew from Munich to Hamburg, having bought a ticket for that flight. He then managed to reenter the plane and continue on to

---

1. Excerpt from the translation by Kurt Lipstein in B.S. Markesenis, W. Lorenz & G. Dannemann, *The German Law of Obligations* vol.1 *The Law of Contracts and Restitution* (1997).

1. Excerpt from the translation by Kurt Lipstein in B.S. Markesenis, W. Lorenz & G. Dannemann, *The German Law of Obligations* vol.1 *The Law of Contracts and Restitution: A comparative Introduction* (1997).

New York. He was refused entry because he did not have a visa. Again without having purchased a ticket, he was returned to Munich. The plaintiff airline, which had transported him to New York and then back again to Munich, sued for the price it would have charged him for tickets.]

"[I]t seems entirely appropriate and even necessary, to transfer those principles which decide whether or not the enrichment has survived, and to apply them to whether there has been an initial enrichment, provided the interests involved are the same. This is at least necessary if such a transfer can solve inconsistencies within the law of unjust enrichment, which would arise if one were to apply different requirements to the survival of an enrichment on the one hand, and to the existence of an initial enrichment on the other, even if no convincing reasons can be found for such different treatment. In these situations, considerations of equity alone — which have a particularly strong influence on the law of unjustified enrichment (cf. BGHZ 36, 232, 235)—require that necessary adjustments be made.

It has been set out above that an enriched party who is aware of the lack of a legal cause when receiving the enrichment, is generally not allowed to rely on a subsequent disappearance of this initial enrichment. In this situation, there seems to be no reason why the same person, under the same conditions, should be allowed to deny the very accrual of an enrichment. This should at least not be permitted if the enrichment in question—as in this case—consists in the saving of expenses for extraordinary matters which the enriched party would or even could not otherwise have afforded."

Bundesgerichtshof, 14 July 1956, BGHZ 21, 319

The defendant continually parked her car in a public parking lot. The parking lot had posted a sign indicating the charge for parking was 25 DM. The defendant insisted she should be allowed to park for free. The court held that she was liable for the parking fee but on a strange ground.

"Principally, in his essay 'On Contractual Relations Based on Fact,' (Festschrift der Leipziger juristischen Fakultät für Siber Band II S 1), in a partial reversal of a concept that often works correctly in commercial life— that a contract can only come into existence through an offer and acceptance—he showed that there are contractual relation based on facts, which do not depend on the conclusion of a contract, but on a relationship of social performances of which a good example is the obligations of drivers on the highway to each other."

[The court held the defendant liable because a contract had been formed in this way here.]

Note: Part of the problem in the last case is how to hold the defendant liable, not for the amount he was benefitted, or would have been willing to pay, but for the amount the defendant knew the plaintiff would charge. The court solved the problem by finding there was a contract—even though the normal requirements for a contract were not satisfied. American courts have sometimes done something similar.

Louisville Tin & Stove Co. v. Lay, 65 S.W.2d 1002 (Ky. 1933)

Mrs. Lay operated a store. Her husband, who was insolvent and without credit, operated another business. He ordered goods from the plaintiff to be delivered to his wife's store. When she was informed that the goods had arrived at the railway depot, she "became angry and said it was her husband's doings." She ordered a drayman to take the goods to his shop. The court held that her acts in taking control over the goods constituted the acceptance of a contract.

Index

account, action of, 15
Accursius, 37, 168, 448–9, 462
actio in rem verso, 555
acts of God, 498
Addison, Charles, 243, 311, 467, 468
adversarial procedures
  confusion with criminal procedure, 80
  depth of evidence, 82–4
  equality of arms, 80–1
  false conflicts, 79–80
  German v American procedures, 66,
    79–84
  and prejudgment, 81–2
  shortcomings, 79–84
  United States, 74, 79–84
  and witnesses, 73
adverse possession
  English law, 148–9
  French law, 150–1
  German law, 151
  Roman Law, 148
  US law, 149–50
advocates
  England, 8–10, 117–20
  France, 105–10
  Germany, 108–9
advowsons, 14
Agostini, Christolphe, 260
Alaric, 31
Ambrose, Saint, 214
American Law Institute, 164
animals
  possession of wild animals, 141–4
  strict liability, 383, 384, 391–2
appeals
  France, 100, 103
  Germany, 91–2
    appeal courts, 88
    disclosure of grounds, 91
    review *de novo,* 91–2
    safeguards, 92
    specialized courts, 87[n100]
  Italy, 100
Appius Claudius, 24

Aquilian liability, 213, 237, 238, 239,
  335–6, 382
Aquinas, Thomas, 45, 215, 238, 350,
  383, 416, 417, 462, 463, 495,
  504, 556
Aristotle, 44, 45, 214–15, 238, 354,
  383, 416, 417, 449, 462, 463,
  495, 504
assault, 241, 245, 246, 341
assize, 6
assumpsit, 10, 15, 421, 466, 527
astreinte, 532–3
Aubry, Charles, 52–4
Augustine, Saint, 349, 503
Augustus, Emperor, 19, 25, 26
Azo, 37, 43, 237

Baldus de Ubaldis, 44, 169, 238, 415,
  449–50, 503–4
Balkans, 33
Bartolus of Saxoferrato, 42–4, 169,
  414, 415, 449
Basilica, 32–3
Bassianus, Johannes, 37
battery, 241, 244, 246, 247, 338, 341,
  344, 352
Baur, Jürgen, 158
Beale, Hugh, 430
Beale, Joseph, 342[n11]
Beatrice, Marchioness of Tuscany,
  35
Belisarius, 30
Berlier, Théophile, 464, 465
Bermann, George, 121–37
Bermuda, 114
Berr, Claude, 188
besaiel, 10
Bigelow, Melville, 244
Bigot-Préameneu, Félix, 47, 500
Blackstone, William, 10, 14, 17, 84,
  160, 168, 242, 243, 349
Bluhme, Friedrich, 31
Bologna, 35–6, 38, 40–2
Boniface VIII, Pope, 39, 64

Lightning Source UK Ltd.
Milton Keynes UK
UKOW07f1140160715

255221UK00005B/155/P